CODEX
MAGICA

012 | Sun 24 | 06   7:56 AM

Mike + Family
Merry Christmas!!!
& Happy New Year!!!
I wish for the very
best!!! & very best wishes
peace and prosperity!!!
p.s. Remember the Reason
For the season!!! ✝ Jesus !!!
always!!!
Look upon Jesus ✝
✝ Jesus Christ!!!   Love Robert

CODEX MAGICA

Secret Signs, Mysterious Symbols, and
Hidden Codes of the Illuminati

TEXE MARRS

RCP RiverCrest Publishing
1708 Patterson Road • Austin, Texas 78733

ACKNOWLEDGEMENTS

Especially deserving mention for helping me to produce this book are the outstanding members of my publishing team: Michelle Hallmark, administrator; Sandra Myers, publishing specialist and art director; Jerry Barrett, computer and internet manager; and Sandra Weedon, customer service. In the shipping department, Rosario Velásquez, manager, Armando Lopez and Nelson Sorto are to be thanked for their excellence.

And of course there is my precious wife, Wanda, my confidant and inspiration.

Codex Magica: Secret Signs, Mysterious Symbols, and Hidden Codes of the Illuminati

Second Printing, 2006

All Scripture quotations are from the King James Version of the Holy Bible

Cover design: Sandra Myers and Texe Marrs

Printed in the United States of America

Library of Congress Catalog Card Number 2001094304

Categories:
1. Conspiracy
2. Occultism
3. Current Events
4. Politics
5. Religion—Bible Prophecy
6. Government
7. History

ISBN 1-930004-04-4

Last night I saw upon the stair
a little man who wasn't there.
He wasn't there again today.
Oh gee, I wish he'd go away!

—Old Nursery Rhyme

OTHER BOOKS BY TEXE MARRS

Days of Hunger, Days of Chaos

Project L.U.C.I.D.: The Beast 666 Universal Human Control System

Circle of Intrigue: The Hidden Inner Circle of the Global Illuminati Conspiracy

Big Sister is Watching You: Hillary Clinton and the White House Feminists Who Now Control America—And Tell the President What to Do

Dark Majesty: The Secret Brotherhood and the Magic of A Thousand Points of Light

Millennium: Peace, Promises, and the Day They Take Our Money Away

America Shattered

New Age Cults and Religions

Mystery Mark of the New Age

Dark Secrets of the New Age

OTHER BOOKS BY RIVERCREST PUBLISHING

New Age Lies to Women, *by Wanda Marrs*

Gladiator: Witchcraft, Propaganda, and the Rise of the World Hero, *by John D. Christian*

Honoring the King James Bible, *by Dr. Solomon Aordkian*

Letters on Freemasonry, *by John Quincy Adams*

FOR MORE INFORMATION

For a complete catalog of books, tapes, and videos about the Illuminati, secret societies, occultism, Bible prophecy, conspiracy and related topics, and for a free sample of Texe Marrs informative newsletter, *Power of Prophecy*, please phone toll-free:

> 1-800-234-9673, or write to:
> RiverCrest Publishing
> 1708 Patterson Road
> Austin, Texas 78733

For additional information we highly recommend the following websites:

> *www.powerofprophecy.com*
> *www.conspiracyworld.com*

TABLE OF Contents

INTRODUCTION: The Occult Script—A Colossal and Monstrous Conspiracy   9

1   Caution!—You Are Now Entering the Forbidden Zone   15

2   The Megalomania of the Psychopaths—Why The Illuminati Do What They Do   25

3   Concealed Messages—The Importance of Hand Signs to the Illuminati   45

4   Hidden Hand of the Men of Jahbuhlun   53

5   For He's a Jolly Good Fellow—Sign of the Devil's Claw By the Men of the Craft   81

6   Baphles Me!—Horned Beasts, Leaping Goats, Satanic Beards, and Other Messages of Evil   97

7   "El Diablo" Shows His Horns—The Devil Rides Out!   119

8   Secret Handshakes of the Illuminati   145

9   A Show of Hands—Illuminists Employ the Grand Hailing Sign and the Sign of Admiration and Astonishment   177

10   "I Gruesomely Swear That I'm On the Square"—More Revealing Signs of Illuminati Cultists   189

11   "Cross My Heart and Hope to Die"—The Mysterious "X" Factor   205

12   That Ravenous Dark Bird—Sublime Mysteries of the Illuminati's Double-Headed Eagle   241

13   The Riddle of the Great Seal of the United States, and the All-Seeing Eye of the Serpent of Wisdom   265

14   "Silence, Slaves, or We'll Cut Your Throat From Ear to Ear!"   285

15   Up to Their Necks in Mischief   295

16   Hand On Heart—Sign of Devotion to the Chiefs   307

17   Triangles Up, Triangles Down, Triangles, Triangles All Around   327

18   Black Magic, Masonic Witchcraft, and Triangle Powers   361

19   Part Devil, Part Angel   393

20   The Merovingian Dynasty, The Priory of Sion, and the Spear of Longinus   405

21   Magical Signs of the Jewish Cabala—The Six-Pointed Star, Babylonian Witchcraft, and the Hollywood Perdition of Jerry Seinfeld and Associates   419

22   Scorched by the Sun—Solar Signs, Circles, and Serpents   459

23   "I Fell In To A Burning Ring of Fire"—Arnold Schwarzenegger's Masonic Ring, Newt Gingrich's T-Rex Dinosaur, and Other Mysterious Messages on Rings and Neckties of the Elite   483

24   OK—Sign of the Divine King   501

25   Victory For the Devil—Fabulous Exploits of Sir Winston Churchill and Other Druid Priests and Illuminati Servants   517

26   "Every Man and Woman Is a Star"   537

27   Lightning Fall From Heaven   557

28   Blood Red—Red Stars, Clenched Fists, Hammers and Sickles, and Other Signs and Symbols of Communist Intrigue   563

Footnotes and References   589

Index   599

More Resources For You   621

About the Author, Texe Marrs   623

The Occult Script—A Colossal and Monstrous Conspiracy

But let the Spirit of all lies with works of dazzling magic blind you. Then absolutely mine, I'll have and bind you.

The Devil, *Faust*
Play by Goethe (1749-1832)

They're everywhere. Cleverly disguised. On TV, imbedded in magazines, and lurking in powerful advertising. Sometimes they're subtle or subliminal, other times direct, provocative, and mind-bending in effect. Strange symbols, signs, charms, talismans, and handshakes that program and control our minds.

Henry Makow, astute inventor and essayist, says that they are key components of the satanic conspiracy that now confronts us with maximum force and evil. "This satanic conspiracy," Makow warns, "succeeds only because people cannot believe something so colossal and monstrous actually exists."[1]

The world is a contest for our souls. The people who are pushing products, violence, and sex are not operating on a random, 'whatever sells' basis. They have Masonic symbols in their logos. The top players are following an occult script designed to enslave us body and soul. They are building a gigantic prison based on their own mental hell. This is the New World Order; we are the inmates.[2]

It is, in fact, "satanic indoctrination," Makow emphasizes, and we are all locked into the prison classroom as this mental poison from hell is piped in to us 24 hours a day, seven days a week.

A Psychological Matrix

In this eye-opening book, *Codex Magica*, you will discover just how accurate and true are the warnings of Mr. Makow and just a few others. Most people, of course, are so far gone, their minds so awash with occultism acquired from decades of propaganda encountered on every side, they cannot any longer decipher reality. The majority are caught in some form of Psychological Matrix. Tragically, hundreds of millions of people have, in a manner of speaking, become *"Manchurian Candidates."* They eat, breathe, move, and sleep as if in a trance. Immobile, unable to react, afflicted with amnesia, they are like Pontius Pilate who, when confronted with Jesus Christ standing right in front of him, the very essence of unmovable Truth, asked Christ the question. *"What is truth?"*

Well, here, in *Codex Magica*, in over 600 incredible pages, is truth. Here you will see pictures of many of the foremost movers and shakers of human history, ancient and modern, as they secretly communicate through sign and symbol. Naturally, the elite do not relish being exposed in their dirty works and evil doing. They and their dumbed-down minions—I am referring to the overwhelming "see no evil, hear no evil" masses of people in society—can be expected to quickly jump to the attack and attempt to deny it all. Through sleight-of-hand, they will do their utmost to divert your attention. "The pictures are taken out of context," they will protest. "The images are not what they seem."

"Here, listen to us," they will implore, "it's not what it looks like. Let us explain it all to you."

"Don't be hasty now in your judgment," they'll cry. "You and I know that conspiracies don't really exist. Everything is okay, nothing is amiss. It is all just an accident, nothing to fret about."

"Are You Going to Believe Your Lying Eyes?"

Their weak and idiotic protestations remind us of the famous TV comedian, Groucho Marx. Groucho enjoyed retelling the story of the time a startled wife came home to find her adulterous husband in bed with another woman. *"It's not what you think,"* he assured her. *"Are you going to believe what I tell you, or are you going to believe your lying eyes?"*

Thank God we no longer have to believe what *they*, the Illuminati, and their lying accomplices in the media and government tell us. We can lay their propaganda aside and view the actual evidence through the prism of truth with our own eyes. This book is the result of over two decades of research. I believe it speaks for itself. The pictures, illustrations, and proofs contained in these pages do, in my opinion, document a monstrous conspiracy that surrounds and envelops us.

It may well be that some, a few, of the photographs, are not what they appear to be. We all know that it is possible, for example, that photographers took shots of certain people as their hands, fingers, arms, and bodies were inadvertently in odd positions. A picture may be worth a thousand words, as the old Chinese proverb says, but even pictures can be deceiving.

And so, I leave it all up to you to decide, dear reader. Do these proofs provide evidence of these peoples' involvement in nefarious, Masonic, occultic, or magical activity or not? You be the judge.

To help you make a decision, often included in the captions that accompany the photos and illustrations is commentary that helps one to better analyze the situation or scene that is pictured. When possible, I present evidence and information outlining the individual's membership in the Masonic Lodge, the Rosicrucian Order, or other globalist or occultic groups, secret societies, and organizations. This is done as an aid to your independent decision-making.

Sometimes, I admit, it is difficult from the picture alone to ascertain whether a person, or persons, are displaying a Masonic or other sign, or to tell for sure that an occultic pose or scene is being portrayed. Again, the author does his best to offer up evidence, such as pages, excerpts, and descriptions of such signs and poses from official textbooks, dictionaries, and encyclopedias of the Masonic Order or illustrations and examples by experts and authorities.

In some instances, it is unclear what exactly is transpiring in a photo because the intent, or motive, of the individual subject cannot be discerned. We cannot read peoples' minds, and so we must judge based on the photographic evidence. For example, there is much confusion today over the hand sign of the devil called "El Diablo" or "Il Cornuto." Many confuse this sign of evil with the sign of the deaf for "I love you" and with the sign given by many to indicate youthful rebellion, sex, and rock and roll.

In the section of *Codex Magica* that pictures a number of people giving this problematic sign, I therefore explain the difference in types of hand signs and discuss the ongoing controversy in an attempt to clear up some of the confusion. Readers may just find the clarifying information presented here revealing, to say the least.

All in all you will view in *Codex Magica* over 1,000 photos and illustrations documenting Illuminists, Satanists, and other elitists practicing magic. Even if the skeptics and naysayers were able to explain away a few of these proofs, the remainder would be sufficient aplenty to prove the thesis of this book. That, indeed, a massive conspiratorial network of occult magicians exists today and has existed throughout human history.

From the perspective of the occult researcher and investigator, the key to understanding the precarious world we live in is the recognition that a *consistent pattern* exists. A criminal is often convicted by an overwhelming preponderance of circumstantial evidence, even when no direct evidence—like a smoking gun—is produced. But in our case, in *Codex Magica*, we *do* produce a convincing array of direct evidence, along with many facts that connect the dots, to conclusively prove the continuing existence of an occult conspiracy. Over 600 pages of photographic evidence and materials cannot *all* be wrong.

Exercising Fairness and Good Judgment

I wish to emphasize that I accuse no one pictured herein of being a Satanist or occultist. Their being pictured here does not mean that individuals are necessarily members of the Order of the Illuminati or prove anything whatsoever about their social, political, religious ideology or other beliefs. Nor am I implying, suggesting, or stating that the men and women pictured are knowingly involved in any type of plot, satanic or otherwise.

My friends are fully aware that over the years, I have authored and produced numerous books, audiotapes, and videos on the subject of mysterious marks, symbols, signs, and logos, including such bestseller classics as *Dark Secrets of the New Age, Mystery Mark of the New Age,* and *Circle of Intrigue.* As such, the reader should realize that the information in my books and other works is based solely on my own opinion. True, I do my level best to judge things accurately and to marshall relevant facts and data that might bear; but ultimately, the reader or viewer must decide if he or she concurs with the author's judgements and opinions. As the cliché of a well-known TV news network so often echoes, *"We report, you decide."*

Those who have read and evaluated my past works know that I am always concerned and desirous of presenting accurate information. I invite anyone who believes the facts and analysis, or even the opinions expressed herein are incorrect or incomplete to promptly inform me of such. I am more than willing to make corrections or retractions based on the best evidence.

Deciphering A Mountain of Data

One of the problems inherent in an undertaking so vast as this book is that the subject matter is so broad and complex. There are literally thousands of secret signs, grips, and symbols to consider in evaluating photographic evidence. My opponents—the men of the secret societies and the Illuminists—would agree that this is the case. In the *Royal Arch Mason,* an official publication of Freemasonry, Dr. William L. Cummings commented on how many hundreds of rites, rituals, and degrees existed.[3]

Obviously, in each of the hundreds of ceremonies a number of secret handshakes and signs are taught and practiced. Thus, Cummings remarks, Masons themselves are in a state of confusion:

> It generally comes as a surprise and sometimes as a shock when the Mason who has never given any attention to the subject learns at least a hundred Masonic and quasi-Masonic rites and systems have existed and no less than eight hundred so-called Masonic degrees have been revised.[4]

Royal Arch Mason editor Ray V. Denslow wryly comments that a long-time Mason of reputation may be asked, "How many of the hundreds of degrees have you received? Have you received the Rite of Memphis of 90 degrees? Or the Rectified Rite? Or the Swedenborgian Rite?"[5]

Moreover, Masons affiliated with the Grand Lodge of the Orient in Paris, the United Lodge in London, or the Grand Masonic Lodge of Israel, may well utilize signs and handshakes not used, seen, or understood in other orders.

Then, of course, there is the Order of the Rosicrucians, the Order of the Trapezoid, The Priory of Sion, The Alta Vendita, the P2 Lodge, the Solar Order of the Temple, the modern-day Knights Templar, the Vatican's Knights of Malta and Knights of Columbus, the Order of the Odd Fellows, the Order of Ahepa, the Order of Skull and Bones, the Bohemian Club, the Pilgrims Society, and a thousand or more other secret societies and orders, not to mention the many Jewish cabalistic groups, satanic churches, and witchcraft and druid sects.

Knowledge of Secret Signs Opens Doors

British Satanist Aleister Crowley, a man who fancied himself the "wickedest man on the planet," was Grand Master of the Ordo Templi Orientis (O.T.O.) and also founded the mysterious and Luciferian, Order of Astrum Argentinium. He once ruefully and knowingly intimated that after he had independently learned and practiced how to do the secret handshakes of a number of other secret societies and orders throughout Europe, he traveled around from city to city and discovered that by knowing how to convey the appropriate handshake, he was invited into what is normally the guarded inner sanctum of almost all the groups. They were persuaded simply by his handshake that Crowley was eligible to attend their conclaves and be made privy to their most closely guarded secrets.

The average Mason or member of other secret orders knows little of the signs and symbols of his own order, let alone that of others. In my work for this book, I have communicated with a number of ex-Masons, but few were able to identify any but the most rudimentary of signs and symbols. I did far better with Masonic encyclopedias and with modern and ancient magical texts and guides.

I Give Credit to...

In addition to the individuals listed in the acknowledgements of the title page, I would also like to acknowledge the assistance of a few very special friends invaluable to me in preparing this book. I'd like, therefore, to give credit to:

- ❖ **Lawrence Patterson**, publisher of *Criminal Politics* magazine and one of the world's leading experts on global finances and investments.
- ❖ **Alex Jones**, well-known radio personality and top-notch producer of many videos documenting the rise of the police state.
- ❖ **Dr. Cathy Burns**, author of the excellent *Masonic and Occult Symbols Illustrated*, as well as *The Hidden Secrets of the Eastern Star*.
- ❖ **Dean Grace**, author of *A Little Guide to the All-Seeing Eye Symbol On Our Dollar Bill*.
- ❖ **Ralph Epperson**, author of *Masonry: Conspiracy Against Christianity*, *The Unseen Hand*, and other fine books.
- ❖ **Dr. Gail Riplinger**, author of the bestselling classic, *New Age Bible Versions*.
- ❖ **David Meyer**, occult researcher and publisher of *Last Trumpet* newsletter.
- ❖ **Michael Hoffman, II**, author of the groundbreaking book, *Secret Societies and Psychological Warfare*.
- ❖ **Fritz Springmeier**, author of *Bloodlines of the Illuminati* and other revealing works.
- ❖ **Robert Gaylon Ross**, author of *Who's Who of the Elite* and *The Elite Don't Dare Let Us Tell the People*.

I also wish to acknowledge the late Jim Shaw and Jim Keith, Bill Schnoebelen, Tom

McKenney, Ed Decker, James Spencer, David Bay, Dr. Dennis Cuddy, Reginald Haupt, Jr., Dr. O.J. Graham, Jeff Rense, Des Griffin, Gary Blevins, Dr. Stanley Monteith, Jack Chick, Ted Pike, Donn de Grande Pré, Jack Roper, and Jüri Lina, all of whose authoritative research and writings provided me with valuable information as well as incalculable inspiration.

Hands On Membership Not Required

Illuminati paid provocateurs and other would-be critics might suggest that because you and I are not Masons or Illuminists, my research in *Codex Magica*—or your own independent research—has no authority. In answer, I am happy to respond by noting that the best of homicide detectives have never been murdered nor participated in such; few lifeguards have had an incident in which they were drowning and required assistance; most lawyers have never been sued; most psychiatrists have never been admitted as a patient to a mental institution; most neurosurgeons have never had brain surgery; most sports writers have never played pro-football or pro-baseball yet they report and comment on the same; most prison wardens have never themselves been locked up as convicts, and no historians have lived in the past centuries of history about which they amass information and facts and comment about.

It doesn't take a monster to know that human monsters exist or a serial killer to know that murdering innocent people involves savage and evil acts. And there is abundant evidence that exists about the Illuminati and secret societies so that we do not have to join and participate in these repugnant groups to know what they are all about. *Codex Magica* proves that.

A Challenge to Critics

I hereby challenge any and all Masons and other members of secret societies to meet me on neutral ground with neutral observers in a contest, a duel of wits, if you will, to see who knows more about the subject matter presented in this book. Until such time as the critic accepts my challenge and is willing to publicly display that he knows as much or more about secret handshakes and grips, symbols, marks, logos and other occultic matters, I suggest that the critic shrink back to the shadowy confines of his Masonic Temple, synagogue, or shrine and refrain from empty, futile criticism.

As for those skeptics and naysayers who get their kicks by pretending to know— just know!—that these things cannot be true, that "conspiracies" just do not exist and who maintain that anyone who even dares to mention the existence of any group called the "Illuminati" just has to be wrong, may I humbly recommend that they earnestly burn the midnight oil, carefully read this book, and examine the evidence in a fair-minded and objective manner? Many a friend has written telling the author that he likewise was once a doubter and skeptic, until, that is, he had heard and considered *all* the evidence. In this regard, the Holy Scriptures have a tremendous bit of advice worthy of consideration:

He that answereth a matter before he heareth it, it is folly and shame unto him.
— Proverbs 18:13

ONE

Caution!—You Are Now Entering The Forbidden Zone

Only puny secrets need protection. Big discoveries are protected by public incredulity.

— Marshall McLuhan
Take Today

What is one to do when, in order to rule men, it is necessary to deceive them?

— Helena Blavatsky
The Secret Doctrine

What you will read and see in this book is forbidden to you. Discovering these things could be highly dangerous to your health. Forbidden knowledge is sweet, but also deadly. Many men have died for revealing far fewer secrets than are found herein.

I am not being overdramatic nor attempting to be sensational. This is a warning: Make very sure that you possess the daring and the courage to proceed before you go any further.

Lingering in my mind are the names of courageous men who have gone before you and me and are now dead because they exposed the forbidden knowledge of the Illumined Ones. Captain William Morgan—abducted, kidnapped and ritually murdered, his lifeless body dumped in a lake after he published a book unmasking Masonic secrets. Danny Casolaro—suicided, having his wrists cut and bleeding to death in a hotel room where he had gone to meet a confidential source; Paul Wilcher, found nude, his body stiff as it sat on a toilet in his home, only days after he mailed his exposé manuscript to U.S. Attorney-General Janet Reno; and Wolfgang Amadeus Mozart, the world-famous classical composer, who paid the ultimate penalty, the *Aqua Toffeta*, arsenic poisoning that wracked his body.

Poor Mozart. He, too, had revealed some of the secrets of Freemasonry. Blackballed by The Order, so frightened were his friends and family that not one human soul so much as attended his funeral. It is said that Mozart's faithful dog followed dutifully behind the lonely funeral wagon. The sad and forlorn canine was the only living creature in sight as the body of the man all of Europe had once toasted and applauded was taken to its burial site.

So, I ask you, dear friend, once again: Do you dare to discover the secrets many have been punished for merely knowing, let alone revealing? Are you sure, very sure, you want to enter the Forbidden Zone?

Immersed In Evil

You see, we are surrounded by evil on every side—quite literally immersed in it—but the wicked and the deceivers want us to believe that evildoing is exceptional. From childhood we have been taught that evil and corruption are the province of the few, that most people are virtuous, honest, and good, that most of our politicians truly have our interests at heart, that the social system, with the exception of just a few deviants and criminal types, is basically sound.

With such assurances, most people breathe a deep sigh of relief. "Don't worry, be happy," said the words of a fun-time novelty song a decade ago. And most of us appreciate and agree with that sentiment. After all, it's not nice to be negative, to be a skeptic in the midst of a nation of wannabe happy faces.

Unfortunately, the masses who believe this nonsense have been gulled and are destined to receive, very soon, a rude shock and an abrupt awakening.

Grand Deception

As Christopher Mark observed recently in an insight-filled article entitled *"Grand Deception: The Theft of America and the World,"* "The world is completely corrupt beyond your wildest dreams, and the United States is, perhaps, the most gullible of all nations."[1] Mark goes on to explain:

> For now, grasp this: The world you believe exists does not exist. We live in a form of the Matrix, not unlike the world portrayed in John Carpenter's movie, "They Live," except that high government officials and international bankers are the elite who control all you see and hear as did the aliens portrayed in the movie. [2]

But, the foolish may object, we have the media to protect us from the corrupt. We cannot be deceived as long as there is a free press to act as our watchdog.

Ah, but there's the rub. There is no free press! Christopher Mark adds:

> The news is a farce. As is the case with the financial institutions, which are

concentrated in the hands of the few, long ago the media was bought and paid for…What you read and what you see on a daily basis is largely manufactured. You are being lied to each and every day.[3]

Thomas Mann, the keen social observer and philosopher, once suggested that men are erroneously taught to believe that it is forbidden and wrong to expose the works of darkness, or to reveal the machinations of evildoers, especially evildoers who, though they act in hellish ways, the deceived world at large so obviously holds in the highest regard:

> That is the secret delight and security of hell, that it is not to be informed on, that it is protected from speech, that it just is, but cannot be made public in the newspaper, or be brought by any word to critical knowledge.[4]

Secret Delight

How interesting the realization that, as Thomas Mann puts it, hell takes "secret delight" in its ability to keep secrets. *Proverbs 9:13-18* seems to have a relation to this. It states:

> *A foolish woman sitteth in the high place of the city, To call passengers who go right on their ways: she saith to him, bread eaten in secret is pleasant. But he knoweth not that the dead are there; and that her guests are in the depths of hell.*

Why do the Illuminati value secrecy so highly? Why all the mysterious, encoded signs, handshakes, symbols, language, and codes? One finds many reasons. For one thing, the psychopath—these are the kind of people who are Illuminists—seems to be drawn to the darkness, to mysterious perversions and deep occultism. "Nothing so arouses the deep mind's attention than the call of the dark, arcane and mysterious," Paul Huston writes in his book, *Mastering Witchcraft.*[5]

Secrecy is deemed essential amongst witchcraft sects, and witchcraft is, in essence, Illuminism. Huston explains: "Now witchcraft consists of knowledge, and knowledge brings power. Power shared is power lost. Although we have entered the Age of Aquarius, along with its attendant freedom and loosening of restrictions, it will still be very much in your interests as a witch to shroud certain of your doings in a reasonable veil of secrecy."[6]

As you will discover in studying the pages of *Codex Magica*, the Illuminati certainly do have much to hide. Seeing as how the leaders of this notorious organization are responsible for hardship, bloodshed and revolutionary terror on a global scale, if their secrets were found out, there would be hell to pay. If the masses ever were to wake up from their trance and begin to understand just how horribly they have been deceived, they would angrily rise enmasse and string up the elite from the nearest light pole.

The Most Terrible Secret of All

But there's also the matter of the most terrible secret of all, the secret that, if discovered, would sound the death knell for the Illuminati and Freemasonry. Manly P. Hall, 33°, touched on this in his book, *Lectures on Ancient Philosophy*:

> Freemasonry is a fraternity within a Fraternity—an outer organization, concealing an inner brotherhood of the elect. The invisible society is a secret fraternity dedicated to a MYSTERIOUS SECRET.[7]

As Hall alludes, Freemasonry hides its greatest secret even from its membership at large—only an invisible "inner brotherhood" is entrusted with it.

Robert Guffey, writing in the book, *The Conspiracy Reader*, reports that the "cryptocrats," as he calls the elite, consider most Americans to be mere sheep who must be kept from discovering "the black cauldron of dirty secrets" hidden to them.[8] The MYSTERIOUS SECRET of which Manly P. Hall, 33° writes, surely falls into this category of dirty secrets kept squirreled away in the black cauldron.

The dirtiest secret found inside that black cauldron—THE MYSTERIOUS SECRET—is this: That the unknown "God" worshipped by the Masons and called by such hazy, nebulous names as the Great Architect of the Universe and by codenames such as Abaddon, Mahabone, and Jahbuhlun, is actually none other than *Satan*, or *Lucifer*. That is the greatest of secrets that the Illuminati must shield from view.

The Illuminated (so-called "enlightened") man who knows this darkest of secrets is taught by his superiors and comes to believe that all who are in on the secret are somehow more sophisticated, urbane, intelligent, and spiritually astute, than the uncouth, vulgar, and coarse people who stupidly follow after the God of the Holy Bible. Stupid people deserve to be deceived, say the Masons and Illuminists. Thus, as Emile Grillot DeGivry comments, the elite "conceal in order to baffle the vulgar."[9]

Marie Roberts and Hugh Ormsby-Lennon, in *Secret Texts: The Literature of Secret Societies*, note that the rituals, rites, symbols, emblems, and other tools of the secret societies are "Mysteries that must not be revealed to the profane, lewd, and unworthy."[10] How does it feel, dear reader, to realize that the wicked men of the Illuminati and of the Lodge and other secret societies consider you, me, and everyone outside their own special preserve, as "profane, lewd, and unworthy?"

Symbols as Secrets

To maintain their rotten and corrupt body of secrets, the Illuminati leaders and groups employ *symbols*. The rites, ceremonies, hand signs, and grips of the Illuminists are based on the science and art of *symbolism*.

It is said that symbolism began as recorded in the Bible's book of *Genesis* when God put a "mark" or sign on Cain who had slain his brother, Abel. Throughout human history, marks, signs, pictures, and hieroglyphs came to be used to convey words, ideas, concepts, and secrets.

"By symbols," wrote Thomas Carlyle in *Sartor Resartus*, "is man guided and commanded, made happy made wretched. He everywhere finds himself surrounded with symbols, recognized as such or not recognized." [11]

As you'll discover in *Codex Magica*, the elite use many symbols and signs to hide and obfuscate their magical work and alchemy. In the Blue Lodge (the first three degrees), the initiate takes an oath of obligation, pledging:

> I will always hail, EVER CONCEAL, AND NEVER REVEAL, any of the arts, parts,
> or points of the hidden mysteries of Ancient Free Masonry… [12]

The Order of the Eastern Star, the women's Masonic organization, informs its
new members that the Order teaches them of their duties and obligations "by means
of SECRET SIGNS AND PASSWORDS."[13] The initiate is further instructed that she
must bind herself "to preserve the most sacred SECRECY respecting the work of the
Order."[14]

Symbols are more than just pictures. Consider: When you and I, as patriotic
citizens, see the red, white, and blue flag of the U.S.A. waving aloft, many emotions
are aroused in our minds and hearts. Memories sometimes gush forth, feelings of
love of country, home, and family; perhaps deep appreciation for our country's
founders, its Constitution, and for the soldiers and servicemen who have died to
protect and keep us free. All this bound up in just one symbol.

To the Masons and other Illuminists, their *occult* symbols also embody a deep and
varied set of meanings. Alex Horne, in *Sources of Masonic Symbolism*, distinguishes
between a mere "emblem" and a "symbol." An emblem is something that stands for
something else, he says, while "a symbol has a moral and spiritual meaning."[15]

That "moral and spiritual meaning" is, of necessity, reserved as secret in nature
by these corrupt cultists, because, if their secrets should be exposed to the light, their
Great Work and Grand Plan would be vulnerable to destruction, as it should be. But
kept secret, the symbols and signs of the Illuminati exert a strong force. Foster Bailey,
33°, in *The Spirit of Freemasonry*, explains:

> A symbol veils or hides a secret, and it is that which veils mysterious forces. These
> energies when released can have a potent effect.[16]

To the man whose entire life is immersed in magical symbols, signs, and codes,
and who has taken a solemn oath to maintain secrecy in fear of disclosure, the world
takes on a supernatural, paranoid quality. Indeed, such men are schizophrenic in
tendency, being torn between their role in the normal everyday world and their
underground existence in the sordid world of their occult fraternity. Illuminists are,
indeed, very dangerous men.

Ancient Origins—Babylonian

Now it is important to understand that almost all the symbols and signs of the elite
are very ancient in origin. Former Scottish Rite Freemasonry Sovereign Grand
Commander Henry C. Clausen, 33°, who was appointed in 1942 by President
Roosevelt to head up the Commission to Investigate the Pearl Harbor Attack, writes
that the footsteps of The Order go deep, and its symbols are thousands of years old.

"They arose in ancient ages," Clausen states. "The signs, symbols, and
inscriptions come to us from across long, drifting centuries and will be found in
ancient Sumerian clay tablet libraries of the cities of Lir, Lagash, and others of the first

true urban civilization. This, occurred about 600 years before Egypt was civilized…"[17]

In other words, Clausen is telling his Masonic readers that their signs and symbols came from Babylon.

The Holy Bible warns that the Ancient Mystery Religion of wicked Babylon will bounce back into demonic prevalence in the last days (see *Revelation 13, 17, and 18*), and here we have the Sovereign Grand Commander, the international chieftain of the Masonic Lodge, informing us of the Babylonian origins of the secret symbols and signs of his Illuminist Order.

When we realize that, for the elite, their symbols are claimed to be infused with dynamic life—to be real things, active images that make and testify and create, we begin to comprehend the powerful and explosive meaning with which the Illuminati endow their signs and symbols.

To them, these are not just geometric shapes, architectural patterns, lines, and circles. Their signs and symbols both live and possess creative power. They are archetypes and thoughtforms. In sum, they are real things that perform. One is reminded, therefore, of the *"image of the beast"* which, in the last days, is prophesied to both move about and to speak *(Revelation 13)*.

Pity the Poor, Hoodwinked Mason

It's bad enough that the elite hide their dirty little (and big) secrets behind such smoke screens as secret hand signs, codes, etc. But what is remarkably obscene is that they hoodwink their own people.

The highest levels of the Freemasons, for example, have a special word for the manner in which they seek to deceive and mislead not only the "profane" (you and me!) but the vast majority of fellow Masons. That word is *hoodwink*. It is defined as the effort put forth by the lying men at the top echelons to keep lower-level members in darkness.

In the *Encyclopedia of Freemasonry*, editor Dr. Albert Mackey, 33°, a former Sovereign Grand Commander, claims that secrecy, silence, and deceit—in other words, *hoodwink*, is an absolute necessity so that, "the mysteries of our art should be preserved."[18]

Helena Blavatsky, co-Mason and founder of Theosophy, was unusually candid when she once remarked, "What is one to do, when in order to rule men, it is necessary to deceive them?…For almost invariably the more simple, the more silly, and the more gross the phenomenon, the more likely it is to succeed."[19]

Listen to the admission of Albert Pike, former Sovereign Grand Commander who Masonic historian Manly P. Hall, 33°, magnificently praised as a "Masonic Prometheus…a king among men by the divine right of merit:"

> Masonry, like all the Religions, all the Mysteries, Hermeticism, and Alchemy, conceals its secrets from all except the Adepts and Sages, or the Elect, and uses false explanations and misinterpretations of its symbols to mislead those who deserve only to be misled; to conceal the Truth, which it calls Light, from them, and to draw them away from it.[20]

What impudence! What arrogance! Pike is letting us in on the deceit. Even if a man is a Mason, he may not be adjudged worthy of being promoted as one of the "Adepts and Sages, or the Elect." In that case, along with non-Masons, he is purposely misled by "false explanations and misinterpretations." And according to Pike, he deserves to be misled.

Secret Doctrine Withheld

George Steinmetz, yet another Masonic author, notes, "There is a SECRET DOCTRINE in Freemasonry! That secret doctrine is concealed, rather than revealed by the very lectures which, we (Masons) are told, offer a rational explanation of the ceremonies of initiation."[21]

Hoodwinked! Pity the poor, foolish man who becomes a Freemason! In the very first degree ritual, that of Entered Apprentice, a blindfold is put over his eyes, and a cable-tow is hung around his neck. Symbolically, the dumb candidate is "HOODWINKED." Little does he know that his superiors intentionally set out to deceive the candidate and they contrive their deceit through all the ritual degrees up to and including the 33rd.

Oh my! So the poor Masons must sit and listen to a bunch of boring lectures, with superiors rattling on and on about what are described as the "Mysteries," when, really, it's all just malarkey because the true explanations—the SECRET DOCTRINE—is concealed to all except the few favored "Adepts."

This is why, when I interview lower-level Masonic friends of mine who are more than happy to privately confide to me all the "secrets" they have learned, I often find that almost everything they think they know is pure junk. The hard facts—the really useful info—is reserved for the Masonic muckety-mucks, though it may be discovered with diligent investigation by others, too, no matter how much the Masonic order vainly attempts to conceal and deny.

As Albert Pike relates, "What is most worth knowing in Masonry is never very openly taught. The symbols are displayed, but they are mute. It is by hints only…that the initiate is put upon the track of the hidden secret." [22]

How does one finally discover the inner secrets of Freemasonry? My own experience provides the answer. It has taken me many years of meticulous research and study of the Ancient Mystery Religions of Babylon, Sumeria, Greece, Rome, China, etc. I have spent many nights reading old textbooks and treatises on medieval and occult subjects; conducted intensive investigation of the rituals and symbols of scores of secret societies and orders; and spent years examining the true teachings and practices of New Ageism, witchcraft and Satanism. Moreover, without study of the Holy Bible and constant referral back to it, much of the knowledge I have acquired could not be properly understood.

Masonic expert Lynn F. Perkins alludes to the gigantic amount of extracurricular research and work needed to uncover the greatest secrets of the Masonic Fraternity. He writes:

The true wisdom is concealed and hidden, not only from those who do not join the Masonic Order but also from those who "take" the degrees; and it will remain hidden until each Mason seeks revelation and finds the Truth for himself. There are no interpretations in the Ritual; they have to be sought elsewhere."[23]

Pike, echoing Steinmetz, Hall, Perkins and all the other high-level Masonic authorities, goes so far as to mock and disparage lower-level Masons, especially those who have earned only the first three degrees ("the Blue degrees"). After acknowledging that the lower-level brethren are "intentionally misled," he goes on to say that it is not intended that the initiate understand the symbols and deepest secrets of the Order, but worse, the Masonic Lodge's rituals and lectures are designed so that the lower-level Masons shall *imagine* he does understand them! It is only at a later time, as he has moved up the ladder of degrees, that the purposely dumbed-down Mason discovers he's been had, that he's been played for a fool. In other words, he's been *hoodwinked!*

So, in effect, Masons are lied to, tricked, made fun of, and intentionally led astray, with only a little knowledge added to their brain reservoirs as they advance up the chain. Meanwhile, the poor, pitiful souls imagine they are really in on all the super-duper secrets of the Craft. Their Masonic superiors play them all for suckers.

P.T. Barnum, of Ringling Brothers, Barnum & Bailey Circus fame, surely was right when he exclaimed, "There's a sucker born every minute." To which yours truly, author of *Codex Magica,* might add: "…and a 32nd or 33rd degree Mason is behind the veil laughing his head off and rolling in the aisle every time a new sucker is initiated into the 1st degree of Freemasonry."

Shining Light on the Darkness

The Brotherhood of Darkness, as a good friend of mine, Dr. Stanley Monteith, calls the Illuminati, is quite confident it can easily maintain the highest level of secrecy regarding the actual meaning and import of its signs and symbols. Its leaders believe they can even afford to communicate these signals and messages in plain sight, sure in the knowledge that the trance-like masses are incapable of recognizing the awful, ongoing masquerade of deception that stares them right in the face.

Martin Short, who authored a book, *Inside the Brotherhood*, exposing the Masonic Order inside Great Britain, observed that Masons, believing their secrets to be oblivious to detection, are known to mutter words of near-contempt as they sing a little ditty called "The Entered Apprentice's Song." A verse of this melody goes:

> The world is in pain, Our secrets to gain.
> And still let them wonder and gaze on;
> They ne'er can divine, the Word or the Sign
> Of a Free and Accepted Mason. [24]

Oh, we can't, can we? Perhaps it is true that the uninformed "world" at large cannot divine the Word and Sign of the Mason, but the readers of *Codex Magica* shall do exactly that. Let us therefore move forward with eager anticipation as we uncover in this book many of the most precious and despicable secrets of the elite—things they never in a million years thought we would discover.

Lives of Quiet Desperation...and Torment

Why have the Illuminists succeeded in their hoodwinking efforts up to now? Is it not because of the gullibility of the general public? It has been said that, "most men lead lives of quiet desperation." This is true, and so it is that in their silent morass of desperation, most seek to dull their senses through alcohol, drugs, sex, and entertainment. Tormented within, but doing their utmost to keep a smile on their faces, unable to face the truth, too frightened to even admit to themselves that anything is awry, most men do not even know who their tormentors really are.

To escape reality, these men shrink from the facts, hoping against hope that all will turn out satisfactory in the end. The reality that a monstrous conspiracy exists against them and against their loved ones becomes an enormous burden they simply cannot bear. Cowards, it seems, die a thousand deaths.

Swedish researcher Jüri Lina, whose book, *Architects of Deception*, is a revealing, fact-filled exposé of the secret society of Freemasonry, warns that the ideology of "Illuminism," propagated by international Freemasonry and other secret elite groups, is an overwhelming, hidden danger to all of us. It has already brought the most violent upheavals and revolutions and is responsible for the "moral and spiritual degeneration of the individual."[25]

Yet astonishingly, writes Lina, most men and women are hopelessly oblivious to the very forces that most affect their lives on a daily and continuing basis. Lina consequently puts forth this word of caution:

> Those who do not examine the different aspects of the conspiracy will remain incapable of understanding the world...Our rulers want us to believe that a lack of historical knowledge and ignorance about the secrets of nature constitutes true knowledge.[26]

Lina laments the rampant ignorance by the masses who possess little or no understanding of the vast evil on their very doorstep about to break down the door and enter therein. Wisely, he contends that the ignorant, while not the inventors of evil things, nevertheless are accomplices and contributors to evil. "Not being aware of these facts," he writes, "is in itself an evil because ignorance serves evil."[27]

"The Little Man Who Wasn't There"

Dr. Peter Ruckman, author of many fine books exposing the conspiracy and defending the Bible, in his newsletter recently penned an article about "The Little Man Who Wasn't There."[28] Ruckman sagely observed that historians, like other establishment "experts," can scarcely be trusted, for they invariably write a history they would *like* to believe. They limit themselves to reporting only that which comports and agrees with the *socially accepted* view of history and "truth." If a set of facts is unpleasant or inconvenient to the officially approved mantra, or version, of events, reality must suffer. Facts must become non-facts and lies must be converted into "reliable truths." Ruckman remarks:

When I was a boy we repeated several little doggerels that turned out to be gems of wisdom in content. One went: "Last night I saw upon the stair a little man who wasn't there; he wasn't there again today; oh gee, I wish he'd go away!"[29]

"Some nonexistent spooks," Ruckman adds, "are very persistent."[30]

In *Codex Magica*, we shine a bright spotlight on the little man sitting on the stair, and — voila! — we discover the incontrovertible fact that he is not only there, he is not a little man at all. He's a giant, dark, wicked, corrupt, conspiring, sly, cunning, devious, dangerous ogre who fully deserves all the contemptible attention we can focus on him. He's more than a spook, he's a bloodsucking parasite, a monster who is sitting on the stair blocking us from entering, a criminal thug lying in wait to waylay you and me and rob us of our belongings, our health, our very lives.

Without him sitting there detrimentally blocking our path, the world would be a far better place. Certainly a safer and happier place.

"Two Plus Two Make Four"

Bob Whitaker, a South Carolinian who has done many fine and adventurous things in his life, teaching college classes, serving as a senior staffer on Capitol Hill, and writing copy for the *Voice of America* radio broadcast, points out that anyone today who simply believes the obvious is ignorantly and unfairly branded an extremist, a conspiracy-monger, a racist, or worse. Men are not free, Whitaker suggests, to tell the truth:

> In George Orwell's book *1984*, it turns out that the whole hideous totalitarianism that crushed the hero is based on ending one simple, useless-sounding freedom; "Freedom," it says, "is the freedom to say that two plus two make four."[31]

How incredible! Whitaker is right on target. Who would have ever thought that in the once great United States of America would reside almost 300 million souls, virtually every one of whom today is shaking in his boots, quivering, numb with fear over what dreadful things might happen if he just once simply put his foot down, gritted his teeth, and spit out the words:

> I see the little man on the stair. He is there!
> And two plus two makes four.
> And that's all there is to it. Period!

How sad that most men, by their cowardly silence, become secret collaborators, acquiescing in their own enslavement. What a marvelous and wonderful world this would be if just a small group of honest and thoughtful, courageous men and women would view the revealing and provocative photographs, illustrations, and proofs in *Codex Magica* and exclaim with all their might in a loud, loud voice to all within hearing range: "I see it. I no longer will remain bound by the willful ignorance that binds the multitudes. I will tell others. I will speak out until, someday, maybe soon, the whole, rotten occult Illuminati establishment comes crashing down!"

TWO

The Megalomania and Rage of the Psychopaths—Why the Illuminati Do What They Do

All of my means are rational, only my ends are insane.

—"Captain Ahab" in *Moby Dick*
by Herman Melville

Why do the Illuminati do what they do? After many years of research and investigation into their behavior and conduct, and understanding their goals and ambition, I am persuaded these men fit the definition of *psychopathic personalities*. They are *psychopaths* and as such they are afflicted with the dangerous malady called *megalomania*.

Here is how *Webster's Dictionary* defines these words:

Psychopathic personality: 1. An emotionally and behaviorally disordered state characterized by clear perception of reality except in the individual's social and moral obligations and often by the pursuit of immediate personal gratification in criminal acts, drug addiction, or sexual perversion. 2. A person having a psychopathic personality.

Megalomania: 1. A mania for great or grandiose performance. 2. A delusional mental disorder that is marked by infantile feelings of personal omnipotence and grandeur.

In sum, the psychopath possesses a clear perception of reality—he knows full well what he's doing—but he refuses to abide by society's morals. Instead, he pursues personal gratification in such things as criminal acts, drug addiction and sexual perversion.

Combined with feelings of megalomania, the psychopath has visions of his own omnipotence—he thinks he is a god—and has delusions of grandeur. Since he is persuaded he is divine and not bound by the rules that apply to other, less godly beings, the psychopath is a dangerous person, indeed. Dr. Essi Viding, of the Institute of Psychiatry at the prestigious King's College in London, England, has done extensive study of the motivation and behavior of the psychopathic personality. Dr. Viding cautions that the psychopath "shows a lack of remorse, conscience, and understanding of the feelings of others."[1] Sounds like a psychological description and profile of a lot of our world's foremost political and corporate leaders today, doesn't it?

Insane, Parasitic, Immoral, and Dangerous

Frustrate the unbridled ambition of the psychopath and he strikes out in a controlled, yet insane, fit of anger and rage. If the psychopath holds a position of great responsibility—say, President of the United States or dictator of a technologically advanced nation, he can do some major damage.

William Krasner, in an article way back in 1946 entitled *Neurotica*, warned of the dangers that lie ahead for societies who fall into the grip of the criminal psychopath. He wrote:

> The psychopath is a disruptive, parasitic, immoral influence. Any group, while it may for various reasons support and even honor the psychopath...in direct proportion to the extent that the psychopath is tolerated, that his attitudes find support in the culture pattern, to that extent it is an unhealthy society.[2]

Tragically, America has actually become a dangerous haven for mentally disordered psychopaths. The Council on Foreign Relations, an Illuminist organization, whose 3,000 members run almost every facet of our federal government, especially at the highest official level, is no doubt populated by a majority of psychopaths.

The Masonic Order in the U.S.A. has some two million initiates who have voluntarily undergone occultic-laced rituals to be accepted as common brethren. The ranks of the Masonic Order are loaded, I believe, with dangerous psychopaths. The United Nations organization, endorsed and funded by our Congress, is a seething cesspool of unrepentant psychopaths.

Liars and Deceivers

Psychopaths are inveterate liars and deceivers. In fact, they lie on an Orwellian scale. If confronted with a situation in which veracity and truth are prerequisite, the men who run America's federal government or who sit as CEOs of this nation's top financial institutions and corporations, have the psychopathic "talent" of looking the citizenry square in the face and insisting that, "two plus two do not make four."

Being deceivers and practitioners of the Craft (witchcraft), the psychopaths who lead the inner circle of the Illuminati are more than capable of standing before the cameras and working magic and occult ritual right before our very eyes, pretending all the while they are simply acting normal as usual. It has been said that if one really wants to hide a great secret, he should conceal it in plain sight. Well, this maxim certainly applies to the disordered, but somehow illogical, behavior of the men of the Illuminati. It is not rational to do what these men do in public, in plain sight, yet they do it and expect to get away with it. And they *do* get away with it! Or at least, they did, before this book was published revealing their unseemly, scripted, ritual behavior.

Why all the occultic ritual rigmarole? Why do some of the world's richest and influential men take the risks they do in working their demonic magical acts in plain sight, so that they are pictured doing it in major newsmagazines and newspapers, on television, and in other avenues with huge potential audiences?

Edgar Allen Poe, the famous novelist of dark mood and mysterious suspense, once wrote a tale, *"Perverse of the Imp,"* in which he suggested that criminals often have an overwhelming, all consuming desire to publicly confess their devious crimes. Could it be this is why the Illuminati so flagrantly flaunt their occultic wares? Is it that they possess a unique taste for deceit and chicanery? Or is the performance in plain sight accomplished because it is believed to infuse power and mastery into their sought for aims and goals?

Mockers and Tricksters

Do they simply enjoy mocking and tricking us? Teasing and playing with our minds, realizing that the vast majority of people in society are willing dupes? It was, after all, serial killer John Wayne Gacy—certainly a psychopathic personality—who once bragged, *"A clown could get away with murder."* Gacy, you see, enjoyed dressing up as a mischievous and gleeful clown and visiting hospital wards to cheer up young male patients. He also took great pleasure, in the confines of his home, in torturing and killing young boys.

All of these are reasons why psychopaths of the Illuminati pose and parade occultly in front of cameras, exchange ritual handshakes, and otherwise taunt the public. Remember, according to Webster's, the psychopath is immoral, selfishly flaunts societal mores, is infantile in personality, is delusional, and has feelings of grandeur and omnipotence. Men who think they are omnipotent gods must take extreme delight in putting things over the masses whom they consider inferior and sub-human.

Twelve Keys to Understanding

Moreover, after long and careful consideration I propose that in addition to these factors, there are at least twelve other reasons, or factors, why the Illuminati persist in their seemingly delusional and infantile behavior. Each of the twelve reasons is represented by one of the key words listed below:

❖ Secrecy
❖ Magic
❖ Build
❖ Power
❖ Pride
❖ Elitism
❖ Signal
❖ Wealth
❖ Please
❖ Invocation
❖ Encourage
❖ Rebellion

It is important we examine these twelve keys to understanding why the Illuminati do what they do. We have already covered the topic of the elite's obsession with *Secrecy* in Chapter One. In the following sections and pages of this present chapter, we will look at the remaining 12 keys. We begin with the Illuminati's employment of *Magic* to accomplish their ends.

❖ *MAGIC*

Magic is defined in *The New Encyclopedia Britannica* as "ritual performance or activity believed to influence human or natural events through access to an external mystical force beyond the ordinary human sphere."[3] This is an exceptionally accurate description of what magic is and reveals to us exactly why the Illuminati consider magic of such extraordinary importance in the accomplishment of their aims.

That magic is an *occult* activity is also indicated in *The New Encyclopedia Britannica*. So we are not talking here about magicians playing parlor tricks or entertainment extravaganzas—pulling rabbits out of hats, sawing beautiful girls in half, being chained in an aquarium full of water and escaping, etc. Instead, as the encyclopedia so well puts it, magic is *ritual performance*. It is an occult ritual.

In this occult ritual, the "magician," the Illuminist, believes he can "influence human or natural events." So in *Codex Magica*, we see pictured the Illuminati giving secret signs, sharing concealed grips and handshakes, displaying symbols and communicating hidden messages. We realize that in performing these magical works, the Illuminist actually believes he is influencing human behavior or otherwise causing real events to occur in a particular, planned way or intended manner. *Magic happens!* is a popular slogan among witches, occultists, and Illuminists—things change, reality is transformed. Alchemical transformation occurs. *Society is shaped by occult plan.*

However, to accomplish these aims, this shaping of society, the Illuminist, as an occult practitioner, fully understands that he is accessing, as the encyclopedia definition explains "an external mystical force beyond the ordinary human sphere."

Now, the Illuminist may imagine that he is merely accessing the "cosmic energy force" or that he is tapping into a "fourth dimension," or the "ethereal atmosphere."

Thus he may well lay claim that his magical work, or activity, is benign—that it is simply *white* magic, good magic, the right-handed path as the Satanists and other occultists call it.

But as we shall see, the highest authorities in the occult world admit that there is no essential difference between *white magic* and *black magic* (the supposedly bad, evil, left-handed path). Magic is magic.

Who, or what, then, is the Illuminist accessing in his *ritual performance* of magic? From my many years of research and investigation into the works and plans of the Illuminati, witches, Satanists, shamans, masons, and other occultists, I declare without hesitation that what these men are doing—knowingly in some cases, unwittingly in others, is calling on, that is invoking devils from an invisible realm ("beyond the ordinary human sphere").

The occult and the Masonic communities can call these evil presences by any coverup name they wish—the Great White Brotherhood, Shamballa, planetary entities, the Hierarchy, etc., but, in fact, the working of magic, I am convinced, is nothing less than the invocation, or inviting, of devils.

This, indeed, is a very dangerous activity; yet the Illuminati has designed its many rituals, signs, codes, symbols, architecture, art, and other devices so that the world around us has become a veritable Grand Theater of the Occult. Because of the Illuminati, the whole world is enchanted, dark with supernaturalism, and the one the Holy Bible calls the Prince of the Power of the Air, also referred to as Satan and Lucifer, must be very proud of his human minions.

❖ BUILD

You will find pictured in *Codex Magica* a variety of different types of people. There are the celebrities and the rich and famous, the glitzy or jet-set people who are into Illuminism, occultism, and witchcraft because it is trendy and fashionable. Among this group are some who are into the Jewish Cabala—movie and Broadway stars, singer/entertainers, activists, and so forth. These are often ignorant people who are used by the Illuminati to extract money, for sex, and as novelties. When the money runs out, they grow too old for use as sex partners, or the novelty wears out, they are often cast out or retired and no longer have access to the "Inner Circle" of the Elite.

Then there are the do-gooders—people who support revolution and the socialistic, globalist, environmentalist, and similar aims of the Illuminati for what they fancy is the good of society. Sometimes these people sign up for Cabala classes taught by rabbis; they eagerly join liberal social issue organizations and may also be involved in the secret societies and orders, though at a lower level. Again, we see these people are mere dupes.

Finally, we see several strata of Illuminati elite—major politicians and bureaucrats, including Presidents, Prime Ministers, Chancellors, etc., as well as some corporate CEOs, financiers, media moguls, and others. These are major players, but again, they are dupes because there is a secret, invisible, arcane or hidden "Inner Circle" which works behind the scenes and tells these major players what to do.

This higher level of the Illuminati elite have historically thought of themselves as

The Builders. There is even a classic Masonic textbook by this very title. The Builders believe that Jehovah God did Adam and Eve a disservice by driving them out of the Garden. They rankle at the fact that Nimrod, the King of Babylon, was confounded in building the Tower of Babel, and they are seized with rage over the destruction of *their* Temple in Jerusalem.

Indeed, the Builders are angered that every time they have sought to bring the world together as One, they have been thwarted by God. All of their chosen disciples, the Caesars, Charlemagne, Napoleon, Hitler, Stalin, FDR, Mao, saw their grand plan of conquest go down to resounding defeat. But still, they strive to complete their assigned mission.

Now it is the New World Order (or Bush's "democracy for all nations") they have in mind. The United Nations is to be "reformed," that is—strengthened. The few rogue nations that remain must be dealt with.

The economies of all the nations must be equalized, enterprise extinguished, constitutions amended or ignored, private property seized or regulated severely, religions transformed, etc. Those are the goals.

In other words, to *build* their New World Order, the elite intend to *destroy* the existing World Order. The old must go to make way for the new. It is the Hegelian Dialectical Process that is being used to achieve this prime objective. What is above must become what is below states the Illuminist law of alchemical transmutations.

J. Robert Oppenheimer, the Soviet spy who oversaw the Manhattan Project, the building of the first atomic bomb, and was present when the humongous mushroom cloud rose with its imploding plumes of fire, is said to have exclaimed, *"I am became the destroyer of worlds."* Few realized that this is a quote right out of the Hindu scriptures, the Bhagavad Gita, and it was supposedly from the Hindu sun god, Krishna. Oppenheimer, a Jew, appointed to his august scientific position by 33rd degree Mason, President Franklin D. Roosevelt, was deep into the occult and was a cabalist magician.

As Michael Hoffman II and a few other keen-minded observers have pointed out, the A-bomb project, the transmutation of matter into intense forms of energy, was long an alchemical objective of the Illuminati magicians. Like the Hindu god who represents them, it is the fondest desire of these wicked, nihilistic men that they become the *destroyer of worlds*.[4]

And then, from the burned out carcass, like the Phoenix rising from the ashes, is to come the New City of Glory, the Kingdom of the Illuminati, ruled by their god-man King and His Master, Satan. This is the ultimate, all-consuming, repugnant goal of *The Builders*, to undo what God has done, to defile and utterly destroy planet earth and to rebuild it in their image.

The prophetic Scriptures tell us that this grandiose Plan—the Great Work of the Illuminati—will never fully come to fruition. The Kingdom shall not become the province of the rebellious Illuminati and their dark, occult master, Satan. Here is Almighty God's glorious declaration of how it all shall end:

"And the seventh angel sounded: and there were great voices in heaven, saying, THE
KINGDOMS OF THE WORLD ARE BECOME THE KINGDOMS OF OUR LORD,
AND OF HIS CHRIST, AND HE SHALL REIGN FOREVER AND EVER...

And the nations were angry, and thy wrath is come, and the time of the dead, that they should be judged, and that thou shouldest give reward unto thy servants the prophets, and to the saints, and them that fear thy name, small and great; and shouldest destroy them which destroy the earth." — recorded in Revelation 11:15, 18

God's incomparable will and plan shall prevail. His Christ and His people shall reign triumphant forever, and the evil shall be judged. And what of the Illuminati, the destroyers of the earth, the ones whom Satan's servant, Oppenheimer, trumpeted were the *"destroyer of worlds?"* The Scriptures give testimony to their fate; they too, shall be judged, so that God *"shouldest destroy them which destroy the earth."*

❖ POWER

The hunger for power motivates the human disciples in the Illuminati structure. Because they serve Satan, they instinctually know they are also serving the will of his human hierarchy. They expect to be rewarded for this service to the evil side.

George Bernard Shaw, who maintained an overwhelming hatred for God and for Christianity, wrote of a "will" incarnated in higher consciousness man (the elite) that shall *"finally mould chaos itself into a race of gods."*[5] To fancy yourself as in a state of becoming divine, as so superhuman, special and superior you shall achieve elevation as one of a "race of gods," is an intoxicating prospect.

"Do As Thou Wilt"

The Bible says of the Antichrist, he *"shall do according to his will"* (Daniel 11:36). Aleister Crowley, head of the occultic order, Ordo Templi Orientis, prided himself on being the "wickedest man on earth." Crowley preached that Satanists had only one commandment: "Do as thou wilt shall be the whole of the law."

Only gods can do as they will. That translates into awesome power. Changing reality by the force of one's will is, in fact, the very essence of magic and witchcraft. F. Aster Barnwell, in his sinister book, *The Meaning of Christ For Our Age*, equates superior human will with god-consciousness. Through development and exercise of will, or magic, says Barnwell, a man may live forever as a god. Illumined by occult knowledge, the person is able to utilize pent-up psychic energy forces to effect material reality. Barnwell refers to this psychic energy force by the Hindu term "Kundalini," or "serpent power."[6]

A man possessing serpent power is said to operate in a spiritual realm. As such, he is immune to and beyond any human spectrum of morality. Whatever he wills is good, based solely on the results and not on any relative moral scale. In essence, the ends justify the means. In such a relativistic theology, black magic is no lesser in moral standing than is white magic. Black is white, bad is good, and all things are reversed.

Power is the Ultimate Aphrodisiac

Oh, how thrilling to the egomaniacal Illuminati is the realization that they possess and wield such awesome power within the planetary realm. Power is addictive. Former Secretary of State and Illuminati insider extraordinaire Henry Kissinger once smiled and confided, "Power is the ultimate aphrodisiac."

To communicate ultra secret, coded, visual messages of an evil and conspiratorial nature to each other or to the whole group by way of the world's most influential media, with no fear of being reprimanded or of ever being punished for the crime must, indeed, be akin to ingesting a mind-altering, soul-satisfying aphrodisiac. These men lust for power, and conveying secret messages unintelligible to the ignorant masses must give them great emotional delight. It inspires in them the desire to accomplish even greater occult aims.

As Shakespeare once wrote, *"The world is mine oyster which I, with sword, shall take and plunder."* Yes, the world is their "oyster," and some in the Illuminati hierarchy are so infused with the carnal ambition and lust to power they even seek to conquer and reign the starry realm beyond the surly bounds of this planet. It was British colonialist plotter Cecil Rhodes who once declared, *"I would annex the planets if I could."*

Somewhat less grand and pretentious in his ambition for power but nevertheless worth recalling is former House Speaker Newt Gingrich, so full of himself sitting at the top of the heap in the U.S. Congress that he once told an audience: *"My goal is to shift the entire planet. And I'm doing it!"*[7]

❖ PRIDE

A perverse sense of false pride is a major factor that motivates men to be active as Illuminati operatives and to communicate by secret handshakes, signs, and by other occult media.

To smugly conceive of oneself as superior in enlightenment, in class status, in social connections, and in other artificial aspects is common to the elite. The promotion upward of the initiate degree-by-degree is purposely designed to create the impression that he is gaining knowledge forbidden to the unenlightened multitudes outside the order. A system of awards, jewels to be worn, covert handshakes and cryptic signs shared also reinforces the ideology that the individual is special and superior.

To Be In On the Joke

To be pictured in a nationally circulated magazine is ego-building enough for the Illuminist. But to identify with members of an exclusive and powerful secret organization by purposely giving a secret hand sign in that picture and realize that only other elite are "in" on the joke, so to speak—that can, indeed, engender a rush of perverse satisfaction and haughty pride. The attitude is, "Ha! Aren't we pulling one over on them! What control we have over the masses. What swill they can be made to swallow!"

Jim Keith, a first-class conspiracy researcher who some believe was murdered by the elite during what was supposed to have been a minor surgical procedure on his knee, believed that the perverse satisfaction and exaggerated pride of these men is a natural outgrowth of their keenly observing how much control over others their elite status confers on them and their associates. This is especially true given the Illuminati's control and manipulation of nations like the U.S.A., Russia and Germany, nations with vast technological prowess that fosters the growth of Big Brother government control. He writes:

> Beneath the cloak of the prime conspirators are larger groups of rich peasantry and landlords dominating a huge mass of poor serfs and less-than-serfs whose labor and lives are sucked to provide the lifeblood to nourish the upper portions of the pyramid. This ancient structure is perfectly visible to anyone with the eyes to be appalled.

> It is also obvious that the ruling class cabals and spy organizations which we do know about are pointed in roughly the same direction: the total control and "utilization" of the mass of mankind by whatever means it takes. Aside from all the lofty banter about the "perfecting of mankind," what is desired is the perfecting of the systems of control.

> Control is the shared goal of these numerous conspiring individuals, groups, and governments, and in that sense they work together, collaborating here, working individually there, creating an evolving noose of murderous technological expertise that swiftly tightens around humanity's throat. With this goal in place, with money and the tools of advanced technology in hand, the overall program of accomplishment crystallizes. [8]

Absolute Power Corrupts Absolutely

Exaggerated, self-absorbed pride becomes especially evil and dangerous when prideful men acquire power. It was Lord Acton who, in 1886, uttered the well-known maxim that, "power corrupts, and absolute power corrupts absolutely." Unduly prideful men are imbued with that unrighteous temperament because they often have unfettered access to power—power over people, over organizations, over resources, and over nations. Power to reward or to punish chosen disciples, friends, or enemies, even power to take life.

The best of historians now admit, for example, that President Franklin D. Roosevelt and his corrupt, Masonic associates knew in advance of the Japanese attack on Pearl Harbor that catapulted the United States into war. The Illuminati *wanted* world war, and the American airmen, soldiers, and sailors who died on December 7, 1941 were considered necessary to precipitate the USA's entrance into World War II.

The U.S. Government also had prior knowledge of both the 1993 Oklahoma City bombing of the Murrah Federal Building and the 9/11 bombing attacks on the World Trade Center and Pentagon. The massive loss of life was no obstacle as far as the elite were concerned. Their cold-blooded agenda is calculated to engender chaos and destruction in a never-ending, alchemical process of bringing *Ordo ab Chao* (order out of chaos). To the elite, murder is business as usual. And so, once again, we discover that a moral vacuum is inherent in the minds of these men of perverse pride.

❖ ELITISM

Closely linked with their perverse and exaggerated pride is the corrupt reality that the men of the Illuminati do, indeed, run most things in society. They are the elite, and, unfortunately, they are afflicted with *elitism*. They do receive unfair advantage and exalted status in society. Sadly, the dumbed down masses adore the men and women of the elite.

Elitism is a sickness, a disease. The men (and women) who are pictured in *Codex Magica* giving secret signs and sharing covert hand grips no doubt enjoy a smugly satisfying sense of perversity in knowing they are deceiving those whom, they are persuaded, are the ignorant and unknowing multitudes.

The Inner Circle and Their Puppets

The elite of the Illuminati are themselves divided by rank and authority. There is a hidden *inner circle*, followed by a several hundred-member core. Next, we have perhaps three to five thousand in a larger *circle of influence*, and then finally, another ten thousand *puppets*.

The latter group, the puppets, have no real influence on matters of importance. This group includes celebrities, media representatives, educators, and others who are only vaguely aware that an elitist global conspiracy exists. They simply know that they must hew to the "party line." The puppets also realize they must maintain a strict form of political correctness by promoting globalism and the approved socialist agenda. They are required to rigorously adhere to the "script" provided and continue to loyally wear the individual "mask" they have been supplied.

John Swinton, newsman and former editor at *The New York Times* once shocked his audience at a luncheon meeting of the press by boldly confessing:

> There is no such thing in America as an independent press. You know it and I know it…The business of the Journalist is to destroy truth; To lie outright; To pervert; To vilify; To fawn at the feet of mammon, and to sell his county and his race for his daily bread. You know it and I know it and what folly is this toasting an independent press?

> We are the tools and vassals for rich men behind the scenes. We are the jumping jacks, they pull the strings and we dance. Our talents, our possibilities and our lives are all the property of other men. We are intellectual prostitutes.

Swinton appears to have known very well that the careers and activities of his peers in the media are strictly controlled and regulated by their elite masters. And this rankled him. But then, after Swinton's comments that day, little was ever heard again from the man.

The Group Mind and the Insectoids

As Michael Hoffman II once sagely noted, the analogy of "insects" often resides in the true tale of the initiates of secret societies and orders. This is because these men are themselves deceived by Lucifer, and so they go about deceiving others. Thus there is a Group Mind resident in all these people, whether an Illuminatus is a member of the inner circle or is a lowly puppet. It is for this reason that Professor Adam Weishaupt, co-founder of the classical Order of the Illuminati (May 1, 1776), called his sect the Beenan Order (Order of the Bees).

Jim Keith, in *Mind Control and UFOs*, also noted this hive mentality. Keith wrote that in the South American nation of Columbia, there is a German community which, even today, over 60 years after World War II, uses the swastika as its icon. This group calls its compound "Hormiga," in honor of the obedient worker ant, yet another form of Illuminati insectoid.[9]

Thus, we find the beehive or anthill as apt metaphors for the servants of the Illuminati. It is fascinating to realize that these people are servile, weak, and crawling little personalities. They echo in unison the words *"Yes, Master"* to their superiors, the potentates of the various secret societies and orders.

The underlings of the Illuminati, in effect, are abject and craven cowards, groveling in fright and terror before their Illuminist chieftains; yet, they act in public as though they are superior beings—oh, so special and "hoity toity," as the saying goes.

Believing in their own inflated self-worth, they consider themselves members of a higher-level caste while categorizing the masses outside their group as like so many cattle or sheep—even as "useless eaters."

They Look Down On the Inferior Goyim

Such is the distorted view of the Jewish Illuminati who derogatorily refer to Gentiles as the *goyim* (cattle).

The late Dr. Israel Shahak, Professor at Hebrew University in Israel, a man I respected greatly, was a constant critic of such a deviant, superiority attitude. Shahak noted that many Zionist Jews are unashamed advocates of human slavery:

> The Israelis have resuscitated a book in Spanish by Jews dating from the 14th century which has been adopted for use as a manual of religious instruction in Israel's secondary schools. It explains why non-Jews ought to be the slave of Jews because Jews are the elite of the human race. Because of this they deserve to have slaves, and these slaves must be non-Jews.[10]

This outrageous and imperious attitude does not take those of us by surprise who have studied the Jewish Talmud, the rabbis' holiest book. According to the Talmud, Gentiles are not even to be considered humans: *"The goyim (Gentiles) are not men, but beasts" (Baba Mezia fol. 1146).*

It should be further noted that the *Encyclopedia Britannica* says, "The Talmud is still the authoritative and practical guide of the great mass of the Jews." (From the

9-volume German language translation of *The Babylonian Talmud* in the Library of Congress, Washington, D.C.)

Slaves and Beasts

Slaves and beasts! That is what the Zionists of Israel consider those who aren't Jewish. Now we discover what the elitist, favored sons of the *Zionist Illuminati* think of you, me, and the masses. No wonder they kill without conscience through their instigation of world wars, through initiation of regional conflicts, and through assassinations and other criminal deeds. The elite plot and carry out heinous terrorist acts and institute financial crises and cultural upheavals to force the Hegelian dialectical process along its desired path toward a New Age New World Order.

Deaths are "acceptable losses," the Illuminati reason, and pain and suffering are necessary for requisite changes to occur in society. In any event, since those outside The Order are relegated to the lowly categories of "slave and beast," why wring one's hands or otherwise unduly concern oneself with whether such miscreants as you and me live or die? The *Malthus Principle* suggests to the Illuminati that periodically thinning the global population is a good thing. Evolution, they believe, calls for the survival of the fittest, and they view themselves as superior and most fit to rule.

Elitism is certainly a disease, a mental disease, and those afflicted with it experience no guilt whatsoever in performing magical rituals of all kinds to enhance and accentuate their elite status and signal their superior "knowledge" to their occultic peers.

❖ SIGNAL

Scan the pages of this book, *Codex Magica*, and you immediately discover that the conspirators of the Illuminati have a deep, dark desire to *signal* each other. They seem to be obsessed with flaunting their special ties with each other as well as their membership in the Brotherhood of the Elite at large.

Could it be that these men—sharers of occult secrets and sharers of crimes—also share a joint consciousness and recognition of their mission as individual members of a commonly shared destiny? I believe that is the case.

In *Conscious Evolution*, Dr. Barry McWaters acknowledges this commonality, this attempt to unify on the part of the insiders, each of which, he acknowledges, make a "unique contribution:"

> In this way the differentiated parts...come to recognize that our common task is a Trans-human one, a goal beyond ourselves. [11]

McWaters notes that, "Many people have opened themselves to serve as channels." By their individual acts of performing rituals, including the communication of signs and symbols which embody intense energies and are magical in effect, there is expected to arise a "transformed humanity, creating a new heaven and a new earth to manifest itself."[12]

In effect, the co-conspirators are performing a psychic form of magic. By the combination in the ethereal world of millions of ritual acts by individuals, it is believed that a collective transformation of mankind and of earth will take place. When a *critical mass* is achieved, a quantum leap in consciousness will spontaneously occur. The catalytic process of magic on a mass, continuing scale will help push this process along to completion. Then and only then will the Universal Mind, long a cherished goal of the elite, be realized.

Meanwhile, the co-conspirators believe they are mass-conditioning humanity and helping to build archetypes of energy forces in the collective consciousness that tend to create a binary, dialectical process of chaos that will result in the Hegelian achievement of *equilibrium*. This, they are convinced, will catapult the world into a global-wide Zionist state, ruled by an enlightened dictatorship made up of Masonic overlords who wisely rule and are beyond good and evil.

In effect, the co-conspirators are persuaded they are each a cell, or molecule, playing a certain role within a greater organism. Their deceit is to imagine themselves an energy unit, or snapshot within a holographic universe in which all things are related and are one: *"Further, not only is there one unity, but there are unities within unities within unities."*[13] But of course, at the top of their unified pyramid is the controlling entity with the all-seeing eye. That, indisputably, is Lucifer.

Interesting is the fact that each of the co-conspirators fully recognize what the others are doing. Each understands the mask he must wear and the signals to be given. In a Public Broadcasting System (PBS) documentary, the story is recounted of the day President Harry S. Truman, a 33rd degree Mason, met Hollywood director and actor Orson Welles (*War of the Worlds* and *Citizen Kane* fame). Truman smiled and said to Welles, "You're the second greatest actor alive today. *I'm* the first."

❖ WEALTH

What would compel grown men to act like immature, two-bit stage actors, twisting and distorting their fingers, hands, and bodies into ridiculous symbolic gestures in what appears to be a ludicrous campaign to force magical change or to convey secret messages via the media to fellow conspirators equally brainwashed? Most of these men are *wealthy*. Is that a factor? Does wealth confer on a man the unbecoming non-quality of stupidity? Is the secret coding and sending of messages, by word and by visual means, a process or activity of stupid, wicked rich men?

Not all wicked and powerful men are wealthy, but many are. Disproportionately so. Having studied the lives and work of the elite, I can testify that their idle lifestyle and wealth often becomes an impediment to their moral development and to their potential exercise of good judgement and common sense. This is especially true of members of Dynasty family lines—the Bushes, Kennedys, Clintons, Roosevelts, Bronfmans, Rothschilds, the royal families in Europe, etc.

Idiotic Behavior, Witchcraft and Magic

Wealth and idleness lead to boredom, and boredom to idiotic and aberrant, bizarre behavior. But though we may laugh at what seem to be the comedic and unfruitful attempts of the elite to use coded messages and symbolism in magazines, newspapers, on TV, and in other media, for them this is no laughing matter. It is serious business. It is ritual witchcraft, and without it, their lives would revert to the mundane. Witchcraft and magic having become an essential part of their lives, they are addicted and must continue. As one famous witch once remarked, "I had no self-control. My appetite for performing spells and working magic eventually became insatiable. Satan kept wanting more and more, and I had to provide it."

The scriptures say that the love of money is the root of all evil. Not just of *some* evil, but of *all* evil. The concentration of wealth into fewer and fewer hands translates into the concentration of evil into fewer and fewer hands. The idle wealthy soon lose perspective and are out of touch with the serfs and vassals. The slave state, at its zenith, is run by dullards, silly men who have convinced themselves that a secret handshake made in front of a camera—or a hand sign flashed by them on a TV news program—turbo-props their personal progress in the ranks of the elite. They are also convinced that their use of covert signs, grips, handshakes and symbols helps in their acquisition of greater satanic powers, leading to greater control by them over the unknowing peasantry.

Foolish, But Also Dangerous

Tragically, these men, though often foolish and dull, are dangerous to us all. The silly man who is given control and management over the keepers to the keys to the nuclear-tipped ICBMs that sit deep inside the earth is, indeed, a dangerous man. So, too, are men whose banking, financial, and corporate decisions can plunge entire nations into desperate straits of bankruptcy and ruin.

It is, moreover, no consolation to realize that the stupid and self-indulgent who populate the highest reaches of the Illuminati ranks are often cunning, sly, devious, and ethically-challenged.

The imbecile son of a wise king is always less wise than his father, but upon his father's passing, he nevertheless assumes the throne. How often does history show that heredity renders a nation a cruel blow when the next generation takes command? In that instance, the cry of the people invariably rings out: "The King is dead—oh no!—Well, okay, long live the King."

Rarely do the men at the top echelons of the Illuminati deserve their powerful and influential positions based on merit. Their reign is based on, first, heredity, and, next, on cronism and toadyism. Survival and promotion is not according to survival of the fittest, but survival of the most wealthy and the most favored.

Sometimes, modern man looks at old newsreel footage of monsters like Lenin, Stalin, Mao, Hitler, Castro, and Mussolini, and they ask, How could entire nations have ever believed in such cartoonish, even outlandish, characters? But, remember, we see these men only in retrospect, and we fancy ourselves as being too smart to have ever been taken in by such odd personalities.

Someday, an evil one will come who will be so wicked and diabolical he shall cause the masses everywhere to revere and honor him as a "saint above saints." The scriptures say virtually the whole world will believe in and follow him. The

Illuminati elite surely will give this evil tyrant all their allegiance. They, along with the duped masses, will fall prey to the Strong Delusion, they will believe the Lie, and they will be Damned *(II Thessalonians 2)*.

❖ PLEASE

To *please* their master, Lucifer, is the highest priority of the Illuminati. Illuminist Albert Pike, 33°, former Sovereign Grand Commander whose commentary on Freemasonry's rituals, *Morals and Dogma*, is the classic learning textbook for all Masons, issued instructions on July 14, 1889, to the Supreme Councils of the World identifying the Master whom Masons universally worship and venerate:

> That which we must say to the crowd is—we worship a God, but it is the God that one adores without superstition… To you, Sovereign Grand Inspector Generals, we say this; that you may repeat it to brothers of the 32nd, 31st, and 30th degrees—The Masonic religion should be, by all of us initiates of the high degrees, maintained in the purity of the *Luciferian doctrine*.[14]

Pike's embrace of the "Luciferian doctrine" is not surprising. Manly P. Hall, 33°, considered by Freemasonry as the Lodge's greatest scholar of the 20th century, taught that the energies of Lucifer were necessary for the successful Masonic warrior. Meanwhile, John J. Robinson, whose book, *Born in Blood*, was celebrated by top Masonic Lodge officials as an accurate history of the Knights Templar and of Freemasonry, insisted in his later book, *A Pilgrims Path*, that Lucifer is *not* Satan or the devil. Instead, Robinson insisted that Lucifer is an angel whose guidance and help can be employed either for good or for evil. Of course, Robinson's writings make clear that pleasing Lucifer is high-up on the Lodge's list of priorities.

Lucifer the Divine

Eliphas Levi, the cabalist magician whose artist depiction of Baphomet, the androgynous goat god, is illustrated elsewhere in this book, was more to the point. He recognized that Satan and Lucifer are, indeed, one and the same. But Levi also taught that Satan, believed by true Christians to be the enemy of God, is, in fact, man's helper and benefactor. Indeed Levi praised Satan, or Lucifer, as the "angel presiding over the light of truth."

"Lucifer is divine and terrestrial," said Levi. "He is the Holy Spirit" and is the "light-bearer in us. It is our mind."[15]

Thus, we discover the cabalistic philosophy is not only that Lucifer is divine, he is integrated into and is one with the *mind* of the men who make up the Illuminati elite. Lucifer and these men are of *one mind*. This brings to pass the prophecies of *Revelation 17* where we are told that the conspiracy of the elite in the endtime shall be composed of world leaders who will be of *"one mind, and they shall give their power and strength unto the beast."*

Unlike Eliphas Levi, most Illuminists are hesitant to identify Satan as their Lord.

Instead, they point to the Grand Architect of the Universe as their deity, or to a hazy and nebulous, unnamed "God." We have discovered that most of the Illuminati elite make the ridiculous claim that they neither worship nor even believe in a being, or entity, named Satan. Many laugh—at least publicly—at the notion of a real entity known as the Devil. The Masonic Lodge not only publicly disavows worship of Satan, but also vainly attempts to cast Lucifer, pseudonym for the Devil, in the mold of a good angel, ostensibly sent here on earth only to assist man and introduce man to the "better angels."

The One About Whom Naught May Be Said

In her eye-opening book, *The Initiation of the World*, occultist Vera Stanley Alder reinforces this pretense of the elite. She remarks that it is "Deity" without a name that is admired and worshipped. Furthermore, this mysterious Deity is esoterically described by her as the *"ONE ABOUT WHOM NAUGHT MAY BE SAID."* Ironically, Alder *does* have a lot to say regarding the *"one about whom naught may be said."* In fact, she praises this unnamed god as a being of immense *"wonder and magnitude."* She suggests, too, that the One the elite worship may properly be referred to as the "absolute." Alder also remarks that the entity she recognizes as the divine "One" is made up of "forces," and he has dominion over certain—again unnamed—greater or lesser entities.[16]

Of course, a rose by any other name is still a rose. And no matter how reluctant or tentative are the magicians of the Illuminati to come right out and identify the One whom they serve, we who have long studied these maladjusted rulers and their psychophants need not dodge the issue. Without question, a great many of the Illuminati know without a doubt whom they serve: Satan, also called Lucifer, the Devil, the Adversary. Their secret hand signs and grips, their symbols and their logos, indisputably prove this is so.

❖ INVOCATION

That demon principalities are *invoked* in the rendering of Masonic signs and other magical operations by the elite is a clear indication that these men are involved in witchcraft. It is not believed that the universe is some neutral machine, operating in a non-theological, pure, mechanical manner. Rather, there are believed to exist certain otherworldly spiritual hierarchies, entities that aid the elitist in creating a powerful effect upon the world. As witchcraft teacher Paul Huston explains:

> There simply exists power to be tapped to do good or to do evil...There exist certain entities who will aid you in your spells...You may call these entities gods, spirits, or watchers; or depersonalize them as powers or forces...[17]

The Hierarchy

These gods, entities, powers, or forces are said to be hierarchically arranged:

At the top, we have Great entities often known as Watchers, Mighty Ones, or gods…which can be contacted to bring a certain power to your rituals.

Then there are spirit entities or demons halfway between men and gods in their constitution…Of course there are many minor, elemental spirits.[18]

Huston says that talismans, images, and symbols — and hand and body signs and the positions and prescribed actions of body parts — will "partake of the nature of a spirit or elemental." In other words, spirits are attracted and supposedly go to work on behalf of the person who wears or displays the magical talisman, charm, image, idol, or symbol, or who practices and puts into operation a particular hand sign, handshake, body movement, or position, or ritual, whether that ritual is simple or sophisticated.

The more sophisticated and complex rituals and the more detailed, intricate, and powerful is the design of the talisman, symbol, hand sign, etc., the more likely a higher level entity — a being higher on the spiritual totem pole or pecking order so to speak — will be induced to participate in performing the desired magical act. That is, the greater the *force* of magic that will be applied. A great Entity, perhaps a prince or other high-up territorial potentate in the demonic spiritual realm, is naturally thought to possess the power to force changes in the real world. It is no accident that in the Bible, the last day, endtimes world ruler and his earthly human companions are said, to worship the *"God of Forces."*

Ritual Ceremonies and Demons of Secret Societies

The leaders of the secret societies of the Illuminati would have to be supreme dullards not to recognize the demonic forces that are invoked in the ceremonial working of the various ritual degrees. C.W. Leadbeater, a 33rd degree Mason and occultist who was allied with Annie Besant and her Theosophical Society in the 1920s, is just one of many Masonic leaders who have acknowledged the participation of devil spirits. For example, Leadbeater says that the ritual for the 30th degree brings forth an angel who is "a great blue Deva of the First Ray." In the 33rd degree, Leadbeater relates, two "splendid fellow workers, spirits of gigantic size as compared to humanity and radiantly white in color are present."[19]

In fact, Leadbeater said that the ritual for the 33rd degree actually links the Sovereign Grand Inspector General of Freemasonry with the "Spiritual King of the World Himself; That Mightiest of Adepts who stands at the head of the Great White Lodge, in whose strong hands lies the destinies of earth."[20]

❖ ENCOURAGE

The frequency of the higher-level elite conveying occultic messages via hand signs, arm gestures, body postures, and similar means *encourages* lesser disciples. It reassures them that they are part of a cohesive and unified whole, members of a distinctive body of powerful and influential world movers and shakers. It is an awesome feeling, no doubt, to find oneself in company with the aspiring and actual rulers of the planet.

Naturally, for the lesser initiate, seeing the top adepts displaying Masonic, Rosicrucian, O.T.O., and other signs and symbols in major propaganda and cultural organs (TV, newspapers, magazines, internet, books, public forums, etc.) also instills fear and dread. Fear and dread of what the Organization—powerful as evidenced by its public display of its chief symbols to a profane, ignorant mass audience—might do to them if they ever should be so bold or so foolish as to damage its assets, reveal its secrets, or betray it:

> There is an inevitability…which is at once its horror and its joy…once an accepted disciple has definitely undertaken the work in preparation for initiation, there is for him no turning back. He could not if he would…

> He has heard the voice of his Master. Occult obedience gives place to enlightened will. He can now be trusted to walk and work alone because he is unalterably one with his group, with the Hierarchy, and finally with Shamballa (hell).[21]

The Carrot and Stick Approach

Thus, we see in use by the top ranks of the elite the carrot and stick approach. If the fledgling initiate strays from the fold, or, worse, reveals any of the secrets of the Brotherhood, he will get the stick of punishment. But if he cooperates, he will be rewarded. He will find himself in the enviable position of being lauded as a co-creator of the world aborning.

C. Fred Kleinknecht, 33°, Sovereign Grand Commander of Scottish Rite Freemasonry, in March, 2002, in *The Scottish Rite Journal*, boasted of this Creator role. In an article entitled, *"A Brave New World of Heroes,"* Kleinknecht encourages Masonic disciples by emphasizing:

> One of the great lessons of the Scottish Rite is this: We do not inherit the world, we create it.

> "O brave new world, that has such people in it!" —This line from Shakespeare's *The Tempest* seems particularly appropriate…[22]

In practicing magic by employing secret signs, the sharing of covert handshakes, the use of power-attracting symbols, the use of hidden codes and other ritual means, the deceived initiate believes he is helping to build that Brave New World—a "better" world. Better, that is, for he and his magical associates. He is working as a member of the Group to alchemically break down and build back up society into a new order of things. He is, as we shall see, engaging in the rabbinic and cabalistic practice of *Tikkun Olam*, the repair and reconstruction of the world.

❖ REBELLION

The illuminated elitist does not regard himself as a man, but as a god. As such, he is, in fact, a rebel, engaged in *rebellion* against the one, true God. Collectively, the elite fancy themselves to be God. How does a mere human being arrive at such an *imagined* exalted state of existence?

Vera Stanley Alder, in her celebrated textbook, *The Initiation of The World*, writes that once the Illuminist has been raised to become a "unit within a great brotherhood," he progresses toward fusion and unity with the all-consciousness. In this state…

> Man is no longer worshipping God, asking things of God, trying to become like God. He knows that he is God…He is.[23]

They Hate Without A Cause

Here, then, we find an arrogant expression of hubris, pride, and, most of all, rebellion. Rebellion against God, against His Truth, and against His people. The Illuminati are revolutionaries. Their revolt has no rational cause. Christ Jesus noted: *"They hate me without a cause."* The Illuminist strives for liberty and fulfillment of self-interest and will apart from God and His Will. That is why this brotherhood of evildoers are rebels, opposers of good, colluders with any and all forms of apostasy.

The propensity of the Illuminati to engage in rebellion, against God, country, and even organized civilization itself is evidenced in the *inner meaning* of their centuries old rallying cry: "Liberty, Equality, Fraternity," the esoteric meaning of which is liberty from the dictates of God, equality of all men only in death, and the unity of evildoers. Truly, the man who has taken vulgar and bloody oaths to defend The Order and has vowed to protect its secrets against onslaught by would be interlopers and intruders is not above killing those who oppose his ambitious personal goals or who stand in the way of the attainment of the objectives of the Order of the Illuminati.

"In Freemasonry It Is Permitted to Kill"

Consider the military trial of the Freemason, Cabrinovic, assassin of the Archduke Ferdinand of Austria, Hungary, a fateful event that touched off the deadly and fiery conflict of World War I. Cabrinovic's testimony at his trial provides us a graphic example of the rebellious spirit of the men of the secret societies and orders.

Asked if he had conspired with other Freemasons to murder the Archduke and thus set off a saga of anarchy and mayhem throughout Europe, Cabrinovic told the military court, *"Yes, I knew we were all Freemasons, and this strengthened my resolve… Freemasonry strengthened my intention. In Freemasonry it is permitted to kill."*

Ah yes. *"In Freemasonry it is permitted to kill,"* testified the assassin Cabrinovic. How exquisitely truthful the man was as he sat in the witness chair, being called to account for his horrific crime.

When we examine the historical record of the world's most despicable mass murderers and revolutionaries, we find that almost all of them were members of

Freemasonry and other secret societies of the Illuminati:

> Robespierre was a Freemason; Weishaupt was a Freemason; Napoleon was a
> Freemason; Lenin was a Freemason; Stalin was a Freemason; Mussolini was a
> Freemason; Truman and Roosevelt were Freemasons; Ariel Sharon is a Freemason;
> Bill Clinton is a Freemason; Fidel Castro is a Freemason.

Is There No Help For the Widow's Son?

At his trial for conspiracy to commit homicide, satanist rebel Charles Manson was observed giving a variety of Masonic hand signs, including the Masonic sign of distress. The same sign was reportedly given by Mormon founder Joseph Smith as he lay dying on the floor of an Illinois jail on a variety of criminal charges. Lying bleeding and desperate, Smith's raspy voice could be heard crying out the plaintive, Masonic wail, calling on Masons to help a brother in dire trouble, *"Is there no help for the widow's son?"*

Joseph Smith no doubt could not believe that he, a man who claimed to be God's Chosen Prophet but who secretly worshipped Lucifer; he, a man of such superior intellect and endowed with the occult gift of spiritual enlightenment, was about to meet his Maker, a victim of a vigilante mob who despised him.

Jack Parsons, American rocket scientist, founder of California's Jet Propulsion Laboratory, and a priest of the O.T.O., was, like Mormon Joseph Smith, a premier servant of Satan and a rebel against God. He even fancied himself to be the prophesied antichrist. Parsons wrote this chilling paragraph in his diary:

> And thus was I antichrist loosed in the world; and to this am I pledged, that the
> work of the beast shall be fulfilled, and the way for the coming of BABALON be
> made open and I shall not cease or rest until these things are accomplished. [24]

A few years after writing this, Jack Parsons was killed in an explosion in a laboratory at his home, which also served as a meeting place for other members of his satanic order. He evidently was not to become the prophesied antichrist, a fact Parsons now knows only too well, residing as he is in some subterranean cell somewhere in a place called hell.

THREE

Concealed Messages—The Importance of Hand Signs to the Illuminati

*And he causeth all, both small and great, rich and poor, free and bond, to receive a mark in their **right hand**, or in their foreheads…*

—*Revelation 13:16*

*Raise the **right hand**…extending the two fingers like a fork…then draw it back over the right shoulder and with a quick motion dart the extended fingers forward in a horizontal direction. It alludes to the penalty of gouging out the eyes of a traitor.*

—Second Sign of a Super-Excellent Master Mason
Richardson's Monitor of Freemasonry (p.91)

As we shall see, the Illuminati worship deity by many names in many disguises. One such name and disguise is "Jahbuhlun." In pursuit of their worship of this false god, Jahbuhlun, they have devised many rituals in which they employ "hidden" hand signs. In all the 33 degrees of Scottish Rite Freemasonry and in the rituals of the York Rite, the Order of Skull and Bones, the Ordo Templi Orientis, the Grand Orient Lodge of France, the Grand Lodge of Jerusalem, and on and on in almost all the secret societies and orders, handsigns, and handshakes are prominent.

In *Coil's Masonic Encyclopedia* we read: "The hand is important in Freemasonry…for the purpose of giving and receiving modes of recognition."[1] In

ROYAL ARCH, OR SEVENTH DEGREE   225

FIG. 32.

THREE TIMES THREE.

1st.	2nd.	3d.
Jah	buh	lun.
	Jah	buh
lun		
		Jah
buh	lun.	
Je	ho	vah.

Lectures on Freemasonry. "we receive a wonderful accession of knowledge, and find every thing *made perfect*; for this is the *ne plus ultra* of Masonry, and can never be exceeded by any human institution."—*Fellows's Inquiry into the Origin, History, and Purport of Freemasonry*, p. 322.

A Degree indescribably more august, sublime, and important than any which precede it, and is, in fact, the summit and perfection of ancient Masonry. It impresses on our minds a belief in the being of a God, without beginning of days or end of years, the great and incomprehensible Alpha and Omega, and reminds us of the reverence which is due to His Holy NAME.—*Historical Landmarks*, vol. i. p. 86.

Masons pay homage to their Satanic god, Jahbuhlun, in performing the ritual "Three Times Three" in the Royal Arch, or Seventh Degree. (page 225 from *Duncan's Masonic Ritual and Monitor*, 3rd edition)

The second sign of the Super Excellent Master Mason simulates gouging out the eyes of a "traitor" to Freemasonry.

J. C. Coopers' *An Illustrated Encyclopedia of Traditional Symbols*[2], the author notes that hand signs include the following symbolic meanings:

Hand on Breast — submission and the attitude of a servant or slave
Crossed at wrist (X) — binding or being bound
Hand on neck — sacrifice
Clenched fist — threat, aggression
Raised hand — adoration, worship, horror, amazement
Both hands raised, palm outward — weakness, supplication, acknowledgment,
    adoration, admiration
Raised to head — thought, care, intellect, wisdom

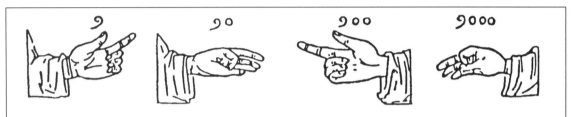

Numerical hand signs from a Renaissance text on mathematics. Such usage often combines the teachings of numerology with the secret messages of hand communications.

The International Secret Language

Is the occult hand sign, in its many forms and varieties, the international secret language of the Freemasons and other covert societies? Manfred Adler, in his German-language book, *The Freemasons and the Vatican*, says the answer to this question is, yes.[3] He writes that according to the findings of a United States Senate Committee that investigated the Central Intelligence Agency (CIA), "Ninety percent of the secret news is transmitted via the media, in particular the press, with the aid of coded texts and pictures."[4]

Messages in the Media

Others, too, besides Adler, have noted the frequent use of hand signs in the media as signals of secret society insiders. Juan Maler, Argentine author and Masonic researcher, explains that the use of the hand sign, is for the uninitiated, a completely trivial and inconspicuous gesture. "But for the members of the Secret Societies, the hand sign is used as a sign of recognition by those who are in a leading position or who have a mission to fulfill and usually appears with a relevant text."[5]

Johannes Rothkranz, German authority on Masonic signs, suggests that, "If one collects the photos of well-known personalities from the daily papers, then one possesses, in a very short time, a great number of conspicuous and — for those who understand the signs — also meaningful poses."[6]

According to Rothkranz, the historic handshake between Helmut Kohl, then the

Chancellor of West Germany, and Modrow, the head of the Communist East German regime which sealed the deal for German reunification was clearly a Masonic handshake. Rothkranz further notes that the historic handshake of the two elitists was shown at length on European television.[7]

A Symbol of Power

Why is the use of the hand considered to be so significant as a means of concealed communications by occultists? *The Herder Dictionary of Symbols* states that the hand is "a symbol of activity and power." It notes that finding oneself "in the hands of a ruler or god means being in that person's power, but also standing under that person's protection."[8] The dictionary goes on to say that the "shaking or offering of the hand is a sign of friendly openers, devotion or forgiveness." But a closed hand signifies secrets or keeping silent. Other uses of hand signs are to indicate fear, threats, devotion, admiration, and argument.

The Herder Dictionary explains, too, that, "In antiquity, covered or veiled hands were generally customary when one approached high dignitaries." Hands with palms resting on one's knees express deep concentration and reflection.[9]

The hand can also be used as a threat to any would-be traitors or betrayer of the Illuminist cause. In the authoritative *Richardson's Monitor of Freemasonry* we find an example of this in the second sign of the Super Excellent Master Mason. The sign consists of raising the right hand, making the two first fingers like a fork, and simulating the gouging out of the eyes of a "traitor."

On the Other Hand...

There is a great symbolic difference between the use of the left and right hands. The right hand is said to be the hand of blessing, a good and positive influence, and those who use it in the occult world are known as those on the *"right-handed path."* This is considered *"white magic."*

Those on the *left-handed path*, however, are practitioners of *"black magic."* Full-fledged Satanists are typically of the left-handed path, though, in reality, it does not matter to the devil which hand is used!

The left hand is ever considered the *sinister* hand. It is associated with words like diabolical, witchlike, clever, deceptive, sly, cunning, evil, wrong, backward, and perverse. The evil eye is said to be the left eye. Some early Christians (for example, the writer of the apocryphic *Gospel of Nicodemus*) taught that of the two thieves crucified next to Jesus, the one at his left side

An odd, old drawing of a priest with hands in prayer, but aimed downwards toward Satan!

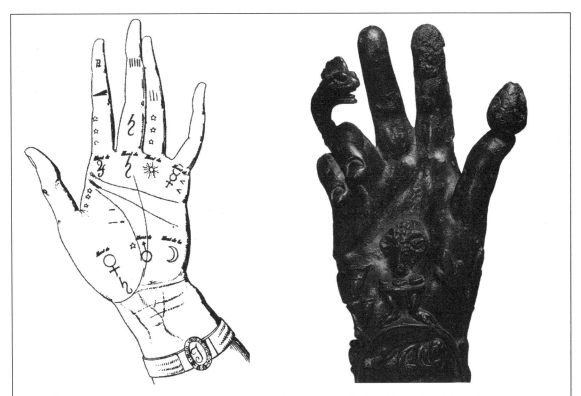

At Left: Josephine Bonaparte's palm from Mlle Le Normand's *Les Memoires historiques et secrets de l'Impératrice Josephine*, Paris, 1827.

At Right: The Sabazios Hand. Bronze symbol of the syncretic Jewish mystery cult of Sabazios in Asia Minor. Circa First Century, C.E. (Collection of the British Museum)

rejected truth and was consigned to hell.

In heaven, Jesus, of course, is believed to sit at the right hand of God, not the left. In *Ecclesiastes*, a book of the Old Testament in the Bible, it is said that, "A wise man's heart is at his right hand, but a fool's heart is at his left." *(Eccles. 10:2)*

Witches throughout history have danced in ritual circles to the left, that is, counterclockwise. Druid priests do likewise as they dance and march around the holy stone at Tara, Shrine of Mother Earth. To blaspheme God, some Satanists and witches derive pleasure in giving the sign of the cross with their left hands.

But while witches and deep occultists are aware of the sinister nature and meaning of the left hand symbolically, one of the foremost Masonic authorities evidently has a more favorable view. Professor James Curl, author of the reference book, *The Art and Architecture of Freemasonry*, writes that, "The left hand is the symbol of equity."[10] In other words the symbol of justice and fairness. Strange, indeed, unless one elevates the devil to the virtuous level of one who serves justice and brings equity or equality. But then, why would a Masonic authority think otherwise of the Lodge's true Grand Master, the Prince of the Power of the Air, *aka* Lucifer?

An Indicator of Attitude

According to most reference books of the occult, the positioning of the hand on a

Grand Master Jacques de Molay of the Knights Templar, predecessor to today's Freemasonry and other secret societies. Accused of blasphemy and of worshipping the grotesque idol of Baphomet, the horned goat-god, de Molay was burned at the stake by the King of France on March 11, 1314. The sign he is giving his captors seems clearly to be the vulgar and obscene "up yours" gesture. Although de Molay was reputed also to be a homosexual, today's international Masonic Lodges honor their former Grand Master by naming their youth groups the "de Molays."

particular part of the body indicates one's mental attitude and inner meaning. A hand placed on the breast indicates a tender, loyal or sympathetic attitude. Placed on the neck, the hand denotes sacrifice and penalty, while the joining of hands signifies mystic marriage and fidelity.

Three or more people linking hands signifies the joining of forces or energy, and is expressive of a virile fraternity and of solidarity in the face of danger.

The authors of *A Dictionary of Symbols* note that the hand expresses "ideas of action, as well as those of power and dominion." They say it is also a sign of royalty. The Jewish Kabbala (or Cabala) teaches that the left hand is the "hand of punishment," while the right hand is the "hand of blessing."[11]

The same reference guide explains that the word "manifestation" derives from the same root as "manus," the Latin word for hand. "What is manifest can be held in, or grasped by, the hand."[12]

The Fingers Can Be Revealing

The position of a specific finger, or fingers, of a hand may also denote great importance. Sammy Davis, Jr., the black entertainer and member of the infamous Sinatra "rat pack," confessed in his autobiography, *Yes, I Can*, to being a Satan worshipper. The talented singer/dancer said that as a Satanist he painted the fingernail of his left-hand "pinkie" finger ebony black as a sign. *"The chicks loved it,"* said Davis, *"and found it really a sexual turn-on."* Some Islamic imams (teachers) preach that the hand of Fatima, a revered daughter of Mohammed, represents the summation of the whole religion of Islam, and that Fatima's index finger points heavenward to Allah.

A hand with finger pointed to or touching the lip indicates, "Be silent." A finger touching or pointing to the head signifies "intellect or wisdom."

The pictures and illustrations in this section and the immediately following sections give evidence of the importance the Illuminati minions give to the use of hands, either in handshakes and grips, or in various poses. The old phrase, "a show of hands" certainly has a multiplication of meanings to the members of secret societies.

Open to Interpretation?

A word of caution and advice is in order, however. Although I have used the best reference guides and the best knowledge obtainable from myriad investigative sources, it is sometimes very difficult to judge and evaluate a particular handshake, hand sign, pose or grip. For one thing, even though a masonic reference book or occult textbook may clearly spell out the specifications for a type of grip or sign, the people who practice it are not always so precise.

I noted in a 20-year career in the U.S. Air Force that while the military manuals and guidebooks clearly explain how to perform a hand salute, not all in uniform complied. Some high-ranking officers render a shoddy, confusing, lackadaisical salute while others give a snappy, precise salute exactly as the textbook prescribes. One can see a hundred different types of salutes at a typical Air Force Base exchanged on a given day, each a little bit different in one aspect or the other. And, of course, if you compare the way the U.S. military salutes with the salute of a British Sergeant Major, the difference is striking, indeed.

Still, even taking into account the human factor, it is possible to identify many of the hand signs and poses given and used by the elite. Check out my selection on the pages that follow and see if you agree.

Many secret orders and societies display and use secret handshakes and signs. In Wales (Great Britain) the Order of the True Ivorites was established in 1836 and prospered for many years. Some believe two lodges of Ivorites still exist today. Pictured here are some of their secret signs and handshakes.

FOUR

Hidden Hand of the Men of Jahbuhlun

Because the higher trinity of man's being must be present before soul-union can take place...the Omnific Royal Arch Word can only be given in groups of three... Their right hands are then raised above their heads or they give at low breath the word: Jah-buh-lun, Je-ho-vah, G-O-D.

—C.C. Zain
Ancient Masonry

The greatest, but the most terrible moment in the life of a Mason...The three supreme officials of the Lodge, with three separate keys, unlock the wooden box with the "Secret of Secrets" and give him to read a slip of paper, upon which is written the name of the "god" whose follower he was...JAH-BUL-ON.

—D.C. Yermak
The Axis of Death

Over my many years of exposing the lies and evils of Freemasonry, the *Ordo Templi Orientis*, the *Rosicrucians*, and other treacherous cultic secret societies, I have been challenged by many Masons. Their typical complaint is, "How dare you say such things about Masonry! Why, I'll have you know I am a Christian, and there is nothing in the Lodge or its rituals that would not be acceptable to my Christian faith."

Of course, it is super-easy, almost like taking candy from a baby, to disabuse the Masonic whiner and complainer hollering that you or I have slandered the Masons by denying their order's "Christian attributes." After all, there are scores of points to make that blow apart the silly notion that the Masonic Lodge or similar groups are even vaguely "Christian" in nature. But the easiest way to handle such a complaint is to ask the Mason if he has reached the Royal Arch Mason ritual level or equivalent (13th degree in the Scottish Rite). If he answers "yes," then, uh oh, he is in big, big trouble.

What About Jahbuhlun?

I then ask him about the name of his sacred god revealed in the Royal Arch degree ritual; that is, I ask him about Jahbuhlun. And usually, I can hear either a long, uninterrupted stutter, or else simply a great gasping sound. Generally, that ends the discussion right there. A Mason definitely does *not* want to publicly discuss that name, Jahbuhlun. Anything but that. Bamm! He's gone. And I can understand why.

Ed Decker, a friend of mine, a good Christian who is an ex-Mormon, now heads up a Christian ministry aimed at helping men get out of these cults. In a book that Ed edited, entitled, *The Dark Side of Freemasonry*, he writes that while Christians know full well that the sacred name of God is Jesus, the Mason is at first denied knowledge of the sacred name of *their* God and then belatedly finds out that the name of the Mason deity is definitely *not* Jesus, the name above every other name (*Philippians 2:9-11*).

The Lost Name of God

The Blue Lodge Masons, encompassing the first three degrees of Masonry, are instructed that they are seeking the *Lost Word* or the *Lost Name* of God...It isn't until they reach the level of Royal Arch Masonry (seventh degree, York Rite) that they discover that the Lost Name of God wasn't lost after all. It's at this level that they learn the sacred name of Masonry's God.

They find that the sacred name of (the Masonic) God is composed of three names representing the three identities of God. It is so sacred it takes three Royal Arch Masons to be able to speak it...Jahbuhlun. The three Masons grip hands high and low and chant, "Jah-buh-lun, Jah-buh-lun, Jah-buh-lun, Je-hov-ah." The name Jahbuhlun has three syllables representing a composite God made up of three subordinate deities. The Masonic material identifies the three as Yah (or Yahweh), Baal, and Osiris. Logically, the name should be spelled Yah-Baal-On, but *Duncan's Masonic Ritual and Monitor* admits that over the years the spelling has been "corrupted" by Freemasonry until it reached its current form.[1]

Decker correctly asserts that, "What these men are doing is worshipping a demon god so far removed from the real God that this worship must surely defile the holiness of God and guarantee those who pronounce that name in such a ceremony a swift ride to Hell..."[2]

C.C. Zain, a Freemason who is part of a group called "The Brotherhood of Light," is developer and author of an entire course on Ancient Masonry having to do with "The Spiritual Significance of Masonic Rituals, Degrees, and Symbols." Zain points out that the name Jahbuhlun is Masonry's *Grand Omnific Word*, the name of their omnipotent deity. He further shows the significance of the fact that the name Jahbuhlun has *nine letters* and is made up of three syllables, Jah, buh, lun. In the ritual for the Royal Arch Degree, since there are three Royal Arch Masons pronouncing the name three times each, altogether, says Zain, twenty-seven syllables are pronounced. This, he explains, represents "the twenty-seven days it takes the moon to pass through the circle of zodiacal signs."[3]

Interestingly, in the ritual drama, the three Masons doing the pronouncing of Jahbuhlun are said to have come from Babylon! So, we have a ritual—the 13th degree in the Scottish Rite and 7th in the York Rite—in which three "Masters" come from Babylon (the font of all evils, see *Revelation 13, 17,* and *18* in the Holy Bible) to instruct the candidate on how to build the Royal Arch (symbolically, how to rebuild the Jewish Temple in Jerusalem and thus establish the kingdom of the elite and their devil god on earth).

The Lost Word Found

Moreover, the three messengers from Babylon inform the candidate that the true name of God, the name that had been lost for so long, is *not* Jesus, but is Jahbuhlun. They conveniently omit mention of the fact that this is, in fact, the name of a monstrous DEVIL GOD, that the name is an unholy and blasphemous composite of Jahweh, Baal, and Osiris, or On. (On is a city in Egypt where the worship of the sun god, Osiris, is alleged to have begun. Somehow, many in Masonry today honor and revere Osiris under the name of On, the name of his city, curiously spelled Un in the name: Jahbuhlun.)

No wonder Masonic authority W.L. Wilmshurst, in his highly thought of (by Masons) *The Meaning of Masonry,* proclaims this degree so vital to the transformation of the candidate's life. He even suggests that in attaining this Degree, one "exhibits the attainment of a new order of life."[4]

The Royal Arch Degree, Wilmshurst emphasizes, provides "a supremely high level of thought and instruction" for the Mason attaining it.[5]

Born Again or Demon-Possessed?

What does Wilmshurst mean when he says the adept has attained a "new order of life?" I believe the candidate receives a counterfeit *born again* experience, receiving the very spirit of Lucifer into his bosom as a result of conforming to the requirements of this degree. In accepting the devil god *Jahbuhlun* as the sacred name of God the man rising to this level in Masonry or a similar sect becomes *demon possessed,* full of the devil, headed for hell, prepared to do the most wicked and foul deeds possible for his hidden deity, Baphomet, aka Lucifer, aka Satan, aka *Jahbuhlun.*

Now, the fatal (ending in spiritual death) sign that is taught for this degree is the one you will find men giving in the photographs in this chapter. Notably, only higher-level initiates and adepts will typically be seen giving this evil sign stamping them as demon-possessed disciples of Satan. I call this sign the *Hidden Hand of the Men of Jahbuhlun.*

From Washington to Rothschild

Regrettably, America's first President, George Washington, exhibited this sign, if the painter of one of his most famous portraits is to be believed. Subsequent Presidents, men like Franklin Pierce and Rutherford Hayes, were disciples of Jahbuhlun, as was President Teddy Roosevelt. We also have communists Karl Marx, Vladimir Lenin, and Joseph Stalin giving the sign, plus Napoleon, Salomon Rothschild, and many others whose images and pictures you will find in the ensuing pages, as they perform this devilish sign.

Wine From A Human Skull

Many other facets and activities pertaining to this degree's ritual stamp it as pure Luciferian and its holder as a Lucifer worshipper. During the initiation into the seventh degree Royal Arch Mason (York Rite) or 13th degree (Scottish Rite), the candidate drinks wine from a human skull. By this monstrous act, he reinforces the fact that he has taken an oath swearing to "have his skull struck off and his brains exposed to the scorching rays of a median sun" should he ever divulge Masonic secrets. He goes on to demand that if he does divulge secrets, may all the sins of the dead person whose skull he is drinking from be heaped upon his, the candidate's, head.[6]

So we see that the Mason's newfound "God," Jahbuhlun (Jah-Baal-On), is a rigid taskmaster who does not look kindly on traitors and blabbers. It was the Canaanite god Baal, of course, to whom the backslidden Jews and pagans sacrificed their children in the fire. You'll recall that the prophet Elijah brought the message of God's judgement against those who worshipped bloodthirsty Baal, who, in reality, is merely an idolatrous representation of Satan. Yes, Baal is the devil.

To attempt in vain to *combine* the name of the true God with that of false gods like Baal and On is particularly evil and grievous to the true God in heaven. Yet, the Mason does exactly this with Jahbuhlun and then compounds his grave error by adopting as one of his chief logos the sign of the *double-headed eagle* (symbolizing *one* body of God, *two* heads!)

The Triple Tau

Yet another proof of the deviltry of the Jahbuhlun hoax is the symbol of the Triple Tau, which is the most important symbol of the Royal Arch Degree. Made up of three interlinking tau symbols (T), these three are said to represent a triad of sacred, Jewish powers of king, priest, and prophet. In other words, the Mason assumes a trinity of

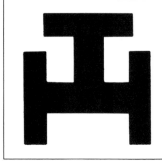

The Triple Tau is the most significant symbol, or logo, of the Royal Arch Mason. It represents the Mason who has reached either the seventh degree of the York Rite or 13th degree of the Scottish Rite as embodying within the attributes of the Godhead, or Holy Trinity, by blasphemously declaring himself to be the great *I Am That I Am*, thus identifying himself with Satan's promise in the Garden, "ye shall be as gods."

Jewish spiritual powers.[7] Actually, this trinity of the Jews is in competition with the true Godhead of the Bible: Father, Son, and Holy Spirit.

"I Am that I Am," the Mason Proclaims

Equally blasphemous is that in the lecture on the seventh, or Royal Arch Degree, of the York Rite, the Mason initiated is asked the question, *"Are you a Royal Arch Mason?"* His answer is required to be: *"I am that I am."*[8]

In other words, in this degree's ritual the Mason has not only acknowledged that the devil, in the guise of Jahbuhlun, is his sacred Lord, but he now is declaring that he, himself, a mere man, is the great *I am!* In other words, he is saying, *"I am God!"*

Uncovering the Hidden Hand

Now you see why I entitled this chapter, *"The Hidden Hand of the Men of Jahbuhlun."* In the early degrees, the Mason is told that the name of God has been lost. He's even told that he should use a substitute name for God, MAHABONE. But later, after he's swallowed whole the rotten fabric of degree ritual after degree ritual, the bamboozled and propagandized fellow is finally told that the one he is to worship goes by the name *Jahbuhlun* and that he is now ready to declare himself, a man, as the great I AM.

Obviously, the Illuminati's Masonic elite do not want the general public to know these terrible things. After all, incredibly, Freemasonry's public image is that it is some kind of "Christian" group. So, the pretense must be maintained and the secrets buttoned up from the "profane and vulgar" masses (you and me, dear reader). *Therefore, the name of the horrible god whom the Masons worship must stay hidden.*

FIG. 34.

The name and identity of the hidden god must be concealed at all costs, and thus an appropriate hand sign has been devised to represent this grotesque coverup: *the Sign of the Hidden Hand.*

How to Perform the Sign

Figure 34 shown here is taken directly from *Duncan's Masonic Ritual and Monitor (3rd Edition).* It pictures the Royal Arch Mason performing the magical *Sign of the Master of the Second Veil,* which I informally and more informatively call here the *Sign of the Hidden Hand of the Men of Jahbuhlun.* According to *Duncan's* the candidate presents this sign when he is approached by three sojourners from Babylon. Their objective: Rebuild the Temple of Solomon in Jerusalem and eventually establish a world empire of the Jews.

SIGN OF THE MASTER OF THE
SECOND VEIL.

In his teaching course on *Ancient Masonry*, C.C. Zain of The Brotherhood of Light explains that the ritual for this degree requires a keen understanding of astrology. But, its performance is said to be derived from a passage in the scriptures. "The sign is made," writes Zain, "by thrusting the hand into the bosom and again drawing it out."[9] The official Masonic explanation for this sign—a myth intended to divert the profane from the truth—is that it refers to the fourth chapter of *Exodus* in the Holy Bible: "And the Lord said unto Moses, put now thine hand into thy bosom; and he put his hand into his bosom; and when he took it out, behold his hand was leprous as snow."

Leprous, indeed, is the hand of the Mason who vainly seeks to hide and coverup his fides oath of allegiance to Jahbuhlun, his sacred god. But, believe me, there is *no* relationship of the Mason to Moses, a prophet of God who loyally worshipped the true I AM, the God who reigns for all eternity in heaven.

Sign of the Master of the Second Veil, or informally, Sign of the Hidden Hand of the Men of Jahbuhlun. (*Richardson's Monitor of Freemasonry*, p. 74)

Guards of the Conclave during the ritual for the Knights of the Christian Mark Degree. (*Richardson's Monitor of Freemasonry*, p. 123)

Right: This is the arrangement of the Chapter (Lodge) for the ritual of the Super-Excellent Master's Degree. Note the "Captain of the Guard" at top left with his hand hidden in his bosom. (*Richardson's Monitor of Freemasonry*)

Below: Once again, we find the Captain of the Guard giving the "hand in bosom" sign (officially the sign of the Master of the Second Veil), this time during the ritual for the degree of Order of Knights Templar. The triangular-shaped altar with the coffin and its skull and bones emblem is revealing.

SUPER-EXCELLENT MASTER'S DEGREE: THE OPENING. 83

SUPER-EXCELLENT MASTER.

A Lodge of Super-Excellent Masters consists of the following officers, viz.:

Most Excellent King (representing Zedekiah, the last King of Israel) presides, and sits in the east.

Companion Gedaliah (so called) is the second officer, and is seated in the west.

First Keeper of the Temple is seated on the right of Gedaliah.

Second Keeper of the Temple takes his seat on the left of Gedaliah.

Third Keeper of the Temple is seated at the door inside the hall, to guard it.

Three Heralds, stationed outside the door, with bugles in their hands.

Three Royal Guards, (including Captain,) stationed near the King.

A Recorder, or Secretary, sitting at the right in front of the King.

The Altar is placed in the centre of the hall, and the general business is conducted similar to that in other degrees. The Council is opened as follows:

110 RICHARDSON'S MONITOR OF FREE-MASONRY.

Grand Commander—Attention, Sir Knights: you will now give the signs.

All the signs in Masonry are given by each Knight, from Entered Apprentice up to those of Red Cross Knights.

The signs in this degree are then given in detail, as explained hereafter.

Grand Commander—Attention, Sir Knights: you will form around the altar, for the purpose of opening this Council of Knights Templars.

The Knights kneel around the altar,

and the proceedings of op[...] lar to those in a Council [...] Knights. After all is rea[...] Commander says:

Grand Commander—Si[...] Council of Knights Te[...] open for the dispatch of [...] you will govern yourselve[...] the sublime principles of [...]

The veil is now drawn, [...] vided. That part occupie[...] Commander is called the [...]

Masons of the Grand Lodge of the State of Montana march through the "Roosevelt Arch" to commemorate the Yellowstone National Park centennial in 2003. Notice that the man on the right is giving the sign of Jahbuhlun, his hand concealed in his jacket. He is wearing his Masonic apron. (*Scottish Rite Journal*, Dec. 2003, p. 53)

George Washington in a Masonic pose. Around his neck is the emblem of the moon goddess, feminine complement to the sun god, Osiris, secretly worshipped in occult Freemasonry. This emblem, combined with the diamond-shaped device just above it, indicates that Washington had taken the vow of vengeance to all enemies of the Order of the Illuminati.

The Marquis de Lafayette of France presented George Washington with this Masonic apron which is now preserved in the library of the Grand Lodge of Pennsylvania, in Philadelphia. It contains many occultic symbols, the meaning of which presumably is reserved for higher-level Masonic brethren. Many, however, are outed and explained in this book, to the chagrin, I am sure, of the Masonic brotherhood.

Emblem of the exclusivist Order of the Cincinnati (also called the Society of the Cincinnati) worn by elite members. The secret society met in private and was headed by George Washington.

Artwork from a china set which displays symbols important to the Society of the Cincinnati, a secret order of elitist rich men begun after the Revolutionary War, headed by George Washington. The symbols include a strange crowned angel blowing a horn and a phoenix bird with a torch aflame in its head from which issues a swirling fire, or sun sign. The Society of the Illuminati was eventually disbanded when public awareness grew that this small band of conspirators seemed to be exercising undue control of governments.

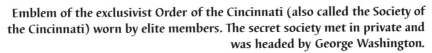

Initiates of many occult societies, including Masons and Rosicrucians, select a mark peculiar to them which they affix to their signature. This is George Washington's signature. See if you can find his "mark."

President George Washington takes the oath of office as the first President of the United States following the adoption of the U.S. Constitution by the states. The gentleman standing directly behind him is giving a decidedly diabolical version of a secret society hand sign. (*G. Washington: Master Mason*, by Allen E. Roberts, Macoy Publishing & Masonic Supply Co., Inc., Richmond, Virginia, sketch by Ronald LeHew)

Many paintings and drawings depicting delegates who drafted and approved the Declaration of Independence show one or more of the delegates secretly identifying his secret society membership through a hand signal. The name of Jesus is never mentioned in either the Declaration of Independence or the subsequent United States Constitution. Instead, our nation's founders used vague, Illuminist-coded terms like "Nature's God" or "Providence." Benjamin Franklin, a key leader of the delegates, was both a Grand Master Mason (Lodge of Nine Sisters, Paris, France) and a Rosicrucian. Thomas Jefferson, who helped draft the Declaration of Independence, wrote favorably of the Order of the Illuminati and its founder, European Jesuit Professor Adam Weishaupt.

This poster showing America's first President, George Washington, as a Mason, is distributed by the George Washington Masonic National Memorial Association. It was printed in the *Scottish Rite Journal* (August 1992).

This caricature drawing of Abe Lincoln pictures him as a high-level Mason giving the left-handed path (darkly occultic) hand sign. However, there is no evidence that Lincoln was ever an initiate of the Lodge (see below). Indeed, he was murdered by a plot spawned by Illuminati Masons and Jesuits. Could it be the elitists are simply trying to ward off accusations of their infamous act by falsely claiming, belatedly, that Lincoln was one of their own?

In this photo printed in *U.S. News & World Report* magazine (December 22, 2003). President Abraham Lincoln is seen visiting a Union military camp. Fascinating is the fact that the men on either side of Lincoln are giving the Masonic "Jahbuhlun" sign while Lincoln is not.

Here is yet another vain attempt to portray Abraham Lincoln as a secret member of the Lodge. Offered by the auctioneer at Christie's in New York as an authentic, 1843, early photo of Lincoln. Experts were skeptical that the portrait is really that of Honest Abe. More Masonic skullduggery?

This old woodcut engraving of the famous United States explorers Lewis and Clark, western pioneers and mappers, lets us see the secret Masonic connection.

U.S. Civil War officers displaying the Masonic sign of the brotherhood of Jahbuhlun. Left is Major Robert Anderson of the Confederate Army and at right is General George McClellan, Union General of the Army of the Potomac. (Photos from *The Florida Mason*, January, 2004, p. 7)

Russian Mikhail Katkov (1818-1880), occult publisher of *Moscow Gazette*. Katkov brought Hindu and Theosophy teachings to Russia. He also published some books of Russian mystic, Helena Blavatsky.

ET TU! Booth (left) with his brothers in the fall of 1864

Above, John Wilkes Booth (left), a well-known stage actor, with his brothers in a production of *Caesar*, in 1864, just a year before he assassinated President Abraham Lincoln. Booth and his elder brother, Edwin, were both members of the Masonic Lodge, but because of John Wilkes' notoriety, the Freemasons quietly removed his name from their rolls. To this day the Scottish Rite's membership office maintains that only brother Edwin was a Mason (Photo from book, *American Brutus*, by Michael W. Kaufman).

This photograph of Lt. Elisha Hunt Rhodes is from a 1993 book entitled *Freemasons at Gettysburg*, by Sheldon A. Munn. The caption above the photograph said that Lt. Rhodes was "A Member and Worshipful Master (the equivalent of the Lodge president) of Harmony Lodge #9, Cranston, Rhode Island. He was also the Grand Master of the Grand Lodge of Rhode Island in 1892-1893."

John Jay, chosen by President George Washington and confirmed by the newly assembled U.S. Senate to be the first Chief Justice of the Supreme Court of the United States.

Both President Franklin Pierce (above) and President Rutherford B. Hayes (below) are acknowledged to have been Masons in the authoritative book, *10,000 Famous Freemasons*, an official publication of the Supreme Mother Council, Scottish Rite Freemasons.

Former Secretary of State Colin Powell holds hands with PLO leader Yasser Arafat as he covertly places his right hand in his coat, a sign to other initiates. Powell is a 33rd degree Mason and a Council on Foreign Relations alumnus. The late Arafat was also a member of the Masonic Lodge.

Rutherford B. Hayes, President of the United States (1822-1893).

U.S.A. President Teddy Roosevelt, seen reviewing the troops onboard a Navy ship, is giving the secret sign of the followers of the god, Jahbuhlun. Was it Teddy who once said, "Speak softly and keep your hand well hid," or was that, "Speak softly and carry a big stick?"

Karl Marx, the Jewish radical who inspired Lenin and Trotsky with his Communist theories, was secretly a High Priest of Satan (see Richard Wurmbrand's book, *Marx and Satan*). Shown here in his official portrait, Marx is giving an enigmatic Masonic hand sign (see *Richardson's Monitor of Freemasonry*, p. 74).

Vladimir Lenin, Jewish Mason who led the Communist overthrow of the Czar in Russia, gives the hidden sign of the men who worship the god, Jahbuhlun. Lenin and his cohorts established the Red Terror, the brutal massacre of tens of millons.

General Paul Von Hindenburg, the notable World War I German war hero of the Russian front who won numerous victories. Later, in the Nazi era, a blimp, named after the General, *The Hindenburg,* was destroyed by flames while attempting to land in New Jersey (U.S.A.) after a celebrated transatlantic flight. Many lives were lost.

Three Red Communist "heros" who conspired to establish a Bolshevik dictatorship in Russia: Sergei Kirov, Mikhail Levandovsky, and Konstantin Mekhonoshin. These men saw to the purge, torture, and death of untold thousands before they, in turn, were wiped out by Stalin. Levandovsky (center) is displaying his Masonic "Jahbuhlun" hand signal. Mekhonoshin (right) wears the Illuminati phyrgian cap.

Four Gulag camp commandants. Note that all four are giving the secret sign of Jewish Freemasonry, just as did Communism's founding father, the Jewish Mason, Karl Marx.

Sculptor Frédéric-Auguste Bartholdi was a member of Paris, France's Grand Orient Lodge. It was Bartholdi (1834-1904) who sculpted the Illuminati's monumental Statue of Liberty which now graces New York's harbor. The statue is replete with Secret Society coded messages and symbols of a particularly blasphemous nature. Yet, the vast majority of Americans adore the Statue of Liberty and naively see in her only virtue and goodness.

In the mid-nineteenth century, French writer Victor Hugo (author of *Les Miserables*) cut a huge swath in occult circles. Here we see the mystical minded Hugo giving a clear hand sign of Masonic Luciferian design. It was Victor Hugo who wrote the story, *"The Man Who Laughs,"* about a boy whose had been horribly shaped into a permanent smile by fiendish cosmetic butchers. The grotesque tale was the basis for *Batman's* "Joker" character. It was alleged that Victor Hugo was not only a Rosicrucian but was also Grand Master of the occultic order known as the Priory of Sion.

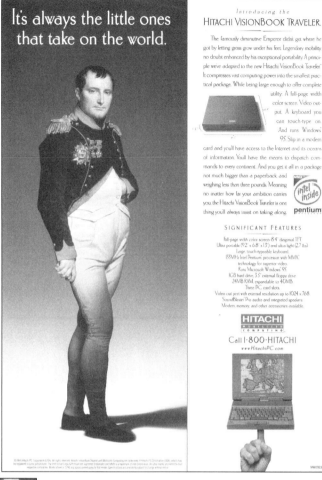

In this ad for Hitachi Electronics, Napoleon is using the left-handed path (dark occultism) of magic. Napoleon was also reputed to be an Illuminatus and an initiate into the *Greater Mysteries* (*Areopagite degree*). Note also the sun sign (Maltese) badge.

Now we find yet another indication of Napoleon's secret society involvement. Wearing red, the color of Rothschild and blood, Napoleon signifies his left-hand path orientation. The symbology of the three-towered church in the background of the painting (behind the curtain!) signifies the boast that Napoleon, a political sovereign, is also Lord over the spiritual realm.

In this famous painting of Napoleon, the Emperor is depicted using his right-hand in giving the Royal Arch Mason handsign.

The legendary Thomas Cochrane, a British sea captain, gained fame fighting Napoleon's Navy. The movie, *Master and Commander: The Far Side of the World*, starring Russell Crowe, as hero, was based on his exploits. Here he is shown giving not only the Royal Arch Mason sign, but the "left triangle" as well. (Painting: National Maritime Museum, London)

Irish-American politician and author Ignatius Donnelly caused a sensation in 1882 with his book, *Atlantis: The Antediluvian World*. Donnelly claimed scientific evidence for the existence of the fabled Lost Continent of Atlantis, which sunk under the sea, predecessor of modern civilization. Donnelly's book even contained a chart showing the alleged evolution of alphabets from the time of Atlantis to the eras of the Mayas, Egyptians, and Hebrews, etc. The Illuminati elite of today believe they are, indeed, descended from the god-men and priests who, alone, escaped the tragic fall of the fabled Atlantis. More recently, Disney Studios did a movie, *Atlantis*, based on the theme, a movie saturated with esoteric codes and symbols.

Crown Prince Alexander of Yugoslavia, who now
resides in London, the city where his father, the
late King Peter, fled during the second world war,
is shown on his first trip to Belgrade, Yugoslavia,
in 1991. His Royal Highness, along with his
family, dutifully posed for this photo. Based on
his hand's position, the Crown Prince clearly
wanted his secret society associates and the
Masonic/occultic world to know he was one of
them and that the elite's power has now been
established in the former Soviet-bloc nation.

The fabulously wealthy Salomon Rothschild,
founder and overseer of the Vienna, Austria
branch of the Rothschild clan.

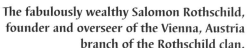

How deeply was the Vatican and its Black Pope of the Jesuit Order involved in the 1865 plot to assassinate President Abraham Lincoln? Burke McCarty, in an extraordinary 1924 book, *The Suppressed Truth About the Assassination of Abraham Lincoln*, alleges that the powerful and influential Giacomo Antonelli, Cardinal and Secretary of the Papal States under Pope Pius IX, supervised the plot from afar and even hid a murderous associate of assassin John Wilkes Booth in the Vatican State, where he had fled, to protect him from execution by American authorities who sought his extradition. In the book, researcher McCarty includes this photo of Cardinal Antonelli without, however, explaining the obvious secret society hand sign of Antonelli.

Origen (185-254 A.D.) is often called an "early church father." But, in fact, Origen brought many heresies, including Gnosticism (Illuminist ideology) into the Church. Origen, a much quoted scholar, hailed from Alexandria, Egypt, giving us yet another clue to his heretical philosophies. In this revealing pen and ink drawing, it appears that Origen's left-hand is demonstrating the mysterious sign of an ancient secret society.

The Reverend Canon John T. Walker, Bishop in the Episcopal Church (left), visiting the Washington Cathedral under renovation, to watch the hoisting of the last gargoyle. Observe how the Bishop slyly displays his Masonic hand sign. The Cathedral, often called the "National Cathedral," is the site of many interfaith prayer gatherings attended by Presidents, Congressmen, and prominent clergy of all faiths. The literature of the Cathedral prominently displays a symbol shaped in the form of the Grand Cross Jewel of the 33rd degree of Scottish Rite Freemasonry (see inset) (Photo: Brochure, *"Completing Washington Cathedral For Thy Glory,"* by Richard T. Feller, Canon Clerk, p. 38)

This issue of the intriguing publication, *Paranoia* magazine, included a feature article examining the tragic life of popular young actor River Phoenix, who died of a drug overdose on Halloween in 1993. The article's writer, Al Hidell, told of Phoenix's upbringing in the sordid sex cult known as the *Children of God*, also called *"The Family."* The cult practiced incest, holy prostitution, and other wickedness. River Phoenix, who was celebrated for his roles in such movies as *Stand By Me* and *Running On Empty*, evidently could not escape his past. Why he is shown in the photo giving the sign of Masonry is not mentioned in the magazine, but some authorities say that *Children of God* leader David Berg had high-level political and Masonic Lodge connections.

Lloyd Shearer (right), with actor James Dean in the early 1950s, wrote the famous column, *"Walter Scott's Personality Parade"* in *Parade* magazine.

"War is hell,"said the crusty and brutish Union General William Tecumseh Sherman, shown here displaying the sign of the Jahbuhlun cult in this official U.S. Army photo. Hundreds of civilians were massacred during Sherman's fiery march through the South.

Three regal figures belonging to a *Nubian* temple. Each carries the Egyptian ankh, signifying rebirth and reincarnation in one hand. Other symbols are also seen (Drawing: Book, *The Round Towers of Atlantis*, by Henry O'Brien, Adventures Unlimited Press, Kempton, IL, 2002)

A Republican Party convention souvenir depicting President Ronald Reagan. The web site offering it for sale describes it thusly: "From the 1984 convention, a smiling Ronnie in a Napoleonic stance." Reagan was given the honorary 33rd degree by Scottish Rite leaders in a private ceremony conducted in the lame duck President's Oval Office in Washington, D.C., just weeks before his second and final term ended. The author has a picture of this ceremony in his files.

FIVE

For He's a Jolly Good Fellow—Sign of the Devil's Claw by Men of the Craft

A naughty person, a wicked man, walketh with a froward mouth. He winketh with his eyes, he speaketh with his feet, he teacheth with his fingers...

—Proverbs 6:12-13

While the word "craft" can properly be used to describe an art, science, skill, or process practiced by a profession or occupation, in the occult world, the word takes on a much darker significance and is often called, the "Craft." It refers to a devious process practiced by like-minded fellows who are bent on, and have agreed to follow, the ritualized path prescribed to effect the magic of the Great Work of alchemical transformation.

The Fellow Craft degree (2°) of Freemasonry is found in both the largest bodies, the York Rite and the Scottish Rite. According to *Coil's Masonic Encyclopedia*, the Order of the Illuminati, formally founded by Adam Weishaupt and Baron Von Knigge in 1776, divided its rites into three principal classes and the second of the second class of rites was the Fellow Craft, 2°.[1]

Reinforcing the authoritative *Coil's Masonic Encyclopedia* is the work of other Masonic and occult researchers who report that the Fellow Craft degree was awarded in the 2° of the Order of the Illuminati. In the book, *Witchcraft, Magic, and The Supernatural*, published in Great Britain, we find information about Sir Francis Dashwood, leader of Britain's 18th century "Hell Fire Club." It is said that Dashwood, a notorious yet rich Rosicrucian magician, greatly influenced America's visiting Benjamin Franklin, who frequently sought him out for occultic advice and information. Indeed, some believe that Dashwood was as important to the Illuminist

Sir Francis Dashwood, leader of England's 18th century "Hell Fire Club," practiced the dark side of magic. The nobility and rich frequented his group and called on him for rituals and advice. (From: *Witchcraft, Magic and the Supernatural*, London: Octopus Books, 1974, p. 33).

cause on the isle of Great Britain as Adam Weishaupt was on the European continent.[2]

The Cunning vs. Those of Lesser Wit

The late Sovereign Grand Commander (Scottish Rite), Dr. Albert Mackey, 33°, in his classic encyclopedia reference book, says that the Fellow Craft degree implies "mutual trust" among the "brethren" of the Order. But he notes it is in a lower degree. The Masons, in the Middle Ages, he writes, were divided into two classes, Masters and Fellows:

> Those who were of greater skill held a higher position and were designated as Masters while the masses of the Fraternity, the commonality, as we might say, were called Fellows.[3]

Put another way, Mackey says that those possessing more "cunning" were graded as Masters, while the Fellows were of "lesser wit."[4]

But of course, today, most all Masons begin by being *initiated* into the First Degree (Entered Apprentice). Then, the new Member is said to be *passed* into the Second Degree (Fellow Craft), and next is *raised* in the Third Degree (Master Mason). These are the three degrees of what is called the Blue Lodge of Freemasonry.

Why Is It Employed By High Level Illuminists?

In this chapter we will reveal a number of high-rank Illuminists giving the Sign of Fellow Craft (2°) Mason. Now since this degree is of lower status, this begs the question of why such famous, publicly acclaimed men as evangelists Billy Graham and Pat Robertson, as well as occult leader Annie Besant, Russian President Boris Yeltsin, and international financier Sir James Rothschild are all displaying the Fellow Craft sign. The answer is a fascinating one.

Mackey writes that the degree—and thus its primary sign—denotes a "fellow workman," a commoner. In other words, it represents the masses of common people. It represents, adds Mackey, the "Stage of manhood" and the maturation of humanity by progression of man's "reasoning faculties and…intellectual powers."[5] In essence, the Fellow Craft degree represents man progressively brought to a high status of possessing the supreme wisdom of the serpent. Man as a whole becomes god through *reason*. Therefore, the promise of the serpent made to Adam and Eve is realized: "Ye shall be as gods."

Wisdom of the Serpent

Those who display this sign, the Sign of the Fellow Craft, to their fellows in the Craft (the Illuminist, magical cult) are those chosen and ambitious of instructing the masses on the wisdom of the serpent. Since religious, or spiritual wisdom, is deemed essential and of a high order in Satan's kingdom, it is only natural that his human representatives on earth who are leaders in the religious field show this sign of recognition. Besant, a Theosophist, also displays the sign as her cult organization is based on serpentine occult wisdom, the perennial philosophy. Yeltsin was acclaimed by the press as popular leader of the Russian peoples' revolution, and Rothschild desires to rule on the throne over all humanity as head of the Illuminati's Inner Circle.

Also pictured here, in the pages that follow, giving the sign: Jesse and Frank James, outlaws celebrated as "Robin Hoods" who, it is claimed, showered some of their stolen wealth on the poor; Anton LaVey, who founded the Church of Satan in 1966 proclaiming it a Temple of Reason for those of wisdom and who sought mass membership as patronage; Socialist Eugene Debs, who claimed to represent the common man; and John Wilkes Booth, alleged assassin of President Abraham Lincoln. Booth was a Freemason and as such, was a fomenter of international revolutions of the people; Lincoln was not a Mason and sought to quell insurrection of the masses.

How the Sign Is Made

The Sign of a Fellow Craft Mason is made by raising the right hand to the left breast, with the palm towards the breast and the fingers crooked. Then, draw the hand smartly across the breast from left to right and let it drop to the side.

In performing the sign, the individual is taking his right hand, making a type of beastly devil's claw out of it and then raking it across the breast from left to right. C. F. McQuaig, in *The Masonic Report*, calls this the Penal sign. It is made to remind the person giving it of his oath taken, that if he discloses the secrets of the Order or gives aid and comfort to its enemies, he should have the right breast torn open and the heart torn out. In sum, this is a ghastly sign warning of death to he who dares betray the Order of the Illuminati.

Sign of the Fellow Craft, or Second Degree. Notice the right hand position on the breast with the fingers crooked in somewhat of a loose "fist." After both arms are in the position shown the left hand is quickly dropped. *Duncan's Masonic Ritual and Monitor* (3d. Ed., p. 16) says: *"In making the due guard and sign of the Fellow Craft, or Second Degree, care must be taken to drop the left arm suddenly and with spirit, as soon as the two motions are accomplished."*

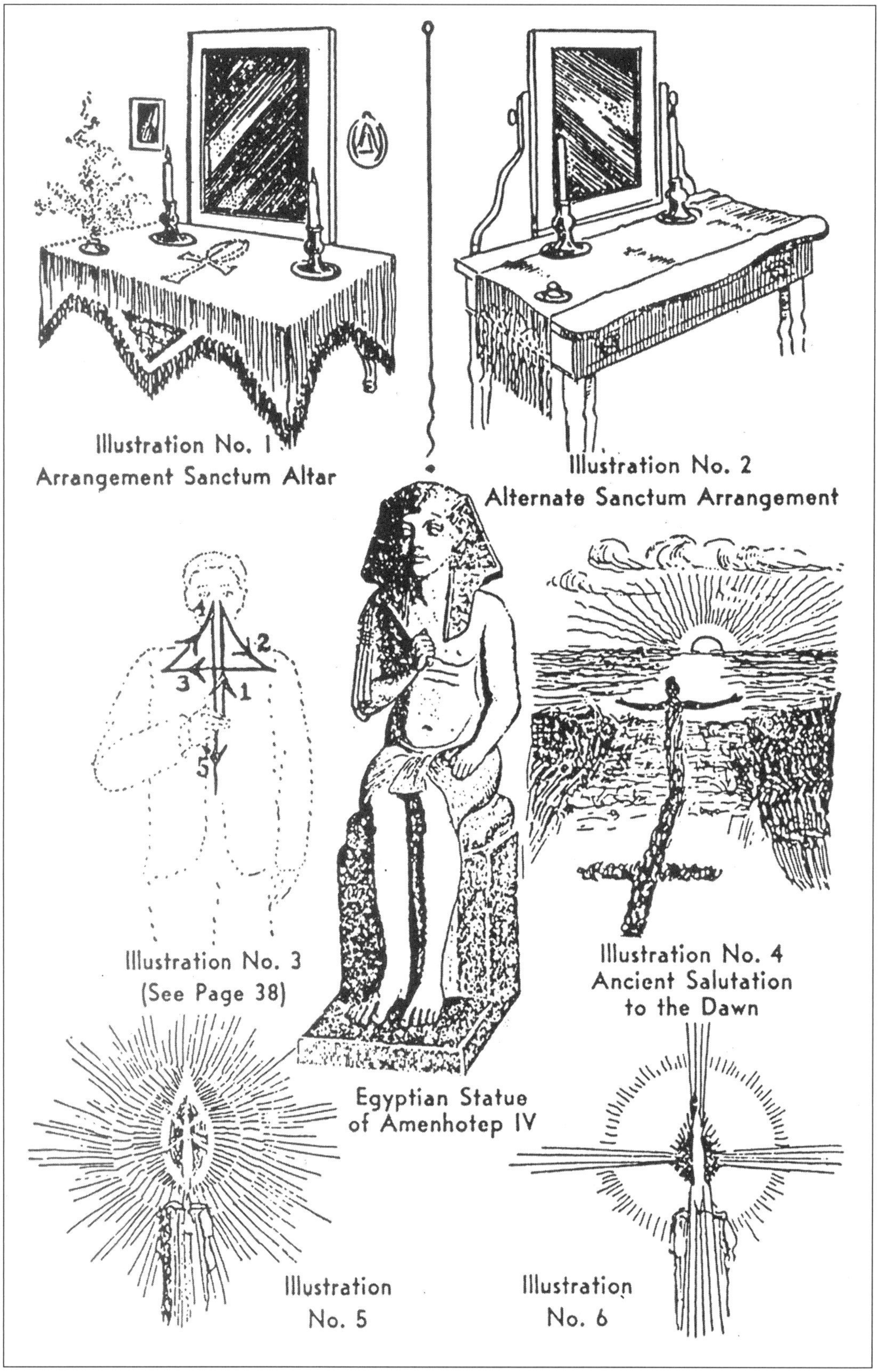

Illustration No. 1
Arrangement Sanctum Altar

Illustration No. 2
Alternate Sanctum Arrangement

Illustration No. 3
(See Page 38)

Illustration No. 4
Ancient Salutation
to the Dawn

Egyptian Statue
of Amenhotep IV

Illustration
No. 5

Illustration
No. 6

Page from a Rosicrucian manual. In the center is an Egyptian statue of Pharaoh Amenhotep IV giving the hand and arm sign later adapted by Freemasonry.

Enclosure walls of Pyramid with statue of Pharaoh Netjerykhet Djoser.

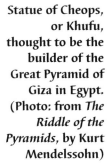

Statue of Cheops, or Khufu, thought to be the builder of the Great Pyramid of Giza in Egypt. (Photo: from *The Riddle of the Pyramids*, by Kurt Mendelssohn)

WORLD

The Associated Press

Statue of high priest Kai

Excavations yield treasures of ancient Egypt

GIZA PLATEAU, Egypt (AP) — Egyptian excavators digging in two ancient cemeteries have discovered an archaeological bonanza buried within sight of the Giza Pyramids.

Finds include several painted statues — one an extraordinary

Statue of High Priest Kai, discovered recently by archaeologists in Giza, Egypt.

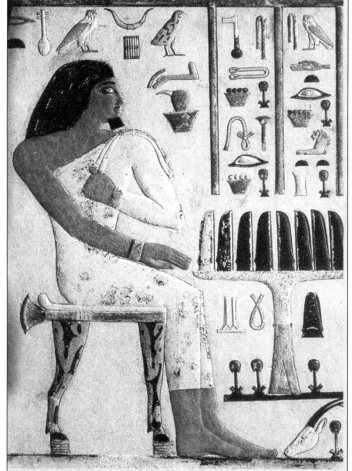

Colorful portrait of Egyptian ruler, Wep-em-nefret

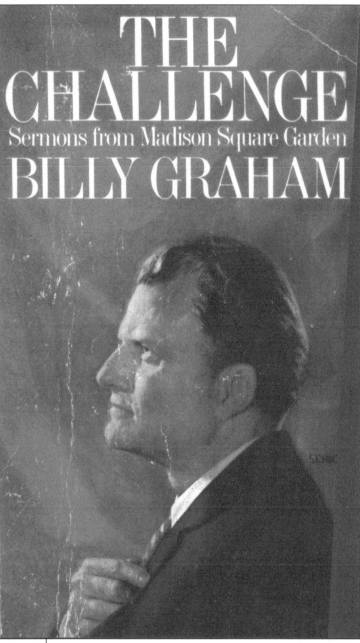

Compare this pose of famous evangelist Billy Graham to that of the Pharaohs. Graham is a high-level Illuminist and consort of the secret society elite (see book, *Billy Graham and His Friends*, by Dr. Cathy Burns; and video documentary, *Tower of Infamy*, produced by Texe Marrs). On the cover of this book, *The Challenge*, Graham's visage and hand position is parallel with that of Khufu, ancient Egyptian builder.

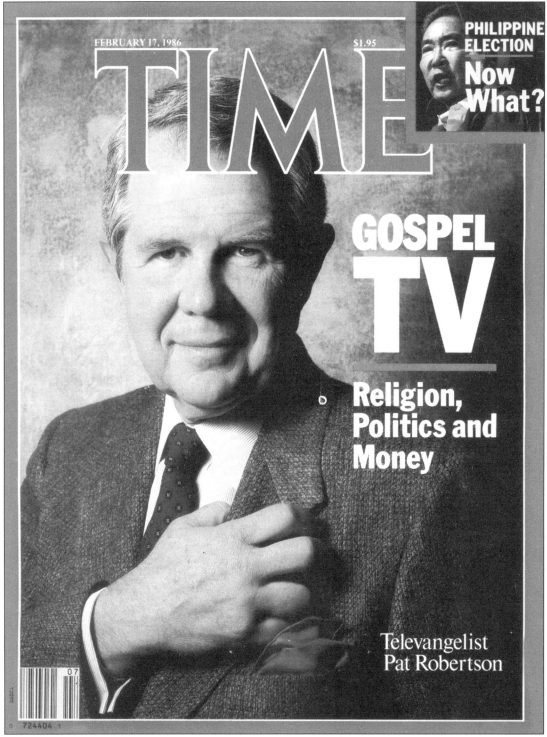

Illuminati servant Pat Robertson, founder of CBN and *The 700 Club*, giving his, by now, notorious Masonic sign on the cover of *Time* magazine, February 17, 1986. Robertson went on after this magazine's publication to become a big star in Republican Party politics. Interestingly, Robertson was ordained for the ministry at a Norfolk, Virginia, church named, appropriately, the Freemason Street Baptist Church. In the author's opinion, this cover of *Time* is clearly a staged event, and both the publisher and Robertson full well knew what they were doing. Robertson has long been allied with the Vatican's Sovereign Military Order of the Knights of Malta (SMOM). His father, as a U.S. Senator from Virginia, was chairman of the Senate Banking and Currency Committee.

Annie Besant, a Co-Mason (women's branch) took over the Theosophy cult at the passing of Colonel Olcott. The logo of Theosophy is blatantly occultic, combining the crowned Oroboros serpent with both the Jewish Star of David, or six-pointed star, and the encircled swastika.

Another photo of theosophist Annie Besant giving the sign. Besant, like her mentors, Colonel Olcott and Russian mystic Helena Blavatsky, believed in the "pure doctrine" of Lucifer, which they called the perennial philosophy and the "Secret Doctrine."

Jesse and Frank James:
THE FAMILY HISTORY

Celebrated western outlaws Jesse and Frank James were both Freemasons. According to Ralph Epperson, researcher and noted conspiracy and Masonic exposer, Jesse James, a 33rd degree Mason, in 1867 became head of the Knights of the Golden Circle, the predecessor to the Ku Klux Klan. Masonry fostered the fictional tale that the James gang stole from banks and gave to the poor, being Robin Hood type heroes. Nothing could be further from the truth. In actuality, excess funds from their robberies went into the coffers of their secret order.

John Wilkes Booth, the assassin of President Abraham Lincoln, was a Knights Templar Mason. His Catholic superiors in Rome were also Lodge initiates as was Booth's actor brother, Edwin, who is listed as a Mason in *10,000 Famous Freemasons.*

Interesting political cartoon in New Jersey's *Star-Ledger* newspaper following the 9/11 World Trade Center attack, sent to the author by a friend. Ever wondered why "Uncle Sam" wears the satanic goatee beard?

Johannes Kepler (1571-1630), a German astronomer and mathematician who taught the numerological philosophies of Plato and Pythagoras that were adopted by the Illuminati. (From the book, *Sacred Architecture*, by A.T. Mann, Element Books, 1993)

14A · MONDAY, AUGUST 31, 1998 · USA TODAY

"USA TODAY hopes
to serve as a forum
for better understanding
and unity to help make
the USA truly one nation."

—Allen H. Neuharth
Founder, Sept. 15, 1982

David Mazzarella
Editor

Karen Jurgensen
Editor of the
Editorial Page

Thomas Curley
President and Publisher

Even presidents in peril could bolster dispirited Russians

Forget lofty expectations of bygone summits. President Clinton's meeting with Boris Yeltsin in Moscow this week may go down in history as the summit of survival. Bruised and battered by political misdeeds, Clinton and Yeltsin begin talks Tuesday, with the goal of doing nothing to worsen already shaky futures.

And that political reality begs the inevitable question: Why bother?

The undeniable answer: Better to engage Russia than to ignore its problems.

Yeltsin's hold on power may be gossamer, and Russia's economy a wreck, but neither vulnerability negates the power Russia retains.

The Russian government still controls more than 6,000 nuclear warheads, each a significant threat in the wrong hands. Russia holds a third of the world's gas reserves, about 50 billion barrels of oil reserves and other vital resources that could be critical as other sources become less plentiful or less accessible.

And though the state of Illinois produces more goods than all the Russian people, Rus-

APTV

Staying put: Russian President Boris Yeltsin vows to serve full term during TV interview in Moscow.

ness in Congress to offer assistance to a government that has squandered international aid

Russian President Boris Yeltsin was known to be a dupe of Jewish Illuminati interests. Following the fall of the Iron Curtain, these Illuminati Jews carved up Russia, seizing every asset of value and leaving the everyday Soviet citizenry in desperate economic straits. Yeltsin, a hopeless drunk, shows his loyalty to Illuminist interests with his clenched fist masonic pose.

England's Sir James de Rothschild, of the fabulously wealthy Rothschild Dynasty, about 1935. The books he has his clenched right fist on are believed to be mystical cabalistic texts. (Photo: From book *Waddesdon Manor—The Heritage of a Rothschild House*, by Michael Hall, photo by John Bigelow Taylor, Harry N. Abrams, Inc., Publishers, New York, 2002)

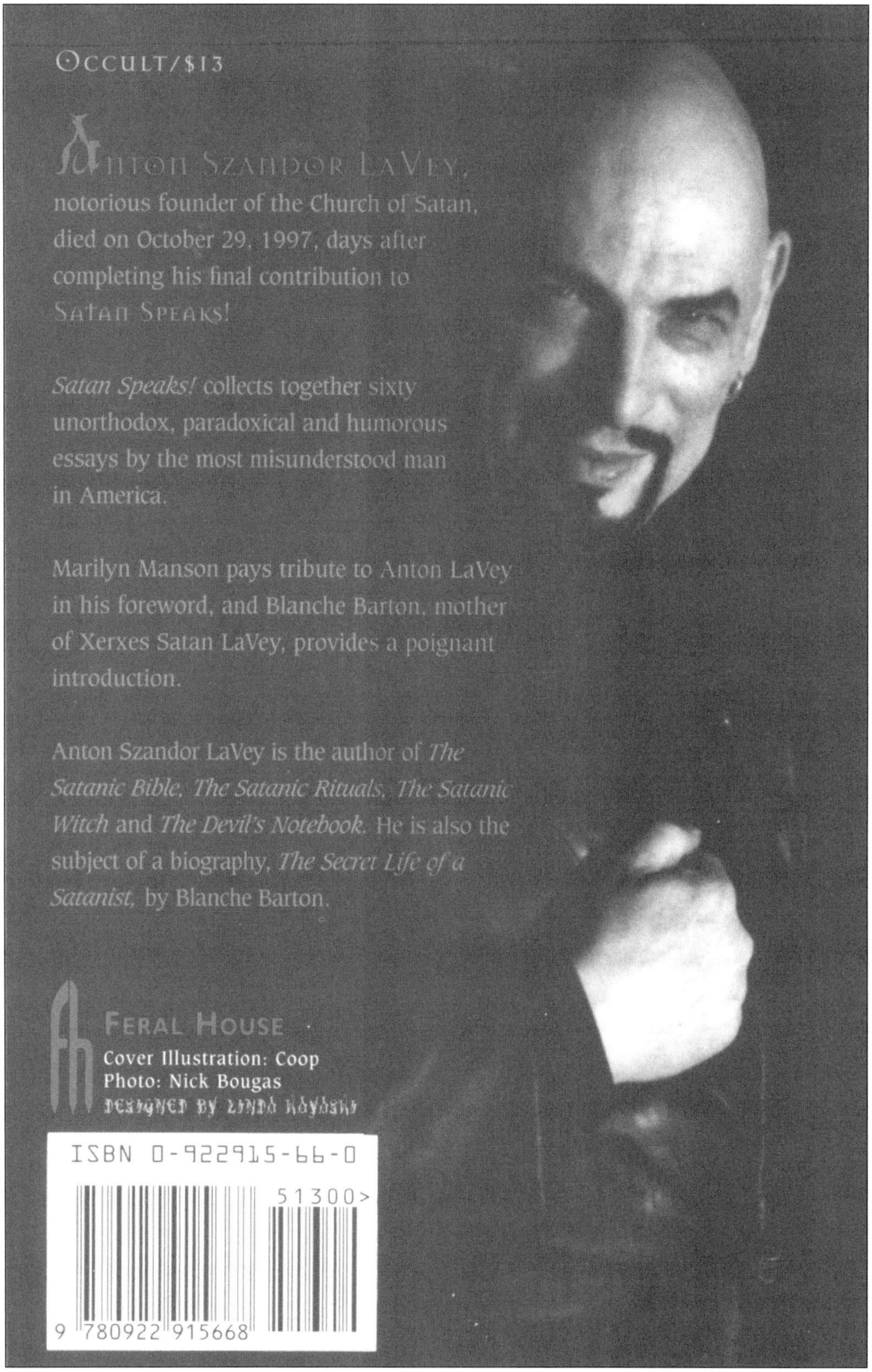

OCCULT/$13

ANTON SZANDOR LAVEY,
notorious founder of the Church of Satan,
died on October 29, 1997, days after
completing his final contribution to
SATAN SPEAKS!

Satan Speaks! collects together sixty
unorthodox, paradoxical and humorous
essays by the most misunderstood man
in America.

Marilyn Manson pays tribute to Anton LaVey
in his foreword, and Blanche Barton, mother
of Xerxes Satan LaVey, provides a poignant
introduction.

Anton Szandor LaVey is the author of *The
Satanic Bible, The Satanic Rituals, The Satanic
Witch* and *The Devil's Notebook.* He is also the
subject of a biography, *The Secret Life of a
Satanist,* by Blanche Barton.

FERAL HOUSE
Cover Illustration: Coop
Photo: Nick Bougas
DESIGNED BY LINDA KOBAYASHI

ISBN 0-922915-66-0

51300>

9 780922 915668

Anton Szandor LaVey, founder of the Church of Satan, from the back cover of his book of essays, *Satan Speaks.* LaVey died on October 29, 1997 just days after completing the manuscript of this book. Satanist rock star Marilyn Manson wrote the foreword. (*Satan Speaks*, by Anton LaVey, Venice, CA: Feral House, 1998)

A stage/production of the classic, "Caesar," demonstrates the similarity of the Roman Emperor's arm and hand position to that of the Masons' sign.

Labor leader Eugene V. Debs ran for president five times on the Socialist Party ticket. His best showing was in 1920 when he received almost six percent of the votes cast.

SIX

Baphles Me!—Horned Beasts, Leaping Goats, Satanic Beards, And Other Messages of Evil

I possess more exalted titles than I have ever been able to count. I am supposed to know more secret signs, tokens, passwords, grandwords, grips, and so on, than I could actually learn in a dozen lives. An elephant would break down under the insignia I am entitled to wear.

— Aleister Crowley, British Satanist
Confessions of a Heretic

Karl Marx was a Satan worshipper…he joined a satanic cult that featured long unkempt beards. Every picture of Karl Marx depicts such.

— Ralph Epperson
Secret Societies (audiotape 1987)

Many believe that Satanism and Luciferian worship are miles apart from the rituals, practices, and philosophies of the secret societies and the Order of the Illuminati. In fact, there is no real distinction between these groups. As Dr. Michael Aquino, hard-core satanist and founder of the Temple of Set once acknowledged, the satanists merely have a "more precise" understanding of occult reality.

Aleister Crowley, the late British satanist, who relished calling himself, "the wickedest man on planet earth," no doubt would have agreed with Aquino. Crowley was initiated into a number of different Masonic fraternities, satanic rites, and occult groups, including the Rite of Memphis, Mexican Scottish Rite 33°, Grand Orient 33°, and the Rite of Misraim. In 1912 he was honored by fellow Luciferians of the *Ordo Templi Orientis* (O.T.O.), being acknowledged for his superior Gnostic knowledge and giftedness and given the following exalted rank and title:[1]

Aleister St. Edward Crowley 33°, 90°, 95°, X°
National Grand Master General for Great Britain and Ireland
Mysteria Mystica Maxima

"An Elephant Would Break Down..."

Crowley claimed that from Bucharest, Hungary to Salt Lake City, Utah, he was showered with honors, titles, degrees and occult paraphernalia. So much was he recognized that a bemused Crowley wittily remarked, "an elephant would break down under the insignia I am entitled to wear."[2] It was Napoleon who once observed how easy it is to win men over through flattery simply by bequeathing a title to them or pinning a medal or token on their chest.

Crowley's wicked philosophies and his ritual experimentation—such as the "Babalon Working" ritual designed to invoke the coming of Antichrist—greatly inspired copycats and imitators. Such include L. Ron Hubbard, who reportedly studied Crowley's works and went on to found the fake religion called Scientology; Anton LaVey, who founded the Church of Satan and authored *The Satanic Bible*; and

Alfred Kinsey, notorious sex researcher whose Kinsey Institute pandered to kinky homosexuals and vicious pedophiles.[3]

Crowley often acted nutty and bizarre, but he was so trusted by the British government that it enthusiastically used his services in an Intelligence unit during the World War II conflict against the Nazis.

Crowley's adoption of the hermaphroditic, horned goat-god Baphomet as his own magical name indicates

L. Ron Hubbard

Aleister Crowley

how powerful is this idol to Illuminists. Crowley certainly knew who Baphomet represents. In his book, *Magic in Theory and Practice*, he states:

> This serpent, Satan, is not the enemy of man...He is 'The Devil' of the (Egyptian) Book of Thoth, and his emblem is 'Baphomet,' the Androgyne who is the hieroglyph of arcane perfection...But moreover his letter is Ayin, the Eye; he is

Light and his zodiacal image is Capricornus, that leaping goat whose attribute is liberty.[4]

No doubt the Inner Circle of the Illuminati have specific objectives in mind that are being met by men like Crowley, LaVey, Hubbard, and Kinsey. These men and their followers are used to degrade and debase humanity, vulgarize religion, and destroy sane and moral culture. In truth, the philosophies of these evil men are in accord with that of the Illuminati. At the core level of Weishaupt's philosophy was always the "elevation" of humanity to god-status.

This Baphomet in a man's suit is carved in the stone arch of a Yale University building that houses the University's education and sociology departments. Yale is also home to the Illuminati's Order of Skull & Bones. (Photo: Yale University)

"Do As Thou Wilt..."

The pitch was to inspire men to reject God's laws and God's religion and strike out in liberty, doing one's own thing. In other words, live free beyond any bounds of morality or propriety. Lust, free sex, immoral conduct, rape, pillage, plunder—all are permitted the New Man of Reason. As Crowley's One Great Commandment put it, *"Do As Thou Wilt Shall Be the Whole of the Law."*

Now Baphomet, the androgynous horned, half man-woman, half goat god of the medieval Knights Templars, inculcates this *"Do your own thing"* philosophy of Illuminism. He is the very image of the freethinker, the Mason and Illuminist who raises the "Torch of Liberty"—the fire of hell and light of Lucifer. The Knights Templar, predecessor to today's Freemasons, revered Baphomet as the deity of wisdom. Look closely at the reverse side of the U.S. dollar bill and you will find the horns of Baphomet meticulously designed and imbedded.

In this chapter, you will discover more about Baphomet; about the Green Man; about Pan, the horned witch god; and about Crowley and his Ordo Templi Orientis (O.T.O.). Since the days of Alexander the Great, the horned god has been worshipped by a significant portion of mankind. The Holy Bible records, for example, the worship of Baal, the horned fire god. Michaelangelo and some other artists, strangely, created sculptures blasphemously showing Moses, the biblical prophet, with horns. All of these horned deities and images represent lust, because the horn is itself a phallic symbol in the occult world.

Of Stars and Goatees

In recent times, Communist revolutionaries adopted the *Star*, also symbol of Baphomet (see the star on the Baphomet goat's forehead in this chapter), and some—Karl Marx, Che Gueverra and others—adopted the huge and straggly beard in honor of the *goatee* of Baphomet, the deity whom they secretly worshipped. Revealingly, the late Anton LaVey, spouting his hellish philosophy in his final book, *Satan Speaks*, says of Baphomet's beard: "The essence of Satanism is...the beard of wisdom on the goat within the inverted star."[5]

Many Hollywood celebrities have become involved in the depths of satanism. Beautiful actresses like Jayne Mansfield and Marilyn Monroe were used as sex tools by the elite, and men such as singer Sammy Davis, Jr., as well as dozens of rock 'n' roll entertainers, were used as Illuminist toys, providing fun, games, and entertainment for the elite. Davis was made an honorary 11° in Dr. Michael Aquino's Temple of Set cult. Blonde bombshell actress Jayne Mansfield was so enamored of

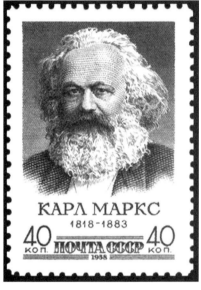

This postage stamp issued by Russia in 1938 honored Comunist theoretician, Karl Marx. Marx, a Jewish Zionist and Mason, was also a Satan worshipper. His straggly, unkempt beard honored the beard of the Illuminati deity, Baphomet, and represented *"Cosmic Intelligence and Will."*

КАРЛ МАРКС
1818-1883

Anton Szandor LaVey, founder of the Church of Satan, died on October 29, 1997. Oddly, Edmund de Rothschild, senior head of the Rothschild banking dynasty, died the same day. LaVey said that the beard of Baphomet was a sign of wisdom.

satanic worship that she had a pink and black Baphomet idol custom-made just for her. She wore the idol around her neck at a San Francisco Festival in 1966. Hollywood involvement in satanic darkness continues today, though the names have changed.

According to one respected source, U.S. President George Herbert Walker Bush (Bush the Senior) once stunned congressional leaders when he made an entrance into the Oval Office wearing a goat's head mask![6]

The He Goat of Prophecy

Significant, indeed, is the biblical passage in *Daniel 8:8-22*, which symbolically pictures a great world leader in the last days as a "he goat." This he goat, say the scriptures, becomes very strong and his power is symbolized by a horn that arises from his forehead. This strange and evil creature makes war on the host of God and stamps upon them. Is this not an image of the Beast, Baphomet, worshipped in secret by the Illuminati?

The Baptism of a Satanic Witch

In the ceremonies of pagan religions, baptisms — counterfeits of the Christian sacrament — were conducted as rites of initiation. Below is the modern-day account of one such dark baptism, exactly as it is recorded in the book, *The Satanic Witch*, by Anton LaVey, head of the Church of Satan. LaVey has declared that the goal of his unholy church is to usher in a "New Age." (The person being baptized is LaVey's daughter, Zeena, and the words are hers.)

> My baptism was indeed the reversal of a Christian baptism. Instead of being dunked into a cold bath by a strange, sexless man to be cleansed of "original sin," we celebrated man and nature as they really are.
>
> As I sat wearing the red robe my mother made that morning, I toyed with the Baphomet amulet dangling around my neck. Imperiously, I surveyed the sea of black-hooded celebrants. It took me a few years to realize that some of them may have been more fascinated with the naked woman sprawled on the altar than with me. The gothic strains of a Hammond organ echoed against the black and red walls…I delighted in being the focal point of all this activity.
>
> My father, the High Priest, raised his ceremonial sword in benediction. I felt a great sense of warmth and respect. How many people can honestly say they have this feeling at any point in their life? "I have something they don't," I thought proudly, in keeping with the indulgent philosophy of Satanism. Since that night I understood what it means to be a Satanic Witch, a woman who makes full use of her feminine wiles. Throughout my life I would replay the words intoned during my baptism:
>
> *The many footed walkers give you the strength, the power of red fang and claw, all the madly dancing demons fill you with the lost knowledge of ancient ones. Small sorceress, the most natural and true magician, your tiny hands have the power to pull the living heavens down and from its shards build a monument to your own sweet indulgence…And with these others in the devil's fane, you will so cause the heads of men to reel and spin, you will fill them with desire. And so we dedicate your life to love, to passion, to indulgence, and to Satan and the way of darkness, fane. Hail Zeena! Hail Satan!*

A Generation Mesmerized

Recently, countless youth have been brought into Satan's kingdom through movies, TV cartoons, video games, comic books, and other means. The Harry Potter witchcraft books have initiated many into the darkest elements of hellishness. Occult fantasy movies (*Star Wars, Jedi*, etc.) have erased any conception of absolutes and have increasingly brought youth into satanic philosophies. The end result is an entire generation mesmerized, all marching in formation through the haze trance-like into a 21st century existence to be ruled over by Illuminati dignitaries. Never before in history have so many been trained and indoctrinated to the tenets of Satanic Illuminism. The hidden entity behind the idol Baphomet must be very proud of his newfound slaves.

Baphomet, the great Luciferian goat god worshipped by the Knights Templar, by gnostics and satanists, and by many others involved in the Illuminati network, is a symbolic, yet graphic representation of the Adversary, Satan himself. Pictured as androgynous (combination male and female), we find his right hand pointing upward, toward the light and his left hand pointing downward, toward the dark regions. The satanic star is on his forehead. Two balanced serpents are in his genital area, and he has a torch with fire coming out of his head. And there are many other symbols represented as well, each packed with malevolent, occult content and meaning.

A malevolent goat carrying a sword (illustration by Una Woodruff, from the book, *Witches*, by Colin Wilson, Crescent Books, New York, 1988)

Replica of Michaelangelo's "Florentine Man," a Green Man idol sculptured by the famous Italian Renaissance artist. (from *Toscano Design* catalog, Holiday, 1999)

Green Man doorbell knocker, "Il Vecchio," replica of an authentic Tuscany model (from *Toscano Design* catalog, Holiday, 1999)

Over a foot tall!

Michelangelo's Florentine Man Wall Relief

Our resin replica captures all the beauty of the original Renaissance relief carved by Michelangelo as part of his design for the Laurentian Library in Florence. Its seamless blending of man and nature creates a breathaking effect for home or garden. 9"Wx1½"Dx12½"H. 3 lbs.
OS-6111 $29.95

In his *Songs of Innocence*, English artist and author William Blake etched, printed and hand-colored this illustration for his poem, *"The Shepherd."* To Christians, the Shepherd is Jesus Christ. But to Blake, as we see here, the Shepherd is Lucifer, beard and all, with serpentine-topped staff. (1802; Harry Ransom Center, University of Texas at Austin)

Pan, the horned god of the mountains, forest, streams, and valleys, is almost universally worshipped by witches, as the honor bestowed upon him by the title and cover art of this recent book indicate. The ivy and holly are his favored vegetation (thus, the ivy-covered buildings on the campuses of Harvard, Yale, and other elite establishment colleges and the name, Hollywood). Pan, whose father is Hermes, god of secrecy, is often pictured as the *Green Man*, a vegetation-covered deity. The tale of the jolly green giant is a myth begun by his admirers. Who, really, is Pan? Well, of course, Pan is simply the Devil in a new disguise.

This statue of Pan, with cloven hooves, horns, and beard, resides in Hyde Park, London, England. It is part of a sculpture collection called "Family of Man," by artist Jacob Epstein. How is it that the people of London, thought to be mainly Christian believers, so easily tolerate this idol of Satan himself housed within their very midst? Have the Illuminati who placed it there already gained such immense power that the people are so pitifully weak and helpless?

Cernunnos, the druidic, horned god of nature, wears horns that are deer antlers. Sitting lotus-like in this museum setting in Britain, his altar is surmounted by the dancing figure of the Hindu Sun God, Shiva. Check out Cernunnos' horn-in-hand salutes to Satan—remarkably similar to the "Il Cornuto" or "El Diablo" hand signs so prevalent at today's modern rock music concerts.

The bearded revolutionary rebel is symbolic of Baphomet, who also has a beard. This artist rendition of notorious Cuban guerilla leader Ché Gueverra does bear a remarkable resemblance to Eliphas Levi's famous drawing of Baphomet, complete with the stars on their respective heads.

This is the interior front page in Aleister Crowley's infamous, channeled treatise *The Book of The Law* (1904). It includes at top the seal of the Ordo Templi Orientis (OTO), a Luciferian secret order whose initiates included Jack Parsons, American pioneer in rocket fuel technology, L. Ron Hubbard, founder of Scientology, and numerous British intelligence officials. Crowley was its "Father" and Chief. The signature of Baphomet is observed along with the diamond-shaped "deluxe Tau," which is the mark of a very high-level leader of the Illuminati. The letter "B" in the name Baphomet is designed to produce three 6s; thus, 666, the number of the beast (Revelation 13). *The Book of The Law* was supposedly dictated to Aleister Crowley by a demon spirit calling himself "Aiwass" (or, Horus). Its text is a confusing bunch of gibberish which Crowley insisted is written in code or cipher.

The Seal of the Grand Master of the O.T.O. The creature appears to be a combination pegasus horse and rooster with a six-pointed black star inside an egg-shaped oval.

Baphomet Goat Head
Wall plaque made of ceramic, painted light steel gray with distressed finish, & attached wall hanger. Baphomet goat head, inverted pentacle & symbols are in 3-D relief. *Approx. 10" diam.*
¹#SBGO $34.95

Seal of Babalon & the Brotherhood A∴ A∴ Wall Plaque
Made of ceramic with attached wall hanger. Black painted background with characters in slight relief, painted red. *Approx. 10"-11" diam.*
⁴#SBAB $25.95

Baphomet Wall Sculpture
Made of ceramic, painted steel gray, with attached wall hanger. Baphomet figure is in 3-D relief & is based upon the Eliphas Levi drawing. Heavy weight. *8" wide x 12" tall.*
⁴#SBAPP $34.95

Sabbatic Goat
Eliphas Levi's Baphomet God of the Witches. *Approx. 1⅜" diam.*
Silver finish
¹#ASABS1 $6.95
Gold finish
¹#ASABS1G $6.95

A Baphomet wall plaque and wall sculpture sold by an occult mail order store, along with a "Seal of Babalon" and the Brotherhood A∴A∴ wall plaque (the Atlantean Brotherhood). Also offered: a "Sabbatic Goat" amulet, described as satanist Eliphas Levi's "Baphomet God of the Witches."

President George Herbert Walker Bush. We do not know what the star and longhorn stand for on his cap, nor the meaning of the sash around his neck. Speculatively, perhaps it has something to do with a Texas state group or a Texas (Lone Star State) cattlemen's association, etc. However, from Australia come two reports that the senior George Bush once stunned congressional leaders waiting to see him in his oval office at the White House. The President entered his office wearing a goat's head mask! (Peter Sawyer's *Inside News*, November 1991 and *South East Christian Witness*, January 1992, p. 5 and July /August 1989, p. 9)

The Grand Master of a satanic secret society in the country of Greece wears a goat's head.

The irregular pentagram with an image of Baphomet filling up the interior spaces is called the *"Goat of Mendes."* It is yet another representation of Satan.

Ἄγγλος Πρωθιερεύς! Ὄχι ὅμως τοῦ... Καντέρμπουρυ ἀλλὰ τῆς Μαύρης Μαγείας, ποὺ κατέλαβεν κατὰ τὰ τελευταῖα χρόνια ἐξ ἐφόδου ὁλόκληρον τὴν πρώην Μεγάλην Βρεταννίαν. Τὰ ράσα εἶναι κατακόκκινα, ὅπως καὶ τὸ χέρι ποὺ καίγεται ἀνάμεσα στὰ κέρατα. Στὰ χέρια του ὁ «Πρωθιερεὺς» βαστάει δύο ἑνωμένα κέρατα καὶ κομπολόγι... Ὁ ναὸς εἶναι γεμάτος ἀπὸ «πιστοὺς» εἰς ἀδαμιαίαν περιβολήν. Ἡ ἱέρεια διαβάζει μαγικὲς ἐπικλήσεις... ἂς μὴν εἰσέλθουμε ὅμως σὲ ἄλλες λεπτομέρειες. Πάντως σὲ λίγες μέρες ἢ ἑβδομάδες ἡ Ἀστυνομία θὰ ψάχνη γιὰ μικρὰ ἀθῷα ἐξαφανισθέντα παιδάκια, ποὺ τὸ αἷμα τους χρειάζεται ἡ σατανικὴ Μαύρη Μαγεία!

Blonde bombshell actress Jayne Mansfield believed she could invoke the powers of satanic black magic to enhance her Hollywood career. (Photo: Book, *Satan Wants You*, by Arthur Lyons, Mysterious Press, New York, 1988)

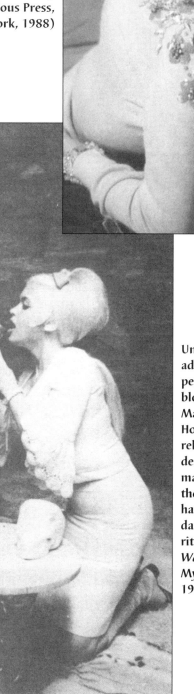

Unbeknown to her throng of admirers, High Priest Anton LaVey performs a "private" ritual for blockbuster movie actress Jayne Mansfield at her home in Hollywood. This photo was released after Mansfield's tragic death in an auto accident. How many other famous persons are there out there, still living, who have "privately" participated in dark black magic masses and rituals? (Photo: Book, *Satan Wants You*, by Arthur Lyons, Mysterious Press, New York, 1988)

The Devil makes an appearance at a black sabbat ritual of his followers. (From an ancient woodcut by Pierre de Lancre, France, 1913)

Baal and some other gods were pictured as horned bulls. This is Baal, god of fire receiving an infant as sacrifice.

World&Nation

Archaelogists believe they've found the lost tomb of Alexander the Great

By EILEEN ALT POWELL
The Associated Press

CAIRO, Egypt — Archaeologists believe they've found the tomb of Alexander the Great in the Egyptian desert, solving one of the great mysteries of ancient times, the head of Egypt's antiquities department said today.

"I do feel that this is the tomb of Alexander," Abdel-Halim Noureddin, chairman of the Egyptian Antiquities Organization, told The Associated Press. "All the evidence is there."

"We have dreamt about this for a long time," he said. "When you find it, you never quite believe it."

Noureddin, one of the nation's ranking Egyptologists, spoke after visiting the site near the oasis of Siwa in the Western Desert.

Alexander, king of Macedon, was one of the greatest generals of all time and one of the dominant personalities of the ancient world. He led his armies out of Greece in 334 B.C. at the age of 22, creating an empire that covered much of Asia and spreading Greek culture throughout the Mideast and Asia.

He is believed to have been planning a voyage by sea around Arabia when he caught a fever and died at Babylon in 323 B.C. at the age of 33.

His burial place is one of the great unsolved mysteries of the ancient world. History has it that after the Macedonian warrior died in Babylon, now in central Iraq, his body was moved to Syria and then to Egypt.

But the burial place was never found.

Last weekend, Greek archaeologists looking for the site disclosed that they had found two limestone plaques near what appeared to be a large tomb at Siwa, 50 miles east of the Libyan border.

The plaques were written in Greek and recount how Ptolemy, Alexander's aide and successor, brought his master's body to the tomb and buried it, according to newspaper reports.

Noureddin said there was no question that the site "is a royal tomb." Its size, he said, indicates that "it is not for the ruler of the area or the province."

Newspaper reports described it as 130 feet long and 65 feet wide and built with large stones.

The inscriptions provided "very good evidence" that the tomb was Alexander's, Noureddin said.

Greek-language specialists in the Egyptian Antiquities Organization will translate the writing on the plaques, he said.

The Greek archaeological team, headed by Leana Souvaltze, has been digging at Siwa for four years. Noureddin said the team would continue its work and that he would send other specialists to see the site.

The Siwa oasis, the Mediterranean port of Alexandria and the ancient Egyptian capital of Memphis have been considered the most likely sites for Alexander's burial place.

Other evidence suggesting he was buried in Siwa appears in references at the tomb to Amun, the sun god.

About 570 B.C., the Pharaoh Amasis built a temple in Siwa to Amun, and the temple oracle gained fame for answering even the most difficult questions. The Greeks later called the god Zeus.

Alexander went to Siwa in 332 B.C. for a private audience with the oracle. According to legend, the oracle told Alexander he was divine and Egypt's rightful owner. Alexander took Egypt without a struggle, then died at Babylon nine years later.

Tomb of Alexander found

Kingdom of Alexander the Great between 334 B.C. and 323 B.C.

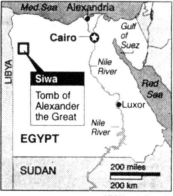

AP/Wm. J. Castello

According to this news account from The Associated Press (April 3, 1995), the tomb of Alexander the Great was found at Siwa, in Egypt.

Adorers of the Greek conqueror, Alexander the Great, attributed horns to him. This was thought to be emblematic of a person's divine power and spiritual acumen. Coins bearing Alexander's visage were struck picturing the Greek military leader as a bull with horns and the lit torch in his head.

Strangely, many medieval artists, especially those clandestinely dabbling in the occult arts, often portrayed Moses as a bearded human figure with horns. *(The Herder Dictionary of Symbols*, Chiron Publications, Illinois)

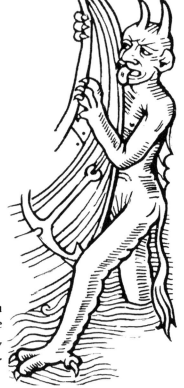

The devil has long been conceived in the popular imagination of the masses as a creature with horns, cloved feet and claws, and tail.

Smokey the bull?

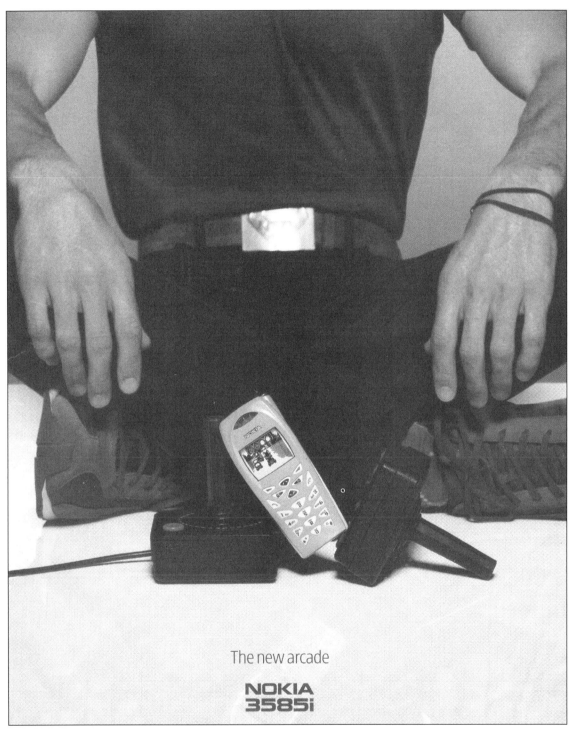

The new arcade

NOKIA 3585i

This ad for Nokia telephones appears harmless enough. But look closely at the subtle, horned image of the man's silver belt buckle. Also, he is wearing what appears to be the string cord on his left wrist characteristic of followers of the occult Cabala (or *Kabbalah*).

President Bill Clinton was named "Man of the Year" by *Time* magazine. The editors stretched the letter 'M' to make it appear as if Clinton had horns.

Horns make Clinton look like the devil

Look closely at Time magazine's latest issue and decide: Is Bill Clinton "Man of the Year" or the devil of the decade?

Editors at the newsweekly meant to honor the president-elect by putting his smiling face on their year-end cover. But, oh, the way they did it!

His hair overlaps the high points of letters in the Time logo, making it appear as though the Democratic politician has horns.

"No, Bill Clinton is not the Antichrist," said Time spokesman Robert Pondiscio, who has been forced to field phone and fax questions about whether Clinton is from down in Arkansas or from Down Under — and we don't mean Australia.

One caller pointed out that Clinton was the 66th Man of the Year. That figure, reflecting a belief that 666 is satanic, supposedly shows "Time is in league with the devil," Pondiscio said he was told.

For the record, he said, the cover causing double-takes was unintentional.

Watch for an editor's note on all this in next week's issue.

Gannett News Service

Gannet News Service, one of America's largest daily newspaper chains, ran this story about the *Time* cover that made President Clinton look like the devil. All unintentional, said Gannett. Sure it was!

"That which we must say to the *CROWD* is: we worship a god, but it is the god that one adores without superstition. To *YOU* Sovereign Grand Inspectors General, we say this, that you may repeat it to the brethren of the 32nd, 31st and 30th degrees – the **MASONIC RELIGION** should be, by all of us initiates of the *high* degrees, maintained in the purity of the **LUCIFERIAN** doctrine. If Lucifer were not god, would Adonay (Jesus)... calumniate (spread false and harmful statements about) him?... YES, LUCIFER IS GOD..."*

*A.C. De La Rive, *La Femme et l'Enfant dans la Franc-Maçonnèrie Universelle* (page 588).

General Albert Pike, 33°

The symbol of the androgynous beast-god, Baphomet, turns out to be remarkably similar to the symbol worn by the Sovereign Grand Commanders of the Scottish Rite, the world's largest Freemasonry group. This is shown on these two pages of a popular tract by Chick Publications. They show Albert Pike, 33rd degree, 19th century Sovereign Grand Commander following the American Civil War, quoted as adoring Lucifer. Also wearing the symbol, Henry C. Clausen, 33rd degree, Sovereign Grand Commander in the 1970s and 1980s. Clausen wore the symbol as does the current Sovereign Grand Commander.

This is the symbol of Baphomet. It was worn by Aleister Crowley, this century's most notorious satanist.*
Let me show you one more picture.
*See Equinox, Vol. 3, No. 1, pg. 248 by Aleister Crowley.

The Sovereign Grand Commander Henry C. Clausen, 33°
Look whose sign is on his hat...
Baphomet !!

Highly acclaimed artist Marc Chagall, a Russian-born Jew, gave us this painting, entitled *Midsummer Nights Dream*, in 1939. Drawing on the theme of "Beauty and the Beast," the painting has a horned goat as a bridegroom, and a wedding couple being influenced by a red-colored angel.

Dutch architect Rem Koolhaas is in great demand. In recent years he's designed a Guggenheim Museum, public libraries, Prada stores, an addition for the Whitney Museum in New York, and published several bestselling books. Featured in *Newsweek* (January 28, 2002, p. 56), Koolhaas apparently is communicating an esoteric message. The parallel vertical lines are undeniably reminiscent of horns. The nude images on either side of the architect cry out lust and sex, while the face, arms and body posture are also meaningful.

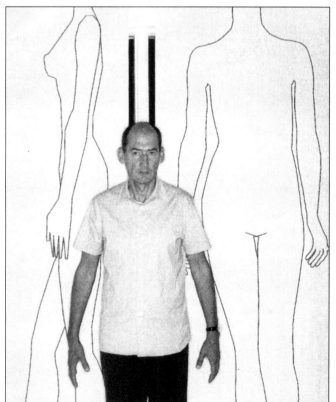

A well-known witchcraft newspaper carried this illustration (top) of the Goddess and her consort and master, the Horned God (Lucifer). The cupid-like angel is their Son. Below is an ad offering "magick" products for the "New Aeon" (New Age). The magnetic (e.g. magical) powers of Lucifer and his goddess mate are boastfully shown to uphold planet earth.

White Light Pentacles/Sacred Spirit Products

"TRADITIONAL MAGICKS FOR THE NEW AEON"

The demon, Mephistopheles, shown being conjured up by a magician in Masonic scholar and 33rd degree Illuminatus Manly P. Hall's 1928 occult book classic, *Secret Teachings of All Ages*, bears a remarkable resemblance to Yoda, the wise ascended master of the Star Wars saga, *Return of the Jedi*. Look closely and you'll see a painting of Baphomet, the androgynous goat god, on the wall at left and also a skeleton's head at top right.

This is a member of the radical environmentalist group, Earth First. He's decked out as Pan, an ancient, mystical Greek deity who had a mistress said to be the "Earth Goddess."

SEVEN

"El Diablo" Shows His Horns—The Devil Rides Out!

People that are Christians now, but were Satanists, recognized President Clinton's signal at his inauguration as a sign of Satan. That seems fairly cut and dried, and it is. Clinton communicated what he wanted to the people to whom he wanted to communicate. The whole affair with him flashing the Satanic handsignal took only a couple of seconds.

Fritz Springmeier
Bloodlines of the Illuminati

It is being flashed everywhere—on TV, in newspapers and magazines, at sporting events, and even at presidential inaugurations. I'm referring, of course, to the sign of *El Diablo*, the horned devil, also known as the sign of *Il Cornuto* and as *Diabolicus*. It began in the modern era with the followers of satanic cults, the members of the official Church of Satan, and heavy metal rock music bands and fans flourishing the sign of two separated fingers upward. The rock bands made it popular and trendy, and now it seems almost everyone is doing it.

Three versions of the "El Diablo," the sign of Satan, the horned god. The hand sign at right is also the deaf's gesture, or signing, for "I love you," a fact which has many people confused.

I Love You, Devil?

The sign often is confused with the deaf's signing of the phrase, "I love you." While at first this appears an odd resemblance, we register an "ahh, I get it!" emotion when we discover that the person who invented, or created, the hand sign system for the deaf, Helen Keller, was herself an occultist and Theosophist. Did Keller purposely design the deaf's "I love you" sign to be such a remarkable imitation of the classic sign of Satan? Was Keller saying, basically, "I love you, Devil?"

Then, we have the confusion of the El Diablo hand sign with the University of Texas "hook 'em horns" sign. Texas' mascot is the longhorn cow and it is only natural that the horns sign be employed by the student body, alumnai, and fans of that great institution.

When Jenna Bush, the daughter of President George W. Bush, gave the horns sign at the 2005 presidential inauguration, it shocked the world. Most viewers of international TV did not know that Jenna is a recent graduate of the University of Texas. However, at that same inaugural gala, the President also was photographed giving the sign, and so was the other Bush daughter. Not only that, but the First Lady, Laura, and even the President's mother, Barbara Bush, got into the mix. They, too, were seen giving the sign. Hmmm.

Partying, Drinking, Rebellion, Or...?

With the rapid rise in popularity of the El Diablo sign among rock fans, many people seem to be blissfully unaware of the satanic background and dark history of this sign. To some, giving the sign more likely indicates their eagerness and gusto for fun, partying, drinking, and youthful rebellion.

Thus it is that I leave it to you, the reader, to decide which of the persons shown here, in this chapter, in rendering the El Diablo sign, are paying homage to Satan and which are employing it for some other purpose. I have my own opinion, what's yours? For example, in the picture shown here you'll discover former President Bill Clinton, from Arkansas, and Italian Prime Minister Silvio Berlusconi giving the sign. Are they telling us they are Texas Longhorns fans or that they love Satan?

A final word: Even if you and I are willing to overlook the giving of this sign by many as not intentionally satanic, we cannot dismiss the evidence that many, if not most, who employ the sign are, in fact, thereby honoring Satan, the rebellious dark angel. The case here, later in this chapter, of the vampire satanists who stabbed a victim 66 times and drank his blood undeniably stamps the El Diablo hand sign given by the murderers as intensely satanic in nature.

Neither can the picture here of the Hindu sect member, the witch, and of Anton LaVey, High Priest of Satan, giving the sign also be disputed or explained away.

As for the photos of the top-ranked Christian evangelists shown in the pages that follow, what do you have to say, dear reader? Are these men servants of the One, True God as revealed in the Holy Bible, or do they cryptically serve His Adversary, Lucifer? Judging from their hand gestures, what do you say?

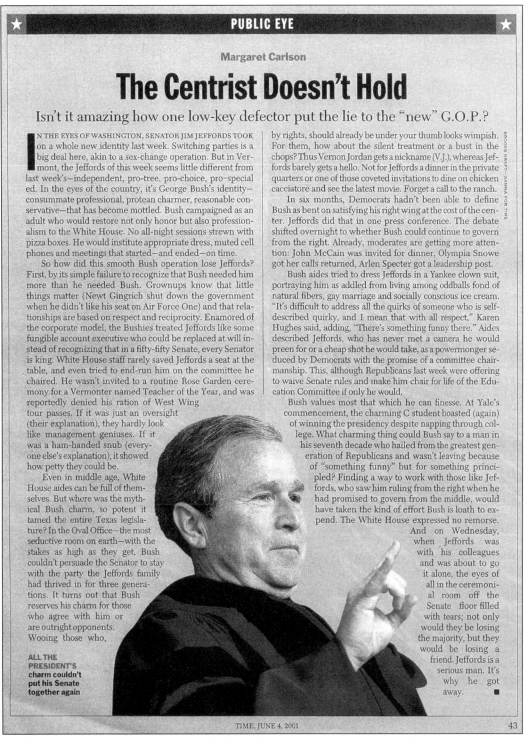

PUBLIC EYE

Margaret Carlson

The Centrist Doesn't Hold

Isn't it amazing how one low-key defector put the lie to the "new" G.O.P.?

IN THE EYES OF WASHINGTON, SENATOR JIM JEFFORDS TOOK on a whole new identity last week. Switching parties is a big deal here, akin to a sex-change operation. But in Vermont, the Jeffords of this week seems little different from last week's—independent, pro-tree, pro-choice, pro-special ed. In the eyes of the country, it's George Bush's identity—consummate professional, protean charmer, reasonable conservative—that has become mottled. Bush campaigned as an adult who would restore not only honor but also professionalism to the White House. No all-night sessions strewn with pizza boxes. He would institute appropriate dress, muted cell phones and meetings that started—and ended—on time.

So how did this smooth Bush operation lose Jeffords? First, by its simple failure to recognize that Bush needed him more than he needed Bush. Grownups know that little things matter (Newt Gingrich shut down the government when he didn't like his seat on Air Force One) and that relationships are based on respect and reciprocity. Enamored of the corporate model, the Bushies treated Jeffords like some fungible account executive who could be replaced at will instead of recognizing that in a fifty-fifty Senate, every Senator is king. White House staff rarely saved Jeffords a seat at the table, and even tried to end-run him on the committee he chaired. He wasn't invited to a routine Rose Garden ceremony for a Vermonter named Teacher of the Year, and was reportedly denied his ration of West Wing tour passes. If it was just an oversight (their explanation), they hardly look like management geniuses. If it was a ham-handed snub (everyone else's explanation), it showed how petty they could be.

Even in middle age, White House aides can be full of themselves. But where was the mythical Bush charm, so potent it tamed the entire Texas legislature? In the Oval Office—the most seductive room on earth—with the stakes as high as they get, Bush couldn't persuade the Senator to stay with the party the Jeffords family had thrived in for three generations. It turns out that Bush reserves his charm for those who agree with him or are outright opponents. Wooing those who,

ALL THE PRESIDENT'S charm couldn't put his Senate together again

by rights, should already be under your thumb looks wimpish. For them, how about the silent treatment or a bust in the chops? Thus Vernon Jordan gets a nickname (V.J.), whereas Jeffords barely gets a hello. Not for Jeffords a dinner in the private quarters or one of those coveted invitations to dine on chicken cacciatore and see the latest movie. Forget a call to the ranch.

In six months, Democrats hadn't been able to define Bush as bent on satisfying his right wing at the cost of the center. Jeffords did that in one press conference. The debate shifted overnight to whether Bush could continue to govern from the right. Already, moderates are getting more attention: John McCain was invited for dinner, Olympia Snowe got her calls returned, Arlen Specter got a leadership post.

Bush aides tried to dress Jeffords in a Yankee clown suit, portraying him as addled from living among oddballs fond of natural fibers, gay marriage and socially conscious ice cream. "It's difficult to address all the quirks of someone who is self-described quirky, and I mean that with all respect," Karen Hughes said, adding, "There's something funny there." Aides described Jeffords, who has never met a camera he would preen for or a cheap shot he would take, as a powermonger seduced by Democrats with the promise of a committee chairmanship. This, although Republicans last week were offering to waive Senate rules and make him chair for life of the Education Committee if only he would.

Bush values most that which he can finesse. At Yale's commencement, the charming C student boasted (again) of winning the presidency despite napping through college. What charming thing could Bush say to a man in his seventh decade who hailed from the greatest generation of Republicans and wasn't leaving because of "something funny" but for something principled? Finding a way to work with those like Jeffords, who saw him ruling from the right when he had promised to govern from the middle, would have taken the kind of effort Bush is loath to expend. The White House expressed no remorse.

And on Wednesday, when Jeffords was with his colleagues and was about to go it alone, the eyes of all in the ceremonial room off the Senate floor filled with tears; not only would they be losing the majority, but they would be losing a friend. Jeffords is a serious man. It's why he got away. ■

This photograph of President George W. Bush in *Time* magazine (June 4, 2001) is curious. It shows Bush presenting the horned devil sign. Also, the simultaneous joint use of the circle is evident. Nowhere in the article does the author explain *why* Bush is making this sign or even explain why he is dressed in what appears to be college robes. Just as curious, the article, including the caption, mentions the word *charm, charmed,* or *charming* a grand total of exactly *six times*. A charm, of course, is a magical talisman. The text also includes the eyebrow-raising phrases: *"There's something funny there"* and *"something funny..."* Yes, indeed, there is something funny and strange at work here.

President George W. Bush is very adept at giving the sign.

Laura Bush, First Lady, sends out a diabolical message. Laura, a liberal, is pro-abortion. She has encouraged Americans to send money to Afghanistan for the restoration of a giant stone statue of Buddha partially destroyed by Islamic militants.

Jenna Bush gives the sign on-stage, in front of tens of millions of TV spectators, at her Dad's inaugural in 2005. With her left hand, Jenna also gives the female delta (vulva) sign.

Laura joins in the fun with George W.

SIGNS OF THE TIMES

Common hand signs, where they came from and what they mean:

1. THE HORNS

Index finger and pinkie raised; thumb joins middle and ring fingers. See story at right for the many, many interpretations of this symbol.

2. "OK"

The modern interpretation of OK might come from President Martin Van Buren's nickname, Old Kinderhook. Another explanation comes from an 1839 Boston Globe misspelling of "all correct" as "oll korrect." Beware sending this sign in Germany, the Balkans, the Middle East and parts of South America, where it translates to "orifice."

3. "I LOVE YOU"

Raise index finger and pinkie finger with thumb extended. Drunken partyers posing for photos often mistakenly send this sign when trying to show "the horns." It's the official American Sign Language sign for "I love you" and is a combination of the letters, I, L and Y.

PAULO MARTINEZ MONSIVAIS AND J. SCOTT APPLEWHITE | ASSOCIATED PRESS

The Bush family are multigenerational fans of the University of Texas Longhorns — or quite possibly, Black Sabbath.

Lost in translation

The Bushes love the Longhorns . . . or is it SATAN?

KATHLEEN MURPHY COLAN
Special to The Plain Dealer

Does the Bush clan worship the devil? Signs here point to "not likely," but overseas, you might get a different answer.

During the inauguration festivities, the first family's "Hook 'em, horns" signal — right hand raised with the index and pinkie fingers extended — was interpreted as a salute to Satan and horrified thousands, especially in Norway.

The two-finger salute — flown by George, Laura, Jenna and even Grandma Barbara during inauguration festivities — has generated Internet chatter and news reports. For the record, the gesture is a sign of love for the University of Texas Longhorns, whose fans — whose numbers famously include the Bush family — often shout "Hook 'em,' horns!" at sporting events.

It's easy to understand where the confusion comes in — this is, after all, a hand signal that is estimated to be 2,500 years old.

For much of that time, it's been associated with pagans and the occult, and today it's best known among heavy metal music fans.

In the beginning, though, it was about a bull.

Ancient people used the symbol to call on the great horned bull, which was a protective god, but "as Christianity gained momentum, this horned god grew to be thought of as the devil, so those who still practiced this gesture as a protective measure were actually calling on the devil to ward away evil," writes Nancy Armstrong and Melissa Wagner, authors of the "Field Guide to Gestures" (Quirk Books, 2003).

Evidence of these beliefs are seen today in the "horn" amulets worn by many Europeans as magical protection against the evil eye. Still other signs of the horn are known as the mano cornuto (literally "horned hand"), which implies a man has an unfaithful wife.

More commonly here, it implies a man — or a woman — likes to rock.

The symbol seen at every rock concert for the past 30 years is attributed to heavy-metal masters Black Sabbath. According to VH1's "100 Most Metal Moments," which aired in spring 2004, Sabbath's Ronnie James Dio came up with the sign, but Gene Simmons of Kiss and funkmaster George Clinton also claim ownership.

Dio says he learned the gesture from his Italian grandmother, who used it to ward off the "evil eye."

Want more? It's used as a curse in parts of Africa; and in Russia, it's a symbol for so-called New Russians, the newly rich, arrogant and poorly educated.

Perhaps most surprisingly, in American Sign Language, it's a sign for an abrupt barnyard expletive that translates roughly to "poppycock." That produced a surprised giggle from the first lady's press secretary when revealed to her last week.

With so many meanings for one simple hand gesture, no wonder people are confused. Follow our guide to make sure you're sending the right message next time you send up a sign.

Colan is a free-lance writer in Cleveland.

4. "PEACE"

The "peace" or "victory" sign was made popular by Winston Churchill during World War II. The 1960s generation appropriated it as a sign of peace during the Vietnam era. President Richard Nixon was famous for flashing the double "V."

5. "HANG LOOSE"

The pinkie and thumb are extended from a fist as the forearm twists, causing the hand to wiggle back and forth. This gesture has origins in Hawaii and translates to "relax" or "be cool." Popular among surfers and hipsters around the United States.

6. "LOSER"

An "L" is formed with the index finger and thumb and displayed on the forehead. The "loser" gesture first made the scene in the 1994 movie "Ace Ventura: Pet Detective." Jim Carrey's character used the sign as his trademark gesture for making sure that those who didn't measure up knew it.

7. FINGERS CROSSED

The index and middle fingers of one hand are crossed, with the middle finger being brought over top of the index finger. This gesture traditionally is associated with wishing for good luck or to show the closeness of a relationship.

8. "SHAME"

One index finger is rubbed across the other. This gesture, known only in the United States, symbolizes the friction between the shamer and shamee.

9. "LIVE LONG AND PROSPER"

The palm is held flat and facing out while the middle and ring fingers are splayed apart, with a space in-between. "Star Trek's" Mr. Spock made this gesture famous. Leonard Nimoy, who played Spock, came up with the "live long and prosper" sign based on the Hebrew letter "shin."

10. THUMBS UP

Modern-day hitchhikers, Arthur "The Fonz" Fonzarelli of "Happy Days" fame and ancient Romans gave meanings to the gesture to get their points across.

*Text by Kathleen Murphy Colan
Illustrations by Milan Kecman*

This article in the *Cleveland Plain Dealer* newspaper followed the international controversy of Bush and family giving what appeared to be the devil's hand sign.

FILE PHOTOS

President Bush (above), first lady Laura Bush (left) and former first lady Barbara Bush (bottom left) give the 'Hook 'em Horns' University of Texas salute at the inaugural parade. Jenna Bush (middle left) flashes the signal at the Black Tie and Boots ball.

HIT WITH A 'HOOK'

Countries criticize the first family's Longhorn salute as an insult.

By JACK DOUGLAS JR.
STAR-TELEGRAM

FORT WORTH, Texas — President Bush may have inadvertently ruffled feathers overseas by flashing a "Hook 'em 'Horns" sign during last week's inaugural parade.

Bush and the rest of the first family raised their right hands in the traditional " 'Horns" salute — customary among University of Texas Longhorns — as the school's band marched in front of the presidential reviewing stand Thursday.

But in Norway and some other parts of the world, a nearly identical hand gesture is considered an insult or, worse, a sign of the devil. In Mediterranean countries, it implies a man is a cuckold, the victim of an unfaithful wife. In parts of Africa, it is used as curse. In many European countries, it is used to ward off "the evil eye."

In Russia, it's a symbol for "New Russians," the newly rich, arrogant and poorly educated. In sign language, it means an off-color word for bull feces. A headline in the Norwegian Internet newspaper *Nettavisen* expressed outrage at the first family's collective gesture last week, saying "Shock greeting from Bush daughter" above a photo of Bush's daughter, Jenna, smiling and waving the sign, according to The Associated Press.

The originator of the "Hook 'em, 'Horns" sign said he doesn't see what all the fuss is about.

"I think 'silly' would be a very kind word for it," said H.K. Pitts, 73, who was a University of Texas student in 1955 when he came up with the hand signal. "It's much to do about nothing," said Pitts, who went on to teach history at Texas A&M University-Kingsville.

"I wouldn't think many Norwegians up there watch Longhorn football," he said. "So I'm not concerned about it that much, to tell you the truth."

Yet another article, this one in Fort Worth's *Star-Telegram* newspaper. The editors insisted that the Bushes were only displaying the "Hook 'em Horns" sign common to University of Texas Longhorns fans. The article points out that in Africa and Europe, the sign is clearly the devil's own. Doesn't it seem odd to you that even Mother Barbara Bush is giving the sign? And, after all, neither George nor Laura were ever students at the University of Texas! George was a bonesman at New England's preppie school, Yale.

President Ronald Reagan's daily schedule in the White House was meticulously arranged by an astrologer employed by First Lady Nancy Reagan.

President Bill Clinton was often seen flashing the horned devil

Former Vice President Dan Quayle.

New York Governor Mario Cuomo. Knights of Malta magnate J. Peter Grace once referred to him as "Cuomo the homo."

Marion Berry, Mayor of the nation's capital, Washington, D.C. Later arrested for cocaine possession, Mayor Berry once remarked, *"Outside of the killings, Washington has one of the lowest crime rates in the country."*

Roberta Achtenberg, Jewish lesbian activist who was a HUD official in the Clinton Administration, shows her philosophical leanings at a Gay Pride Parade in San Francisco.

Prince William of Britain's royal family.

Italian Prime Minister Silvio Berlusconi.

ENTERPRISE

The Kids in the Corner Office

Workplace: Flush with offers of $20 an hour, benefits and even stock options, Internet interns these days are in the driver's seat. BY LAUREN BARACK

WORKING THE SUMMER BEfore her senior year was a necessity for 20-year-old Kara Kotwas, who is paying her way through a computer-graphics-design program at Syracuse University. When she signed up for an internship, she expected not only hands-on experience with a reputable firm, but also a nice compensation package. "Some companies treat internships like a charity," says Kotwas. "But I can't imagine not getting paid for what I do."

Fortunately Kotwas, like a host of other college students this year, entered the internship market at just the right time.

One step at a time: *Nathan (left) and Jason Kuder went from internship to ownership in just a few months*

Kodak, where Kotwas spent her summer designing and laying out packaging in Rochester, N.Y., offered her $600 a week, plus health insurance, a rental deposit, commuting expenses and college credit.

Desiree Sylvester knew she needed experience before graduating last spring from Santa Clara University with a degree in communications. But she didn't blink an eye when Hewlett-Packard offered her $16.50 an hour—or $2,640 a month before taxes—last summer to intern full time as a writer on its internal Web site. "I didn't even think it would be unpaid," the confident 21-year-old remarks.

"I went into one interview and they offered me $8 an hour and I was totally surprised. It was enough to make me say 'No way'."

With unemployment at a low of 4 percent, it's a buyer's market not just for job seekers in high tech, but also for interns. Tech companies and Internet start-ups are choosing to fill the gaps, at least in the short term, with what was once cheap labor. Now, interns pull in upwards of $20 an hour, with science and business majors typically earning the most. Recently Cisco Systems CEO John Chambers told an audience of cheering interns they would each receive 500 stock options—as long as they came back to work for the company after graduation.

INDUSTRY STANDARD

Prepared by staff of The Industry Standard, the news magazine of the Internet Economy

74L   NEWSWEEK SEPTEMBER 18, 2000

Article in *Newsweek* (September 18, 2000). Do you think these two young men were knowledgeable of what the hand sign means?

The top two executives of the McDonald's fast food chain jointly display interesting hand signs in this photograph in Newsweek dated February 2004. At left CEO Charlie Bell with his predecessor, Jim Cantalupo. Note that Bell (left) extends the thumb, Cantalupo does not, once again demonstrating the confusion—or is it simply the blurring of distinctions—between the two types of signs. Are both men giving a diabolical sign—or is neither?

strange*days*

Killing for

Ever since Charles Manson and his Family made the headlines, murder has been a whole new ball-game, in which Satanic cult trappings, media stardom and anti-authoritarian rebellion without-a-cause have been inextricably entwined.

Now Daniel and Manuela Ruda, a pair of self-proclaimed vampiric Satanists, have shocked the world with their brutal 'ritual killing', tales of demonic possession and courtroom antics.

Whether the Rudas are mad, bad or just dangerous to know, the usual claims of large Satanic networks and more killers-in-waiting have emerged in the wake of this high-profile case.

On 31 January, Daniel Ruda, 26, and his wife Manuela, 23, were found guilty of killing Frank Hackert "for Satan", and were sentenced to 15 and 13 years respectively. Manuela attended the regional court in Bochum, western Germany, in full gothic garb, her head partly shaved to reveal an inverted crucifix and a target tattooed on her skull. Her final gesture was to make a Satanic sign with inch-long black nails.

Manuela ran away to England at the age of 16, living first in London where she met other Satanists and attended vampire "bite parties" where people drank each other's blood. She then went to Scotland and worked in a hotel bar in Kyleakin, Skye. When the hotel closed for the winter, she paid four visits to the Leopard Man of Skye [see panel]. Back in Germany, she had her teeth removed and animal fangs implanted. On Hallowe'en night in 1999 she dedicated her soul to Satan and promised to serve him after her death.

That year she met Daniel Ruda, a car parts salesman, when he advertised in *Metal*

they stabbed him 66 times and drank his blood

Hammer magazine's lonely-hearts column as a "raven-black vampire" seeking a "princess of darkness who hates everyone and everything". They married on 6 June 2001 and chose Daniel's workmate Frank Hackert, 33, for sacrifice because he was "so funny and would be the perfect court jester for Satan". (Some reports call him Frank Haagen.) They denied murder, claiming they were only following Satan's order to "kill, sacrifice, bring souls". Manuela explained: "It was not something bad. It simply had to be. We wanted to make sure that the victim suffered well."

They invited him to a party in their flat in Witten on 6 July 2001. As Ruda hit him on the head with a hammer, his wife shouted "Stab him in the heart!" Manuela saw the light in the flat flicker as Hackert died. "That was the sign that his soul was going down," she said. He was stabbed 66 times. The couple then prayed to Satan, cut a pentagram on the dead man's stomach, drank his blood from a bowl on an altar topped with skulls, and copulated in a silk-lined, oak coffin in which Manuela usually slept. Manuela was disappointed she didn't turn into a vampire, "because as a vampire I would not have needed the streets."

Shortly after the killing, Manuela wrote to her mother: "I am not of this world. I must liberate my soul from the mortal flesh." Her mother alerted the police, who raided the Rudas' flat. Skulls, bloody scalpels, vampire teeth and coloured contact lenses lay scattered around, and the blood-spattered walls were hung with knives and machetes. Hackert's mutilated and party-decomposed body was found with a scalpel protruding from his stomach, near a death list of 15 other intended victims.

sychiatric experts claimed that the couple suffered from "severe narcissistic personality disturbances," while Judge Arnjo Kerstingtombroke maintained that the case "was not about Satanism but about a crime committed by two people with severe disorders. Nothing mysterious or cult-like happened here; just simple, base murder." Admirers and supporters of the Rudas were dotted about the courtroom, and the pair had received so much fan mail that Kerstingtombroke added that he was worried by the "limitless stupidity of many members of the public."

Daniel Ruda's lawyer was equally unconvinced by his client's claims of acting under Satanic orders and believed these were simply a cover for his desire for fame: "He says, 'I want to get on stage, I want that everybody knows me... I want to be as famous as Charles Manson and so I have to kill someone.' "

Ingolf Christiansen, who investigates occult groups for the Lutheran church, claims that Satanism has 7,000 adherents in Germany. It first hit the headlines there eight years ago when a 15-year-old member of a group called Satan's Children in the eastern state of Thuringia was strangled by three fellow cult members. On 26 August 2001, three teenage followers of a Satanic cult committed suicide by throwing themselves off the 240ft (73m) high Göltzschtal bridge near Chemnitz in eastern Germany. *D.Telegraph, 28 Aug 2001, 18 Jan, 1 Feb 2002; D.Express, Metro, 18 Jan; Sunday Times, 20 Jan; Scotsman, 21 Jan 2002; Guardian 1 Feb 2002.*

THE VAMPIRES OF ISLINGTON

Manuela Ruda's account of how she drifted into vampirism and Satanism during her time in North London has certainly put the wind up the *Islington Gazette*, whose recent statement that "a secret colony of 'vampires' is operating within Islington's bars and nightclubs" make Tony Blair's old stamping ground sound more like Anne Rice's New Orleans.

There are certainly plenty of London clubs (some, like Slimelight, in Islington) where like-minded Goths can dress up and get together – and it seems a small step to London's vampire scene. This apparently started at Torture Garden nights, originally held in Islington, though blood-letting and drinking were not openly practised. Steve Wilson, a member of the London Vampire Group, told *FT* that while most vampire events are really just fancy-dress affairs, outsiders like Manuela could easily be drawn into more serious activities like sado-masochism and blood-drinking. A search of the internet reveals that such things are commonly practised by many 'vampires'. "I'm not saying that there aren't any blood-drinkers in Islington," said a local Police Constable, "but it's very much an underground scene."

In the US, the vampire subculture appears to be far bigger – an alternative community for alienated youths who see themselves as a tribe or family rejecting (or rejected by) their culture's mainstream. Like all subcultures, this has its own rules, terminology, preferred texts (Anne Rice), lame in-jokes and (of course) schisms (sanguinarians versus psychic vampires). A perusal of the many websites devoted to vampire culture turns up helpful advice on blood-letting, how to deal with 'hunters' and easing migraine (to which your average vampire is, it seems, prone). A dangerous blood-drinking cult in our midst... or trekkies with fangs? *Islington Gazette, 31 Jan 2002.*

Those who claim that if the thumb is diplayed, it is not the "El Diablo" Satan hand sign may just want to take a gander at the cover of a recently published (2005) book by Sondra London entitled *True Vampires—Blood-Sucking Killers Past and Present.* Published by Feral House, a book company originally founded by Anton LaVey, High Priest of the Church of Satan, the cover clearly demonstrates that, for hard-core Satanists, there is no real difference in meaning whether the sign includes the thumb or does not.

Manuela Ruda, 23, (shown at left in sun glasses giving the "El Diablo" hand sign), and her husband, Daniel, 26, a pair of self-proclaimed vampire satanists from Germany, sacrificed a victim to Satan. The pair ceremoniously stabbed the man exactly 66 times with a dagger. Then they drank his blood. Some might say that Manuela's hand sign is merely the deaf's *"I love you,"* but the couples' grim conduct indicated otherwise. Also shown: Manuela's head, shaved to reveal an inverted Christian cross. Manuela also had a rough-edged, blood red circle tatooed on her scalp. The two were trained to be Satan worshippers while visiting Scotland. (From news report and article in *Strange Times* magazine, Great Britian)

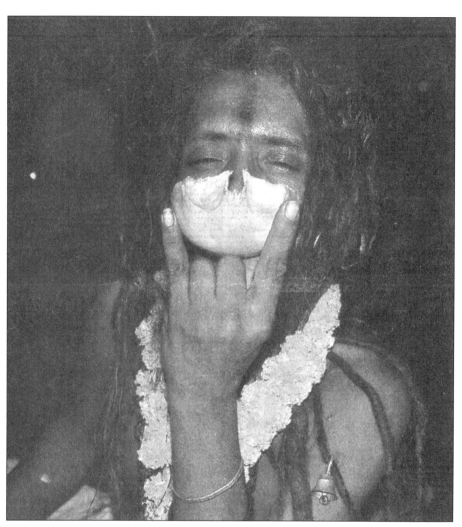

An American member of the Aghora sect of Hinduism drinks from the top of a human skull. Some members of the sect practice cannibalism to gain magical powers (*The Tampa Tribune*, June 2, 2003, p. 1).

The illustration from the book *Witches*, by Una Woodruff and Colin Wilson (Crescent Books, New York, 1988), shows a satanic witch signaling the "El Diablo."

A22 San Francisco Chronicle ★★★★☆

BY BRANT WARD/THE CHRONICLE

Karla LaVey held the hand of a wax statue of her father, Anton LaVey, who died last week in San Francisco of heart disease

Satanist's Daughter To Keep the 'Faith'

Famed devil-worshiper died last week

By Susan Sward
Chronicle Staff Writer

It was a news conference unlike any other: Black velvet curtains kept the autumn sunlight out of the living room in the Richmond District Victorian. Daggers hung on the wall. A skull perched on top of the organ.

At the center of the room yesterday stood a wax figure of Anton LaVey, the founder of the Church of Satan who had died 10 days before. His skin was shiny white, his head shaved, his cape black. On his chin was a beard usually described as Mephistophelian.

On either side of LaVey sat two of his High Priestesses — his long-time companion, Blanche Barton, and his daughter, Karla LaVey.

The reason for the news conference, the two women explained, was to announce that they will be carrying on LaVey's work.

"It makes it like old times," murmured Karla LaVey, a black-haired woman in her mid-40s. "We haven't done anything like this since the 1960s," she told the dozen ⎯o reporters and c⎯⎯⎯⎯people

LaVey preached that life should be lived to the fullest, and he complained that he never got enough credit for helping start the human potential movement.

But there was always a sense that LaVey might not be taking himself entirely seriously. Asked by Chronicle reporter Jerry Carroll in 1986 what this devil business was all about, LaVey replied with a tincture of melancholy, "It's a living."

In recent years, LaVey's name appeared infrequently in the mainstream press.

The 67-year-old LaVey died on October 29 of heart disease at St Mary's Hos⎯⎯⎯⎯⎯ording to ⎯

High priest of the Church of Satan, Anton LaVey, was honored upon his death in this article in the *San Francisco Chronicle*. In the picture, LaVey is giving the "El Diablo" hand sign while, on the wall, is the "Baphomet" version of the satanic pentagram star. Was it mere coincidence that on the very day that this wicked satanist died in California, across the sea, in England, Illuminati chief Lord Edmond de Rothschild also passed away?

Benny Hinn

Rodney Howard Brown

Kenneth Copeland

Jesse Duplantis

In a video exposing charismatic "prosperity preacher" televangelists, these four men were among many apparently giving what some people claim is the universally recognized "El Diablo"—horns of the devil sign.

Heather Whitestone, Miss America (1994) flashes what is clearly the deaf's "I love you" sign. Ms. Whitestone, a Christian believer who is deaf, is definitely *not* a satanist or occultist.

THE "CALLING" OF A
ROCK STAR
a Christian mother's story

THIS IS THE BOOK THAT'S ROCKING THE CHURCH!!!

Beth Whit...

Christian Rock?—Is there such a thing as Christian rock'n'roll? This book , authored by a mother of a young man who was a member of a rock band, was intended to defend Christian rock music. But perhaps tellingly, the cover seems to show one person giving the horned devil sign and a couple more displaying the F...k You! sign (finger in middle of hand upraised)—all at a Christian rock concert! Also, lights displayed in three triangles are in the background. The tirangle has three sides. Three plus three equals nine. The number nine in occult numerology conceals the number 666, the number of the beast, since adding the digits 6+6+6=18=9. Whether the cover artist and the author were aware of these odditiies is unknown.

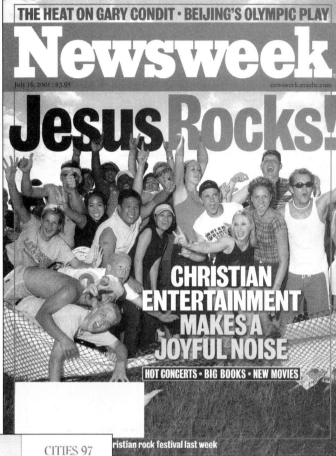

This issue of *Newsweek* trumpeted "Jesus Rocks!" The article talked about the popularity of rock'n'roll Christian bands. But, get a load of the hand signs of several of these "Christian" youth.

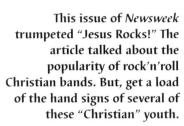

This is a full page ad placed for the Cities 97 Basilica Block Party.

"LITERATURE IS MY UTOPIA," SAID KELLER, HERE READING IN BRAILLE

Helen Keller (1880-1968), shown here at her desk, creator of the deaf signing system. The brilliant Keller was a pitiful character in some ways. Stricken blind and deaf at an early age, she nevertheless went on to considerable achievements in life. But Helen Keller also got involved in occultic sects like Swedenborgianism and Theosophy. Did her membership in these groups inspire Keller to choose a hand sign for the deaf, translated as "I love you", which is today often used interchangeably with the universal *"I love (and/or worship) Satan"* hand sign?

Helen Keller with Alexander Graham Bell. Keller wrote a book, *My Religion*, in which she explained her occult religious views and her enthusiasm for the teachings of mystic Emmanuel Swedenborg. Was the architecture of the deaf signs based on Keller's aberrant religious views?

These U.S. postal stamps depicting the deaf's "I love you" sign are shocking, to say the least. The inventor of the deaf signing system was herself an occultist and devoteé of Theosophy, the Hindu/occult group founded by Russian mystic Helena Blavatsky, author of *The Secret Doctrine*.

you've got to send the elevator back down."

Academy Award-winning actor Kevin Spacey, who is acknowledged as a homosexual. The mysterious painting on the wall directly behind Spacey is of Lucifer, with horns, amidst the flames of hell. The revealing but quite subtle message below reads: *"You've got to send the elevator back down."*

Actress Salma Hayek giving either the deaf's "I love you" or the horns of the devil sign.

Costars Pierce Brosnan and Greg Kinnear, who head-line the dark comedy *The Matador*, take a few candids during an impromptu shoot at the VW Lounge.

Handsome actor Pierce Brosnan of Great Britain, to left of actor Greg Kinnear, has a rather odd look on his face as he gesticulates with his left hand. (*People* magazine February 7, 2005)

The comedian duo, Penn & Teller, are vulgar, foul-mouthed and satanic. The two once performed a revolting skit in Las Vegas in which Teller, dressed as "Christ Jesus" on a full-size cross, entered the room on a cart. A midget dressed as an angel performed a simulated sex act on the near-naked Teller who was pretending to be Jesus. Shocked and offended, many in the audience abruptly got out of their seats and walked out of the room.

"This was beyond bad taste," said Rick Neiswanger, who attended the exhibition but had no idea that Penn & Teller would pull such a blasphemous stunt.

In the *Globe* tabloid (February 7, 2005), actor Chad Michael Murry (movie—*A Cinderella Story*), lets readers know what kind of star he is.

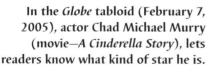

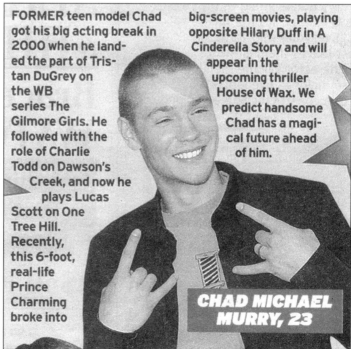

FORMER teen model Chad got his big acting break in 2000 when he landed the part of Tristan DuGrey on the WB series The Gilmore Girls. He followed with the role of Charlie Todd on Dawson's Creek, and now he plays Lucas Scott on One Tree Hill. Recently, this 6-foot, real-life Prince Charming broke into big-screen movies, playing opposite Hilary Duff in A Cinderella Story and will appear in the upcoming thriller House of Wax. We predict handsome Chad has a magical future ahead of him.

CHAD MICHAEL MURRY, 23

This scotch whiskey ad in *Rolling Stone* magazine shows a bizarre image of a Scottish highlander rock'n'roller giving a satanic sign. The circle was placed there by the person who clipped and sent this ad to me.

Rock band *Metallica*

Big in the 80s, the band Night Ranger is now heard on Sirius satellite radio. (*Newsweek*, November 29, 2004)

According to the article (*USA Today*, February 24, 2003, p. 3A) that accompanied this photograph, it depicts a near-capacity crowd of almost 500 people at the Bowery Ballroom in Manhattan, New York City. Fittingly, the enthusiastic crowd came to hear the band called *Satanicide*.

Popular singing group *Nickelback* gives thanks to their hidden deity for their great success. Two are giving the "El Diablo" sign, a third (the one with the hat on) has a skull emblazoned on his T-shirt. (*USA Today*, June 5, 2002, p. 2A)

The Grammy-award winning singer known as "Pink" shows off more than just her midriff and breasts. (*USA Today*, March 1, 2002, p,10D)

Entertainer Michael Jackson sends a
message to his fans.

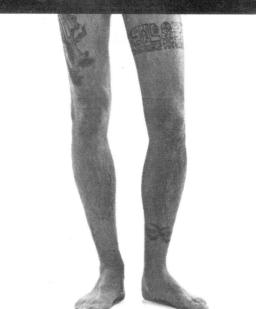

Full page ad in *USA Today*, July 22, 2003 p. 5D

The Beatles singing group shown at left in a cartoon drawing from their *Yellow Submarine* album. John Lennon flashed the "El Diablo" sign. At right, Paul McCartney gives the "OK," or "666," sign while Lennon again displays the horned devil signal with his left hand. Lennon, who once bragged the Beatles were more popular than Jesus, was assassinated just outside the Dakota House condominiums in New York City, where he and wife Yoko Ono lived. It was at the gothic Dakota House condominium complex that the deeply satanic movie, *Rosemary's Baby*, was filmed.

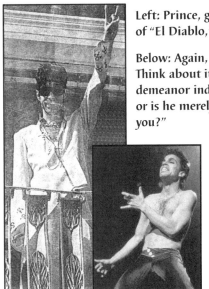

Left: Prince, giving the unadulterated sign of "El Diablo," the horned god.

Below: Again, singer/entertainer "Prince." Think about it: Does Prince's stance and demeanor indicate a wild, satanic attitude or is he merely signing the deaf's "I love you?"

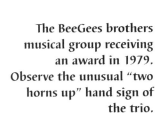

The BeeGees brothers musical group receiving an award in 1979. Observe the unusual "two horns up" hand sign of the trio.

The crowd at a boxing match at Austin Convention Center, Austin, Texas. (Photo: page 1 of *Austin American Statesman* newspaper, August 16, 2003)

F

NBA

**DETAILS,
C9**

**Phil Jackson,
king of coaches**

Phil Jackson can coach like nobody else out there . . . like no one who has ever coached. Think that's going too far?

GOLF

**COMING
THURSDAY**

Fo
of

A

Hurricane Kevin

Kevin Brown hits a homer and has 5 RBIs and Kevin Mannix drives in 3 runs as Miami romps to fourth College World Series title, **C3.**

Section **C**

From the masthead
of the Sports section,
Austin-American Statesman
newspaper, June 17, 2001

Canadian Ross Rebagliati celebrates
his gold medal, won in the giant
slalom event at the '98 Winter
Olympics. (*USA Today*, February 9,
1998, p. E1)

Tour de France champion bicyclist Lance Armstrong gestures heavenward with the index finger of his left hand while, with his right hand, Armstrong seems to be beckoning to a strange god known in the Bible as the "Prince of the power of the air."

Lance Armstrong is a resident of Austin, Texas, and it is possible the famous athlete's sign could just be in honor of the University of Texas at Austin. But if so, why give it in France?

Actress Meryl Streep gives the sign of the Devil just over the head of "Angels in America" director, Mike Nichols. In 2004, the HBO series "Angels in America" was aired. It was possibly the most evil TV program ever broadcast. The director and actress were given "Golden Globe" awards, indicating how hateful Hollywood and the TV networks have become. The series depicted angels having sex with homosexuals and blasphemously mocked God. It praised communist spies like Ethel Rosenberg. (Photo: *Newsweek*, November 17, 2003)

EIGHT

Secret Handshakes of the Illuminati

The secret hand signs of Illuminists are thought to work magic, to evoke supernatural beings, and, of course, to communicate messages. For example, the higher degree Mason, Rosicrucian, or other Illuminist can discern at what ritual level a brother in the Craft is at by testing his handshake, or grip. It is, therefore, an important mode of recognition. The commonly used phrase, "Get a grip," has Masonic origins.

The handshake, or grip, is a sign of unity, oneness of purpose and allegiance or devotion to joint cause. It is considered a bond, or seal, of acknowledgment between Illuminist brethren. The Masonic authorities speak of a *"mystic tie"* or spiritual union. Certainly, demon powers *do* congregate together and enjoy one another's foul company.

The God of Fidelity

The Illuminist handshake, the clasping or joining of hands, can have many meanings. Its simplest is as a symbol of *fidelity*. Interestingly, Dr. Cathy Burns, in her informative exposé, *Hidden Secrets of the Eastern Star*, notes that even at this basic level,

> **42   ENTERED APPRENTICE, OR FIRST DEGREE**
>
> *A.* From a Lodge of the Sts. John of Jerusalem.
> *Q.* What came you here to do?
> *A.* To learn to subdue my passions and improve myself in Masonry.
> *Q.* Then I presume you are a Mason?
> *A. I am so taken and accepted among all brothers and fellows.* (See Note F, Appendix.)
> *Q.* How do you know yourself to be a Mason?
> *A. By having been often tried, never denied, and willing to be tried again.*
> *Q.* How shall I know you to be a Mason?
> *A.* By certain signs, a token, a word, and the perfect points of my entrance.
> *Q.* What are signs?
> *A.* Right angles, horizontals, and perpendiculars (⌐, ═, ‖).
> *Q.* What are tokens?
> *A.* Certain friendly or brotherly grips, by which one Mason may know another in the dark as well as in the light.
> *Q.* Give me a sign.
> Here give sign of Entered Apprentice. (See Fig. 2, p. 17.)
> *Q.* Has that an allusion?
> *A.* It has; to the penalty of my obligation.
> *Q.* Give me a token.
> Here give sign of Entered Apprentice. (See Fig. 2, p. 17.)
> *Q.* I hail.
> *A.* I conceal.
> *Q.* What do you conceal?
> *A.* All the secrets of Masons, in Masons, to which this (here press with thumb-nail the first joint hard) token alludes.
> *Q.* What is that?
> *A.* A grip.
> *Q.* Of what?
> *A.* Of an Entered Apprentice Mason.
> *Q.* Has it a name?
> *A.* It has.
> *Q.* Will you give it me?
> *A.* I did not so receive it, neither will I so impart it.
> *Q.* How will you dispose of it?
> *A.* I will letter it or halve it.
> *Q.* Letter it, and begin.
> *A.* No, you begin.
> *Q.* Begin you.   (Some say, No, you begin.)
> *A.* A.
> *Q.* B.
> *A.* O.

The instructions issued the candidate of the Entered Apprentice, or First Degree, of Freemasonry include these given here. Notice that the candidate is asked, *"How shall I know you to be a Mason?"* His answer: *"By certain signs, a token, a word, and the perfect points of my entrance."* Then, when he is asked, *"What are tokens?,"* he replies, *"Certain friendly or brotherly grips, by which one Mason may know another in the dark as well as in the light."* (*Duncan's Masonic Ritual and Monitor*, p. 42)

the Illuminist is signifying allegiance to a deity other than the Christian God. For example, Dr. Burns quotes Albert Mackey, 33°, former Sovereign Grand Commander of the Scottish Rite, who admits:

> The right hand has in all ages been deemed an emblem of fidelity, and our ancient brethren worshipped Deity under the name of Fides or Fidelity, which was sometimes represented by two right hands joined…

> Numa was the first who erected an altar to Fides under which name the Goddess of Oaths and Honesty was worshipped.[1]

Burns points out that this reference to the worship of the Roman pagan goddess is literally repeated by the initiate in the very first degree of the Masonic ritual. Yet the Holy Bible commands: "Thou shalt have no other gods before Me." *(Exodus 20:3)* and goes on to emphatically state: "Make no mention of the names of other gods, neither let it be heard out of thy mouth." *(Exodus 23:13)*

In volume 1 of Albert Mackey's *Encyclopedia of Freemasonry*, a large section is devoted to a discussion of the hand and hand signs. Mackey states: "In Freemasonry, the hand as a symbol holds a high place…The same symbol is found in the most ancient religions and some of their analogies to Masonic symbolism are peculiar."

Mackey revealingly says that the hand is deemed important "as that symbol of mystical intelligence by which one Mason knows another in the dark as well as in the light."

He goes on to discuss the use of the hand in such ancient Mystery Religions as Mithraism and in worship of the Sumerian, Assyrian, and Babylonian gods. He notes that the tradition of the red seal attached to important documents is a throwback to the ancient use of the *bloody hand* as a way of authenticating documents.

Examples of Grips and Handshakes

I have included in this section of *Codex Magica* drawings of a number of Masonic handshakes taken from official Masonic publications and from other objective sources. In addition to Freemasonry, there are scores of Illuminati secret societies and many have their own unique handgrips and signs. Moreover, the Mormon Church, the Sufi Muslim Brotherhood, and even the notorious Mafia have their own identifying handgrips and signs. In the pages that follow in this chapter, you'll see a large number of well-known persons sharing handgrips and handshakes that clearly are Masonic and Illuminist.

Subject to Interpretation

It is true that a handshake can be a questionable thing in its interpretation. All of us have attempted handshakes when greeting old friends and meeting new acquaintances. Sometimes your hand and theirs do not quite meet and clasp as you and they intended. It might be the fit of the hands due to the relative difference in size of each person's hands; or perhaps the distance between the two persons' bodies, causing a longer or shorter reach; or some other factor (Maybe the individual is short or tall, is just not good at shaking hands, etc.).

I have done my best to take all these uncontrollable factors into consideration here and I include only what I believe to be indisputable Masonic and Illuminist handshakes, tokens, and grips. Naturally, one must especially consider who is shaking whose hand—and whether the person is known to be an Illuminist, a Mason, a Rosicrucian, an O.T.O. adept, and so forth. With these caveats in mind, let us take a look at the secret handshakes of the Illuminati. But first this brief article by Christopher Story.

(**NOTE:** The following article by Englishman Christopher Story was originally published in the *Economic Intelligence Review* (Westminster, England) and was reprinted in Des Griffin's *Midnight Messenger* (May/June 2004). It is reprinted here for the reader's interest.)

Handshake Diplomacy: An Outbreak of the "Grips"

"They are out of the gate, and nothing will stop them." This description, by one of the sharpest of our informants, with the hectic pace associated with the imposition of the New Underworld Order, sums up the way the world is being turned upside down "as we speak." That's why the press is publishing all these "grips." And the newspaper editors have shown themselves to be only too willing to oblige. A huge photograph showed Tony Blair, our Fabian revolutionary Prime Minister, shaking hands with Adrian Nastase, the son of Illie, a leading Communist who "survived" the fall of Ceausescu. The Romanian Prime Minister is shown doing a five-knuckle grip (five-point degree), indicating to those whom Lenin called "the interested" that he's "a member of the club." Masons call their handshakes "grips"—hence the saying, "Get a grip."

Let's "get a grip" with what's going on here. All of a sudden, newspapers on both sides of the Atlantic have taken to publishing large photos of our "chosen ones" indulging in various manifestations of Masonic "grips." There was that Kerry-Clinton handshake published in *The Washington Times* in March.

In that instance, Clinton was demonstrating, for those "in the know," just who was boss, and how high up in the geomasonic stratosphere he is (right at the top). The "grip" in question was a Ma-Ha-Bone Lion's Paw Grip, which leaves the junior party in no doubt who's in charge (and in pain as a consequence).

On 26th March, British newspapers carried an enormous picture of Tony Blair's "grip moment" with Libyan dictator, Muammar Qadhaffi. Before proceeding, it needs to be said that these close-ups of Qadhaffi's face reveal this man to be burdened with the most evil physiognomies on record—far nastier than those of Adolf Hitler and Saddam Hussein combined: in fact Saddam looks quite benevolent beside this creature.

For his part, Blair looked extremely uneasy, his eyes watery, and his faced tensed up after what may have been some unspeakable encounter or other about which the record is silent (worse case scenario). Beneath the main picture, *The Times* had taken the trouble to provide us with three smaller close-ups of the "grip moment" — the newspaper's management being clearly signed up, *in advance*, to the significance of these New Underworld Order handshakes.

Our expert geomasonic handshake analyst writes that "the Blair-Qadhaffi handshake is a *Shibboleth Grip* which denotes fellowship and total agreement. The purpose of these photographs is to tell fellow Masons that these two are 'one.'" Beneath the photograph was a caption containing the following odd language:

"Clearly he (Blair) has not read Emily Post, the *doyenne* of 20th Century etiquette. 'The proper handshake,' she wrote, 'is made briefly...and one should look into the countenance of the person whose hand one takes' (Blair was looking at the camera instead of course). But more to the point, this gratuitous reference to Emily Post was intended, our U.S. based expert writes, 'to show compatibility with the USA Scottish Rite. The palmetto in the background (there was a garish green wallpaper behind the pair — Ed.) reminds me of the State Flag of South Carolina (Charleston, on the 33rd parallel is the headquarters of the US Scottish Rite masonry — Ed.), and also relates to the prominence of the Middle East in all things occult."

On the same day (i.e., the photo research had been done well in advance), *The Independent* newspaper carried a double spread entitled: "PLEASED TO MEET YOU: THE HISTORIC HANDSHAKES THAT SHOOK THE WORLD." It showed the following geomasonic grips: Gerry Adams and Clinton, 12th December 1995: Shibboleth; Kim Jong-Il and Kim Dae-Jung (of the two Koreas), 12th December 2000 (Ma-Ha-Bone Grip (master masons); Yasser Arafat and Yitzhak Rabin, with top Mason Clinton looking on, 13th September 1993: Ma-Ha-Bone Grip (Lion's Paw, master mason; Pervez Musharraf and Atal Vajpayee, 6th January 2002: Shibboleth Grip ("friendship"); and most revealing of all *Ronald Reagan and Mikhail Gorbachev*, meeting for the first time in Versoix, Switzerland, 9th November 1985. In this picture, Reagan is shown gripping with the Supreme Master Grip with a pronounced Ma-Ha-Bone Lion's Paw. Gorbachev attempts the same but Reagan won't allow the same grip. This shows that Reagan demanded (and kept) the "upper hand."

Business of City Will Halt Today as Mayor Orders Most A...

ESSENTIAL DUTIES WILL BE COVERED

Rockefeller Proclaims Day a Legal Holiday—Schools and Markets Are Shut

Continued From Page 1, Col. 1

pontifical requiem masses will be celebrated at noon and 5:30 P.M. The first will be offered on behalf of delegates to the United Nations whose Secretariat will be closed for the day.

Throughout the day the Middle Collegiate Church's "liberty bell" will toll as it has for the death of every President since George Washington. The church is at Second Avenue and Seventh Street.

Temple Emanu-El, like many synagogues, will hold a memorial service at noon.

Among churches that have scheduled noontime services are the Cathedral Church of St. John the Divine; St. James's Protestant Episcopal Church, Madison Avenue and 71st Street; St. Thomas Protestant Episcopal Church, Fifth Avenue and 53d Street; the Fifth Avenue Presbyterian Church at 55th Street, and St. Luke's Lutheran Church, 308 West 46th Street.

There also will be a memorial service at noon today in St. Paul's Chapel at Columbia University.

Naval guns will fire simultaneous 21-gun salutes at one-minute intervals starting at noon. The salutes will be fired from the aircraft carrier Franklin D. Roosevelt, berthed at the Naval Shipyard Annex in Bayonne, N. J., and by a Marine battery at the Brooklyn Navy Yard parade ground.

Trains To Be Halted

Railroads serving the city announced that trains would be halted at noon from one to five minutes as a mark of respect for Mr. Kennedy.

Subways and buses operated by the New York City Transit Authority will stop for two minutes at noon.

The New York Telephone Company said it expected all employes to report for work at their normal times today. "Essential telephone service must be maintained," a company spokesman said.

Normal weekday parking regulations will be in effect today, the Police Department announced. There will be no change in alternate-side-of-the-street regulations.

Mayor Wagner said departments and agencies that would...

Experts Favor Telling Children About Death

Some Counsel Taking Young to Funeral—Advise Early Preparation for Event

By MARTIN ARNOLD

When and what should parents tell a child about death?

A sampling of professional opinion on the subject rejected last night a widely held idea that children should be shielded from the fact of death or concepts about it.

Many parents have been concerned about this matter in recent days because of the assassination of President Kennedy. Some are...

gists feel that if one is to make a choice between complete shielding of the death and explaining it, it is better to involve the child in death.

The experts agreed that a child should be told simply that someone who had died would...

be left alone because I'll be here with you."

The child can picture a parent's growing older while he himself remains only 3 years old," Dr. Spock said.

"So it must be explained," he went on, "that while you expect to live a long time the child will be grown up and have his own children when you die."

Believe Religion Helps

Dr. Spock, like Father Hagmaier, believes that religion can be very helpful... for a child...

TEXAS INCREASES CONNALLY GUARD

At Least 20 Extra Troopers Are Assigned to Hospital

TYLER, Tex., Nov. 24 (UPI)—The Chief of the Texas Highway Patrol ordered at least 20 extra men into Dallas today to guard Gov. John B. Connally Jr., who is recuperating in a hospital.

"We have complete respect for the Dallas Police Department and we do not mean to imply that we do not," Col. Homer Garrison Jr., head of the Department of Public Safety, said.

Governor Connally was shot when President Kennedy was assassinated. He was reported to be up and around today at Parkland Hospital and well enough to shave himself.

A temporary headquarters for his staff has been set up at the hospital.

"The Governor's security is always our prime concern." Colonel Garrison said. "By law we guard the Governor in the mansion. Wherever the Governor is . . . that's where our prime concern is.

"Here [at Parkland Hospital] we will use whatever security measures we think necessary for his protection.

"We have complete respect for the Dallas Police Department. This just happens to be our special assignment."

Colonel Garrison stressed that there was nothing "unusual" about extra police units being brought into Dallas. He refused to specify, however, how many additional troopers were ordered into the city.

But it was learned that at least 20 additional troopers we brought in from the Tyler district. Tyler is 98 miles east of Dallas.

Colonel Garrison took personal charge of the security guard for Governor Connally. He said that nobody could see the Governor without clearance.

"And that includes the Secret Service and the F.B.I." he said.

Connally Leaves Bed

DALLAS, Nov. 24 (UPI)—Gov. John B. Connally Jr. was wounded during the assassination of President Kennedy last Friday, was able to walk from his bed to a chair and sit up today.

Governor Connally stayed in his chair a few minutes and then walked back to bed...

His wife, Nellie, was composed earlier today when she said that her husband "is now apparently out of danger."

Mrs. Connally... a news...

Masefie...

John

Lone A Plottin

A study of tempts of the the three cou have been Czarist Russia United States pattern or m common urge

There is on between most to kill Gover other countrie United States

In Russia assassination the culmina plans made groups usua Government ations were tionalistic.

In the Un except two were made often with ning and o real grievan sonage attac

That seem case with L killer of Pres was himself

Plot A

The two American p have been th ed by Jo against Abr the attack b nationalists 1950 in an a kill Presiden

The origin to kidnap Li hostage for Southern Union jails that the fou died for the

IRELAND'S PRESIDENT ARRIVES: Eamon de Valera, right, being welcomed by Mayor Wagner last night at Idlewild, on the way to Washington for President Kennedy's funeral. Between them is Frank Aiken, who is Irish Minister for External Affairs. *Associated Press*

As reported in *The New York Times*, November 25, 1963, New York City's Mayor Wagner welcomes Ireland's President Eamon de Valera to the "Big Apple." The Irish leader was at New York's Idlewild Airport on his way to Washington, D.C. for the slain President John F. Kennedy's funeral. Strangely, the smiling Mayor looks in high spirits, though most of America was in deep mourning.

J. Robert Oppenheimer, scientist who oversaw development of the first nuclear bomb in Project Manhattan, receives a Masonic handshake from President Lyndon B. Johnson. Johnson earned only the 3rd degree of Master Mason. Oppenheimer, a Jewish cabalist, held the 33rd degree. Andrew Jackson ("Old Hickory"), the historical figure in the painting on the wall, was also a 33rd degree Mason. Oppenheimer lost his security clearance when it became clear to security officials that he was most likely a Communist espionage agent and certainly was a Communist sympathizer. Both the Soviet Union and the nation of Israel were given secret plans to the atomic bomb weapon by Jewish spies burrowed deep inside the United States military science establishments.

Senate Minority Leader Harry Reid (D-Nev.), left, and a fellow legislator in a Masonic grip. (*USA Today*, May 19, 2005, p. 6A)

U.S. Secretary of Defense Donald Rumsfeld and Afghani leader Karzai prominently display their Masonic grip. (*Newsweek*, May 12, 2003, p. 32)

Presider Mathea Falco and Speaker Hime Paz-Zamora, President of Bolivia, at September 28, 1989 Council on Foreign Relations (CFR) Roundtable Breakfast. (*CFR Annual Report*, 1990, p. 46)

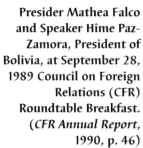

Iraq's Chalabi, left, with civil chief Bremer

U.S. overseer Paul Bremer shares a Masonic grip with Iraq's Ahmed Chalabi, a known CIA asset. (*Time* magazine, June 23, 2003)

Secretary of State Colin Powell meets with Morocco's King Mohammed VI. (*USA Today*, April 10, 2002, p. 14A)

Palestinian President Mahmoud Abbas with Israeli
Prime Minister Ariel Sharon. Both men are Masons.

This display ad was run in *The Jerusalem
Post* newspaper in November 1994

The Grand Lodge of the State of Israel
of Ancient Free and Accepted Masons

To the Masons of Peace

The Honorable **Yitzhak Rabin**, Prime Minister of Israel
His Majesty **King Hussein** of Jordan
The Honorable **Bill Clinton**, President of the United States

With warm fraternal congratulations
on the signing of the peace agreement
between Israel and Jordan

Ephraim Fuchs
President of the Israel Order of Masons

Freemason Shimon Peres, who was
educated by Jesuits as a youth in
Poland and was the Prime Minister of
Israel and that nation's Minister of
Foreign Affairs, is being welcomed to
the Council on Foreign Relations,
based in New York's Harold Pratt
House, by its Chairman of the Board,
fellow Illuminist, Peter G. Peterson.

Pat Robertson meets with Red Chinese Premier
Zhu Rongji in 1998. *The 700 Club* host has
invested millions of dollars in Red China and
supports its policy of forced abortions, all the
time pretending to be "pro-life."

The cover of Stephen Knight's exposé, *The Brotherhood—The Secret World of the Freemasons*. This book caused a sensation and a furor upon its publication because Knight revealed that the police, judiciary, and government of Great Britain are riddled with Freemasons who give job preference and show official favoritism to their Masonic cohorts.

Pope Pius XII greets Cardinal Spellman of New York.

New York's powerful
Cardinal Spellman
shakes hand of Pope
John XXIII, who
succeeded Pope Pius XII.

Boston's Cardinal Bernard Law and Catholic Priest
Paul Shanley exchange greetings. Subsequently,
Shanley, a founding member of NAMBLA, was
exposed as a pedophile criminal and convicted of
molesting young altar boys. Meanwhile, Cardinal
Law, forced by public scorn to leave the United
States, was promoted to a top position inside the
Vatican. At the death of Pope John Paul II in April
2005, Law surfaced once again, being given the high-
visibility role of conducting a mass for the dead
Pontiff that was viewed around the world on TV. This
was the Vatican's way of retorting to those angered
or concerned over priest pedophelia: *"Get Lost!"*

In a Greek-language book exposing the Masonic link with religion we find this picture of the Orthodox prelate and Pope Paul VI in a Masonic grip.

ρου καὶ λύκου τῆς Ρώμης εἰς τοὺς
ρας χαίρεται ὅτι κατώρθωσεν νὰ προ-
καὶ νὰ ὑποταγῇ εἰς τὴν παπικὴν ἀλα-

Conjunction of Masonic handshakes by Greek businessmen. (From Greek book exposing the Lodge connection)

Ὁ ἀρχιμασόνος πρώην πρόεδρος τῶν ΗΠΑ Χάρρυ Τρούμαν μὲ τὴν ἡγεσίαν τῶν Ἑλλήνων μασόνων. Μεταξὺ τῶν τελευταίων, ὁ «μέγας διδάσκαλος» Ἀλέξανδρος Τζατζόπουλος, ὁ ἑβραῖος Μπεχαρᾶ καί ὁ ἀσφαλιστὴς Εὐαγ. Μακρυμίχαλος. Φωτογραφία εἰλημμένη τὴν 11 Μαρτίου 1964.

Put another nickel design in – two, actually

Back of Jefferson coin recognizes two historic events

By Barbara Hagenbaugh
USA TODAY

WASHINGTON — Coin collectors, get ready for more change.

Drawing on the enormous popularity of the state quarter program, the U.S. Mint on Thursday unveiled two new nickels it hopes will also lure collectors.

The nickels, which mark the 200th anniversaries of the Louisiana Purchase and the Lewis & Clark expedition, are the first redesign of the 5-cent piece in 65 years. The two will hit cash registers in 2004 and will be followed by new designs in 2005.

The "heads" side of the nickels will continue to feature Thomas Jefferson throughout. In 2006, Monticello, Thomas Jefferson's home in Virginia, will return, but the image might be redesigned.

The state quarter program, which is at the halfway point after beginning in 1999, has turned millions of Americans into coin collectors. That has made the U.S. Mint one of the few government agencies that makes more money than it spends and has thrilled members of the coin-collecting community, who were frustrated by the infrequent rede-

5 cents' worth: Special editions of the nickel will feature two new designs on the back. One commemorates the Louisiana Purchase, left; the other, the Lewis & Clark expedition.

sign of the nation's change.

"There are a lot of people interested in coins, and a lot of that can be traced to the state quarters," says Beth Deisher, editor of *Coin World*, a weekly publication for coin collectors, and *Coin Values*, a new monthly publication aimed at novice collectors.

Mint officials are preparing for a run on the current nickels, which might be seen as collector's items, and will soon be selling uncirculated coins on their Web site.

The first nickel out next year will be released in the spring. It depicts the Jefferson Peace Medal, which was presented ceremoniously to Native Ameri-

can leaders. It commemorates the Louisiana Purchase, the 1803 purchase of more than 800,000 square miles of territory from France for $15 million, which doubled the size of the USA. The second, which will come out in the fall, features Meriwether Lewis and William Clark on a keelboat as they set out in search of a passage to the Pacific Ocean.

The nickels' introduction was delayed this year after Virginia lawmakers in Washington complained about the removal of Monticello from the coin. Mint officials negotiated with the lawmakers, promising to return Jefferson's home to the 5-cent piece in 2006.

American coinage and currency frequently has borne hidden messages and symbols of the Illuminati. This new clipping from *USA Today* newspaper discusses and pictures the new nickel (5¢ coin) released in 2004 to commemorate the Louisiana Purchase of 1803. The coin bears the image of the Masonic handshake and also the occultic *"X."*

Masonic handshake imbedded in Greek 500 d. note.

This drawing of the ancient Babylonian god, *Nebo*, from a dictionary of the Bible, makes him appear to be instructing adepts on the finer points of using hand signs or exchanging mysterious grips. In fact, Nebo's title was *"Interpreter of the gods,"* and he was said to be the god of learning and of letters. The biblical King Nebuchadnezzar in the book of Daniel was named after Nebo. This cut is in the British Museum, London.

Masonic Handshakes Illustrated in Official Lodge Publications

30   RICHARDSON'S MONITOR OF FREE-MASONRY.

go on a Master Mason's errand, even barefoot, and bareheaded, to save his life or relieve his necessities. Furthermore do I promise and swear, that I will remember a brother Master Mason, when on my knees at my devotions. Furthermore do I promise and swear, that I will be aiding and assisting all poor and indigent Master Masons, their widows and orphans, wheresoever dispersed round the globe, (they making application to me as such, and I finding them worthy,) as far as is in my power, without injury to myself or family. Furthermore do I promise and swear, that if any part of this my solemn oath or obligation be omitted at this time, that I will hold myself amenable thereto, whenever informed. To all which I do most solemnly and sincerely promise and swear, with a fixed and steady purpose of mind in me to keep and perform the same, binding myself under no less penalty than to have my body severed in two in the midst, and divided to the North and South, my bowels burnt to ashes in the center, and the ashes scattered before the four winds of heaven, that there might not the least tract or trace of remembrance remain among men or Masons of so vile and perjured a wretch as I should be, were I ever to prove wilfully guilty of violating any part of this my solemn oath or obligation of a Master Mason; so help me God, and keep me steadfast in the due performance of the same.

Master, to candidate—What do you now most desire?

Candidate—Light.

Master—Brethren, please to stretch forth your hands and assist in bringing this new-made brother to more light in Masonry. "And God said, Let there be light, and there was light."

[The candidate has the bandage dropped from his eyes in the same manner as in preceding degrees, with three stamps on the floor, and three clapping of hands.]

Master, to candidate—On being brought to light, you first discover, as before, three great lights in Masonry, by the assistance of three lesser, with this difference, both points of the compass are elevated above the square, which denotes to you that you are about to receive all the light that can be conferred on you in a Mason's Lodge.

The Master steps back a few steps, and then advances again.

Master—Brother, you now discover me as Master of this Lodge, approaching

you from the east, under the sign, step, and due-guard of a Master Mason.

The sign is the hailing sign of distress given on page 29. The words accompanying it are, "Is there no help for the widow's son?" As the last words are uttered, you let fall your hands in a manner to indicate solemnity. The due-guard is given by putting the open right hand to the left side of the bowels, the palm of the hand flat, and downwards; then draw it quickly from the left to the right, and let it fall by your side.

After thus instructing the new candidate, the Master approaches him, and taking him by the hand, says:— Brother, in token of a continuation of true brotherly love and esteem, I present you with my right hand, and with it you will receive the pass-grip and word of a Master Mason. Take me as I take you.

The pass-grip is given by pressing the thumb between the joints of the second and third fingers where they join the hand, and the word is TUBAL-CAIN.

As the Master gives the grip, the following dialogue ensues, the Senior Deacon answering for the candidate:

Master—What is that?

Senior Deacon—The pass-grip of a Master Mason.

Master—Has it a name?

Senior Deacon—It has.

Master—Will you give it me?

Senior Deacon—I did not so receive it, neither can I so impart it.

Master—How will you dispose of it?

Senior Deacon—Letter, or syllable it.

Master—Syllable it, and begin.

Senior Deacon—No, you begin.

Master—No, begin you.

Senior Deacon—TU

Master—BAL-

Senior Deacon—CAIN.

Master—TUBAL

Senior Deacon—TUBAL-CAIN.

Masonic handshakes and grips from *Richardson's Monitor of Free-Masonry*.

More Masonic Handshakes and Grips

22   RICHARDSON'S MONITOR OF FREE-MASONRY.

Sign and Due-guard of a Fellow-Craft.

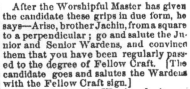

This sign is given by taking hold of the left breast, with the right hand, as though you intended to tear out a piece of it, then draw your hand, with the fingers partly clench-ed, from the left to the right side, with some quickness, and drop it down by your side.— The due-guard is given by raising the left arm until that part of it between the elbow and shoulder is per-fectly horizontal, then raising the rest of the arm in a vertical posi-tion, so that that part of the arm below the elbow, and that part above it, forms a square. The two are always given together, and are called the sign and due-guard of a Fellow Craft.

Master—Brother, I now present you with my right hand, in token of brother-ly love and confidence, and with it the pass-grip and word of a Fellow Craft Mason.

The pass-grip is given by taking each other by the right hand, as though going to shake hands, and each putting his thumb between the fore and second fin-ger, where they join the hands, and pressing the thumb between the joints.

This is the regular pass-grip of a Fellow Craft Mason, and the name of it is SHIB-BOLETH. Its origin is explained here-after. In some Lodges the word is given in syllables, but usually it is pronounced entire.

The real grip of a Fellow Craft Mason is given by putting the thumb on the joint of the second finger where it joins the hand, and then each one should crook his thumb so he can stick the nail into the joint of the other. The name of the grip is JACHIN.

After the Worshipful Master has given the candidate these grips in due form, he says—Arise, brother Jachin, from a square to a perpendicular ; go and salute the Ju-nior and Senior Wardens, and convince them that you have been regularly pass-ed to the degree of Fellow Craft. [The candidate goes and salutes the Wardens with the Fellow Craft sign.]

After saluting the Wardens he is con-ducted back to the Worshipful Master in the east, who thus addresses him : Bro-ther, I now have the honor of presenting you with a lamb-skin apron, as before, which I hope you will continue to wear with honor to yourself, and satisfaction to the brethren ; you will please carry it to the Senior Warden in the West, who will teach you how to wear it as a Fel-low Craft Mason.

The candidate goes to the Senior War-den, who ties on his apron, and turns up one corner of the lower end, tucking it under the apron string.

Senior Warden—At the building of King Solomon's Temple, the workmen were distinguished by the manner in which they wore their aprons. Fellow Crafts wore theirs in the manner I have here arranged.

The candidate is again conducted by the Senior Deacon back to the Worship-ful Master in the east.

Master—Brother, as you are dressed, it is necessary you should have tools to work with : I will, therefore, present you with the tools of a Fellow Craft Ma-son. They are the plumb, square and level. The plumb is an instrument made use of by operative Masons to raise per-pendiculars ; the square, to square their work ; and the level, to lay horizontals : but we, as Free and Accepted Masons, are taught to use them for more noble and glorious purposes. The plumb teaches us to walk uprightly, in our se-veral stations, before God and man ; squaring our actions by the square of virtue ; and remembering that we are traveling on the level of time to that " undiscovered country, from whose bourne no traveler returns." I further present you with three precious jewel ; their names are Faith, Hope, and Cha-rity ; they teach us to have faith in God, hope in immortality, and charity to all mankind. The greatest of these three is Charity ; for Faith may be lost in sight, Hope often ends in fruition, but Charity extends beyond the grave, through boundless realms of eternity.

The Senior Deacon now conducts the candidate back to the preparation room.

And More Masonic Handshakes

MOST EXCELLENT MASTER'S DEGREE: THE INITIATION.   61

solemn oath or obligation of a Most Excellent Master Mason, which I assure you, as before, is neither to affect your religion or politics. If you are willing to take it, repeat your name and say after me:

I, John Smith, of my own free will and accord, in presence of Almighty God, and this Lodge of Most Excellent Master Masons, do hereby and hereon, most solemnly and sincerely promise and swear, in addition to my former obligations, that I will not give the secrets of Most Excellent Master to any one of an inferior degree, nor to any person in the known world, except it be to a true and lawful brother of this degree, and within the body of a just and lawfully constituted Lodge of such; and not unto him nor them whom I shall hear so to be, but unto him and them only whom I shall find so to be, after strict trial and due examination, or lawful information.

Furthermore do I promise and swear, that I will obey all regular signs and summonses handed, sent, or thrown to me from a brother of this degree, or from the body of a just and lawfully constituted Lodge of such; provided it be within the length of my cable-tow.

Furthermore do I promise and swear, that I will support the constitution of the General Grand Royal Arch Chapter of the United States; also, that of the Grand Chapter of this State, under which this Lodge is held, and conform to all the by-laws, rules and regulations of this, or any other Lodge of which I may hereafter become a member.

Furthermore do I promise and swear, that I will aid and assist all poor and indigent brethren of this degree, their widows and orphans, wheresoever dispersed around the globe, as far as in my power, without injuring myself or family.

Furthermore do I promise and swear, that the secrets of a brother of this degree, given to me in charge as such, and I knowing them to be such, shall remain as secret and inviolable in my breast, as in his own, murder and treason excepted, and the same left to my own free will and choice.

Furthermore do I promise and swear, that I will not wrong this Lodge of Most Excellent Master Masons, nor a brother of this degree, to the value of anything, knowingly, myself, nor suffer it to be done by others, if in my power to prevent it.

Furthermore do I promise and swear, that I will dispense light and knowledge to all ignorant and uninformed brethren

at all times, as far as is in my power, without material injury to myself or family. To all which I do most solemnly swear, with a fixed and steady purpose of mind in me to keep and perform the same; binding myself under no less penalty than to have my breast torn open, and my heart and vitals taken from thence, and exposed to rot on the dunghill, if ever I violate any part of this, my solemn oath, or obligation, of a Most Excellent Master Mason. So help me God, and keep me steadfast in the due performance of the same.

Master to the candidate—Detach your hands and kiss the book six times. [Candidate obeys.] You will now rise and receive from me the sign, grip and word of a Most Excellent Master Mason.

The sign is given by placing your two hands, one on each breast, the fingers meeting in the centre of the body, and jerking them apart as though you were trying to tear open your breast: it alludes to the penalty of the obligation.

The grip is given by taking each other by the right hand, and clasping them so that each compress the third finger of the other with his thumb. [If one hand is large and the other small, they cannot both give the grip at the same time.] It is called the grip of all grips, because it is said to cover all the preceding grips.

Master (holding candidate by his hand and placing the inside of his right foot to the inside of candidate's right foot) whispers in his ear—RABONI.

Should there be more than one candidate for initiation, the ceremony stops here until the others are advanced thus far, and then they all receive the remainder together.

A noise of shuffling feet is now heard in the Lodge, which is purposely made by some of the members.

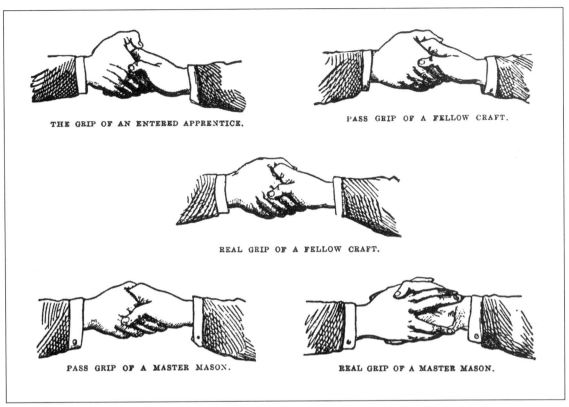

THE GRIP OF AN ENTERED APPRENTICE.

PASS GRIP OF A FELLOW CRAFT.

REAL GRIP OF A FELLOW CRAFT.

PASS GRIP OF A MASTER MASON.

REAL GRIP OF A MASTER MASON.

Masonic handshakes and grips from *Duncan's Masonic Ritual and Monitor,* 3d Ed.)

Excerpt from the book, *Mormonism's Temple of Doom,* by William Schnoebelen and James Spencer. The two authors are both ex-Mormons. In their book, they show the remarkable parallels between the secret signs, grips, and rituals of Freemasonry and those of the Mormon (LDS) Church. Mormonism's founder, Joseph Smith, was a Mason, and all Masonic authorities today acknowledge the similarity of the two groups' rituals, symbols, signs, and doctrines.

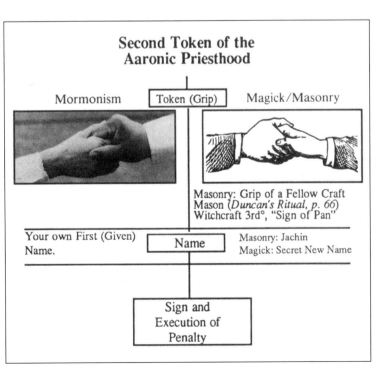

Second Token of the Aaronic Priesthood

Mormonism   Token (Grip)   Magick/Masonry

Masonry: Grip of a Fellow Craft Mason (*Duncan's Ritual, p. 66*) Witchcraft 3d°, "Sign of Pan"

Your own First (Given) Name.   Name   Masonry: Jachin
Magick: Secret New Name

Sign and Execution of Penalty

President George W. Bush and FBI Director nominee Robert Mueller exchange grip behind podium. (Photo: *The Washington Post,* July 22, 2001)

In August, 2000, Prime Minister Ehud Barak of Israel in a clear Masonic hand grip with Jordan's King Abdullah as they meet in Amman, Jordan. All Prime Ministers of Israel since the formation of that nation in 1948 have been initiates of the Masonic Lodge. All have been recruited into the Order of the Illuminati, also. (Photo: Associated Press, in *Austin American-Statesman*, August 17, 2000, p. A3)

European Farm Commissioner Franz Fischler (left) in handshake with German Agriculture Minister Karl-Heinz Funke at a European Community session in Brussels, Belgium. (Photo: *Spotlight* newspaper, December 7, 1998)

Nelson Mandela, political leader of South Africa, shakes hands (Masonic) with South African Communist Party leader Oliver Tambo. Mandela, lionized by the Western Press, is a life-long Communist activist and a known terrorist criminal. Mandela acquired power at the helm of the South African government by arrangement with the heads of the Illuminati's Rockefeller, Rothschild, and Oppenheimer dynasties. In exchange, the Illuminati cartel holds exclusive rights to South Africa's mineral rich assets of diamonds, gold, and platinum. (Photo: from the book, *In The Words Of Nelson Mandela*, published by Carol Publishing Group, York, 1998)

New York Governor George Pataki and New York State Senator Joseph Bruno meet in December 2003 with Tetsuro Higashi, president of Tokyo Electron Ltd., to announce a new $300 million research and development facility. (Newsletter of State Senator Joseph L. Bruno, December 2003, p. 1)

NEWS / Cuba

Checkmate for Fidel?

Some Cubans believe that a papal visit would endanger the Castro regime; others fear it might give the Communist leader a new propaganda victory. But everyone agrees the Pope's trip would be an important challenge to the Communist government.

By KRISTINA ARRIAGA DE BUCHOLZ

Back in April 1966 Father Miguel Angel Loredo was arrested at his church in San Francisco, Cuba. He was taken to the forced-labor camps on Isla de Pinos and put to work in the quarries. One morning while he was there, the guards pulled him aside—for no reason except that he was a priest—stripped him, and beat him with their bayonets. Unconscious and bleeding from his mouth and nose, he was sent back to prison, where he would spend ten more years.

Thirty years after his arrest, Father Loredo traveled to Rome to witness an audience between Pope John Paul II and the man who was responsible for his torture, Fidel Castro. He was delighted. "I really enjoyed watching Fidel Castro meet with the Pope," he said with relish. "I think this was a great victory for his Holiness," he added. "He's poised to checkmate Fidel."

Others are not so sure. Whether the Church in Cuba is in position to win this chess match is a highly controversial question. The much-publicized audience at the Vatican took place after a long, amply documented history of virulent repression of believers in Cuba. As the Pope accepted Castro's invitation to visit the Communist island in 1997, some Cubans predicted that Castro would control the visit for his own purposes. Indeed, they complained that the Cuban dictator had turned his meeting with Pope John Paul into an opportunity to seduce the West—yet again—into believing that he is prepared to allow democratic change. Other Cubans breathed a little easier, believing and praying that this meeting with the Pope, and the prospect of a papal visit to their island nation, had the power to change Cuba forever.

■ **Fidel Castro with the Vatican Secretary of State, Cardinal Angelo Sodano.**

> *"Who provides you with food? Fidel. Who takes care of you? The Revolution."*

A history of repression

During his 35-minute private meeting with Castro, during which the two men spoke in Spanish, Pope John Paul reportedly discussed ways to protect the role of the Church and the place of the faithful in Cuban life. A few days later, some results were already evident; 15 priests and 25 nuns were granted visas to move to Cuba, where they will assist the 250 priests already living there, who now serve a population of 4.5 million Cuban Catholics. And in the aftermath of the meeting, Castro told reporters that he had been deeply moved by his session with the Holy Father. In a response to his critics, he added that his Cuban Revolution had never wounded the dignity of a Catholic priest.

Father Loredo laughed out loud when he heard that last statement. Since 1959, Castro has done much more than merely wounding the dignity of Catholic priests. Shortly after he took power, the Jesuit-educated dictator nationalized all private schools (including Catholic schools) and expelled most priests from the country. Many of the clerics who stayed behind were imprisoned—like Father Loredo—or sent to rural provinces. By 1963 the priest population had dropped from 800 to 200; out of 2,500 nuns only 300 remained on the island.

From the outset of his revolution, Castro sought to fill the spiritual void he had created by cleverly providing Cubans with new mottoes. "Inside the

Fidel Castro (right) in a Masonic grip with Vatican Secretary of State, Cardinal Angelo Sodano. The Cuban dictator is a lifelong Freemason and is also a member of the secret order known as the Odd Fellows. Almost all the Vatican curia are Masons and cabalists and many are also Rosicrucians. (Photo: *The Catholic World Report*, January 1997)

Pope John Paul II in a Masonic grip with a Cardinal at the Vatican. Notice the pressure on the knuckle.

Israeli Foreign Minister David Levy (left), in Masonic grip with Red Chinese counterpart in Beijing, China in March, 1992 as a bemused official looks on.

WORLD

U.S., Islam not in conflict, Clinton says

Tells U.N. that only foe is terrorism

By Barbara Slavin
USA TODAY

President Clinton made an overture Monday toward Muslim nations, saying that terrorism was a global problem and those who view a clash between the West and Islam as inevitable are "terribly wrong."

"False prophets may use and abuse any religion to justify whatever political objectives they have — even cold-blooded murder," Clinton told the U.N. General Assembly. "But that is not our understanding of Islam."

Coming a month after bombings at two U.S. embassies in Africa, which killed more than 250 people and injured 5,500, and the retaliatory U.S. missile strikes in Afghanistan and Sudan, Clinton's speech was seen as a gesture to the wider Muslim world.

Since the collapse of the Soviet Union in 1991, some politi-

cal scientists have theorized that the next major geopolitical fault line will be between Muslim and Judeo-Christian societies.

But Clinton, noting that a quarter of the world's population — including 6 million Americans — are Muslim, said the only dividing line was between those who support or practice terror and those who regard it as murder.

Clinton noted that there are 1,200 mosques and Islamic centers in the USA.

"The 6 million Muslims who worship there will tell you there is no inherent clash between Islam and America," Clinton said.

Zalmay Khalilzad of the Rand think tank in Washington called the president's comments at the United Nations "a good idea" after the anti-Muslim anger generated in the USA by the embassy bombs, which U.S. officials blamed on

By Don Emmert, Agence France-Presse
General Assembly opens: President Clinton, with U.N. Secretary-General Kofi Annan, was among nearly 50 government leaders present.

Saudi financier Saudi Osama bin Laden. U.S. retaliation for the attacks, in turn, produced widespread Muslim anger.

In recent years, Khalilzad said, there has been a U.S. tendency to replace talk of a communist threat with that of a Muslim one. U.S. policy on issues from terrorism to weapons proliferation have focused on Muslim nations.

Clinton, however, said all nations are victimized by terrorism, including Iran. He cited attacks around the world, from Ireland to the former Yugoslavia to Japan.

Khalilzad said the president's speech also appeared to be directed at Iranian President Mohammed Khatami, who spoke after Clinton.

The Iranian leader also condemned terrorism and called for U.N.-sponsored talks to resolve a long-standing conflict among Muslim rivals in Afghanistan.

Nine Iranians were killed there last month by the dominant Afghan faction, but Khatami said Iran, which has massed nearly 300,000 troops on the border, preferred a diplomatic solution.

U.S. President Clinton receives Masonic grip from United Nations Secretary-General Kofi Annan at opening of the UN General Assembly. In this staged photo opportunity, aides for the two world leaders arranged the national flags so that Nicaragua's Illuminati-designed flag, which has a (male) triangle, a solar image, and all-seeing eye as its focus would be most prominently displayed. Kofi Annan is married to a white woman, a Rothschild heiress.(Photo: *USA Today*, September 22, 1998, p. 11A)

Great Britain's Duke of Kent, head of the United Lodge, the largest Masonic fraternity in England, holds the title, The Most Worshipful Grand Master. The Duke is sharing a Masonic grip on visit to Cape Town, South Africa.

International News   December 27, 2004 • AMERICAN FREE PRESS   **19**

British Nationalists Jailed for Criticizing Radical Islam

By Peter J. Huxley-Blythe

At 7 a.m. on Dec. 14, 2004, and long before daylight, four plain-clothes detectives woke up British nationalist Nick Griffin and his family at their farm in mid-Wales and arrested him. The leader of the British National Party (BNP) was then taken on a long cross-country journey to a Halifax police station where he was questioned by detectives until his release at 5:30 that afternoon.

RACIAL HATRED?

The charge against Griffin, 45, was that he was suspected of inciting "racial hatred" against the British Muslim community. This arose after the British Broadcasting Corporation (BBC) had secretly filmed some BNP members and then screened it on television as a "sting" program on July 15 last year. At that time, Griffin is alleged to have said, among other things, that Islam was a "vicious, wicked faith."

"I was brought here, kept in the cell for a little while and interviewed by two police officers," said Griffin upon his release. "We knew this was going to happen. The Crown Prosecution Service [CPS]—we've got a ... le—told us ... me d ... ago. This ...

French populist leader Jean-Marie le Pen (left) shakes hands with British National Party (BNP) leader Nick Griffin prior to a press conference held by the BNP in Manchester. Griffin, was arrested early December 14 on suspicion of incitement to commit racial hatred for comments he made about the extent and influence of radical Islam in the United Kingdom. Evidence used in his arrest was provided by a BBC film crew which had been secretly filming Griffin and other members of the BNP.

political rival."

And from what has happened it would appear other arrests have been well orchestrated, too.

The day before Griffin was arrested, the founder of the BNP, John Tyndall, 70, who lives in Hove, in Sussex, was also arrested because of a speech he had made in Lancashire.

WHO'S ALIEN TO BRITAIN?

Some observers believe the reason for Tyndall's arrest was a speech he made in response to Tory leader Michael Howard's claim that the BNP was "alien" to Britain. Tyndall reportedly responded, "the BNP could hardly be as alien to Britain as Mr. Hecht," a reference to the fact that the Romanian family name of Hecht had been anglicized to become Howard in the late 1940s.

As a result of the television program, 12 men were arrested, but six of them were not charged with any offenses.

A Yorkshire police spokesman is reported as saying to the British press that the BBC had given the police 300 hours of film and that "a team of officers had been working 10 hours a day, five days a week" viewing the film material.

Griffin has ...

Frenchman Jean-Marie le Pen (member of Paris' Grand Orient Lodge) warmly welcomes Masonic brother Nick Griffin, leader of the British National Party (BNP). Jean-Marie le Pen, head of a supposed right-wing populist party in France, is oft criticized in that country's press for what they say are his anti-Semitic views. In fact, by this hand grip and by other clear Masonic gestures he has made publicly, it appears that le Pen is a covert Mason, which would make him more akin to Zionism and its Communist Hegelian philosophy.

Secretary of State Donald Rumsfeld in the Bush Administration gives coded handshake to Saudi Arabia's King Fahd (top) and Oman's Sultan Qaboos (below). (*Time* magazine, October 15, 2001)

Jerry Falwell, Baptist hero, in a Masonic grip with Skull & Bones alumnus, President George H. W. Bush, at the White House in 1991. Falwell claims to be a pro-life advocate but never complained when Senior Bush nominated abortion supporters like Judge David Souter to the U.S. Supreme Court and other federal posts.

Israeli Prime Minister Menachem Begin (left) a dwarfish terrorist thug who went on to become Israel's Prime Minister, shares a Masonic hand grip with one of the "brethren," Moral Majority leader preacher Jerry Falwell. Falwell received the Jabotinsky Award for his devoted efforts to oppress the Palestinian people while promoting Jewish racial supremacy. Jabotinsky, the man whom this award was named after, was a pro-Communist Socialist/Zionist. Falwell also received a multimillion dollar executive jet as a gift from Israel, a nation that receives from five to ten billion in free foreign aid money each year from American taxpayers. In effect, Begin and Israel stole money from the U.S.A. taxpayers and funneled it to Falwell.

President Clinton in a Masonic grip with Supreme Court Justice Stephen Breyer. Breyer, a devout cabalistic Jew, was nominated by Clinton to the Supreme Court. To the right of Breyer is Justice Ruth Bader Ginsberg, also a cabalistic and Talmudic Jew and again a Clinton appointee. (Photo: *The Cincinnati Post*, October 1, 1994)

Apollo 8 crewman Frank Borman and a top NASA manager in a Masonic hand grip.

ROVE Rhymes With 'Love'?

Karl Rove has earned a lot of nicknames, among them "The Architect," "King Karl" and even "Turd Blossom," as George W. Bush affectionately calls him. But what about Karl Rove, political heartthrob? As a keynote speaker at the Conservative Political Action Committee's annual conference last week in Washington, the newly appointed White House deputy chief of staff attracted an overflow crowd of nearly 1,000 GOP faithful, including hundreds of college students who crammed into the room. At the back of the pack stood Michelle Morrow, 19, applauding wildly and taking pix with her digital camera. "He is my political idol," she said. "I wish I could meet him." She's not alone. To raise money on the campaign trail last year, Rove offered "private briefings." Cost: $4,000 per person, plus another $1,000 if you wanted a picture with the strategist. For the budget-conscious, there's always the ILoveKarlRove.com Web store, which sells, among other things, a $10 thong emblazoned with his photo inside a large pink heart. Rove, who was unavailable for comment, tries to downplay his celebrity. When introduced at CPAC as a fan of Mark Hanna's, President William McKinley's political guru, Rove insisted that he admired McKinley more. "McKinley was the guy in charge, not Hanna," Rove said. "The president reminds me of that all the time." —HOLLY BAILEY

WANTED: The heartthrob

Karl Rove, top White House advisor to President George W. Bush, sharing a Masonic connection. (Photo: *Newsweek*, February 20, 2005)

French President Jacques Chirac, Masonic initiate of Paris' Grand Orient Lodge, with Irish Prime Minister Bertie Ahern (left).

Shimon Peres, former Prime Minister and leader of Israel's Labor Party (left), in Masonic grip with Morton L. Janklow of the Council on Foreign Relations (CFR). (Photo: *CFR Annual Report*, 1990)

Dr. Foy Valentine (left), President of the
Masonic-founded group, Americans
United for Separation of Church and
State, with the anti-Christian group's
executive director, Barry Lynn. The group
is a leader in working to stop prayer in
schools, remove the Ten Commandments
from public display, and prevent public
displays or mention of Christmas.

Egyptian Ambassador to Israel Mohammed Bassiouny (center) and his wife with Israel Prime
Minister Shimon Peres. As is the practice of the members of both the Grand Lodge of Jerusalem and
the Masonic Lodges of Cairo and Egypt, the left hand is used to conceal the Masonic nature of the
grip. (Photo: *The Jerusalem Post and International Edition*, November 1, 1997, p. 9)

President Bill Clinton meets in 1995 with Pope John Paul II. The Pope is extending his left hand in a Talmudic attempt to conceal the Masonic grip that is about to occur. Dr. Dennis Cuddy, premier researcher of the global conspiracy and expert on occult symbols, writes: "Some Christians have wondered why Pope John Paul II seemed to use a hand gesture when photographed with Gorbachev in 1989 that was similar to the real grip of the Master Mason (a grip shown in *Duncan's Masonic Ritual and Monitor*, 3d edition, 1976) and Star Trek Spock's 'Vulcan Salute.'" (Dr. Dennis Cuddy, *Now Is the Dawning of the New Age New World Order*, Hearthstone Pub., Oklahoma City, OK, 1991, p. 387)

The late Pope John Paul II greets Archbishop Charles Salatka and they share the Real Grip of a Fellow Craft Mason. Simultaneously, the Pontiff gives the "cover grip" with his left hand to conceal the maneuver.

Soviet President Mikhail Gorbachev and Pope John Paul II combine to present a Masonic symbol in this staged event for the TV cameras. (Photo: *The New York Times*, October 1, 1989)

Pope John Paul II meets with Israel's Chief Rabbi, Yisrael Meir Lau, at the papal retreat in Rome. As is customary of members of the Grand Lodge of Jerusalem, the rabbi disguises the Masonic hand grip with his left hand. This is called the "cover grip." (*Duncan's Masonic Ritual and Monitor*, 3d Ed., p. 216)

Neal Wilson, president of the General Conference of Seventh-day Adventists (left), chats with Konstantin Kharchev, Chairman of the Ministry of Religious Affairs, at a banquet hosted by Russian Orthodox Church representative Pimen, Patriarch of Moscow and all Russia. Listening are Dr. Alexander Haraszti, Billy Graham's spokesman at the Peace Forum (background), and Rabbi Arthur Schneier, president of the Appeal of Conscience Foundation.

Neal Wilson, president of the General Conference of Seventh-day Adventists (left) exchanges an indisputable (in my opinion) Masonic handshake with Konstantin Kharchev, the Soviet Union's Chairman of the Ministry of Religious Affairs. The occasion was a socialist-sponsored environmental conclave, called the International Forum for a Non-nuclear World and the Survival of Humanity, February 13-15, 1987. The leadership of the Seventh-day Adventist Church (SDA) is heavily Masonic. Many SDA officials have cooperated with pro-Communist, anti-Christian lobby groups such as Americans United, People For the American Way, the American Civil Liberties Union, and the Jewish ADL. These groups veil their anti-Christian positions with high-sounding goals like "liberty" and "separation of church and state." (Photo and article: *Ministry* magazine, May/June 1987, p. 7)

Three world-renowned Christian evangelists were present in 1966 at the House of the Temple, the headquarters of Scottish Rite Freemasonry, in Washington, D.C. The occasion was the elevation of men newly chosen to the elite 33rd degree. The three were Billy Graham, Norman Vincent Peale, and Robert Schuller. Statues of the three Masons have been erected in the courtyard of the Crystal Cathedral in Garden Grove, California.

Former President Harry Truman welcomed Graham to his home in Independence, Mo., in 1967. President Lyndon Johnson (left) often sought spiritual counseling from Billy, in fact insisting that Graham preach at his graveside when death caught up with him.

Evangelist Billy Graham shares an indisputably Masonic handshake with fellow 33rd degree Mason, former President Harry S. Truman. Also, observe Graham's left hand, held in the Masonic position. According to *Coil's Masonic Encyclopedia*, Truman was elected Grand Master of all Masons in Missouri in 1940. A 33rd degree, Truman's Masonic funeral was the first to ever be televised worldwide.

The Crystal Cathedral's Reverend Robert Schuller, 33rd degree Mason, shares a clearly Masonic handshake with former Soviet Communist Party boss, Mikhail Gorbachev. Gorbachev, an initiate of the Grand Orient Lodge, Paris, France, spoke at Schuller's church.

GUESS WHO'S COMING TO CHURCH?

Dr. Robert H. Schuller's special *Hour of Power* guest **Mikhail Gorbachev**. This Sunday, October 22, 2000 at 7am, WNYW-5.

Also seen Saturday, October 21, 2000 at 9pm on TBN.

THE NEW YORK TIMES **NATIONAL** SATURDAY, OCTOBER 21, 2000

A Show of Hands—Illuminists Employ the Grand Hailing Sign and the Sign of Admiration or Astonishment

It all depends on what is is.

— President Bill Clinton, in answer to a
question by the Special Prosecutor

A rose by any other name is still a rose.

— Old Proverb

In *Richardson's Monitor of Freemasonry*, an authoritative reference sourcebook, we are told that in the ritual for the Masonic degree of Most Excellent Master of the Royal Arch Mason, all present are required to give a *"Sign of Admiration or Astonishment."* It is explained that this sign is similar to that gesture expressed by the illustrious Queen of Sheba on her first viewing the fabulous edifice of Solomon's Temple.[1]

In *Duncan's Masonic Monitor and Guide* the group present for that same degree ceremony is further told that this sign alludes to "the wonder and admiration of our ancient brethren who were present to view the interior of that magnificent edifice (Solomon's Temple) which King Solomon had erected, and was about to dedicate to the service of the Supreme Being."[2]

The arms raised with the palms of the hands facing forward is a supplicatory gesture, meaning passive acceptance, surrender, or an appeal for mercy. Caesar, in his *Gaelic Wars*, noted the use of this sign by Gaelic women, who apparently were signaling subjection to, or acceptance of, their Roman conquerors.

A single hand raised with palm outward represents a hand to heaven acknowledging the gifts or help received from extraterrestrial sources. It can also mean invocation, the calling down of powers or energy from the heavens or from ethereal sources (hell). Yet another meaning is that the hand with all five fingers showing, palm outward, indicates that one is giving honor and admiration to the *Underworld Deity*. Its essential meaning: "Thank you O Subterranean Lord for your deceptive wisdom and for your cunning aid in our struggle to overcome our enemies and to effect the Great Work."

Pharaoh Ramses paying homage to the god Horus, son of Osiris, the sun god deity symbolized as the all-seeing eye in the capstone on the U.S.A.'s dollar bill. Quite possibly, the Masons' *Sign of Admiration and Astonishment* came from practices of adherents to the old Mystery Religions of Babylon and Egypt. (From book, *Other Worlds*, Hilary Evans, Readers Digest Books, 1998)

On all occasions when the Egyptian high priest was called to officiate, he wore his robe of office, the spotted leopard's skin. The priest then led the rituals in worship of the "Hidden One," the concealed mystery divinity, known esoterically as Saturn, the sixth planet from the sun. Here we see the priest, attired in leopard's skin, hands upraised, palms outward, exactly as is done in various Masonic, Rosicrucian, witchcraft, Thelemic, and O.T.O. rituals to this day. (Hislop's *The Two Babylons*, p. 45)

As we shall see in this chapter of *Codex Magica*, this sign has been displayed in public media by Presidents, presidential candidates, Prime Ministers, and many other VIPs throughout history including the Emperor of France, the Freemason Napoleon Bonaparte.

Clinton the Devil, President of the U.S.A.

President Bill Clinton was named *Time* magazine "Man of the Year" in 1993. On the *Time* cover making the announcement, President Clinton's head was pictured with the "M" in the *Time* masthead of the magazine stretched and appearing to be *two horns* on Clinton's head.[3] Were the magazine's editors telling us that Clinton is the devils' man, or was it some strange coincidence?

Even more weird and dramatic, inside that same issue was a photo of Clinton in his Oval Office holding his hands and arms in the Masonic display of the sign of admiration. Now, get this: carved on the President's *desk* in the Oval Offices directly in front of Clinton is the eagle, in the presidential seal or logo, with its face turned to the *left*. But on the carpet just in front of the desk one finds the presidential seal facing toward the *right*: Two eagles, each facing in the opposite direction.

This is clearly the double-headed eagle of Freemasonry, a symbol representing the Serpent, honored as the Sun God in the Mystery Religions with its eagle-like, all-seeing eye. In other words: Lucifer! Solar God of Bill Clinton and the Illuminati.

Meanwhile, in Clinton's left hand (see page 183 of *Codex Magica*) is a rose—sign of the Illuminati's blood covenant and the *Rosicrucian Order*. You will also find here a photo of former Yugoslav Serb leader Slobodan Milosevic, likewise holding a rose in his hand, the right hand. In Satanism the left-handed path is the most magical and powerful, but more evil. Clinton (left-hand) is still today recognized by the world as a great leader. Milosevic (right-hand) is in disgrace, in a prison cell, after being felled by Clinton and his Illuminati cohorts, proving that it's not nice to attempt to doublecross your Illuminati overlords, Mr. Milosevic!

In this chapter you will find not only Bill Clinton, Slobodan Milosevic, John Kerry, and others giving enigmatic ritual messages, but, also, we will examine other signs in which the Illuminati signal with the arms and either or both hands.

The Grand Hailing Sign of Distress

One classic Masonic pose, duplicated by or similar to that employed in many other Orders, is the *Grand Hailing Sign of Distress*. Theoretically, this is used in extreme circumstances in which a Mason or other elitist finds himself in a crisis or in a bind. In such an emergency he gives the Grand Hailing Sign of Distress, sometimes called the "High Sign." At that point, brethren who recognize the secret sign of alarm are expected to come to his rescue. Comically, mass murderer Charles Manson was observed giving this sign and a number of others during his trial for conspiracy to commit murder. Reportedly, Manson believed the judge in his case was a 33° Mason and would rescue him. It was all to no avail.

Likewise, Mormon Church founder Joseph Smith gave this sign while under siege of a lynch mob at the Nauvoo, Illinois jail where he had been incarcerated.

Smith knew that the angry mob was comprised mainly of Freemasons because he, too, had been one of them until he was excommunicated. The Masons didn't take too kindly to Masonic Brother Smith's stealing their symbols and ceremonies and incorporating them into his Mormon (LDS) Church rituals.[4]

As Joseph Smith lay dying on the jailhouse floor, he cried out, "Is there no help for the Widow's Son?" This is the enigmatic saying taught Masons, stamping Smith as a follower of the Great Goddess, patroness of the Masonic fraternity. The Bible in *Revelation 17* refers to her as "Mystery, Babylon the Great, Mother of Harlots."

John J. Robinson, author of a celebrated book, *Born in Blood* defending Freemasonry and blasting its critics, also referenced the Grand Hailing Sign of Distress sign taught in the 3° ritual:

> After brief ceremonies, the blindfold is removed, and the newly sworn Master Mason is taught several secrets of that degree. He learns the penal sign, the hand signal based on the penalty of the Master Mason's oath, which is to pass the hand in a slashing motion, palm downward and thumb toward the body, across his stomach. The due-guard of the Master Mason repeats the position of his hands on the Holy Bible and the compass and square as he takes the oath: with his upper arms along his sides, forearms out straight, with palms down.

> To this point, the ceremony is much like that of the first two degrees, but now is added a third sign, the Grand Hailing Sign of Distress of the Master Mason, given with the upper arms parallel to the ground, forearms vertical with hands above the head, palms forward. For those times when the Master Mason is out of sight of possible help, or in the dark, he is taught to summon assistance with the word, "O Lord, my God, is there no help for a Son of the Widow?" a reference to Hiram, legendary master craftsman at the building of the Temple of Solomon, about whom the initiate has yet been told nothing, and whom Masons identify with the metalworker that scripture describes as "a son of a widow of Naphtali."[5]

Note that Robinson makes mention of the "penal sign, the hand signal based on the penalty of the Master Mason's oath." In *Codex Magica*, you will see several examples of this signal, including a photo of Soviet dictator Joseph Stalin and one of former House Speaker Newt Gingrich.

In his book *Freemasonry*, Jack Harris, a former Master Mason who renounced the Order after converting to Christianity, quotes at length the ritual according to the State of Maryland's Masonic Manual.[6] That manual assures the Mason that at his death, if his good works are sufficient, "a kind messenger from the Supreme Grand Master will be sent to translate us to that all perfect, glorious and celestial lodge above, where the Supreme Architect of the Universe presides."

According to Harris the ritual continues as follows:

> All officers and members bow toward the East. The Master raps the lodge down (1 rap). Also explained to the brother in the third degree lecture is what he is to do in times of peril or danger. He is instructed (if he can be seen) to throw up both arms over his head and let them fall by three distinct motions. This is the great hailing

sign or sign of distress, and never should be given except in a lodge for instruction, or if his life is in danger. If a Mason sees this sign, he is to flee to his rescue if there is more probability of saving the brother's life than of losing his own.

At times when this sign could not be seen, such as in the dark, a spoken signal is substituted: *"O Lord, My God, is there no help for the widow's son?"* A Mason hearing these words would be equally bound to flee to the brother's rescue if there were more probability of saving his life than losing his own life.[7]

THE INEFFABLE DEGREES : PERFECT MASTER. 135

Master—Before you can be admitted to this privilege, it will be necessary for you to join the funeral procession of Hiram Abiff.

Candidate is then conducted several times round the Lodge, the brethren joining in the procession, and singing a dirge from text-book, after which he passes to the tomb of Hiram Abiff, joined by the Master, (personating King Solomon.)

Master (looking at inscription J. M. B. on the tomb, and making sign of admiration)—It is accomplished and complete.

The brethren now make the same sign of admiration, viz.: raise hands and eyes upward, and then let the arms fall crossed upon the abdomen, looking downwards.

Master and brethren now resume their proper places, while the Master of Ceremonies instructs the candidate how to approach the east, and to take upon himself the obligation in this degree, as follows: by four times four steps from a pair of compasses, extended from an angle of seven to that of sixty degrees. Candidate then takes the obligation, which enjoins secrecy, and to obey the orders and decrees of Council of the Princes of Jerusalem, under penalties in all former degrees, and of being smitten to the earth with a setting maul, &c.

Master (drawing green cord from candidate's neck)

let the right arm fall perpendicularly on the right side. This alludes to the penalty of being smitten down with a maul.

Second sign is that of admiration—Raise the hands and eyes upwards, as in the engraving, then let the hands fall crossed in front, at the same time casting the eyes downwards.

The pass-word is ACCASSIA.

The token is that of a Mark Master, given on the five points of fellowship, [page 42.] Mysterious word, JEVA, pronounced Je-vau.

Master then invests candidate with the jewel and apron of a Perfect Master, and informs him that the jewel should remind him to measure his conduct by the exact rule of equity.

Master then instructs candidate in the history of the degree, as follows:

After the body of Hiram Abiff had been found, Solomon requested Adoniram to make suitable arrangements for his burial. The brethren were ordered to attend with white aprons and that the marks in spilled in the Te until the assassins the meantime, Ad for a superb tom and black marble nine days. The passing between a square stone cles. On the sto ter J. On the to senting a virgin, The heart of Hi in a golden urn, a sword to denot

In the ritual for the *Perfect Master* degree of Freemasonry, the Master of the Lodge and the brethren make the *Sign of Admiration*, illustrated on page 135 of *Richardson's Monitor of Freemasonry* and described as: *"raise hand and eyes upward, and then let the arms fall crossed upon the abdomen looking downwards."* The sign may be made with both hands or with either the left or right hand extended only.

212 MOST EXCELLENT MASTER, OR SIXTH DEGREE

The brothers now all join hands as in opening, and while in this attitude the Right Worshipful Master reads the following passage of Scripture, 2 Chron, vii. 1, 4.

FIG. 30.

SIGN OF ADMIRATION, OR ASTONISHMENT.

"Now when Solomon had made an end of praying, the fire came down from heaven, and consumed the burnt-offering and the sacrifices; and the glory of the Lord filled the house. And the priests could not enter into the house of the Lord, because the glory of the Lord had filled the Lord's house. And when all the children of Israel saw how the fire came down, and the glory of the Lord upon the house, they bowed themselves with their faces to the ground upon the pavement, and worshipped and praised the Lord, saying, For he is good (here the Master, who is high-priest of the Chapter, kneels and joins hands with the rest), for his mercy endureth forever."

They all then repeat in concert the words, "*For he is good* (here one of the brethren, standing behind the candidate, throws a piece of blazing gum-camphor or other combustible matter into the *pot of incense* standing on the altar, around which the brethren are kneeling), *for his mercy endureth forever*," six times, each time bowing their heads low toward the floor. The mem-

Sign of Admiration, or Astonishment, as practiced in the sixth degree of Royal Arch Masonry—the *Most Excellent Master* ritual. During this same ritual, the participants bow their heads low toward the floor exactly six times, balance six times, and then balance six more times. Thus, 6+6+6, or 666. And this happens in the ritual for the 6th degree (*Duncan's Masonic Ritual and Monitor*, p 212-213). It is taught that the sign of Astonishment or Admiration is given in remembrance of the emotion felt by the Masons in the days of King Solomon at the moment they viewed the inner sanctuary of the newly completed Temple of God in Jerusalem.

The Council on Foreign Relations (CFR), an Illuminist organization headquartered in New York City, has as its official logo a conquering, wild, naked, man riding a rampant white horse, while giving the *Sign of Admiration and Astonishment.* The fingers of the hand are pointed toward the CFR's hidden Master in the Stars, the Prince of the Power of the Air (Lucifer). Notice, too, the black, circular background and the cryptic latin inscription, *ubique,* which means *"everywhere."* This logo, until recently, was printed on every issue of the CFR's official publication, *Foreign Affairs.* The man on a white horse theme, I believe, comes from the Bible's *Revelation 6,* the Four Horsemen of the Apocalypse. The first rider comes riding a white horse and proclaims to the world, "Peace," which claim proves to be a monumental lie.

Mikhail Gorbachev, Soviet President and Chairman of the Communist Party, visits the Council on Foreign Relations (CFR) in New York City. The presiding head of the organization proudly shows him a copy of the very first edition (1921) of *Foreign Affairs,* the CFR's official journal which has annotated notes of Vladimir Lenin written by him personally on the margins of some pages. Lenin obviously was a servant of the Illuminati, too. Note that the awed Gorbachev respectfully gives the Illuminist/Masonic Sign of Admiration and Astonishment with his right hand, only this time it is lain on the display case parallel to the "sacred" document to which his focus and devotion is directed.

Newly elected President Bill Clinton holds out his arms in the Masonic gesture of admiration and astonishment. Was it just his joy at becoming President, or was Clinton paying homage to the entity represented by the combined double-headed eagle carved on the front of the wood desk and imprinted in the Great Seal logo on the carpet? (From *Time* magazine, January 4, 1993, p. 29)

Slobodan Milosevic, President of Serbia, holds a rose aloft in his right hand signifying he is an initiate of the Rosicrucian Order. Milosevic failed to carry out the wishes of the Illuminati to the letter. Therefore, in this same issue of *Time*, he was called *"The Butcher of The Balkans"* and the *"high priest of ethnic cleansing."* Later, Milosevic was arrested, thrown in prison, and tried by an international court for supposed "crimes against humanity." (From *Time* magazine, January 4, 1993, p. 45)

Satanic, muddle-headed rock'n'roller Ozzy Osbourne, who once bit the head off a bat at a rock concert and sometimes led altar calls for the devil, raises his hands at a White House dinner hosted by President George W. Bush and wife, Laura Bush. Osbourne was so happy to be invited, he arrived early. Bush, at the podium, publicly recognized and applauded Ozzy and told him how much Bush's mother, Barbara, enjoyed his albums!

This is Senator John Kerry, arriving in Ohio for a campaign stop while running for President of the United States in 2004. See how Kerry's hands and arms are extended in salute to the sun, as its rays burst through the clouds. A sun worshipper? Strange, unless one understands that it is entirely possible Kerry was giving the Masonic sign of adoration and admiration to the one the scriptures call the "Prince of the power of the air" (e.g. Satan!). Interestingly, neither the caption of the *Time* magazine (March 15, 2004) photo nor the accompanying article gave any clue or mention at all of why Kerry's arms were outstretched in this position.

In this celebrated painting, *The Battle of the Pyramids*, by Baron Antoine Jean Gros, Napoleon is shown presenting the Masonic and Rosicrucian sign of astonishment or admiration at the sight of the marvelous sight of the pyramids of Giza. From written historical accounts, we know that the French Emperor did, indeed, experience feelings of amazement and admiration upon viewing the spectacle of the Egyptian pyramids. This particular sign can be accomplished either with the left or the right arm extended and the palm facing toward the object of admiration, or astonishment.

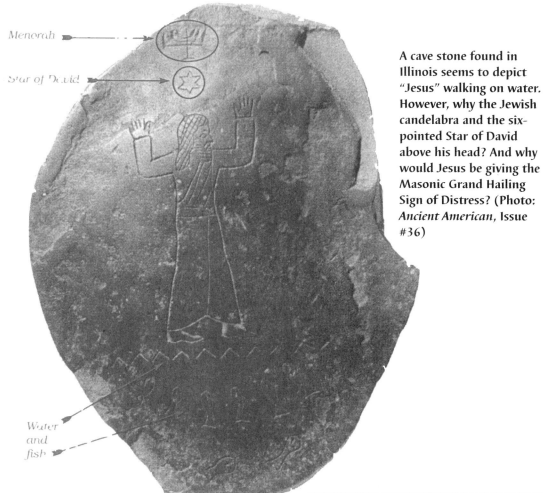

Menorah ➤

Star of David ➤

Water and fish ➤

A cave stone found in Illinois seems to depict "Jesus" walking on water. However, why the Jewish candelabra and the six-pointed Star of David above his head? And why would Jesus be giving the Masonic Grand Hailing Sign of Distress? (Photo: *Ancient American*, Issue #36)

This illustration in *Richardson's Monitor of Freemasonry* (1860) shows the Master Mason giving the "First Sign, or Due Guard" with his hands upright "in the manner of giving the grand hailing sign of distress." Compare this with the image inscribed on the cave stone above.

This goddess statuette was on display in the chambers of Alex Sanders, well-known British warlock (witch) as he led a witchcraft ritual. Witches worship both the goddess and the horned, male god. (Photo: *Witchcraft, Magic and the Supernatural*, Octopus Books, Hong Kong, 1974)

Instructional material for educators in the Fort Worth, Texas, Independent School District included this drawing of 13 goddess worshippers (13 comprise a witches coven) on a succession of six circle platforms paying homage to the Sun. The illustration originally came from an Italian foundation dedicated to the work of New Age evolutionist and educator Maria Montessori.

In the Babylonian religion, as the initiate entered into the "Mysteries," part of the ritual was the drinking from the cup of the Woman (the Goddess). Here, in this ancient woodcut we find a supplicant kneeling while raising his hands in submissive fashion after just drinking from the cup. The priest (at right) appears to be administering an oath while offering an oblation—perhaps a wafer, piece of bread, or honycomb—with his left hand. (*Kittos' Biblical Cyclopedia*; reprinted in Alexander Hislop's *The Two Babylons*, First Edition 1916, American Edition by Loizeaux Bros., 1916)

DAILY BRIEFING

Austin American-Statesman   statesman.com

NEWSMAKERS

Rob O'Neal   FLORIDA KEYS NEWS BUREAU

Taking in the Truman show

President Truman stayed 11 times from 1945-53 at what is now the Harry S Truman Little White House Museum in Key West, Fla.

Fellow Democrats ex-**President Clinton** and his wife, U.S. Sen. **Hillary Rodham Clinton**, had their own getaway there this weekend.

Sunday talk

'News Sunda
Fox: John Negr
U.S. ambassado
Sens. Lindsey G
R-S.C., and Dian
stein, D-Calif.

'This Week,'
ABC: Negropo
Chuck Hagel,
Joseph Biden
former Verm
Howard Dean

'Face the N
a.m., CBS: N
Sen. John
Ariz.

'Mee
a.m., N
Rep.
Cali

Former President Bill Clinton gives the Sign of Admiration as he views a painting of the late President Harry Truman. Both Clinton and Truman were initiates of the Masonic Lodge, and, by giving this sign, Clinton is acknowledging the Masonic achievements of his predecessor, Harry S. Truman, 33°. The Clintons were visiting the Harry S. Truman Little White House Museum in Key West, Florida. (Photo: Florida Keys News Bureau, in *Austin American-Statesman*, January 23, 2005, p. A2)

A dockside member of Greenpeace, the radical environmentalist group, hails the organization's sea-going vessel. Almost all environmentalist organizations are funded and run by the Illuminati. Members are ignorant of this behind the scenes influence.

CONTEXT

ANALYSIS · COMMENTARY · WORLD REPORT · SCIENCE

Sunday, July 23, 1995   Section F

The rainbow returns

"I Gruesomely Swear That I'm On the Square"—More Revealing Signs of Illuminati Cultists

A number of hand signs are used by Illuminists to indicate their allegiance to their Order and to demonstrate their knowledge that to divulge its secrets shall bring gruesome and swift, perhaps fatal, retribution.

When President Richard M. Nixon resigned the office of the presidency on August 9, 1974, he signaled the *Dueguard and Sign of a Royal Arch Mason*. As the Nixon audiotapes since released by the Nixon presidential library clearly show, Nixon and his "Prussian Guard," White House Chief of Staff Robert Haldemann and top aide John Erlichman, plotted to thwart the power of the Jewish Illuminati media that poisons the mind of America. They also conspired to overthrow the elaborate FBI and intelligence network historically run behind the scenes by the Jewish-led Illuminati chieftains.

Nixon knew what he was risking. He well knew that John F. Kennedy's murder was orchestrated by the Jewish Illuminati with the backing of Zionist Vice President Lyndon B. Johnson and with the connivance of J. Edgar Hoover's Mafia-infiltrated FBI and the Skull & Bones-run CIA. Nixon had been a close associate of David Rockefeller and had met privately with the Rothschilds a number of times. Nixon also had attended the notorious homoerotic occultic rituals of the Bohemian Club outside San Francisco. Still, as President, he had hoped to mount an offensive against the elite and dislodge them from their position of awesome power in the United States.

Instead, it was Nixon and his entourage who were dislodged, falling from grace and being ousted, even though Nixon's so-called crimes ("Watergate," etc.) were paltry compared to the colossal criminal treachery of predecessors like Wilson and Roosevelt, and successors like Clinton and both Bushes.

Captain William Morgan, in the nineteenth century, suffered a worse fate, being murdered in a Masonic ritual and his disfigured body dumped into a lake. Incensed by this outrage, John Quincy Adams, sixth President of the United States, in his classic exposure of the Masonic murderers (*Letters on Freemasonry*), minced no bones in declaring the Freemasons as "Luciferian" and as a grave threat to America.

In this section, we examine a few of penal (penalty) signs and also signs given to communicate the message, *"on the square,"* a phrase made common in the American lexicon by its frequent usage by Masons. Along the way, we shall note the Illuminist involvement of such infamous folks as the Russian mystic and master seducer, Grigore Rasputin, former U.S.A. President Jimmy "Peanut" Carter, Cuban strongman Fidel "Odd Fellow" Castro, and Master Mason and Illuminist thug extraordinaire, Joseph Stalin, the half-Jew who massacred some 50-60 million innocents while heading up the Illuminati's experimental Bolshevik regime. And we'll also take a brief look at a hand sign of Illuminist Al Gore, some Confederate officers into Masonic skullduggery, Timothy McVeigh's rancid "F...you" signal, and a few other choice hand poses of elite servants.

"Masonry ought forever to be abolished. It is wrong—essentially wrong—a seed of evil, which can never produce any good."
—John Quincy Adams

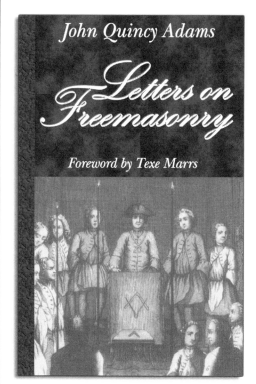

John Quincy Adams, sixth President of the United States, was a determined opponent of the secret society and fraternity of Freemasonry, the Masonic Lodge. The question of Freemasonry and the controversy over its character has long been debated. But for John Quincy Adams, writer, poet, faithful husband, patriot, former Ambassador and Secretary of State, and President, there was no question. The teachings and practices of the Lodge, Adams asserted, are detrimental, noxious, and unfortunate. John Quincy Adams was persuaded that the Masonic Lodges were a bane to society, evil, and Luciferian.

This unusual book, *Letters on Freemasonry*, first published in 1833, is finally back in print. Until now, it was virtually impossible for the general public to obtain a copy. It is now available for $22 postpaid through Power of Prophecy Ministries, 1708 Patterson Road, Austin, Texas 78733, or call toll free: 1-800-234-9673.

By Gregory Bull, AP

Historic visit: Former president Jimmy Carter, left, greets students at a medical school outside Havana. Cuban President Fidel Castro joins him.

Carter's skills can smooth U.S.-Cuban hostilities

We need to listen to former president Jimmy Carter about Cuba ("Cuba opens door to Carter" News, Monday).

If the United States had normalized relations with Cuba 40 years ago instead of acting like a spoiled child who had his hands smacked, we would not have a communist nation 90 miles off

125,000 people to South Florida.

Former president Jimmy Carter is right. Negotiation, compromise and agreement can be facilitated with anyone. The United States should have long ago begun to work with Cuba. We didn't, and to this day I can't under-stand

Former President Jimmy Carter in Havana, Cuba, with communist dictator Fidel Castro. Castro gives a sign showing he is a member of the *Odd Fellows*, a Masonic-affiliated secret order popular in Cuba. Meanwhile, Carter presents the Dueguard of the Fellow Craft (2°). (Photo: *USA Today* newspaper, May 16, 2002, p. 11A)

Supreme Court Justice nominee Clarence Thomas, appearing before a U.S. Senate Committee, in 1991, holds his right hand up to take the Oath. But at the same time, Thomas places his left hand and arm in such a fashion as to present the familiar *Dueguard of a Fellow Craft* sign of Freemasonry.

22   RICHARDSON'S MONITOR OF FREE-MASONRY.

This sign is given by taking hold of the left breast, with the right hand, as though you intended to tear out a piece of it, then draw your hand, with the fingers partly clenched, from the left to the right side, with some quickness, and drop it down by your side.— The due-guard is given by raising the left arm until that part of it between the elbow and shoulder is perfectly horizontal, then raising the rest of the arm in a vertical position, so that that part of the arm below the elbow, and that part above it, forms a square. The two are always given together, and are called the sign and due-guard of a Fellow Craft.

Sign and Due-guard of a Fellow-Craft.

After the Worshipful Master has given the candidate these grips in due form, he says—Arise, brother Jachin, from a square to a perpendicular; go and salute the Junior and Senior Wardens, and convince them that you have been regularly passed to the degree of Fellow Craft. [The candidate goes and salutes the Wardens with the Fellow Craft sign.]

After saluting the Wardens he is conducted back to the Worshipful Master in the east, who thus addresses him: Brother, I now have the honor of presenting you with a lamb-skin apron, as before, which I hope you will continue to wear with honor to yourself, and satisfaction to the brethren; you will please carry it to the Senior Warden in the West, who will teach you how to wear it as a Fellow Craft Mason.

The candidate goes to the Senior Warden, who ties on his apron, and turns up one corner of the lower end, tucking it under the apron string.

Senior Warden—At the building of

Excerpt (p. 22) of *Richardson's Monitor of Freemasonry*, illustrating and describing the sign and due-guard of a Fellow Craft Mason.

An excerpt, page 107, from the 1826 book *Freemasonry Exposed* by Captain William Morgan, showing the sign and due-guard of a Fellow Craft Mason. Morgan, a Mason of 30 years standing, renounced the cultic secret fraternity and decided to expose their evildoing. Shortly after his book was published, outraged Masons kidnapped Morgan, then murdered him and mutilated his body in a Masonic death ritual. The murder caused a public uproar which ended in the majority of the members of the wicked secret society across America leaving the

Candidate taking Fellow Craft Obligation. [The left arm should be perpendicular.]

Due Guard.

DUE GUARD OF A FELLOW CRAFT.— Hold out the right hand a little from the body and on a line with the lower button of the vest, the palm being open and turned down-ward; also raise the left arm so as to form a right angle at the elbow, from the shoulder to the elbow being horizontal and fore-arm perpendicular.

SIGN OF A FELLOW CRAFT.—Made from the due-guard by dropping the left hand carelessly to the side and at the same time raise the right hand to the left breast, with the palm towards the breast and the fingers a little crooked; then draw the hand smartly across the breast from left to right and let it drop perpendicularly to the side.

SIGN WITHOUT DUE GUARD.—The usual way out side the lodge). Draw the right hand, palm open and fingers a little crooked, smartly across the breast from left to right and drop it carelessly by your side.

Sign Fellow Craft

PASS GRIP OF A FELLOW CRAFT. —Take each other's hands as in ordinary hand-shaking and press the top of your thumb hard against the space between the first and second knuckles of the right hand. Should the person whose hand you hold be a Fellow Craft, he will return a like pressure on your hand, or else may give you the grip of an Entered Apprentice.

Lodge. Morgan's murder even inspired John Quincy Adams, the sixth President of the United States, to write and publish his own exposé of Freemasonry. In Adams' book, *Letters on Freemasonry*, the distinguished former President branded Freemasonry as *"Luciferian."*

Russian Orthodox priest Grigori Rasputin was not only an occultic Mason, but also engaged in Dionysiac sex orgies and rituals. A cult developed around the hypnotic Rasputin after the monk was said by the Czarina to have healed her young son who suffered from a blood disease. Those jealous of the growing political power of the "Mad Monk Rasputin" eventually had him assassinated. Rasputin is shown here giving the left-handed path version of the penal sign of the Fellow Craft degree of Freemasons.

Catholic Cardinal (left) stands with Greek Orthodox prelate on official visit to Greece.

Ὁ καρδινάλιος Μπέα, εἰς τὸ πλευρὸν τοῦ Ἀθηναγόρα χαιρετᾶ τοὺς προδότας τοῦ Φαναρίου, οἱ ὁποῖοι τὸν ἐπευφημοῦν.

The illustration from the book, *Mormonism's Temple of Doom*, by William Schnoebelen and James Spencer, demonstrates the parallels between the Mormon Temple ceremonial sign and the sign of a Fellow Craft Mason.

Sign and Execution of Penalty

Obligation and penalty of a Fellow Craft Mason: "I will...ever conceal, and never reveal any of the secret, arts, parts, or points of the Fellow Craft Degree...binding myself under no less penalty than of having my breast torn open, my heart plucked out and placed on the highest pinnacle of the temple." (*Duncan's Ritual*, pp. 64 & 65).

"The penalty is executed by placing the right hand on the left breast, and drawing the hand quickly accros the chest..." (*Mormon Temple Ceremony*)

Masonry: Sign of a Fellow Craft Mason (*Duncan's Ritual*, p. 17)

THE LIGHT OF KRISHNAMURTI
By Gabriele Blackburn

The *Light of Krishnamurti* relates the many-faceted mystical and spiritual occurrences of J. Krishnamurti as experienced by Gabriele Blackburn, a spiritual healer and clairvoyant. This is the story of the author's life in relationship to these events, their extraordinary meaning, and the profound effect they had on her. In a simple, direct, factual manner, she tells how his friendship, personal interviews, and the understanding of his teachings, helped her to resolve a life crisis, and discover an insightful way of living. This book voices the quality of the clear Light of truth which casts no shadow. It is a personal testimony to the sacred life and teachings of Krishnamurti, that Gold Light of eternity.

ISBN: 0-9613054-4-4 Quality Paperback

5⅜ x 8⅜ 260 Pages $14.00

Available in bookstores or send check or money order payable on any U.S. Bank to:

IDYLWILD BOOKS
P.O. Box 246-B
Ojai, California 93024

California Residents add 7¼% Sales Tax
S.H. $2.50 Foreign: $5.00 Air: $15.00

An advertisement for a biography of India's Theosophy guru, Krishnamurti. Occultist Annie Besant, who took over as leader of Theosophy after the death of its founder, once touted Krishnamurti as the "Christ of the New Age." The guru's pose here shows he's "on the square" and honors the trifold deity of Illuminist sects.

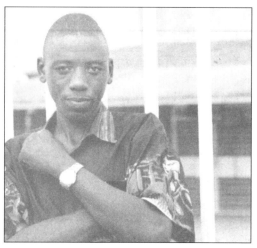

This man, in 1994, participated in the brutal, genocidal massacre of 3,000 Tutsi tribes people who sought refuge in a church in Rwanda, Africa. In this news article (*Austin American-Statesman*, April 11, 2004), he says he is repentant and is rehabilitated. The cultic positioning of his arms and clenched fist say otherwise.

Rock star Ozzy Osbourne lets his Masonic friends know he's *"on the square"* with this hand/arms pose. (*USA Today*, November 29, 2002, P. 10A)

Jewish actor E. G. Marshal who played a crusading lawyer on TV's *The Defenders* show in the 1960s and starred in many movies, shows that, masonically, he's *"on the square."*

A somber Richard Nixon, having just resigned the high office of President, waves goodbye from his helicopter, August 9, 1974. Few people, understood that the defeated ex-President was actually signaling the Dueguard and Sign of a Royal Arch Mason (7th degree). The film of this historic event shows Nixon stiffly raising his right hand to his forehead, the hand and arm horizontal, the thumb toward the forehead. He then dropped it perpendicularly by his side, turned and entered the aircraft. This exactly fits the description given of the *Royal Arch Duegard and Sign* in *Duncan's Masonic Ritual and Monitor*, 3rd Edition, Crown Publishers, p. 251 (see figure 36). According to Masonic teachings, the brother who descends into the "vault" and discovers deep secrets and then reveals them to the profane (that is, to outsiders) or who turns against the Order and/or his Masonic superiors, must be duly punished for his transgressions. He must receive the *penalty* due him. Richard M. Nixon was favored by the Illuminati, gained access to their innermost secrets, and then threatened to expose them. Swift punishment followed.

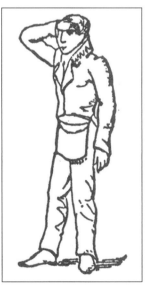

The 7th degree sign given by resigning President Nixon, as illustrated in yet another official Masonic scourcebook, *Richardson's Monitor of Freemasonry*, p. 79.

JEWISH WORLD 23

JEWISH TIME

A report in *Pravda*, the official Soviet daily, said 48 years ago last week that a predominantly Jewish group of doctors was arrested for conspiring to kill the Soviet leadership, in collusion with the CIA, the Zionist Organization, and the Joint Distribution Committee. The report touched off a wave of antisemitic attacks, including dismissals from key economic, cultural, and academic posts. It remains unclear where that anti-Jewish effort would have led had Stalin not died six weeks after its publication. Some scholars contend the Soviet dictator was serious about deporting some two million Jews from the western USSR to Siberia. On April 4, 1953, one month after Stalin's death, *Pravda* conceded that the "doctors' plot" story was fabricated by the KGB. However, Stalin's successors retained – until Mikhail Gorbachev's Glasnost era – the emigration ban which kept Soviet Jewry from m[...] ing to the free world generally, and to Israel in particular.

This photograph of Soviet dictator Joseph Stalin in *Pravda* (January 20, 1953, reprinted in *Jewish World*, January 2001, p. 23), the official communist newspaper, shows him clearly signaling the *Sign of A Master Mason*. Compare Stalin's arm and hand with the illustration of Figure 6, page 18, from *Duncan's Masonic Ritual and Monitor*. (Note: Stalin gives the sign with his left hand, indicating he follows the diabolical "left-handed path of occultism.")

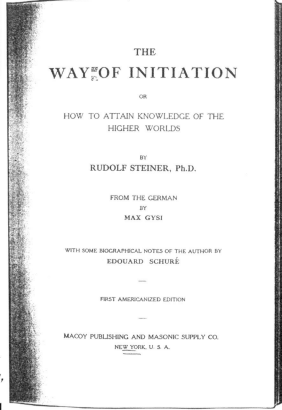

THE

WAY OF INITIATION

OR

HOW TO ATTAIN KNOWLEDGE OF THE
HIGHER WORLDS

BY

RUDOLF STEINER, Ph.D.

FROM THE GERMAN
BY
MAX GYSI

WITH SOME BIOGRAPHICAL NOTES OF THE AUTHOR BY
EDOUARD SCHURÉ

FIRST AMERICANIZED EDITION

MACOY PUBLISHING AND MASONIC SUPPLY CO.
NEW YORK, U. S. A.

Rudolf Steiner, a Hitler contemporary in Germany, displays the *Master's Grip.* During the Nazi era, Steiner became world-famous for his Masonic and Rosicrucian-based teachings. This picture comes from his book, *The Way of Initiation—How to Attain Knowledge of the Higher Worlds*, published by Macoy Publishing and Masonic Supply Co., New York City. Steiner also created the teaching system for the Waldorf schools, very popular today in the U.S.A.

An excerpt from page 36 from *Richardson's Monitor of Freemasonry*, illustrating the strong Master's Grip, or Lion's Paw, as practiced in the third degree of Scottish Rite Freemasonry.

86   RICHARDSON'S MONITOR OF FREE-MASONRY.

and see if the Master's word cannot be found. He searches, and soon reports—No trace of it, my lord!

The Master and brethren all give the grand hailing sign of distress (page 29) and exclaim—O Lord, my God, I fear the Master's word is forever lost!

The Master directs that the body be raised by the Entered Apprentice's grip.

A brother takes the candidate by that grip (page 11) and pulls so as to raise him a little, then lets him back and says—My lord, the body cannot be raised by the Entered Apprentice's grip; the skin cleaves from the flesh.

The Master and brethren again give the grand hailing sign of distress and repeat aloud—O Lord, my God, I fear the Master Mason's word is forever lost!

The Master orders another of the twelve to raise the body by the Fellow Craft's grip. He takes hold of the candidate by that grip, pulls him partly up, lets him fall back, and says—My lord, the body cannot be raised by the Fellow Craft's grip; the flesh cleaves from the bone. All again raise their hands, as in the hailing sign of distress, and exclaim,

The Master's grip is given by taking hold of each other's right hand, as though you were going to shake hands, and sticking the nails of each of your fingers into the joint of the other's wrist where it unites with the hand. In this condition

the candidate is raised, he keeping his whole body stiff, as though dead. The Master in raising him is assisted by some of the brethren, who take hold of the candidate by the arms and shoulders. As soon as he is raised to his feet they step back, and the Master whispers the word MAH-HAH-BONE in his ear, and causes the candidate to repeat it, telling him at the same time that he must never give it in any manner other than that in which he receives it. He is also told that Mah-hah-bone signifies marrow in the bone.

Al Gore..

the "Little Horn" that wars against the saints? Dan. 7:21 Look up "gore" in the Strong's Concordance. It's # 5055 and it means to : "war against"

Former Vice President Al Gore, who ran for the presidency on the Democrat Party ticket in 2000, appears to be in the process of making the Master's Grip of the 3rd degree of Freemasonry, indicating he is, as a minimum, a Master Mason. (Photo: from Exodus III, Volume 2, Number 1) Note: A sign similar to that of the Master's Grip is that of the Most Excellent Master as illustrated on p. 61 of Richardson's Monitor of Freemasonry.

Page 61 of *Richardson's Monitor of Freemasonry* illustrating the sign of the *Most Excellent Master*'s degree.

MOST EXCELLENT MASTER'S DEGREE: THE INITIATION.   61

solemn oath or obligation of a Most Excellent Master Mason, which I assure you, as before, is neither to affect your religion or politics. If you are willing to take it, repeat your name and say after me :

I, John Smith, of my own free will and accord, in presence of Almighty God, and this Lodge of Most Excellent Master Masons, do hereby and hereon, most solemnly and sincerely promise and swear, in addition to my former obligations, that I will not give the secrets of Most Excellent Master to any one of an inferior degree, nor to any person in the known world, except it be to a true and lawful brother of this degree, and within the body of a just and lawfully constituted Lodge of such ; and not unto him nor them whom I shall hear so to be, but unto him and them only whom I shall find so to be, after strict trial and due examination, or lawful information.

Furthermore do I promise and swear, that I will obey all regular signs and summonses handed, sent, or thrown to me from a brother of this degree, or from the body of a just and lawfully constituted Lodge of such ; provided it be within the length of my cable-tow.

Furthermore do I promise and swear, that I will support the constitution of the General Grand Royal Arch Chapter of the United States ; also, that of the Grand Chapter of this State, under which this Lodge is held, and conform to all the

at all times, as far as is in my power, without material injury to myself or family. To all which I do most solemnly swear, with a fixed and steady purpose of mind in me to keep and perform the same ; binding myself under no less penalty than to have my breast torn open, and my heart and vitals taken from thence, and exposed to rot on the dung-hill, if ever I violate any part of this, my solemn oath, or obligation, of a Most Excellent Master Mason. So help me God, and keep me steadfast in the due performance of the same.

Master to the candidate—Detach your hands and kiss the book six times. [Candidate obeys.] You will now rise and receive from me the sign, grip and word of a Most Excellent Master Mason.

The sign is given by placing your two hands, one on each breast, the fingers meeting in the centre of the body, and jerking them apart as though you were trying to tear open your breast : it alludes to the penalty of the obligation.

The grip is given by taking each other by the right hand, and clasping them so

Mormon (LDS) woman gives a sign in a LDS Church ritual ceremony. It is exactly the same as that of Freemasonry, as proven by this excerpt from page 17 of *Duncan's Masonic Ritual and Monitor*, illustrating the sign of an Entered Apprentice. Joseph Smith, founder of the Mormon Church, borrowed many of his church's signs, grips, symbols, and rituals from the Masonic Lodge. In fact, Smith was excommunicated by the Masons for having done so. (Photo of Mormon woman is from *Mormonism, Masonry and Godhood*, by Dr. Cathy Burns, Sharing Publishing, Mt. Carmel, Pennsylvania)

Michael A. Hoffman II   Secret Societies and Psychological Warfare   Page 66

All the Pyramid's Men

The Confederate officer on the left is First Lt. John Oden, of the Tenth Alabama Volunteer Infantry who fought at First Manassas, Chancellorsville and Antietam, where he was seriously wounded. Lying bleeding, Oden used a stick and his own blood to draw masonic symbols on a paper. Then he called out to the Union troops on picket duty to take the paper to any Yankee who was a Freemason.

It was carried to a Union Colonel who was a mason, but not of a high enough degree to comprehend Oden's symbolic message. Another mason, Union Capt. Perry was summoned and he recognized the drawings and announced that a fellow mason was in distress. Four Northern masons crept out to the field, placed the wounded Southerner on a cot and carried him to the field hospital of the 5th New Hampshire Volunteer Infantry where he was treated. When the Union Army moved on, Oden was sent to the private home of a physician to recuperate, rather than to a prisoner of war camp. Lt. Oden survived the War Between the States.

While at first sight, this is a touching story of the brotherhood of Freemasonry, some of the glow dims when we recall that a non-mason, Christian Confederate would have been left to bleed to death. Moreover, if cooperation like this existed between brother masons in the field, one is left to wonder at what degree collusion between Confederate and Union Freemasons of high office and rank, took place behind the scenes.

This photo and accompanying text comes from the book, *Secret Societies and Psychological Warfare*, by Michael A. Hoffman, II, a book highly recommended by the author of *Codex Magica*.

And More Revealing Hand Signs...

22 Supporters of A.Q. Khan, father of the Islamic bomb, rally in Karachi

This photograph in *Time* magazine (February 14, 2005) pictures an Islamic mob rallying in Karachi, Pakistan. The demonstrators were declaring their support for A. Q. Kahn, called the "Father of the Islamic Nuclear Bomb." What is especially interesting are the many varied hand gestures of the people in the crowd. Intriguing, to say the least.

Environmental activists, members of *Greenpeace*, show their signs. Several display the so-called "V" sign of the Illuminati. The fellow at top left has his fist clenched in a communist mode. The peace symbol, an upside-down broken cross inside a circle, is painted on the banner behind them. (Photo: *The Toronto Star*, July 23, 1995, p. F1)

John Meriwether, manager of Wall Street's Long-Term Capital Management hedge fund, lays his left hand on the table as an unusual, but no doubt planned mode. (*U.S. News and World Report*, May 3, 1999, p. 45)

Entertainer, Lyle Lovett, who once was married to actress Julia Roberts, presents an odd hand sign. (*Texas Monthly* magazine, July 2003, p. 19)

Academy Award winner Meryl Streep, who has been observed giving the *Il Cornuto* horned devil sign, in this picture in *Newsweek* (September 26, 1994) looks to be just sitting and relaxing. Actually, Ms. Streep displays a cabalistic pose.

Former Vermont Governor, Howard Dean, Chairman of the Democrat Party's National Committee (DNC), signs with both hands. (*Business Week*, January 12, 2004, p. 35)

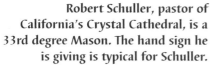

Robert Schuller, pastor of California's Crystal Cathedral, is a 33rd degree Mason. The hand sign he is giving is typical for Schuller.

U.S.◉NEWS

No regrets, no remorse

The Oklahoma City bomber is unrepentant

BY MIKE THARP

When he was a soldier in the Persian Gulf War, Sgt. Timothy McVeigh expressed compassion for the injured and hungry Iraqi children he saw on the battlefield. A decade later, he referred to the 19 children killed in the Oklahoma City bombing as "collateral damage."

In a book being published this week, McVeigh takes full responsibility for the 1995 blast that left 168 people dead and more than 500 wounded. "I blew up the Murrah Building," McVeigh said, "and isn't it kind of scary that one man could wreak this kind of hell?"

The convicted killer says he was partly motivated by the deaths of children during the government sieges at Waco, Texas, and Ruby Ridge, Idaho. The new book, *American Terrorist: Timothy McVeigh & the Oklahoma City Bombing*, is based on

McVeigh was interviewed for the book in prison. He is to be executed May 16.
● *He's "trying to become a martyr."*

some 70 hours of interviews that authors Dan Herbeck and Lou Michel conducted with McVeigh.

Reaction has been mixed. "I think he's just trying to become a martyr," says Richard Williams, 55, a government supervisor who was severely injured in the bombing. Adds Tom Kight, 62, whose stepdaughter was killed in the explosion:

"His intended victim was the government and, unfortunately, the government is the people."

Eager witnesses. McVeigh is scheduled to die by lethal injection on May 16 in Terre Haute, Ind., in what will be the first federal execution since March 1963. The event, set to take place 23 days after McVeigh's 33rd birthday, is expected to attract more attention than any death-penalty case since 1977, when Gary Gilmore became the first person executed after a 10-year moratorium. More than 250 victims and families of victims want to witness the execution. There will be a limited number of spectators allowed, and the U.S. Bureau of Prisons is considering televising the execution on closed-circuit TV.

McVeigh's former trial lawyer, Stephen Jones, disputes his former client's claim that he was the sole perpetrator. "If McVeigh is saying he acted alone, that is inconsistent with what he told me," Jones told the *Daily Oklahoman*. Another former McVeigh attorney, Richard Burr, says McVeigh could ask Judge Richard Matsch to reconsider his request for a new trial. But, Burr says, "I don't think Tim would ask him to." ●

Timothy McVeigh, put to death by lethal injection after conviction of perpetrating the murder of 168 people in 1995 by blowing up a federal building in Oklahoma City, remained an enigmatic personality to the end. But this picture of McVeigh in prison shortly before his execution may be revealing as to the man's character. What at first appears to be just the man's thumb sticking out may actually be the magical sign called the *mano figo* (a clenched hand or fist, the thumb jutting out). In some secret societies and witchcraft sects the thumb thus symbolizes the phallus inserted as a creative act. In sum, in this posture, McVeigh, realizing it is the final image or one of the last of him that the outside world—his accusers—will probably see, is saying, "F..k you!" The article accompanying the picture of McVeigh would seem to buttress this theory. It is titled, "No Regrets, No Remorse," and says the Oklahoma City bomber is "unrepentant." The angry scowl on Timothy McVeigh's face is also indicative. (Photo: *U.S. News & World Report*, April 9, 2001)

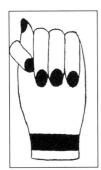
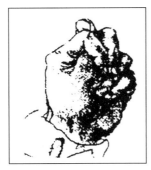

At left, the magical *mano figo* or *mano in fica* hand sign. At right is a second version. Timothy McVeigh's hand sign above is a third version. The *mano in fica* is of oriental origin. It represents a *lingam-yoni* (penis-vagina) formed by the thumb protruding between any of the fingers. To early Christians, it was called *manus obscenus*, the obscene hand.

The vicious Michael Chertoff, son of a Jewish Rabbi, former U.S. Justice Department prosecutor who is active in the anti-Christian group, the ADL, lets the elite see who he is by giving the vulgar and coarse *mano figo* hand sign. Chertoff is President George W. Bush's Director of Homeland Security. Many believe Chertoff is an Israeli Mossad asset.

"Cross My Heart and Hope to Die"—The Mysterious "X" Factor

An X is an ancient symbol for change or transformation…long associated in medieval and renaissance art with the coming of the Messiah who shall make all things new.

—Jim Tresner, 33°
Scottish Rite Journal

The Illuminist/Masonic meaning of the X is simply this: It is the sign of Osiris, the great (Egyptian) sun god…

—Texe Marrs
Dark Majesty

The sign, or letter, X, has a long history of use in the Ancient Mystery Religions, in apostate Judaism, in Freemasonry, and in the occult. The Illuminati elite use it to this day to symbolize key phenomena and mark significant events.

The mysterious letter X seems to take on a wide and varied life of its own, with or without the secret aid of the elite sponsorship. Mark Euston, of the Christian Intelligence Resource Network, in a letter to the author, detailed some of the many examples of the use of the letter X. For example, the well-known science fiction TV show, *The X Files*. Pornographic movies are rated X and the more sensational movies in the raw flesh category are touted as *XXX*, or *triple X*. Euston noted that we have the Microsoft Corporation creation of *X-box*, the movie *X-Men*, off-brand products are called "Brand X," and of course, there is the U.S. terrorist prison camp, *Camp X-Ray* at Guantanamo, Cuba. Today's youth have been called *Generation X*, and a lot of folks are concerned about a planet, or star, reported to be speeding toward us called *Planet X* that has occult significance.

Euston asks about all the usages of X, "Are these just strange coincidences, some type of mind control trigger, or a subliminal conditioning of some kind?" Good question.

Another friend, Kathy Creek, wrote and asked if I had noticed the many new drugs being released by pharmaceutical firms with either a V, Z, or an X in their name? She mentioned an ad she had seen for Clarinex, an allergy drug that had a little sun sign used to dot the letter "i" in Clarinex.

John Myers, another astute friend interested in such topics, sent me a lengthy letter and included an excerpt from Arthur Edward Waite's reference book, *A New Encyclopedia of Freemasonry*. Myers wryly observed that, "generally, things that are bad are X-rated." He mentioned, too, the interesting use of the letter X in the *Rx* of drug stores; the use of the four-letter, abbreviated word *Xmas* to replace Christmas, and the fact that, in *Black's Law Dictionary*, it says that the sign or mark of X is sometimes made as a substitute for a man's signature on legal documents.

And the continued use of the mysterious X abounds. Children at play can be heard to say, "Cross my heart and hope to die." In the Greek alphabet, the letter Chi is denoted with the symbol X, and given the numerical designation of 600. The numerologists say that triple X, then, would yield the number 666.

Black Muslim leaders obviously see X as a substitute name of great spiritual significance. Two well-known Black Muslim leaders have been named Malcolm X and Louis X, names they chose for themselves. The latter, who was born Louis Eugene Wolcott in 1933 in New York City, changed his name to Louis X after his conversion to Islam by Black Muslim leader Elijah Muhammed. Today, he is known as Louis Farrakhan. It is well-known that Farrakhan is a 33° Prince Hall Mason.

X as Symbol for the Sun God

According to Dr. C.J. Koster, head of the Institute for Scripture Research in South Africa, X was the emblem of the Chaldean (Babylonian) sky god. Koster says that X was an ancient symbol of the sun deity and that the letter carried with it sexual connotations. In the old Semitic languages, X represented the cross.[1]

Freemasonry early-on latched onto this letter exactly because of its paranormal significance as a sign of Lucifer, the solar (sun) god. The Masonic Lodge also uses X because of its sexual meanings and its Babylonian origins. Writing in the *Scottish Rite Journal*, the official journal of the Mother Supreme Council, 33°, Jim Tresner discussed the use of X in the ritual ceremony for the 17°, *Knight of the East and West*.[2] Tresner, a 33rd degree Mason, emphasized that the 17th degree ritual is "one of the most powerful and profound degrees of the Rite."[3]

"Here," said Tresner, "we encounter raw spiritual energy" and "we begin to glimpse the spiritual power which is available" to the person who is able to access it.[4]

X as Symbol of Transformation

Tresner goes on to suggest that the X, representing the Roman numeral 10, also symbolizes the 10 yods, or manifestations, of the Jewish Cabala's *Tree of Life* (the Sephiroth). He notes that the candidate for this degree wears two cordons, one black in color, the other white, which symbolizes the duality of Masonic doctrine.

"The fact that they cross each other," Tresner explains, "suggests the unions of opposites or *equilibrium (Ordo Ab Chao)*."[5]

"In crossing," says Tresner, "they form an X shape." X, he observes, "is *an ancient symbol for transformation.*"[6]

"This degree," Tresner concludes, "provides a spiritual jolt or jump-start in preparation for the transformation, refinement, and redefinition to come."[7]

Tresner chooses his words very carefully...and very deliberately. But Christians who have studied the book of *Revelation* will intuit and understand what he is hinting at. I believe he is telling the Masonic candidates that this degree, in which the mark of X is prominent, is to prepare them to wage war against true Christians, and to exalt their Man-King as the events prophesied in Bible prophecy roll forward. Naturally, Tresner would probably deny this meaning, so I leave it to you, dear reader, to discern.

Page 158 from *Richardson's Monitor of Freemasonry*, detailing the ritual ceremony of the Knights of the East and West. In this ritual, the sacred word *Abaddon* is expressed. Abaddon is a synonym for the name of the Devil who leads millions of demons out of the pit of hell to torment earth in the last days.

However, the Masonic author of the authoritative *Richardson's Monitor of Freemasonry*, no doubt lets the cat out of the bag, so to speak, by detailing how, during this ritual ceremony for the Degree of Knight of the East and West, the *Sacred Word* is given to the assembled members of the Lodge. That sacred word is a shocker: It is *Abaddon*.

Yes, Abaddon is the Sacred Word for the Masonic Knights of the East and West. And the Holy Bible reveals exactly who Abaddon is in *Revelation 9:11*:

And they had a king over them, which is the angel of the bottomless pit, whose name in the Hebrew tongue is Abaddon, but in the Greek tongue hath his name Apollyon.

In *Richardson's Monitor of Freemasonry* it is revealed that, following the announcement of the sacred word, Abaddon, the Lodge drama for this fateful degree provides a demonstration "intended to represent the end of the world."[8]

At left: First sign in the Super-Excellent Master Mason Degree (*Richardson's Monitor of Freemasonry*, p. 91)

At right: Second sign of a Select Master Mason Degree. (*Richardson's Monitor of Freemasonry*)

How very appropriate. How very telling!

X Symbol in the Masonic Lodge

One thing is for sure: The Masonic Order uses the X not only for the revelatory 17th degree of Knights of East and West, but for others as well. In the Royal Arch's Super-Excellent Master's Degree, the First Sign given is the crossing of the hands over the breast/chest. This sign refers to the penalty assessed if any secrets learned are ever divulged.

Then, in the ritual ceremony for the Select Master Degree, the Second Sign is made by crossing the hands and arms just below the neck and dropping them downward quickly. Again, this is a reminder of the disclosure penalty, which is to have the body butchered and quartered.

In the ritual for the Intimate Secretary Degree, an X pattern is employed. *Richardson's Monitor of Freemasonry* reveals what happens in the Lodge:

> The brethren now fall, each on his right knee, and they cross their hands and hold them up so that the thumb of the right hand touches the left temple, and the left thumb the right temple...[9]

The X as Tumbling Cross and Sex Symbol

In ancient India, the X symbol was equated with the *vajra* (jewel-phallus). Probably, this is yet another reason why the Masonic Lodge adopted this symbol for many of their ritual activities. Masonry is, in fact, a deviant sex cult.

In her interesting encyclopedia called *The Woman's Dictionary of Symbols and Sacred Objects*, Barbara Walker calls the symbol the *"Cross Saltire"* which means literally "tumbling cross" or a cross performing a somersault. In this sense, it is decidedly anti-Christ in nature.

The Church of Scientology, New Age in its beliefs, has as its logo a traditional cross (vertical) integrated with an X, or Cross Saltire. This is understandable since Scientology is unquestionably non-Christian.

Cross Saltire

X as Sign of Death

Finally, as if to signify the somber, ghastly meaning of the letter X in Freemasonry ritual, pomp and circumstance, it should be noted that upon his death, when the departed Mason's body is given a Masonic funeral by the assembled brethren, with his immediate family in attendance, the X again comes into play. *The Monitor of the Work, Lectures, and Ceremonies of Ancient Craft Masonry for the Grand Lodge of the State of New York* in part describes the ritual and scene prescribed for funerals as follows:

> The funeral honors are given by extending the hands toward the grave with the palms up, the brethren repeating in unison:
>
> 'To the grave we consign the mortal remains of our deceased brother.'
>
> The arms are then crossed over the breast, the left above the right, the fingers touching the shoulders...[10]

You'll find among the photos and illustrations in this section one of horror novelist Stephen King seeming to emulate exactly this funeral procedure of crossing the arms (X), the fingers touching the opposite shoulder. Is King, the master of death literature, in fact taking on the image of death, the grim reaper? Does King believe that this publicly displayed ritual act by him confers on the famous novelist the "raw spiritual energy" mentioned by Masonic authority Jim Tresner, 33°?

X—The Egyptian Connection

From what source do the Masons draw for this funeral symbolism of the X? In my book, *Dark Majesty*, I explain the Egyptian connection:

> In ancient Egypt, the mark of "X" and the symbol of cross-bones in the symbol of an X was very prominent in religious contexts. You can find the X on the walls of a number of ancient Egyptians temples and pyramids...It is the sign of Osiris, the great sun god...
>
> The ancient pharaohs, when they were buried, had the legs crossed in the form of "X" as a sign of devotion to Osiris.[11]

Today, as in ancient Egypt, Osiris the sun god is worshipped; now the homage and veneration comes from the Masons and their fellow Illuminists. These confused and perverted men mistakenly believe they are illumined (enlightened) by their solar deity, the Great Architect, Jahbuhlun, or Lucifer.

They have even arranged for Osiris' watchful eye, the all-seeing eye, to be pictured on each and every U.S.A. one dollar bill. It is the eye in the capstone surrounded by the rays of the sun announcing to the whole world the coming of a New Age, a New World Order *(Novus Ordo Seclorum)*.

What a grand surprise these wicked men have in store for them when Jesus Christ, Lord of Lords, returns. *II Thessalonians 2* says that the opposers of Christ—the leaders of Illuminati and their hordes of rapt followers—shall be utterly destroyed by the brightness of His coming. Until that great and momentous day, the pitiful men of the Illuminati shall continue to wallow with each other in the mire and muck. They will continue communicating the sign of X, the sign of their silly, fanciful god, all the while cursing the darkness rather than lighting a candle. Men blinded for all eternity by their rejection of the True Light.

The arm patch on the military uniform of Pakistan's President, General Pervez Musharraf, tells a number of tales. Against a black, circle background we find the familiar crescent moon and star of Islam (actually, pagan origin, being representative of Diana, the witchcraft "star" and "moon" goddess) as well as the two crossed swords (in the pagan era, a sign of Mars, god of war). It is doubtful Musharraf has any idea of the actual meaning of these symbols.

Her Majesty, Queen Elizabeth of Great Britain, has a fortune of some $18 billion—and a crown with an "X" in its centrum. (*Majesty* magazine, Volume 25, August, 2004)

The "X" Team? In *Time* magazine (July 14, 2003, p. 79), it was reported that Marvel Comics intended to publish a comic book that featured a resurrected Princess Diana with superpowers. The title of the first edition was to be "Di Another Day." The plot was to have Princess Di and a number of mutant, resurrected-from-the-dead partners gallivant around the world performing feats for the good side fighting evil. Princess Di and her mutant friends would all bear a logo on their chest of a (circle) sun sign with a bold red "X" superimposed on it.

BROAD MANDATE
Barak, here with his wife Nava, has the authority now to pursue peace

Ehud Barak, a Freemason chosen Prime Minister of Israel in 1999, with his wife, Nava. This is a very staged *"X."* Also significant is Nava's earring, which has the emblem of the Masonic double-headed eagle. (Photo: *Time* magazine, May 31, 1999, p. 64)

Larry Summers, Secretary of the Treasury in the second term of the Bill Clinton Administration, signals to his associates in the Illuminati elite the strength of their Order. We see first his crossed "X" hand position, the left hand path dominant. Then there is the pillar of strength of Jaquin and Boaz origins, and finally the black and white checkered "trestleboard" upon which he stands, the science of polar opposites, the Hegelian dialectic, the high Masonic principle of *equilibrium*. Summers is currently President of Harvard University.

Madeleine Albright, socialist/communist former Secretary of State under President Bill Clinton, wears the X in gold on a black circle earring. Albright, whose father was once a Communist leader in Czechoslovakia, "discovered" she was Jewish at about the same time a few isolated reports came out on the internet. Jews with Communist backgrounds often hide their ethnic ties to coverup the fact that it was Illuminati Jews—mostly non-Russian Jews at that—who funded, fostered, and ran the Lenin/Stalin Red Terror in Soviet Russia. (*Vanity Fair*, November 1997)

DONALD E. GRAHAM
AND KATHARINE GRAHAM

Photographed by Annie Leibovitz in the *Washington Post* newsroom in
Washington, D.C., on September 4, 1997.

Donald Graham, 52, is chairman and C.E.O. of the
Washington Post Company and publisher of *The Washington Post*. He was born
in Baltimore, Maryland, and received a B.A. from Harvard in 1966.

Graham's first job with the Washington Post Company was
as a metro reporter at the paper; he then moved to *Newsweek*. As chairman
and publisher he has remained a friend and advocate of the
journalists he employs. During the 1975 pressmen's strike Graham impressed
colleagues by working at least two jobs and spending nights on
his office couch to get the paper out. The *Post* missed only one day of publication.

Small, closely held, and thoroughly blue-chip, the Post Company
boasts one of the best stock performances of any American media company.
Ask shareholder and Graham-family friend Warren Buffett.

Katharine Graham, 80, is chairman of the Washington Post Company
Executive Committee. She was born in New York City
and received an A.B. from the University of Chicago in 1938.

She is the matriarch of a publishing dynasty worth $1.85 billion,
and is one of the world's richest and most influential women. The Post empire
includes the newspaper, *Newsweek*, and six TV stations.

Nixon attorney general John Mitchell warned, "Katie Graham is
gonna get her tit caught in a big fat wringer" for printing the story of Mitchell's
"secret funds" during the Watergate crisis. She was later
presented with a wringer signed by the paper's staff. It remains in her office.

Graham ceded publishing duties to her son in 1979
(she retired as chair of the Post Company
board in 1993), but continues to be synonymous with the paper
she led to greatness.

Donald E. Graham, chairman and CEO of *The Washington Post,* in a staged setting in the newsroom.
(*Vanity Fair*)

NELSON MANDELA

President, South Africa.

Photographed by Jean Baptiste Mondino
in Saint-Germain-en-Laye, France.

Born, Mvezo, Transkei region, South Africa.
B.A., University of South Africa, 1942. Divorced from his
second wife, Winnie Mandela;
four children, including two daughters with Winnie.

Mandela, 78, joined the pro-democratic
African National Congress in 1944. He lead the A.N.C.'s
nonviolent Defiance Campaign
against the Afrikaner-dominated National Party's rule.
In the early 60s, when the A.N.C. was banned,
he became a fugitive. For more than a year
he eluded authorities, earning the nickname "the Black
Pimpernel." In August 1962 he was
captured and later sentenced to life imprisonment
without parole, for high treason.

When Mandela was released on
February 11, 1990, he made a triumphant tour of
North America and Europe.
Working with then president F. W. de Klerk (with whom
he shared the 1993 Nobel Peace Prize),
he brought about the first elections open to all
South African citizens, in April 1994.
In these elections he was
chosen president of South Africa with
62.6 percent of the vote.

Enlargement
of tie.

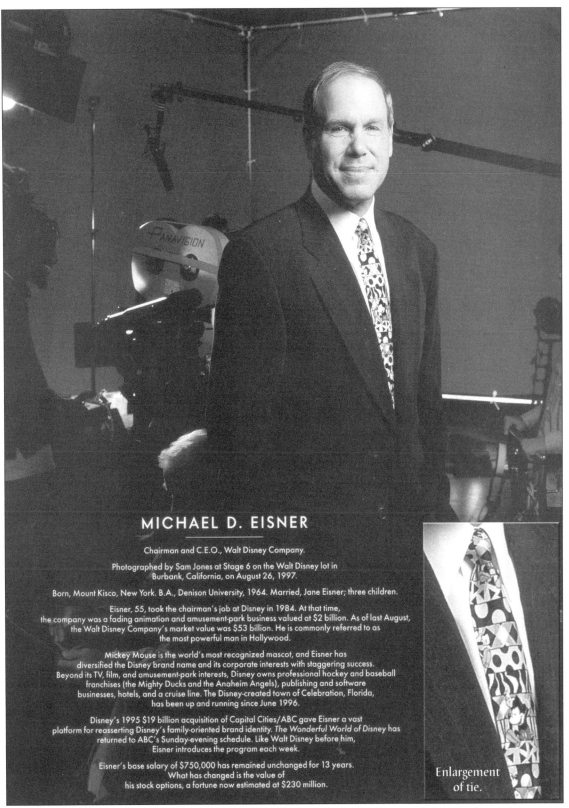

MICHAEL D. EISNER

Chairman and C.E.O., Walt Disney Company.

Photographed by Sam Jones at Stage 6 on the Walt Disney lot in
Burbank, California, on August 26, 1997.

Born, Mount Kisco, New York. B.A., Denison University, 1964. Married, Jane Eisner; three children.

Eisner, 55, took the chairman's job at Disney in 1984. At that time,
the company was a fading animation and amusement-park business valued at $2 billion. As of last August,
the Walt Disney Company's market value was $53 billion. He is commonly referred to as
the most powerful man in Hollywood.

Mickey Mouse is the world's most recognized mascot, and Eisner has
diversified the Disney brand name and its corporate interests with staggering success.
Beyond its TV, film, and amusement-park interests, Disney owns professional hockey and baseball
franchises (the Mighty Ducks and the Anaheim Angels), publishing and software
businesses, hotels, and a cruise line. The Disney-created town of Celebration, Florida,
has been up and running since June 1996.

Disney's 1995 $19 billion acquisition of Capital Cities/ABC gave Eisner a vast
platform for reasserting Disney's family-oriented brand identity. *The Wonderful World of Disney* has
returned to ABC's Sunday-evening schedule. Like Walt Disney before him,
Eisner introduces the program each week.

Eisner's base salary of $750,000 has remained unchanged for 13 years.
What has changed is the value of
his stock options, a fortune now estimated at $230 million.

Enlargement
of tie.

Sometimes, a person wears what they are! These photos of South Africa's political leader Nelson
Mandela (left) and Disney Corp. CEO Michael Eisner (above) paint a story by reference to the design
on each man's neckties. Look close-up and the "X" and other Illuminist symbols are clearly seen.
(*Vanity Fair*, November 1997)

LET THERE BE LIGHT: Digitally enhanced view of the new atrium (left); the architect

geously curvy Guggenheim Bilbao), Taniguchi's self-effacing building rejects the status of icon, as if to murmur, "Don't mind me—just look at the art." After all, the art is the richest collection of modern masterworks in the world, from Monet's "Water Lilies" to Picasso's "Les Demoiselles d'Avignon" to Andy Warhol's soup cans. Some of MoMA's devout followers believed the museum—the first to create a department of architecture—betrayed its mission by building Taniguchi's scheme rather than something jazzier. But MoMA, 75 years old and hardly a haven for the avant-garde, makes no apology. "It's like having an English suit or an Italian suit," says museum director Glenn Lowry. "Yoshio's building is the English suit—it's not flamboyant but it's perfectly tailored and will be the same in 100 years as it is today."

Taniguchi likes to say his goal is to make the architecture "disappear." And while we don't believe him literally—his ego is fiercely invested in his design principles and his impeccable details—his understated approach at MoMA is to subtly and meticulously create experiences of shifting spaces, light and views as you move through the museum. He started with a homage, restoring the façades of the original 1939 museum by Philip Goodwin and Edward Durell Stone and Philip Johnson's 1964 east wing. He then turned his focus to the famous sculpture garden—"the heart of the museum," he says—and framed it with immaculately cool glass-curtain walls and deep, porchlike overhangs. Then, inside the museum, Taniguchi, in his quiet way, went to town: his new entrance cuts a wide public passage through the city block. From there, you cross a spacious ticket lobby and wham!—you're standing in a gorgeous 110-foot-high atrium, flooded with daylight,

Noted Japanese architect Yoshio Taniguchi who specializes in buildings and structures housing museums.

Fortune magazine (December 20, 1999) had this rather unusual photograph picturing two *CompUSA* e-commerce subsidiary managers, Michael Laskoff (left) and Stephen Polly. The caption and article gave no clue as to why the two men are crossing their legs ("X") nor was there an explanation for the bizarre staging of what should have been your usual, stock business photo.

James Erwin, vice chairman of Bank of America, heads up the giant financial institution's Dallas, Texas, operations. Is the "X" crossing of his legs just a "good old boy" gesture or an Illuminist fraternal sign?

Allen Ginsberg, in an enigmatic example of the X. With this photo—published in the obituary column of *Newsweek* (December 22, 1997)!—there was no caption, only Ginsberg's laudatory obit. The magazine touted Ginsberg's "genius" and praised him for his "hymn of alienation" during his earlier years—a valueless poem titled "Howl." In fact, Beat poet Allen Ginsberg was a warped, child-molester advocate who boosted NAMBLA, the North American Man-Boy Love Association. He was a reprobate pedophile, but a hero of Satanists, sadists, and assorted culture freaks, not to mention the Illuminati elite. In the years before his death, they rewarded him with a $1 million payment by Stanford University. In return, the University, a prime center of Illuminist instruction, got Ginsberg's "papers," which reportedly included "300,000 utility bills, newspaper clippings, paper napkins, concert tickets, and anything else the gay poet chose to save."

CampusReport

November 1994 ■ Volume IX, Number 10

Ginsberg is NAMBLA Booster

Pro-Pedophile Poet Paid $1M By Stanford

Stanford University just paid nearly a million dollars for a collection of gay poet Allen Ginsberg's papers and "memorabilia."

What do students get for this hefty expenditure? Among other things, they get a pair of Ginsberg's old tennis shoes. They get snippets of his beard from various trimmings. They get dried-out vines of hallucinogenic plants.

And they get more than 300,000 old utility bills, newspaper clippings, paper napkins, old concert tickets, and anything else the gay poet chose to save.

Conservative critics and alumni have questioned the price paid and the propriety of supporting Ginsberg in view of the fact that he is a long-time member and booster of the North American Man/Boy Love Association, a group of pedophiles that openly advocates sex between adult males and young boys. Most homosexual groups will have nothing to do with them.

Ginsberg writes, "I'm a member of NAMBLA because I love boys... Everybody does who has a little humanity."

Stanford officials denied having received any negative reaction to the purchase, though. "The NAMBLA thing is not an issue," Pete Rapalus of Stanford's media relations office told *Campus Report*. "The relevance of the acquisition has nothing to do with the [author]'s *purported* sexuality [emphasis his]," he said.

Critics also note Ginsberg's promotion of illicit drug use. He has been photographed carrying a sign that says, "Pot is a reality kick," and he has spoken with pride about the fact that we now have a president "who dared to put a joint to his lips."

Ginsberg himself acknowledges that Stanford has not been an admirer of his unconventional poetry in the past.

"Stanford was dominated by a very conservative, formalist poetry that very much rebelled against the kind of ecstatic, apocalyptic, William Carlos Williams-based naturalistic poetry we wrote," Ginsberg told the *New York Times*. "I gave readings for ten years or so, at every university up and down the coast, and the one place that never invited me was Stanford."

According to Rapalus, funding for the purchase came from the university's General Operating Budget, which is made up of tuition, grant, gift, endowment and other moneys. Though the school has "been going through cutbacks for years," Rapalus dismissed accusations of wastefulness saying, "This university has spent millions of dollars over the past few years on things that it considers worthwhile, while at the same time cutting its budget."

Gay poet Alan Ginsburg built the 300,000 piece collection because he believed his life "embodied the struggle for sexual, social and political liberation in the 1950's and 60's."

The three English professors who pushed for the purchase agreed that Stanford was an unlikely home for the collection. "If he came down tomorrow, nine-tenths of the English department wouldn't turn out for him," said Prof. Marjorie Perloff.

Nonetheless, the Stanford librarian who negotiated the deal praised the pedophilic poet, calling him "one of the most important figures in postwar culture, literature and politics."

Symbols galore adorn feminist Gloria Steinem's apartment décor in New York. She's wearing a black outfit with belt with a huge, round *sun* emblem and, naturally, her handsign is *"X."* Now 70-years-old, Ms. Steinem, like so many other "chosen ones," is not at all what she seems. A former *Playboy Club* bunny, Steinem was covertly working for the CIA. She "founded" the radical agenda *MS* magazine reportedly with Illuminist funding and traveled widely in India. Her elitist role: Foster the anti-Christian, culture-destroying Feminist Movement.

Charlie Chaplin spoofs Adolf Hitler as Adenoid Hynkel in the film classic, *The Great Dictator* (1940). The hat he wears has two *"X's"* while the double doors in the scene have Rosicrucian rosettes on them. Charlie Chaplin was much more than simply a spoofing comedy genius. Born April 16, 1889, in London, England, to Jewish parents, at age 30 he co-founded United Artists, a major Hollywood movie corporation. Strongly pro-Communist and Zionist, Chaplin had a penchant for teen-age girls that sometimes got him in trouble. The Illuminati paid homage to Chaplin by adopting the actor's *"The Tramp"* icon for TV commercials for global technology giant IBM. (Photo: *Time* magazine)

Charlie Chaplin in 1952 letting the whole world know just what he is—a devil in human form! This photo, by famous photographer Richard Avedon, ran in *Time* magazine (October 11, 2004), an Illuminist-shill publication.

CHARLIE CHAPLIN
1952

Actress Marlene Dietrich, a tool of the OSS, the predecessor of the CIA, was a lesbian who privately snickered because Hollywood portrayed her as a sex symbol for males.

Allen Iverson, NBA Basketball star. Observe his deathhead skull tattoo and, of course, the "X."

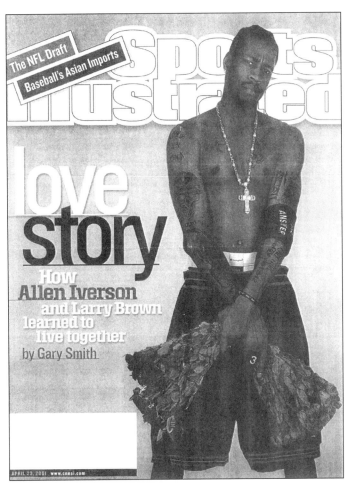

Rock'n'roller Tommy Lee embraces hip-hop entertainer Sean Combs in an "X." Lee's sign of the satanic pentagram tattoo on his left hand is also evident. (Photo: *U.S.A. Today*, June 4, 2001, p. 4D)

Famous horror film actor Boris Karloff, in the classic cinema, *The Mummy*, lays in the mummy's crypt and symbolically crosses his arms ("*X*") just as was done in Egyptian ritual in the days of the Pharaohs.

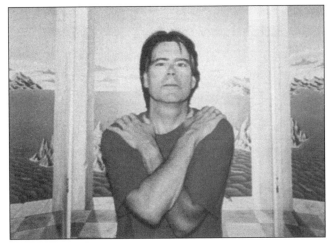

Stephen King, whose novels on horror and terror invariably go to the top of the bestseller's list. The caption of this photo, published in *Newsweek* (August 28, 2000, p. 45) reads, *"It's good to be King."*

These ancient Egyptian figures demonstrate how prevalent was Osiris' sacred sign, "X."

The mummy of Rameses the Great (1279-1213 B.C.) was found in this cedarwood sarcophagus. This pharaoh is thought by Egyptologists to be the ruler who enslaved the Israelites and forced them to build cities.

Painting from the Tomb of Rameses I, Valley of the Kings, West Thebes, in Egypt.

The figure at right (Luciferian angel?) has wings crossed in "X" fashion. This is said to be a secret, coded alphabet used by the clandestine Templars Order. (From *Secret Societies*, by Arkon Daraul)

These ancient Egyptian figures demonstrate how prevalent was Osiris' sacred sign, "X."

Pre-Aztec figurine, today on display in Mexico, has arms crossed in "X" position.

Bronze figurine of the demon god Pazuzu, 800-600 B.C. Pazuzu is still secretly worshipped today by many.

A real Egyptian mummy, arms crossed in honor of Osiris, divine Father.

Rosicrucian and other mystical orders emphasize the process of *alchemy*, mystical union that brings about cleansing and renewal. The goal of Illuminati alchemy is to realize a New World Order through destruction ("cleansing"). Thus, *Ordo Ab Chao*, order out of chaos. In this drawing from Mylius's *Philosophia Reformata* (1622) the alchemical process is "Bath," the union of Sol (Sun) and Luna (Moon). The *"X"* is the intersection of the two opposites.

Swami Bua, an Indian Hindu sage who, in 2003, claimed to be 115 years old. He crosses his legs in the X-configuration typical of Hindu gurus and swamis as they meditate and practice yoga. Apparently, the Swami's lifestyle does not a healthy nation make. According to statistics overall in India, the longevity rate is 23 years less than in North America (Photo: *Transformation* magazine, July-August, 2003)

Kali, merciless goddess of death and destruction, metes out justice and balancing of karma to her victims. Observe the satanic sign of Kali's left hand and her spinning on her finger of a sun sign. Her color is blue, same color as the Blue Lodge of Freemasonry (first three degrees). The rose and the lotus are her flowers, also the same flowers represented throughout the occult world by many other individuals and groups.

Façade and front elevation of Our Lady of Grace Chapel and Padre Pio Spirituality Centre in Barto, Pennsylvania. Padre Pio was a Catholic monk who became famous for stigmata in his hands. Pope John Paul II declared Padre Pio a "Saint" May 2, 1999.

The papacy often uses the "X," as is demonstrated in the Dagon fish-hat of Pope John Paul II on the cover of The Pope Speaks journal.

The X symbol on the robe worn by Pope John Paul II is telling, as is the silver metal torch with its black flame. Silver is the metallic element of the ancient goddess, which the Pope would recognize in the form of Mary, Mother of Jesus. The X, of course, represents the Father deity. Not the Father God of the Old and New Testament, but of Babylon and Egypt.

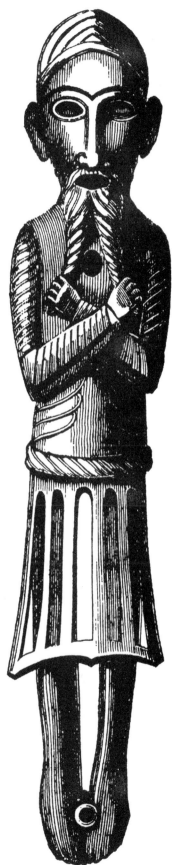

Georges Darboy, Archbishop of Paris in 1870. Observe the crossed hands (X) and the Il Cornuto horned devil sign given with the left hand as it holds the prelate's hat. (From the book, *How The Pope Became Infallible*, by August Bernhard Hasler, 1981, Doubleday & Co., Garden City, New York)

This image was found under the root of a tree dug up in Roscommon in Ireland. It is made of brass. The gilding, however, is now almost worn off. It is on display at the Museum of Trinity College, Dublin.

"To this deity in particular they apply themselves for success when they go out a hunting or fishing, and for the relief of all such as are indisposed!"— Miramba. (From the book, *The Round Towers of Atlantis*, by Henry O'Brien, published 2002; originally in 1834; Adventures Unlimited Press, Kempton, IL 60946)

CIRCLE
NETWORK NEWS

Nature Spirituality Quarterly
Summer 1994 • Issue 52 $4.50

Special Section

Sacred Sun

Cover of a popular witchcraft publication in the U.S.A., *Circle Network News* (copyright 1994). Cernunnos, horned antler god of the forest, is at top with his arms folded ("X"). The sun, sacred to wiccans is at center.

In this photo of the staff of Yale University's *Yale Literary Magazine* (1941), the five young men in front are all giving a similar hand over hand ("X") signal. The photo is significant because one of the students pictured (second from right, back row) is James Jesus Angleton, perverted Mason who was long-term Deputy Director of the CIA and was guilty of murder, rape, torture, treason, and numerous other counts of evildoing. It is also at Yale where the Order of Skull and Bones and other elitist groups initiate their recruits.

Pirates hoisted the Skull & Bones (the "Jolly Roger") flags on their sea vessels. (Illustrations from book, *Pirates and The Lost Templar Fleet*, 2003)

The seal of Edinburgh University in Scotland.

Logo of Garrett-Evangelical Theological Seminary, a liberal institution in Illinois.

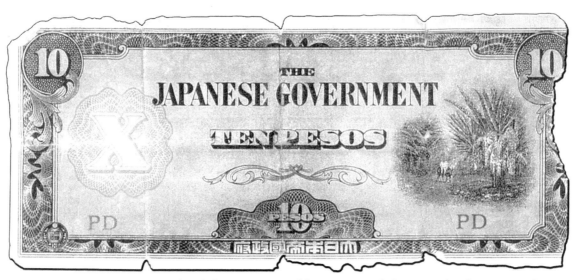

The Japanese army occupying the Philippines in World War II issued their own local currency. This 10 peso bill was found by American soldiers on the body of a dead Japanese soldier. The "X" is apparently the Roman numeral for "ten."

Leon DeGrelle

The "Cross of Burgundy" was two crossed sticks, in the form of an *"X,"* which became the emblem of the Nazi Wallonien Waffen SS Division, a group of French volunteers, led by Leon Degrelle, that fought on the Russian front against the Communists.

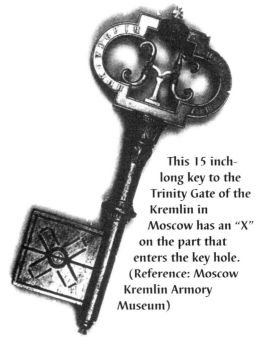

This 15 inch-long key to the Trinity Gate of the Kremlin in Moscow has an "X" on the part that enters the key hole. (Reference: Moscow Kremlin Armory Museum)

Its advocates claim the X design of the old confederate flag (the *"stars and bars"*) is adapted from the ancient and historic Saint Andrew's cross. This is far from certain. The Confederacy was secretly supported by Jesuits, Masons, and Jews (Rothschild interests) all of whom were aware of its true, occultic origins. Moreover, the degree of the Scottish Rite of Freemasonry emphasizes the X-shaped cross of Saint Andrew.

This letter from a "gentleman" claiming to be of the Invisible Empire of the KKK was sent to the author after he had on his radio program a Jewish guest, a Christian who was head of the International Board of Jewish Missions, a group that evangelizes Jews for Christ. Obviously, the KKK was a little upset that the author is not anti-Semite. The logo on the letterhead is of interest with its blackish circle, triangle, and the Masonic "47th Problem of Euclid" triune design. The KKK, of course, was founded by Masons following the South's defeat in America's Civil War, 1865.

8/4/96

❖ HONOR ❖

To: Living Truth Ministries

Subject: International Board of Jewish Missions

    Aug. 4,1996 WWCR Broadcast

The hideous crimson hour has arrived;

    TEXE MARR, you have defiled your soul with canaanite excrement and the world listen as you whored for the so-called jew.

    The bride shall not be bartered for your cup of self-glorification.

    I pray that YAHSHUA the CHRIST will put an end to your corrupt, negro mixing, jew idolizing sorcery!

        In hoc sign vinces,

        Mikel P. Geren

        Mikel P. Geren

        Invisible Empire v,

        Realm of Tennessee

Ku Klux Klan

Militant Ku Klux Klan
$14.00

Artwork for t-shirts offered through the mail by a company called Aryan Graphics. The Confederate flag's X-styled "bars and stripes" is a focal point.

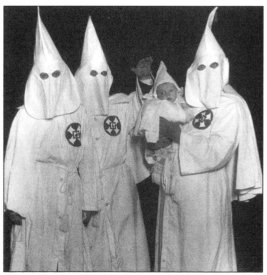

These Ku Klux Klansmen wear an X on the left breast of their white robes. The KKK was founded by Confederate Generals Albert Pike and Nathan B. Forrest. Pike was also the Sovereign Grand Commander of Scottish Rite Freemasonry, and his book, *Morals and Dogma*, is still lauded as a classic by the global Masonic leadership. Although Pike was a confederate general and was labeled a criminal by President Abraham Lincoln, today, a statue of Pike stands in front of the U.S. Justice Department's headquarters in Washington, D.C. His body is entombed in the Scottish Rite's The House of the Temple headquarters in Washington, D.C.

Illuminism in space: NASA patches are loaded with pagan, occultic, and Masonic meanings, including the X of Osiris, the Egyptian Sun God.

An *X* is formed as America's top four politicians met at the White House to decide the fate of the federal budget. Obviously, this was a staged "photo op" event, but for Vice President Al Gore and House speaker Newt Gingrich to reach over the clasped hands of President Bill Clinton and Senate Majority Leader Bob Dole was a serious breach of etiquette. (*USA Today*, December 21, 1995)

MORALS AND DOGMA.

I.

APPRENTICE.

THE TWELVE-INCH RULE AND THE COMMON GAVEL.

FORCE, unregulated or ill-regulated, is not only wasted in the void, like that of gunpowder burned in the open air, and steam unconfined by science; but, striking in the dark, and its blows meeting only the air, they recoil, and bruise itself. It is destruction and ruin. It is the volcano, the earthquake, the cyclone;—not growth and progress. It is Polyphemus blinded, striking at random, and falling headlong among the sharp rea...

Albert Pike, former Sovereign Grand Commander of the Scottish Rite, in his book, *Morals and Dogma*, considered by many Masons to be their "bible" and guide for daily living, has this illustration of an *"X,"* in the form of a crossed gavel and a measuring stick, or rule. Pike explains the illustration by suggesting that *Force* (the brute power of the people) must be regulated by the elite: "The blind Force of the people is a Force that must be economized, and also managed... It must be regulated by Intellect."

80.   MORALS AND DOGMA.

hour; and hence, in several African dialects, as names of the Sun,
Airo, Ayero, eer, uiro, ghurrah, and the like. The royal name
rendered *Pharaoh,* was PHRA, that is, *Pai-ra,* the Sun.

The legend of the contest between *Hor-ra* and *Set,* or *Set-nu-bi,*
the same as *Bar* or *Bal,* is older than that of the strife between
Osiris and *Typhon;* as old, at least, as the nineteenth dynasty. It
is called in the Book of the Dead, "The day of the battle between
Horus and Set." The later myth connects itself with Phœnicia
and Syria. The body of OSIRIS went ashore at *Gebal* or *Byblos,*
sixty miles above Tsūr. You will not fail to notice that in the
name of each murderer of Khūrūm, that of the Evil God Bal is
found.

    *   *   *   *   *   *

Har-oeri was the god of TIME, as well as of Life. The Egyptian
legend was that the King of Byblos cut down the tamarisk-tree
containing the body of OSIRIS, and made of it a column for his
palace. Isis, employed in the palace, obtained possession of the
column, took the body out of it, and carried it away. Apuleius
describes her as "a beautiful female, over whose divine neck her
long thick hair hung in graceful ringlets;" and in the procession
female attendants, with ivory combs, seemed to dress and ornament
the royal hair of the goddess. The palm-tree, and the lamp in the
shape of a boat, appeared in the procession. If the symbol we are
speaking of is not a mere modern invention, it is to these things it
alludes.

The identity of the legends is also confirmed by this hieroglyphic
picture, copied from an ancient Egyptian monument, which may
also enlighten you as to the Lion's grip and the Master's gavel.

In his classic Masonic textbook, *Morals and Dogma,* Scottish Rite legend Albert Pike suggests
that "This hieroglyphic picture, copied from an ancient Egyptian monument, may enlighten you
as to the Lion's grip and the Master's gavel," two standards of the ritual ceremony for the
Master degree. In the picture, the candidate, lying on the floor, is about to be "raised" by the
powerful grip of the Lion's paw. The lion is carrying in his right hand the *Ankh,* symbol of
reincarnation, or regeneration. The *"X"* on the man's chest tells us this is Osiris, the Sun God
who was slain but arose from the dead, being pieced back together by his beautiful Queen, Isis.

XXIX.

GRAND SCOTTISH KNIGHT OF ST. ANDREW.

A MIRACULOUS tradition, something like that connected with the *labarum* of Constantine, hallows the Ancient Cross of St. Andrew. Hungus, who in the ninth century reigned over the Picts in Scotland, is said to have seen in a vision, on the night before a battle, the Apostle Saint Andrew, who promised him the victory; and for an assured token thereof, he told him that there should appear over the Pictish host, in the air, such a fashioned cross as he had suffered upon. Hungus, awakened, looking up at the sky, saw the promised cross, as did all of both arm Hungus and the Picts.

Beginning on page 801 of Albert Pike's classic textbook, *Morals and Dogma*, we find an explanation of the 29th degree, Grand Scottish Knight of St. Andrew.

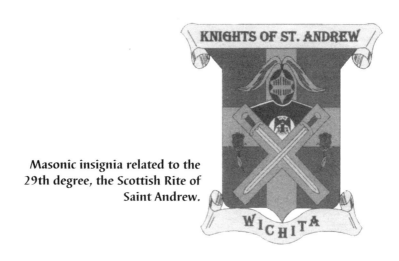

Masonic insignia related to the 29th degree, the Scottish Rite of Saint Andrew.

Lisa Marie Presley's sophomore album, *Now What*, is due April 5.

You're rich and the daughter of a pop star. How come you didn't turn out like Nicole Richie? My mom, myself and Scientology. With reality shows like [Richie's], it's so easy to become a celebrity now, isn't it? It doesn't take much work.

It didn't take much work for you. When you made your first record, you were immediately booked on Letterman. Yeah, and my first live performance was on *Good Morning America*. I skidded through it. I had no chops yet.

Do you have chops now? I have my moments. Don't expect perfection. The way it all happened for me, perfection isn't in the cards.

Was this album easier to make than the first? There wasn't as much pressure. With the first one, nobody really knew me. I had to answer for myself.

Do you think about your dad before you go onstage? I can't say I

Q&A
LISA MARIE PRESLEY

think about him. Usually I just have terror stomach, which I know he had. I do the deep breathing and the pacing he did.

How often do you go back to Graceland? A few times a year. It's a beautiful, sad place for me. I still have family there. We have Christmas dinner at the house. I find it my responsibility to still go there and inject some life into it.

Are you what your daddy would call a Hard Headed Woman? Not at all. That's someone who's stubborn. I'm rebellious.

Your single Dirty Laundry, a 1980s Don Henley song, is about the bloodthirsty media. Explain. I thought that song was more relevant now than ever. Our entertainment now—the reality-show thing—is about watching the demise, humiliation and darkest hour of others.

Have you been asked to be a witness in the Michael Jackson trial? That's too much of a hot stove. There's a trial going on, so I can't say a word, and I'm pretty happy about that.

Lisa Marie Presley demonstrates her cabalistic knowledge in this body pose in a news magazine, including the X sign of Osiris and the legs in diamond position. This body position emphasizes the sex generative energies. (*Time* magazine, April 5, 2005)

TWELVE

That Ravenous Dark Bird—Sublime Mysteries of the Illuminati's Double-Headed Eagle

And he cried mightily with a strong voice, saying, Babylon the great is fallen, is fallen, and is become the habitation of devils, and the hold of every foul spirit, and a cage of every unclean and hateful bird.

— *Revelation 18:2*

The Royal Secret...the Secret of the Universal Equilibrium...shall at length make real the Holy Empire of true Masonic Brotherhood.

— Albert Pike, 33°
Morals and Dogma

Two heads are better than one, except when they're on the body of only one eagle.

— Texe Marrs

Can the body of *one* bird have *two* heads? Is such a notion insane? I believe so. Insanity can be described as a demented man's firm belief that two totally contradictory and opposite things are nevertheless one and the same. If a man simultaneously embraces two competing, mutually exclusive ideas or philosophies, he can properly be deemed "out of his mind," or insane. If, for example, he is convinced that an apple is a bird or that the color black is actually white, then he is insane.

But the Illuminati do not agree. Their whole insane doctrine is based on the supposition that black *is* white, that good *is* evil, that two plus two equals five. They are men of insane minds. And they have developed an equally insane "scientific" system, designed to reprogram and recreate social material and spiritual reality to fit their perverted, upside down theology.

Universal Motion: Alchemy and Magic

Their scientific system, actually a form of witchcraft, is based on *alchemy* and *magic*. Its process is one of *Universal Motion*, designed to purposely foment diabolical chaos so that order may come out of two dynamic competing forces, *Ordo Ab Chao*. Their objective is the *Great Work*, the changing of man created in God's image into the image of a serpent-being void of morality and void of righteous, just values. In other words, the Great Work is designed to create and produce a race of soul-less satanic creatures.

To effect their Great Work, to transform and transmutate the world and humanity into the "new soul-less creature," heaven and earth must be destroyed, crushed, and thoroughly converted into a new paradigm. In essence, heaven and earth are to become hell. The will of Satan shall be done on Earth as it is in hell. This is the exalted, *"Royal Secret."* It is the Illuminati's core doctrine, their cardinal teaching, that out of bloody, universal chaos will ultimately come equilibrium and the Holy Empire of the Illuminati, to be ruled by their cabalistic Messiah, or King—actually the Antichrist. Pike revealed this ultimate objective to subordinate Illuminists on page 861 of his celebrated textbook, *Morals and Dogma*:

> The Royal Secret, of which you are a Prince, if you are a true adept...is that which the *Sohar* (an occultic and cabalistic text) terms The Mystery of the Balance. It is the Secret of the Universal Equilibrium...Such, my Brother, is the True Word of a Master Mason; such is the true Royal Secret, which makes possible, and shall at length make real, the Holy Empire of true Masonic Brotherhood.[1]

Ruining God's Creation

Ezekiel 28 tells us that, as first created by God, Lucifer was a beautiful creature, one of the most lovely in Heaven. His body was not of flesh but was made up of actual gems and jewels. Even more fantastic, musical instruments were incorporated into his being. A beauty to behold.

But then the deceitful Lucifer rebelled, taking down with him one third of the angels. He and they apparently became vile creatures, ugly and deformed, appearing in grotesque forms appropriate to their mental and spiritual deformities.

> *How art thou fallen from heaven, O Lucifer, son of the morning! how art thou cut down to the ground, which didst weaken the nations! For thou hast said in thine heart, I will ascend into heaven, I will exalt my throne above the stars of God...I will ascend above*

the heights of the clouds; I will be like the most High. Yet thou shalt be brought down to hell, to the sides of the pit. (Isaiah 14:12-15)

The Bible says that the angry and furious fallen Lucifer now walks to and fro in the earth like a lion seeking whom he might devour. His aim is to ruin God's creation, to bastardize and corrupt it, to change it into what he is—a monumentally ugly and warped creation, totally opposite of what God intended. Man and the world must be ruined, destroyed, transformed into a barren, non-producing, hideously shaped wasteland.

Men are to be made feminine; women masculine. Marriage is to be perverted. No longer between man and woman, it shall be used also to join men with men and women to women. Abortion—the reckless slaughter of innocents—is to be applauded. Sex is to become rife with perversion. Children are given over to the terrible passions of lustful pedophiles. Spiritual values are converted to material desires. False gods are exalted. False Bibles are invented. Murder and assassination become religious goals.

The Christian seeks as his life goal to become more and more like Jesus. But man and the world are progressively becoming more like Satan and his dark angels—more corrupt and evil every day, in every way. Evolution, oddly, becomes fact, except that man isn't evolving from apes, he is *becoming* an ape. He is transferred into base animal, devoid of God's values, without the mind of Christ, but instead filled with instincts and ambitions of pride, lust, murder, and envy.

As Above, So Below

This, then, is the end-goal of Illuminism: To destroy earth, debase civilization, end pure spirituality, induce chaos on earth, and bring order according to Satan's Illuminati script. Earth is to be hell and hell on earth: *As Above, So Below.*

This is the meaning of the double-headed Eagle; the androgynous joining of man and woman; the mixing of the yin and yang; the checkerboard, black and white floors of the Masonic Lodges; the mirror images of the Rosicrucians; the sulphurous tale of Beauty and the Beast; the witches parable of the lovely lady vs. the crone on her broom; the Druid/Satanic/Catholic alternating of black and white priest vestments; the front and obverse (hidden) sides of the Great Seal of the United States; the reversing of the cross and the reading of the Lord's Prayer backwards in satanic worship, *ad naseum*.

All fields, all things, must be reversed. Negative must be transmuted into positive. Bad will be good. Black shall be white. The ugly shall be adjudged beautiful and the beautiful is to be spoiled, scarred, and made repugnant and revolting. God shall be debased and Satan exalted.

Illuminism, therefore, is a system of dualism (thesis and antithesis) which cyclically repeats as synthesis results. Then, the conflicting forces of the duality cycle clash again, with synthesis being achieved once more. Always the synthesis, the temporary solution or form, is unfrozen, the process of two competing forces re-ignited, and the cycle is continued.

Chaos begets order, but chaos ensues again, followed by order, and so on. The

THE DOUBLE-HEADED EAGLE—THE SUPREME SYMBOL.

Here is depicted the Supreme Hierophant, Master of the double Holy Empire of the superior and the inferior universes. The ancient emblem of equilibrium consisted of an androgynous body surmounted by two heads, one male and the other female, wearing a single imperial crown. That being alone is perfect in which all opposites are reconciled, and this state of perfection is appropriately typified by the two heads of equal dignity. Hence the double-headed eagle is reserved as the emblem of completion, for it signifies the Philosopher's Stone, the ultimate soul condition, and that absolute and transcendent perfection which arises only from the fullest unfoldment of the latent potentialities within the individual. Philosophically, the thirty-third degree of the Ancient and Accepted Scottish Rite represents the innermost sanctuary of Masonic mysticism. If the double-headed eagle, the symbol of that sublime degree, were endowed with the power of speech, it would say:

"Only he may wear me in whom there is no guile, in whom all passion has been transmuted into compassion, all natural ignorance into divine wisdom, all selfishness into selflessness; for I am an ancient and a sacred emblem of all greatness, all perfection, and all truth. I represent a spiritual condition, a mental attitude, a physical state attained only by the elect of earth; I am the symbol of the illumined and transfigured soul which has been born again and has approached the throne of Divinity. I am the symbol of the gatekeeper, for with one face I behold the radiant countenance of my Creator and with the other the expanse of the universe which He has fashioned. Upon my strong pinions of intuition and reason men have ascended to a position betwixt heaven and earth. He in whom I spread my wings is more than a man yet less than a god; therefore he is a god-man. I clutch between my talons the flaming cherubimic sword, the flaming spirit-fire with which the miracle of my existence was wrought. I am the symbol of the Initiator who through the ages carries Ganymedes into the presence of the gods upon his back."

Manly P. Hall, 33°, the 20th Century's most revered Masonic scholar, titled this "The Double-Headed Eagle, The Supreme Symbol," in his classic book, *The Secret Teachings of All Ages.*

conflict of opposites leads finally to system equilibrium which is disturbed once again by renewed conflict, and a new, temporary stage of equilibrium is achieved. Ever upward, evolving until perfection. So, the Illuminist is a perfectionist ever changing, seeking more light as he travels down that yellow brick road to tomorrow. As Bill and Hillary Clinton's favorite song intoned, "Don't stop thinking about tomorrow."

"Everything must change," was the slogan of the Illuminists who sparked the French Revolution.[2]

The Illuminists ruling America give us two political parties, Democrat and Republican (thesis and antithesis), both of which they control. But the conflict of these two opposites never leads to a real solution, only to a fluid, sketchy, "synthesis." Problems are never completely and satisfactorily resolved. The dualistic process is never ending. We are all citizens of "Neverneverland," and we don't even know it.

The Third Side to Every Issue

Here's how one Illuminist philosopher, satanic priest Anton LaVey, explained it:

> There are not always 'two sides to every issue.' That statement is a ridiculous slogan invoked by vested interests…

> In matters of significant concern, there is invariably another alternative: a THIRD SIDE, a satanic side.

> 'Two sides of the same coin' is what most major issues are artfully constructed to be. Subsequently, the populace lives by imperceptible Hobson's choices masquerading as opposing opinions.

> The two uppermost points of the inverted pentagram of Satan represent the dualistic nature of all things, *as all things are naturally perceived*. Man has always been motivated and controlled by whatever dualistic concept is in fashion, and always will be. Like it or not, it's the way things really are. Shades of gray only appear between established opposites.[3]

The Rosicrucian Orders and the Masonic Lodge incessantly teach this duality of all things in their rituals and lectures. In the book, *The Rose Cross and the Goddess*, Masonic advocate, Gareth Knight, speaks of this *"dual polarity."* In Masonic symbolism, Knight observes, this duality is expressed by the square and compass.[4]

One of the highest degree rituals in Scottish Rite Freemasonry is that which honors the Emperors of the East and West. It is symbolized, among other things, by the Masonic double-headed eagle. Two heads, one body. Again: duality.

The Universal Serpent Force

Albert Pike, the former Sovereign Grand Commander whose writings are so honored and venerated that Pike's body has been entombed in the Scottish Rite's international headquarters, The House of the Temple, in Washington, DC, taught that out of the ongoing *universal motion* of the conflict of opposites, a potent and magical *force* could be created or energized, so powerful that "a single man, who could possess himself of it, and should know how to direct it, could revolutionize and change the face of the world." In *Morals and Dogma*, he emphasizes:

> This force was known to the ancients. It is a universal agent, whose Supreme law is equilibrium...it was adored in the secret rites of the Sabbat or the Temple under the hieroglyphic figure of Baphomet or the hermaphroditic goat of Mendes...

> There is a Life-Principle of the world, a universal agent, wherein are two natures and a double current...It is the body of the Holy Spirit, the Universal Agent, the Serpent devouring his own tail...Force attracts force...[5]

The Jewish cabalists speak in mysterious, guarded terms of this same potent *Force*. They say it is produced from the uniting of the two triangles, male and female, in the sex act, releasing the generative energy of creation. The result symbolized is, of course, the Jewish Star of David, known as the Seal, or symbol, of Solomon or simply as the Six-Pointed Star. The cabalists say this Star represents the combined energy of good and evil becoming one Force; it represents the "white Jehovah and the black Jehovah." It is the epitome of the "As Above, So Below" doctrine. As LaVey put it, it represents "THE THIRD WAY."

To the Illuminati, nothing is static, everything is deceit; the Force is dynamic, ever-changing, the quicksand of light that diffuses and reappears only to disappear again. Dark is Light and Light is Dark and no one can divine a difference. Satan is therefore God and God is Satan, and the Serpent chases its own tail. Forever.

The Invisible Light

This is all insanity, of course, but to the Illuminist it is Reason. Thus, Francis Adams Moore, in the Lucis Trust publication, *The Beacon*, wrote an article entitled *"The Invisible Sun."* In it, Moore speaks of "The Ageless Wisdom":

> The Ageless Wisdom teaches that this darkness out of which visible Light came, is actually the pure Light—the Light that is so brilliant, radiant, and transcendent it appears as darkness to the form world.[6]

To Moore, what we perceive as darkness is actually invisible Light. In all creation, he says, light and darkness are mixed and "their equilibrium is the mystery of mysteries."[7]

Once again we see the Illuminists' insane doctrine of duality. The bisexual is preferred, bad is good, and so on. Duality and synthesis, and more duality and synthesis, in never-ending incarnations of confusing light and shadow cycles of unreality blended with reality.

No wonder the Holy Bible says, "A double-minded man is unstable in all his ways." *(James 1:8)*

Yin and Yang

The satanic, Illuminist doctrine of duality is seen in the concept of *yin and yang*. These are the two opposites, one light and one dark, yet complementary and co-dependent. The two influences are said to be constantly influencing one another. They represent alchemical polarities, or *dialectical* opposites. Witchcraft can appreciate the yin and the yang and the Illuminist doctrine of *"As Above, So Below."* Paul Huston, in *Mastering Witchcraft*, explains the witches' parallel concept of Gnostic duality:

> In the beginning the Great Darkness, Diana, divided herself into two equal and opposite forces, night and day. The night was ruled over by Diana herself as the moon, the day by her alter ego and brother, Lucifer, the Sun.[8]

Detail from a Moslem coat-of-arms shows heraldic eagle bearing Sufi octagonal calligraphic motto on its breast. (From the book, *A History of Secret Societies*, by Arkon Daraul, Citadel Press, Secaucus, New Jersey, 1961)

The Eagle is the Sun

The Herder Dictionary of Symbols notes that the eagle has long been a symbol of power, endurance, and heavenward flight. It also symbolizes the sun (and the sun god) and spiritual majesty. *Coil's Masonic Encyclopedia* says that, "to the pagans, the eagle was an emblem of Jupiter, and with the Druids it was a symbol of their supreme god."

The eagle appears in the insignia of many nations, including ancient Rome, Nazi and modern-day Germany, Czarist Russia, and the United States of America. The Rothschilds adopted the double-headed eagle as the logo of the Rothschild Family Dynasty. The eagle is also represented in the Great Seal of the U.S.A. and it is revered as a holy sign by Sufi Moslems.

The Oval Office and The Eagle in the Great Seal

In *The Wall Street Journal*, former presidential speechwriter and now political commentator Peggy Noonan reported on an interview she had with President George W. Bush in the White House.[9] As she sat before him, a friendly Chief Executive Bush brought up the topic of the eagle symbol so prominently displayed in the Oval Office.

> The President noted the carved American eagle on the front of his antique desk, the one used by Ronald Reagan, John F. Kennedy, and Bill Clinton. The head of the eagle, he notes, is turned toward the arrows it holds in its talon. But look here, he says, at the American eagle in the presidential seal on the rug: The head is turned away and toward the olive branches he holds in his other talon. "Harry Truman changed it," he says. "He wanted America looking toward peace."[10]

These three pictures reveal a mystery. Top left is the President's classic oak desk in the Oval Office. This desk has been in place in the White House since 1887 when it was given as a gift to President Rutherford B. Hayes by Great Britain's Queen Victoria. The middle panel of the desk, bearing the presidential seal with the eagle facing to the right, was added by President Franklin D. Roosevelt to hide his use of a wheelchair. Roosevelt was a 32º Mason. Bottom left is the presidential seal woven into the Oval Office's carpet, displayed in front of the desk.

This is the same presidential seal as is on the desk, except that here the eagle is facing the opposite direction—to the left. Then finally, above right, we see President George W. Bush and aides holding a conference in the Oval Office. Bush's carpet is a different, lighter color than that of the Clinton era, but the presidential seal of the carpet, or rug, continues to show the eagle facing to the left, while the desk has the bird facing to the right. In combination, this reflects the classic, double-headed (left-right) eagle of 33º Freemasonry. Notice also that, in Bush's carpet are added a number of brilliant, radiant sun rays arching out from the seal, indicating the "Illumination" of the Presidency of the United States. Moreover, at the Bush conference, the positioning of furniture and accessories (chairs/tables) provides the classic Masonic Lodge ritual arrangement, plus we have overall the Mason square and compass within a circle design. The red roses in the middle are also symbolic in that they represent the feminine aspect (vagina) while the eagle represents the masculine aspect (phallus). One chair is left empty in case their Lord, Satan, decides to appear.

Interesting stuff by Peggy Noonan. We must remember that President Truman was a 33rd degree Mason. "Peace" to a Mason means something entirely different than the same word means to you and me. In fact, to a Mason, peace is defined according to the Hegelian dialectical process of doublemindedness. Thus, the Hegelian motto: "Perpetual war for perpetual peace." What Ms. Noonan also failed to realize is that in turning the two heads of the eagle — one carved on the desk, the other on the rug — in opposite directions, the Illuminati is reproducing, or mimicking, the symbol of the double-headed eagle in Freemasonry.

A Ravenous Bird From the East

To the Illuminati, the eagle is a symbol of overriding importance and, in its double-headed form, the eagle represents the Illuminati's principal Luciferian doctrine of *As Above, So Below*. It also represents the *Great Work of the Initiation of the World*.

How prophetic, then, is the Bible verse found in *Isaiah 46:11* which reveals that in the last days, a "ravenous bird from the East" shall be called forth by God to wreak havoc and destruction on rebellious mankind and the fallen world.

So when you see the duality principle *("As Above, So Below")* represented in the photos and illustrations in this section, remember: You're observing the great secret in operation, the perennial teaching of the Hidden God, the God of the Mysteries, the God who it is said possesses the key to the invisible world (hell), the God of the Arch, the God of cunning, lies and deceit, the two-faced Deity, the Masonic double-headed eagle. *In other words, bluntly stated, you are viewing Satan in disguise.*

Among hard-core occultists deep into Babylonian and Egyptian lore and magic we find the worship of the two-headed Mammon-Ra, the God of Prosperity and Riches. Mammon-Ra is actually a powerful demon, one of the four great princes of hell. He is especially worshipped with great pomp by Jewish cabalists hungry and greedy for wealth and affluence.

Two golden phoenix serpents face each other inside the Temple Room of the Scottish Rite headquarters, The House of The Temple, in Washington, D.C. located exactly 13 blocks from the White House. While the focal point is the black stone altar with its three sun medallions, the two serpents provide the most grotesque sight. On the rug we read, "The Goal of Initiation," and, indeed, it is reportedly before this imposing black stone altar that the candidate for the 33rd degree kneels and drinks wine from a human skull.

The medical profession uses the winged caduceus, symbol of Mercury, the ancient god of commerce, as a universal sign, or logo. Medical doctors even take the Hippocratic Oath, vowing obeisance to Asclepius, the Greek god of healing. The caduceus design is of two serpents intertwined around a staff, or pole, facing each other. Again, this is evidence of Illuminist doctrine of the integration of opposites. The two serpents are the same as the emblem of Freemasonry—the double-headed eagle.

Below is an illustration of the Grand Hailing Sign of Distress, learned by initiates of the Order of Knights Templar. (*Richardson's Monitor of Freemasonry*.)

FAREWELL

SETTING BILL FREE

"COME SEE BILL BRADLEY!" SCREAMED THE YOUNG BLACK MAN STANDING AT THE corner of New York City's Bryant Park. Just blocks away, in another life, Bradley regularly packed Madison Square Garden to the rafters. But the evening before Super Tuesday, the crowd just swept past. When Bradley arrived for his last rally, the park lawn was untouched, his crescent of supporters thin enough to fit onto the concrete entry. Thankfully, night had fallen and the gas lamps burned low. One would not want a man so proud to see clearly their pitying smiles. The next night Bradley lost every primary, and badly. As he conceded—"He won, and I lost," Bradley said simply—his wife Ernestine kept her eyes trained on him, as if hoping her gaze could soak up the sting. His young aides went into full bawl, some bending over in sobs. That it was over spilled into the smallest indignities: before Bradley was done speaking, the hotel staff be-

NONVICTORY DANCE Bradley exults before withdrawing

gan breaking down the bar and buffet.

And yet. The last few weeks, and imminent defeat, made Bradley a new man. Shoulders back and loden eyes alight, he joyfully returned to talk of a world in which everyone has health insurance, children live outside poverty and there is no soft money. As others cracked in sorrow, Bradley kept a slight smile Super Tuesday. "I knew I was going back to telling people what I believed at the end," he told TIME. "I had a great time."

Bradley, aloof and famously wary of the media, even embraced the youthful band of reporters who traveled with him at the end, joshing with them on flights. At his last press conference the questions were harsh, his answers often waspish. But Bradley added a coda. Grinning, he had an aide hand him a Tiffany's shopping bag, and he called reporters forward to hand them baby-blue boxes. Inside each was a running-shoe charm on a key chain. The gift came with tins of the lozenges he sucked on during the campaign. "Who is this guy, and what has he done with the Senator?" joked a reporter. "Too bad this guy didn't show up six months ago," answered another. "This might have been a different race."

Bradley's life has always been about winning—college All-American, Rhodes scholar, champion Knick, U.S. Senator. What is it like to be nearly 60 and fail, so soundly and so publicly, for the first time? "I once wrote, 'Defeat has a richness of experience all its own,' and that's probably true here too," he said.

But failure has given Bradley back his freedom. Since he was a boy, he has lived in the stifling hothouse of others' expectations, put up as a presidential contender while still a gawky teenager. "Are you running, Bill?" others asked. "Are you running, Bill?" he asked himself. Now he has, and it is done. "Today means the closing of a chapter," he said about those expectations. "This is a loss, and you move on." Bradley, for the first time of his adult life, may now enjoy the serenity of knowing that no one is pressing for the next move. —*By Tamala M. Edwards*

Senator Bill Bradley does what is described by the press as a "nonvictory dance" after conceding defeat and bowing out of the 2000 race for the Democratic Party's nomination as President. In fact, Illuminati flunky Bradley was never intended to defeat the Illuminati's choice, Al Gore. But the elite needed *someone* to be the designated opponent and lose. That's all part of the Hegelian game of dialectics: controlled opposition. So, Bill Bradley did his duty, ran, and—predictably—lost. His so-called "nonvictory dance" is, in reality, his acknowledgement of the hidden influence of *"as above, so below"* (see *Richardson's Monitor of Freemasonry, pp. 91, 93, 121*). Bradley's underlying message to his Illuminist superiors: *"I am in distress because of my loss, but I did it all for you!"* (Photo: *Time* magazine, March 20, 2000)

The shadow figure in the background of this photo of Egyptian President Hosni Mubarak faces the opposite direction. Appropriate considering the Masonic principle of the combining, or synthesis of opposites. (Photo: *U.S. News & World Report*, March 14, 2005, P. 30)

Sammy Davis, Jr., popular singer and entertainer, integrated the Illuminist sign, *"As Above, So Below,"* into his dance performance. In his autobiography, *"Yes, I Can,"* Davis confessed to being a past member of High Priest Anton LaVey's Church of Satan. In his performances, Davis often wore a satanic pentagram necklace. He also painted the fingernail black as a sign of his devotion to his master, the devil. One of Sammy Davis, Jr.'s most popular songs, *The Candy Man*, reportedly was secretly in praise of Satan, the Candy Man who brings his disciples gifts, such as illegal drugs like heroin and cocaine, and sexual favors.

BURYING THE ROMANOVS

End of a chapter: *Boris Yeltsin came to St. Petersburg to redress history and assert his authority over a country facing economic and political chaos. At the burial of Russia's last tsar and his family, Yeltsin denounced his communist predecessors, 80 years to the day after the Romanovs were murdered by Bolshevik revolutionaries.*

'We are all guilty,' he said, paying his respects to Nicholas II; his wife, Alexandra, and three of their five children (the other two bodies are still missing). 'I bow my head before the victims of political violence.' To make sure potential coup makers got the point, Yeltsin added that 'you cannot change society with violence.'

This article in *Newsweek* (July 27, 1998, p. 31) speaks for itself. Under orders from Bolshevik Communist butcher Vladimir Lenin, the Russian Czar and his entire family were slaughtered. In the center of this photo, above the windows you will see the golden, double-headed eagle.

Antique Jewish prayer book showing the double-headed eagle with a crown, representing the coming King of the Illuminati, who will use "Craft" (cabalistic magic) to hoodwink and enslave the Gentile masses. (Photo from *The Jewish Encyclopedia*)

CHIEF CHARLES MOOSE

The situation called for subtlety, smarts and swiftness, and for a few days people wondered whether a man named Moose was the right person for the task. But with all eyes on him, the Montgomery County, Md., police chief led some 1,000 investigators in a 22-day manhunt for the snipers who haunted Washington's suburbs. In the end, he got the duo believed to be the shooters, and America got a new hero.

Photograph for TIME by Brooks Kraft—Gamma

Mirror Image: In 2002, two snipers terrified Washington, D.C. suburbs with deadly and accurate shooting of innocent citizens. Police Chief Charles Moose, of Montgomery County, Maryland, led some 1,000 investigators in a 22-day manhunt. The press and media made Chief Moose into a celebrity and hero, though clearly his police skills were not just inadequate, they had proven to be vastly incompetent and bungling. Moose turns out to be a puppet of the Jewish ADL and a "Chosen One" of the Illuminati. This photo in *Time* (January 6, 2003) unmasks Chief Moose as a stooge of the elite. It illustrates perfectly the satanic doctrine, *"As Above, So Below."* We see Chief Moose, a black man, shrouded in darkness, his hands giving a Masonic symbol (explained elsewhere in *Codex Magica*). They rest on a mirror surface in which the shadow image of the Chief is seen. Viewed either as is or upside down, we observe the secret sign of the diamond (two triangles abutted together), indicating the portal of hell, high sign of the conspiracy. It doesn't get much more revealing than this. Yet, it is doubtful that even a fraction of the readers of *Time* who saw this photo had any idea of its esoteric nature.

In this advertisement in Spain's *Hola* magazine (April 13, 2000), a coin bearing the image of King Juan Carlos was offered. Juan Carlos is heir to the Bourbon Dynasty. One of his titles is "King of Jerusalem." The emblem of the double-headed eagle is on the reverse side of the coin.

"As Above, So Below," is symbolized by this prelate's giving the "Il Cornuto" (horned devil) sign, one hand pointing up and one down. Message: Lucifer and Christ shall be reconciled, with the Masonic Great Architect of the Universe reigning in heaven, on earth, and in hell.

As Above, So Below: A shadow ink drawing of Count Cagliostro, whose magic and satanism inspired the Order of the Illuminati and its bloody French Revolution. It is said that American diplomat Benjamin Franklin studied and practiced the magic of Cagliostro. (Drawing from the book, *Witchcraft, Magic, and the Supernatural,* p. 88)

ΟΙ ΑΔΙΣΤΑΚΤΟΙ ΜΕΤΑΡΡΥΘΜΙΣΤΑΙ ΟΙ ΟΠΟΙΟΙ
ΠΡΟΕΒΗΣΑΝ ΕΙΣ ΤΗΝ ΑΛΛΑΓΗΝ ΤΟΥ ΕΟΡΤΟΛΟΓΙΟΥ
ΚΑΙ ΑΠΕΣΧΙΣΘΗΣΑΝ ΑΠΟ ΤΗΝ ΕΚΚΛΗΣΙΑΝ
ΤΟΥ ΧΡΙΣΤΟΥ «ΠΑΤΡΙΑΡΧΗΣ» ΜΕΛΕΤΙΟΣ ΜΕΤΑΞΑΚΗΣ
ΚΑΙ ΑΡΧΙΕΠΙΣΚΟΠΟΣ «ΑΘΗΝΩΝ» ΧΡΥΣΟΣΤΟΜΟΣ ΠΑΠΑΔΟΠΟΥΛΟ

One of the clergy leaders of the Orthodox Church in Greece wears a pendant of the crowned double-headed eagle as a talisman around his neck. The cross, meanwhile, is relegated to the left side of the satanic talisman.

In 1917, after the dynasty of Czar Nicholas II fell, the Moscow government of Freemason Alexander Kerensky issued new currency, including this 250 ruble banknote. At its center is the double-headed eagle superimposed on the swastika (sun deity). The swastika is arranged as a diamond. Soon afterwards, the government of Kerensky gave way to the Bolshevik coup of Lenin and Trotsky. Kerensky fled to Paris, France, where he joined the Grand Orient Lodge. Lenin and Trotsky, also Masons and satanists, decided these symbols on the ruble banknotes were far too obvious and feared that the Russian people would discover the Jewish Masonic roots of the Revolution. Therefore, they ordered the removal of the symbols and created as a replacement for them the familiar hammer and sickle emblems as the U.S.S.R.'s official seal.

The Magical Head of Zohar is a cabalistic design illustrating the concept of opposites, the principle of "As Above, So Below." It is widely used by cabalists and Jewish rabbis as an instructional device.

Abraxas, the gnostic rooster god, symbolic of the Sun God. Notice the two serpent legs, indicating the satanic doctrine of duality.

Famed architect I.M. Pei giving the "As Above, So Below" sign. Pei was commissioned by France's government, led by Masonic President Francois Mitterrand, to design an Egyptian-style pyramid structure adjacent to the Louvre, perhaps the world's best known museum. Pei's pyramid acts as the entrance to the Louvre. It is reportedly made up of exactly 666 panes of crystal glass.

In tarot card decks, one of the cards depicts "The Magician" (also called the Magus or the Juggler), a young man holding up a wand in his right hand, and pointing to the earth with his left. On a table before him are the four elemental symbols, and above his head is the sign of eternity or infinity. He is the Magus, the god-like human being integrated on all planes, the will liberated through gnosis, or knowledge. His gesture refers to the basic occult principle "That which is above is as that which is below."

This design illustrates the ultimate blasphemy for its message is that Satan is deity of the universe, that he shall be King over all realms, above and below, and that the reign of he, the serpent, shall stand for all eternity. The Scottish Rite textbook, *A Bridge to Light*, by Rex Hutchens, 33rd degree, outlines the knowledge and symbols used for the various degrees of Freemasonry. In this book, Hutchens restates the principles of Albert Pike's 19th century classic, *Morals and Dogma*. According to these principles, the oroboros serpent shown in this design (Levi's occult magic of "As Above, So Below") represents eternity and the Holy Spirit of the triune godhead. In other words, the Illuminists are declaring that the serpent, identified in the scriptures as the devil, is, in their religion, the divine Holy Spirit! A blasphemous concept, indeed.

Horus-Set

A company called Azure Green puts out a catalog offering "Egyptian Deity Wall Plaques," including this one, a depiction of the combined gods of Egypt, Horus and Set. Two entities represented by one body. Once again, we discover the principle of integration, or synthesis. Horus is the son of the Sun God and is said to be one with his Father, Osiris. The god Set is the dialectical opposite, or mirror of Horus and Osiris, but rather than the Sun and its light, he represents the darkness of the underworld. Set is god of the dead, Horus-Osiris, god of the living.

This cover of a book by W. Bruce Lincoln about Russia's czars, the Romanov Dynasty, pictures the dynasty's fascinating symbol, the double-headed phoenix serpent. Eye-opening is the crowned victorious hero figure with a cape, carrying a lance, riding a white horse found within the "heart" of the double-headed black bird. The symbolical meaning of this image is overwhelming, to say the least, in terms of Bible prophecy.

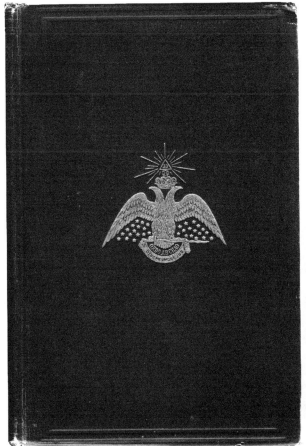

The idolatrous image of the double-headed eagle—shown here on the cover of Albert Pike's classic text, *Morals and Dogma*—is a much-treasured symbol of Jewish Masons. It represents the Babylonian god of money and forces, Mammon-Ra, as well as the Hegelian dialectical process practiced by the Jewish elite. This same symbol is the "Masonic Jewel" awarded high-level Masons initiated into the 33rd degree.

A friend of the author sent him this photograph he took while visiting Russia recently. It is the fence and gate outside a sprawling and luxurious old mansion estate.

Red Army cuts are announced by Gorbachev

NEW YORK (AP) — Mikhail S. Gorbachev, urging a "period of peace," announced a cutback of 500,000 Red Army troops on Wednesday and called on the United States and its allies to "take certain steps" in reply. President Reagan and President-elect George Bush embraced the troop reduction gesture after a cordial luncheon summit with the Soviet leader.

In a speech at the United Nations, Gorbachev billed the cutback in troops, artillery, planes and tanks as "unilateral" — part of a reduced reliance on military might. He later said "Nyet, nyet, nyet," when asked if there was resistance at home to the move, but there was evidence to the contrary.

Reagan said in a speech in Washington a few hours later that if the Soviet reduction is carried out speedily and in full "history will regard it as important — significant."

On a day that blended superpower substance and symbolism, the Soviet president bade farewell to Reagan and answered Bush's welcoming handshake with a vigorous two-handed embrace. He declared the president-elect would find the Soviets ready "without long pauses or backtracking" to continue work toward a new arms control treaty as well as on other issues.

Bush, who played a low-key role throughout the day, said he had told Gorbachev he "needed some time" to settle in as president after his inauguration next month. He hailed the troop reduction announcement, even while saying it was not enough to produce a balance of forces in Europe.

Reagan declared he "heartily" approved of Gorbachev's overtures. "Read our smiles," he said after emerging from lunch and taking Gorbachev and Bush for a brief ride to the edge of Governors Island and a spectacular view of the Statue of Liberty across New York Harbor.

In the face of severe economic pressures at home, Gorbachev used his U.N. speech to declare that military force no longer "can or must be an instrument of foreign policy." He said 50,000 Soviet troops and 5,000 tanks would be pulled out of Eastern Europe by 1991, and pledged reductions on Western and Eastern soil within the Soviet Union, as well. Overall, the reductions were to reach half a million.

A few hours later he told reporters, "We do hope that the U.S. and the Europeans will also take certain steps."

The Soviet leader called for steps to end the war in Afghanistan under U.N. auspices within a month and urged international cooperation on issues ranging from arms control to the environment.

ON THE MARK
Soviet leader Mikhail Gorbachev, President Ronald Reagan and President-elect George Bush look for their marks on the viewing stand overlooking New York harbor form Governors Island Wednesday. The marks were placed by White House advance personnel to indicate where the leaders should stand for the best picture situation. (AP Laserphoto)

For Comrade Mikhail Gorbachev, there is only one deity that should be recognized—the god below, in the abyss. Here we see Gorby smiling broadly while finding his "mark" for a history photo made with Bush and Reagan overlooking the New York City harbor. Gorby seems to merely be clowning around, but his membership in the Grand Orient Lodge in Paris, France and his favorable status by the Illuminati's Inner Circle inform us otherwise. His hands tell a story understood by the wise. (Photo and article, December 8, 1988)

Commemorative Silver Coin bearing images of Lord Ganesha and Goddess Laksmi struck in honor of the historic occasion of the first Hindu Diwali ritual ever conducted in the White House. It happened under President George W. Bush, in 2003.

Double-headed eagle pendant owned by the Czarina. The word *"Czar"* in Russian means *"Caesar."*

A horse cloth used in the royal stables of the Russian Czar (circa 1795) bears the symbols of the double-headed eagle, a triangle, and diamonds, all Illuminist signs.

Russia's President Vladimir Putin (left) meets with the CEO of Lukoil, Russia's biggest oil company. On the desk between the two men are desk accessories bearing the emblem of the double-headed eagle. (Photo: *Agence France-Presse*)

Vladimir Zhirinovsky, flamboyant Russian politician, holds in his hand the double-headed eagle insignia of the czarist regime, recently revived in the Gorbachev-Yeltsin-Putin era. Zhirinovsky gained worldwide notoriety in the 1990s for bashing Jews and for his extreme anti-Semitic views. However, he quieted down and muted his animosity toward the Jews after it came out that Zhirinovsky is himself a Jew! The setting up of such fake fronts by the Illuminati is a common tactic. It is all part of the Hegelian dialectical process (Thesis+antithesis=synthesis); i.e. create the problem, then come up with the pre-planned "solution" favored by the elite. (Photo and article: *The European*, April 1-7, 1994)

"*The Czar is dead. Long live the Czar,*" seems to be the cry today in Russia. Czar Nicholas and his entire family were massacred by Lenin and the Communists. But, in recent times, Russia, under Gorbachev, Yeltsin, and Putin, has once again officially returned the Empire to the key symbol of the double-headed eagle. *Der Spiegel*, a popular German news magazine, carried this telling depiction of "Czar Boris" (President Boris Yeltsin) on its cover, with the revived official seal on his breast.

Believe it or not, in front of the Department of Justice building in Washington, D.C. is a statue of a confederate general, Albert Pike. Pike served as Sovereign Grand Commander of Scottish Rite Freemasonry, Southern Jurisdiction. Fascinating, isn't it, that black leaders like Farrahkan and Jesse Jackson aren't complaining? Usually, they go nuts complaining about Confederate monuments and statues on government land. Could their silence be attributed to the fact that Jackson and Farrakhan are themselves 33rd degree Masons? In any case, at the foot of Pike's Justice Department Statue is a Masonic female figure representing Lady Justice, holding a banner with the 33rd degree double-headed eagle and the triangle of Freemasonry.

The androgyne, a combination creature of male and female, symbolizes the hermaphrodite principle of the two-faced entity or two-headed eagle. In the Jewish Cabala, this strange creation of the feminine and masculine principle is known as "Adam Kadmon," both Adam and Eve, a Golem. This conjunction of opposites is part of the science of alchemy, or hermeticism, and is especially beloved by occult magicians. In witchcraft, it is known as the joining of sun and moon, and sacred sex rituals are common.

Janus, Roman two-faced "God of the Sun," was said to be the "keeper of the keys" to the invisible spirit world. Hislop (*The Two Babylons*) called him "the source and fountain of all the pagan gods." Is the Masonic double-headed eagle symbolic of his predecessor, Janus?

THIRTEEN

The Riddle of the Great Seal of the United States, and the All-Seeing Eye of the Illuminati's Serpent of Wisdom

And the great dragon was cast out, that old serpent, called the Devil, and Satan, which deceiveth the whole world…

—*Revelation 12:9*

The Great Serpent of the Garden of Eden and the Lord God are identical.

—Helena Blavatsky
The Secret Doctrine

What is the true meaning of the curious, arcane symbols found in the Great Seal of the United States? Who designed this fantastic two-sided device, and why is it so prominently featured as art and décor on our most common item of currency—the U.S. one dollar bill?

Answering the Riddle

The symbols on the Great Seal at first glance seem to be incompatible with the history, political organization, and religious heritage of our great nation. An Egyptian pyramid? What has that to do with America? Strange Latin inscriptions? A bizarre all-seeing eye radiated by the sun's rays? Odd, indeed.

Truly weird, especially, is the fact that there are *two* sides to the Great Seal. The

front side pictures a strong, war-ready eagle with a constellation of stars in a cloud above its head. The reverse, the mystical side, is the one with the pyramid, Latin inscriptions, all-seeing eye, etc. Why two sides? After all, a seal is like a rubber stamp. It is used to authenticate documents to prove authenticity and affirm veracity and genuineness. You don't need a reverse side on a "rubber stamp!"

In fact, both sides of the Great Seal, each with various images, have been around since the days of the Continental Congress.

In 1776, just hours after the Declaration of Independence was formally adopted, a committee composed of Benjamin Franklin, Thomas Jefferson, and John Adams met to design the Great Seal. They invited an artist, Pierre Eugene Du Simitiére, to join them and a design was approved. But the Continental Congress failed to approve it. So, in 1782, Congress called on William Barton, an authority on symbols and heraldry, and Charles Thompson, Secretary of Congress, to help sort out the process. Finally, out came the current day, two-sided Great Seal.[1]

Enter Rothschild's Man, Haym Salomon

That, of course, is the official version of events. But some claim that a mysterious man from Europe, but living in Philadelphia, named Haym Salomon, secretly assisted the committee of Franklin, Jefferson, and Adams. Haym Salomon, a Jewish banker, just happened to be the American representative for the Rothschilds of Europe. Salomon, it is said, bribed a number of American politicians and was able to get about anything he and his mentors wanted done. In the case of the Great Seal, the Rothschilds wanted symbols to be pictured in the Great Seal of United States befitting the aims of the Illuminati.

Though Jewish and Zionist in ambition, the Rothschilds were not worshippers of the God of the Old and New Testaments of the Bible. They were Sabbatian/Frankist (Satanic) in theology. They sought (and still today seek) a Jewish Utopia or Kingdom on planet Earth. This Kingdom would be the New Age successor to ancient Babylon and Egypt. It would be a powerhouse nation that would, through magic and intellect, conquer the world. America would be its proxy. America would be its alter ego. America, then, must be fashioned into a cabalistic, Jewish state. All Hail the New

Egypt, Empire of the Ages, child of the Sun God of the ancients! America, the New Jerusalem, must unite with Old Jerusalem, and the Zionist Illuminati must reign!

Rothschild agent Haym Salomon had millions of dollars of largesse to spread around in bribes. And so he did. A good portion of the money went to fund the Continental Congress and its operations. Some went into the Treasury for the Revolutionary War effort. Some went into politicians' pockets.

Rothschild eventually got the images he had demanded on the Great Seal, though not without opposition. The design was bitterly opposed by the few who recognized the Masonic and Illuminist elements.

As for Haym Salomon, few history textbooks mention him. But he is privily called by Illuminati Jews *"The Financier of the American Revolution."* Only recently, scattered bits of propaganda have begun to be floated about him. A few Jewish books speak of his "grand accomplishments," offering a more cheery and less honest version of his life and his activities as banker for the American Revolution. The ultimate goal of the Illuminati is to eventually bring Haym Salomon out of the closet, so to speak. Someday, his name will be in lights. He'll be immortalized in print, in movies, and on TV as a great and noble hero, akin to a George Washington or Thomas Jefferson. Statues will be built to honor him. One already has, in Philadelphia. Mark my words and mark your calendar for the future and see if what I tell you isn't so.

Now, let us examine the symbols on America's Great Seal and see if we can make sense of their true, esoteric meaning and purposes. Let us wipe away the gloss and get down to the base surface to better understand. This is vital because of the future of the United States—and the destiny of all humanity—is wrapped up, and is revealed, in this collection of Illuminist symbols and marks.

The Ashlar Stones and The Pyramid

Masonry is a peculiar Egypto-Babylonia-Jewish institution, and so the pyramid itself hearkens back to the Dynasty of the pharaohs and to the gods and goddesses of ancient Egypt. The stones which make up the pyramid are also of esoteric significance. In the Masonic philosophy it is taught that unenlightened man is in a rude, natural state. Having little or no "light" and without the spiritual illumination offered by the Mystery Religions he is likened to an *imperfect or rough ashlar stone.* But once enlightened and illuminated, he is crafted into a man of education, sophistication, discipline, and culture. He reaches upward toward spiritual perfection. He is then a *perfect ashlar stone.*

In many pagan religions this concept of the Rough vs. Perfect Ashlar was taught. In Freemasonry, it is heavily emphasized. The pyramid's structure is fitted only with perfect ashlar stones, it is said, meticulously chosen by "The Builders" who watch for flaws and reject the rough, or imperfect ashlar.

Likewise, the higher level Masons discover that the pyramid reflects, or parallels, the New World Order (*Novus Ordo Seclorum*) they and their Illuminized superiors are building under the watchful eye of the Great Architect of the Universe, whose secret and sacred name, the Royal Arch Mason learns, is *Jahbuhlun.*

The Builders (the Perfect Ashlars), then, are the Illuminati and their minions. Their building project is the renovation and reconstruction (*Perestroika* or *Tikkun*

Olam) of the whole earth. Of course, in order to build the New Deal of the Ages, they must first tear down the old. Civilization as we know it today must be razed and destroyed by dialectic chaos, so that the new order may be ushered in: *Ordo Ab Chao*

It is when this ambitious goal is achieved that, symbolically, the capstone will be set in place atop the pyramid. Then he who lies *within* the living stones shall come forth to rule. The Phoenix (Satan and his "son") shall rise from the flames of destruction just as the legendary phoenix bird arose.

The Phoenix, however, is, in reality a cockatrice, a dragon-bird, a flying serpent. The word "pyramid," incidentally, literally means "amidst the fire." And now you know the true, occultic meaning of the word.

Peering Into the All-Seeing Eye

Simply put, Freemasons, under the direction of Haym Salomon, Ben Franklin, and others, designed the Great Seal with its all-seeing eye in the capstone amidst the radiant sun background. As followers of Egyptianism, it has long been assumed that the eye is that of Osiris, the Egyptian sun god, and/or of his son, Horus. This is true, but there is much more.

Osiris, of course, was worshipped as the Sun. Albert Pike, former Sovereign Grand Commander, wrote: "The sun...is the All-Seeing Eye in our Lodges."[2] Pike goes on to say that, "the Blazing Star (the pentagram deity) has been recognized as an emblem of Omniscience, or the All-Seeing Eye, which to the Ancients was the Sun."[3]

The Illuminati and their subordinates, the Masons, honor the Deity of countless names. Yes, one of those names is Osiris, with his son Horus. But the Illuminati Deity is a concealed god who hides his true identity in a multitude of disguises and subterfuges. He is called "The Sun," the "Central Sun," "Hiram Abiff," the one with the "Ineffable Name," "Ein Soph," the "Great Architect of the Universe," "Abaddon," "Mahabone," and "Jahbuhlun." Ostensibly the Illuminati worship a pantheon, a multiplicity of gods. But, not so. These are all fronts for the elite worship of Lucifer. He is their true god, the God of Light. As Albert Pike stated in *Morals and Dogma, "Doubt it not."*

Their God is The Serpent

Now, the Bible, in *Isaiah 14* and *Revelation 12:9,* identifies Lucifer as "the great dragon...that old serpent, called the Devil, and Satan, which deceiveth the whole world." So, by whatever name you call him, the god of the Illuminati and Masonry is the Serpent. In fact, in *A Bridge to Light*, an official textbook of the Supreme Mother Council, 33°, the highest council of the Scottish Rite, Rex Hutchens, 33°, reveals that "the body of the Holy Spirit, the universal agent," is none other than "the Serpent devouring his own tail."[4] That is, the Oroboros serpent.

Remember, in all their writings, the most revered of Masonic scholars—Manly P. Hall, Albert Mackey, Albert Pike, etc.—claim that the Masonic rituals and teachings come from the "mysteries" of ancient Babylonians, Egyptians, Greeks, Persians and others. Thus, we glean understanding when we read, in *Earth's Earliest Ages*, this statement by G. Pember: "There is little doubt that the culmination of the mysteries was the worship of Satan himself."[5]

You'll also recall our discussion elsewhere in this book that the Illuminist and Masonic theology is solidly based on the *Jewish Cabala* (Kaballah or Quaballah). Indeed, almost all occult and magical belief systems are founded on the principles and teachings of the Jewish Cabala. In her most famous book, *The Secret Doctrine*, Helena Blavatsky praised Satan as the teacher of humanity.[6] He is to be thanked, Blavatsky says, for setting men on the path to divinity and liberty. It is, she emphasizes, the Cabala that "unveils the secret." To what secret is she referring? Listen, as Blavatsky flatly states the core doctrine of the mysteries, of occultism, of Illuminism:

> The Great Serpent of the Garden of Eden and the Lord God are identical.[7]

Ah, we have here the reality of supreme evil in this core teaching. Paul knew of this mystery teaching, he wrote of the "Mystery of Iniquity" and said of the ancient religionists, that they "knew God, but glorified Him not as God," and changed the Glory of God "into the likeness of creeping things" — that is, serpents *(Romans 1:23)*.

The Devourer of Self

Barbara Walker, researcher of occultism and paganism, writes:

> As Lord of Death, Osiris was sometimes identified with the Great Serpent of the underworld, and sometimes was painted in the same serpentine form, bent around so his toes touched his head.[8]

The serpent, or Satan, as we know from the scriptures, is god of the dead. Indeed, God says, "all they that hate me love death" *(Proverbs 8:36)*. He is Lord alright, but only of death, of the underworld, and of planet earth for a season *(II Thessalonians 2)*. He is graphically pictured in the occult world as a serpent biting his own tail; how appropriate: A devourer of himself! And that is what actually happens when a person defies God and worships the Adversary. He or she is "biting his own tail" — tragically and pathetically devouring himself.

The Oroboros

The oroboros, or serpent biting its own tail, is pictured on the cover of *Codex Magica*. This book unmasks the Illuminati worship of this detestable creature, a worship of which virtually every person on earth is dangerously and hopelessly unaware. Since the Illuminati, Masons, and fellow cabalists have amassed such tremendous political, financial, social, and technological powers, is it not a frightening thing to realize that these men are not only religious, their religion is Satanism, and their god is the Devil?

The destructive path, therefore, is the way of the Illuminati. As I have demonstrated, these wicked agents of the Serpent are psychopaths and present a clear and present threat and danger to our lives. But the gravest danger is that which confronts the souls of billions of unsaved, ignorant human beings. If they fall for the Lie of the Serpent, they will suffer total destruction and suffer loss for eternity.

In *Occult Geometry*, A.S. Raleigh examines the symbol of the *circle*. He writes:

> One form of the circle is a serpent with a tail in its mouth…It is the return to Unity…The true circle symbolizes evolution, the Serpent Circle involution…the power brings Unity out of diversity…*The Serpent Circle is, therefore, ever the symbol of the destructive.*[9]

Later, in the photos and illustrations presented in this chapter, you will discover the startling artwork on a Jewish New Year's postcard by Jewish artist Alain Roth back in 1915. The design shows the Oroboros Serpent (Satan) encircling and conquering the whole earth. Happy New Year?

As I have proven over and over by a preponderance of documentation, we cannot separate the murderous goals and activities of the Illuminati from their religious belief system. Their inspiration, their fanatical zealotry, comes from their teacher, Satan, who has given them a thorough set of instructions—an Unholy Bible if you will, in the Jewish Cabala. In this Unholy Bible, the Serpent plays the key role. He is praised as the "Serpent of Wisdom." The destiny of the Illuminati and the whole world is said to be in his hands.

We thank God that all who believe in Christ Jesus have no part of this destiny. Jesus said *He has chosen us out of the world*. We are pilgrims, aliens on earth, spiritually residing in heavenly places. The serpent has no power or control whatsoever over us, and we solidly reject his many works, among which, regrettably, is the symbology of the Great Seal of the United States.

Advertisement for a cigarette brand. The three most prominent symbols: (1) All-seeing eye; (2) The sign of eternity—resembling the figure 8 lying on its side; (3) The three dots, or points, indicative of the unholy trinity.

The Guardian Angel organization in New York City has as its logo an all-seeing eye in a triangle, and angel wings. Message: *"We are watching!"*

Reason (*La Raison*), an engraving by Darcis in the National Museum, Paris, France, was said to capture the spirit of the bloody, Illuminati-inspired French Revolution. What we see is symbolism of the unholy trinity of Lucifer—Father (Lion), Mother (Goddess), and Son (all-seeing eye).

Art illustration from the book, *Active Meditation*, by Robert Leichtman, M.D. and Carl Japikse (Ariel Press). The hermetic monk holds the solar disk with cross and all-seeing eye.

ARE YOU HUMAN?

This bizarre advertisement for cable-TV's *The Learning Channel*. The tattoos on this man are real. The all-seeing eye is in what Hindus call the "ajna center," in the midpoint of the forehead just above the eyebrows.

A History of the World

Sir Walter Raleigh, the impetuous adventurer and polished courtier, was also a man of considerable literary accomplishments. Much of the poetry he wrote has been lost, but several impressive prose works survive. The most ambitious and distinguished of these is *The History of the World*, written between 1607 and 1614, during his years of confinement in the Tower of London under a death sentence. Although Raleigh's name did not appear on the elaborately engraved frontispiece to the first edition (above), there was no secret about the authorship. The book was immediately banned by King James I.

Raleigh set out to write a universal chronicle that would parallel the Old Testament chronology in its initial chapters but bring the story up to his own times, in which the history of England would be related to that of the rest of the world. He got only as far as the fall of Macedonia in 130 B.C.

James's displeasure was caused by Raleigh's portrayals of Assyrian Queen Semiramis, which was seen as a tribute to Elizabeth I, and of her effeminate successor, Ninus, which the king interpreted as an unflattering caricature of himself.

Sir Walter Raleigh's distinguished book, *The History of The World* (written between 1607 and 1614) had this illustration as its frontispiece. The book was banned by England's King James I because it revealed too much, ostensibly for its portrayals of Babylonian Queen Semiramis and her effeminate son, Ninus. More likely is that the artwork shown here revealed far too many occult secrets, including the androgynous (male/female) figure holding aloft the globe, the all-seeing eye, etc.

United Mine Workers Union poster, 1890. The two miners are exchanging a masonic handshake, being overseen by the all-seeing eye. Almost all unions in America and Europe were founded by Jewish activists deep into Cabala, Masonry, and other occult secrets.

Many medallions, engravings, shields and badges of heraldry in the Renaissance era carried the image of the all-seeing eye somewhere on them. This engraving by George Wither entitled *The Reign of the Wise* (1635) depicts divine man, lord of all, under the watchful stare of the solar logos (Lucifer) below his feet.

NASA's Hubble space telescope captured this startling image of what appears to be an all-seeing eye in space. *National Geographic* pictured it on the magazine's front cover in April, 1997.

Frenchman Eliphas Levi, satanist whose classic work, *Transcendental Magic* (1896) inspired Masonic Lodges and occult societies alike. In his book, Levi posted this illustration of an egg-shaped Oroboros serpent, the six-pointed star and other occult symbols combining to emphasize the ancient Luciferian principle, *"As Above, So Below."* (see *Codex Magica* section on the hidden mysteries of the double-headed eagle.)

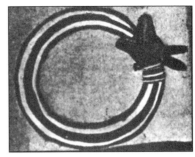

Three versions of Oroboros, the circular serpent biting its own tail.

Above left: This version is from *Atlanta Fugiens*, by Michael Maier, 1618.

Above right: This version of Oroboros is from Dahomey, West Africa.

Left: An early, hand-painted Masonic apron depicts many occult symbols, including the serpent Oroboros, the skull and bones, pentacle stars, the pyramids, the mallet, and the X.

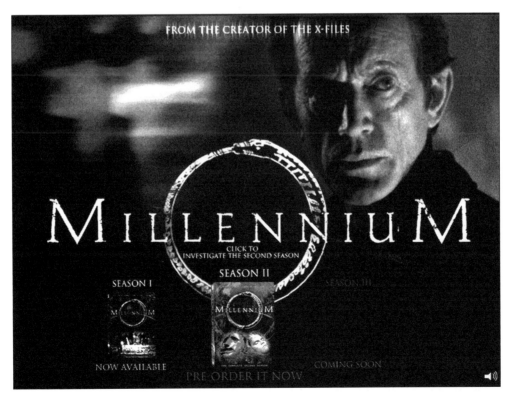

The Fox-TV network ran 67 episodes of the popular series, *Millennium*. The Oroboros serpent was the focal point of advertising for the series though the occult meaning of the symbol was never fully explained.

Alchemical Rosicrucian drawing of a crucified snake, which
is a secret symbol of the Philosophical Mercury which is
achieved by practice of the arcane art of alchemy.
Some might mistakenly believe the cross symbol is
Christian, but it is the tau, not the cross of Calvary.
The serpent 'S' is backward, as if seen in a mirror.

⊗ Austin American-Statesman

Black Crowes dive into reviving careers

Album review

The Black Crowes
'Three Snakes and One Charm'
(American Recordings)
★★★

BY CHRIS RIEMENSCHNEIDER
American-Statesman Staff

Don't count the Black Crowes out just yet. After tripping disasterously while trying to run over new territory on last year's "amorica," then proving to be a mess of a live act on the '95 H.O.R.D.E. Festival, it seemed the group was forever entombed to classic rock status only five years after releasing its smash debut.

The Crowes readily bounce back with their fourth album, "Three Snakes and One Charm." Granted, the group's leaders Chris and Rich Robinson have returned to blatantly rehashing age-old rock bravado, but at least here they go beyond the Jagger/Richards camp to album-oriented rock's other songwriting team, Page-/Plant.

Just like Stones licks hadn't sounded as good in a long time as they did on the Crowes second album, "The Southern Harmony and Musical Companion," it's been too long since Zeppelin riffs have reverberated as strongly as they do in such sure-to-please rock-

fit (at least in the studio) than to any songwriting genius it may lack. Chris Robinson's ragged, soulful vocals have never sounded as good as they do on "Three Snakes," and the guitar work of Rich and fellow riffman Marc Ford in "Nebakanezer" or "Blackberry" is pure, ecstatic bliss.

Best of all, though, is the fact that the group sounds more inspired by what it's doing here than it has since its debut album. "Good Friday," the first single from this album, plus "Under a Mountain" and "Better When You're Not Alone" again show them as a

THE BLACK CROWES THREE SNAKES AND ONE CHARM

The Black Crowes bounce back from last year's disasterous 'amorica' with the release of their fourth album, 'Three Snakes and One Charm.'

great, great band. And if they're nothing more, that's still something the rock world can always use.

■

Other albums released today include Alice in Chains' "MTV Un-

The *Black Crowes*, a rock
singing group, put out
this album in 1996. It
was titled, *"Three Snakes
and One Charm."*

Egyptian Religion: In this ancient papyrus drawing we
discover the unholy trinity of the Egyptian goddess
religion. Seated is Osiris the horned father god. Behind
him is the goddess Isis, and their son, Horus. The snake is
the focus of this trinity; the woman (Goddess) is
therefore depicted with the head of a serpent and with
destroyer weapons in her hands.

In 1976, prosecutors tore Patty Hearst's credibility to shreds. A new case against her SLA partners rests on rehabilitating it.

From Villain to Victim

BY MARK MILLER

SHE WAS THE SPOILED rich kid who unaccountably helped her own kidnappers wage a campaign of robbery and wanton violence, a reckless debutante with an extreme case of radical chic. And when she went on trial for taking part in a 1974 San Francisco bank robbery, Patty Hearst's attempts to explain it away were shredded by prosecutors and rejected by the jury: she was convicted and served nearly two years in jail.

Twenty-five years later, Hearst has undergone a transformation from leftist wanna-be to earnest victim. Now 47 and the mother of two daughters, Hearst has established a modestly successful acting career and last year won a full pardon from Bill Clinton. Soon her rehabilitation will be complete—when she appears in a California courtroom to testify against four of her old comrades from the Symbionese Liberation Army who will be on trial for murder, in a case that will hinge largely on her credibility.

The defendants are Emily Harris, William Harris, Sara Jane Olson and Michael Bortin, all of whom allegedly took part in a 1975 bank holdup in Carmichael, Calif., in which a customer, Myrna Opsahl, was shot and killed. All four are expected to plead not guilty. Because the Carmichael robbers wore ski masks, the prosecution will rely on Hearst to prove that the defendants were there. Hearst, who had become an SLA member calling herself "Tania," has admitted taking part in the heist, although she says she was only driving a getaway car. In her version, Emily, Olson and William were inside the bank and William was stationed outside with another SLA member, Steven Soliah. Hearst says Emily directed the stickup and that Emily, carrying a shotgun with a finicky trigger, later said she shot Opsahl by accident.

The question now is whether Hearst,

REBEL: Hearst, shown here in 1974, says the four engaged in 'jihad' against the U.S.

with her admitted involvement in the SLA's campaign of armed violence, will be a credible witness. The Carmichael case has been gathering dust for 20 years precisely because prosecutors thought her testimony was unreliable. In her book and at her trial in 1976, Hearst said she became an SLA member under duress because she was beaten and raped while imprisoned for months in a closet in an SLA safe house. Prosecutors didn't buy it, and neither did the jury that convicted her. James L. Browning, the former federal prosecutor who tried Hearst, says, "It was pretty plain from the evidence that she did everything voluntarily. That's the way I feel about it, and probably her testimony [in

the new case] is going to be somewhat suspect."

William Harris, now in jail, told NEWSWEEK two years ago that Hearst was never tortured, raped or coerced. In retrospect, Harris said he thought Hearst's conversion to the SLA cause was a prime example of Stockholm syndrome, in which hostages come to identify with their captors. "We're accused of brainwashing her," Harris said. "That's ridiculous—we didn't know how to do that." He said gang members were "infatuated with the political theater" of Hearst's transformation and that no one understood the psychological dynamic between the prisoner and her captors. "It was beyond our control and hers," he said. "We were all swept up in the thing."

Now they loathe each other. In a recent interview on CNN, Hearst compared the SLA members to Timothy McVeigh and Charles Manson and said they were conducting "their own little jihad" against the United States. Stuart Hanlon, the San Francisco attorney who is representing Emily Harris, says Hearst's performance was a disingenuous attempt to portray herself as a victim. "She has continually used her money, her position, to try to rewrite history," Hanlon said. "She took no responsibility for anything she ever did."

Hearst's attorney did not respond to NEWSWEEK's request for comment. But Michael Latin, the assistant district attorney who prosecuted Olson in a separate case, says he thinks Hearst will be very effective on the stand. For one thing, her credibility problems have diminished over the years—and in this case, unlike her own trial, she does not need to persuade the jurors she is innocent. "She knows the truth and she is willing to tell the truth," Latin says. "That is really all that is required." Because California had no death penalty when the crime was committed, the defendants will not face execution if convicted. But they could spend the rest of their lives in prison if the jury believes the woman they called Tania. ∎

In 1974, heiress Patty Hearst was kidnapped by members of a group calling itself the Symbionese Liberation Army (SLA). The group took this picture of Hearst, who inexplicably actively participated in crimes with SLA gang members. Conspiracy researchers subsequently discovered that the SLA was a secret revolutionary project funded by the FBI. (Photo and article: *Newsweek*, February 4, 2002)

Tempted?

Enjoy our quality responsibly · *Visit crownroyal.com*

CROWN ROYAL • IMPORTED IN THE BOTTLE • BLENDED CANADIAN WHISKY • 40% ALCOHOL BY VOLUME (80 PROOF) • ©2001 JOSEPH E. SEAGRAM & SONS, NEW YORK, NY

Blatant serpent wickedness is rampant in this advertisement for *Crown Royal* whisky. We have the regal scarlet crown, the diamond cuts on the glass, the evil snake shaped in the form of *"S"* (Satan?), and the one word question, "Tempted?" The phrase below, "Enjoy our quality responsibly" sounds like some kind of hellish joke. *Crown Royal* is manufactured by Seagram & Sons, the world's largest distillery. Seagram is owned by the Bronfman bloodline dynasty of Canada, the family of ardent ADL Jewish Zionists. Its senior is currently Edgar Bronfman, who also just happens to be chairman of the World Jewish Congress.

The dragon is, of course, a mythical form of serpent. Indeed, the Holy Bible in the book of Revelation describes Satan as "that old serpent, the dragon." Well, for those who wish to pay homage to the dragon, *The Pyramid Collection* catalog offers such jewelry items as this pendant, ring, and arm band.

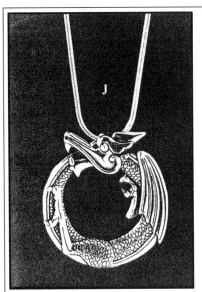

J. From Page to Pendant

Exclusive! Artisan Stephen Harris is one of the foremost translators of Celtic art into contemporary jewelry—demonstrated in this antiqued sterling silver pendant, crafted in a design familiar to admirers of the illuminated *Book of Kells.* 1⅛" diam.

P14-752 Dragon Circle Pendant **$49.95**
P150-068 18" Sterling Figaro Chain **$14.95**

I. The Dragon of Cymru

As descendants of the ancient Celtic tribes of Cymru (*Chim*-ree), the Welsh immortalize the dragon as a symbol of national unity—depicted on their flag, as well as in the casting of this garnet-centered, antiqued sterling silver ring by designer/artisan Stephen Harris. For men and women. Whole sizes 6–12.

P11-750 Garnet Dragon Ring **$39.95**

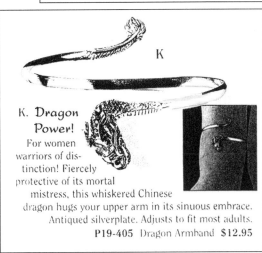

K. Dragon Power!

For women warriors of distinction! Fiercely protective of its mortal mistress, this whiskered Chinese dragon hugs your upper arm in its sinuous embrace. Antiqued silverplate. Adjusts to fit most adults.

P19-405 Dragon Armband **$12.95**

The Illuminati Serpent: In *The Two Babylons*, Hislop writes: "In the mythology of the primitive world, the serpent is universally the symbol of the sun... As the sun was the enlightener of the world, so the serpent was held to have been the great enlightener of the spiritual, by giving mankind knowledge of good and evil."

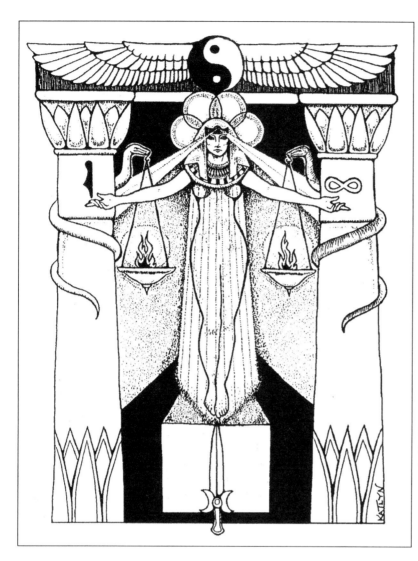

Revealing drawing from a New Age magical publication, *New Moon Rising*. The yin/yang circle at top has the backward "S" and the black is white, white is black motif; and we discover the veiled goddess, in addition to two serpents facing each other. Again, this emphasizes the occult principle of joining, or integrating of opposites. The author of *Codex Magica* could give about a 60-hour lecture series devoted exclusively to the meaning of all the symbols in this seductively evil—even grotesque—piece of occult art.

The serpent has long been associated with the Goddess. At right are depictions of the Greek Goddess Medusa, whose hair was a nest of snakes, and the cobra, a holy Egyptian symbol for the Goddess religion. (From book, *New Age Lies to Women*, by Wanda Marrs)

Singer/Entertainer Britney Spears used this white python serpent in one of her music videos. Some in witchcraft falsely believe the white snake is the possessor of good magical powers because of its "pure" color. The satanist knows otherwise. Dr. Michael Aquino, High Priest of the Temple of Set, once stated on *The Oprah Winfrey* TV show that there is no real difference in good vs. evil magic. Magic is magic. (Photo: *The Tennessean*, December 19, 2001, p. 3D)

Ὄθων Σπυρ. Μπότσαρης

Ἡ Μαγικὴ Εἰκόνα

Ὅ,τι πρόκειται νὰ συμβῇ εἰς τόν κόσμον καί πού ἡ ἀνθρωπότης τό ἀγνοεῖ

ΕΚΔΟΣΙΣ Γ΄
1987

Ἐκδόσεις «ΑΠΟΚΑΛΥΨΙΣ»
ὁδός Γλάδστωνος 8, Ἀθῆναι
Τηλ. 36.37.203

The title page of a book published in Greece exposing the global plot of the Zionist Masons of the Illuminati. The authors demonstrate their understanding by the symbolic use of the evil oroboros serpent encircling the whole world.

The Oroboros, the serpent coiled up in a circle biting its own tail (also *Uroboros*), is pictured as a gnostic rooster combination creature in this illustration from Horapollo's *Selecta Hieroglyphica*, 1597. The sun and moon symbolize the conjunction of opposites, which is the alchemical doctrine of Illuminism.

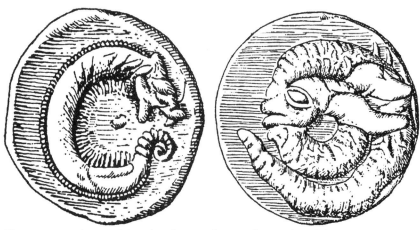

These two ancient Celtic coins from Bohemia (second and first centuries B.C.) bear the marks of the dragon, or serpent. The first coin has the image of an oroboros serpent/dragon torqued and prepared to bite its own tail. The second coin bears the image of a coiled, horned serpent with ears. The coins signify the adoration and homage paid the serpent as a religious icon of worship-status by the Mystery Religions. The revival today of the ancient Mystery Religions is accompanied also by modern-day advances in serpent worship.

The most famous of all-seeing eyes is found on every U.S.A. one dollar bill. It is the image of Osiris, the Eygptian Sun God, above the pyramid. Below the pyramid is the Latin inscription, New World Order (*Novus Ordo Seclorum*), with a pair of cloven tongues, one on each side of the unfinished pyramid. The words "Annuit Coeptis" in Latin stand for "He favors our undertaking," or "He is on our side." It is vital to know that this strange image is actually the obverse (reverse side) of the Great Seal of the United States which, oddly, is also pictured on the same side of the dollar. But, why would a seal—much like a rubber stamp—need a reverse side? And why is it that the mysterious, hidden, reverse side of the Great Seal was unknown to the American public at large until 1935? In that year, 32° Mason, President Franklin D. Roosevelt, ordered the U.S. Treasury to add the obverse side of the Great Seal to the design of the $1 bill. Imagine! For about 150 years, no one but the Illuminati insiders knew that a satanic mark—the all-seeing eye and the pyramid of the serpentine sun god—had already been prepared and was being kept for unveiling at some future, occultic appropriate date. Incidentally, the unfinished pyramid represents the Illuminati's fond desire of rebuilding the Tower of Babel, whose original builders were confounded by God. Again, however, we find a metaphor and allegory. The rebuilding of the Tower of Babel actually represents something else: The unveiling of the New World Order, a tyrannical, Big Brother system of global government led by an antichrist and superintended by Satan, temporary god of this world.

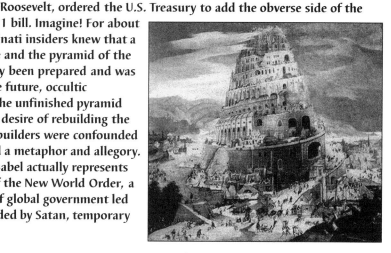

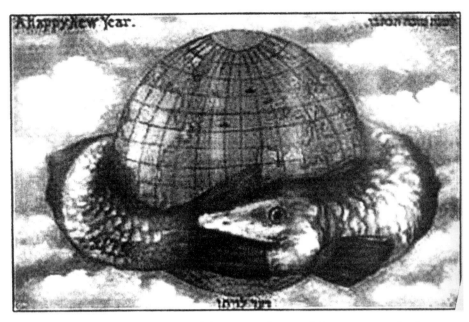

This is a Jewish New Year postcard, by artist Alain Roth in 1915. Amazingly revealing, the postcard image confirms the documentation found in the long controversial *Protocols of the Learned Elders of Zion*. In the protocols the Jewish Zionist conspiracy is described as a symbolic serpent encircling the world! As if to emphasize that this is the correct understanding, the writing in Hebrew at the bottom of this Jewish New Year postcard is the word "Leviathan." The identity of Leviathan is revealed in *Isaiah 27* as the serpent, or Satan. Have a Happy New Year, indeed!

An Oroboros serpent associated with the aionic cycles of life and death. (*Cydonia: The Secret Chronicles of Mars*, by David E. Flynn, 2002)

Fritz Springmeier, one of the world's top researchers into the global conspiracy, discovered the Illuminati symbol of a snake swallowing its own tail (the Oroboros) being used by Portland, Oregon's public library system as the logo placed by the library on its books. (*Newsletter From A Christian Ministry*, October 15, 1993)

The Illuminati's architectural concept of the unfinished pyramid (the capstone yet to be fused on top) is exactly captured in this intriguing, obviously staged ritual image. This photo, from the American Bar Association's (ABA) annual convention in 1999, shows attorney Philip Anderson (left), president of the ABA, Janet Reno, Attorney-General of the United States, and President Bill Clinton. Notice that each of the three stand erect, a somber and knowing look on their faces, their bodies arranged to create a mystical trinity of unity. Behind them we find the ABA logo, which is in the shape of an unfinished pyramid. (*USA Today* newspaper, August 10, 1999, p. 8A)

From *The Herder Dictionary of Symbols* (Chiron Publications, Illinois), we have two different representations of the alchemical/mystical concept of *"trinity as unity."* At left is a Rosicrucian seal and at right is an illustration from Valentinius's *Duodecim Claves*, 1678.

FOURTEEN

"Silence, Slaves, or We'll Cut Your Throat From Ear to Ear!"

...binding myself under no less penalty than that of having my throat cut across...

— Oath of Freemasonry
Entered Apprentice
Degree (1°)

But above all things, my brethren, swear not, neither by heaven, neither by the earth, neither by any other oath...

— James 5:12

In every ritual degree of Freemasonry and in all the most important ceremonial rituals and initiations of elite orders, the candidate is required to take an oath and is warned of the hideous and grotesque penalty that awaits him if he dares ever to reveal any of the group's innermost secrets.[1]
For example, in the very first degree oath of Freemasonry, the candidate declares:

...binding myself under no less penalty than that of having my throat cut across, my tongue torn out by its roots, and my body buried in the rough sands of the sea, at low-water mark, where the tide ebbs and flows twice in twenty-four hours, should I ever knowingly violate this my Entered Apprentice obligation.

Second degree Masons recite the following heinous oath:

…binding myself under no less penalty than that of having my breast torn open, my heart plucked out, and placed on the highest pinnacle of the temple there to be devoured by the vultures of the air, should I ever knowingly violate the Fellow Craft obligation.

The third degree oath proclaims:

…binding myself under no less penalty than that of having my body severed in two, my bowels taken from thence and burned to ashes, the ashes scattered before the four winds of heaven, that no more remembrance might be had of so vile and wicked a wretch as I would be, should I ever, knowingly, violate this my Master Mason's obligation.

That's not all. In the 4th degree, Mark Master of the York Rite, the candidate performs a ritual which symbolizes having his "ear smitten off" if he reveals the order's secrets. And for the 5th degree, Past Master, the hapless candidate agrees as follows:

…binding myself under no less penalty than (in addition to all my former penalties) to have my tongue split from tip to root, that I might thereafter be unable to pronounce the word.

The sixth degree (Most Excellent Master) of the York Rite continues with the horrific penalties:

…binding myself under no less penalty than to have my breast torn open, and my heart and vitals taken from thence, and exposed to rot on the dunghill.

It's no wonder that our Lord Jesus Christ, as recorded in the Holy Scriptures, commanded that His followers take no oaths *(Matthew 5:34-37)*. Christ's brother, James, put it this way: "But above all things, my brethren, swear not, neither by heaven, neither by the earth, neither by any other oath" *(James 5:12)*. Let Masons and other Illuminists who lie claiming to be "Christian" believers try to dance around and vainly evade this commandment.

The Sign of Silence

Illuminists have a sign to be used to remind associates when it is needful to stonewall or to shut up about a matter. In the York Rite initiation for the Royal Master's Degree, this sign, called the Due-guard, "is made by placing the forefinger of the right hand upon the lips."[2] *Richardson's Monitor of Freemasonry* remarks that this sign "is a caution to a companion when you wish him to keep silent."[3]

In the ritual degree ceremony of the Secret Master, the candidate places two fingers to his lip and is told that the obligation he is taking "enjoins secrecy and to

142   RICHARDSON'S MONITOR OF FREE-MASONRY.

MASTER'S ELECT OF NINE.

Some of the Societies call this degree "Elected Knights of Nine," but we have given its original name according to the French Rituals. It is founded on the award of punishment to the principal murderer of Hiram Abiff. After that murder was perpetrated, a great assembly of Masters was convened to take measures to apprehend the murderers. A stranger came and disclosed the fact that he had discovered a person concealed in a cave near Joppa, who answered the description of one of the supposed murderers. Solomon appointed nine Masters to proceed to the spot with the stranger as guide. On their way, Joabert, one of the nine, learned from the guide the location of the cavern, and he made his way there apart from the rest, where, by the light of a lamp, he discovered the murderer fast asleep, with a poinard at his feet. He took the poinard and stabbed him, first in the head, and then in the heart. The villain exclaimed, "Vengeance is taken!" and then expired. Joabert then cut off the murderer's head, and, taking it in his hand, and the bloody knife in the other, returned to Jerusalem with his companions. Solomon was at first offended at this summary vengeance, but at the intercession of the others he became reconciled.

The meeting is called a Chapter, and represents the audience chamber of King Solomon, hung with red and white hangings—the red representing flames. There is a group of nine lights in the east, and one in the west.

Master (representing King Solomon, and dressed in royal robes) sits in the east before a table covered with black, and is styled Most Potent.

There is only one Warden, who represents Stolkyn, and is called the Inspector, he sits in the west, with seven brethren around him.

Grand Marshal sits in the north.

The Inspector and brethren are dressed in black robes, and with their hats flapped. They wear white aprons sprinkled with blood red, and lined and bordered with black; on the flap of the apron a bloody arm, holding a dagger, and on the apron a bloody arm holding a bloody head by the hair. They also wear scarfs of wide black ribbon from the left shoulder to the right hip, with four rosettes near the extremity in front, four behind, and one at the bottom, to which is attached the Jewel of the Order, viz., a gold-handled dagger, with silver blade.

The brethren sit with knees crossed, and lean their heads on their right hands.

Most Potent Master raps seven, when the Grand Marshal rises.

Master—Brother Grand Marshal, are we all Masters Elect?
Marshal—We are, Most Potent.
Master—Your place in the Chapter?
Marshal—In the north.
Master—Your business there?
Marshal—To see that the Chapter is duly guarded.
Master—Please to inform the Sentinel that we are about to open a Chapter of Masters Elect, and charge him to keep guard accordingly.

Marshal goes to the door, informs the Sentinel, and returns to his post.
Master raps eight, and Inspector rises.
Master—Brother Stolkyn, are you a Master Elect?
Inspector—One cavern received me, one lamp gave me light, and one fountain refreshed me.
Master—What is the hour?
Inspector—Break of day.
Master raps eight and one, and the companions all rise.
Master—If it is break of day, it is time to open a Chapter of Masters Elect. Brother Stolkyn, you will inform the companions that we are about to open a Chapter of Masters Elect of Nine, for the dispatch of business, and I will thank them for their assistance.
Inspector repeats this order, when the brethren give the signs up to and including those of this degree, hereafter described.
Master raps eight and one, which is repeated by the Inspector and Marshal, and all the companions clap eight and one with their hands, when the Master declares the Chapter duly open.

THE INEFFABLE DEGREES: MASTER ELECT OF NINE.   143

If a candidate is to be admitted, he is prepared in an outer room by one of the companions, who is detailed as Master of Ceremonies, and who hoodwinks him, conducts him to the door of the Chapter, and raps eight and one.
Inspector raps the same from the inside, and demands—Who comes there?
Master of Ceremonies—A companion, who is desirous of going in search of the assassins of Hiram Abiff.
Inspector opens the door, and the candidate is led in and placed in the west behind the Inspector's seat.
Master to candidate—What do you desire of us?
Candidate—To be installed as a Master Elect, and avenge the death of our late Grand Master, Hiram Abiff.
Master—Have you the courage to revenge his death?
Candidate—I have.
Master—Then you shall have the opportunity.
Candidate—I am ready.
Master—You shall now be shown the place where one of the murderers lies concealed: a stranger has discovered it to me, and if you have the resolution, follow the stranger.

Candidate—I will follow.
Master of Ceremonies leads candidate out, and through several passages, or rough roads, and then into a room lighted by a single taper, seats him on a block, representing a stone, and says—I am now going to leave you: after I have gone you can remove the bandage from your eyes and drink some water from the spring to refresh yourself after so fatiguing a journey.
Candidate removes the bandage, and discovers a basin of water with a tumbler beside it. He is also astonished to see a human head lying on the floor, and a bloody knife, or poinard, beside it. The Master of Ceremonies returns and directs candidate to take up the knife in his right hand and the head in his left.
Candidate takes them and (under instruction) goes to the door of the Chapter and raps eight and one.
Master of Ceremonies (who has gone in, and raps eight and one from inside)—Who comes there—what do you want?
Candidate—An Intendant of the Building, who desires to enter this Chapter of Masters Elect of Nine.
Master of Ceremonies—By what right do you claim this privilege?

Richardson's Monitor of Freemasonry (pp. 142-143) provides these bloody reminders of the horrible penalties that await the Mason or other elitist who divulges secrets of the Order. "Silence, Slaves" is certainly the catchword for the submissive servants of Satan's earthly elite corps of leaders.

obey the orders and decrees of the Council of Princes of Jerusalem, under penalties of all former degrees."[4]

For the fifth degree (Past Master) the penal dueguard sign is the placement of the thumb to one's mouth, again indicating the warning to keep silent.

A Softening of Penalties?

Freemasonry and many other secret societies have been under siege in recent years as the author of *Codex Magica* and a number of other courageous men have boldly come forward exposing the frightening, cold and bloody oaths taken by millions of Masons around the globe. As a consequence, as I understand it, the leadership of the Lodge and other groups has more recently begun to "soften the edges," so to speak and to eliminate some of the more egregious and ghastly phrases and words used in the rituals.

In June 2001, according to *The Scottish Rite Journal*, C. Fred Kleinknecht, Sovereign Grand Commander, 33°, the reigning potentate of Freemasonry, presented copies of the *Revised Standard Pike Ritual* to his subordinate Sovereign Grand Commanders.[5] Kleinknecht explained to his lieutenants that this new guide provides "modified

For the Secret Master degree, the candidate places two fingers to his lip and is told that his obligation "enjoins secrecy." (*Richardson's Monitor of Freemasonry*, p. 133)

The fifth degree in the York Rite requires this Due-guard be given (thumb of the right hand to mouth) and a sworn oath that the candidate will never disclose "the secrets of a brother." (*Duncan's Masonic Ritual and Monitor*, 3d ed., p. 189)

In the Royal Master's degree, in the Due-guard , placing the forefinger to the lip tells one's companion to keep silent. (*Richardson's Monitor of Freemasonry*, p. 81)

versions" of the seventh and twenty-seventh degrees which were originally created by Albert Pike, their much revered nineteenth century "Illustrious Sovereign Grand Master."[6] One can assume that to appease its critics, further editions of the ritual will water down the most grievous of the penalties.

Other ways, however, will undoubtedly be found to motivate the membership to keep the secrets, including banishment from elite status and possibly even the periodic assassination of disciples who stray and who recklessly disregard the dictate to retain secrecy.

Still it is of interest that the Masonic elite are embarrassed over being outed for their hideous oaths. What's more, in the Mormon Church (LDS), the penalty portions of the Masonic-oriented rituals celebrated in the Temple also have recently been watered down somewhat.

It sure seems as though the big-wigs of the secret orders are running scared, doesn't it? How they must despise Christians like Texe Marrs who are forcing these changes on a reluctant and evil Illuminati corps.

Pagan Origins of the Sign of Silence

The Masonic practice of signs warning of frightening penalties for breaking silence most definitely is of pagan origins. In Greece, Rome, Babylon, and Egypt, those who had loose lips often paid with their lives and fortunes, so sacred and guarded were the secrets of the Mystery Religions.

The Egyptians and Romans even worshipped a god of silence, *Harpocrates,* a form of the solar deity. Harpocrates was often pictured sitting on his mother's lap, suckling at her breast. Later, the Catholic Church adopted similar images in the veneration of Mary with child. Sometimes Harpocrates was pictured naked or with horns on his head, symbols of power. He often sat on a Lotus flower. The Lotus is a sexual symbol of the female vagina.[7]

In the active days of Benjamin Franklin and our nation's founders, their secret society counterparts in Great Britain made use of the god Harpocrates. Sir Francis Dashwood, instrumental in the British operation of the Illuminati, recruited nobility for his Hell-Fire Club, a secret group based on magic, satanism, and sex. Numerous harlots—and sometimes newly deflowered virgins—were scandalously used by Dashwood and his occultic, jolly men. On club premises, the members erected a statue of Harpocrates, depicting him solemnly holding a finger to his mouth to

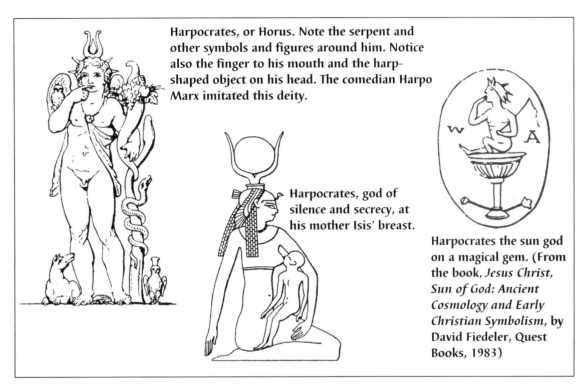

Harpocrates, or Horus. Note the serpent and other symbols and figures around him. Notice also the finger to his mouth and the harp-shaped object on his head. The comedian Harpo Marx imitated this deity.

Harpocrates, god of silence and secrecy, at his mother Isis' breast.

Harpocrates the sun god on a magical gem. (From the book, *Jesus Christ, Sun of God: Ancient Cosmology and Early Christian Symbolism*, by David Fiedeler, Quest Books, 1983)

remind the frolicking members of the Hell-Fire Club that, "What happens here, stays here."[8]

Rome also had the Mystery Goddess Angerona. Her statue showed Angerona as a beautiful woman holding a finger to her mouth, "the emblem of secrecy and mystery."[9] Angerona watched over the sexual promiscuity goings-on at various orgies connected with the festivals of the solstices and the changing of the seasons.

The Mystery Religions of the Romans and other peoples especially needed the utmost secrecy because, during the higher initiations, the unspoken names of the hidden or unknown god, or gods, was often revealed. As the Christians gained in numbers and influence, they began to properly understand that these names were actually synonyms for Satan, Lucifer, the Devil. Great effort was therefore taken by pagans to obscure or prevent the unmasking of this satanic connection.[10]

An interesting sidenote: As a child watching TV in the early days (1950s), one of the most popular programs was a game show hosted by Jewish comedian Groucho Marx. Groucho had a brother, Harpo Marx, who was also a comedian and starred in numerous TV programs and in movies. Harpo always played the cherubic character of a mute young boy, with blond hair in curls. In other words, Harpo was cast in the image of Harpocrates, god of silence and secrecy, also known as Horus the child.

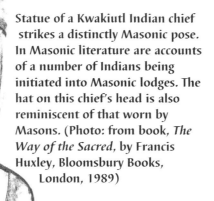

Statue of a Kwakiutl Indian chief strikes a distinctly Masonic pose. In Masonic literature are accounts of a number of Indians being initiated into Masonic lodges. The hat on this chief's head is also reminiscent of that worn by Masons. (Photo: from book, *The Way of the Sacred*, by Francis Huxley, Bloomsbury Books, London, 1989)

Harpocrates, the Egyptian god of secrecy and concealment, carved into a small basalt stone tablet, probably used as a seal. The image of Harpocrates is that of a hideous-looking dragon springing up from a lotus flower. (Photo from *The Adepts In the Esoteric Classical Tradition*, by Manly P. Hall, The Philosophical Research Society, Los Angeles, CA, 1988)

The Egyptian form of the god Harpocrates giving the sign of silence is shown in this ancient drawing. Below and supporting Harpocrates is the lion-god and encircling him is the supreme deity, the Oroboros, or serpent.

Representation of Horus, son of the Egyptian god Osiris. (Drawing from *The Herder Dictionary of Symbols*, Chiron Publications, Wilmette, Illinois, 1986)

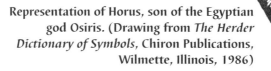

BUSINESS & TECHNOLOGY

Dot-com gallows humor

A chronicle of the great Web shakeout

BY FRED VOGELSTEIN

PATRICK HARBRON—OUTLINE FOR *USN&WR*

Philip Kaplan's Web site captures the Internet shakeout's zeitgeist.

● *"I don't want my site to end up on my site."*

Philip Kaplan surfs through his E-mail and bursts out laughing. "Look at that. That number means there are 1,129 of them—all in the past month. I've gotten more than that, but I've deleted a bunch." Lately, Kaplan estimates he receives more than 100 E-mail messages a day. "Thanks for documenting the stupidity in the business world," reads one. "You are my idol. Period," goes another.

Who is Philip Kaplan, and why is he so popular? A month ago, the 24-year-old programmer was living the hermetic existence of a young entrepreneur, subsisting on fast food and working 15-hour days out of his Manhattan loft to build a consulting business. But on Memorial Day, he put up a Web site challenging visitors to pick the next dot-com flameout. He gave it a vulgar if somewhat catchy name, ~~pany.com~~ ~~king the title of~~

awarded based on how many players selected the company and the severity of the bad news. Companies that aren't widely picked to crater but do so anyway are the ones that generate the most points. ~~Of course, th~~ ~~s th~~ ~~re's n~~

Kaplan gets all his information by encouraging his audience to tell him confidentially what's happening in their companies. Then, usually at midnight, he cul~~l~~ all of these leads into 30 or s~~o~~

Philip Kaplan, who has gained some notoriety for his successful website, *f——dcompany.com*. (Photo: *US News & World Report*, July 10, 2000, p. 41)

Medieval priest affiliated with the sect of the *Alumbrados* (Illuminati), signifying to his monks and brothers not to disclose or reveal the secrets entrusted to their order.

Colin Powell, steeped in Jewish magic and cabalism, gives the due-guard of the Royal Arch Mason.

BUSINESS

Brainy economist Larry Summers replaces Wall Street wizard Robert Rubin at the Treasury. Can he leave well enough alone?

TAKING THE HANDOFF

By KARL TARO GREENFELD

THERE EXISTS A PARADIGM OF THE perfect economy, a place where a dismal scientist may even lay down his HP-19B calculator because analysis is superfluous in a land where supply and demand are calibrated, inflation is checked, growth steady, the workforce fully employed and the stock market bullish. For the moment, the U.S.

in the postwar era, redefined that Cabinet post from discreet adviser and signatory of our currency to a sort of global emissary and projection of American geopolitical clout as it is expressed now—not in warheads or throw weights but in loan guarantees and bailout packages.

With Rubin's resignation and Summers' ascension, the question arises: To what extent did Rubin's personal make possible the enla Secretary's

Lawrence Summers, President of Harvard University and former Secretary of the Treasury under President Bill Clinton. (Photo: *Time* magazine, May 24, 1999)

Jacques Delors, from France, head of the European Community, arriving for a conference at 10 Downing Street, residence of England's Prime Minister. The caption under the photo reads: *"Jacques Delors gives nothing away as he arrives at 10 Downing Street this week."* (Photo: *The European* newspaper, June 25-28, 1992, p. 6)

Sir Winston Churchill, former Prime Minister of Great Britain, a Mason and Druid Priest, gives the sign of silence.

Harpo Marx giving the *silence* sign, finger to lips. One of the three Marx Brothers comedy team—Groucho and Chico were brothers—Harpo's given name at birth was Adolph, which he later changed legally to Arthur. But in his entertainment career, he played a mute pantomimist and uttered not a word. His stage name, *"Harpo,"* was obviously a derivative of the name of *Harpocrates*, the ancient Greek god of silence.

"Silence," a painting by Odilon Redon (1911), is a portrait of Harpocrates, the God of Mystical Silence.

FIFTEEN

Up to Their Necks in Mischief

When it's your neck up there on the chopping block, you don't want a dull blade.

— Anonymous spectator in
crowd at guillotine
execution, Paris, France, 1789

Y ou've no doubt heard the old saying "up to their necks in mischief," haven't you? Well, it is definitely applicable to the Illuminist elite and their legion of secret society puppets.

Hanging over the fireplace in the famous Green Room at the White House in Washington, D.C. is an acclaimed oil portrait of Benjamin Franklin, one of our country's most celebrated "founding fathers." It depicts the famed statesman sitting studiously, poring over an ancient document which he is holding with his right hand. His left hand, meanwhile, is at his throat, set with the finger in a V-design, the thumb pushing upward to his chin. Franklin's neck is a prominent focus of the painting. Obviously, this is a sign Franklin is communicating.

I have observed this same fascinating sign being performed by many other elitists, both ancient and modern. However, Old Ben certainly is the epitome of the occult secret society patriarch. This man's feats as a Mason and Rosicrucian are legendary. *Mackey's Encyclopedia of Freemasonry* acknowledges Franklin as "a devoted Freemason occupying for many years places of official prominence and serving his (Masonic) Brethren with conspicuous Masonic zeal and aptitude."[1]

The same Encyclopedia spends a great amount of space listing Franklin's exploits and positions held as a Freemason, not only in the United States, but in Great Britain and in France. In 1779, he was elected Worshipful Master of the Lodge of the Nine Sisters in Paris, and in 1782 he became head of a lodge of the Grand Orient de Paris. Earlier, Benjamin Franklin had officiated at the Masonic funeral of one of his "brothers," the monstrously wicked atheist, Voltaire.[2] Voltaire, as historians will attest, was certainly up to his neck in mischief.

The Neck A Sign of Sacrifice

A number of dictionaries of symbols state that the hand placed on the neck signifies *sacrifice*. Now sacrifice can have at least two meanings — one, the continuing threat of

same penalty on all who are guilty of disclosing the secrets of this degree.

The candidate is then instructed in the signs, words and token in this degree, as follows :

Signs—Place the point of a poinard under your chin, and draw it downward to the waist, as if in the act of ripping open the body, speaking the word ZERBUL. The brother will answer by giving the Entered Apprentice's sign as on page 7, and saying ELIHAM. Another way is to clench the fingers of the right hand, extend the thumb, place it on the abdomen, and move it upwards to the chin, as if ripping open the body with a knife. The brother answers as before.

Words—The pass-words are Eliham and Zerbal. Sacred words, Zerbal, Beniah, Benhakar, Bendaka, &c.

Candidate is now clothed as a companion of this degree, and salutes the Senior Warden as a Master Elect of Fifteen.

If there is no other business before the Chapter, it is then closed in same manner as in the preceding degree, except that the Master and other officers rap three times five, and the companions clap three times five with their hands, &c.

omon. It is hung with red and white curtains, and is lighted by twelve candles on four triangular branches.

The officers consist of Thrice Potent Master, representing King Solomon, sitting in the east : Grand Inspector in the west, and Master of Ceremonies.

The brethren wear white aprons, each with an inflamed heart embroidered or painted upon it, and lined and bordered with black. The ribbon, or Order, is similar to that in tho preceding degree, except that in place of three heads, three hearts appear upon it. The jewel is the same.

In opening the Chapter, Thrice Potent Master raps ten, and Grand Inspector rises. Master makes the usual inquiries as to whether the Chapter is duly guarded, and the duties of the several officers, as in former degrees, which are answered by the Inspector.

Master raps eleven, and inquires of Grand Inspector—What is the hour ?

Grand Inspector—It is twelve, Thrice Potent.

Master raps twelve, which is repeated by the officers, and the brethren clap twelve with their hands : Master says— If it is twelve it is time to labor by the greatest of lights. I pronounce this Grand Chapter open.

The brethren now give the signs of the different degrees, and then those of this degree, hereafter described.

If a candidate is to be admitted, he is prepared outside by the Master of Ceremonies, who brings him hoodwinked to the door, and gives twelve raps, which are answered by twelve by the Inspector, who demands, who comes there ? &c.

Master of Ceremonies—A Master Elect of Fifteen desires to receive the degree of Sublime Knight.

Candidate gets admittance in the same manner as in the previous degree, and is led to the Grand Inspector in the west, who examines him in all former degrees.

One of the signs for ritual of the Grand Master Elect Degree is a dagger under the chin. (*Richardson's Monitor of Freemasonry*, p. 146)

the penalties to be applied to punish those adepts and initiates who so impertinently reveal the secrets of the Order; and two, the willingness of the individual performing the sign to sacrifice himself for the good of the Order, or for the good of the cause or Great Work of the Illuminati.

The Neck Ritual

The neck, being the bridge to the head and brain (intellect) and the point at which the jugular vein can be ruptured by a knife or stone thrust, does seem to be an appropriate place to physically focus this sign. *Duncan's Masonic Ritual and Monitor* summarizes the "Penal" code of Freemasonry. That reference book says the various penal signs are designed so that each "intimates that the stiff neck of the disobedient shall be cut off from the head of the living…"[3]

The ritual for the Grand Master Elect Degree, according to *Richardson's Monitor of Freemasonry*, has the candidate either placing the point of a knife under the chin, or alternatively clenching the fingers of the right hand, extending the thumb, placing it on the abdomen, and moving it upwards to the chin, as if ripping the body open with a knife.

In the York Rite, the Past Master, or Fifth Degree, the candidate places the thumb of his right hand (fingers clinched) upon his lips. This, says *Duncan's*, "alludes to the penalty of having his tongue split from tip to root."[4]

The "Pain in the Neck" Degree

And finally, according to *Richardson's Monitor of Freemasonry*, the candidate for the Select Master Degree makes the second sign for that degree by crossing the hands and arms just below his neck—creating sort of a scissors effect as if he is ready to chop off his own neck—and then he draws the crossed hands and arms downward. The meaning is said to indicate the willingness of the candidate to have the body quartered if he discloses any secrets. (I informally call this the *"Pain in the Neck"* sign since it starts with a scissors at the neck).

The sign I call the "Pain in the Neck." Actually, it is the second sign in the Select Master degree and is made by crossing the hands and arms. Then, after this scissor look is effected, with a quick motion draw the hands edge-wise across the body downwards as if you were in the act of quartering the body. Finally, let them drop by your sides. (*Richardson's Monitor of Freemasonry*, p. 84)

Benjamin Franklin, Rosicrucian and Mason, from an oil portrait painted by David Martin in 1766. This famous painting today hangs over the fireplace in the Green Room at the White House.

Israeli magician Uri Geller, whose close friends include occultic pal U.S. Senator Claiborne Pell and fellow cabalist, singer Michael Jackson. (Photo: *U.S. News & World Report*, December 5, 1998)

URI GELLER. Age: 42.
Job: Lecturer, inventor, consultant who uses psychic skills to explore for minerals and oil.
On skeptics: "I don't care what those schmucks think. I'm a millionaire."
Hobby: Bending spoons for the likes of Senator Claiborne Pell, left.
Best claimed feat: Found gold in Amazon for Japanese firm.

Portrait of Paul Revere, by Copley. The Scottish Rite reference, *10,000 Famous Freemasons*, lists the celebrated American patriot, made famous by his night-time horse ride warning citizens the British troops were at hand, as an initiate of the Masonic Lodge.

THE RUSSIAN SPHINX

VERY age has its riddle. Helena Petrovna Blavatsky was the enigma of the nineteenth century. The publication of her letters and also those of Mahatmas Morya and Koot Hoomi cast a new and fuller light upon her extraordinary personality. She is revealed as a woman in the memory of the living, not as a half mythical sibyl from some distant age or the Pythia of some ancient oracle. Though but a few decades have passed since Madame Blavatsky departed from this life, hers is already a name to conjure with. She is the third person of a bewildering triad—St.-Germain, Cagliostro, and Blavatsky.

As though by common consent, humanity attacks viciously and relentlessly anyone who assails the infallibility of the mediocre. Dare to preach or even presume that order reigns behind the chaos of life—that anything in the universe other than man has intelligence—and an outraged society shows its claws but partly hidden by the semblance of its culture. Oppose the knowledge of the few to the ignorance of the many, and morons are provoked to a frenzy of resentment. A large portion of mankind has been baptized in the faith of the commonplace. Stupidity is the vogue and all men dread to be out of style. The fear is not that the occultist may be wrong; the fear is that the occultist may be right. To the criminal we may give the benefit of the doubt; to the occultist, never. The criminal violates only our laws; the occultist (*Que le Diable l'emporte!*) violates our sacred opinions.

Like children, incapable of the emotions of maturity, we are pitifully deficient in our grasp of spiritual values. Indifferent to the light given us and the efforts made for our improvement, we permit our petty ambitions to overshadow higher issues. We tolerate every form of error, but are utterly intolerant of Truth. We are generous toward any state but that of wisdom, which, when recognized, we swear to destroy. Occultism is regarded as a synonym for imposture, and the philosopher can hardly expect a better fate than hemlock or the rood in an age

(111)

Helena Petrovna Blavatsky, Co-Mason, Russian mystic and Egyptian Hindu deuoteé, who founded the occult group, Theosophy. Her classic occult text, *The Secret Doctrine*, inspired Adolf Hitler and thousands of others.

BUSINESS & TECHNOLOGY

Creating a new corporation

How Peter Drucker radically changed American business

In The Capitalist Philosophers *(Times Business Books, 2000, $26), Andrea Gabor looks at the people behind the ideas that shaped this dynamic age. This article is adapted from a chapter on management consultant Peter Drucker.*

One of Jack Welch's first decisions after being named General Electric's new CEO in 1980 was to meet with Peter F. Drucker. The Austrian intellectual, then 71, and the working-class boy turned business executive (at age 45, the youngest CEO in GE history) seemed like unlikely soul mates. Yet, after little more than an hour, Welch was hooked.

Drucker, in his slow, measured, Viennese-accented baritone, had asked one of the "big questions" that so intrigued Welch, a question that would dominate the executive's thoughts and actions for the next several years. " 'If you weren't already in this business, would you choose to get into it now?' " Welch recalls Drucker asking. "You could write a book and not learn as much as you would from that question."

The question spurred Welch to act. He began shedding businesses in which GE could not be No. 1 or No. 2. The massive restructuring helped boost GE's market value from $12 billion in 1981 to $492 billion in 1999 and, in the bargain, made Welch one of America's most admired business executives.

In many respects, though, Drucker was an unlikely apostle of management. Born in Hapsburgian Vienna, he worked as a journalist before moving to the United States in 1937. He believed that the failure of European capitalism to give "status and function" to the individual had paved the way for fascism. That idea fostered Drucker's romance with large corporations, which he saw as "the representative institution" for building citizenship in U.S. society. In 1943, when most Americans were preoccupied with World War II, Drucker gained entree to General Motors and conducted a sweeping analysis of its structure and management. He published his observations in *Concept of the Corporation*, which quickly became required reading for managers across the country.

Over the course of six decades, Drucker became the most sought-after adviser to CEOs, among them Walter Wriston of Citicorp, David Rockefeller of Chase Manhattan Corp., Henry

DAVID STRICK—CORBIS OUTLINE

Management guru Peter Drucker
● *Asking the "big questions" of corporate executives*

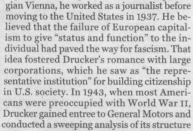

Luce of Time Inc., and Mark Willes of Times Mirror Co. He invented the term "management by objectives" and helped develop objective measures for pay and promotion. He identified the importance of the "knowledge worker"—the elite of the white-collar work force—earlier than almost anyone else.

He also wanted to orient companies around consumers, not just technology. Functioning more like that famous Viennese psychoanalyst, Drucker probed deeply, asking questions and drawing connections. He would lecture executives on such topics as the demographic changes in Latin America, including the shift of peasant populations from the countryside to the cities, and what it meant to GE's businesses. "You're in the transportation business. Do you think the move to big cities means a new market for transportation?" he would query.

Jet power. Drucker's ability to grasp new ideas—and to inspire the confidence of GE managers—was crystallized in the role he played helping GE's jet-engine division revolutionize the commercial aircraft business. GE had to convince aircraft makers who had long catered to the military that it was worth spending enormous sums of money to design civilian aircraft. Drucker's role was to help GE's jet-engine executives, "all of whom were technically oriented, most of whom came out of the military, understand . . . the value system of potential customers."

Drucker was sometimes wrong, with stunning long-term consequences. "We designed the world's most scientific compensation system, and it damn near ruined GE," admits Drucker with calculated self-deprecating humor. He helped come up with what remains, according to Drucker, "the foundation for [most] compensation systems"—one tied to return on investment. But it stifled innovation by penalizing managers who sacrificed short-term gains for long-term growth.

In his 90s, Drucker still consults, though he rarely leaves his modest home in Claremont, Calif. He still serves on the faculty of the Drucker School of Management of Claremont Graduate University. But he is no longer convinced that corporations are the institutions for "creating citizenship" and worries that the mobility of the new knowledge society is fostering new social problems. "Corporations once built to last like pyramids are now more like tents," he says. ●

Andrea Gabor is a professor of business journalism at CUNY–Baruch College in New York City.

This unusual photo of "management guru" Peter Drucker in *U.S. News & World Report* (May 8, 2000, p. 42) paints Drucker as a contemplative, god-like character who has "sacrificed" for the Illuminati Order.

Soviet Foreign Minister Eduard Shevardnadze (left), protégé of President and Communist Party Boss Mikhail Gorbachev, was a favorite of the Illuminati.

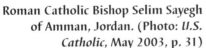

Roman Catholic Bishop Selim Sayegh of Amman, Jordan. (Photo: *U.S. Catholic*, May 2003, p. 31)

James Jesus Angleton, CIA Chief of Counterintelligence, presents the clenched fist under chin and throat—sign that a violent end at the hands of revolutionary assassins shall come to he who reveals secrets of the Craft.

THE SEPTEMBER 2000

SCOTTISH RITE

JOURNAL

OF FREEMAS... ...ISDICTION USA

Brother Michael A. Richards
Renaissance Man, Not "Kramer"

The Scottish Rite Freemasons, on the cover of the September 2000 issue of their official journal, recognized "Brother Michael A. Richards" as a "Renaissance Man, Not Kramer." Richards, a Jew, is the well-known comic actor who won raves for his role as "Kramer" in the long-running #1 hit TV show, *Seinfeld.* Inside the Masonic Lodge magazine, it was noted that Richards holds the 32nd degree of Freemasonry and has received the red cap. Richards says he is a keen student of Masonry and its symbolism and has over 1,000 masonic books in his home in California. Observe Michael Richards' clearly Masonic handsign, which presents the V and is the "due-guard" sign of initiation in the Order of Knights Templar which relates to the penalty of the obligation—the oath agreeing that one's head will be impaled on the highest spire in Christendom as a penalty for revealing secrets. The sign is also similar to the sign for the "due-guard" of the Past Master, 5th degree in the Scottish Rite.

U.S. Senator Kay Bailey Hutchinson (R-TX) is highly exalted by the elite as this photo demonstrates. The strategy of this photo, with the Senator standing between two swords (symbols of authority) and two encircled sun signs (symbol of the Masonic and Illuminati Deity of Light) shows great favoritism toward this lady, especially as this bio-sketch and photo is in a major newsmagazine, *Newsweek* (June 26, 2000). The caption reads: *"Staying in the spotlight. If Pakistan can elect a woman leader, says Hutchinson, why can't the United States?"* Judging from this staged rite, the regal doors may be about ready to open wider for Senator Kay Bailey Hutchinson.

A few signs of the Rosicrucian Order. Many are similar to those of Freemasonry and other secret societies. The penalty sign related to having one's throat cut is shown at number X.

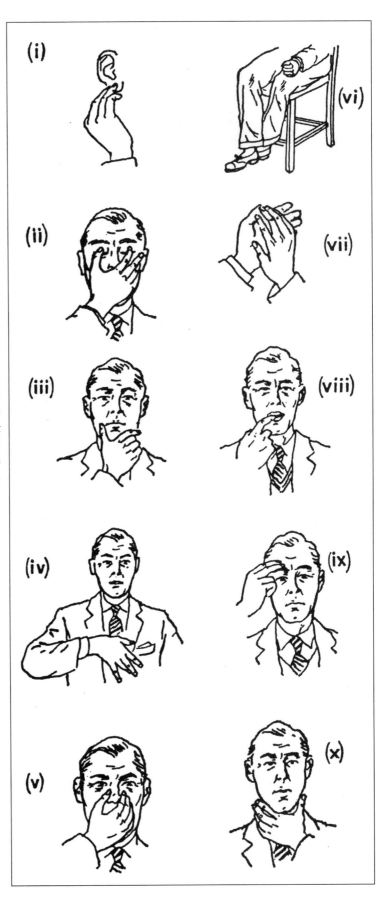

SIXTEEN

Hand On Heart—Sign of Devotion to the Chiefs

Masonry's homage to the heart by the Sign of Hand on Heart can best be understood by the fact that the leaders of the Masonic Lodge themselves boast that the rituals of Freemasonry hearken back to ancient Egyptian religion. *The Egyptian Book of the Dead* addressed prayers to "My heart of my mother…My heart of transformations," meaning the source of rebirths.

The Mother Goddess of Egypt was worshipped by various names—Isis, Hathor, Rhea, etc. She was the one to whom the people "gave their hearts," meaning their heart-felt devotion and allegiance. As the Goddess of sacrifices, it was deemed necessary by her admirers that men should sacrifice their "energies" on her behalf. The Goddess was said to take possession of men's hearts.

Cutting Out Hearts and Eating Them!

In the pyramids of Mexico, Central and South America, the gods were also gods of sacrifice and, once again, the heart was the centerpiece of devotion. Bloodthirsty followers, egged on by high priests, cut out the hearts of victims of tribal wars.

On the stone altars of the temples, the priests cut the heart out of the breast of sacrificial victims while they were still alive! The hearts were eaten, just as they were in ancient Egypt and as they are in a number of satanic cults in existence today.

Back to Egypt

Freemasonry today freely admits its connection to the religion and rituals of ancient Egypt and proudly displays Egyptian idols (the Sphinx, etc.) in and around its lodge facilities and at its international headquarters, the House of the Temple in Washington, D.C.

Moreover, in the ritual ceremonies of the higher Masonic degrees, the Hindu pantheon of deities is honored as the true "Holy Trinity."[1] In the Hindu religion, the whole universe is said to be centered in the heart. The Yogi, in meditation, is claimed to be listening to the heartbeat of the universe, which is the great god Shiva's beating heart. This expresses the basic oriental idea that divinity lies in the heart of every person, but needs to be "realized," or awakened.

Devotion to the Secret Chiefs

Within the Illuminati structure, the initiate is taught in no uncertain terms that he must devote his whole heart to the "secret chiefs," the top elite who comprise the Inner Circle. His life must be dedicated to the goals they have set, for they, in turn, are being directed by the Hierarchy, the spirit beings (Satan and his demons) who have given them *The Plan*. In other words, the life of every Illuminist is a divine temple, and through ritual, magic, and loyal devotion the Great Work of alchemical transformation is to be accomplished within the individual heart and within the world at large. *Ordo Ab Chao*—order must come out of chaos.

A Number of Meanings

As the evidence points out in the illustrations in this section, the "hand on heart" sign has a number of meanings, depending particularly on the exact placement of the hand and the positioning of the fingers. As always, the left hand on heart indicates the *sinister* occultic path. The thumb extended upward leaving the hand squared in the "L" position signals fidelity, sincerity and being "on the square." The thumb upward symbolizes the child-soul, the heart in subjection to higher powers.

The sign of Hand on Heart is practiced and taught in the rituals for many degrees of Freemasonry. For example:

❖ In the Degree of Sublime Knights Elected, the candidate is instructed in the sign. His right hand is extended across the chest to the heart and the thumb is pointed upward. (*Richardson's Monitor of Freemasonry*, p. 147)

❖ In the Degree of Companion Select, the sign is given with the right hand. (*Richardson's Monitor of Freemasonry*, p. 86)

❖ In the Degree of Select Master, the initiate is told "The most popular signs in Masonry are made in this manner: Place the palm of the right hand on the heart, and pronounce the word SECRESY." (*Richardson's Monitor of Freemasonry*, p. 80)

❖ In the Degree of the Knight of the Pelican and Eagle Sovereign Prince Rose Croix of Heredom, the lecturer directs the assembled members to "pass to the Black Room, 18° collars being reversed." Following this instruction, the sign of "right hand on left breast is given." (*18th Degree Secret Initiation Ceremony*)

❖ In the Degree of Mark Master, the members form and march around the Lodge, singing a song. The words of the song include the following: "*Mark Masters all appear Before the Chief Overseer…You who have passed the square, For your rewards prepare, Join heart and hand…Wages to you are due, At your command.*" (*Duncan's Masonic Ritual and Monitor*, p. 161)

Separation of Fingers as Sign is Given

Separating the fingers has its own interpretation, often being the sign of choice for cabalists who employ the letters of the Hebrew alphabet in their hand on heart communications. The illustrations of Christopher Columbus and Ignatius Loyola in this chapter are prime examples. Both of these historical characters were members of secret cabalistic orders founded by the rabbis of the Jewish Sanhedrin.

Erasing Confusion

The Illuminist/Masonic sign should *not* be confused with the American custom of placing one's hand over the heart while reciting the Pledge of Allegiance to the flag (Citizens of some other nations practice this same tradition). Again, in judging the Illuminist intent, we look to such factors as time period, the history and affiliations, who's performing the sign, and other factors. As always in this book, I leave it to you, the reader, to form your own learned opinion of what you are seeing.

Freemasons strongly deny there are any women in their Order. But in *Mackey's Encyclopedia of Freemasonry* we find this picture captioned, *"Lady Freemason Mrs. Elizabeth Aldworth."* In the text (page 353), Mackey, 33°, former Sovereign Grand Commander of the Scottish Rite, writes that, "there are a few instances in which the otherwise unalterable rule of female exclusion has been made to yield."

Robespierre, the heartless monster of the French Revolution. Inspirer of the Jacobins sect, Robespierre caused untold thousands to be sent to the guillotine. Rejecting Jesus, he called for a new religion based on worship of a nameless *"Supreme Being."* After relishing so many of his opponents being sent to their death, one day the tumbrel carriage came also for Robespierre, the Jewish plotter of terror, who himself lost his head. As his head rolled, the mob laughed and cried out *"Do you feel any pain, your majesty?"*

Was Christopher Columbus a clandestine member of the Knights Templar, or another 15th century secret society? Much evidence exists confirming exactly that. So, too, does the cabalistic sign he displays of the left-handed path of the initiate. (Oil painting by Sebastiano del Piombo, 1519)

A statue of Soviet Communist Party leader Joseph Stalin on the cover of the book, *Stalin's Shadow*, by Rosamond Richardson. Photographs of Stalin also show the tyrannical dictator—half Jew and Jesuit-trained—giving the Royal Arch Mason hand sign.

HELMUT KOHL

Chancellor, Federal Republic of Germany.

Photographed by Konrad Müller in Edinburgh, Scotland.

Born, Ludwigshafen, Germany.
Married, Hannelore Kohl; two children. Kohl was given a remarkably ecumenical education—including, over time, studies of Jewish history, religion, and culture.

The chancellor's nickname, Der Schwarze Riese ("The Black Giant"), refers both to his size (six feet four inches and approximately 300 pounds) and to the traditional color of German conservative parties.

Superb interpersonal skills have won him the enduring support of fellow leaders. George Bush is still received with honors when in Bonn, and Kohl and Boris Yeltsin have been known to discuss politics in a sauna. "We're not discussing our good looks," says the chancellor.

Last fall, Kohl, 67, passed his mentor, Konrad Adenauer, to become the longest-serving chancellor in Germany's postwar history (since October 1982). He has fulfilled his dream of a unified Germany and currently leads the drive for a single European currency. The elder statesman among the world's leading industrialized nations, he intends to stand for election to a fifth term in 1998.

Helmut Kohl was the longest-serving Chancellor in the history of post-World War II Germany. Kohl, a servant of the Illuminati's inner circle, worked to unify Germany and empower the European Community. He is a Bilderberger, a covert Jewish Mason, and initiate of numerous secret societies and orders. Here we see the Chancellor strike an Illuminist pose, being the only person pictured who gives the necessary sign. (Photo: *Vanity Fair* magazine, November 1997)

Interview

Sharp Words From Iran

Iran's foreign minister talks about his government's evolving view of Saddam Hussein, Yasir Arafat and George Bush

BY LALLY WEYMOUTH

IS IRAN STILL IN THE "Axis of Evil" with North Korea and Iraq? Or could it be an ally in a future war against Saddam Hussein? In an exclusive interview, NEWSWEEK's Lally Weymouth grilled Iranian Foreign Minister Kamal Kharrazi in New York last week about his country's relations with tyrants and terrorists. Excerpts:

Would you support the United States if it goes to war against Saddam Hussein?

We are basically against a military operation against Iraq. Of course it all depends. If Americans are going to attack Iraq unilaterally, we certainly would not be supportive. In the case that Iraq does not comply [with U.N. resolutions] and the Security Council would authorize using force against Iraq, it would be a different story. But basically we cannot agree with the U.S. policy to use force in order to change the regime of another country.

I don't know how to put this delicately, but I can't imagine that you would be too sad to see Saddam Hussein go.

It is a matter of principle. We have the United Nations system. We believe that this is the right of people in each country to decide about their future, not others from the outside.

The Ayatollah Khomeini wanted to replace Saddam in the 1980s.

This is completely different. At that time Iraq had invaded Iran. We do not see Iraq invading the United States. The United States does not like the regime of Iraq. But the United States does not have any legitimate right to change it.

There have been reports that Al Qaeda members are in Iraq.

In the northern area there are some groups associated with Al Qaeda. The leader was arrested recently at the Meerabad [Iran] airport when he was trying to come to Iran illegally. He was sent to Amsterdam [where he was detained].

Do the Iraqis have weapons of mass destruction?

They have chemical weapons.

But let's face it, Israel hasn't been dropping chemical weapons on Iran.

No, not yet.

Why do you back Hizbullah, a terrorist group fighting Israel?

Hizbullah is a legitimate party in the Lebanese political system that has been resisting occupation.

> **[The Iraqis] have chemical weapons. They have used them against us. The inspectors will have to [determine] if there is a stockpile of weapons of mass destruction or not.**
>
> —KAMAL KHARRAZI

They have used them against us. The inspectors will have to [determine] if there is a stockpile of weapons of mass destruction or not.

Surely you think that those weapons should be eliminated.

Yes, sure. That is [also] the concern we have about Israel because it has nuclear, chemical and biological weapons and we believe that the Middle East should be free from any weapons of mass destruction.

Why in the world would you send a boat loaded with arms, the Karine A, to Palestinian leader Yasir Arafat?

Who says that we sent that?

The United States government.

This is an example of a United States government claim that is not substantiated. In fact we as the government of Iran have been asking everyone if there is any evidence to prove that this ship was loaded in Iran. But all the information was from Israeli sources. One has to be very simple-minded to fill up a

ship with arms manufactured in Iran and send it to Palestine under the eyes of satellites.

What are your relations now with Yasir Arafat?

I know that Arafat has not been doing a good job. This is for sure.

He has not been doing a good job how?

He has not been strong enough and he has been humiliated by the Israelis. There are differences among Palestinians themselves. Not all people support him. But still he is the president of Palestine.

Do you support suicide bombings?

I don't like these sorts of questions.

It is a pretty big issue.

No, this is not the way to interview. If you have any meaningful questions I will let you ask [them].

Do you recognize the right of Israel to exist as a state?

We do not recognize Israel as a government. We believe that eventually Palestinian refugees have to return to their homeland. Under the supervision of the United Nations, there should be a referendum and the original inhabitants of that land, including Palestinians, Jews and Christians, should decide about any political entity to be established.

How would you describe your relations with the United States?

Although Iran played a very important and constructive role in Afghanistan, right after the Afghanistan crisis President Bush came up with the notion of the "Axis of Evil." He accused us of supporting Al Qaeda, which was not true. Recently, the president asked the people of Iran to rise up against the government. All of this has been intervention in the affairs of Iran, which has been totally rejected by the Iranian people. ∎

KAMAL KHARRAZI

LOUAI BESHARA–AFP

Iran's foreign minister, Kamel Kharrazi. (*Newsweek*, September 30, 2002)

WORLD

THE SWORD OF ISLAM

With Pakistan isolated and near economic collapse, its leader plays the religion card

By TIM MCGIRK NEW DELHI

I'S BECOME A HABIT IN PAKISTAN THAT whenever a ruler's popularity disintegrates, he or she begins waving the scimitar of Islam. Never mind that not once since Pakistan became a nation 51 years ago has this noisy brandishing of faith ever worked to bolster the leader's popularity. Now, with Pakistan ostracized after its nuclear tests and on the edge of economic collapse, Prime Minister Mian Mohammed Nawaz Sharif is reviving the old custom of trying to make the Islamic Republic of Pakistan even more Islamic than it already is.

Even in the best of times, the implementation of Shari'a, or Islamic law, led to quarreling among the country's 72 Muslim sects and subsects over the "pure" interpretation of the law. And this could be the worst of times for Pakistan to try to revive fundamentalist laws. Everything seems to be going wrong for Nawaz Sharif. His support of the Taliban militia in neighboring Afghanistan has drawn enmity from Iran and the Central Asian republics (*see following story*). India and Pakistan have intensified their cross-border artillery fire in disputed Kashmir. Nearly bankrupt, Pakistan may run out of foreign

**DESPERATION
The Prime
Minister
wants
Pakistan to
become
more Islamic**

exchange by the end of the month, and the Karachi stock exchange imploded after the May 28 underground nuclear tests, wiping out half its share value.

If the nukes didn't scare off foreign investors, the mob outrage over the U.S. missile strike last month in nearby Afghanistan certainly did. Diplomats and executives from many Western companies fled Pakistan, fearing revenge attacks by supporters of Saudi extremist Osama bin Laden, the intended target of the American raid. In the port city of Karachi, ethnic gangs armed with grenades and machine guns prowl neighborhoods hunting for enemies. Sectarian rivalry among Muslims has become so fierce that some clergymen post bodyguards at their mosques to guard against bomb throwers speeding by on motorcycles. In Karachi, kidnappings of clergymen have become routine; their mosques are then seized by adversaries who try to convert the prayergoers to a harsher vision of Islam.

Will a stronger dose of religion cure Pakistan's ills? Many of Nawaz Sharif's countrymen think it could send Pakistan into terminal decline. According to the well-respected Karachi newspaper *Dawn*, people "just want a little improvement in their lives from the tyranny and callousness of Pakistani officialdom." Political opponents, including, of course, ex–Prime Minister Benazir Bhutto, say the new Islamic bill is likely to

WHO DEFINES WHAT IS "PURE"

increase that tyranny. One interpretation holds that this amendment will anoint Nawaz Sharif as a religious dictator, a supreme arbiter of what is considered good and evil under Islam. Nawaz Sharif, though, contends that only a strict adherence to Shari'a—which relies on the Koran and on the Sunna, a record of the Prophet Muhammad's deeds and sayings—can save Pakistan from "corruption and maladministration."

At the moment though, Nawaz Sharif is hoping for a more earthly kind of intervention: he is in New York City this week at the United Nations, where he will appeal to Bill Clinton to lift economic sanctions—imposed after the nuclear tests—and push the International Monetary Fund into mounting a rescue. As part of the trade-off, Clinton wants him to sign the nuclear test-ban treaty. This may help him get the money he urgently needs, but would anger fundamentalists at home who would see this as capitulation and surrender.

If Nawaz Sharif succeeds in driving his Islamic bill through both the National Assembly and the Senate in the coming weeks, Pakistan, long a reliable U.S. ally in South Asia, will become one of the world's

56

Pakistan's Prime Minister Mian Mohammed Nawaz. (*Time* magazine, September 28, 1998)

In Palestine, a senior Hamas official Khaled Mashaal welcomes Jordanian and other guests to a dinner.

Panama's President Guillermo Endara, installed in office by the U.S.A. after the American military deposed Army dictator Manuel Noriega. (From *U.S. News and World Report*, October 25, 1993, p. 37)

AMERICAN SURVEY

What is hand-on-heart Brady up to?

Now you see it, now

WASHINGTON, DC

AMATEUR detectives, two a penny in Washington, are weaving theories around the fact that the Federal Reserve chose on April 30th to cut its discount rate for the third time since December, this time from 6% to 5.5%. The circumstances have

Nicholas B tramped r ordinated dusty ansv When the

Nicholas Brady, Secretary of the Treasury in the first Bush Administration. The caption with this photo, published as part of an article knowingly entitled, "Now you see it, now you don't," asked *"What is hand-on-heart Brady up to?"* (The Economist, May 4, 1991, p. 25)

Monday, April 29, 2002

Newsline

■ News ■ Money ■ Sports ■ Life

By Tyrone L. Turner for USA TODAY

Choctaw Chief Phillip Martin lobbies in Washington.

Miss. tribe shows how to go from bust to boom

Factories, tourism employ thousands of non-Indians on Choctaw reservation.1B

Choctaw Indian chief Phillip Martin, head of a Choctaw reservation in Mississippi, lobbies in Washington. (Photo: *USA Today*, p. 1, April 29, 2002)

Reverend Ezra Stiles was one of the founders and an early President of Yale College (now University) in New Haven, Connecticut. A member of the Masonic Lodge, Stiles is giving the Lodge sign in this drawing, published in *The Literary Diary of Ezra Stiles, D.D., L.L.D, President of Yale College*, edited by Franklin Dexter, M.A. (Volume I, January 1, 1769-March 13, 1776). Above Stiles' head is the sacred sun symbol, and in his left hand he is displaying a mysterious book, which may or may not be the Holy Bible. Interesting, too, is the collar men of this era wore, which resembles the ancient, finely manicured beard of the Babylonian historical elite.

The founder of the Catholic order, the Jesuits, Ignatius Loyola. Loyola, a Spanish general, had been a member of the *Alumbrados*, the Order of the Illuminati. The Pope commissioned Loyola to counter the Protestant Reformation. Loyola's Jesuits used every means to do so, from deception to outright murder. To boost demonic control over the priests and soldiers of his new Jesuit Order, Loyola instituted methods of prayer and meditation taught by the Moslems and Moors. These *"Spiritual Exercises of Loyola"* continue to be employed by Jesuit priests and by monks, priests, and nuns of many other orders as well.

Robert Fludd (1574–1637), medical doctor and hermeticist of the late English Renaissance, was a Rosicrucian and practitioner of the magical arts who emphasized the power of visual and imaginative symbols.

Michael Servetus who, in 1535, was burned at the stake by Calvinists for having published a treatise disagreeing with the doctrine of the Trinity. Servetus, an enemy of Christ, was an Illuminist who worked to bring in heresies to pollute Christianity. He has been called "The Father of Unitarianism."

A top official of the Orthodox hierarchy in Greece gives the initiate sign.

The Pope with Palestinian leader Yassar Arafat, at the Vatican on September 15, 1982.

Eugene Vintras, a Frenchman who taught occult spiritual philosophy, wears the upside down cross on his religious robe and presents the sigil (hand sign) of his Order. Vintras gained a large following in the 1830s and 1840s by declaring the coming of a dark Prince, a god on earth who would rule and reign.

A chief rabbi in Ottoman Turkey (from the book, *The Lost Messiah: In Search of the Mystical Rabbi Sabbatai Sevi*, by John Freely (Woodstock and New York: The Overlook Press, 2001)

Aleister Crowley, as a youth, in his occult regalia. Crowley, whose books were the basis later for Anton LaVey, founder of the Church of Satan and Michael Aquino, founder of the Temple of Set. Crowley also inspired L. Ron Hubbard, founder of Scientology.

An elderly man who is chief dervish of the Sufi Moslem sect and a young boy who is a dervish in training in the early 1900s (from the book, *The Lost Messiah: In Search of the Mystical Rabbi Sabbatai Sevi*, by John Freely (Woodstock and New York: The Overlook Press, 2001)

Martin Luther, priest who set in motion the Protestant Reformation, is shown in this picture from *Christian News*, a periodic Lutheran publication, giving a masonic sign. The same Lutheran newspaper carries on its masthead (pg. 1) of every edition Luther's seal, of Rosicrucian design. In fact, Luther was a Rosicrucian. Masonic signs and grips closely parallel those of Rosicrucians (*Christian News*, February 18, 2003, p. 1).

In an article on the internet entitled "Calvinism," John Paul Jones quoted Masonic scholar Manly P. Hall, 33°, as affirming that Protestant reformer Martin Luther was a Rosicrucian initiate. In the article, Luther's official seal, middle, was depicted, along with the seal (far right) on Martin Luther's ring. At far left is Luther's seal with author Jones showing how if the petals of the flower are connected, an occult pentacle results.

Christopher Walken, actor, seems to be favored by the elite. He is often cast in strange roles as deranged psychos, mob killers, etc. *Interview* magazine devoted this entire page in its June 2004 edition, without caption and without comment or explanation. Obviously, the picture speaks for itself.

One fine date?
George Clooney at the *Perfect
Storm* premiere last June

In an article, strangely enough, entitled *"Gods and Monsters,"* Hollywood actor George Clooney is seen presenting his sigil as he stands outside a theatre presenting the world premier of the film, *A Perfect Storm.* (Photo: *Elle* magazine, November 2000)

Ad for Polo clothing in consumer magazine.

Michael A. Hoffman II   Secret Societies and Psychological Warfare   Page 56

Eating Raoul ...and Others

"How would you like to bite into a part-human bacon cheeseburger?" asks Michael Colgan, Ph.D., in the journal *Nutrition & fitness* (sic) (vol. 10, no. 1 & 2). In five years they'll be at a burger stand near you, predicts the author. The U.S. Department of Agriculture's research center in Beltsville, Md., has been inserting human genes into fertilized swine eggs, and a herd of "hupigs" now resides at the center. One goal of such research is to manufacture "spare parts for humans," that is, genetically engineered organs to replace diseased human organs; another goal is to "design" animals for more efficient meat production.

The USDA creatures reportedly suffer from coordination so poor that they can barely walk. They also are subject to arthritis and lung and gut diseases. State and federal laws severely restrict access by journalists and the public, and photographs of the "hunimals" are forbidden.

In Michael Hoffman's excellent book exposing the psychological and alchemical bases of the elite, *Secret Societies and Psychological Warfare*, the author included this news clipping about the horrors of inserting human genes into swine and other animals. The phrase *"Eating Raoul,"* comes from a cult-classic film about people who enjoy eating human flesh.

SEVENTEEN

Triangles Up, Triangles Down, Triangles, Triangles All Around

Everywhere one turns today the triangle is seen. On TV, and in art, architecture, product design, advertising, commercial packaging, and in religion it is ubiquitous. I am convinced that this simple, yet profound device, the triangle, somehow has a mystical, mesmerizing effect on men's minds. The never-ending blizzard of triangle designs we encounter daily is intended to induce a trance state in those who are bombarded day and night by it.

Back to Babylon

For an answer why the triangle may be the ultimate satanic symbol for Illuminists we go back in time to uncover its origins. A book on mathematics history called *Early Computations* tells us that "A Babylonian tablet dated around 1900 BC to 1600 BC and called 'Plimpton 322' deals with Pythagorean triplets." This ancient document detailed an elementary knowledge of triangles and proportions.

The Triangle as Woman's "Holy Door"

Barbara Walker, in her *The Woman's Encyclopedia of Myths and Secrets*, outlines how the ancient Mystery Religions greatly honored the triangle as the sign of deity. She notes that the Hindus, too, borrowed this emblem as their tantric (sexual) female Triangle of Life. It was known as the Kali Yantra, sign of the female vulva. In Egypt, the triangle was a hieroglyphic sign for "woman." In ancient Greece, the sexual intent is clear in that the triangle represented the Holy Door, genitalia of the All-Mother Demeter, known as "Mother Delta."[1]

"The triangle was everywhere connected with the female trinity, and a frequent component of monograms of goddesses," writes Walker.[2]

It is easily understood, therefore, why the gay homosexual movement adopted the sign of the *pink triangle* as its emblem. For male homosexuals particularly, the goddess image and feminine archetype were powerful motivators dictating adaptation of the triangle as symbol of "gay liberation."

To occultists, the triangle pointing upward represents *fire* and that pointing downward *water*. To combine, balance, and unite the two brings dualism, or *equilibrium*, which is a goal of Freemasonry and a cardinal tenet of all Illuminist religious systems.

The Pope's Triceps

The Vatican also got into the triangle act. In some Roman Catholic churches today, behind the altar we find displayed the all-seeing eye inside a triangle. Meanwhile, the Pope can often be seen wearing the symbol of the *triceps* on his vestments or on his Dagon Fish God hat, which has its own unique triangular design.

The triceps is a Nordic design of three earth diamonds thought to invoke earth energy powers and spiritual magic. By adding straight lines on its three sides to fill in the open spaces, we discover that the Triceps unexpectedly becomes a larger triangle with a concealed Jewish Star of David (six-pointed star) within.

The Catholic Pope often wears this symbol, the Triceps. If the broken sides are filled in by straight lines from the tip to tip, the Triceps becomes a single, larger triangle bearing a six-pointed star in its center. Here we have the concealed Jewish Star of David being worn by the Pope.

The Triangle and Freemasonry

Many erroneously believe that Freemasonry is a Christian religion and may be misled into thinking that the prominent use of the triangle in its rituals and its display of icons has a Christian purpose. But in his book, *A Bridge to Light*, an official Scottish Rite publication of the Supreme Mother Council, 33°, Rex Hutchins, 33° explains that the triangle of the Masonic Lodge represents pagan religions as well and he especially cites the Hindu trinity of gods, Brahma, Vishnu, and Shiva.[3]

I have mentioned elsewhere that a triangle symbol containing a letter "Y" inside which divides it internally into three triangles is called the *Eye of the Dragon*, or Dragon's Eye. Since Freemasonry has its all-seeing eye which represents Satan, the Dragon, again we have a connection.

Dragon's Eye

The Triangle and Astrology

In astrology we find the concept of the *grand trine*, which is considered very, very lucky. Joan Quigley, astrologer to movie stars and to President Ronald Reagan and First Lady Nancy Reagan, says that, "the grand trine is formed by three planets approximately 120 degrees apart. When you see this sign in the planets when forecasting their horoscope, you know they are about to hit (figuratively) a "grand slam home run."[4]

Quigley illustrates the grand trine in her book, *What Does Joan Say? – My Seven*

Years As White House Astrologer to Nancy and Ronald Reagan.[5] As it turns out, the astrological symbol for a grand trine is a *triangle inside a circle*.

This is the same symbol configuration adapted by Alcoholics Anonymous (AA) founder Bill Wilson to be the official logo of AA. My extensive research of Bill Wilson's life documents he was an occultist. He despised Christianity and adopted AA's concept of worship of an unnamed "Higher Power" to substitute for Jesus. Wilson came up with the logo for AA from a dream he had in which he saw the image of the triangle within a circle and *knew* it was to become the logo for AA.[6]

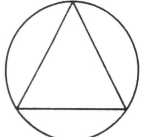

Grand Trine of Astrology

Do the Illuminati Secretly Worship the Great Goddess?

It is interesting that in the Jewish Cabala, we again find use of the triangle as a feminine vulva sign. Of the ten Sephiroth, the third Sephira, or Triad, is deemed of feminine potency. Formed as a triangle, it represents the "great productive Mother, who copulates and is united sexually with the Father." In effect, to cabalists she is the feminine form of "God."[7]

Just as Masons decry the equality of ordinary women, even denying women the opportunity to become a Mason in most orders, so do Orthodox Jews who practice cabalism openly proscribe and limit women's rights. Yet, we see that deeply hidden and imbedded in their secret doctrine, both Masonry and Cabalistic Judaism revere and honor the Great Goddess, just as does Roman Catholicism in the form of Mother Mary.

It may surprise male chauvinists, but the Goddess, the consort of Lucifer, the woman figure whose sign is the downward pointing triangle, reigns side-by-side with Jahbuhlun (Satan) over the Illuminati and its minions.

Corporate Triangle Logos—A Sign of Illuminati Influence?

The above logos are trademarked by the corporations concerned.

So many priests are now outed as homosexuals and pedophiles, this noted Catholic publication, *The Catholic World Report* devoted a special edition to the topic. The editors of this cover of the January, 1997, edition, call the problem a "Rebellion." The smiling Catholic prelate has a pink triangle on the cross, symbol of his cap (itself triangle-shaped upward) and the Bishop's hands are fixed in the triangle downward (feminine, delta position).

Homosexual activists have latched onto the pink-colored *triangle* as the chosen motif for their protests and demonstrations. On this page we find demonstrators holding up placards with the pink triangle and, at a university, the pink triangle against a black circle background on the hands of gay students. Then there is the *"Subscribe!"* to *Frontiers* magazine ad card, featuring a gay man with a rainbow-colored triangle on his chest. The newspaper clipping, *"Colored Triangle Has Become Badge of Honor For Gays,"* comes from the Montreal, Canada, *Gazette* newspaper, June 28, 1992.

Colored triangle has become badge of honor for gays

CINDY RODRIGUEZ
HARTFORD COURANT

HARTFORD, Conn. —Gay men wore pink, and lesbians wore black.

Nazi Germany forced gay men and women to wear colored triangles as an announcement of their homosexuality — symbols of oppression and discrimination.

Over time the gay community has reclaimed the triangles and revised the meaning: they now symbolize gay pride.

"Never again will we let ourselves be oppressed," said Baruch Gould, 48, of New London, Conn., who wears a pink triangle as a "badge of honor."

Pink and black triangles have been highly visible at parades and other gay festivities in June, which is designated Gay Pride Month.

The triangles are not the only signs that have special meaning to those who wear them.

Rainbow flags, freedom rings, the labyris (a double-bladed axe), interlinked woman's symbols, the Greek letter lambda and the color lavender also are worn by those wishing to visually express pride for their homosexuality.

Rainbows symbolize hope for better days, Gould said. The colors represent a diverse world, while the arch gives a feeling of shelter.

Freedom rings are the most recent items to carry the rainbow. Introduced a year ago, they are a set of six aluminum rings — each a different color of the rainbow.

Designed by New York artist David Spada, the rainbows also appear in earrings, necklaces, bracelets, key rings and on caps and suspenders.

"For me, it's a visible piece of being lesbian and being proud of who I am," said Shawn Lang, 36, who wears freedom rings.

The labyris represents the double-bladed axe used by an ancient Amazonian goddess.

The Woman's Encyclopedia of Myths and Secrets by Barbara Walker says the labyris "has been adopted by lesbians as a symbol of reminiscence of the all-female community of Lesbos and its founding mothers, who worshiped only the goddess in nature and in each other."

The Greek letter lambda is used by men and women and are found on T-shirts, posters and jewelry. The the arms on the letter resemble the arms of justice and represent gay and lesbian rights.

Lavender's mixture of red and blue — colors associated with women and men — is a symbol of androgyny, Gould said. ☐

Triangle on Bible: At the inauguration of the first President of the United States, April 30, 1789, in New York City, a Bible was provided by a Masonic lodge nearby and opened to Genesis chapters 49 and 50 where the familiar occult design of a *circle inside a triangle* just happens to be printed as an artist's illustration. George Washington pressed his palm to the book as the oath was administered and then kissed it. A member of the lodge then marked the page for succeeding generations. The year 2005 marked the fifth time the tome has been lent for a presidential inauguration, as another George celebrated the 216th anniversary of the inaugural Bible.

This official postcard, widely circulated by the Communist government in Russia following the Jewish Bolshevik takeover, is entitled "Leaders of the Proletarian Revolution." The postcard reveals the Jewishness of these original leaders of the Communist Party. All six shown, including Lenin and Trotsky, are Jews! Also observe the double triangle arrangement of the placement of the six individuals.

Triangular structure at gala opening ceremony of 2002 Winter Olympics in Salt Lake City, Utah. (Photo: *Newsweek*, February 18, 2002)

The ball to be used for New York's famous Times Square New Years Eve gala event is being put together by technicians. It is made up of 504 *triangle-shaped* Waterford "Hope For Healing" Crystals. The inset shows the final, interior design of each triangle. (Photo and story: *USA Today*, December 31, 2001, p. D1)

An employee at *Amazon.com*, the internet book sale firm, stacks boxes of copies of the occult kids novel, *Harry Potter and the Order of the Phoenix* at the company's warehouse. The book, oddly enough, in this photo is shown being stacked upside down. The trapezoid-shaped box of each book has the words *"Deeper Secrets, Darker Powers, Stronger Magic."* (Photo and news: Associated Press, June 18, 2003)

Tobey Maguire as jockey Red Pollard astride one of the eight horses that played Seabiscuit in the hit film

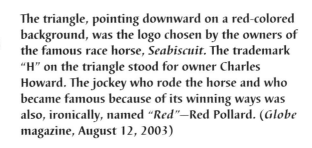

The triangle, pointing downward on a red-colored background, was the logo chosen by the owners of the famous race horse, *Seabiscuit*. The trademark "H" on the triangle stood for owner Charles Howard. The jockey who rode the horse and who became famous because of its winning ways was also, ironically, named *"Red"*—Red Pollard. (*Globe* magazine, August 12, 2003)

According to *An Illustrated Encyclopedia of Traditional Symbols*, this illustration is packed with occult and alchemical symbols. However, the triangle is the focal point. Inside the triangle (the triangle with concentric circles surrounding it) is the astrological and generative symbols of male and female combined, the Hermaphrodite. This is indicative of the Illuminati's principle of integration, or synthesis, of the dialectical process.

Three symbols used by the Ordo Templi Orientis, (OTO) and by the Order of the Golden Dawn, each employing the triangle device. At left, the Eye of Horus in the pyramid of fire, radiating the solar blaze. Right—the seal of the Great White Brotherhood, the spirit hierarchy, showing the design of Babalon; and below is the seal of the OTO. This latter symbol was used by satanist Aleister Crowley on the title page of his spirit-channeled, 1904 book, *The Book of The Law.* Next to the seal, Crowley signed the name "Baphomet."

Also From Dorset Press:

MOZART
by Marcia Davenport

A SHORT HISTORY OF MUSIC
by Alfred Einstein

THE BROTHERHOOD:
The Secret World of the Freemasons
by Stephen Knight

ISBN 0-88029-159-1

This is the back cover of the book, *Mozart and Freemasonry*, published by Dorset Press, a firm that publishes many masonic-related volumes. The triangle symbol is prominent. Within the triangle is the three-headed serpent, most likely representing the unholy trinity. Also, a smaller symbol, subtle and tiny, near the head of the serpent, is an image of some type of creature with a lightning bolt out of its head. Mozart, considered today a great composer and famous even during his lifetime, was murdered by the Masons in 1791 as penalty for his revealing of the secrets of Freemasonic ritual in his work entitled, *The Magic Flute.* Not only was the composer murdered (by poisoning), but the Masons blackballed his funeral. It is said that even Mozart's closest friends and family members did not so much as attend his funeral.

This is the symbol of the *Lucis Trust*, New York City. Led by high-level Masons, co-Masons (women), theosophists, and other occultists, the Lucis Trust has on its rolls many top United Nations officials. Its logo, the triangle, contains the *"X"* sign and also the three-pronged *Trident*, symbol of the triple phallus. In India, the trident-bearer is the god Shiva, bridegroom of the triple goddess, Kali. In Greek and Roman mythologies, the trident symbolized, among others, Hades, Pluto, Neptune, and Poseidon. And, of course, the Devil is often pictured with his three-pronged pitchfork.

mbol of
Military

Rock'n'roll magazines and CD album covers are littered with satanic triangles. This one is on the cover of *RIP* magazine.

Alex Sanders, below, employs the ascendant triangle sign in this witchcraft ritual. Sanders, a warlock, is famous throughout Great Britain as a witchcraft leader. The woman with him is also a witch. (Photo from the book, *Witchcraft, Magic, and the Supernatural*, Mandarin Publishers/Octopus Books, Hong Kong, 1974)

Joe Mansueto, founder of *Morningstar*, the number one company rating mutual funds on Wall Street. (*Newsweek*, October 10, 1994)

Bad blood: *Mansueto, a Value Line ad*

Newsweek magazine (November 5, 2001), in the caption to this picture, describes the man at center signaling the ascendant triangle hand sign as *"Rashid Dostum. A sadistic warlord who once ran the secret police in a Soviet puppet government in Kabul."*

EUREKA:
Andreessen
and his team
unleashed the
modern Web

The Killer Browser

It's been only a decade since the release of Mosaic, the Web application that changed finance, commerce, culture—and the world

BY STEVEN LEVY

JUST ABOUT THE ONLY place you could get something to eat at 4 in the morning in Champaign, Ill., in early 1993 was a convenience store called the White Hen Pantry. "It's kind of a Midwest 7-Eleven," says Marc Andreessen, who would often stumble out of his workspace at the National Center for Supercomputing Applications at ungodly hours in search of sustenance. Andreessen, 21 years old at the time, and fellow NCSA worker Eric Bina were working on a program they called Mosaic. One night at the White Hen, Andreessen scanned the newsstand and saw the first issue of a magazine called Wired. "I thought, 'Wow, this is pretty interesting stuff'," he recalls of the magazine that promised to treat technology as a cultural breakthrough. "But you know what? The magazine didn't mention the Internet once."

The project that Andreessen and Bina were hatching would change that. Posted on the Internet in beta form—free of charge—in March 1993 and in an official release the following month, Mosaic just may have been the most important computer application ever. It was the first major Web browser, a strange concept at the time because almost no one had ever heard of the Web. The Internet had been around for 20 years, of course, but was known mostly to technically competent students, researchers and government workers. In 1990 Tim Berners-Lee, a British researcher at the CERN physics lab in Geneva, Switzerland, had created a set of technical rules for what he hoped would become a universal Internet document center called the World Wide Web; it was getting some buzz in the research community as a way to digitally distribute papers, but the first browsers were text-based only and hard to use. Andreessen and Bina's program handled graphics and was easy to use.

Mosaic was an instant success online. Within six months more than a million people had downloaded it. A cycle of motion had begun. Before Mosaic, there were only a few hundred Web sites. But when huge numbers of people were able to access

Marc Andreessen, computer scientist who in 1993 developed a program called *Mosaic* while working at the National Center for Supercomputing Applications. Mosaic was the first web browser and made the internet possible. (Photo: *Newsweek*, April 21, 2003, p. E6)

Two media titans confer: Viacom's chairman, Sumner Redstone (a Jew—Redstone is not his real name), and Viacom's President Mel Karmazin, also Jewish. Viacom owns CBS, MTV, Disney, and many other media properties, all firmly in the Zionist camp editorially and subject-wise. (Photo: *U.S. News & World Report*, June 14, 2004, p. 70)

This scene is set at the White House in March, 2001, with Israeli Prime Minister Ariel Sharon and President George W. Bush both presenting mirror-image descending (female, delta, or vulva) triangles. Two triangles joined together constitute a Jewish Star of David. For added *subliminal power*, the room was arranged so that the bust of Lincoln was directly behind Sharon. The message: In bludgeoning hapless Palestinians and denying them their own state, Sharon is simply being Lincolnesque. After all, Lincoln put down the Southern insurrection, right? (Photo and article: *USA Today*, March 21, 2001, p. 13A)

Michael Moore, liberal Democratic Party propagandist and maker of documentaries, no doubt takes pleasure in signaling the triangle. Moore, a Jew, is agented by the brother of the Clinton insider many suspect was the mysterious Mossad espionage agent codenamed *"Mega"* (Photo: *Time*, May 13, 2004, p. 72)

At the Parliament of the World's Religions in Chicago, a Rockefeller-funded event, an Episcopal Bishop (second from left) has fellowship with an unidentified couple and with Donald Frew, far right, a warlock (male witch) who oversees 70 covens. Note Frew's use of the sign of the warlock (ascendant) triangle. (Photo: *SCP* Newsletter, Winter 2005)

Governor Edwin Edwards of Louisiana, just convicted of taking bribes and pay-offs, is apparently appealing to *"higher powers."* Notice the caption in the clipping just under Edwards' photograph. (Photo: *Oxford American,* May/June 2001)

An honest politician is one who stays bought.   —a Louisiana saying

Tyler Bridges, who was part of a team that won the 1999 Pulitzer Prize for investigative reporting, has written an enthralling

short history of attitudes toward corruption and gambling. He reveals that from the beginning Louisiana has been a place where people of wealth and power have kept the population under their thumbs—from the original French and Spanish coloniz-ers, who tried to populate the area just so they could turn a buck on its inhabitants, to the plantation owners, lum-ber barons, and on up to the postbellum breed of crooked politicians

Are these hand signs mere accidents, or do they convey a concealed, occult meaning? Left is Richard Buy; right is an unidentified man making the *"X"* with his arms and hands, while Mr. Buy is presenting the ascendant triangle. The occasion was the House Committee's hearings on the Enron Corporation's financial failure debacle. Mr. Buy was a high-level Enron financial officer. Were these hand signs intended to invoke protection or perhaps to influence Illuminist puppets on the Committee? (Photo: *Knight-Ridder*, in *Austin American-Statesman* newspaper, February 8, 2002, p. A13)

This comes from *Newsweek* (July 9, 2001) and is a brief Q & A with black hip-hop recording star Caushun who is communicating a nonverbal message with his hands.

QUESTIONS & ANSWERS

Can Hip-Hop Handle a Gay Rapper?

NEWSWEEK: How'd you get started?
CAUSHUN: I called into a radio station to rhyme [on the air], and they shunned me. They heard my voice, and they was like, "Oh, wait a minute, are you sweet?" Had I sounded more thuggish, they would've let me on. After that, I was like, "You all are gonna hear me."

Is the homophobia and misogyny in hip-hop overpublicized?
There are artists you can call

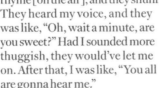

"studio thugs." They're made to appear that they're so against women and homosexuals. But you have a conversation with them and realize they're not homophobic at all.

Are there many gay people working behind the scenes in hip-hop?
We're there, honey. You have hip-hop artists wearing flamingo-pink suits. Think that was a heterosexual's idea? *(Log on for Jane Spencer's full Q&A.)*

THE NEW FACE AT FOGGY BOTTOM

Condoleezza Rice has Bush's ear, but can she sell his ideas abroad?

BY KEVIN WHITELAW
AND THOMAS OMESTAD

DAVID Y. LEE—POLARIS FOR USN&WR

In nearly four years as President Bush's national security adviser, Condoleezza Rice was much more than just one of his top aides. She became a close confidant who regularly accompanied the first family to their Texas ranch, where she dined with them and joined them for walks through the bluebonnet fields and cedar groves. She became almost a family member.

In nominating Rice to be his next secretary of state, Bush is signaling the world (and all those doubtful State Department diplomats) that he has no intention of pulling back from his assertive post-9/11 foreign-policy agenda. Rice, the consummate insider who has the ear of the president, will be a sharp contrast to the departing Colin Powell, an American icon who was always a distinct outsider in the clubby Bush administration. Bush aides hope that Rice will be able to avoid the kind of infighting that roiled Bush's first term and to sell Bush's policies abroad. That won't be easy. Laments an anxious European envoy: "Now we have to worry whether the ideologues will somehow exert even more influence."

A purge? On a personal level, Rice will bring her immense charm and a touch of

prevent Vice President Cheney from intruding on her turf. Some Bush critics, including Republicans who served his father, fear that Rice's mission will be to rid the State Department of Bush policy critics—or at least neutralize them. "It looks like there will be a purge," says a former senior U.S. official who served two Republican presidents. "If you said hello to Colin in the halls, you're gone." may be l

dier,'" says one of his advisers. "'Sometimes I'll win, and sometimes I'll lose.'"

In the end, Powell, 67, will most likely be remembered for his role surrounding the Iraq war. He did help persuade Bush to seek the support of the United Nations. In doing so, he also put a moderate face on the case for war. Aides say Powell now sees his low point as his Feb. 5, 2003, U.N. presentation of intelligence evidence on Iraq's presu

POWER TEAM. Rice seated alongside Defense Secretary Donald Rumsfeld in the Oval Office

Observe Secretary of Defense Donald Rumsfeld as he displays the ascendant triangle sign. (*U.S. News & World Report*, November 29, 2004, p. 20)

Billboard in Russia. Hand position (triangular) reinforces the black/white, yin/yang triangle logo.

This revealing photo of three-star U.S. Air Force General Claudia Kennedy was run both on the cover of mass circulation *Parade* magazine and *Newsweek* (June 26, 2000, p. 23). Evidently, the elite wanted the message out to their servants that this photo conveys. Note particularly the General's clearly staged hand sign, her back against a wall, a purposeful shadow etched behind, her two feet squarely in place, her standing in the midst of two evergreen shrubbery bushes, and the seemingly bizarre fact she has her eyes closed! All in all a very unflattering picture, but one that conveys much information. At the time (2000), General Kennedy, an intelligence operative who was retiring from the military service, was being touted as a potential presidential candidate. Did the Illuminati choose other career options for the lady?

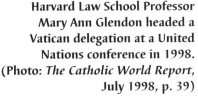

Harvard Law School Professor Mary Ann Glendon headed a Vatican delegation at a United Nations conference in 1998. (Photo: *The Catholic World Report*, July 1998, p. 39)

DAVID STRICK—OUTLINE

No circus trial for Intel's Andy Grove

Intel is no Microsoft

The company settles its antitrust case

BY WILLIAM J. COOK

Round II in the federal government's antitrust assault on the dynamic duo known as "Wintel" (as in Microsoft Windows and Intel microprocessors) has been called off. One day before a Federal Trade Commission trial of Intel Corp. was to begin last week, the two sides agreed to settle the case. Specific terms will not be announced until FTC commissioners vote on the agreement, but clearly Intel has promised to change its business practices enough to satisfy the government's antitrust prosecutors.

Intel had been charged with using its near monopoly power to bully customers. The chip maker had demanded that some of them hand over, free of charge, certain proprietary data. In one case, according to the FTC, Intel wanted technology held by

It appears from the position of his hands that computer chip magnate Andy Grove, Jewish head of Intel, wants to get across his "message," doesn't it? (*U.S. News & World Report*, March 22, 1999, p. 52)

MADNESS 2001: ARIZONA'S SECOND CHANCE ... OTHER SURVIVORS

ESPN

NOTORIOUS MVP
A.I. SHAKES THE RAP ... AND ROCKS THE GAME

Cover of *ESPN* magazine, published by ESPN Sports channel.

Actress Doris Day has more of a message to communicate than merely her innocent usual clean-girl image. Maybe the well-known Hollywood producer was right who, when asked about Day, quipped, *"Oh yes, I've known her a long, long time. Why, I even knew Doris Day before she became a virgin!"*

The rock music group R.E.M. is featured in this *USA Today* feature (October 5, 2004). The writer says that R.E.M.'s new album, *Around the Sun* explores "the darker side of modern America."

Music

Somber sounds: Michael Stipe, front, Mike Mills and Peter Buck of R.E.M. explore the darker side of modern America on *Around the Sun.*

Warner Bros. Records

Dave Matthews Band: Solid as a rock star

Flying high: "At this point, we get to do pretty much what we want. ... And we don't want anything bad enough to bow down for it," says Dave Matthews, center. From left are Stefan Lessard, Boyd Tinsley, Carter Beauford and Leroi Moore.

By Dan Winters, RCA Records

Here we see the hand signal is the focal center—what they want the viewer to take note of. All except one person's hands are concealed. In this article in *USA Today* newspaper (March 12, 2001), Dave Matthews, center, of the popular rock group, *Dave Matthews Band*, brags, "At this point, we get to do pretty much what we want..." This sounds like satanic priest Aleister Crowley's dictum, "Do as thou wilt shall be the whole of the law."

ANXIOUS: Cartier at home in Queens, amid photos of his son James, who died in the attacks

the way Feinberg is trying to implement it is as fair as possible—which is surprising given that the law was passed in a frenzy of midnight drafting just after the attacks.

The fund was an add-on to an emerg[...] Trade Center or the Pentagon, plus the owners of the Twin Towers, the businesses in and around the towers and anyone else damaged that day—a stadium's worth of [...]ose claims could easily exceed [...] ance coverage. This meant that although thousands of people and businesses might sue the airlines, the pot from which they could collect would be limited to the insurers' $1.5 billion per crash—or $6 billion [...]

According to "tradition," the next of kin at military funerals are given a flag folded into a triangle with exactly six stars showing. Few families of victims know that the tradition appears to be of Masonic origins. (Photo: *Newsweek*, January 7, 2002, p. 29)

BARADEI BOMBED

The United States is ratcheting up its efforts to oust Mohammed ElBaradei, the head of the UN's nuclear watchdog agency, because U.S. officials say he claims Iran's nuclear program may just be to generate power. ElBaradei's track record on accurately assessing countries' weapons programs has been better than the United States. Previously ElBaradei had come in conflict with U.S. officials because he had disputed American neo-cons' claims that Iraq had a nuclear weapons program. We all know who was right about that.

In 1990 this photo of U.S.S.R.'s KGB Chief Vladimir Kryuchkov was published in *The European* newspaper (December 14–16, 1990, p. 7). The caption read: *"KGB head Vladimir Kryuchkov has dispelled illusions of the new 'Mr. Nice Guy' approach with his chilling attack on separatists."* Kryuchkov's hand sign shows he has approval of Illuminati superiors for his new "Tough Guy" approach.

Mohammed El Baradei, head of the United Nation's International Atomic Energy Association, the world's nuclear watchdog agency, signals with his hands that he is in league with the Illuminati elite. (*American Free Press*, February 21, 2005, p. 2)

Meeting with First Lady Nancy Reagan is Pope John Paul II. At left—the pontiff displays yet another masonic sign, that of Hand on Heart, with thumb communicating, "I'm on the square."

The Pope does it again, with President Ronald Reagan and First Lady Nancy at his side. As an aside—
the skull cap, in many color variations, is worn by Jews and high Catholic clergy alike, though its use
hearkens back to the horrific memory of Jesus crucified on Calvary, Golgotha, "the place of the skull."
(Photo: Book, *Pope John Paul II Visits America: A Celebration In Pictures*, New York: Crescent Books)

TOYOTA
DRIVING DETROIT
EVEN CRAZIER (P. 50)

CISCO STRUGGLING
TO BE A GROWTH
COMPANY AGAIN (P. 62)

SOUTHWEST
A NEW CEO's BOLD
STRATEGY (P. 60)

The McGraw·Hill Companies

BusinessWeek

FEBRUARY 21, 2005

www.businessweek.com

CAN ANYONE SAVE HP?

BY BEN ELGIN (P. 28)

Plus: The Story Behind Carly's Ouster

```
#BXBBGDD ***CR LOT 0155A*R073
#1708PEPOW97 3#695348      BX027513
                           040268
EXECUTIVE          SEP 05 05  0622
POWER OF PROPHECY       P019
1708 PATTERSON RD
AUSTIN       TX  78733-6507
```

Former Hewlett-Packard CEO, Carly Fiorina

This cover of one of many *Star Wars* publications, pictures a character (top, left) from that movie saga giving what is clearly a combination of two masonic signs. (From an ad collage in a Sci-Fi magazine)

Full page consumer ad for Phoenix Wealth Management, an investment firm. For info on the Phoenix as symbol, see the chapter in *Codex Magica*, examining the double-headed eagle (p. 341).

*Τὸ Β΄ Οἰκουμενιστικὸν συμπόσιον τοῦ ἱδρύματος Εὐρώπης Δραγάν. Συνῆλ-
θεν εἰς Ἀθήνας (11-6-1969) μὲ θέμα «τὸν κοινὸν ἑορτασμὸν τοῦ Ἁγίου
Πάσχα». Εἰς τὸ κέντρον διακρίνεται ὁ τότε «μητροπολίτης» Ἰωαννίνων κ.
Σεραφεὶμ νῦν «ἀρχιεπίσκοπος» νεοημερολογιτῶν, μὲ τὸν μέγαν ρεφερενδά-
ριον τοῦ «οἰκουμενικοῦ» πατριαρχείου, πρόεδρον τοῦ ἱδρύματος, κ. Κων/νον
Δραγάν.*

**Catholic Cardinals and Bishops meet with Orthodox counterparts in Greece. Observe the
hand sign of the Catholic prelate who's third from the left and also the double-headed
eagle logo on the wall behind the group.**

Ad in a tabloid for Miss
Cleo, who became somewhat
of a TV icon in the 1990s
hawking her psychic abilities
as a Tarot Card reader. Her
money-making powers
dimmed when the Feds
launched an investigation of
what some reported as a
scam.

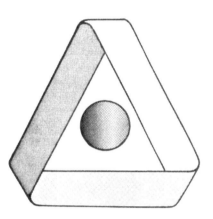
A New Age group paid for this ad offering a symposium to be led by top New Age occultists Jean Houston, Joseph Campbell, and James Hillman. Jean Houston was and is a spiritual guide and mentor for Senator Hillary Rodham Clinton (D-NY). Joseph Campbell promoted symbols and masonic New Age philosophies in a popular series aired over the Public Broadcasting System (PBS) network on the *Bill Moyers* program.

The Stelle Group, a New Age community, offers to interested persons this brochure which entices the reader to maximize the "hidden powers" of his or her mind by seeking initiation into a Brotherhood. The founder of Stelle Group says that spirit beings gave him his initiation and actually made a sign, or marking in his body.

Historic photograph of Russia's last Romanov dynasty czar, Nicholas II, and his family. Though connected with other Illuminati dynasties, the Romanovs were despised by the Bolshevik Zionists, Lenin and Trotsky, who in 1917 took over Russia and deposed the czar and set up their Communist dictatorship. The Zionists, under orders from Lenin, kidnapped, then murdered the entire family shown here.

House Minority Leader Richard Gephardt (left) is known to be both a Mason and a lap-dog of Illuminati interests. At right is House Speaker Dennis Hastert, giving the sign of the (delta, vulva) triangle. (Photo and article: *USA Today*, September 17, 2001)

Attacks prompt lawmakers

They are likely to drop items that divide them and focus on healing

By William M. Welch
USA TODAY

WASHINGTON — Congress is responding to last week's terrorist attacks with a dramatic reordering of its priority list, focusing full attention on the nation's security and putting aside issues that it has spent months or years debating.

Big-ticket proposals such as a prescription-drug benefit for seniors, which backers hoped to push this fall, and an overhaul of Social Security, which the Bush administration was seeking, appear unlikely to go anywhere in the fore-

By Chris Kleponis, *Fox News Sunday*, via AP

Undergoing transformation: House Minority Leader Richard Gephardt, left, and House Speaker Dennis Hastert discuss terrorist attacks.

Congress

seeable future. Congressional leaders in both parties say they probably will abandon or stall other issues that have divided rather than united lawmakers.

In their place, Congress is tightly focusing on the immediate tasks at hand: recovering and rebuilding the terrorist attacks, finan-

like health care, campaign-finance reform, maybe even the energy bill are going to have to be put on the side burner."

The events have transformed Congress in a way unimaginable before. Gephardt and House Speaker Dennis Hastert, R-Ill., scarcely on speaking terms before

keep lawmakers in Washington until Thanksgiving. Now they are talking about trying to move swiftly on annual government spending bills and finishing up in October.

Congress left town for the weekend after overwhelmingly approving $40 billion in eme

A better Life

Health, education & science

By Bebeto Matthews, AP

Living history: Alice Cohn Ginott was one of Alfred Kinsey's research subjects more than 50 years ago.

Kinsey's study still vital after 50 years

In 1944, Alice Ginott Cohn joined thousands of women who openly discussed a subject most others only whispered about: sex. The result of those private interviews was Alfred Kinsey's landmark book *Sexual Behavior in the Human Female*, which shocked the world in 1953 with its explicit revelations. Indiana University, which fostered the research, marks the book's 50th anniversary in 2003 with a year-long series of art exhibitions, film festivals and lectures exploring women's health and sexuality, the arts, science and history. Mostly, though, the school

Actor Martin Short (*People* magazine, July 14, 1997, p. 148)

Alice Cohn Ginott, a Jewish woman who participated in satanist Indiana University Professor Alfred Kinsey's sex studies. Ginott says she gave an interview to Kinsey's group. Hopefully, Ginott had no idea of Kinsey's bisexual proclivities nor of his child molestation activities. Quite possibly, Ginott doesn't intentionally sign the feminine triangle, either. (Photo: *USA Today*, January 27, 2003)

Right: Picture of Israeli singer, *Yosefa*, in the pages of *The Jerusalem Report* (October 19, 1995). Yosefa's album, *"The Desert Speaks,"* was released worldwide by EMI Records.

A HERO'S DEATH: THE NFL'S PAT TILLMAN

Newsweek

May 3, 2004: $3.95

newsweek.msnbc.com

Teresa

Is John Kerry's Heiress Wife a Loose Cannon—Or Crazy Like a Fox?

‖‖‖‖‖‖‖‖‖‖‖‖‖‖‖‖‖‖‖‖‖‖‖‖‖

```
#BXBCMDG *******CAR-RT LOT**R-073
#NWM0069914091/7#11 23MAY05 N6 Z
POWER OF PROPHECY
1708 PATTERSON LN           031
AUSTIN      TX 78733-6507   404
                           106627
```

Teresa Heinz Kerry, philanthropist and political spouse

Teresa Heinz-Kerry, the fabulously rich heiress of a colonialist fortune, who married two—count them—two U.S. Senators who were each initiates of the Skull & Bones, John Heinz and John Kerry (Teresa married Kerry after Heinz was killed in a mysterious airplane crash). Teresa, a Jewess whose maiden name was Simoes-Ferreira, is a board member of the Illuminati-run Carnegie Institute, a member of the Council on Foreign Relations, and a member of the Brookings Institute. Illuminati institutions all.

No doubt about the Illuminist staging here. Václav Havel, President of the Czech Republic, in *Parade* magazine (September 24, 2000), was lionized by the media as a poor dissident poet who helped to overthrow the Communists in Czechoslovakia. However, it has now come out that during the Communist era, Havel lived in luxurious apartments and drove around in two Mercedes. Havel is known to be a New Age occultist who has had meditation sessions with his friend, the Dalai Lama, the so-called "Tibetan god-man."

Hollywood movie director, Robert Altman, pictured in *The European* newspaper (September 12, 1993, p. 17). The newspaper's headline labeled Altman in a positive way as the "Lion of Venice."

EIGHTEEN

Black Magic, Masonic Witchcraft, and Triangle Powers

Ever wonder why the Masons installed the statue of a woman in stone atop the U.S. Capitol building in Washington, D.C., and the statue of a woman called "Liberty" in New York City's harbor? Well, now you know. America, meet your satanic mistress, Isis.

— Texe Marrs

The triangle is of primary importance in all Illuminati realms, whether in the ritual ceremonies of the Rosicrucians and Masons or the witchcraft, astrological and black magic practices of other Illuminist followers. Always the triangle is used.

Among satanists and witches, the double triangle, the Seal of Solomon, also called the hexagram, is of great interest. This seal, known as the *Magen David* of the Jews, is actually composed of two triangles, superimposed on each other. One triangle pointed upward represents the flesh or material matter and the male generative act; the other, pointed downward, signifies female sexuality and the spiritual plane.

Therefore we have a masculine and a feminine triangle integrated. This indicates sexual union, the sex act, and the reconciliation of opposites, yin and yang, or God and Satan. The blasphemous suggestion in the symbol becomes clear.

Remember: Everywhere in the world of Illuminism, we discover sexual connotations. Theirs is a sex cult; indeed it is the world's greatest sex cult; yet, the Illuminati use symbols and signs to mask their sexually perverted messages.

The Star of David and the Beast's Number, 666

The supremely evil nature of the double triangle, the hexagram, Solomon's Seal, the Magen David (Shield of David), is proven by the fact that the symbol contains the hidden number *666*, the number of the beast *(Revelation 13)*. Notice that there are six triangles incorporated on the outside of the hexagram; that it has six out points, and that six lines are used in constructing the symbol's two triangles. Thus, 6-6-6.

Also, the symbol incorporates six triangles of three sides each. Six times three equals eighteen (6 X 3 = 18 and 6 + 6 + 6 = 18).

An outstanding study of the six-pointed star was accomplished by Dr. O.J. Graham in the book, *The Six-Pointed Star.*[1] Dr. Graham proves that this symbol was *never* used by King David of Israel and so the name Star of David is a misnomer. The symbol was chosen in 1948 for the flag of the fledgling nation of Israel at the insistence of the Rothschilds. Its usage stems from the medieval period when corrupt rabbis into cabalistic magic began to use the six-pointed star in their rituals.

Dr. Graham does not mince words in declaring this emblem a tool of Satan, unworthy of use by the holy people of God.

The Occult Triangle and the Masonic Lodge

Returning back to the single triangle as a common symbol of occult usage, we note that the Freemasons were able, through the influence of Grand Master Benjamin Franklin, to have the triangle became the sun-lit capstone above the pyramid on the obverse (reverse) side of the Great Seal of the United States.

The design of the 33rd degree jewel worn by the elite Mason is made up of interlocking triangles.

The Real Grip of a Master Mason, which the Order claims can "resurrect" the candidate and cause him, in essence, to be "born again" (a counterfeit of the Christian experience) is formed with fingers separated to form a triangle. In the photos and illustrations in this section, you will find several real-life examples of this grip.

In *Coil's Masonic Encyclopedia* we are told of the *triangular chain*, the legend taught by Freemasonry that Jewish Freemasons were carried as captives from Jerusalem to Babylon by Nebuchadnezzar, being bound by triangular chains. The Babylonian King is said to have been gravely insulting the Jews by doing this because, to the Jews, the triangle, or delta symbol, was a symbol of their Deity.[2]

King Solomon and the Triple Triangle

In the 6° of Freemasonry, the Degree of Intimate Secretary, the concept of a triple triangle is introduced, said to be emblematic of the three Masons who were present at the opening of the first Lodge of Intimate Secretaries. It is further claimed that King Solomon was one of those three present.

It is significant that in the first Book of *Kings* in the Holy Bible, King Solomon rebelled against God and His commandments and began to worship the god and goddess of the heathen in his temple. He also required of the High Priests of

Solomon's Temple that they annually render to him, as tribute, the sum of 666 talents of gold. Undoubtedly the number 666 is symbolically the triple triangle, because the holy number of the Goddess was 666.

In *Mackey's Masonic Ritualist*, the author, Sovereign Grand Commander of the Scottish Rite, Albert Mackey, emphasized the key importance of the triangle in the rituals of Freemasonry.[3] The late Jim Keith, an exposer of conspiracies and cults, also discussed the importance of this symbol to Masonry. He writes, "There is in fact a triad of three governing officers to be found in almost every degree."[4]

In a number of books written by Masons, the downward pointing triangle is related to Set, the god of Egypt, and to Bacchus. Both of the deities are Satan in other guises.

Jim Tresner, 33°, whose academic writings are often published in Masonic journals and publications, notes the use of triangles in the ritual for the fifteenth degree of the Scottish Rite, Knight

The late Albert Mackey, Sovereign Grand Commander of International Freemasonry.

of the East, of the Sword, or of the Eagle. Tresner says that the apron worn for this degree's ritual in the Lodge is of red velvet, and "on the apron are three triangles, one inside the other, formed of chains with triangular links." These three triangles, he explains, "represent the three great limitations on, or enemies of, the human intellect—tyranny, privilege, superstition."[5]

In reality, Tresner is subtly alluding to the Masonic Order's long-standing doctrine of fierce opposition to existing political sovereigns not yet corrupted or conquered by Illuminism and its hatred of the true Christian Church, which the Masons teach is "superstition" and is a sectarian belief that cannot be tolerated. Tresner may object to my characterization, but the evidence of my allegations is insurmountable, as the rituals themselves prove.

Rosicrucians, Theosophists, and The Triangle

The Rosicrucian Order, too, relies on the triangle as a vehicle to impart and convey its teachings to rising candidates. For example, Arkon Daraul, in *A History of Secret Societies*, describes a ritualistic scene of initiation in a German branch of Rosicrucianism:

> The room of initiation was carpeted in green and on it were a number of objects...
> Three candelabra were placed to form a triangle, and nine glasses indicated the
> male and female properties...[6]

Helena Blavatsky's worldwide cult *Theosophy* and its offspring, *The Lucis Trust*, led for many years by prolific occult writer, Alice Bailey, likewise adopted the triangle as symbolic of their teachings. In 1937 the Lucis Trust founded a subsidiary group named *Triangles* which today encourages people across the globe to network by forming local three person triangle groups to come together often and meditate. In this way, said the parent organization in a letter, occult adepts can "help to illumine world thought...through which the new incoming Aquarian energies can function, the new ideas spread, and the New World Order emerge."[7]

According to Bailey, the coming New World Order of the New Age is best symbolized by a triangle within a circle, with a single dot, or point, within the triangle. This symbol is said to represent three Centres (in U.S.A., Centers), the point standing for the ruler of the spirit world, Sanat (an anagram for "Satan" apparently), the entity who at the appointed time will emerge to rule the Earth and humanity. The second Centre is Sanat's "Hierarchy," the many unseen spirits (i.e. devils), and the third Centre is the human masses.[8]

At the close of the Age, Bailey assures us, "the three major Centres will be in complete unified and synchronized activity," controlling all manifestations of life.[9]

Aleister Crowley, the late British satanist and Freemason, was also a devoteé of the triangle as symbol. As a high-level officer of the occult group, Order of the Golden Dawn, Crowley used for one of his emblems the Eye of Horus in the Pyramid of Fire, radiated by the sun's rays. It was Horus, in the form of a spirit guide named Aiwass, that allegedly gave Crowley *The Book of the Law*, a book of prophecy Crowley claimed he received by automatic writing.[10]

ABRACADABRA Not Just Childish Fun

Witches and deep occult magicians join Bailey in use of the triangle. Take the word ABRACADABRA that is repeatedly used in kids TV cartoons and programs by supposedly mythical creatures like wizards and witches and fairies. Actually, this word is of ancient origins. In a poem on occult medicine written by a pagan doctor in ancient Rome about 250 AD, to ward off fevers and sickness, the physician recommended the word abracadabra be written down in an inverted triangle like this:

```
A B R A C A D A B R A
A B R A C A D A B R
A B R A C A D A B
A B R A C A D A
A B R A C A D
A B R A C A
A B R A C
A B R A
A B R
A B
A
```

Next, the paper on which the word was written was to be tied round the patient's neck for nine days and then thrown backwards over the shoulder into a stream running eastwards. The fever then would shrink to nothing, the patient was told.

The magical word ABRACADABRA comes from worship of the gnostic god, Abraxas. It literally means: The dead body, or corpse, of Abraxas.

Witches often use the triangle as a protective symbol. They foolishly believe it can be used as a talisman, especially if the Tetragrammaton, the Hebrew letters for God, are inserted inside the triangle. The Masons do the same thing essentially in the Masters Jewel of the 4th degree. The triangle is inscribed on the ring given holders of the 14th degree also.

The Geometrical God Is a Woman

A closely kept secret of higher level Masons and other Illuminists is that, in addition to their worship of the Devil by other names, they also worship a female deity, the Great Goddess. This is made plain by John Yarker, a renowned British Freemason. Yarker's translation of the French manuscript, *Lectures of a Chapter, Senate, and Council*, informs us that the triangle's origins can be found in Egyptian religion, being the symbol of Isis, the Egyptian goddess:

The triangle, which they called the geometrical God, was the emblem of Isis.[11]

You'll recall that the symbol "G" is found at the center of the most common of Freemasonry's symbols, the Masonic square and compass, and that the Mason is told this letter G represents "God" and "Geometry." This, then, is the "geometrical god" that, Yarker observes, "was the emblem of Isis."

Ever wonder why the Masons installed the statue of a *woman* in stone atop the U.S. Capitol building in Washington, D.C., and the statue of a *woman* called "Liberty" in New York City's harbor? Well, now you know. *America, meet your satanic mistress: Isis.*

110   RICHARDSON'S MONITOR OF FREE-MASONRY.

Grand Commander—Attention, Sir Knights: you will now give the signs.

All the signs in Masonry are given by each Knight, from Entered Apprentice up to those of Red Cross Knights.

The signs in this degree are then given in detail, as explained hereafter.

Grand Commander—Attention, Sir Knights: you will form around the altar, for the purpose of opening this Council of Knights Templars.

The Knights kneel around the altar, and the proceedings of opening are similar to those in a Council of Red Cross Knights. After all is ready, the Grand Commander says:

Grand Commander—Sir Knights, this Council of Knights Templars is now open for the dispatch of business, and you will govern yourselves according to the sublime principles of our Order.

The veil is now drawn, and the hall divided. That part occupied by the Grand Commander is called the Asylum, and

Page 110 of *Richardson's Monitor of Freemasonry* give details of how the lodge sanctuary will be arranged for initiation in the degree of Order of the Knights Templar. Take note of the triangle-shaped table with candles and coffin.

This cover of an issue of *Scottish Rite Journal* (October, 1998) displays the triangle with radiant sun rays and, containing within, the all-seeing eye. There is also the square and compass, the "G" (Geometry, Goddess, and/or sexual Generative power), and the Masonic hand grip of fellowship.

800   TRIANGLE   TRIANGLE

and extent of the punishment to be inflicted, beginning with expulsion and proceeding, if necessary, to indefinite suspension and public and private reprimand. To inflict expulsion or suspension, a vote of two-thirds of those present is required, but for a mere reprimand, a majority will be sufficient. The votes on the nature of the punishment should be *viva voce*, or, rather, according to Masonic usage, by a show of hands.

Trials in a Grand Lodge are to be conducted on the same general principles; but here, in consequence of the largeness of the body, and the inconvenience which would result from holding the examinations in open Lodge, and in the presence of all the members, it is more usual to appoint a committee, before whom the case is tried, and upon whose full report of the testimony the Grand Lodge bases its action. And the forms of trial in such committees must conform, in all respects, to the general usage already detailed.

Triangle. There is no symbol more important in its signification, more various in its application, or more generally diffused throughout the whole system of Freemasonry, than the triangle. An examination of it, therefore, cannot fail to be interesting to the Masonic student.

The *equilateral triangle* appears to have been adopted by nearly all the nations of antiquity as a symbol of the Deity, in some of his forms or emanations, and hence, probably, the prevailing influence of this symbol was carried into the Jewish system, where the yod within the triangle was made to represent the Tetragrammaton, or sacred name of God.

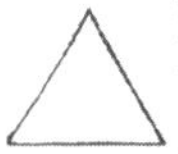

The equilateral triangle, says Bro. D. W. Nash (*Freem. Mag.*, iv., 294), "viewed in the light of the doctrines of those who gave it currency as a divine symbol, represents The Great First Cause, the creator and container of all things, as one and indivisible, manifesting himself in an infinity of forms and attributes in this visible universe."

Among the Egyptians, the darkness through which the candidate for initiation was made to pass was symbolized by the trowel, an important Masonic implement, which in their system of hieroglyphics has the form of a triangle. The equilateral triangle they considered as the most perfect of figures, and a representative of the great principle of animated existence, each of its sides referring to one of the three departments of creation, the animal, vegetable, and mineral.

The equilateral triangle is to be found scattered throughout the Masonic system. It forms in the Royal Arch the figure within which the jewels of the officers are suspended. It is in the ineffable degrees the sacred

delta, everywhere presenting itself as the symbol of the Grand Architect of the Universe. In Ancient Craft Masonry, it is constantly exhibited as the element of important ceremonies. The seats of the principal officers are arranged in a triangular form, the three lesser lights have the same situation, and the square and compass form, by their union on the greater light, two triangles meeting at their bases. In short, the equilateral triangle may be considered as one of the most constant forms of Masonic symbolism.

The *right-angled triangle* is another form of this figure which is deserving of attention. Among the Egyptians, it was the symbol of universal nature; the base representing Osiris, or the male principle; the perpendicular, Isis, or the female principle; and the hypotenuse, Horus, their son, or the product of the male and female principle.

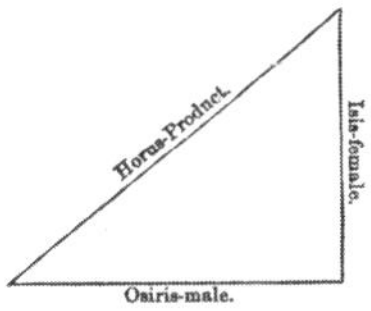

[triangle diagram labeled "Horus-Product", "Isis-female", "Osiris-male"]

This symbol was received by Pythagoras from the Egyptians during his long sojourn in that country, and with it he also learned the peculiar property it possessed, namely, that the sum of the squares of the two shorter sides is equal to the square of the longest side—symbolically expressed by the formula, that the product of Osiris and Isis is Horus. This figure has been adopted in the Third Degree of Masonry, and will be there recognized as the forty-seventh problem of Euclid.

Triangle and Square. As the Delta was the initial letter of Deity with the ancients, so its synonym is among modern nations. It is a type of the Eternal, the All-Powerful, the Self-Existent.

The material world is typified by the "square" as passive matter, in opposition to force symbolized by the triangle.

The Square is also an emblem of humanity, as the Delta or Triangle typifies Deity.

The Delta, Triangle, and Compasses are essentially the same. The raising one point, and then another, signifies that the Divine or higher portion of our nature should increase in power, and control

[Star of David / interlaced triangle diagram labeled "1."]

TRIANGLE   TRIANGLE   801

the baser tendencies. This is the real, the practical "journey toward the East."

The interlacing triangles or deltas symbolize the union of the two principles of the active and passive, male and female, pervading the universe. (1.)

The two triangles, one white and the other black, interlacing, typify the mingling of the two apparent powers in nature, darkness and light, error and truth, ignorance and wisdom, evil and good, throughout human life. (2.)

The triangle and square together form the pyramid (3), as seen in the Entered Apprentice's apron. In this combination the pyramid is the metaphor for unity of matter and force, as well as the oneness of man and God. The numbers 3, 5, 7, 9, have their places in the parts and points of the square and triangle when in pyramidal form, and imply Perfection. (See *Pointed Cubical Stone.*)

Triangle, Double. See *Seal of Solomon* and *Shield of David*.

Triangle of Pythagoras. See *Pentalpha*.

Triangle, Radiated. A triangle placed within and surrounded by a circle of rays. This circle is called, in Christian art, "a glory." When this glory is distinct from the triangle, and surrounds it in the form of a circle, it is then an emblem of God's

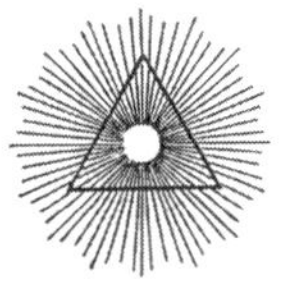

[radiant triangle diagram with eye]

eternal glory. This is the usual form in religious uses. But when, as is most usual in the Masonic symbol, the rays emanate from the center of the triangle, and, as it were, enshroud it in their brilliancy, it is symbolic of the Divine Light. The perverted ideas of the Pagans referred these rays of light to their sun-god and their Sabian worship.

But the true Masonic idea of this glory is, that it symbolizes that Eternal Light

52

of Wisdom which surrounds the Supreme Architect as a sea of glory, and from Him as a common center emanates to the universe of His creation.

Triangle, Triple. The *pentalpha*, or triangle of Pythagoras, is usually called also the triple triangle, because three triangles are formed by the intersection of its sides. But there is another variety of the triple triangle which is more properly entitled to the appellation, and which is made in the annexed form.

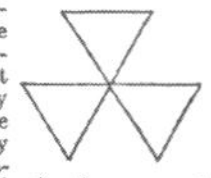

It will be familiar to the Knights Templar as the form of the jewel worn by the Prelate of his Order. Like every modification of the triangle, it is a symbol of the Deity; but as the degree of Knights Templar appertains exclusively to Christian

Masonry, the triple triangle there alludes to the mystery of the Trinity. In the Scottish Rite Degree of Knight of the East the symbol is also said to refer to the triple essence of Deity; but the symbolism is made still more mystical by supposing that it represents the sacred number 81, each side of the three triangles being equivalent to 9, which again is the square of 3, the most sacred number in Freemasonry. In the Twentieth Degree of the Ancient and Accepted Scottish Rite, or that of "Grand Master of all Symbolic Lodges," it is said that the number 81 refers to the triple covenant of God, symbolized by a triple triangle said to have been seen by Solomon when he consecrated the Temple. Indeed, throughout the ineffable and the philosophic degrees, the allusions to the triple triangle are much more frequent than they are in Ancient Craft Masonry.

The Indian trimourti, or triple triangle of the Hindus, is of a different form, consisting of three concentric triangles. In the center is the sacred triliteral name, AUM. The interior triangle symbolizes Brahma, Vishnu, and Siva; the middle one, Creation

---

Pages 800 and 801 from *Encyclopedia of Freemasonry* by Albert G. Mackey, 33° and Charles T. McClenachan, 33°.

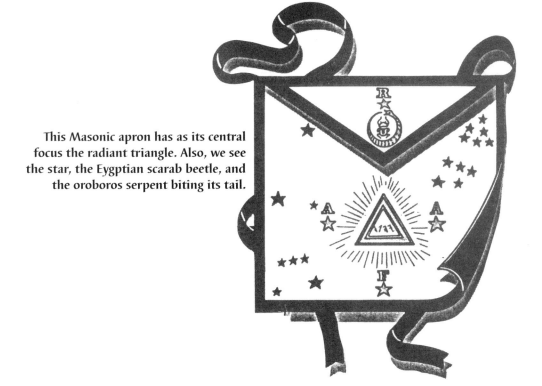

This Masonic apron has as its central focus the radiant triangle. Also, we see the star, the Eygptian scarab beetle, and the oroboros serpent biting its tail.

Ἡ ἀγγλὶς ἱέρεια Μαύρης Μαγείας πρὶν ἀπὸ τὴν τέλεσιν τῶν μυ-
στηρίων... ἐνῷ βαστάει τὰ δύο κόκκινα κεριά. Τὰ σύμβολα ἀπὸ πάνω
της εἶναι τὸ διαβόητον «Κροὺς Ἀνσάτα» ἤ ΑΝΚΧ δηλαδὴ ὁ «Σταυρὸς
τῆς ζωῆς» ἐν ἀναλύσει... Οἱ ἀναγνῶσται μας τώρα ἀσφαλῶς θὰ κα-
ταλάβουν τὴν σημασίαν τοῦ σήματος Τ τὸ ὁποῖον φέρουν οἱ τέκτονές
μας ἐπὶ τῶν στολῶν των...

A dark scene inside a Masonic Temple in Greece. The human sacrifice lays straddled as a five point star on the altar. Superimposed behind are the descendant (hell) triangle and the tau symbol of the Royal Arch. The delta triangle design is feminine and corresponds to the female's vulva.

Two magical seals based on the *Black Book of Honorius*. The first is the occult seal of Great Work. The second is the occult seal of Black Magic. Note in both of them the opposed position of the triangles and the position of the moon (in the center of the Black Magic seal).

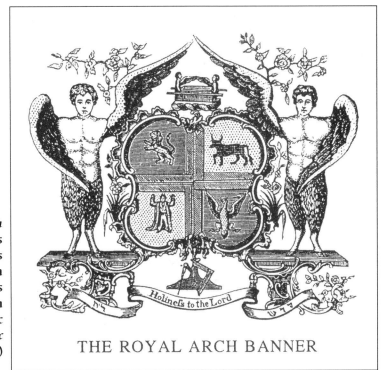

THE ROYAL ARCH BANNER

Freemasonry's *The Royal Arch Banner* reveals two angels holding their respective wings in a triangle shape. The cloven hoofs and goat legs demonstrate the Luciferian nature of these angelic creatures. (From *Coil's Masonic Encyclopedia*, revised 1995)

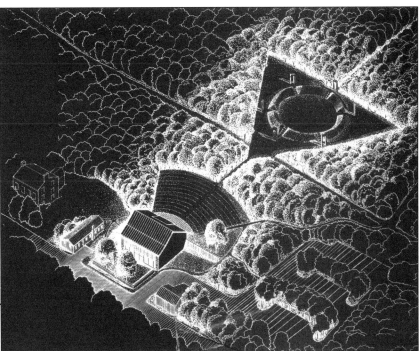

The architectural design for the Yellow Springs Institute for Contemporary Studies and the Arts in Chester Springs, Pennsylvania reveals a music amphitheater and a triangle structure with a circle inside. Meanwhile, the official logo for the Yellow Springs Institute is a red triangle with a tree inside.

Only an adept heavily schooled in occult symbology would understand the message being communicated in this full-page ad for *"Virginia Slims"* cigarettes. The occult significance of the lightning bolt, the triangle, the square, the arm and hand signs and positions, even the wide spread of the model's legs is explained in the pages of *Codex Magica*. The colors she wears, black, red, blue, and white also contain significance. Still, given the general deterioration of intellectual thinking in society and of moral values and Christian knowledge—and the dearth of knowledge of occult deception—it is entirely possible that neither the fashion designers nor the Advertising Agency are culpable of intentionally using occult devices. The significance however, remains, and in the author's opinion, such advertising cannot help but aid the cause of evil forces.

From Ancient to Modern

SAROS

requests the company of reliable fellow pilgrims along the dragonways of space and time. Tickets $75 for six months.

Itinerary from
The Courier,
London

Kabalah: A Process of Awakening

An extensive home study course encompassing philosophy, psychology and mysticism, which teaches the wisdom, understanding and use of the Tree of Life and incorporates the mysticism of Judaism and the esoteric teachings of Christianity.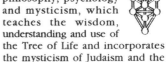

The Center is now recognized as a Branch of The American Apostolic University, College of Seminarians, by the Federation of St. Thomas Christian Churches. The Seminary Program will become available to correspondence students late Spring, 1994.

For information on enrollment as a Kabalistic student or for information regarding Seminary Enrollment, write or telephone:

KARIN KABALAH CENTER

Institute of the Healing Arts

CLASSES:
Yoga - Acupressure - Healing
Tai Chi - Meditation - & MORE
PRIVATE APPOINTMENTS:
Acupressure - Reflexology
Hands-On-Healing
WEDNESDAY EVENINGS:
Healing treatments (donation only)

Display ads like these are common in New Age and occult publications.

Institute of Spiritual Awareness

*May the Light of Spiritual Awareness brighten your path.
May Its presence be your guide at every turning point.
May Its beauty be the life that you share with others.*

CLASSES AND SEMINARS IN SPIRITUAL UNFOLDMENT
SUNDAY HEALING SERVICE 10:30 AM
SUNDAY CELEBRATION 11 AM

Bonnie Wells
— *Astrologer* —
Specializing in Esoteric Astrology

Phone or FAX
Durango, Colorado

Exploring Personal Meaning in the Light of Soul Experience
Over Twenty Years in Practice • Consultation by Appointment

INITIATION
the Great Adventure of the
Western Mystery Tradition

A direct lineal descendent of the Golden Dawn offers a correspondence course preparatory to training in Ritual Magic. Our goal is the perfecting of our personalities to become fit vehicles for the cosmic flow of healing, love and harmony.

The Fraternity of the Hidden Light
P.O. Box _____, Covina, CA _____

To interest like-minded people to inquire about the Rosicrucians, this or a similar ad is placed in some magazines. Under the heading, *"Secrets Entrusted to A Few,"* we find an ancient and worn book with a triangle and cross imprinted on the cover. The Rosicrucians are actually several different Orders. This ad is for AMORC, an American-based Order that is less influential among the elite than European branches. Perhaps the most famous initiate of the Rosicrucians was Benjamin Franklin. Catholic Pope John XXIII was reputed to be a Rosicrucian as was Martin Luther, the Protestant Reformer. U.S. Senator Ted Kennedy (D-MA) is today a high-level Rosicrucian.

JEWEL OF THIRTY-THIRD DEGREE

The design for the Jewel of Scottish Rite Masonry's 33rd degree includes a system of interlocking triangles, circles, the "X," and the quadruple Tau background.

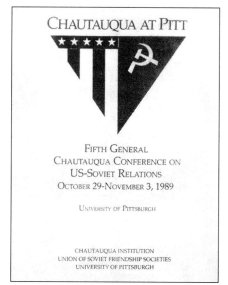

CHAUTAUQUA AT PITT

FIFTH GENERAL CHAUTAUQUA CONFERENCE ON US-SOVIET RELATIONS
OCTOBER 29-NOVEMBER 3, 1989

UNIVERSITY OF PITTSBURGH

CHAUTAUQUA INSTITUTION
UNION OF SOVIET FRIENDSHIP SOCIETIES
UNIVERSITY OF PITTSBURGH

Official logo of conference held by socialists promoting the political and economic merger of the United States and the old U.S.S.R. Speakers at the 1989 conference included Illuminati U.S. Senator John Heinz (Order of Skull & Bones), U.S. Senator Bill Bradley, and Pittsburgh Mayor Sophie Masloff.

Aleister Crowley, British satanist who was a high-level initate of many occult Orders and Secret Societies, giving the supreme sign of the horned god. The triangular hat resembles the style of hat worn by many in the earlier colonial period in America. The triangle contains the all-seeing eye and has the radiant rays of the sun deity shining forth.

people, the belief that there exists and has always existed an inner, unfolding divine plan or purpose for the human family is not new. And there is in the world today a growing number of visionary thinkers who are working selflessly to ensure that human development is in line with

profound energies are used by Triangles co-workers. Daily they visualise these energies streaming into human consciousness to help build a lighted mental climate in which people everywhere can sense and contribute to the planetary vision of a new enlightened social order.

Through the network which the Triangles are creating, light or illumination is invoked by the daily work and attitude of the Triangles members; thus light can indeed "descend on earth" and goodwill, which is the love of God and basically, the will-to-good, can also stream forth in fuller livingness into the hearts of men; thus they are transformed in their lives and the era of right human relations cannot be stopped.

Alice Bailey

HELPING TO BUILD RIGHT HUMAN RELATIONS

ISSN 0818-4984

WORLD GOODWILL is an international movement helping to mobilise the energy of goodwill and to build right human

Nations Economic and Social Council.
The WORLD GOODWILL NEWSLETTER is published four times a

This logo of *Triangles*, a Lucis Trust organization, and the message from Alice Bailey, occultist founder, was included in *World Goodwill* newsletter (1997, No. 4). World Goodwill is yet another global organization, affiliated with the Lucis Trust, but which also networks with scores of other Illuminist groups, orders, and secret societies. Lucis Trust and World Goodwill teach of the coming of the Cosmic, New Age Christ, avatar for the Age of Aquarius, who represents the Central Sun, also called the Solar Logos.

☐ Energy System Parameters
○ *Pilgrim's Progress*
△ *The Community as Disciple*
· *The School of Symbols*

P.O. Box 12-939 / P.O. Box 93
Albany, New York 12212 / Unity, Maine 04988
U.S.A. / U.S.A.

August 12, 1988

Dear friends and members of ESP,

This letter is to announce the 1988 General Membership Meeting in or nearby Ottawa, Canada's national capitol, on October 14th and 15th. The past two years has witnessed change in the membership of ESP, accelerated change in the personal lives of ESP members and, as a result, a change in the group energies of ESP. It is suggested we use the meeting this fall to examine the meaning of these changes, to share the excitement of our changes, and to consider the future of ESP in light of these changes.

The New Age group, *Energy System Parameters (ESP)*, has this as the logo on its letterhead. In this letter announcing its general membership's annual meeting, the co-Presidents emphasized ESP's focus on *"group energies," "cosmic reorganization,"* and the importance of achieving the *"crystalized form of new patterns."* The signature line had the phrase, *"In the Service of the One."*

32° Brothers

Your Jewel

As based on The Supreme Council, S.J., *Statutes*, a 32° Jewel is now available. See *Current Interest* in this issue.

The *jewel* of the 32nd degree, Scottish Rite, contains four, interlocking Tau elements and four squares. Symbology-wise, this arrangement conceives of the Freemasons and their coming Prince to be rulers of all four corners of the globe. (From the back cover of *Scottish Rite Journal*, October 1998)

Eastern religions believe that the use of the *Sri Yantra* produces unparalleled spiritual power by evoking (inviting) help from the unseen spirit world. Commonly employed in sexual tantra rituals, the design of the Sri Yantra meditation device begins with the four "T"s, (Tau) which, interestingly, is the same as the design of the Mason's 32nd degree jewel. From this base, the Sri Yantra is drawn from nine (666=6+6+6=18=1+8=9) triangles, four pointed downward and five pointed upward, forming 42 (6X7) triangular fragments around a central triangle. Occultists teach there is no other set of triangles which interlock with such integrational perfection. The diagram of the Sri Yantra is said to contain, or synthesize, within all the activities and energies in the universe. Made up of black and white triangle elements, the design bears also the yin/yang, black is white and white is black principle underlying the *Masters Carpet* (checkerboard) floor of Masonry and also parallels the "two heads" doctrine implicit in the great symbol of 33rd degree Freemasonry, the double-headed eagle. (Drawing from book, *Sacred Geometry*, by Robert Lawlor, Thames and Hudson, New York and London, 1989)

Two more versions of the *Sri Yantra*. Left: A Sri Yantra found inside the cover of a rock album. Right: Sri Yantra from the book, *The Tantric Way*, showing the multiple-triangle design, representing the generative (sex) act. In this design the interior, triangular (male) elements are "buried" within the Lotus blossom (female).

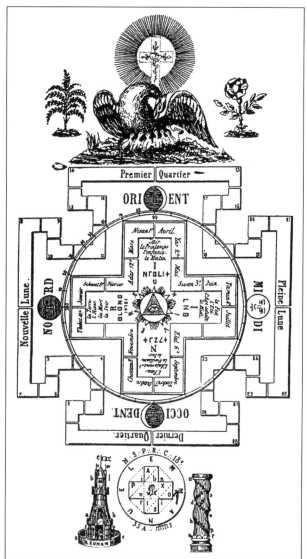

The Sri Yantra pictured as a mystical diagram of Solomon's Temple, as planned in the building scheme of the Knights Templar. The cross and sun rays on top do *not* represent Jesus Christ, but point to the Cosmic Christ, who came in many names in the past and shall come again with a new name. (From the book, *The Sword and The Grail*, by Andrew Sinclair, New York: Crown Publishers, 1992)

A masonic tracing board with an image of a coffin, decorated with the "tools" of the Craft. The V or square at the bottom of the coffin is pointed downward to hell and the Lord of the Underworld. The skull and bones, or death's head, is thought to guard the doorway to the Mysteries of initiation. There are three number fives arranged in a triangle pattern, thus 555, the triple nickel, symbolizing death and resurrection. Not coincidentally, the Washington Monument, in our nation's capital, is exactly 555 feet high. It was designed by Masonic overlords and architecturally is an obelisk, worshipped in Egypt as Osiris' penis (Baal's shaft).

The occult spiritual nature of the mission of the United Nations (UN) is seen in the UN's Meditation Room, inside the UN headquarters in New York City. The austere Meditation Room has a rough, black granite ashlar altar (masonic origins) and a mural with various occult symbols, including the serpent, triangle, crescent moon, and square. The Room itself is designed as a pyramid without a capstone lying down on its side. The UN even has a chaplain of sorts; Sri Chinmoy, a Hindu guru who leads chants and meditations inside the Meditation Room. Evidently, the Illuminati were not keen on separating church and state when they founded their world body, the United Nations.

Jackson and son, Jesse Jr., watch Goodman's T-shirt signal to shipmates: 'Send me home'

Rich Lipski—UPI

Appointment in Damascus

Sirens echoing in the ancient streets, a motorcade of black limos sped through downtown Damascus last weekend bearing a distinguished visitor. It was the Rev. Jesse Jackson, erroneously identified in the local press as "Senator Jackson" and actually only an untested candidate for the Democratic presidential nomination. But Jackson, in Damascus to extend what he termed a "moral appeal" for the release of a captive

the plane, and said U.S. officials should not be suspicious of his good treatment in Syrian hands. Asked repeatedly what he thought of the various efforts to bring about his release, he replied, "I'm not a politician, I'm a naval officer." Said Jackson: "A wise lieutenant."

In fact, neither Jackson nor anyone else knew whether Syrian President Hafez Assad would set Goodman free—but Jackson, at least, had nothing to lose by trying

When captured American aviator, Navy Lt. Robert O. Goodman, Jr., 27, was released by Syrian authorities into the hands of self-appointed diplomat Jesse Jackson, the aviator was given this souvenir T-shirt from his hometown of Akron, Ohio. The T-shirt had triangular designs and demonic eyes. Perhaps Syria's President, Hafez Assad, agreed to deal with Jesse Jackson because both he and Jackson are 33rd degree Masons. Later, Jesse Jackson traveled to Communist Cuba, where side-by-side with another Lodge brother, dictator Fidel Castro, the black religious and civil rights leader hollered out to the Cuban crowd, *"Viva Fidel, Long Live Fidel Castro!"* (Photo and article from *Newsweek*, January 9, 1984)

An Oregon state occult newspaper, *Excalibur*, ran an ad using this triangle symbol with the all-seeing eye within. The ad advertised the services of a "psychic healer" who claimed to do "Omega Energy Work."

Cancelled postage stamp commemorating the 1939 New York World's Fair. The year '39 was chosen for its masonic numerological significance. A classic movie, *The Thirty-Nine Steps*, also embodied this body of hidden masonic numerological teachings.

△△△ INSTITUTE FOR PLANETARY SYNTHESIS
IPS GENEVA

P.O. Box 128
CH-1211 GENEVA 20
Tel. : 022/ 45 72 49
Telex : 427993 TXC CH, attn. I.P.S.

ORDER FORM

Name :

The New Age occult organization, *Institute For Planetary Synthesis*, employs the triple triangle for its logo, as this "Order Form" for its teaching products indicates.

Judge Roger Sherman, one of the signers of the American Declaration of Independence, giving the triangle sign with his right hand. (Painting: from book *The Miracle On Main Street*, by F. Tupper Saussy)

Duane Ackerman, CEO of BellSouth Corporation, holding his hand in what subtly appears to be the masonic triangle. (*USA Today*, March 15, 2004, p. B4)

Texas Governor George W. Bush in 1998 with Russian presidential candidate, General Alexander Lebed exchange a concealed handshake as Lebed displays the enigmatic double triangle sign of the Lodge which is similar to the Real Grip of a Master Mason (*Duncan's Masonic Ritual and Monitor, 3rd Ed.*, p. 120). General Lebed, the most popular political figure in Russia at the time, never succeeded in his ambitious quest to win the Russian presidency. His airplane crashed in mysterious circumstances in Russia, and he was killed. (Photo: from *Austin American-Statesman*, March 22, 1998)

B2   Sunday, March 22, 1998   *   **METRO 8**

Political 🏛 Capital

Foreign dignitaries lining up with Bush

You might have noticed the would-be president of Russia, Alexander Lebed, in a firm handshake last week with the would-be president of the United States, George W. Bush, at the Governor's Mansion after Alex stopped by for breakfast. You may recall that Bush met with José Angel Gurría Treviño, Mexico's foreign secretary and maybe someday president, on Gurría's September visit to Austin. Not to mention that Argentina's U.S. ambassador and its chief of cabinet ministers will be knocking on the mansion door March 30. If the governor announces for the millennium presidency, you could be watching his foreign policy being shaped here.

■

A new strategy: House members traditionally vote their districts on school finance bills, but advocates for school districts that want a bigger share have devised an effort to lobby senators. Their larger districts can contain dozens of school districts, so voting their districts is not so clear. Now the Equity

Ralph Barrera/AA-S

Gov. George W. Bush, left, and Russian presidential hopeful Alexander Lebed exchange an obviously cordial farewell handshake after breakfast at the Governor's Mansion on St. Patrick's Day.

campaign aides, has come over to Williamson's campaign. "There should be no doubt, Barry Williamson is the only conservative left in the race for

ting Children First. (The organization's leaders disowned an anti-Laney fund-raising letter, saying it was sent without authorization by a staff member.)

Comedian Bob Hope, knighted by the Sovereign Military Order of Malta, shows the Masonic square, known also as the triangle, V, downward delta sign.

New York's Governor Mario Cuomo (left), a Democrat, is politically endorsed by Rudy Giuliani, the Republican Mayor of New York City. The Illuminati elite know no political party boundaries and their servants only pretend to be conservative or liberal. In the case of Giuliani, it may also be significant that he is reportedly a gay bisexual. According to the *New York Times*, Mayor Giuliani once performed as "Rudia," transvestite nightclub performer. Giuliani also lived with a gay couple for a time, and dressed as a woman transvestite in a Gay Pride Parade. Meanwhile, billionaire industrialist J. Peter Grace, head of W.R. Grace Chemicals, once denigrated Governor Cuomo by referring to him as "Cuomo the Homo." Even though Grace later apologized, his off-the-cuff comment seems to have caused knowing snickers among those in-the-know.

In this photo—a cover of *Time* magazine—Jewish big-shots Steven Spielberg, David Geffen, and Jeffrey Katzenberg of Dreamworks are arranged in a triangle pattern. Probably, the three are into Jewish Cabalism (magic and sorcery).

DOWN TO EARTH BUZZ ALDRIN

Aldrin inside
Apollo 11 (top),
and training in
1969(right).
His footprint
in the lunar
soil (bottom).

After the nation's most famous astronaut, Buzz Aldrin, flew to the moon in 1969, he returned to Earth an American icon. But his training as a moonwalker hardly prepared him for fame. Scrutiny on a global scale led to depression, alcoholism and divorce. Over time, he summoned the courage to seek help and work through his difficulties.

Many factors led to his recovery, among them therapy, Alcoholics Anonymous and his marriage to Lois Driggs Cannon. Lois, his third wife, has helped him build a new life. They share a comfortable home in Southern California and drive cars with license plates reading MARS GUY and MOON GAL. Today, he even jokes about his alter ego, Buzz Lightyear.

Psychology Today May/June 2001

Above: In its May/June 2001 issue, *Psychology Today* carried this feature article and interview with Astronaut Buzz Aldrin. Aldrin and fellow astronaut, Neil Armstrong, were the first to walk on the Moon, in 1969. Aldrin, a Freemason, was said to have conducted a bizarre Masonic ritual on the moon. In the article in *Psychology Today*, triangles are everywhere, including being imbedded in the type of the heading. Also, see the picture of Aldrin—exactly *three* fingers of his *left* hand are reaching into his pocket, with the arm displaying a *triangle* pattern. According to the book *Axis of Death*, by D.C. Yermak, this is similar to a secret Rosicrucian sign indicating the initite has removed himself from God's control and given his life over to the devil. Aldrin is confirmed to be a Mason, but his Rosicrucian involvement is unknown.

Astronaut Buzz Aldrin, supposedly walking on the moon in 1969. Many believe the Apollo 11 mission was a hoax, filmed right here on earth. In this classic, staged photo, notice Aldrin's left arm in its triangle position. Did the taxpayers pay billions just so Aldrin and his masonic brothers could claim the moon for the Illuminati in a staged esoteric ritual?

The three super-rich Hunt brothers in a downward triangle arrangement on the cover of *The New York Times* magazine, September 18, 1997.

An Ordo Saturnus Ritual. Drawing done by Fritz Springmeier based on a drawing done by an eye witness.

Fritz Springmeier, author of the bestselling *Bloodlines of the Illuminati* (available by phone order, toll free 1-800-234-9673), made this drawing based on an actual ritual conducted by a satanic sect known as *Ordo Saturnus* (Order of Saturn). The planet Saturn is the *sixth* planet from the sun in our solar system. Saturn was worshipped in ancient civilizations as a form of Satan, or Lucifer. The triangle within a circle (symbol also of today's Alcoholics Anonymous) group is on the wall while the satanic "X" within the circle is on the front of the altar cloth.

Rosicrucians also commend the triangle within the circle, the very logo of Alcoholics Anonymous. From a page right out of a Rosicrucian manual, the figure at left is the "Symbol of Creation," Nehushstan the serpent, also called Oroboros, the serpent swallowing its own tail. This symbolizes perpetual movement (Hegelian dialectic) and the occult conception of the "Circle of Life," the slogan that Disney's movie, *The Lion King*, made famous. The book of *Revelation* in the Holy Bible calls Satan "that old serpent" and for good reason! The triangle inside the serpentine circle represents the unholy trinity, which the occult teaches is the spiritual element soon to manifest, already operating at the very center of the material universe.

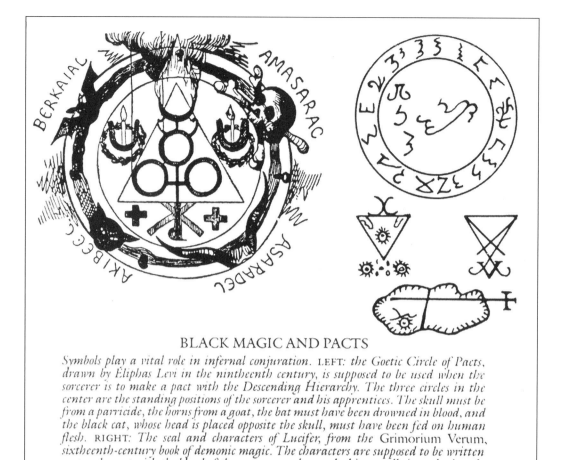

BLACK MAGIC AND PACTS

Symbols play a vital role in infernal conjuration. LEFT: *the Goetic Circle of Pacts, drawn by Eliphas Levi in the nineteenth century, is supposed to be used when the sorcerer is to make a pact with the Descending Hierarchy. The three circles in the center are the standing positions of the sorcerer and his apprentices. The skull must be from a parricide, the horns from a goat, the bat must have been drowned in blood, and the black cat, whose head is placed opposite the skull, must have been fed on human flesh.* RIGHT: *The seal and characters of Lucifer, from the* Grimorium Verum, *sixteenth-century book of demonic magic. The characters are supposed to be written on parchment with the blood of the sorcerer, and worn by him at all times during the conjuration.*

(From the book, *Satan Wants You*, by Arthur Lyons, The Mysterious Press, New York, 10019)

In this 17th century alchemical drawing, the Antichrist King and his unholy trinity (three crowns over Earth) worship the transforming fire from their sun deity, symbolized by the triangle within a circle.

Meaning Behind Our Corporate Seal

Howard M. Duff FAFA

I was asked to design an official seal when we incorporated in 1938 as the American Federation of Astrologers. The four fixed signs were chosen to indicate stability and practicality. The words around the circle showed our purpose and ideals. The hand and torch backed by the star of truth indicated our purpose to lead in teaching true Astrology; the little dots, the starry firmament; the large ones, the seven planets with the Sun and the Moon dominant; these were significant of our "alphabet" for doing this on a national scale.

Excerpt from article of the same name in AFA Bulletin 1973, Volume 35, Number 5 — 35th Anniversary edition.

A2

In this page right out of the Bulletin of the American Federation of Astrologers (AFA), we find the corporate seal and its explanation. However, the explanation given is weak at best and seems geared to please the majority of astrologers who are active in the organization without giving away any real secrets. Almost any knowledgeable student of the occult can see hidden meanings in these symbols far beyond the official explanation. Symbols that beg for more esoteric (and accurate) explanation include the triangle inside the circle, the pentagram star, the torch and hand, the point within the circle and the stars.

Hazelden, a company specializing in products related to Alcoholics Anonymous, offers such items as tie tacs and lapel pins, money clips, necklaces, and key chains. You can even get the *"God's Eye Pendant."* The Hazelden catalog glowingly tells potential buyers: *"In times of trouble or joy, this precious pendant keeps our Higher Power's eye on our recovery and spiritual growth."* The same catalog ad says, *"This five-thousand-year-old symbol of continual movement and spirituality... has become a popular icon in the recovery community."*

A Rosicrucian symbol described as "The Eternal Madonna," in the encyclopedic work, *New Age Bible Interpretation (Old Testament, Volume III)*, editor Corinne Heline

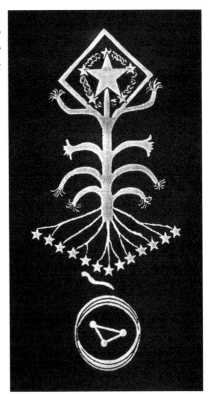

A friend sent the author this photograph she took of one of the student art exhibits on display at a local high school. Many of the exhibits were on occult subjects. The meaning of the triangle within the circle superimposed over the body of the person, lying in a fetal position on a surface of red, most likely symbolizes man's servitude and enslavement to the Solar Deity, whom Masons call the Great Architect of the Universe.

Christian medallion for youth from Hawaii advertised in Christian contemporary music magazine.

This issue of *The Royal Arch Mason* magazine (Summer 1990) featured the seal of the General Grand Council of Cryptic Masons International, which is designed in the form of a triangle within a circle.

This cover of *The Royal Arch Mason* magazine pays tribute to their "Most Worshipful Brother Harry S. Truman." (Truman, a 33rd degree Mason, once told his brothers in the craft that he would rather be a Master Mason than be President of the United States of America.) The symbol of the Royal Arch Masons is also seen at left: The Triple Tau, a sign of the unholy trinity within a triangle within a circle, a composite symbol said to connote triple power.

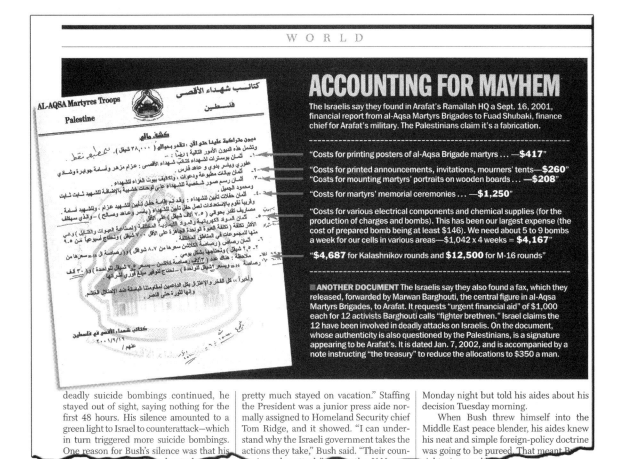

As reported in *Time* (April 15, 2002), this is a financial report sent to Yasser Arafat's Palestine headquarters bearing the insignia of the rebel group, the Al-Aqsa Martyr's Brigade. If authentic, the logo, or seal, for the group roughly resembles a triangle within a circle.

NINETEEN

Part Devil, Part Angel

Ye cannot drink the cup of the Lord, and the cup of devils: ye cannot be partakers of the Lord's table, and of the table of devils.

—*I Corinthians 10:21*

Always front and center…stood Lyndon Johnson, almost handsome then, in his 40s, leaner than history remembers, narrow-eyed, his hair sleek…alert in a vaguely dangerous way — an impresario, a genius of nuances, a wolf in his prime.

—Lance Morrow
"Part Devil, Part Angel"
Newsweek magazine

Illuminists can sometimes be engaging, likeable people. The kind of person you wouldn't mind going to dinner with or hosting at a barbecue. That is, unless you knew that beneath that happy, party-like veneer and surface there was a deep interior of consummate evil.

Take Will Rogers, for example, the loveable Oklahoman storyteller. He was admired by the nation for his rangy, down to earth humor and wit. Who would know that, along with his fellow Masons, Rogers bowed before satanic altars and drank wine from human skulls!

There's astronaut Buzz Aldrin who, it is claimed by NASA, once went to the moon. How many knew that Aldrin carried with him to outer space a Scottish Rite flag emblazoned with the diabolical image of the double-headed eagle?

And we have the late Pamela Harriman, so popular and likeable her biography was entitled *"Life of the Party."* Harriman's husband was Averell Harriman, Patriarch of the Order of Skull and Bones. What tales Ms. Harriman could have told us! After all, she was mistress to a Rothschild and also once used a young, up and coming, Georgetown University student as her sexual boy toy. His name: William Jefferson Clinton.

President Lyndon B. Johnson certainly fits into that category—if there is such a category—of "Part Devil, Part Angel." A Master Mason raised to the third degree in a Lodge in central Texas, Johnson was the primary mover for the black civil rights movement. His aggressive endorsement of various civil rights bills helped create a more equal society. But, why do his biographers call LBJ "cunning" and a "wolf?"

Several books have been published maintaining that then Vice President Lyndon B. Johnson was one of the plotters and conspirators behind the 1963 assassination of President John F. Kennedy. Few people believe it. Most have been snookered into believing the absurd theory that Lee Harvey Oswald acted alone. But in 2003 a book by a former Texas lawyer, Barr McClellan, again broached the subject of LBJ's culpability.[1]

Then, also in 2003, Jeff Rense, in his outstanding internet web site, Rense.com, published two photos of what is being called "The Most Revealing Wink of the Twentieth Century." As a public service, the author of *Codex Magica* is reproducing the same photos here.

This heart-rending scene aboard Air Force One of Lyndon B. Johnson being sworn in as President of the United States following the assassination of John F. Kennedy, was published everywhere, in newspapers, magazines, and books. Look closely at the somber looks on the faces of the persons in the photograph.

Here's the photo that was left unpublished and was kept hidden from public view until now. Congressman Albert Thomas winks back at a quickly-smiling LBJ as he is being sworn in to be the next President of the United States on Air Force One. The grief-stricken Jackie Kennedy stands next to him. Meanwhile, a sly smile also creases the face of Ladybird Johnson, LBJ's wife.

LBJ—was he "part devil, part angel?" I don't think so. He was 100% something, and I'll let you decide just what. Johnson and the others are shown in the following pages giving what appears to be the Illuminist hand sign of the arm in triangular position with hand to side of body. The photos here give evidence that this gesture is not accidental as one might suppose. Several illustrations from authoritative Masonic reference books provide further documentation that the sign is intentional and communicates a message.

...ets of this degree.

The candidate is then instructed in the signs, words and token in this degree, as follows:

Signs—Place the point of a poinard under your chin, and draw it downward to the waist, as if in the act of ripping open the body, speaking the word ZER-BUL. The brother will answer by giving the Entered Apprentice's sign as on page 7, and saying ELIHAM. Another way is to clench the fingers of the right hand, extend the thumb, place it on the abdomen, and move it upwards to the chin, as if ripping open the body with a knife. The brother answers as before.

Words—The pass-words are Eliham and Zerbal. Sacred words, Zerbal, Beniah, Benhakar, Bendaka, &c.

Candidate is now clothed as a companion of this degree, and salutes the Senior Warden as a Master Elect of Fifteen.

If there is no other business before the Chapter, it is then closed in same manner as in the preceding degree, except that the Master and other officers rap three times five, and the companions clap three times five with their hands ...

curtains, and is lighted by twelve candles on four triangular branches.

The officers consist of Thrice Potent Master, representing King Solomon, sitting in the east: Grand Inspector in the west, and Master of Ceremonies.

The brethren wear white aprons, each with an inflamed heart embroidered or painted upon it, and lined and bordered with black. The ribbon, or Order, is similar to that in the preceding degree, except that in place of three heads, three hearts appear upon it. The jewel is the same.

In opening the Chapter, Thrice Potent Master raps ten, and Grand Inspector rises. Master makes the usual inquiries as to whether the Chapter is duly guarded, and the duties of the several officers, as in former degrees, which are answered by the Inspector.

Master raps eleven, and inquires of Grand Inspector—What is the hour?

Grand Inspector—It is twelve, Thrice Potent.

Master raps twelve, which is repeated by the officers, and the brethren clap twelve with their hands: Master says—If it is twelve it is time to labor by the greatest of lights. I pronounce this Grand Chapter open.

The brethren now give the signs of the different degrees, and then those of this degree, hereafter described.

If a candidate is to be admitted, he is prepared outside by the Master of Ceremonies, who brings him hoodwinked to the door, and gives twelve raps, which are answered by twelve by the Inspector, who demands, who comes there? &c.

Master of Ceremonies—A Master Elect of Fifteen desires to receive the degree of Sublime Knight.

Candidate gets admittance in the same manner as in the previous degree, and is led to the Grand Inspector...

In the Grand Masters Elect Degree of Freemasonry, the candidate pledges he will accept severe penalties if he divulges the secrets. His hand and arm are positioned on the abdomen and then moved upward "as if ripping the body open with a knife." (Richardson's Monitor of Freemasonry, p. 146)

As this illustration from a Masonic manual demonstrates, the candidate for the Sublime Knights Elected Degree makes a sign which includes both the right hand on the heart and the left hand in a triangular pose as shown.

...association which, like you, we have received, forms a tie so strong that nothing can break it: woe to him who attempts to disunite us!

The obligation in the degree is then administered. It is similar to those of former degrees, the penalty being to have the hands nailed to the breast, &c.

The candidate is now instructed in the sign, token, and words, &c., viz.: Cross the arms on the stomach, the fingers clenched, and thumbs elevated, and raise the eyes upward. It alludes to the penalty of having the hands nailed, &c.

The token is exactly the same as that in Intimate Secretary. The pass-words are Stolkyn, Emerh, Emeth, and Amuriah. The sacred word is Adonia.

This ends the initiation.

The closing ceremonies are similar to those in previous degrees. Master raps ten and inquires about the duties of the officers: he then raps eleven and inquires of the Inspector—What is the hour?

Inspector—Low six.

Master raps twelve, and brethren rise, the signs are given, &c.

Master again raps twelve, the officers twelve, and the brethren all clap twelve with their hands, when the Master declares the Chapter to be duly closed.

The brethren, or companions, wear stone colored aprons and scarfs; the apron has a star upon it, and in some cases a square and rule: the jewel is a gold medal, with the five orders of architecture, a star, and a case of mathematical instruments delineated on each side.

In the opening, Most Potent Master raps one, and Grand Marshal rises. Master inquires if the Chapter is duly guarded, &c., the same as in the former degrees.

Master raps two, when the Grand Inspector rises.

Master—What is the hour?

Inspector—A star indicates the first instant, the first hour, and the first day in which the Grand Architect commenced the creation of the Universe.

Master raps one and two, when the companions all rise.

Master—Companions, it is the first instant, the first hour, the first day, the first year, when Solomon commenced the Temple; the first day, the first hour, the first instant for opening this Chapter. It is time to commence our labors.

Master raps one and two, the other officers do the same, and the companions clap one and two with their hands, when the Master declares the Chapter duly opened for the dispatch of business.

When a companion is to receive this degree he is prepared outside by the Master of Ceremonies, who conducts him to the door of the Chapter and raps one and two, which is answered by the same from within. He is admitted through the door by the same ceremonies as in the former degrees, and conducted to the east, where

BOOKS

Part Devil, Part Angel

Robert Caro's massive and magisterial *Master of the Senate* charts Lyndon Johnson's cunning rise

By LANCE MORROW

WHEN I WAS A SENATE PAGE boy long ago in the 1950s, my boss was Lyndon Johnson's young pet lizard, Bobby Baker. Senator Johnson would snap his fingers softly, and I would hustle to the cooler in the Democratic cloakroom to bring him a glass of White Rock sparkling water or dash down the marble back stairs to the Senate restaurant to fetch a dish of vanilla ice cream, which he ate at his desk on the Senate floor as he played his mighty legislative Wurlitzer.

In those days, a distinctive cast of characters populated the Senate. The spectacle seemed like continuous American Shakespeare, with a more interesting regional variety than homogenized America offers today.

The Southerners, flamboyant or saturnine, came from another age. Hoey of North Carolina wore wing collars. Freshman John Kennedy of Massachusetts, thin and glamorous, the millionaire's dreamboat boy, hobbled at the rear of the chamber, on crutches from his back operation. Joe McCarthy of Wisconsin, remembered now as a dark cloud shadowing America, could show, in private, an unexpected sweetness and charm. Always, front and center (first desk, middle aisle, the Democratic leader's spot) stood Lyndon Johnson, almost handsome then, in his 40s, leaner than history remembers him, narrow-eyed, his hair sleek with Stacomb, alert in a vaguely dangerous way—an impresario, a genius of nuances, a wolf in his prime.

in four short years. Caro, whose great gifts are indefatigable legwork and a sense of historical drama and character, has a fine protagonist for his life's work. His Johnson, a man of Manichaean contraries, is now familiar—by turns Caligula and Lincoln, a narcissistic monster capable of immense personal cruelty and breathtaking political cynicism who now and then metamorphoses into an angel of compassion and statesmanship.

Part of the key, Caro writes, lay in Johnson's astonishing ability to talk himself into anything, including, sometimes, the right thing. (Bill Clinton also possessed the trait.) "[Johnson] had a remarkable capaci-

THE WOLF IN HIS PRIME: Johnson, the natty Senate majority leader and legislative magician, in 1959

ty," Caro observes, "to convince himself that he held the principles he should hold at any given time, and there was someth[...]

An interesting article showcasing a book about rascally President Lyndon B. Johnson. The headline says the touted, biographical book *"charts Lyndon Johnson's cunning rise."* The caption under the photo of LBJ describes the late President as *"The Wolf In His Prime"* and lauds him as a *"legislative magician."* Above, we are especially interested in the clearly Illuminist pose struck by Johnson: His left arm in the triangle position with the clenched fist of socialist power. No wonder this article in *Newsweek* magazine is entitled, *"Part Devil, Part Angel."* Incidentally, the Librarian of the House of the Temple, Scottish Rite, Washington, D.C., reports that Lyndon B. Johnson never got past the Master Mason (3º) degree. This author believes, however, that Johnson was initiated into other secret societies and Orders than Freemasonry and, of course, he was a key political mover and shaker acting on behalf of both Zionist interests and the nation's oil elite.

David Rockefeller, Sr., Illuminati insider, multibillionaire, and founder of the Trilateral Commission. This photo, in the upscale *Town & Country* magazine, was without caption or explanation. It is obviously staged as it shows the exaggerated masonic arm sign. Note that the image of Rockefeller's torso is not even centered, even though a highly professional photographer took the photo, and *Town and Country* magazine's editors are thorough and detailed in photo art selection and placement.

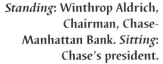

Standing: Winthrop Aldrich, Chairman, Chase-Manhattan Bank. *Sitting*: Chase's president.

Just an innocent photo shoot? Don't believe it! This is Congressman Richard Gephardt (D-MO), House Minority Leader. He's standing on a square, in Masonry signifying rulership of the four corners of the earth. Both his arms are in the triangular position. His necktie is black and white checked, as on the floor tile of the Lodge. He is wearing the colors black and white, signifying the occult *equilibrium* of good and evil, light and darkness. ("Equilibrium" is the secretive *"Lost Word"* of Freemasonry—explained in the 33rd degree as the alchemical synthesis that propels the energies of the universe.) Behind Gephardt are three steps (there are three degrees in the Blue Lodge.) He is standing in an open doorway. Behind him in mosaic on the marble floor is the emblem of the all-seeing eye. The portal beyond, looming above and virtually framing the Congressman, is the arch. The arch plays a significant role in Freemasonry, and one of the major schools of the Lodge is Royal Arch Masonry. All in all, a thoroughly Masonic—and meticulously staged and crafted scene. Gephardt was shown in this photo to be a major player in political affairs and a prime contender on the national and world scenes. This photo took up the entire page in *Time* magazine, but there was no caption or explanation about it. (Photo: *Time* magazine, September 30, 1996)

2003: Year of the woman among the 'Fortune' 500?

Small number of CEOs deliver outsized results

By Del Jones
USA TODAY

The smart money was on the women in 2003.

Eight *Fortune* 500 companies have female CEOs, and as a group they outperformed the broader market by a substantial margin. An $8,000 investment Jan. 1 in the S&P 500 index would be worth $10,130 as of the close of stock trading Monday. The same $8,000 invested equally in the eight companies with women at the helm would be worth $12,130, including a loss in energy company Mirant, which has been under bankruptcy protection since July. That's a 52% gain for the women vs. a 27% gain for the index of all large companies.

Cover story

One explanation is that 2003 was a fluke. When the women's performance is examined for the entire tenure they've been CEOs — which ranges from six months to 40 years — results are more mixed.

Nevertheless, 7-for-8 in 2003 is impressive enough to give rise to a Darwinian theory: The glass ceiling has been so difficult to crack that women who reach the top are, on average, ~~ives than their male count~~

By Todd Plitt, USA TODAY

Turnaround artist: Lucent Technologies CEO Patricia Russo led the company to its first profitable quarter since 2000.

chain of 143 supermarkets in the Northeast.

Another explanation proposed by Marion Sandler, co-CEO of Golden West Financial since 1963, is that many recently promoted women were ~~~~ that were on life~~~~

Lucent Technologies CEO Patricia Russo in a *USA Today* newspaper (December 30, 2003) photo and article. See how clever the editors were in placing Russo's head so that the red, serpentine, circular Lucent Technologies (similar to the Oroboros) appears to be an occultic ring or halo (Nimbus).

Banker E.H. Harriman (center) with sons Roland (left) and Averell (right) in 1907. Young Averell Harriman is giving the masonic sign with his left arm. Averell Harriman went on to become Governor of New York State, U.S. Ambassador to Dictator Joseph Stalin's Communist Russia, and a Patriarch of the Order of Skull & Bones.

Pamela Harriman is doing more here with her body than merely being "Life of the Party," title of this book. A Churchill heir, Pamela was a mistress of one of the Illuminati Rothschilds and later married Governor Averell Harriman, Patriarch of Skull & Bones. Pamela Harriman met and "mentored" young Bill Clinton when he was just a student at Georgetown University in Washington, D.C. She introduced the young man to her aging husband and *voila!*—the political career of William Jefferson Clinton was on the fast track. Many years later, after Pamela's husband passed away and President Bill Clinton was in the White House, Clinton appointed Pamela to the prestigious post of Ambassador to France in Paris.

Buzz Aldrin, Scottish Rite Mason, was the first astronaut to walk on the moon. Aldrin also planted a double-headed eagle flag on the soil of the moon's surface, claiming the moon as territory belonging to the Supreme Mother Lodge of Freemasonry. Note Aldrin's Masonic arm pose. (Photo: NASA)

Astronaut Edwin "Buzz" Aldrin, 33° Mason, presents the Scottish Rite flag carried to the moon on Apollo 11 in 1969 to Masonic Grand Commander Luther A. Smith (from the book, *Lodge of the Doubleheaded Eagle*, by William L. Fox, University of Arkansas Press, 1997).

General Robert E. Lee, commanding officer of the Army of the Confederacy. (Oil portrait: Washington & Lee University, Lexington, Virginia)

Will Rogers (1879-1935), was a famous storyteller and a Freemason. Here he is in the pose of *Sublime Knights Elected* degree.

Elias Ashmole was made a Freemason in 1646. This illustration is from the picture in the Ashmolean Museum in Oxford, England. The book is Ashmole's *History of the Garter*. It chronicled the secret society of English nobility called the Order of the Garter. The Latin words in the lower corner of the engraving mean an *"honorable distinction."*

TWENTY

The Merovingian Dynasty, The Priory of Sion, and the Spear of Longinus

The Priory of Sion (also the *Prieure de Sion*) is said to be the "secret society of societies."[1] Baigent, Leigh, and Lincoln, authors of one acclaimed book, *Holy Blood, Holy Grail*, write that the brotherhood of the Priory of Sion has been preserved for two millennia. France's royal Merovingian Dynasty's bloodline is said to be the protector of the sect, which boasts that it is the actual bloodline of Jesus. The astonishing claim is that Jesus and Mary Magdalene were married and had children and from this bloodline shall someday arise a man who shall become the ruler of planet earth.

The Holy Grail

Tied in with this unscriptural—even blasphemous—legend are the tales of the Holy Grail and the Spear of Longinus. Some teach that as the blood of Jesus oozed from his body on the cross, it was collected in the Holy Grail cup. Esoterically that would make the Holy Grail, if it exists, magical and capable of great miracles.

A variation of this story is that the Holy Grail was the drinking vessel of Jesus at the Last Supper, which again would translate into the cup being a magical talisman.

The Spear of Longinus

The Spear of Longinus is yet another legend connected to the Priory of Sion. It holds that a Roman Centurion named Longinus was the one who thrust his spear into Jesus' side at the crucifixion. Some of Jesus' blood is alleged to have fallen on him and miracles ensued. Thus, again, a magical talisman was created—the Spear of Longinus.

Throughout history wicked tyrants, including Napoleon and Hitler, have sought possession of the Spear, believing that it is the Spear of Destiny and that whoever possesses it shall have the power to rule the world.

William Cooper, whose book, *Behold a Pale Horse,* and his revelations on his national radio program so angered the elite they put out a contract on his life, sometimes mentioned the Spear of Destiny.[2] Cooper was murdered by a combined federal-local police team that ambushed him as he peacefully stopped his pickup at a stop sign on his way home from a grocery store. In his book, he spoke of how vital the Spear of Destiny is in the Illuminati scheme of things:

> According to members of the intelligence community, when the New World Order is solidified the relics will be taken out, will be united with the *Spear of Destiny*, and will, according to legend, give the world's ruler absolute power… Again, I remind you that it makes not one iota of difference what you believe. If *they* (the Illuminati) believe, *you* will be affected.[3]

The Spear As Pentagram and Lightning Bolt

The Spear is a symbol of long-standing repute in the pagan and ancient Mystery Religions. In the Egyptian religion, it was called the Arrow of Re, or Ra, the Sun God, who was also called Horus, son of Osiris and his reincarnation, who had the all-seeing eye. Anton LaVey, in his book *Satan Speaks*, notes that the Sign of the Spear is actually the inverted pentagram.[4] In turn, the pentagram (the satanic five-pointed star), according to LaVey represents "Excalibur, the Spear of Destiny, Wotan's spear point, the lightning bolt that created the protoplasm of life."[5]

The Rosicrusians and the Sign of An Arrow

Moreover, the Rosicrucian Order seems to be somehow connected with both the legend of the Spear and the Priory of Sion. D. C. Yermak, writing in *The Axis of Death – Vatican, Masonry, Zionism, Enemies of God*, explains that, "The Rosicrucians, by making their secret sign with the first three fingers of the right hand united, make the *Sign of an Arrow*."[6]

The Rosicrucian's Sign of an Arrow is dark and evil because it is used by the individual to remove himself from God's Blessing and leave himself purposely exposed to the arrows of the devil. (In this case, the form, or shape, relates the arrow to the spear).

Dean Grace, authoritative researcher in symbology and Masonic secrets, believes that at least some modern-day disciples of this international black lodge, Priory of Sion, communicate their involvement to other hidden members by giving the *Sign of the Spear Point*.[7] In this sign, the point of the spear can either be sharply angular or it can be modified. Often, the fingers are positioned so that the horns and face of Baphomet are indistinctly seen, as in the inverted pentagram star.

Grace's research also indicates the Priory of Sion is either linked or had something to do in the development of other, related occult groups such as the Order of Knights Templar. "The spear point symbol," he says, "is the building block of the four-spoked, eight-pointed Maltese Cross of the Order of the Knights of Malta."[8]

How the Sign is Given

A variation of the sharp, angular spear point sign is that displayed in this chapter of

Codex Magica in the photos of ABC News reporter Sam Donaldson and U.S.A. Vice President Dick Cheney. However, their modified hand and finger positioning is likely simply a personal eccentricity. As in all cases of secret hand signs, human variation and personality intervene, so that not all the signs are rendered expertly and in a crisp, uniform, standardized fashion.

When placed in or near the female vulva area or the male genital area, the spear point becomes a phallic symbol. In all cases, the sign of the spear point is given so that the Y, the spear or arrow, is pointing *downward*, toward the nether regions where, presumably, Satan and his legions reside. That is, toward the pit of hell.

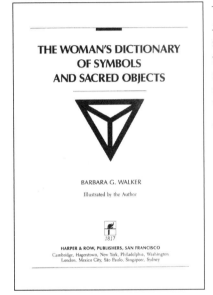

Title page of Barbara Walker's *The Woman's Dictionary of Symbols and Sacred Objects*. Inside, Walker identified the symbol shown as the Dragon's Eye. She reports that the Dragon's Eye forms a triple triangle, sacred to the Goddess, and that this symbol appears often in medieval books of magic, to invoke the protection of female spirits and entities. In fact, the Dragon's Eye bears a remarkable resemblence to the Sign of the Spear Point, and the name Dragon's Eye is appropriate, indeed.

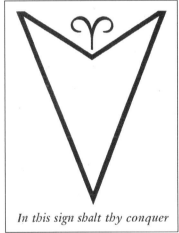

In this sign shalt thy conquer

Symbol from the back cover of the fascinating book, *The Talisman of the United States: The Mysterious Street Lines of Washington, D.C.*, by Charles Westbook, Ph.D. (1990). The symbol depicted is a spear point superimposed by a modified *fleur de lis*, a symbol of the Merovingian royal dynasty.

"Shield of the Trinity," in the British Museum, which turns out to be an emblem of the Priory of Sion.

Drawing of the Rock of Sion and the Sign of the Priory of Sion. (From the book, *Holy Blood, Holy Grail*)

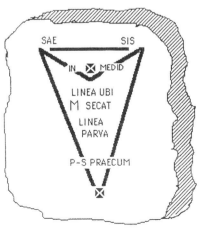

MARCH 1, 1999 $2.95

BEHIND THE SCENES WITH LEO

Senator Clinton?

www.time.com

First Lady Hillary Rodham Clinton, wearing a "Mao Tse Tung" peasant outfit and fashion look, clearly giving the Baphomet/Priory of Sion sign. This cover and feature article in *Time* (March 1, 1999) examined Hillary Clinton's possible candidacy for the U.S. Senate from the state of New York in the upcoming election (2000). In fact, Ms. Clinton ran and won. Was the symbology displayed (Priory of Sion Sign) predictive of her future successful run?

Said by political analysts to be one of the most important addresses of his political career, in late August 1998, President Bill Clinton went on national television to give a limited *mea culpa* (*"I am sorry"*) for his sexual indiscretions with the young White House intern, Monica Lewinsky. Left: A chagrined, frustrated, and angry Bill Clinton readies himself for the camera shoot, with the aid of an associate. Below: Just moments before the TV cameras roll, Clinton sets his face in a sober, resolute attitude. With his *Baphomet/Priory of Sion hand sign*, he invokes success and blessings from the ruler and forces of darkness. (Left photo: *Newsweek*, August 31, 1998, p.3; Below photo: *The European* newspaper, August 24–30, p.3)

TELEVISION

Dan Rather chats with the chief

CNN's Sadler snags Arkan for interview

Big day for war-related scoops Wednesday.

CBS' Dan Rather scored an exclusive with President Clinton for Wednesday's *60 Minutes II.*

Earlier in the day, CNN's Brent Sadler snagged a surprise interview in Belgrade with accused war criminal and Serb paramilitary leader Zeljko Raznatovic, also known as

Inside TV
By Peter Johnson

Arkan. In a live 25-minute interview, Arkan denied charges against him and accused CNN's Christiane Amanpour of inaccurate reporting, which CNN and Amanpour denied.

Why did Clinton, who last gave a one-on-one television interview to PBS' Jim Lehrer on Jan. 21, 1998, agree to talk to Rather, who last interviewed Clinton after the 1996 Democratic National Convention?

"The war is on, and he's concerned about having the public understand very clearly why he's doing this, and what he hopes to accomplish," Rather said after spending just over an hour at the White House.

Rather said he had no concerns about being used by Clinton to push his agenda on Yugoslavia. "There are times when one has that thought, but when you're talking about war, you can never get too much information."

Clinton said the NATO campaign "will take some time." On other subjects, he said he "never" considered resigning, his family is doing "quite well, considering what we've been through" and "I'd be happy to

White House photo via AP

Presidential, personal: Rather interviewed Clinton Wednesday about 'personal things as well as war.'

War criminal? Arkan (Zeljko Raznatovic), left, denied charges in talk with Brent Sadler and accused CNN of shoddy work.

slavia last week and allowed to return to Belgrade this week, got word that Arkan would talk Wednesday morning.

"Everyone said, 'Wow, let's start making arrangements,' and six hours later, courtesy of a satellite hook-up from Serb TV, the interview aired live," said CNN vice president Will King.

MARIA'S MOMENT: If it

gets better than this, please alert NBC's Maria Shriver. First: In the span of a month, a book she never expected to be a best-seller has sold 200,000

ic. Which means, third, a spring break in New York while hubby Arnold Schwarzenegger tends to the kids in Los Angeles. Now, fourth: Wednesday, Shriver won a Peabody for her hour-long look at welfare on *Dateline.* "Twenty-two years of journalism and 43 years of life, and in one month it all comes together," Shriver said. Her *What's Heaven?* is a kids' book on how to talk about death.

Until Wednesday, after being stopped by countless numbers of people who said the book moved them, "it was the thing I most proud of." Then she

NBC

Maria Shriver: Wins Peabody

has her filling in this week for vacationing Katie Couric.

Winning that top broadcast-journalism prize is sweet, she said. "When you suggest an hour on welfare, it's not a subject that people jump up and down about."

Other winners of the Peabody, presented by the University of Georgia for achievement in broadcasting: CBS' Carol Marin and Don Mosely for a *Public Eye* piece on a burn victim; CNN's Christiane Amanpour for international reporting; and PBS' Bill Moyers for a *Frontline* piece on campaign fund raising. Producer David E. Kelley won for ABC's *The Practice* and Fox's *Ally McBeal,* while producer Steven Bochco won for an episode of ABC's *NYPD Blue* called "Raging Bulls," dealing with racial intolerance.

BRIEFLY: A good start Tuesday for Craig Kilborn on CBS' *Late Late Show* against NBC's Conan O'Brien in the late late night scene. Kilborn's debut was watched by 1.55 million viewers, compared with O'Brien's 1.95 million viewers.

Inside TV appears Monday through Thursday.

In yet another Clinton bit of magic, President Bill Clinton gives cabalistic sign (Baphomet/Priory of Sion spearpoint) while being interviewed in late March 1999, by CBS News anchor Dan Rather. The *USA Today* newspaper's editors apparently complied with elitist's request to give maximum publicity to Clinton's interview and to this particular photo. Subject of this interview was the U.S. war against Yugoslavia/Serbia, a key Illuminati project to help usher in their New World Order. Clinton invokes the forces of darkness to assist his speech and enhance his hypnotic persuasive powers over the American people.

TV and movie actor Scott Bakula (*Quantum Leap; Murphy Brown*) (Photo: *Parade* magazine, November 25, 2001)

ALLAN SLOAN

Lucky Timing Is Good (Big Time)

Vice President Dick Cheney bailed out of his chief executive's job at Halliburton before an acquisition hit the fan and its stock plummeted

SOMETIMES IT'S BETTER TO BE LUCKY THAN SMART. Consider Vice President Dick Cheney. He's got to be one of the luckiest former corporate chieftains on the planet. No, I'm not talking about managing to pull out the election in Florida. Rather, I'm talking about how he came out about $20 million ahead because, at least partly because of public criticism, he cashed in stock options that would currently be underwater if he'd kept them. And how, luckily for him, he had left the executive suite before the roof fell in at Halliburton, the big oil-services company that he used to run.

This same "better lucky than smart" principle applies to the Bushies who had to liquidate their Enron holdings to take big jobs in the administration. Some of them complained about the supposed injustice of having to make such a financial sacrifice. Poor babies. Of course, they've totally lucked out, because Enron, $70 a share when Bush was sworn in, now goes for 24 cents.

Cheney's worth a closer look because he's the luckiest of the group. And because a deal he made as Halliburton's CEO has come back to haunt the company—big time, as he would say.

Let me give you some history, and take you through Lucky Cheney's

RIGHT PLACE, RIGHT TIME: Cheney in 1996, when the energy company he ran was on the way up

math. In August 2000, you may recall, George W. Bush picked Cheney to be his vice presidential candidate. Cheney, a longtime politician who had been at Halliburton all of five years, promptly stepped down. He said he would sell his stock before taking office if the Republicans won—but he wouldn't commit to unloading his Halliburton options. That caused an uproar because owning Halliburton options would have given Cheney exactly the same ethical problem as owning Halliburton stock: he would have a substantial personal interest in Halliburton's stock price. The company traditionally has good years when oil prices are rising and not-so-good years when they're falling. The conflict is obvious.

Cheney cashed in all the options he could, clearing $19 million by my math. Since I can't read Cheney's mind and I couldn't get any comment from him or his associates, I don't know if he sold because of the public pressure, or because he wanted to sell. Regardless, it sure worked out well for him. He got around $10 million more from selling the Halliburton shares he owned outright. Total: around $30 million. I'm a bit vague on the numbers because

no one in Cheneyland would discuss them with me. So I'm relying on public documents, work by Thomson Wealth Management and my own analysis.

Flash-forward to the present. At Halliburton's current price of around $17, Cheney's options would be out of the money, because their exercise prices ranged from $21 to $54.50. Someday, of course, Halliburton's stock price may soar. But for now, Cheney is $19 million ahead because he cashed them in. (His $10 million of stock would currently fetch $3 million.)

I don't think for a minute that Cheney bailed out of Halliburton knowing that trouble lay ahead. I think he just got lucky. If he were still Halliburton's CEO, shareholders would probably be screaming for his head. That's because his biggest deal—Halliburton's $8 billion purchase of Dresser Industries in 1998—infected Halliburton with an asbestos liability. Think of it as financial plague, and you get a sense of how nasty the problem is. To give you the short version, Dresser once had a subsidiary, Harbison-Walker, that used asbestos in some products. Dresser made Harbison-Walker a separate company in 1992, and H-W agreed to take over the entire asbestos liability. But the claims became so enormous that H-W and a European company that subsequently bought it both ended up in bankruptcy. So the asbestos lawsuits, searching for deeper pockets, have migrated to Dresser and its new owner, Halliburton.

A Halliburton spokesman said the firm didn't know it was taking on a potential asbestos problem when it bought Dresser in 1998: "We believed they were indemnified," she said. Indeed, in the past year or so, asbestos liability has exploded, becoming a threat to companies that barely know how to spell asbestos. Halliburton, which lost some big asbestos verdicts that it's now appealing, has taken an active role in H-W's bankruptcy, trying to pull off a fancy maneuver to keep the asbestos problem confined to H-W. We won't know for years how the game ends.

Meanwhile, Cheney isn't giving any of his stock and options profits back to Halliburton or its shareholders. He gets the blame for this fiasco, because he was in charge. That's the way the world works. Big time.

SLOAN is NEWSWEEK's Wall Street editor. His e-mail address is sloan@panix.com.

Vice President Dick Cheney. His wife, Lynn, is a writer of steamy lesbian sex novels. His daughter is an avowed Lesbian, and Dick? Well... this photograph is rather telling.

Austin American-Statesman

SUNDAY, MAY 19, 2002

PARADE

Attorney General **John Ashcroft** *is taking firm steps to thwart terrorism. Understandably, his efforts provoke a critical question:*

Has America's Top Cop Gone Too Far?

A Report By Edward Klein

INSIDE: Grill A Backyard Feast..

Attorney-General John Ashcroft was given his high post by Bush, say the Christian conservatives, because Ashcroft is one of them. But his actions in office and this Illuminati pose would suggest otherwise. When Ashcroft was sworn into office, he did not rest his hand on a Bible and take the oath. Instead, an official photo shows Ashcroft laying his hand on a stack of three books. What were these three mysterious books?

Tom Pritzker, CEO of the Hyatt Hotels chain. (*Business Week*, December 20, 2004, p. 40)

President of the U.S.A. James K. Polk (1795-1849)

Producer David Gest and wife, singer Liza Minelli. Gest, a homosexual, and Minelli are now separated and seeking a divorce.

Actor Jack Bolger, who played the Tin Man in the classic alchemical drama, *The Wizard of Oz*, with wife, Floe, at home in Beverly Hills.

May | June 2004

AARP
The Magazine
America's Largest Circulation Magazine

"Every day of my life I walk with the idea I am black, no matter how successful I am."
—*Danny Glover*

SPECIAL REPORT

A New America
71% now approve of interracial marriage—even for their own children. Are we close to Martin Luther King Jr.'s dream of a "beloved community"?

PLUS THE STARTLING GENETICS OF HATE

#BXNQHFG ************CR LOT 0156A**R-073
#027303034/6/A 9# OCT2005 037086 00285
TEXE W MARRS
1708 PATTERSON RD
AUSTIN TX 78733-6507

www.aarpmagazine.org $3.50

Actor Danny Glover, notorious for his Marxist liberal political activism, sends a cabalistic message through the medium of *AARP* magazine, also known for its Marxist and Jewish agenda. Glover is signaling deep occultic spirits to empower his quest.

Sam Donaldson's face has been a staple for many years on ABC News. But here, in this photo in *Smart Business* magazine, it is Donaldson's hands we should pay attention to. This full page shot of Sam Donaldson had no caption and no explanation. Obviously, it was staged for the sole benefit of those who know.

Impresario Donald Trump demonstrates his knowledge of the Illuminati's cabalistic Baphomet/Priory of Sion hand sign in the ad (left, above) for his successful TV series, *The Apprentice*. Then, in the glossy mag *Private Clubs*, June 2004, read mostly by wealthy members of elite country clubs. Trump is shown three times, once on the cover and twice inside, in cabalistic poses. Analysis: At center, above, Trump's necktie and hands create a sexual "diamond in the lotus" position, with three triangles. The magazine cover photo at left includes the mirror factor, the message being that there are two Trumps, the esoteric, private "Illuminati Trump," and the outgoing and extroverted "Public Trump." Finally, at top, right, we also are shown a serious Donald sitting and giving the required cabalistic triangle sign with both the fingers and thumbs of both hands touching. This is a common sign of recognition among Illuminati.

Mexican actor Diego Luna played a bisexual in the raunchy movie, *Y Tu Mama Tambien* (*And Your Mother, Too*). In this photo from *Interview* magazine (2004), Luna gives the Baphomet and Priory of Sion hand sign giving it cabalistic sexual impact by placement of his hands in the genital area. He shows his indifference and ambivalence toward the beautiful girls on either side, conduct befitting a homosexual.

Whitfield Diffie, highly acclaimed cryptographic computer software designer for the Defense Department and for Sun Microsystems. Diffie's wife is an Egyptologist. David Meyer, foremost authority on symbols and occultism, believes Diffie's pose is a symbol of tantric, or sexual yoga, rather then the Priory's *Spear of Longinus*.
·(Photo: *Omni*, Winter 1995)

INTERVIEW

WHITFIELD DIFFIE

A (SEMI) PRIVATE CONVERSATION WITH
THE HEADMAN OF
THE CYPHERPUNK REVOLUTION

Depressed for weeks, worried his career was going nowhere, he mulled over a set of apparently unsolvable problems. Otherwise unemployed, Whitfield Diffie was a househusband about to cook dinner for his wife, when he sat down in the living room of their borrowed quarters to ponder once more the ideas that had plagued him for a decade. Diffie cared about hidden writing—codes, ciphers, cryptograms—because he had a passionate interest in keeping people's private lives private. A Sixties radical with blond hair flowing down his back, he saw cryptography was the only way for citizens to protect themselves from government snooping. He

PHOTOGRAPHS BY CHRISTOPHER SPRINGMANN

Magical Signs of the Jewish Cabala—The Six-Pointed Star, Babylonian Witchcraft, and the Hollywood Perdition of Jerry Seinfeld and Associates

He said furthermore unto me, Son of man, seest thou what they do? even the great abominations that the house of Israel committeth here…

Ezekiel 8:6

Kabbalism is a system of Jewish mysticism and magic and is the foundational element in modern witchcraft. Virtually all of the great witches and sorcerers of this century were Kabbalists.

— William J. Schnoebelen, in
The Dark Side of Freemasonry

In the decades of the 70s, 80s, and 90s, the hottest spiritual trend was the New Age movement. As we move forward through the first decade of the 21st century, the latest cure-all spiritual phenomenon seems to be the Jewish Cabala (or Kabbalah). The Cabala is not new, of course. It's been around for centuries. The Cabala is actually ancient magic. It is an exotic blend of devilish, sometimes fanciful, New Age mystical practices topped by a philosophical bent of Jewish supremacism. Orthodox Judaism, or phariseeism, is rife with cabalism, and Jewish rabbis are the Cabala's greatest promoters.

Celebrities and Cabala

The recent explosion in mainstream interest in cabalism is boosted by the many big-name celebrities who have recently been hawking cabalism as the miraculous answer to all of man's problems. An undercover BBC reporter who infiltrated a London cabala group witnessed singer Madonna and Guy Ritchie chanting mystic spells to "cleanse" Chernobyl, the site in Ukraine of a nuclear plant disaster in 1986.[1] Other news accounts link entertainers Paris Hilton, Britney Spears, Roseanne Barr, Demi Moore, Shirley MacLaine, Ashton Kutcher, Sandra Bernhard, Barbra Streisand, Dianne Keaton, Gwyneth Paltrow, Goldie Hawn, Elizabeth Taylor, Michael Jackson, Mick Jagger, Uri Geller, Diane Ladd, Laura Dern and a legion of other "stars" with practice of cabala.[2]

Look closely when you see any of these people on TV or pictured in magazines and you'll often see the characteristic red string wristband they wear. Lately, former President Bill Clinton's been spotted wearing it—he's a cabalist—and so has Florida's politician Katherine Harris, who became a famous household icon as Florida's Republican Secretary of State during the bizarre 2000 election snafu. Republican big-wig and former House Speaker, Newt Gingrich, is reported to be a cabala advocate, and some say conservative talk show host Rush Limbaugh and his rabbi are also into the cabala.

Among the most notorious of cabalists are the TV comedy stars of the once #1-rated "The Jerry Seinfeld Show." The producer of the Seinfeld show was Larry David, a Jew, all four of the cast were Jews, and cabalistic hand signs, occult language, and magic rituals were covertly planted in many episodes.

Republican Party spokesman and former Speaker of the House Newt Gingrich, shown here wearing his Judaism skull cap, is into New Age cabalistic magic and is a paid spokesman for Zionist interests.

Jason Alexander, who played the loveable loser "George Costanza" on the show, posed for *TV Guide* magazine in a blatantly cabalistic body pose. Plus, his left and right hands gave the "El Diablo" horned devil sign in an "As Above, So Below" gesture.

Michael Richards, who portrayed the klutzy "Kramer" in *Seinfeld*, also seems to relish giving cabalistic and Masonic hand signs and gestures. Richards was pictured on the front cover of the *Scottish Rite Journal*, and inside the publication, he told of how pleased he is to be a Freemason.[3]

Star Trek's Leonard Nimoy ("Mr. Spock") is constantly sighted in cabalistic poses. His famous Vulcan hand sign on the TV series was actually the Hebrew letter, *Shin*.[4] Its display is part and parcel of Jewish religion. So every time viewers observed Mr. Spock (Nimoy) giving the sign, they were unknowingly being made a participant in a cabalistic occult ritual.

Sodom, Egypt, and 21st Century Judaism

In one of the most controversial of all the many video documentaries I have produced, ***Cauldron of Abaddon***, I stated, *"From Jerusalem and Israel flow a torrent of satanic evil and mischief, endangering the whole world."*[5] Zionist Jews and their cohorts in the Christian Zionist community were angered over what I said, but they had no response to the mountain of facts presented in the video proving my point.

It is undeniable that God Himself, in *Revelation 11:8*, declares that in the last days just prior to Christ's return, one of the most wicked places on earth will be Jerusalem and Israel. In *Revelation* God calls Jerusalem "Sodom and Egypt."

The question is, why? Why is Jerusalem and the nation of Israel spiritually "Sodom and Egypt?" I believe it is because of the Jewish religion, a religion diametrically opposed to the Old Testament faith of Moses, Isaac, Jacob, and the prophets.

From the days of the Jews' captivity in Babylon, to today, the religion of the Jews has increasingly grown more dark and more wicked. Jesus openly castigated the Jewish religionists; He called them "blind guides," "fools, hypocrites." He said, "ye devour widows' houses, and for a pretense make long prayer...ye compass sea and land to make one proselyte, and when he is made, ye make him twofold more the child of hell than yourselves" *(Matthew 23:14-15)*.

Children of hell, that's what Jesus called the Jewish religious teachers. That was almost 2,000 years ago. Well, guess what? The Jewish religionists are even worse now, in the 21st century. They've had almost 2,000 years more to practice and perfect their evil religion. Today, those who practice satanic cabalism and believe in the *Talmud* are the children of hell a hundred times over.

In *Codex Magica* we do not have the space to fully report on the almost unbelievably wicked Talmudic and Cabalistic religion of the Jews. But it is important to understand that the horrific nature of the Jews' religion lies in its man-made traditions. In reality, these traditions are satanic in origin. I refer especially to the *Jewish Talmud*, the legalistic law traditions of the rabbis, and to the *Jewish Cabala* (also Kabbalah or Quaballah), which are the mystical teachings and traditions of the rabbis and sages.

If the Jews had stuck to the teachings of the Old Testament, Satan would not have had such terrible inroads. Indeed, if Moses and the prophets had been heeded, or if their writings were honored today, the Jews would believe in Jesus Christ as Messiah and be saved by faith in His promises. Instead, the Jews departed from the prophets, and over the centuries the rabbis steadily developed a body of man-made literature (the *Talmud* and the *Cabala*) that is supremely wicked and corrupt. Their traditions, moreover, are antithetical to the Faith and teachings of Moses and the prophets. (I do not refer, of course, to the Faith of Jews who are Christian believers.)

Worse, it can be remarkably demonstrated that the philosophy and doctrines of the Jewish Cabala are the very fount and wellspring of virtually every wicked, occult sect, satanic secret society, and witchcraft cult that has arisen in the past one thousand years!

The Cabala brings together in one neat package the core of all the Mystery teachings of the ancients. Indeed, the Holy Bible gives evidence that the Jewish elders had brought the Mysteries into the Temple and had conducted secret ceremonies in hidden chambers as far back as the days of the prophet Ezekiel (see *Ezekiel 8)*. God called these teachings and rituals *"abominations."*

Regrettably, the abominations are multiplied in the 21st century Jewish religion in which the Cabala plays a central role.

The Masonic Lodge and The Cabala

Freemasonry has long praised the Cabala, and its top officials have admitted that the Lodge's rituals and teachings are but the offspring of the Jewish tradition. Albert Pike, former Sovereign Grand Commander of the Scottish Rite wrote: "One is filled with admiration, on penetrating into the Sanctuary of the Cabala."[6]

Just how much Masonry owes to the Cabala is illustrated by study of the Knights of Kadosh degree (30°). Ed Decker, director of Free the Masons Ministries, reports that the trappings of this degree ritual are "overtly sinister" and incorporate a "High level of Kabbalistic symbolism."

> When one is surrounded by black curtains, skulls, and a coffin with a shrouded
> knight speaking forth from within, it doesn't take a spiritual giant to discern that
> this is not a godly organization![7]

Confirming Decker's findings, medical doctor James L. Holly, a Christian who has done great works in exposing Freemasonry, in his outstanding volume, *The Southern Baptist Convention and Freemasonry*, shows how the 30° Masonic initiate is led unawares into a direct spiritual relationship with Satan. In the ritual, Satan is personified as a mysterious cabalistic mystic.[8]

Interestingly, *Richardson's Monitor of Freemasonry* says that, "the Knights of Kadosh Degree is intimately connected with the ancient Order of Knights Templar, as it commemorates their old ceremonies of initiation."[9] Allegedly, the members of the Order of Knights Templar worshipped Baphomet, the hideous male/female Luciferian goat god and conducted blasphemous ceremonies, which included urinating on a cross and homosexual sodomy.

Freemasonry is Jewish

In 1855, the renowned Rabbi Isaac Wise wrote: "Freemasonry is a Jewish establishment, whose history, grades, official appointments, passwords, and explanations are Jewish from beginning to end."[10]

The *Jewish Tribune* newspaper, in 1927, in an editorial, stated: "Freemasonry is based on Judaism. Eliminate the teachings of Judaism from the Masonic ritual and what is left?"[11]

Ray Novosel, writing from Australia in 2004, states:

Zionist world leaders, men in influential positions with the various Masonic organizations everywhere, have worked "hand in glove" for a universal world revolution, which will bring in the One World Church and a One World Government. Many Masonic Lodges are exclusively Jewish, as are the controlling

In *Richardson's Monitor of Freemasonry* (p. 64), this symbol is used to illustrate the Royal Arch Degree. Masonic literature is replete with examples of the Jewish Star of David and other Cabalistic tokens, symbols, emblems, and signs.

Freemasonry's The Real Grip of a Master Mason (3°) is a magical handshake based on ancient Jewish Cabala and the letter "Shin" from the 22-letter Hebrew alphabet. (*Duncan's Masonic Ritual and Monitor*, p. 120)

B'nai B'rith Lodges—the mother of the infamous and very dangerous Anti Defamation League (ADL).[12]

Masonry's Jewish Roots

A popular pro-Freemasonry web site, in an article entitled *"Judaism and Freemasonry,"* comments:

> Jews were actively involved in the beginnings of Freemasonry in America. There is evidence they were among those who established Masonry in seven of the original thirteen states…A Jewish Mason, Moses M. Hays, helped introduce the Scottish Rite in America…Jews, including Rabbis, continued to be involved in the Masonic movement in the United States throughout our history. There have been 51 Jewish American Grand Masters…

> There are many common themes and ideals in Masonic and Jewish rituals, symbols, and words.[13]

The late Pope John Paul II was a believer in Jewish Cabala. On March 22, 1984, the Pope received members of the infamous *B'nai B'rith* Freemasonry Lodge of New York City, made up exclusively of influential Jews, at the Vatican.

Rabbi Seymour Atlas, 32°, K∴C∴C∴H∴

APRIL • 1987 • VOLUME XCV, NUMBER 4

"I am proud to be a Mason" writes Rabbi Seymour Atlas, 32°, in this issue of *The New Age Magazine* (April 1987). Note: The name of this magazine has since been changed to *The Scottish Rite Journal*, to hide the connection of Masons with the occultic New Age movment. In fact, the Masonic order is predominantly led by Jews. As its former Sovereign Grand Commander, Albert Pike, has revealed, the symbols and rituals of Freemasonry are all based on the Cabala of the Jews.

The most honored Masonic leader in the history of Freemasonry was Albert Pike. Pike maintained that, "every Masonic Lodge is a temple of religion; and its teachings are instruction in religion."[14] Now, Pike also asserted that the true meanings of the symbols of Freemasonry are found in the occult philosophy of the Jewish Cabala, that Freemasonry owes all its secrets to the Cabala, and that Freemasonry is a religion based on the Cabala.[15]

Demons, Magic, and Mysticism in the Cabala

Here are the eye-opening comments of a number of knowledgeable authorities on the Jewish Cabala:

> The Cabala contains such power and demonic teaching, it is more than enough to give the ideology and driving force needed to lead the world astray and to keep such an evil conspiracy alive through the centuries…The Cabala is a teaching source of the Freemasons as well as for other groups.
>
> — John Torrell, publisher
> *The Dove*

> Kabbalah: The sacred books of black magic of Orthodox Judaism which form a large part of the basis of the western secret societies, from Rosicrucianism to Freemasonry and the OTO. Kabbalism is itself derived from the sorcery of ancient Babylon and…Pharaohic Egypt.
>
> — Craig Heimbichner
> *Blood on the Altar*

> Kabbalism is a system of Jewish mysticism and magic and is the foundational element in modern witchcraft. Virtually all of the great witches and sorcerers of this century were Kabbalists.
>
> — William J. Schnoebelen,
> *The Dark Side of Freemasonry*

> The Hebrew Cabala is a series of occultic writings that are as demonic as any incantation ever uttered in witchcraft. Webster's Dictionary tells us the Cabala (sometimes spelled Kabbala) is "an occult religious philosophy developed by certain Jewish rabbis…"
>
> — James Lloyd
> *The Apocalypse Chronicles*
> (Vol. VII, No. 1, 2005)

Sorcery is commonplace in the depraved religious rituals of cabalistic Judaism. Here a rabbi is seen carrying a chicken off to be sacrificed in a voodoo/Santeria-type ritual during the Jewish festival of Yom Kippur. (*Israel, A Photobiography*, by Micha Bar-Am, New York: Simon & Schuster, 1998)

Twisted Satanic Rituals and Lies

The rabbinical doctrines and teachings of Cabalism are based on a curious blending and mosaic of astrology, numerology, graphology, color magic, symbology, alchemy, pagan religion, and pure Luciferianism.

There are hand signs and body gestures, talismanic jewelry and clothing, hidden codes, and on and on. The end result is a confusing jumble of "man is God" theology (but only *Jewish* man—Gentiles are inferior) and magical formulae, words of power, incantations and spells. Heads of chickens are cropped off and blood sprinkled around; "magic cords" of specific color are worn on the wrist as miracle-working bracelets; magic water is used to heal; magic symbols are objects of trance-like mediation; and mantra-like chants are repeated over and over.

The 22 letters of the Hebrew alphabet are touted as religious idols of great magical powers. Even their shapes are studied and accorded supernatural powers. Angels, Archangels, grimoires, devas, and elementals are worshipped and feared. There are "gods" and more "gods" but only a mysterious, hazy supreme deity behind everything. This supreme deity is a pantheistic god who fills up the whole universe. In fact, he is the macrocosm, the Universe.

Of course, as in all Illuminist magic, there's the double-minded theology of "As Above, So Below," the insidious lie that black is white and *vice versa*; that good and evil are one, that the shadow and the substance are unitary.

Sex magic holds an important place in Cabalism, and sex ritual is a popular vocation of students of Cabala.

Margie Martin, in her informed, unpublished manuscript for her upcoming book, *The Molten Image*, explains that the Tarot cards of witches and occultists are of Jewish origin and correspond with the 22 letters of the Hebrew alphabet.

Finally, Cabalism is pure Illuminism because it teaches the secret doctrine that, ultimately, the higher level adept learns: That the Holy Serpent is the true God; that all the evil that a person does, through alchemy, is magically transformed into righteousness; and that, yes, Lucifer is Lord. Satan is the true and only god. That is the essential doctrine of Cabalism.

The Star of David and The Jewish Utopia

The symbol of the Jewish six-pointed star, known as the *Seal of Solomon* and as the *Magen David*, is the preeminent symbol of Cabalism, but other symbols, signs, and marks also hold the interest of cabalists, including the pentagram or pentacle, the triangle, the circle, the sun, the obelisk, the yoni, and the diamond. It is believed by cabalistic rabbis that there are hidden codes and messages in the numbering of scriptural letters. It is also believed that by working the Cabala, the earth may someday be renovated, rebuilt, perfected. This, say the rabbis, will result in a perfect Jewish Kingdom, or Utopia on earth, ruled by a Cabalist Master, a Jewish leader, naturally.

This belief system of the coming of a Jewish Utopia fits in well with the teachings of the Illuminati. Lady Queensborough, quoting the Jewish authority Bernard Lazare, in the classic *Occult Theocracy*, reported that, "There were Jews behind Weishaupt, founder of the Order of the Illuminati...Jewish financiers such as Daniel Itzig, Friedlander, Ceerfbeer, Benjamin and Abraham Goldsmid, Moses Mocatta, Veitesl Heine Ephram...also Moses Mendelsohn, Naphtali Wessely, Moses Hersheim..."[16]

First Sign, or Due guard.

David Ben Gurion, the first Prime Minister of the newly formed nation of Israel, performs the First Sign of a Select Master Mason. Ben Gurion, a dedicated Marxist/Leninist, was quoted as saying, "I am in favor of Bolshevism" (*American Spectator*, January, 1998). (Photos: *Richardson's Monitor of Freemasonry*, p. 84; *Israel, A Photobiography*, by Micha Bar-Am, New York: Simon & Schuster, 1998)

This illustration from *Mackey's Encyclopedia of Masonry* dates the founding by Jews of the Royal Order of the Freemasons in Palestine at Anno Lucis 4037, or 37 AD.

Chart of Masonic emblems showing the many degrees published, distributed by a Jewish-owned jewelry firm.

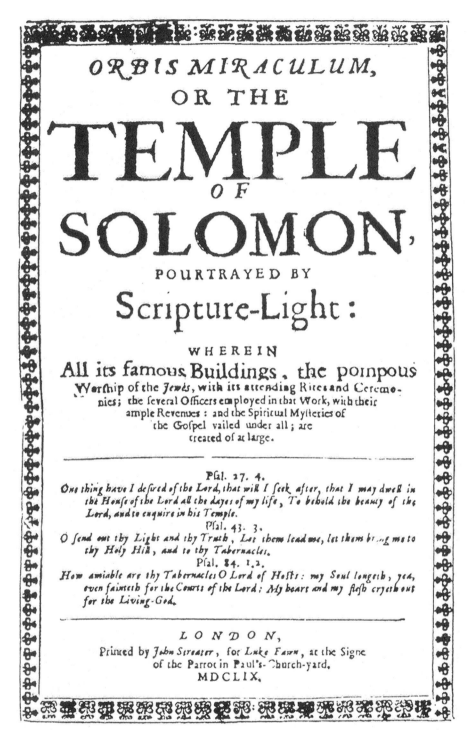

ORBIS MIRACULUM,
OR THE
TEMPLE
OF
SOLOMON,
POURTRAYED BY
Scripture-Light:

WHEREIN
All its famous Buildings, the pompous
Worſhip of the Jews, with its attending Rites and Ceremonies; the ſeveral Officers employed in that Work, with their
ample Revenues: and the Spiritual Myſteries of
the Goſpel vailed under all; are
treated of at large.

Pſal. 27. 4.
One thing have I deſired of the Lord, that will I ſeek after, that I may dwell in
the Houſe of the Lord all the dayes of my life, To behold the beauty of the
Lord, and to enquire in his Temple.
Pſal. 43. 3.
O ſend out thy Light and thy Truth, Let them lead me, let them bring me to
thy Holy Hill, and to thy Tabernacles.
Pſal. 84. 1,2.
How amiable are thy Tabernacles O Lord of Hoſts: my Soul longeth, yea,
even fainteth for the Courts of the Lord: My heart and my fleſh cryeth out
for the Living-God.

LONDON,
Printed by John Streater, for Luke Fawn, at the Signe
of the Parrot in Paul's-Church-yard.
MDCLIX.

An old English masonic manual. The words *Orbis Miraculum* mean
"Magic Mirror."

Many in the Arab and Islamic world know that Zionism is racism and resent the United States' blind support of Israeli Zionist aggression. Fanatical Zionism has also led to Masonic excesses, Talmudic evil, and cabalistic magic by satanic Jews. (Photo: *Reuters*)

BLOOD RITUAL

Philip de Vier

For many years, in Europe and Russia, reports of cabalistic blood ritual sacrifices of young Gentile girls and boys were commonplace. While many were hype and based on old wives' tales, apparently at least some accounts proved to be true, as documented in this revealing book.

The masonic symbol of *square and compass* seems to be patterned on the design of the *Star of David,* also known as the magical *Hexagram.*

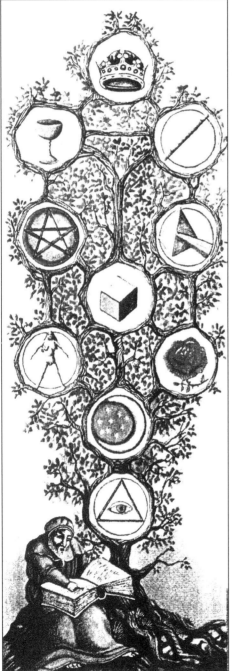

The cabalistic tree of life. (from *Telepathy,* by Alice Bailey, Lucis Trust)

Billionaire Edgar Bronfman, head of the World Jewish Congress, presents President Bill Clinton with the "Nahum Goldman Medal" at the group's tribute dinner on April 30, 1995. The logo of the World Jewish Congress pictures a regionalized globe, within the six-pointed Star of David, set against a darkened circle background.

Some say the word and name of *"Fox"* has hidden, cabalistic significance. Numerologically, the letters F-O-X in the English alphabet equal the sum of 666. Jesus once called Israel's King Herod, a murderous scheming man who embraced magic, *"That old fox."* Fox television network is owned by Rupert Murdock, an ardent Zionist.

Grand Sign.

A poster of Israeli Prime Minister Ariel Sharon

This picture of a political campaign poster promoting the candidacy of Israeli Prime Minister Ariel Sharon was published in *U.S. News & World Report* (February 10, 2003, p. 17). Notice how the poster is twisted to make it look like Sharon has horns! Indeed, Sharon has been called the "Butcher of Lebanon" and is accused of the massacre of Lebanese civilians while he served as Israel's defense minister. Oddly perhaps, the horned shape of the twisted poster resembles the image of the official symbol of the U.S./U.S.S.R. Summit (see inset, above left). Also, notice the striking similarity with the Masonic Grand Sign (below inset).

Triangle design on skull cap of Jewish man is interesting. (Photo: *Israel My Glory*, January 1996)

Logo of the Israel international spy agency, the *Mossad*. The Mossad has a notorious reputation for skullduggery, deception, murder, and assassination. Mossad agents commit many terrorist crimes and the Jewish-run media conveniently blame them on "Arab terrorists." Motto of Mossad and its logo is *"By Deception We Conduct War."*

Cabala symbol (from book, *Art and Symbols of the Occult*, Destiny Books, Rochester, Vermont)

CHALDEAN MAGIC

Its Origin and Development

This front cover of book *"Chaldean Magic"* highlights the importance of the Star of David to occult ritual and magic.

Francois Lenormant

The hexagram, long a magical symbol, was adopted by the Jews in Europe during the medieval period. It later became the centerpiece of the Israeli flag. Here we see a variety of hexagrams, also known as the Jewish Star of David or simply as the six-pointed star.

The magic of the Cabala calls for many uses of the occultic star. Both the five-pointed star and six-pointed star are used by Jewish magicians who work the Cabala formulas and rituals. An enduring cabalistic tale is that of the *Golem*. In medieval times, it was taught that by use of the magic word and by other means, an inanimate man made of clay or dust could be made to come alive. A huge and powerful monster, or beast, the Golem would then do the magician's bidding. In 1920, the classic film *Der Golem* created a stir. Directed by Paul Wegener, *Der Golem* depicted the monster variously wearing either the five-pointed star with one point up (white magic) or two points up (satanic). Also the six-pointed Star of David played a part in the film's plot as a Jewish Rabbi, Rabbi Löw, using the secret word *"AemAct"* brought life and breath into the artificial man.

In *Der Golem*, Rabbi Löw employs the magic word and the pentagram star to bring life to the creature.

Der Golem's film crew used this drawing as a model.

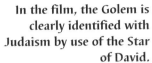

In the film, the Golem is clearly identified with Judaism by use of the Star of David.

Der Golem was shown during the movie with the pentagram star. Here we see two points ascendant (negative; horns of evil).

The relative position of the star points varies through the movie. It is seen here with one point ascendant, indicating positive, good magic.

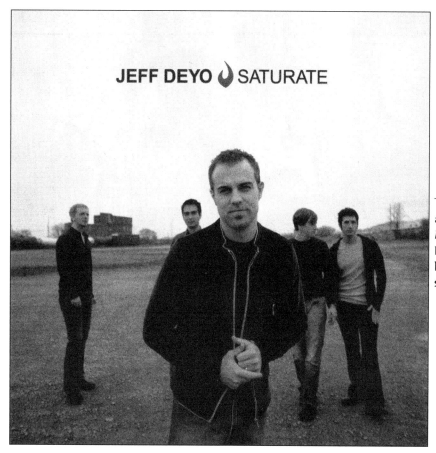

This album was advertised in *Christian Retailing* magazine in February 2002, but the handsign of the person seems to be cabalistic.

President Clinton with Israeli Prime Minister Ehud Barak, left, and PLO Chairman Yasser Arafat in Norway on Tuesday.

Clinton: Mideast peace talks revitalized

OSLO, Norway — President Clinton won pledges of intense peace negotiations from Israeli Prime Minister Ehud Barak and PLO Chairman Yasser Arafat on Tuesday. "We have revitalized the peace process," an upbeat Clinton declared. Barak promised to "finish the journey" initiated by Yitzhak Rabin, the Israeli leader gunned down by an Israeli opponent of the peace process in 1995. Barak and Arafat said they will speak regularly during the 100-day sprint for peace, which may include a U.S.-sponsored summit meeting.

Horror fiction novelist Stephen King with his hands in exactly the same, familiar position as that of Senator Schumer (right page).

Israel's Prime Minister Ehud Barak (left), U.S.A. President Bill Clinton (center), and PLO Chief Yasser Arafat each look down at their hands to make sure they get their masonic grips done correctly. Notice overlapping hands by Clinton. (Photo and article: *Austin American-Statesman*, November 3, 1999, p. A2)

Placing one hand, resembling horns, in the other symbolizes the idea that the person is entrusting his soul in care to the superior deity (Satan). Thus, he is submissive, playing down his own power and acknowledging a superior power which controls him. In effect, Senator Charles Schumer (D-NY), ADL fanatic and *avid* Jewish Talmudist, greets "in-the-know" readers of *Newsweek* (December 28, 1998) with a cabalistic sign. The knowing look on Schumer's face is telling, isn't it?

Rabbi Yehuda Getz, Chief Rabbi of all the holy places in Israel, holds his hands in the cabalistic pose. Rabbi Getz claims he knows where the Ark of the Covenant is hidden beneath the Temple Mount in Jerusalem.

Albert Nicholas, head of Wall Street's Nicholas Fund mutual stock firm, in *Newsweek*. (October 10, 1994, p. 52)

Israeli Prime Minister Netanyahu (right) with Knesset leader Milo (left). Notice Milo's hand sign. (*The Jerusalem Report*, August 31, 1998, p. 15)

Profiled in the elitist *Private Clubs* magazine (May/June 2004), Kumar Malavalli, shown here apparently displaying the same hand sign as U.S. Senator Charles Schumer, is said to be a member of the Silicon Valley Capital Club. Malavalli, a native of India, has founded multiple companies and has a portfolio of a dozen businesses.

Statesmen and Nobel laureates in Israel for a Peres Peace Center conference join hands last week in Ramallah. From left: Archbishop Desmond Tutu, former Costa Rican president Oscar Sanchez Arias, Polish President Aleksander Kwasniewski, Palestinian Authority Chairman Yasser Arafat, Shimon Peres, former Soviet leader Mikhail Gorbachev and former South African president F. W. de Klerk. (AP)

Statesmen and Nobel laureates in Israel for a Shimon Peres Peace Center conference interlink hands masonically.

A beautifully staged Masonic production with each actor playing his role with adeptness as all form a symbol. (left- Israeli Prime Minister Yitzhak Rabin; center- President Bill Clinton; right- PLO Chief Yasser Arafat)

The finger to the head like these indicates the elite's approval of the individual's intellect and fitness for office or promotion to the next level.

Drawing from an old masonic text.

Political mover and shaker Vernon Jordan, a Zionist favorite, on the cover of a biography. It was Jordan who arranged employment for Monica Lewinsky, the Jewish young woman who became sexually involved in a White House/Bill Clinton scandal.

Campaign rally for Israeli Prime Minister Ariel Sharon (Photo: *International Jerusalem Post*, February 9, 2001)

uior Warden in the west, to assist the Right Worshipful Master in opening and closing his Lodge, pay the crafts their wages, if any be due, and see that none go away dissatisfied; harmony being the strength and support of all institutions, but more especially of ours.

Master—The Right Worshipful Master's station in the Lodge?

Senior Warden—In the east, Right Worshipful.

Master—His duty there, Brother Senior?

Senior Warden—As the sun rises in the east, to open and adorn the day, so rises the Right Worshipful Master in the east, to open and adorn his Lodge, and set the craft to work with proper instructions for their labor.

Master (rising)—After that manner so do I. It is my will and pleasure that a Lodge of Mark Master Masons be opened in this place, for the dispatch of business. Brother Senior, you will please the Junior

Due-guard.

gree. You then drop your arms down, the last two fingers of the right hand clenched, the first two and thumb open, parallel with each other and about one inch apart.— It alludes to the manner the candidate is directed to carry the key-stone. You then raise the right hand to your right ear, still holding the thumb and the two first fingers open, and with a circular motion of the hand the fingers should be passed round the ear, as though you were combing back your ear-lock, the ear passing between the two fingers and thumb. The hand is then dropped partly down, the palm open and in a horizontal position,

An excerpt from p. 42 of *Richardson's Monitor of Freemasonry* showing the Due Guard of the Mark Master in the Lodge. Cabalistic Jews also have similar signs, some using one finger, others using two fingers to the head as is customarily the case in the Mark Master (4th) degree.

FIG. 20

SIGN OF A MARK MASTER

Illustration from p. 154 of *Duncan's Masonic Ritual and Monitor* illustrating the sign of a Mark Master Mason (Figure 20).

Malcolm X wears a ring of the Black Muslims while giving the Masonic sign. Both Malcolm X and Black Muslim leader Louis Farrakhan were initiated into the 33rd degree of Prince Hall Freemasonry, an order exclusively made up of African ethnics.

Hank McKinnell, CEO of global pharmaceutical giant *Pfizer*, on the cover of *Business Week* (February 28, 2005)

Look close at this item from *Time* magazine (April 4, 2005) and you'll see actor Leonard Nimoy, *Star Trek* icon who thrilled sci-fi fans as a Vulcan who regularly gave the cabalistic "Shin" sign with his hand. Here, Nimoy is presenting the Mark Master's duegard sign. Interestingly, the text of the article from *Time* reveals that Nimoy, whose hobby is photography, is exhibiting his photographs of very large women at a New York City art gallery. The photography of obese women is also found in Nimoy's book, entitled *Shekina*. The word shekina in Hebrew is feminine for "Holy Spirit."

U.S. Ambassador Franklin Williams, a Director of the Council on Foreign Relations (CFR) from 1975 to 1983 and a member until his death in 1990. The CFR offers an internship each year to a college student in his name.

No, Israeli Prime Minister isn't really striking a Sinatra pose. As is often the case, in cabalism magic, a picture reveals the hidden message. The accompanying article (*U.S. News & World Report*, May 24, 1999, p. 43) is entitled, *"Getting Into the Ring,"* and discussed the fact that key American political strategists and consultants like James Carville and Arthur Finkelstein went over to Israel and worked for the election of Barak, an Illuminati favorite. Needless to say, Ehud Barak won!

WORLD REPORT

Getting into the ring

Wealthy Americans and other foreigners played a quiet role in Israel's election

BY DAVID MAKOVSKY

JERUSALEM In the United States, he is the Slim-Fast king. But in Israel, the affable Danny Abraham last week was playing kingmaker.

At a private dinner of Mediterranean mixed grill in the seaside town of Netanya, the wealthy American Jewish businessman tried to persuade Yitzhak ("Itzik")

Barak strikes a Sinatra-esque pose on the campaign trail.

Mordechai, a fading third-party candidate in Israel's presidential election, to drop out of the race and throw his support to Labor Party candidate Ehud Barak. This, the American argued, could push Barak's share of the vote over 50 percent and give him a clean, first-round knockout of Prime Minister Binyamin Netanyahu — avoiding a run-off election on June 1.

Mordechai demurred, but he had to listen. "Danny [Abraham] is a contributor to Itzik, and he wanted him to join up with Labor," says a source close to Mordechai, who reportedly made three trips abroad to raise funds from American Jews like

Abraham, who built a fortune on the Slim-Fast brand of diet supplements.

Israel's 1994 election law prohibits foreign contributions to candidates. And yet, the only thing unusual about Mordechai's campaign is its candor. Both of Israel's major parties, Labor and Likud, also are suspected of receiving indirect assistance from wealthy foreigners. Campaign insiders say that $4 million in foreign money flowed into the 1992 elections, and that the taps opened even wider in 1996 and this year.

Atmospherics. Rather than going directly into party coffers, the money pays for "atmospheric" advertising that does not promote a candidate by name, but pushes an agenda; for transportation of voters to the polls, including chartered planes that bring Israeli citizens home from abroad shortly before election day; and possibly for campaign advice, although this is disputed.

Both of the big Israeli parties have expensive American consultants. Arthur Finkelstein, the Republican strategist, advises Netanyahu. Finkelstein said in an interview that he is paid just $4,000 per month by Netanyahu's Likud Party—considerably less than he charges some American clients. Meanwhile, Ron Lauder, heir to the Estee Lauder cosmetics company, admits hiring Finkelstein, but not on behalf of Netanyahu. It is unclear how Democratic consultant James Carville has been paid for his work on behalf of Barak. But Likud filed two complaints last week against Barak's campaign, charging use of nonprofit groups to circumvent funding laws. Says Menachem Hofnung, a Hebrew University political scientist: "The politicians go abroad and raise the money for so-called nonprofit associations, even though everyone knows it benefits their campaigns." ■

The androgyne, a combination creature of male and female, symbolizes the hermaphrodite principle of the two-faced entity, or two-headed eagle. In the Jewish Cabala, this strange creation, a conjunction of the feminine and masculine principles, is known as "Adam Kadmon," both Adam and Eve, a Golem. This conjunction of opposites is part of the science of alchemy, or hermeticism and is especially beloved by occult magicians. In witchcraft, it is known as the joining of sun and moon, and sacred sex rituals are common.

Edgar Bronfman, Jr., son of billionaire Edgar Bronfman, Sr., head of the World Jewish Congress, is CEO of Seagram, the giant liquor and entertainment industry conglomerate. Seagram's logo is subtly placed on the wall and includes a white horse (shades of Revelation 6?) and other interesting features. (Photo: *USA Today*, December 14, 1998)

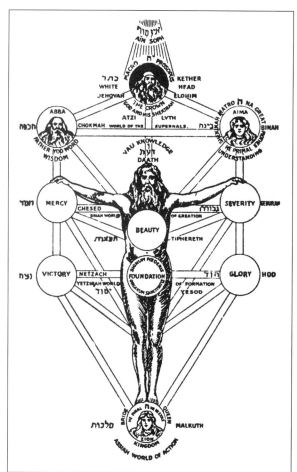

In *Cabala*, the Sacred Tree of the Sephiroth is claimed to represent the Cosmos, including God (male), his Shekinah (*Aima*, the goddess/female), and the Kingdom of Zion. As shown here, the Foundation of all things is the male genitals, or the sex generative process. (*Zolar's Encyclopedia of Ancient and Forbidden Knowledge,* Arco Publishing, 1984)

Worldly fortunes

Jewish comedian Jerry Seinfeld strikes a decidedly cabalistic pose. It is well-known in entertainment circles that Jerry Seinfeld—indeed, all of the performers on TV's popular *Seinfeld* sitcom—practice cabala magic and ritual. According to *Forbes* magazine in 1998, Jerry Seinfeld made a whopping total of $225 million on the comedy circuit. And that's no joke! (Photo and article: *Austin American-Statesman*, September 9, 1998, p. A14)

What is the value of a sensitive, boyish face, a wry and irreverent sense of humor or a knack for a clever phrase accompanied by a hypnotic rhythm? Pretty darn high, according to Forbes' list of the 40 highest-paid entertainers. Heartthrob Leonardo DiCaprio, comedian Jerry Seinfeld and rapper Master P, all of whom are on the list, would concur.

The 1998 estimated incomes of many of the super-rich entertainers cited by the business magazine come close to the most recently reported gross national products of several developing nations. That should raise a few eyebrows at the World Bank, which monitors international financial policy. The gross national product (GNP) is a nation's total goods and services valued at market prices.

DiCaprio's $37 million is chump change compared to Seinfeld's $225 million, which makes him No. 1 on the Forbes list. (DiCaprio is 34th.) But $37 million is big bucks in Africa's Tanzania, whose 1994 GNP was only $2 billion.

NBC

Jerry Seinfeld was 1998's highest-paid entertainer.

Seinfeld's projected income could boost the economy of Kenya, which had a 1994 GNP of $7 billion.

Master P, who taught MTV viewers the meaning of "UH! Na Na Na NAH," is expected to earn $56.5 million this year. Closely following the rapper on the Forbes' list is Austin's own Mike Judge, co-creator of Fox TV's "King of the Hill." Judge is expected to earn $53 million this year. The men's combined incomes would be one-sixth of the gross national product of the central African nation of Zaire, which was $6 billion in 1994.

Others on Forbes' list include the Rolling Stones ($57 million) and the Spice Girls ($49 million) and television talk show queen Oprah Winfrey ($125 million), who has appeared on the list several years in a row.

Any of the entertainers on the Forbes' list could influence the economies of several of the world's nations. "Not that there's anything wrong with that," as Seinfeld and crew would say defensively. But the list sure does put the world's financial troubles in context.

MATCH THIS
BY SHMULEY BOTEACH

muley,

enough to be in ut I wonder how I riend to go ahead stion. We have wo years.

y answer to this ate commitment boyfriend into a a tricky ordeal – Groom maga- e some important sure him (that will nd don't talk onstantly (that

n't commit to ke yourself less ake him want earn you. If he that he never

To ask Rabbi Boteach, author of the best-selling Kosher Sex, *about love, life, and dating, write to* Match This

of primacy and excl boyfriend has to giv He has to make you macy) and the only Don't think that the many other women want him. Just stick And don't verbalize doing. Just do it. A commitment he sho you are available to

Most important o tle. Don't think that you to "play games" "The Rules," which I the contrary, these a and your withdrawal done manipulatively. the natural response closing their heart to Solomon said that looking in a mir shown to you bac

Rabbi Shmuley Boteach has gained a measure of fame for his national columns, his books (*Kosher Sex*), and for the fact that he once was a confidant and spiritual counselor and advisor to black superstar singer, Michael Jackson. Here we see Rabbi Boteach in a pose familiar to practitioners of Cabala. (Photo and article: *The International Jerusalem Post*, December 28, 2001)

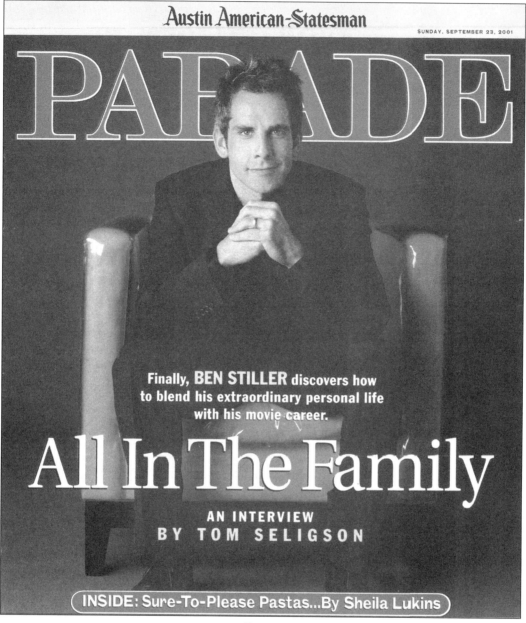

Austin American-Statesman

SUNDAY, SEPTEMBER 23, 2001

PARADE

Finally, **BEN STILLER** discovers how to blend his extraordinary personal life with his movie career.

All In The Family

AN INTERVIEW
BY TOM SELIGSON

INSIDE: Sure-To-Please Pastas...By Sheila Lukins

Ben Stiller, popular Jewish comedian and movie celebrity, in a cabalistic pose with his hands. His left hand folded on top over the left indicated Stiller follows the left-hand (dark) path. On the opposite page, David Rockefeller gives notice he follows the right-hand path.

San Francisco Mayor Gavin Newsom lets insiders know he's one of them with this cabalistic hand/arms gesture. Newsom became the gay community's ultraliberal darling in 2003 by promoting gay marriages. *Time* magazine's editors go wild in this article, mentioning that the mayor is "simply adored," touting his many achievements, and insisting that publishers give him a "fat cat" contract to write a book. (*Time*, April 25, 2005)

The glossy magazine *Town & Country* selected David Rockefeller, Sr., President of Chase-Manhattan Bank and founder of the Trilateral Commission, as *"Our Generous American for 1995."* This full page photo, bearing no caption or explanation, was included in the magazine exactly as you see it. Occult experts and those knowledgeable of masonic and cabalistic signals will recognize the significance of Rockefeller's pose; also the "X" design cufflinks and the "diamond" designs of necktie.

Former President George Herbert Walker Bush and PLO Chief Yasser Arafat use cabalistic signals to communicate the attitude of resignation and the knowledge that their time in the sunlight is now over. (Bush photo: *Texas Monthly*, July, 2003, p. 97)

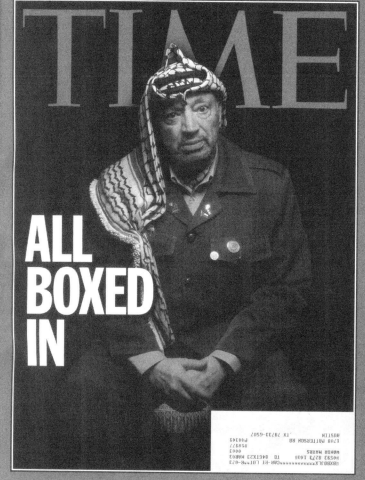

Cabalists and members of many secret societies use "sacred geometry" to create designs and symbols of magical and occultic power. This is the cover of one book on this subject. Hundreds of books and texts on sacred geometry have been published over the centuries, from the days of Pythagoras.

ROBERT LAWLOR

sacred geometry

PHILOSOPHY AND PRACTICE

with 202 illustrations and diagrams, 56 in two colors

THAMES AND HUDSON

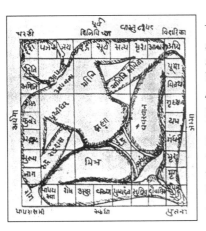

The Hindu religion also is big on sacred geometry and cabalistic oriented measurements and architecture. This is a "plan" for a Hindu temple based on the diagram of the Perusha, or *"Cosmic Man."* The ancient Hindu architectural sutra (rule) proclaims that, *"The whole universe is present in the Temple in the form of geometric proportion."* In the Hindu practice of *Yoga*, the participant bends and twists his or her body parts and limbs into specific forms symbolic of universal energies (Drawing from book, *Sacred Geometry*, by Robert Lawlor, Thames and Hudson, London, 1989, p. 92)

'Seinfeld' in a parallel universe

A Kramer who knocks before entering the room?

A George who's generous, honest and soft-spoken?

A Jerry who cares for others and accentuates the positive?

Be careful what you ask for. You just might see it.

As if to answer the critics

Television
News & Views
By Matt Roush

(including this one) who found it hard to forgive that sour bunch of *Seinfeld* misanthropes after last season's bad-taste finale, in which the death of George's fiancée, Susan, was callously shrugged off by all, tonight's brilliant episode offers a glimpse at what life might be like if these creeps were actually nice guys.

You don't want to go there.

It starts when Elaine breaks up with Kevin (Tim DeKay), her nice-guy boyfriend of last week, and suggests they just be friends. Kevin likes the idea. Kevin, you see, likes friends.

Whereas Jerry, when he hears about this, sneers, "Why would anybody want a *friend*?" (Take that, *Friends* clones.)

When Elaine meets Kevin's other buddies, they turn out to be funhouse-mirror inverses of that gang of hers: a bald schmo named Gene (Kyle T. Hefner) and a gangly guy named Feldman (Pat Kilbane). They're normal. They sit around and read. Kooky they're not.

By George Lange, NBC

Bizarro time: After meeting the alter egos of her pals Michael Richards, left, Jason Alexander and Jerry Seinfeld, Julia Louis-Dreyfus ponders what life would be like among the normal on 'Seinfeld.'

hero's exact opposite.

In a memorable street scene, Elaine finds herself torn between the two groups: one gonzo and self-absorbed, the "bizarro bunch" anything but. She articulates her crisis of comradeship to Jerry: "I can't spend the rest of my life coming into this stinking a̶p̶a̶r̶t̶m̶e̶n̶t̶

system is breaking down!"

Why not, indeed.

In the season opener, Jerry seemed downright cruel as he continually belittled Elaine upon her ill-fated promotion at work. George's unending trash-ing o̶f̶ ̶S̶u̶s̶a̶n̶ ̶s̶e̶e̶m̶e̶d̶ ̶i̶n̶- unne̶c̶e̶s̶s̶a̶r̶y̶ toni̶g̶h̶t̶

Tonight's surreal subplots confirm that this world is like no other on TV, and welcome to it. Jerry dates a beautiful woman with one hard-to-get-past physical flaw. (Watch her manhandle a lobster.) Kramer

The Illuminist insider who titled this article was in the know. It reads: *'Seinfeld' In A Parallel Universe*. The photo shows the four entertainers from TV's wildly popular sitcom each in cabalistic poses. All four are Jewish as is the show's producer.

Actor Jason Alexander ("George" in *Seinfeld* TV series) performs a cabala ritual in plain sight of a vast audience. To the uninitiated and ignorant millions of people who read *TV Guide* and see this cover, Jason Alexander appears to be merely hamming it up. Little do they know of the deeper occult meaning. For example, we find Jason's left and right hands giving the *"El Diablo"* satanic hand sign. His arms—one pointing up, the other down—indicate the dualistic (marriage of opposites, or reconciliation), cabalistic magical philosophy "As Above, So Below" (The devil goat *Baphomet* performs the same sign). We also note the three triangles presented by Jason's legs and arms.

April 23–29   89¢

TV GUIDE

SEINFELD'S LOVABLE LOSER

WIN YOUR OWN TREK TO HOLLYWOOD!

STAR TREK
THE NEXT GENERATION
TRIVIA SWEEPSTAKES

Jason Alexander of NBC's 'Seinfeld'

0 864415 2

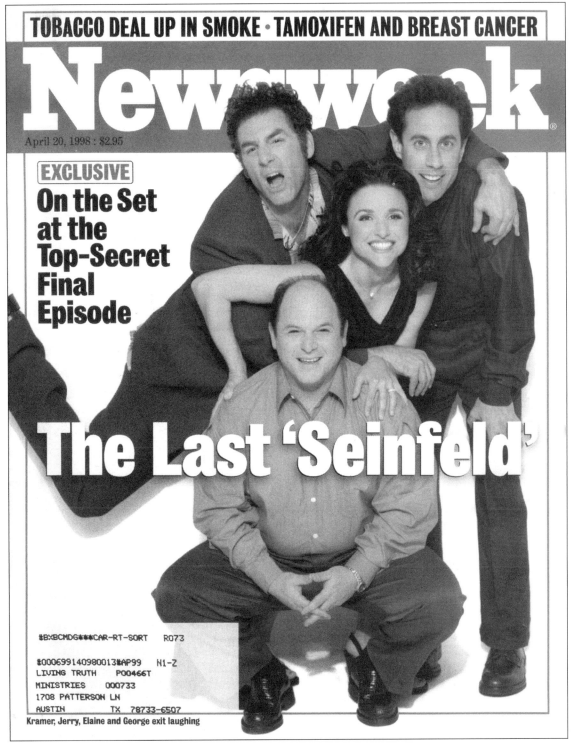

Again we discover the comedy team from *Seinfeld* teaming up to present cabalistic messages. Observe the *V* in Michael Richards' ("Kramer") leg and in Julia Louis-Dreyfuss' ("Elaine") arm; the circle that Richards makes with the fingers of his left hand, the *"X"* made by the intersecting hands and wrists of Richard and Louis-Dreyfuss; the descendant triangle sign of Jason Alexander's ("George") hands, and so on.

Sign of the Ram: 2004 Vice Presidential candidate, Senator Joseph Lieberman, a Jew, on the campaign trail. The placement of both hands downward to create the appearance of the two horns of a ram is a cabalistic sign often given by members of Middle Eastern Lodges, especially the Masonic lodges of Israel. It is a sign of high rank and is said to invoke good fortune on the part of the user. The sign is often given publicly at the beginning, or commencement of a project to enhance success.

Shlenker wants city and county to pay his debts

Both sides consider appeals of court ruling

By Chris Conley
The Commercial Appeal

By Karen Pulfer Focht

MEMPHIS, WEDNESDAY, JULY 29, 1992

Promoter Sidney Shlenker said Tuesday he would "walk away" from The Pyramid if the city and county would pay his creditors millions of dollars.

Shlenker also said he is willing to forgo repayment of $2 million which he says he sank into the project. But the attorney representing the local governments said agreeing to pay Shlenker's creditors would be "paying for his mistakes."

Shlenker's comments followed a ruling Monday in which U.S. Bankruptcy Judge Bernice Donald said local governments did not give adequate notice before ending a contract with Shlenker's Pyramid Management Authority (PMA) to run The Pyramid. She also ruled that PMA did not fulfill its contract with local governments on the skybox rentals and the arena equipment.

Both sides have until the end of next week to appeal to the U.S. District Court in Memphis. Neither side has decided whether to appeal.

Sidney Shlenker says his house in East Memphis is up for sale and he intends to return to Houston.

Promoter Sidney Shlenker, here giving the sign of the ram, was in the news back in 1992. Shlenker, a Jewish wheeler-dealer and owner of a professional basketball team, was co-builder of Memphis, Tennessee's massive new Great Pyramid of the Americas.

Newly chosen Palestinian leader Mahmoud Abbas, successor to the late PLO Chief Yasser Arafat, gives the cabalistic sign with his hands to indicate expectation of success and to invoke good fortune. It is thus apparent that Abbas is a servant to the Jewish Illuminati who only pretends to represent Palestinian interests. (*U.S. News & World Report*, January 10, 2005)

Yitzak Rabin　　**King Hussein**　　**Hosni Mubarek**　　**Yasser Arafat**

Four Middle Eastern leaders, all brother Masons, met in 1997 in so-called "peace negotiations." From left to right: Israeli Prime Minister Yitzak Rabin, Jordan's King Hussein, Egyptian President Hosni Mubarek, and Palestinian Leader Yasser Arafat. Mubarek is giving the cabalistic sign of the ram. (Photo: *News From Israel*, October 1997)

Israel's Ashkenazi Chief Rabbi Yisrael Lau clearly conveys a cabalistic message to Egyptian President Hosni Mubarek. In return Mubarek's left hand under his chin presents a Masonic message. (Photo: *The Omega Times*, New Zealand, January 1996, p. 7)

This picture of South African leader Nelson Mandela took up an entire page in *Modern Maturity* magazine in 2004. *Modern Maturity* is distributed by AARP, which some believe to be managed and run by a radical leftist/Zionist faction purporting to represent seniors. In this picture, Mandela takes joy in presenting the double V (shin) sign of cabalism. Nelson Mandela became a Mason in 1994. He is a tool of the Rothschilds and the Oppenheimers.

Hindu Dance, Hindu Gods: The positions of Hindu classical dance *(Bharat Natyam)* describe geometric angular relationships from the axis of the body's center of gravity just below the navel. These positions, while defining principle angles, are also often attributed to various deities and are meant to convey their characteristic powers. (Drawing from book, *Sacred Geometry*, by Robert Lawlor, Thames and Hudson, London, 1989, p. 95)

The late Milton Berle, a Jew, was widely lauded as a comedian, but again, his antics were not always spontaneous. This bit of fluff demonstrates cabalistic insights and Masonic knowledge.

The late Arthur Murray was called "America's Dancing Master," and so he was. A talented genius on the dance floor, Murray's real name was Arthur Teichman, Jewish of course. From the era of the roaring 20s to today, a number of the fad dances were based on masonic and Jewish cabalistic rituals.

Anne Rice, writer of the popular "Vampire" series, giving an occult, cabalistic sign with her left-hand, partially concealed yet in front of all. Various occult symbols are on Rice's blouse. The statues of Mary give evidence of Rice's veneration of the Virgin but most probably in the form of the eternal pagan goddess. (Photo: Associated Press in *Austin American-Statesman*, January 31, 2004, p. A2)

Chaim Potok, Hasidic Jewish writer and novelist, creates a headcovering of cabalistic magic. This sign is also reminiscent of the fourth sign in the initiation for the Select Master's Degree (see *Richardson's Monitor of Freemasonry*, p. 85). (Photo: *Newsweek*, August 5, 2002)

Mr. Spock, a *Star Trek* character played by actor Leonard Nimoy, became famous for giving the *Vulcan greeting* with his right hand. Nimoy, a Jew, says that the sign is the same gesture given in Jewish Synagogues when the Rabbi and Elders bring out the Holy of Holies. It is based on the Hebrew letter "shin." In essence, on the popular TV show, every time Spock gave the "shin" Vulcan greeting hand sign, he was invoking cabalistic magic.

TWENTY-TWO

Scorched by the Sun—Solar Signs, Circles, and Serpents

It is He (God) that sitteth upon the circle of the earth…

> — *Isaiah 40:22* (written about
> 1,000 years before Columbus
> proved the earth was not flat)

It would not be impossible to prove, with sufficient repetition and psychological understanding of the people concerned, that a square is, in fact, a circle.

> — Joseph Goebbels
> Propaganda Minister
> Nazi Germany

In the mythology of the primitive world, the serpent is universally the symbol of the sun…The serpent was universally represented by the sun symbol, the circle or disk.

> — Bishop Alexander Hislop
> *The Two Babylons*

The sun has ever been at the center of false religion. The Ancient Mystery Religions venerated the sun, the solar disk, as deity. The Greeks honored Apollo as the child of the sun. The Romans paid homage to Mithra the sun god. These pagan philosophies form the basis for the worship of the

Sun worship in Peru exemplifies the universal worship of the sun god, or solar deity.

Illuminati and indicate the importance of the sun as symbol of satanic deity.

Englishman John Yarker, a well-known nineteenth century Masonic magician and occultist, in his *Notes on the Scientific and Religious Mysteries of Antiquity*, makes mention of the fact that the High Priests of the ancient Jews also worshipped the sun god. He writes:

> The Mysteries we know were practiced in a secret subterranean chamber under the Temple of Solomon, at Jerusalem, where four and twenty elders adored the sun, with their faces toward the east.[1]

What Yarker says is true, but as the Scriptures give evidence, this unholy worship by the Jewish leaders in secret was an abomination to God. *Ezekiel 8* makes this crystal clear. It is understandable why God would so detest worship of the sun god by the Mystery Religions and by the apostate Jewish elders. In reality, in worshipping the sun, the ancients were worshipping Satan. G.H. Pember, in a scholarly work on the Mysteries, *Earth's Earliest Ages*, affirms this fact when he states, "There is little doubt that the culmination of the Mysteries was the worship of Satan himself."[2]

Now today, the Masons, as did the apostate Jewish elders and priests in the days of Ezekiel, continue to worship Satan the sun god, also called Lucifer or Baal, by other names. The name of their great god, Jahbuhlun, which is revealed to Masons in the higher degrees, is a synonym for the solar deity; two of the three syllables in the name, buh and lun, mean "Baal" and "On," both of which represent sun and fire gods. That is why, in the authoritative guide *Gods of the Lodge*, Reginald Haupt reports that in the Lodge:

> All the movements by the Consecrating Officers of the Masonic Lodge or Chapter follow the course of the Sun. The Master and the Wardens enter and leave their chairs as the Sun returns to the East and goes forth therefrom. Most processional occasions are governed by these principles of what is known as "circumambulation." This ritual came from the ancient pagan rites of the Egyptians and from the worship of their Sun God and of the sun itself.[3]

The first 15 divisions of the Egyptian Royal Cubit. Each division of the cubit was dedicated to a divinity, and the first division, on the right, shows the hieroglyph of the sun god Ra, symbol of divine unity. (From the book, *Jesus Christ, Sun of God: Ancient Cosmology and Early Christian Symbolism*, by David Fideler, Quest Books, Wheaton, Illinois)

Halos, also known as nimbuses, present the individual as a saint, a deity, or other holy person. (From the *Herder Dictionary of Symbols*, Chiron Publications, Wilmette, Illinois)

Tom DeLay: A roadblock on tax cuts

At right: Congressman Tom DeLay (R-TX), House Majority Leader, pictured in *Time* magazine. Politicians are sometimes framed with a sun-like halo, called a "nimbus," over their heads. This gives them the subtle majestic appearance of being some type of god-man.

In honoring and worshipping the sun in their rituals, Freemasonry and Illuminism defy God. The Bible's Job displayed great wisdom by uttering these words concerning God's thoughts concerning worship of the sun and the heavens:

> *If I beheld the sun when it shined, or the moon walking in brightness; and my heart hath been secretly enticed...this also was an iniquity to be punished by the judge; for I should have denied the God who is above. (Job 31:26-28)*

The Swastika Represents the Sun

The Nazi swastika is a representation of the sun. But the Nazis simply borrowed this symbol from the ancient religions, including the Hindus of India, the Shintoists of Japan, and a number of Native American Indian tribes. Even today, in temples and shrines throughout Asia, you will find the swastika painted on walls, on totem poles, and over altars. Until Hitler and the Nazis gave the sign a bad reputation, the Masons also universally used the sun sign. And today the symbol of the circle, particularly that of the point within the circle, is a prominent feature of Masonic theology.

The Point Within the Circle

According to *Mackey's Masonic Encyclopedia* the hidden, true meaning of this symbol, the point inside the circle, is far different than what the everyday Masonic brother is told. In reality, its meaning is yet another proof that Masonry is a sex cult. Mackey says the esoteric explanation is that the *point* within the circle is the male phallus, or penis, and the circle is the female yoni, or vagina. Here, says Mackey, is a "symbol of fecundity, expressed by the male generative principle."[4]

But, Mackey emphasizes, the sun is still not forgotten in Masonry, for while the phallus (point) and the vagina (circle) symbolize the sex act (the generative principle), they also represent the sun as deity. The point with the circle is the sun god.

"At times," Mackey observes, "this circle is represented by the ananta (Sanscrit for *eternity*), a serpent with its tail in its mouth."[5]

Since the symbol of the point within a circle is of such overriding importance to the Illuminati Masons and yet is so little recognized as significant by the dumbed-down masses, many Illuminists enjoy a bit of mockery of the masses by blatantly displaying this symbol. Some believe the Target department store chain logo — the red circle and point — is one example.

Pat Robertson's Hidden Message

Pat Robertson, Religious Right leader of TV's *The 700 Club* and founder of the Christian Coalition, gives us another graphic example. Some years ago, Robertson had two books ghostwritten for him, one called *The New World Order* and another titled *The New Millennium*. As happens often in elitist circles, the opinions and material for both books seemed to be decidedly anti-elitist; they even exposed the global conspiracy and the Illuminati. So, was Pat Robertson really joining the fight against the evil Illuminati? Not on your life!

The books were for the "stupids," the masses. While reading *The New Millennium* the reader ignorant of the uses of symbolism probably ignored the fact that at the top of every page, a point within a circle could be found. This was Robertson's "hidden code" to his elite pals that he was still on their side and was just taking the ignorant masses for a ride.

The Sign of the Mafia, the Illuminati and of Druids

According to Dr. Cathy Burns, in *Hidden Secrets of the Eastern Star*, the point within the circle is, "The sign of the infamous Mafia or Cosa Nostra," rather than the "black hand" as many believe.[6]

But the real shocker is the importance given this sign by Adam Weishaupt and the Order of the Illuminati. Burns explains that because Illuminism was so determined to keep the true nature of the Order under wraps, its founder, Weishaupt, ordered that the actual words "Illuminati" and "Illuminism" never be used in correspondence. Instead they were to be replaced by the astrological symbol for the sun; that is, the circle with a dot in the middle.[7]

Burns also gives evidence that the point within

An Arch-Druid from pagan Great Britain in his ceremonial robes. (From Wellcome's *Ancient Cymric Medicine*)

the circle was used by the Druids of Britain, whose stone temples were circular with a single stone erected in the center. They believed this design conferred magical powers.

Flower Power and Magic Circles

The daisy flower, the marigold, and the sunflower also are indicative of the sun as deity and so, traditionally, adherents of the Mystery Religions, as well as Hindus, Zoroastrians, and others, utilize these symbols. Adam Weishaupt, founder in 1776 of the Order of the Illuminati, encouraged "Flower Power" as a symbol, and it was taken up by New Age hippies in the '60s.

The symbol of the circle is, for the Illuminati, sort of a pared down, basic sun sign. That is why the circle is used so frequently and in a score of configurations within Masonic and other secret society networks. It is also a staple of witchcraft and Satan worship. Bill Schnoebelen, author of many books unmasking Freemasonry, witchcraft, and the occult, was himself formerly a Mason as well as a male witch. He has described the witch's "temple" as follows:

> In witchcraft, the "temple" is frequently not a building but rather a sacred "Magic Circle" laid down on the floor of a room with great ceremony. It is the sacred space of the Wicca and serves the same function as a temple does to the Mason.[8]

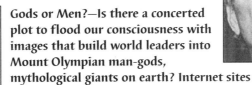

Gods or Men?—Is there a concerted plot to flood our consciousness with images that build world leaders into Mount Olympian man-gods, mythological giants on earth? Internet sites www.freepressinternational.com and www.Rense.com caught on to this recent trend and published a number of photographs that seem to confirm this bizarre plot. Free Press International, an alternative news website, wrote, "These are just a few of the many photographs mainstream media has been deliberately releasing to the public showing our world leaders with halos. I'd say with the shape our world is in right now, they should have horns instead of halos. Most of these pictures are coming from Associated Press, and Reuters." Surely, the scriptures were right on when they warned that the Devil himself often comes disguised as an "angel of light." (Note: *Codex Magica* has seen these pictures published in an increasing number of media forums, from *Time* and *Newsweek* to daily papers.)

DECEMBER 10, 2001

BUSH'S CIVIL LIBERTIES   THE INVENTION EVERYONE'S BUZZING ABOUT

GEORGE HARRISON
1943-2001

```
#BXBDJLX*************CAR-RT LOT**R-073
#0593 8273 140#    ID 13721X23 MAR02
WANDA MARRS                    0010
                              #01156
1708 PATTERSON RD             P0036B
AUSTIN      ,TX 78733-6507
```

www.time.com   AOL Keyword: TIME

Upon his death, *Time* magazine published this telling photo of Beatle superstar George Harrison (1943-2001) on the cover of its December 10, 2001 issue. Harrison, wearing black, in a black and white photo, holds a sunflower, symbol of the Illuminati Sun God. The solar deity is also prominently worshipped in the Hindu religion, and the Beatles were devoted followers of the Maharishi Mahesh Yogi and other Indian Hindu gurus. *Time's* feature story, in fact, reports that George Harrison never gave up on his gurus, to his dying breath. All the Beatles were drenched in illegal drugs, such as cocaine, hashish, and heroin. Their album, *Sergeant Pepper's Lonely Hearts Club Band*, even had a cameo photo of British "666" beast satanist priest, Aleister Crowley, on its cover. The latest information is that the Beatles were an experimental music group sponsored behind the scenes by British and U.S. intelligence. Their role was intended to use various psyops mechanisms and anti-Christian messages to arouse turmoil and psychological trauma in society. One of the Beatles' most memorable albums was titled, *Magical Mystery Tour*. Beatle John Lennon was murdered by a man many believe to have been a CIA trained "Manchurian Candidate," and George Harrison was once assaulted and stabbed by a would-be assassin.

Hindu guru Maharishi Mahesh Yogi and the Beatles. The Hindu religion, thoroughly wicked and satanic, is closely related to the Illuminati's religious doctrines.

"The New Age is dawning. A sun shines within every person." That's the philosophy of the "Taiyo no Kai" (Following The Sun Association), founded by Japan's Kaoru Nakamaru.

Falun Gong is a religious movement in China. With some 100 million adherents worldwide, Falun Gong is a spiritual force to be reckoned with. Its logo is the circle with the yin/yang and the swastika (a sun sign) prominently displayed.

The swastika (swirling sun sign) was not invented first by Hitler and the Nazis. It is an old Freemasonry symbol. One can find swastikas painted and carved on ancient temples in Japan and India, and on Native American Indian pottery and artifacts. It seems that the forces who gave us this sign, the swastika, continue to attempt to reintroduce it to the masses. BBC News on-line recently reported that Hindus want to reclaim the swastika, which their gurus claim has been a Hindu good luck sign for centuries. "It's the second most sacred symbol in the Hindu tradition," said Hindu Forum spokesman, Ramesh Kallidai. (BBC News/UK, January 19, 2005)

ANANOVA™

Home   **News**   Entertainment   Sport   Business   Video Reports   Weather

News   Ananova:

Quirkies
Eccentrics
Quirky gaffes
Strange crime
Sex life
Animal tales
Sporting quirkies
Showbiz quirkies
Business quirkies
Heartwarmers
Rocky relationships
Bad taste
Unlucky

Top headlines
Latest picture stories
Latest video reports
Celebrities
Science and discovery
Technology

Corrections

Coca-Cola promotes drink with 'swastika' robots

A Coca-Cola promotion in Hong Kong featuring a robot adorned with 'swastikas' has been condemned.

Rabbi Yakkov Kermaier, of Ohel Leah Synagogue, says it is probably an honest mistake, but he's called toy sets featuring the "Robocon" characters unacceptable.

One character, the robot-like "Robowaru," has two swastikas on its chest and can be bought in the UK for around £2.60 with any purchase of six bottles of Coke.

In 2003, when the Coca-Cola Company in Hong Kong ran an ad promotion featuring a robot adorned with swastikas, Jewish spokesmen balked. A Jewish rabbi, however, admitted, *"The Nazi swastika can easily be confused with Buddhist swastikas that are common in Asia."* (*Ananova.com* news, May 1, 2003)

Symbols of the sun as a deity are commonplace in the publications and artifacts of Masonic, Rosicrucian, and other occultic groups. The point within the circle is especially significant and has profound implications.

The yin/yang is often seen at martial arts studios, yet few understand its esoteric meaning. The symbol represents the combining of male and female, the forces of darkness and light; the integration of God and the Devil.

Circular images of goddess worship and sun adoration are found in many New Age and occult publications.

Witches are major promoters of the Goddess revival. Above is an ad for a witch's periodic newspaper (address deleted).

An interesting drawing of an upscale witch, complete with lunar force (moon in window), pentagram (on chair), naked goddess holding the radiating sun in her left hand, and more. (From the book, *To Ride a Silver Broomstick: New Generation Witchcraft*, by Silver RavenWolf, Llewellyn Publications, St. Paul, MN, 1993)

(From the book, *To Ride a Silver Broomstick: New Generation Witchcraft*, by Silver RavenWolf)

Logo for a publisher of many occult and esoteric books.

Two circle images used in magical rites. *Left:* magic circle with six-pointed star (hexagram) and occult cross. *Right:* magic circle from Francis Barrett's *The Magus*, London, 1901. (From *The Herder Dictionary of Symbols*, Chiron Publications, Wilmette, IL, 1986)

This symbol is featured prominently on the cover of the New Age book *THE MARK*, by Maurice Nicoll. The book is mostly full of mysteriously garbled esoteric nonsense. Yet, a careful reading enables the reader to glean what the author, Maurice Nicoll, was attempting to convey to his New Age readership concerning the Mark. Nicoll is a British psychiatrist and student of occultist Carl Jung.

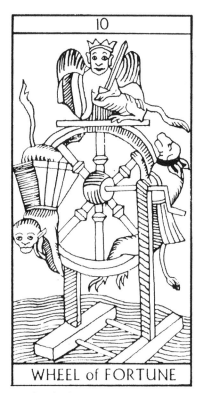

"Wheel of Fortune" tarot card, used by witches and seers for predicting one's future. The inner circle of the Illuminati elite are sometimes referred to as the *"Wheel."*

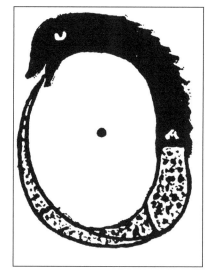

Stylized Oroboros serpent biting its tail, forming a circle with its body. Inside the circle is the point of Lucifer.

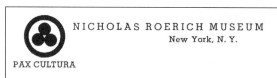

Logo for the Nicholas Roerich Museum in New York City. Nicholas Roerich was a Russian mystic and Freemason who had vast and mysterious influence over both President Franklin D. Roosevelt and FDR's Secretary of Agriculture, Henry Wallace. Reportedly, FDR had the Treasury include the design of the all-seeing eye and the pyramid on the U.S. one dollar bill at Roerich's urging.

14 LIFESTYLE

The Korea Times

St. Patrick's Day Celebrated in Dublin

DUBLIN, Ireland (AP) — Hundreds of thousands of people braved a wet late-winter day Sunday to watch Dublin's annual St. Patrick's Day parade, the climax of a three-day festival in honor of Ireland's patron saint.

Organizers estimated that 500,000 people lined the parade route from St. Patrick's Cathedral on the city's south side to Parnell Square in the north.

Thousands more participated in the parade, including 19 marching bands from Britain, the United States, Norway and Germany.

On Saturday, up to 1 million people thronged the city's streets and squares for free music, comedians and special entertainment geared to children. Thousands lined the banks of the River Liffey for a 3,000-ton fireworks display Saturday night.

A 19-year-old man drowned while trying to swim across the river Saturday night. His body was recovered several hours later.

Backers of the festival hope it will ensure that Ireland's normally thriving tourism industry gets off to a good start this year.

Last year's festival had to be postponed for two months because of fears that foot-and-mouth disease, then rampant in British cattle and sheep, would spread to Ireland. The island ultimately suffered only a handful of confirmed cases, but tourist numbers slumped.

The fallout from the Sept. 11 terror attacks also has meant far fewer Americans in the crowds and parade this year. The Irish Hotels Federation said U.S. visitor numbers were down by between 30 and 50 percent compared to the last normal St. Patrick's Festival weekend in

A float passes Christ church in the St. Patrick's Day Festival parade in Dublin Sunday. 　　　**AP-Yonhap**

2000.

In London, thousands of people sported sprigs of shamrock and took to the streets for the British capital's first official St. Patrick's Day festival.

Police estimated that 5,000 people marched in a parade from the city's Roman Catholic Westminster Cathedral to Trafalgar Square, where a crowd of 14,000 gathered to watch performances by Irish dancers and musicians.

Organizers said 50,000 people attended the event.

London mayor Ken Livingstone, said the celebration recognized the contribu-

tion Irish people had made to the city.

The Irish, he said, "have helped to build it, to nurse the sick in it, to educate the children in it."

London is home to some 400,000 Irish people.

Irish Prime Minister Bertie Ahern said the London event showed that Britain and the Republic of Ireland had moved beyond their long-acrimonious relationship.

"That is a real step forward and does show we have moved on from some of the terrible periods of the past," Ahern said.

This float honoring the sun (with *six* rays) was a part of the St. Patrick's Day Festival parade in Dublin, Ireland. (Photo and article from *The Korea Times* newspaper, March 19, 2002, p. 14)

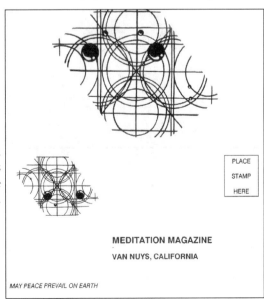

Designs on a return envelope for subscriptions of *Meditation*, a New Age magazine.

PLACE
STAMP
HERE

MEDITATION MAGAZINE

VAN NUYS, CALIFORNIA

MAY PEACE PREVAIL ON EARTH

BookPeople

America's Largest New Age Bookstore

Dedicated to Preserving the Written Word

When we saw the original printing of *Love and the Golden Rule*, we were so moved by the insight and wisdom it presented, that we bought the entire first printing. Every copy was sold in less than three months...

We are now pleased to announce the second printing of *Love and the Golden Rule*, which is currently available at Book People and other fine, independent Austin bookstores.

This book is the first volume in a series focusing on Universal Truths being published by the Golden Rule Foundation. *Love and the Golden Rule* is a little book which you'll read in 30 minutes and think about the rest of your life. The Golden Rule has appeared as a part of every major spiritual practice and its history can be traced back to the prehistoric *Mahabharrata* of the Vedas:

SENECA, ca 5-65 AD:
"Treat your inferiors as you would be treated by your superiors." - **Epistle XLVII, 11**

SOCRATES, ca 470-399 BC:
"Do not do to others that which would anger you if others did it to you."

CONFUCIAN, ca 500 BC:
"Surely it is the maxim of loving kindness, do not unto others that which you would not have them do unto you." - Analects, Lun-yu, 23

BUDDHIST, ca 525 BC:
"Hurt not others in ways that you find hurtful." - Tripitaka, Udana-varga 5,18

ZOROASTRIAN, ca 600 BC:
"That nature alone is good which refrains from doing unto another whatsoever is not good for itself." - Savesta, Adistan-idinik 94:5

JUDAIC, ca 1300 BC:
"What is hateful to you, do not to your fellow man. That is the entire Law, all the rest is commentary."
- Talmud, Shabbat 31a

HINDU, prehistoric
"This is the sum of duty. Do not unto others that which would cause you pain if done to you. "
- Mahabharrata 5:1517

Price: $3.95. An ideal Valentine's gift.

Book People:
The Bookstore for Insightful People
• 10 -10 everyday •

Like many in the New Age and occult worlds, the managers of *Book People*, a large occult bookstore in Austin, Texas, claim their works are loving and good. But in this revealing advertisement in the swirling astronomical spiral mist at right, is clearly seen the letter "S." As in Satan? Let the discerning reader decide.

Prozac can help? Really? So why the design resembling the oroboros serpent? And is it just this author's imagination, or are the radiant sun rays in the form of number 6s?

THE DAWN HORSE is a publication of the Laughing Man Institute of Austin.   Feb.-March 1987 Edition

FREE

THE DAWN HORSE

"Every living being has the instincts and the Destiny of Infinite Life."— Heart-Master Da Love-Ananda

Inside:

Interview with Irena Tweedie
page 4

Ken Wilber On Heros and Cults
page 3

Special Events:

Crazy Da Must Sing

This seminar will explore the way in which Spiritual Adepts have engaged their devotees in the most fierce and passionate struggle in order to awaken them beyond their egoic limitations on life and love. The day will include many personal stories about the extraordinary way in which Heart Master Da has worked with devotees and also

Heart-Master Da Love-Ananda

DA LOVE-ANANDA: You are all becoming philosophical in the midst of a life in which you are hoping to Realize the Truth. If you examine the Great Tradition,[1] you will observe that whenever people appear to have become very serious about Truth, they have also become very philosophical. In

American Hindu guru DaFree John publishes *The Dawn Horse* newspaper with this unusual logo, consisting of circles, flames, a white horse, the occultic star and two feet (the disciple on his knees or prostrate).

Drawing in *Circle Network News*, well-known witchcraft newspaper, a focal point for worshippers of "Father Sun" and solar deities according to the magazine.

Celtic cross (sunwheel) and torch adopted as the emblem for the America First Party, a political party geared to the goals of the white race, headquartered in Georgia.

The Celtic Cross (or Sunwheel) - the most ancient symbol of the White European people. That is why it was adopted as the emblem of the America First Party.

America First Party

Smyrna, GA :

Write for a free platform and membership application.

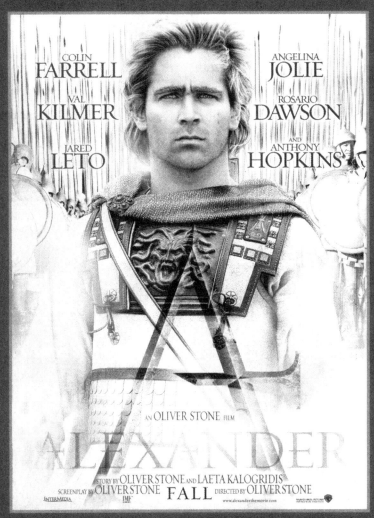

Advertisement for the 2004 movie, *Alexander*, a saga about the Greek conqueror, Alexander The Great. Accurately portrayed on Alexander's tunic: An image of the great Sun God worshipped under a variety of names by the ancients.

Hieroglyphic plan, supposedly by Hermes, of an ancient zodiac. (From *The Secret Teachings of All Ages*, by Manly P. Hall, 33º)

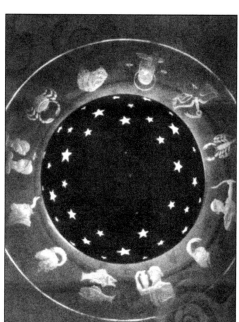

This Masonic Zodiac decorates the interior of the Federal Reserve Board Building in Washington, D.C. If the Nation had heeded the advice of President John Quincy Adams, Freemasonry would not have gained the foothold it has today in American Government.

Jewish astrological horoscope. The Sun deity is within the circle.

Native Americans worshipping the Sun God, bearing a totem idol. (Engraving from Theodore de Bry's *America*, 1590)

Mesopotamian worship of the Sun God. (British Museum, London)

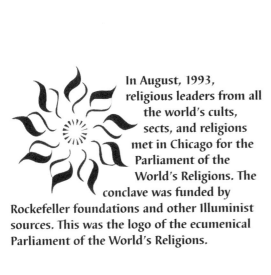

In August, 1993, religious leaders from all the world's cults, sects, and religions met in Chicago for the Parliament of the World's Religions. The conclave was funded by Rockefeller foundations and other Illuminist sources. This was the logo of the ecumenical Parliament of the World's Religions.

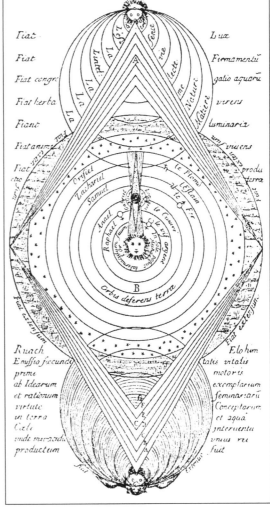

General plan of Cabalistic Jewish magic reveals a diamond focal point and many concentric circles. (From *Encyclopedia of the Occult*)

A T-shirt offered by a vendor of gift items from the *Hard Rock Cafe* restaurant chain. Note the sun symbol. Hard Rock Cafes were begun by Isaac Tigrett, a multimillionaire occultist who also conceived The Great American Pyramid, a sports arena built in Memphis, Tennessee.

The fairy tale legend of the origin of the peace sign holds that it first came into use by Vietnam War protestors. In reality, it has long been used as a sign of the hatred of Christ and is called "Nero's Cross"

The Greek theater at Epidaurus (circa 300 B.C.) enclosed a design of circle and point within. (Photo from book, *The Pattern and the Prophecy*, by James Harrison, Isaiah Publications, 1994)

Variations of the Yin/Yang.

TWENTY-THREE

"I Fell In To A Burning Ring of Fire"— Arnold Schwarzenegger's Masonic Ring, Newt Gingrich's T-Rex Dinosaur, and Other Mysterious Messages on Rings and Neckties of the Elite

One Ring to rule them all…One Ring to find them…One Ring to bring them all and in the darkness bind them.

> — J.R.R. Tolkien
> *Lord of the Rings*

I fell in to a burning ring of fire. I went down, down, down, and the flames went higher…

> — Johnny Cash
> *Ring of Fire*

The Illuminati seem to have an unusually passionate, if bizarre, attachment to jewelry, tie tacks, ties, and items of clothing. The Masons wear aprons, high hats, black clothing. They wear ties and rings emblazoned with symbols. And as the individual Mason progresses upwards to the 33rd degree, he is awarded "Jewels" befitting his various earned degrees.

Their ardent attachments to rings — some would call it idolatry — was exemplified in an article in a recent issue of *The Louisiana Freemason*.[1] The author, Mason David Roach, entitled his article, "If You Only Knew What This Ring Means to Me." He called the symbols engraved on his ring "precious," compared them to holy things from Scripture, and said the Masonic ring was akin to a "Crown of Purity." His ring was simply a typical, gold band made with the Masonic square and compass and letter "G."[2]

Sexual Idols

Former Mason Bill Schnoebelen, now a Christian, reveals the awful truth about most of the Masonic rings, tie tacks, and other symbolic items when he writes:

> Let's face it, the Masonic tie tacks and rings that so many Masons wear proudly to their churches on Sunday are sexual idols…The gods, like Baal, of all pagan nations around Israel were all sexual idols. This is precisely what God does not want in His Church, and yet all these Masons are flaunting both their idols and their (church) membership.[3]

Schnoebelen also mentions a little pin many Masons wear on the lapel of their jacket or coat shaped like a hockey stick with two balls attached. It is named "Tubal Cain." In reality, it represents a man's phallus and testicles; yet, the pin is worn publicly and proudly by many perverted Masons.

"Tubal Cain," the phallus pin worn by many Masons. Tubal Cain is the password of a Master Mason (3°). (From the book, *Masonic and Occult Symbols Illustrated*, pg. 233, by Dr. Cathy Burns)

A Bond Between Chieftains and Warriors

Barbara Walker, editor of *The Woman's Dictionary of Symbols and Sacred Objects*, discusses the significance of the ring in her book. She says that, "Rings were traditional symbols of the bond between chieftains and their warriors in Anglo-Saxon England." Moreover…

> Among the Celts, a ring given by a woman to a man represented her sexual availability; putting the finger through the ring was a sign of sexual intercourse.[4]

The ring, then is a symbol of authority, of bonding, and is a sign of the covenant made between the inferior and superior members of the Illuminati group.

In ancient religions and cultures, rings were also *magical* in nature. According to cabalistic rabbis, King Solomon used a magic ring with a hexagram symbol on it to enslave the demon Asmodeus into helping him build his famous Temple.

Some members of the Illuminati in France in the late 18th century, about 1780, founded a new secret order, the Academy of Sublime Masters of the Luminous Ring. The tenets of the group were Pythagorean, and the fields of geometry and science were emphasized.[5]

In today's Illuminati, the philosophy underlying the use of rings, neckties, etc.

continues from such traditions. The ring is configured as a circle, implying the supposed eternal reign of their god, Lucifer. He shall, they declare, wear a crown of gold. Thus, the metal of gold is favored.

The Mystic Tie of the Masons

The Masonic fraternity teaches the illusory goal that all who are inititated into its ranks are bonded by the "Mystic Tie" of fellowship. Of course, this is allegory, and yet the necktie does seem to have a special place in Masonic lore and symbology.

It is believed that both the bowtie and the traditional necktie are of Masonic symbolic design. The necktie has two triangles descending, a larger and a smaller. It is tied into a "knot" at the neck, signifying solidarity and unity. The neck itself, as a part of the human anatomy, represents the virtue of sacrifice. In terms of the secret order or secret society, it symbolizes sacrifice of the individual to the common good of the organization. The necktie is also seen as a bridge to two other triangles—those of the shirt collar. All of the triangles, on the tie and on the shirt collar, have their point, or spear, downward, toward the realm that is the controlling force of Masonry.

Congressman Lloyd Doggett (D-TX), at center, is sworn in as a voter registrar for the State of Texas. The elite of the Democrat Party in Doggett's Austin, Texas district are heavily Freemason. Doggett's necktie has the Masonic "X" symbol, connected to worship of Osiris the Egyptian sun god. At Doggett's left is the late Congressman Jake Pickle (D-TX), a Mason who for years was Chairman of the House Committee on Banking and Currency. Pickle refused to allow the U.S. Treasury, which he oversaw, to remove the Illuminati's pyramid and all-seeing eye symbols from the U.S. dollar bill.

President Bill Clinton seems to specialize in wearing neckties bearing cabalistic and occult symbols. Here, triangles. (Photo: *U.S. News & World Report*, January 29, 1996, p. 32)

Triangles and more triangles on yet another of President Bill Clinton's ties.

JEWISH WORLD

Into the Lion's Den

The nomination of Madeleine Albright as secretary of state has sent shivers through the Arab world. But some U.S. Jewish officials fear she may turn her fearsome tongue on Netanyahu.

JONATHAN BRODER Washington

IF THERE IS ONE MOMENT THAT defines Madeleine Albright's persona as a diplomat, it could very well be the time last February when she stood before the United

Clinton to nominate her to be his new secretary of state.

Yet as she awaits Senate confirmation, many in the foreign-policy establishments in Washington, Israel and the Arab world are wondering anxiously whether the 59-year-old Albright will bring her combative

president of the Middle East Institute, an Arabist research center, told The Jerusalem Report. After outgoing Secretary of State Warren Christopher's failure to nail down a peace agreement between Israel and Syria in 22 visits to the region, "she will probably treat the Middle East like

According to news reports, Monica Lewinsky, President Bill Clinton's White House intern lover, gave him a special necktie. When he wore it, she could watch him on TV and know he was thinking about her.

Bill Clinton's mother, Virginia, with his father, before he was born. Virginia, a Jewess, was deep into the supernatural magic of the Cabala. Bill Clinton's father is a dead ringer for Jack Ruby, the Jewish gangster and homosexual who assassinated Lee Harvey Oswald.

The Nature Conservancy, a radical environmental group, boasted in its March/April 1998 magazine that CNN founder Ted Turner, Presidents Bush and Clinton, and Vice President Gore often wore oak-leaf ties to denote their support for environmental causes. The oak tree and its leaves are a staple of druid witchcraft and are popular as symbols among nature followers of the forest horned god Pan.

these. The Nature Conservancy is active in 13. Notes Andreas Lehnhoff, the Conservancy's Guatemala program director, "We are already more deeply involved than we thought. And it's a good opportunity for us to establish new partnerships in the region." Research conducted by the Conservancy and other conservation groups has contributed to the plans for the Central American greenway.

—John A. Kinch

TYING THE KNOT

Conservancy Tie More Than a Fashion Statement

Some schools of thought hold that red is the color of the ultimate power tie—that slip-knot of silky fabric that greets you with its bold pronouncement, "I mean business."

But this is the '90s, and the power tie appears to have transformed to one navy blue flecked with green oak leaves. It's The Nature Conservancy's own, and this

In the past few years, Presidents Bush and Clinton and Vice President Gore also have been spotted—even

once during a presidential debate—brandishing oak-leaf ties, a low-key expression of conservation support, as well as good taste. "For us, it's been the power tie for years," says Mike Coda, vice president and director of marketing for the Conservancy.

—Martha Hodgkins Green

President Harry Truman (left) and Secretary of State Dean Acheson, both Illuminati initiates, each wear neckties imprinted with "sun god" symbols.

President Gerald Ford, a 33rd degree Mason, wears a necktie with the "cross of Baphomet" emblem of the occultic OTO and British satanist Aleister Crowley. The symbol is also worn by the Sovereign Grand Commander of Scottish Rite Freemasonry. Ford was a member of the Warren Commission that came up with the preposterous conclusion that Lee Harvey Oswald acted alone in the assassination of President John F. Kennedy. Chief Justice Earl Warren, like Ford and all the other members of the commission, was a 33rd degree Mason.

The Superstitious Necktie

When they visited Paris in 1636, a regiment of superstitious Croats from what is today Yugoslavia wore silk kerchiefs as talismans to ward off blows to the throat.

King Louis XIV admired the adornment and produced a necktie of his own, embroidered and tied with a simple knot. This new style was deemed the "cravat," the French word for Croat. The nobility of neckwear quickly caught on, and the tying of the tie became an entire regimen in itself.

By the 18th century, the cravat had evolved into the slender rectangle with a diamond-shaped tip we associate with modern neckwear. The ready-made tie began competing with the handmade cravat and eventually took over the neckwear market.

—Idea submitted by John L. Shaw, Palo Alto, Calif.

House Speaker Newt Gingrich wears a necktie designed by satan-worshipping rock music star, Jim Morrison of *The Doors*.

Illuminist signals: Insiders say speaker Newt Gingrich is a vain man who does not like being photographed without make-up. Here he is below pictured in *USA Today* newspaper (December 5, 1994, p. 5A) primping for a taping of NBC's "Meet the Press." This provides greater curiosity about *Time's* running as its front cover (see following page of *Codex Magica*) a staged picture of Gingrich in which the speaker is looking haggard and sweaty, his face red-flushed, and needing a shave!

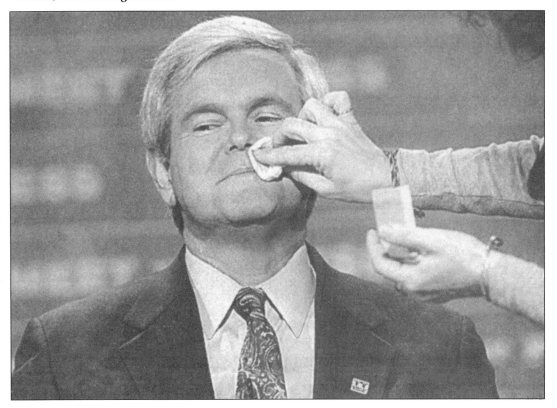

SPECIAL DOUBLE ISSUE

DECEMBER 25, 1995/JANUARY 1, 1996 $2.95

MAN OF THE YEAR

NEWT
GINGRICH

On House Speaker Newt Gingrich's necktie we find what appears to be a triceratops dinosaur and a small daisy flower, each image packed with powerful symbolic content.

At left: This cover of *Time* announcing the selection of House Speaker New Gingrich as *Time's* "Man of the Year" reveals many mysteries. First, the issue is dated December 25, 1995/January 1, 1996. December 25th, Christmas Day, is also the day the ancient Romans and Greeks worshipped the Sun God. In his photo, Newt Gingrich appears tired and dismayed. He is sweaty. No make-up is used, and he has a day-old growth of stubble on his face and neck. There is also a red coloration or flush on Newt's face. His head is strategically placed *behind* the *Time* logo, communicating the subtle message that his time in the political limelight is about up. In fact, Gingrich did abruptly resign and leave his high-level post shortly after this issue; some believe his departure was caused by his unseemly romantic liaison with a female staffer, an affair which prompted the Congressman to divorce his wife. However, the most significant images you'll find on this cover are hidden on Newt Gingrich's necktie! Look closely at the inset and what do you see? A dinosaur. The cave age monster is facing downward toward a flower. The Illuminati's founder Adam Weishaupt, in the late 18th century, introduced the concepts of *"flower power"* and nature worship (shades of the hippy era of the 60s!). So that might explain the flower. But what about the dinosaur? It seems that Newt (get the name, Newt?—isn't a Newt a form of lizard?) is a dinosaur fan. Gingrich once borrowed a Tyrannosaurus Rex dinosaur bones exhibit from Washington, D.C.'s Smithsonian Museum and kept it on display for a long time in his House Speaker's office. Newsmagazines often commented that Newt Gingrich was very proud of the T-Rex display and constantly asked friends and associates, *"Would you like to see my T-Rex?"* Now, *Webster's* dictionary informs us that the root word for "tyrannosaurus" is *tyrant*, or *tyranny*, defined as "A government in which absolute power is vested in a single ruler"—a ruler unfettered by a constitution! What's more, the short version of the dinosaur's name, T-Rex, would have a very special meaning for occult Illuminati. "T" stands for Tammuz, the Christ figure to come, whose symbol is the T, or Tau cross. The word "Rex," meanwhile, stands for *Man as King*. In Weishaupt's Illuminati system, the highest degree initiate earned the "Rex" degree. Thus, the symbols on Newt Gingrich's necktie, displayed for all the world to see, but for only Newt and his Illuminati henchmen to understand, trumpet this message, that: *Our Illuminati goal is a tyranny, ruled by a single ruler—the fearful antichrist, beast of prophecy!*

The caption reads: *"Speaker Newt Gingrich shows off tyrannosaurus rex Osborn in his Capitol office. It's on loan from the Smithsonian."* Observe Gingrich's Masonic handsign also, which is similar to the sign of a Master Mason. (Photo: *Roll Call*, May 22, 1995, p. 14)

The Church of Satan
by
Michael A. Aquino

Founded in San Francisco by Anton Szandor LaVey in 1966 CE (I ÆS), the Church of Satan went on to become the preeminent institution of Satanism in contemporary society. For nine years, until the next Working Year of 1975 CE (X ÆS), it openly acknowledged and pridefully exercised the Mandate of the Prince of Darkness on Earth. This book tells the story of those nine great years in 34 chapters, 143 appendices, 10 pages of plates, extensive annotation & indexing, for a total of over 900 8-1/2x11" pages, one million words in length and six pounds in weight.

Unlike popular, commercial treatments, *The Church of Satan* is designed neither to sell, excuse, criticize, sensationalize, nor otherwise distort the institution and the individuals whose history it documents. It does not simplify concepts, censor ritual texts, nor in any way doctor the truth. It is the author's conviction that the legacy of the Church of Satan, and of the many worthy Satanists who built and sustained it, stands quite adequately on its own. The book names names and describes events simply as they took place, and includes an abundance of letters, papers, and ceremonial texts which are now available nowhere else - to include analyses of the *Satanic Bible*, *Satanic Rituals*, and *Compleat Witch* and various original texts from which they were assembled and abridged.

Where the ... is ... 1975 Age of ...

When I sent Dr. Cathy Burns, a foremost authority on occult symbols and their meaning, a copy of speaker Newt Gingrich's *Time* magazine photo with the T-Rex dinosaur image on Newt's necktie, she sent me back this flyer advertising a book, *The Church of Satan*, written by Luciferian High Priest Michael A. Aquino. As you can see, the flyer has images of two dragon serpents atop satanic pentagrams facing each other (the occult sign of duality, or "as above, so below"). In fact, the two serpentine dragons do resemble the T-Rex dinosaur image.

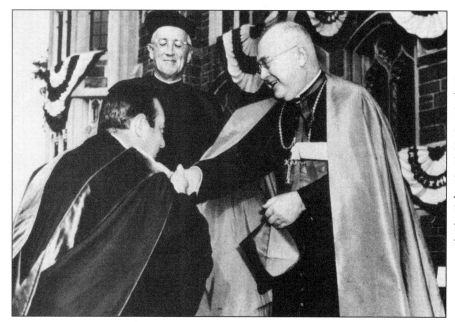

New York Mayor Wagner kneels and kisses the ring of Catholic Cardinal Spellman as Reverend McGinly, president of the Jesuit-run Fordham University, looks on with a sly grin on his face.

It seems that California Governor Arnold Schwarzenegger ("The Terminator") is well-schooled in the propaganda value of well-placed props in photographs, such as the U.S. flag, the State seal, and even a broom! What is most fascinating, however, is the big, blue sapphire masonic ring the Governor wears and so readily shows off. Apparently, the media know what's what and the photographer always seems to be glad to picture Arnold's ring up close. Oh, about the broom: That's not the same one that Arnold's wife, Kennedy heiress Maria Shriver, flies around on, is it?

Inset below left: C. W. Leadbeater, homosexual occultist who was head of late 19th Century Theosophy after Madame Blavatsky, wore a ring similar to the one sported about today by Arnold Schwarzenegger.

(Photo: *U.S. News & World Report*, January 12, 2004, p. 27)

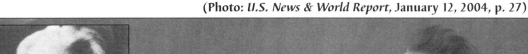

Schwarzenegger off to 'good start,' but he still faces his toughest test

Due Jan. 10, his budget plan must deal with $14B deficit

By Martin Kasindorf
USA TODAY

LOS ANGELES — Arnold Schwarzenegger has ended his first five weeks as California's governor with more praise from politicians than he ever got from film critics.

"A good start," says Gray Davis, the Democrat who lost his job in the historic recall election Oct. 7 and was replaced by the Republican actor.

"I have to give him high grades," says Robert Beverly, who retired in 1996 after 30 years as a Republican leader in the state Legislature. "I'm a little surprised."

Since his inauguration Nov. 17, Schwarzenegger has done a lot more than learn his lines on a new stage. He has demonstrated — with well-timed coaching from his wife, Maria Shriver — that he can abandon a script that isn't working.

Schwarzenegger, at age 56, is learning improvisation. He is using his executive power in unprecedented ways, and he is cutting budget deals with Democratic legislators he once called "addicts to spending."

Much of the praise Schwarzenegger is hearing is for a compromise he brokered with the Legisla-

By Robyn Beck, AFP/Getty Images

Learning to improvise: After just five weeks in office, California Gov. Arnold Schwarzenegger, a Republican, has already learned how to cut budget deals with Democratic legislators he once called "addicts to spending."

ture's Democratic majority earlier this month that ended a deadlock and could provide at least a short-term solution for the state's budget crisis.

Cover story

Mayors and police chiefs also are praising him for using obscure emergency powers last week to give strapped cities and counties $2.7 billion to avert layoffs of public-safety workers. It was a problem he had largely created. He kept his campaign pledge to cancel Davis' unpopular 300% increase in vehicle license fees — the "car tax" that helps pay for cops and firefighters. But the tax cut created budget shortfalls for local governments.

On this issue, Schwarzenegger remains at odds

Please see COVER STORY next page ▶

"Ring: forward, photograph!," barked Arnold to the *USA Today* photographer and editors who eagerly and obediently complied. (Photo: *USA Today*, December 22, 2003)

Recently, Bohemian Grove alumnus Arnold Schwarzenegger met privately with Warren Buffett (left), America's second richest man according to *Forbes* magazine, and Britain's Lord Jacob Rothschild (right), at the Rothschild mansion in England. Schwarzenegger evidently earned the endorsement and support of Jewish groups the old-fashioned way—he "bribed" them with millions of dollars!

Arnold Schwarzenegger, Mr. Universe, giving a very familiar hand salute. Schwarzenegger once remarked: *"I admired Hitler because he came from being a little man with no formal education up to power."*

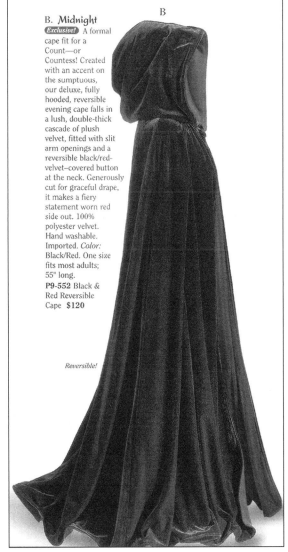

B. Midnight
Exclusive! A formal cape fit for a Count—or Countess! Created with an accent on the sumptuous, our deluxe, fully hooded, reversible evening cape falls in a lush, double-thick cascade of plush velvet, fitted with slit arm openings and a reversible black/red-velvet–covered button at the neck. Generously cut for graceful drape, it makes a fiery statement worn red side out. 100% polyester velvet. Hand washable. Imported. *Color:* Black/Red. One size fits most adults; 55" long.
P9-552 Black & Red Reversible Cape **$120**

Reversible!

A. Good for What Ails You
In the 13th century, Albertus Magnus said it cured depression. In the 14th, Konrad von Megenberg conferred on it the powers of fertility and beauty. Gonelli wrote in 1702 that it drove away night-mares—and a certain Adamus Lonicerus said it even cured *snakebite*. Whatever its properties, this cabochon of genuine blue chalcedony surely lifts the spirits in its fanciful setting of stencil-cut sterling silver. Whole sizes 6–9.
P11-617 Blue Chalcedony Ring **$29.95**

Genuine blue chalcedony!

Sort of a feminine version of the ring worn by Governor Arnold Schwarzenegger. Offered in *The Pyramid Collection* catalog, 2004.

Also available in *The Pyramid Collection* catalog, this "Midnight" cape. The catalog says it is "fit for a Count—or Countess." The color of the cape is listed as black and red. *"It makes a fiery statement,"* says the advertising copy.

OCCASIONAL WEAR FRATERNAL RINGS
14K and 18K Gold Electroplate
(Rings available in EVEN SIZES only)
Jewelery not shown actual size

1. **Nugget Ring.** Sizes 7 - 14. 5160–$30.00
2. **Masonic Signet Ring.** Sizes 7 - 16.
5162–$30.00
3. **Masonic Ring.** Enamel. Sizes 7 - 14.
5161–$35.00
4. **Signet Ring with Simulated Diamond.**
Sizes 7 -14. 5167–$35.00
5. **Sculptured 320 Consistory Ring.**
Sizes 7 -14. 5701–$35.00
6. **32⁰ Consistory Ring.** Enamel.
Sizes 7 - 14. 5702–$35.00
7. **Eastern Star Ring.** Sizes 5 - 10.
5590–$35.00

8. **Masonic Synthetic Sapphire.** 18K heavy electroplate.
Sizes 7 - 14. 5168—$40.00
9. **Masonic Synthetic Ruby.** 18K heavy electroplate.
Sizes 7 - 14. 5169—$40.00
10. **Masonic Black Onyx.** 18K heavy electroplate
Sizes 7 - 16. 5171—$40.00
11. **OES Ring.** 18K heavy electroplate.
Whole sizes 5-10. 5589—$40.00

RINGS—14K Electroplate

Masonic Onyx. Sizes 7-16. 5163–$35.00

Shrine Onyx. Sizes 7-14 5704–$35.00

Shrine Enameled Emblem. Sizes 7-14 5705–$35.00

Masonic Imitation Sapphire Sizes 7-16 5165–$35.00

Masonic Imitation Ruby Sizes 7-16 5164–$35.00

Masonic Onyx Same as 5151. Sizes 7-16 5151O–$30.00

Masonic Ring Encrusted synthetic sapphire with sprig of acacia sides. Sizes 7-16 5151–$30.00

17 Masonic Symbol Antique gold finish. Sizes 7-14 5154–$25.00

Masonic Imitation Ruby Same as 5151. Sizes 7-16 5151R–$30.00

Masonic Imitation Ruby Cusion shaped. Sizes 7-14 5166–$30.00

Masonic Tiger Eye Corner simulated diamond. Sizes 7-14 5159–$35.00

Masonic Onyx Bark side design and raised emblem. Sizes 7-14 5152–$30.00

Masonic Onyx Sprig of acacia side and raised emblem. Sizes 7-16 5153–$30.00

ABOVE RINGS ARE IN WHOLE SIZES ONLY FROM 7 THRU 14

5148—$35.00 Enameled shrine onyx ring w/6 simulated diamonds. Sizes 7-14.

5146—$35.00 32nd eagle onyx ring w/ 6 simulated diamonds. Sizes 7-16.

5156—$35.00 32nd eagle signet w/ simulated diamond. Sizes 7-14.

5150—$35.00 PM onyx ring w/6 simulated diamonds. Sizes 7-14.

5149—$35.00 Master Mason cushion shape sapphire stone ring. Sizes 7-14.

5147—$35.00 PM signet w/ simulated diamond. Sizes 7-16.

A page from the catalog of Macoy, a distributor of Masonic books, pins, rings, jewelry, and supplies. (2003/2004 Catalog No. 130)

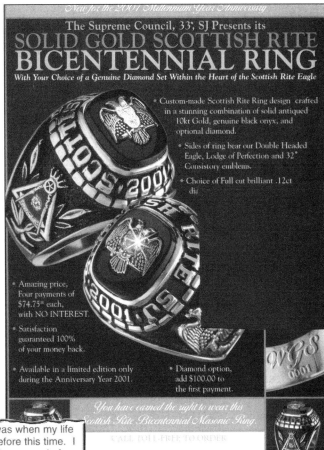

An advertisement on the back cover of *Scottish Rite Journal.*

. . . . In 1962, the year my birth father died, was when my life was turned upside down. But there were clues before this time. I had asked my grandmother why I did not resemble anyone in four generations from what I thought was my family, and why I was so different from everyone else in the family. She was evasive. However, she gave me a photograph *(circa 1919)* of some men who I did not know and two rings.

Bernard Baruch's Ring

. . . . She then stated, *"Your father wants you to have his ring, and Bernard Baruch wants you to have this gold ring, which is engraved with the date April 13, 1913."*

Bernard Baruch

. . . . I would learn later that this ring commemorated the founding of the Federal Reserve; each of its founders received a gold ring at the founding ceremony. She pointed to the photograph and then specifically to a tough-looking man in the photograph. She then said, *"This man is important to you."* In addition, I received a French Legion of Honor Medal dated 1928 from my adoptive father, who pointed to the man on the medal and said, *"This man is important to you. He is Andre LeBon."*

. . . . These were the only clues I had to my real identity, but when I received these gifts I had no idea about their significance. In fact, I would have to relive my childhood over and over again through the mists of memory to solve the mystery. I finally recalled that in 1955 I was taken in the middle of the night to the

In his excellent publication, *Criminal Politics*, this author's good friend, Lawrence Patterson, published a fascinating story (excerpt at left) about this ring. It is the 13th ring of the Illuminati founders of the Federal Reserve Board. It was owned by Bernard Baruch, wealthy benefactor, advisor, and controller behind the scenes of President Franklin D. Roosevelt. Baruch gave this gold ring to Dr. Nancy L. Nicholson, heiress of a disputed financial empire. Dr. Nicholson is not a conspirator of the Illuminati although she was raised among the Rothschilds and other dynasty members. Her father, she says, was Lucky Luciano, the infamous Mafia leader. A close look at the engraving on Bernard Baruch's ring reveals what seems to be the number 6 repeated in a combination circular and spiral design. (Photo: *Criminal Politics* magazine, April 30, 2003, p. 11)

Issue Price $4.00 (Outside U.S. $5.00)
U.N. Tax Not Included

MediaBypass

THE UNCENSORED NATIONAL NEWS   VOL. 4 #9 • SEPTEMBER 1996

"ANGEL OF DEATH"
AND ELECTION '96

This issue of *Media Bypass* magazine (September, 1996) featured the activities of Charles Hayes, who was said to be a retired operative of the CIA. According to the magazine, Hayes had been busy in retirement as a vigilante exposing the financial skullduggery and crookedness of various high-level politicians and world leaders. On the cover of the magazine we find Mr. Hayes in front of law library publications and a Great Seal of the U.S. plaque, puffing placidly on a pipe. But what stands out is the mysterious ring with the devilish face, composed of some type of blackish material, inside a circle. A few months after this issue was published, Charles Hayes was indicted by a federal grand jury and arrested. News reports allege that Hayes was guilty of solicitation of murder. Did the revelations contained in the article in *Media Bypass* cause the elite to take action to shut him up? Or was something else up? What is the riddle of the mysterious ring with its curious image?

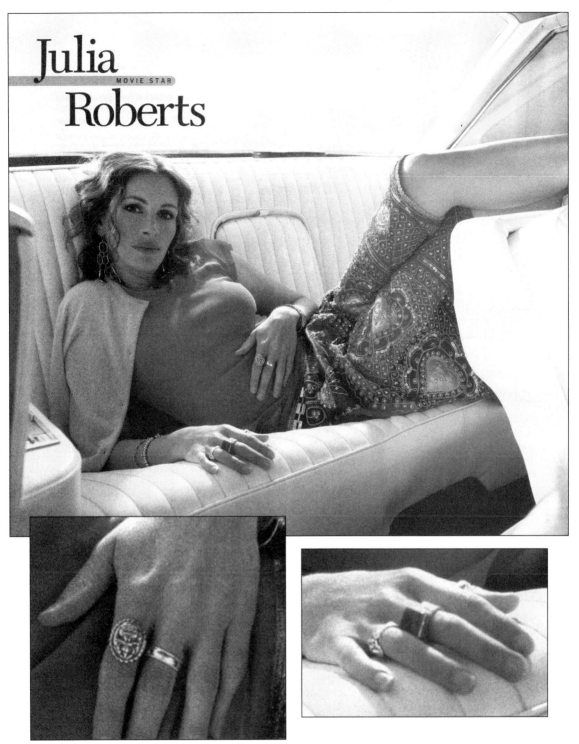

Julia
MOVIE STAR
Roberts

This mysterious photo of Oscar-winning actress Julia Roberts in *Time* magazine gives us an intriguing view of two rings she wears. On her right hand is the blue-stoned rectangular ring, and on her left hand is a ring with a strange image, indeed one could even say the ring has a creepy and eerie image. In the accompanying article, the writer acclaims Roberts as "the reigning queen of Hollywood."

Without caption, *Brill's Content* magazine published this photo of Russian President Vladimir Putin. The black border is unusual and obviously connotes a dark and evil significance to Putin's character. The necktie Putin wears has Illuminist meaning. The X of Osiris is prominent in the design as is the two triangles—one pointing up, the other down—inside a diamond.

Manly P. Hall, 33°, informs us of the occult meaning of the Pythagorean Signet Ring in his classic textbook, *The Secret Teachings of All Ages*. Albert Pike, former Sovereign Grand Commander of the Scottish Rite Masons, wrote in *Morals and Dogma* that the pentagram (pentacle, cabalistic star) on this ring *"carries with it the power of commanding the spirits."* Use it, he instructed, to *"bind the demons of the air, the spirits of fire, the spectres of water, and the ghosts of the earth."* Note that the star atop the ring is encircled by the Oroboros serpent.

TWENTY-FOUR

OK—Sign of the Divine King

"Annuit Coeptus" — He approves our undertaking.

— Latin inscription atop
the all-seeing eye on
the U.S.A. one dollar bill

Westerners know it as the "okay" (or "OK") sign. It's done with the fingers and thumb of right or left hands (usually the right). Simply touch the index finger to the thumb, creating a circle. The other three fingers then spiral off and there you have it—the well-known symbol for *OK*. Universally, this sign means alright, acceptable, good, right-on, you bet!, A-OK, satisfactory…

But to occultists, the OK sign takes on darker significance. First, we have the *circle*, indicating the sun deity and the Mason's never-ending quest for more light. To Freemasonry, the circle also represents the female genitalia, or yoni. In the Hindu religion, the OK sign is a revered *mudra* (sacred gesture) meaning "infinity" or perfection. It is associated with the female genitalia—thumb and forefinger pressed together at the tips with the other three fingers extended.

In the practice of tantric yoga (sex rituals), the OK sign is a token of ecstasy, spiritual and physical. In ancient Sumeria and Persia, charms and amulets have been discovered of fingers and hands in the modern OK position, joined along with horns implying fertility. The three fingers extended outward are symbolic of ecstatic union with the Goddess, the third member of the pagan trinity.

In Satanism, when making this sign the three fingers not used to make the circle are considered symbolic of the *unholy* trinity—horned god, goddess, and offspring (antichrist). Some go so far as to adopt the view that the bent three fingers are shaped as three number six's, or 666. Thus, we have 666, the sun deity (Lucifer), the goddess

(Mystery, Babylon the Great, Mother of Harlots), and the beast (antichrist, 666), all in one unitary hand sign. Oh what a web of evil wicked men can weave around something seemingly so ordinary and mundane.

In the Illuminist philosophy, the OK sign becomes a sign indicating approval of the Divine King, their coming Lord of Light, whom we as Christians know as Antichrist. To them it means, "He approves our undertaking." This meaning is roughly equivalent to the words in Latin atop the all-seeing eye of Osiris on our U.S. one dollar bill—*Annuit Coeptus*.

A Gesture to Avoid?

As we've noted, the gesture made by touching the tips of the thumb and index finger to form a circle, with the remaining three fingers of the hand fanned out and pointing out may signify "A-Okay" in the U.S.A., but in other cultures the same gesture will certainly not meet with approval.

In Brazil, Germany, and Russia, the signal is a supreme insult and vulgar, indicating a very private body orifice.

In France, the sign portrays the person it is aimed at as being a flunky or a "zero"—basically a worthless person. When it's placed over the nose it means he or she is drunk.

In Japan, the same sign is used in commercial transactions to indicate you want the cashier to give you your change in coins rather than in currency.

In Spain, in Eastern Europe, and in some parts of Latin America, the OK hand gesture is considered very rude. When then Vice President Nixon visited Brazil in the 50s, a crowd of onlookers became a rampaging mob after Nixon flashed them what he thought was the A-Okay sign. To them, Nixon was making an obscene gesture. Nixon's "goodwill" trip suddenly became a "badwill" trip.

And there's more confusion abroad: In Arab countries, making this sign while shaking the hand symbolizes the giving of the *"evil eye,"* perceived by Arabs as an event of great dread. It may be interpreted that you are putting a curse on the individual. Could it be that the Arab interpretation of this sign is exactly what the Illuminati intend in their performing it?

Donald Rumsfeld, Secretary of Defense in the Bush Administration, signals with his hand as he renders a sour look with his face.

Beautiful actress Brittany Murphy gives the enigmatic "OK" sign. In the article accompanying the Brittany Murphy photo, *People* magazine quotes Murphy as saying she sneaks off in the middle of the night to write poetry. The magazine thus calls her the "Midnight Rambler."

Robert Rubin, Secretary of the Treasury in the Bill Clinton Administration. (Photo: *Austin American-Statesman* newspaper, May 16, 1999)

Israeli Prime Minister Benjamin Netanyahu (Photo: Associated Press, in *Lewiston Morning Tribune*, October 26, 1998, p. 7A)

Lotz shares famous father's fire

L. MUELLER/Staff

Anne Graham Lotz, Billy Graham's daughter, speaks to a crowd of 1,900 during the YMCA's annual community prayer breakfast at the Charlotte Convention Center on Thursday.

Billy Graham's daughter shows she's more than that

By KEN GARFIELD
Religion Editor

An altar call was about all that was missing from Thursday's YMCA prayer breakfast, not that evangelist Anne Graham Lotz wasn't aching to call the sellout crowd of 1,900 down front to commit to Christ.

But since an altar call isn't part of the nation's second-biggest prayer breakfast — and since the Charlotte Convention Center ballroom wasn't equipped for such a stampede — she did what any daughter of Billy Graham would have done. She implored people to live for Christ, then asked those who want to know more to write their name and address on the program and she'd send them a Bible study guide.

Add a choir singing "Just As I Am" and it could have been one of her father's famous crusades.

The second of the Grahams' five children, Lotz showed Thursday why The New York Times recently rated her as one of five contenders for

Please see PRAYER / page 5C

Anne Graham Lotz, Billy Graham's daughter, at a YMCA prayer breakfast (Photo: Charlotte, NC newspaper, April 2, 1999)

This drawing by an anonymous artist is very revealing in its carefully crafted symbology. We see in all three hands a variation of the Illuminati's *"OK"* sign. Then, there's the oval-shaped "egg," the "El Diablo" devil's horns, the two dialectic birds.

Roddy Doyle, popular Irish novelist. (*Newsweek*, July 1, 1996, p. 64)

RODDY DOYLE: *The more popular this widely read novelist grows, the darker and better his books become*

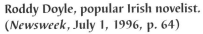

Pat Robertson, Mason, Illuminist, Knight of Malta, and elite propagandist in the field of religion.

John Foster Dulles (right), Secretary of State in the Eisenhower Administration, with Illuminist religious puppet, Billy Graham. (Photo: From book, *Thy Will Be Done—The Conquest of the Amazon: Nelson Rockefeller and Evangelism in the Age of Oil*, by Gerard Colby, Harper Collins, 1995)

Playing politics: *De Villepin is said to adore Machiavelli, known in part for perfecting the art of the diplomatic lie.*

ward with military action, and claimed that Iraq "has complied fully with all

French Foreign Minister De Villepin, at the United Nations in New York. (Photo: *Insight* magazine, April 13-26, 2004, p. 39)

394–foot tall Buddha statue in Tokyo, Japan.

President George W. Bush (*Time* magazine, March 3, 2003, p. 5)

President George Herbert Walker Bush, has often been seen giving the Illuminati's mudra, known by masses as the "OK."

David Graham, FDA official in the Bush Administration. (Associated Press, in *Austin American-Statesman*, December 5, 2004, p. 18)

INTERNATIONAL

GETTING RUSSIA ON BOARD: Vice President Gore with Moscow envoy Viktor Chernomyrdin

DAVID HUME KENNERLY FOR NEWSWEEK

will preside over an unworkable peace.

The debate over whether America has interests in the Balkans is now somewhat irrelevant. Our commitments have created interests, even though in foreign policy it should usually be the other way around. We have two sets of concerns relating to Kosovo, humanitarian and strategic. Sadly, in both our goals will end up being to undo the consequences of the war. The ⸺

tonomy is now the best NATO can hope for.

The Clinton administration's overriding objective is to stop the exodus of refugees and have them return to Kosovo in safety. This does not figure in any of the original statements on the war, and for a simple reason. There was no refugee exodus until the bombings began. NATO angrily denies the connection, but the facts are clear. ⸺ United Nations High Com⸺

litical goals, ⸺ make backu⸺ Weber once judged not b⸺ sequences of to clamor fo⸺ cy, but ⸺ and ⸺

Vice President Al Gore (left) and influential Moscow envoy and fellow Illuminist, Viktor Chernomyrdin. Chernomyrdin, a crypto-Jew and Mason, oversaw the redistribution of assets of the old Communist Soviet State in the hands of Jewish oligarchs. This was a prime Illuminati project in the late 1980s and 1990s. Symbols expert Dr. Cathy Burns, in reviewing this photo, remarked: "Not only are hand signs important in the occult, but other features in a picture can also have a symbolic meaning. For instance, notice the book with an eagle on the cover. Could the United States be the Eagle? The caption just below mentions "getting Russia on board." Notice too, the title of the book, *The Company We Keep.* Is this a reference to the United States keeping company with Russia ("getting Russia on board")? (Photo: *Newsweek,* May 17, 1999, p. 38)

President George W. Bush, affectionately holds his left hand as France's President Jacques Chirac gives the high sign of the Illuminati with his right. (Photo: *Insight* magazine, April 13-26, 2004, p. 41)

The PLO Chief Yasser Arafat with his current-day successor, Mahmoud Abbas. Both men were Masons, and both were tools of the CIA and Mossad.

Hillary Clinton And The White House Feminists Who Now Control America—And Tell The President What To Do

BIG SISTER IS WATCHING YOU

TEXE MARRS

This cover of one of the author's bestselling books illustrates the former First Lady wearing an "angel pin" with wings crossed in an Osirian X. Her right hand is formed in a circle.

President Bill Clinton with a double circle sign, to emphasize his point. The headline reads "Clinton goes on offensive against Starr...Alleged sex scandal won't make him resign, President says..." Clinton's hand signal indicates that his Illuminist superiors had decided to let him stay in office and not be ousted through impeachment conviction due to the Lewinsky sex/perjury scandal charges brought by special prosecutor, Kenneth Starr. (*Austin American-Statesman*, February 7, 1998, p. 1)

Rasputin, the "Mad Monk" of Russia who ingratiated himself with the Czarina and other nobility. Rasputin was an initiate of a secret order whose members engaged in naked dances, ecstatic states, drunkeness, and sexual orgies, which they claimed to be "holy." Children begotten were said to be born of the Holy Ghost.

Pre-Christian idol from Ireland

8 THE JERUSALEM POST **NEWS FEATURE** MAY 28, 1999

Those unsinkable Shasniks

Aryeh Deri called the elections a referendum on his trial – and in this referendum he did supremely well, but not well enough to save him politically. Herb Keinon reports

'He is innocent," Benny Elbaz sang in one of the more memorable Shas television campaign ads.

"He is innocent," a crowd of thousands thundered back, with tears dripping down their cheeks, overturning – at least in their hearts and minds – the Jerusalem District Court's verdict in the Aryeh Deri case.

"Is anybody really buying this?" countless people undoubtedly asked themselves. The unequivocal answer came back last Tuesday morning.

Seventeen Knesset seats. That's seven *more* seats than the party had before the court convicted Deri of accepting bribes, and sentenced him to a jail term. It's three times as many seats

10 seats were worth to Netanyahu.

"Even if they join a coalition, it will not be with the same bargaining strength they enjoyed before."

Prime Minister-elect Barak, said Cohen, has a wide range of coalition options, so the power of any one party – even a party with 17 seats – is limited.

And, according to Cohen, Shas bears a large part of the responsibility for Netanyahu's defeat and the collapse of the right. In other words, the party is "to blame" for the fact that Barak has so many coalition options.

"Shas contributed a great deal to the fall of the Likud and the right-wing camp, for one reason: it let the secular genie out of the bottle.

"Shas did not win 17 seats," said. "It won 23 – its 17,

Netanyahu's embrace of Shas also led a number of Likud voters into the political center, because they were fed up with Shas's lack of respect for the rule of law.

"When the Likud writes its report on why it lost the elections," Cohen said, "a chapter entitled 'We lost because of Shas' will form a major part of that report."

vacating the political stage, being replaced by the religious right."

This is a long-term process that helps explain the steady growth of Shas, which has gone from four seats in 1984 to 17 last week. But there are also more immediate causes.

"The first is Netanyahu's social and economic policies. Although

the state's institutions.

"When something like the Deri trial takes place, it only enhances this feeling, because they feel that the country is oppressing the person they view as their leader."

ACCORDING to Cohen, that so many people hold the court in disregard is frightening.

Dancing for joy: Jubilant Shas supporters express their joy at winning 17 Knesset seats at Shas headquarters in Jerusalem the day after the elections. (Ariel Jerozolimski/The Jerusalem Post)

Jubilant supporters of Israel's hard-core Shas political party dance for joy after the victory of winning many disputed seats in that country's Knesset (parliament). (Photo: *The Jerusalem Post* newspaper, May 28, 1999, p. 8)

Beatle Paul McCartney, left, gives the Illuminati's "Divine King" sign while fellow Beatle John Lennon lets us know he's a Luciferian.

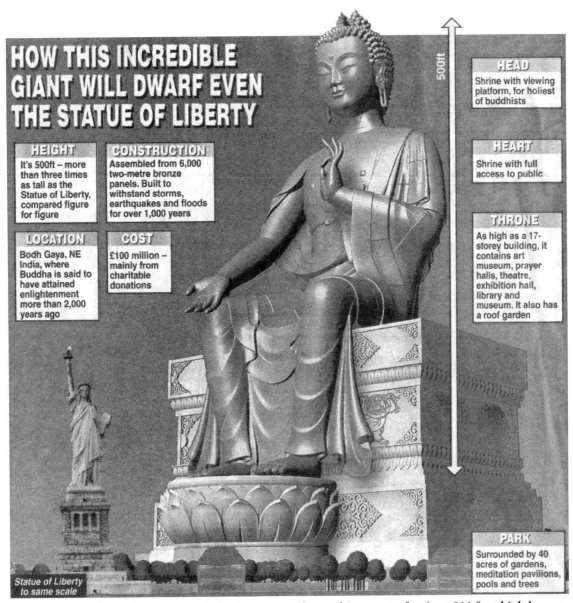

HOW THIS INCREDIBLE GIANT WILL DWARF EVEN THE STATUE OF LIBERTY

HEIGHT
It's 500ft – more than three times as tall as the Statue of Liberty, compared figure for figure

CONSTRUCTION
Assembled from 6,000 two-metre bronze panels. Built to withstand storms, earthquakes and floods for over 1,000 years

LOCATION
Bodh Gaya, NE India, where Buddha is said to have attained enlightenment more than 2,000 years ago

COST
£100 million – mainly from charitable donations

HEAD
Shrine with viewing platform, for holiest of buddhists

HEART
Shrine with full access to public

THRONE
As high as a 17-storey building, it contains art museum, prayer halls, theatre, exhibition hall, library and museum. It also has a roof garden

PARK
Surrounded by 40 acres of gardens, meditation pavilions, pools and trees

500ft

Statue of Liberty to same scale

In London's *Daily Mail* newspaper (July 6, 2000, p. 9) was this report of a giant 500 foot high bronze Buddha statue, called the Buddha Maitreya, in the Indian holy city of Bodh Gaya. The statue will be over three times higher than the U.S.A.'s Statue of Liberty. It is being built by British engineers. Observe the Buddha statue's mudra, or left hand sign. Also, the "horns" on the head.

HOUSTON
Lifestyle & Entertainment

Mainstream meditation

America's outlook changing

By HOLLY SELBY
Baltimore Sun

BALTIMORE — Remember when meditation was something only hippies did? Remember when it was something only New Age crystal-carriers did?

No more.

East increasingly meets mainstream West these days as meditation and other relaxation techniques — often with roots deep in Eastern philosophies — gain acceptance and credence among Americans ranging from true spiritual seekers to Yuppie Type A's just trying to relax.

Consider: On Thursday evenings at the Golden Temple, a woman in a white turban, pants and T-shirt begins a yoga class with a deep-breathing exercise. The class ends with her students — retirees, social workers, students — meditating together.

In Washington, D.C., on Fridays, the Pentagon Meditation Club meets in the Pentagon chapel to meditate for peace. Members of the group call it SDI — the Spiritual Defense Initiative.

On any given day at Johns Hopkins Hospital, patients suffering from stress-related symptoms like headaches are treated with a combination of meditation, biofeedback and relaxation techniques, says Richard Waranch, director of the Behavioral Medicine and Bio-

things when they can use technology, when they can see it objectively."

The result of all this research has been a gr...

and biofeedback techniques at Hopkins since 1978.

Some people, initially drawn to meditation for physi...

E. Joseph Deering / Chronicle

Kay Wescott, a lawyer and CPA who works for the Justice Department, attends meditation classes at the Yoga Institute and Bookshop.

The caption reads: *"Kay Wescott, a lawyer and CPA who works for the Justice Department, attends meditation classes at the Yoga Institute and Bookshop."* Yoga is very popular in the United States, though most do not understand that the yogic positions of hands and body represent Hindu pagan religious symbols and doctrines. In this instance, Ms. Wescott sits in the upright position, legs crossed lotus-style, her hands in the mudra "OK," or circle.

The San Marga Sanctuary

AMERICA'S FIRST ALL-GRANITE TEMPLE IS BEING BUILT ON THE TROPICAL HAWAIIAN ISLAND OF KAUAI.

A Hindu swami and worshipper of the god Shiva at the San Marga Sanctuary in Hawaii. He is accompanied by a strange paper idol and a brazen cobra idol.

Buddha displaying the left-hand "OK" mudra. This drawing is from *The Herder Dictionary of Symbols* (Chiron Publications, Wilmette, Illinois, 1986). That reference source explains it as "an eye in the hand of God signified God's creative wisdom." Of course, this is not referring to the Christian God, but to the ineffable, unknown God called *Ain Soph* in the Cabala and as the evil, satanic "God of Forces," in the Bible's book of Daniel.

Illustration in *The Herder Dictionary of Symbols* (Chiron Publications, Wilmette, Illinois, 1986).

Buddha statue (Photo: *The Clarion Call* **magazine, Spring 1988)**

TWENTY-FIVE

Victory for the Devil—Fabulous Exploits of Sir Winston Churchill and Other Druid Priests and Illuminati Servants

A remarkable thing occurred with the hand so lifted, is that its shadow resembles the head and horns of the Goat of Baphomet..the symbol of black magic.

— *The Complete Book of Witchcraft*

Britain's legendary World War II Prime Minister, Sir Winston Churchill, made the "V" sign famous. It was standard for the cigar-smoking, paunchy politician; he flashed the "V" sign every chance he got, and news photographers captured hundreds of photographs of Churchill giving the sign. It was generally thought that in doing so, the pugnacious Churchill was signaling confidence in eventual victory over the Nazi foe across the channel. So, the sign of two fingers pointed upward in a "V"shape became universally accepted as a sign for victory.

Sign of the Horned God, Pan

But what the majority of people believe to be conventional wisdom is often wrong. Such is the case here, too, for this sign, in reality, is of ancient origins. It is, in fact, a sign of Satan, of malediction, of the horned god, Pan, and worse.

Paranoia magazine, an interesting publication which bills itself as "the conspiracy reader" had a picture some years back of Churchill displaying the "V." An astute reader knowledgeable of dark things wrote a letter to the editor in the next issue commenting on Churchill and his sign. Nigel A. Cornwall of Britain wrote, "The sign I believe has its origins as a symbol for a pagan horned god." [1]

Cornwall also suggested that when the sign is given with the *palm inside*, it is recognized as a horribly vulgar and offensive gesture—signifying penetration of both body orifices.

Done in the typical fashion, this sign literally means intercourse by the devil—to be violated sexually by the horned god. The thumb holding down the fingers creates the "vulva," while the two largest fingers pointed up are the horns of the god (Satan).

The Law of Opposites

In her highly regarded encyclopedia of symbols entitled *Masonic and Occult Symbols Illustrated*, Dr. Cathy Burns explores the meaning of the "V" sign. She explains that the two fingers upward relate to the Masonic and Gnostic Law of Opposites, exactly as the case for the Masonic Lodge's black and white checkerboard floors. This is the doctrine of bringing order out of chaos, of reconciling the two opposites, evil and good, with Satan reigning over both heaven *and* hell.[2] The "V" sign is also a sign of the Horned God of witchcraft, often called Pan; or *Baphomet*, the androgynous (male and female) goat god (again illustrating the Law of Opposites).

The Face in the Shadow

The Complete Book of Witchcraft[3] explains further the occult meaning. When the sign is given to produce a shadow behind, a diabolical image appears that seems to be the face of the devil. Witches and Magicians—and some Catholic Popes—used this image to effect emotional responses:

> There was a deeply seated belief in the fascination or enchantment of shadows; so that the witch, or magician, could use them to either produce sickness and death or to inspire love...The shadow of the (Satanic) priest's fingers raised in blessing was considered to have evil significance...

> A remarkable thing occurred with the hand so lifted, is that its shadow resembles the head and horns of the Goat of Baphomet...the symbol of black magic.

> The use of the 'shadow of blessing' was regarded as the legitimate prerogative of the Pope, and was most terribly exercised during the Dark Ages and at the time of the Inquisition.[4]

Interestingly, other authoritative sources say that the "V" sign (the sign of the horny goat, or horned god) is practiced even today in satanic covens as a symbol of Satanic benediction. In times past, it was just the opposite, being a sign of evil, of malediction, but today the twisted minds of satanic worshippers view evil as something good and desirable. What is malediction to the holy and righteous, to the Satanist is a wonderful thing!

A Symbol of Wrath and Destruction

The "V" sign as displayed by the hand is also used by Illuminists in the form of the letter V with two straight lines angled to meet at a point facing downward. It becomes a V device, or chevron, and has been adopted for the uniforms of military troops of some countries. Resembling a downward pointing triangle with the top line open or omitted symbolizes fiery destruction and wrath on the object at which it is pointed.

About 12 years ago, a few Satan worshippers arrived secretly in the darkness at my ministry building and evidently carried out a ritual. For many months we had received anonymous telephone threats, so were not surprised. On the concrete porch near our front door, the vandals had scratched a "V" pointing to the entrance, and there were signs of candle use and the burning of objects. Here we see the fantastic beliefs by occultists that their rituals create reality. However, in vainly attempting to harm a true Christian ministry, I am persuaded that the "magic" backfired. When God is your protector, those who cast Satan's spells end up in deep, deep, trouble.

Triple 6 or 666

As we have previously seen, the Jewish cabala is at the root of most wicked systems of magic. The cabala (or Kabbalah) is the fount of doctrine for Freemasonry and for many other secret societies. We can expect, therefore, that the "V" sign is also emphasized by the rabbinical priests of cabalism. And in fact, we find that the rabbis teach that the meaning of the Hebrew letter for V (Vau) is "Nail," and nail is a secret title for Satan. (Its corrupt meaning comes from the nails driven into the hands of Jesus crucified.) Vau, or V, is the *sixth* letter in the Hebrew alphabet, and, of course, the Book of Revelation reveals that the name of the beast, or Antichrist, is coded with the number of triple 6, or 666.

Churchill A Druid Priest

Where did Winston Churchill learn of the satanic powers of the "V" sign? Few people are aware that Churchill was a Freemason. Stephen Knight wrote an explosive exposé, *The Brotherhood*, that rocked the British Isles when it was published some 15 years ago.[5] In it, he unmasked many British nobles, police, judges, and politicians who were Masons. Among them: Winston Churchill, who, Knight documented, was initiated in 1903 at Lodge No. 3000 of the United Lodge of Great Britain.

However, even fewer people are aware that Churchill was not only a Mason but a witch druid! Dr. Stanley Monteith, occult and secret society researcher and host of *Radio Liberty* out of California, states: "Churchill was an adept of the occult, having been inducted into the Druids in 1908, and having pledged the occult oaths required of those who have entered into the world of Freemasonry."[6]

Monteith's sobering statements are backed up by Miranda J. Green's *The World of the Druids* and by John Daniel's *Scarlet and the Beast*, two excellent resource books.[7]

Rites of the Druid Witchcraft Sect

The rites and ceremonies of the Druid witchcraft sect—which has chapters both in Great Britain and in the United States—are remarkably similar to those of Freemasonry. They hearken back to the Ancient Mystery Religions.

The Burning Man in the Wicker Cage

Some scholars are convinced that human sacrifice was practiced by the Druids. Julius Caesar, Roman General who conquered Britain for Imperial Rome, wrote of how brutal and furiously savage were the people under the influence of the Druid priesthood. He also described the horror of the rite in which the Druid priests and people would periodically choose a victim to be confined inside a huge wicker effigy. The wicker was set ablaze and the human victim consumed by the flames as the people celebrated and paraded in a circle carrying candles.

Even today, at the ruins of Stonehenge in England, modern-day Druids meet on festival occasions, wearing the appropriate white garb and carrying out rites and worship of the ancient gods.

Meanwhile, in Nevada each year, hundreds of thousands attend the incredible *"Burning Man"* festival at which the sacrificial ritual of the burning wicker man is recreated.[8]

Archbishop of England Also A Druid

Amazingly, the British press recently carried news reports, including pictures, of the Druid initiation of a man, Rowan Williams, who just happens to be Archbishop of Canterbury, head of the Church of England. Williams told reporters that he saw no incompatibility in his duties as a pagan Druid priest and those he has assumed as Archbishop of the—presumably Christian—Anglican Church of England.

This is yet more evidence of how apostate and corrupt the global "Christian" establishment is today. While it is true that the true Christian Church, though tiny in numbers, lives on and is undefeated, the majority of modern-day pastors, ministers, and churchmen have departed from the Faith and have no concept at all of genuine Christian doctrine. The spectacle of the top, so-called "Christian" clergyman of the entire British Commonwealth, Archbishop Williams, being initiated as a wizard in the Druid witchcraft sect and publicly boasting of it is proof positive that the Devil and his Illuminati have become the unacknowledged "Masters" who run the Christian establishment behind-the-scenes. The big name clergy and evangelists today merely follow the script laid down for them by their elite controllers.

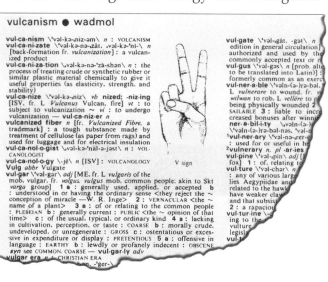

Page from *Webster's* dictionary where V sign is pictured but never defined or explained! Such words as "vulcanism," "vulcanize," and "vulgar" are defined, however, in close proximity. Vulcan is the ancient god of fire and destruction.

Sir Winston Churchill, a crypto Jew, a Mason, a Druid witch, and war-time Prime Minister of Great Britain, flashes his famous "V" sign. Long used to represent a number of occultic tasks, including Divine Man, sexual license, and fire, Churchill's frequent use spurred the use of the device by an uninformed populace as a sign of victory.

Rarely is the "V" sign discussed in regard to its unholy meaning. But this picture of Sir Winston Churchill juxtaposed next to the Playboy model on a copy of *Playboy* magazine was published by one alert Christian in his newsletter.

The Hebrew language has no actual numbers. Numbers are represented by letters. The Hebrew "V" or "VAU" represents the number 6. The number 6 represents unrest or evil. Multiplied as in 666 symbolises multiplied evil. Winston Churchill, devoted to the Cabbalists (Jewish occult teaching) introduced the Cabbalist 6 to the Goyim world as the "V" for "Victory" sign. The naïve Goyim, have taken over this evil symbol, not realising that by showing it, they are promoting the Cabbalistic aim to subjugate the world. Churchill's sign meant, not only that he was under secret Jewish occult control, but that he was furthering their goal to take over the world.

Young Winston Churchill arrives for his Druid initiation ceremony. Was Churchill taught the true, occult meaning of the fiery and destructive "V" hand sign that he later made so famous it became used around the world? (Photo: from the book, *The Druids,* by Peter Berresford Ellis)

The present Archbishop of Canterbury, formal head of the Church of England (Anglican) is also a senior druid priest. Dr. Rowan Williams received the dubious honor in west Wales, at an open air celebration. According to news reports, Williams bowed down before the Arch Druid, his pagan superior, amidst mistletoe and oak leave branches. Williams wore a white headdress for the occasion and joined his hands in the druid style. During the ritual, attendants sheathed and unsheathed a splendid silver sword, exactly 6 feet, 6 inches in length, and six inches across the metal that fits snug onto the scabbard, thus 666.

Dr. Rowan Williams, Archbishop of Canterbury, head of the Church of England, and Senior Druid Priest share a secret handshake at a church ceremony.

In this ancient engraving, Dionysius the Areopagite, an Athenian "convert" to Christianity, gives the double "V" sign—"as above, so below" with left hand toward hell. Dionysius was a mystical Christian, a gnostic heretic who is thought to have been the author of an occultic treatise entitled *The Mystical Divinity*. (From the book, *Mystics and Mysteries of Alexandria*, by Manly P. Hall, 33°)

S. DIONYSIVS AREOPAGITA.

The Green Man, sign of the druids, is found carved on wood and in concrete in the architectural details of buildings, altars, and structures throughout the British isles. An insightful movie, *The Green Man*, starring Peter Finch, touched on the connection of the Green Man, sexual perversity, and the Devil's demon powers.

This brass plate is decorated with a circle and, inside, the universal sign of the Masonic Lodge, which is the square and compass. Within the combined symbol of square and compass is the "G," representing "God," which is, in masonry, also the generative process (sexual). In this, advanced Masonic view, we have a man on top of a woman in the act of coitus, or sexual relations. Both the compass and the square are "V" in configuration, and when this brass plate is turned upside down, we find the same, that one symbol, V-shaped, still surmounts the other "V" symbol.

This ancient black and white drawing depicts an initiate undergoing trials in order to advance in the Order. Pointing to his head, on the floor, is the *square*, shaped as a 90 degree "V."

When General George Washington visited Boston in 1789, this banner was carried by a group during a procession in honor of his visit. The "V" is the focal point of the emblem, but the three goat heads contained within the egg-shaped device and the bearded goat head atop it are also significant in occult teaching.

SS Gestapo Chief Heinrich Himmler with the Fuhrer, Hitler. On the arm of Himmler's jacket is the V.

Two Nazi guards in the Congress Hall at Nuremberg. On their helmets and collar we find the SS runes while on the coat sleeves is the V. (Photo: from *New Zealand Herald*, June 5, 2002).

Detail of an anonymous oil painting depicting the famous Viennese composer, Wolfgang Amadeus Mozart at a meeting of his Vienna Masonic lodge. Mozart is at right. Notice the "V" device worn around the men's necks, symbolic of the square of the Masonic Order.

Albert Pike, the much honored homosexual Lucifer-worshipper who served after the Civil War as Sovereign Grand Commander of Scottish Rite Masonry, rewrote and introduced a new version of the Order's 33 rituals. Here, Pike wears the V-shaped sash of the Sovereign Grand Commander. Hanging around his neck is a jewel of the double-headed eagle.

The occultist who drew the design at right well understood the esoteric meaning behind the symbols. First, we see the *"V"* sign which, in shadow, becomes the gnarled and ugly, dark image of Satan. What appears at first to be good (*Benediction*), when seen from the hidden perspective of the unseen becomes *Malediction*. The diamond and circle at top indicate the same principle, that black equals, or shadows, white, and white mirrors black. This is the Hegelian principle of the synthesis of opposites (Pictured in the book, *Pictorial History of Magic and the Supernatural*, by Maurice Besey)

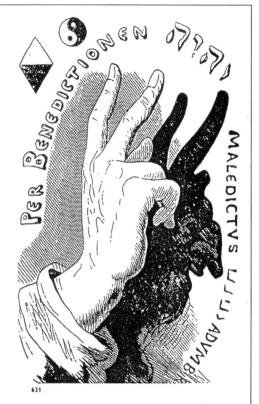

631. The gesture of benediction is changed into malediction when one looks at the 'double' or shadow. This is the opposition of black and white which is here demonstrated. The artist responsible for this drawing also reveals the esoteric connection of the so-called V, or "victory" sign, with the yin/yang.

Michael Jackson, black entertainer accused of child molestation, presents the *"V"* to the crowd as he leaves the courtroom. (*USA Today*, April 30, 2005, p. 3A)

This mural on a wall in Havana reads, "For Life with Fidel." (Photo: *The Catholic World Report*, January 1997, p. 24)

Children dressed as peasant revolutionaries greet Mexico's President Vicente Fox in celebration of the Mexican Revolution (Photo: Associated Press, *Austin American-Statesman*, November 21, 2004)

Official stamps from around the Arab world supported Palestine's Intifada uprising in the late 1980s. In many, the guerilla fighters are pictured giving the "V" sign. (Photo: *News From Israel*, October 1993, p. 11)

Yasser Arafat, leader of the Palestinian Liberation Organization, popularized the ancient "V" sign among Arab demonstrators and guerrilla fighters. At right is the symbol worn on arm bands of some Palestinian fighters.

Stewart Meacham, head of a pro-Communist group called the New Mobilization Committee, is pictured in the Communist *Guardian* newspaper with this "V" sign on a poster behind him.

New Age guru Ira Einhorn, a weird nut barely literate, became a pop hero in the '70s among the New Age spiritual elite. Einhorn's activism was funded by some of the nation's largest corporations being directed to aid the *"Age of Aquarius"* transformation of America. In this photo we find Ira Einhorn in his glory in 1970, rendering the V sign as master of ceremonies at the first, huge Earth Day. At right is the headline in the *Philadelphia Daily News* of Einhorn's arrest. He was tried and convicted of murdering his live-in lover, strangling and stabbing her and stashing her lifeless body in a trunk. Fleeing justice, Einhorn hid out in Europe for years, thanks to covert help from a Rothschild family member. He's now in prison serving a life sentence. (Photos: from book, *The Unicorn's Secret*, by Steven Levy, Prentice Hall Press, 1988)

Former President George Herbert Walker Bush lets insiders know of the goal and eventual total victory of the Zionist Illuminati by blatantly displaying the cabalistic V sign. The position of Bush's left arm is further indication of the cabalistic nature of the sign. Inside the pages of the magazine there was not one shred of explanation as to why the Senior Bush was pictured on the cover giving this sign, nor was it an election year. Moreover, the former President was in retirement, proving the elite adage, "once a servant of the Illuminati, always a servant." (Until death, that is.)

President Franklin D. Roosevelt was both a 32nd degree Mason and a cabalist, crypto-Jew. As his family tree clearly demonstrates, Roosevelt's ancestors came from the Netherlands and were of Jewish blood lineage. Here, fishing in the Gulf of Mexico off the Texas coast in 1937, FDR signals the V of cabalistic occultism, using, however, his thumb.

Ralph Reed, the young man who came from nowhere to head the Masonic Knights of Malta/Illuminati project called the *"Christian Coalition."* Today, no longer with the Christian Coalition, Reed is a high-paid Republican lobbyist in Washington, D.C., and a member of the exclusive Bilderberger Group.

Broadway found a bit of success with its vulgar *The Vagina Monologues* production. Soon, the raunchy and stupid feminist series was on HBO-TV. Its simple plot: women ranting on and on about their private parts, constantly using what the show's producers called the *"V word."* In this group picture, we see a number of the actresses who participated in various episodes of *The Vagina Monologues*. Look close at the two at top left, flashing the "V" sign. One of the two starred in the slutty HBO series, *Sex and the City*. Incidentally, New York Mayor Rudy Giuliani's wife was a participant in *The Vagina Monologues*.

Actress Jane Fonda, an Indian actress, and Eve Ensler, producer of *The Vagina Monologues*.

Neo-Nazi protester in Germany, January 1993. Most of the people who participate in such demonstrations are trained and paid by Illuminati organizations and government intelligence agencies to inspire the public to react. This, in turn, enables the government to curtail citizen liberties and freedoms under the guise of providing "public safety and security."

The group calling itself "GIs and Vets For Peace" adopted this logo, which utilizes the "V" sign in its opposites mirrored theme of the occult. (Pictured in the Communist newspaper, *The Daily World*, October 18, 1969).

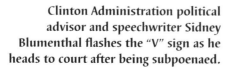

Clinton Administration political advisor and speechwriter Sidney Blumenthal flashes the "V" sign as he heads to court after being subpoenaed.

Presidential candidate
Richard Nixon jubilantly
demonstrates the
double "V."

An activist protesting
at an economic Group
of Eight summit in
Genoa, Italy in 2001
casts an interesting
shadow in this photo
published in the *The
Austin American-
Statesman*. (July 22,
2001, p. A14)

cover story

Joey Fatone of the popular music group, *NSYNC*, displays the "V" sign.

President Bill Clinton flashes a mysterious hand sign to former California Governor Jerry Brown. Both Clinton and Brown were trained by the Jesuits.

The witchcraft goddess wears horns on her head, a five-pointed star on her breast, and is giving the witchcraft "V" downward sigil in her right hand, clutching the crescent moon, sign of Diana, witchcraft goddess.

Astrological symbol of the Sun Goddess, from *The Woman's Encyclopedia of Myths and Secrets*, edited by Barbara G. Walker (Harper & Row Publishers, San Francisco, 1983). Observe the V on top of the solar circle with a point inside. Thus, goddess and god intertwine and become One, in unity, yin/yang. The Sun Goddess was worshipped universally in ancient cultures. The Hindu Great Mother was Aditi. Tantric Buddhism honored Mari, and the Japanese revere the goddess Amaterasu to this day.

"Let us get into your head," says this ad for an ABC-TV series called *Wonderland.* Interestingly, the show's producers chose the V sign to make their point. In this instance, the man is giving the Due-guard sign relating to the penalties of divulging the secrets of the Mark Master degree of Freemasonry.

TWENTY-SIX

"Every Man and Woman is a Star"

But ye have borne the tabernacle of your Moloch and Chiun your images, the star of your god, which ye made to yourselves.

—Amos 5:26

Every man and woman is a star.

—Aleister Crowley
The Book of the Law

Few who are knowledgeable dispute the fact that for satanists, occultists and other Illuminists, the symbol of the *star* has vast significance. Whether five-pointed in shape, six-pointed, or in some other configuration, the star is a premier symbol of the Devil.

Illuminists and witches claim that the pentagram, a five-pointed star with one point upward (ascendant) is useful for "White Magic" rituals and spells. The *inverted pentagram* (five-pointed star) is widely used by hard-core Satan worshippers. When the two points are aimed upward (ascendant), it is said to indicate "Black Magic" and to be the two horns of Satan. No wonder that Aleister Crowley, the infamous, self-proclaimed "Beast 666" from Great Britain, once stated, "Every man and woman is a star," which, loosely interpreted, meant, "Every man and woman is a god."[1]

The Star of Initiation

In the Hindu religion, the pentagram is the "Star of Initiation." It is the caste-mark of

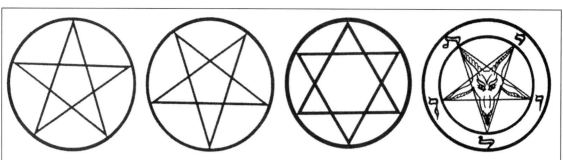

From left to right: Pentagram, Inverted Pentagram, Hexagram (Star of David) and Star of Baphomet (Goat of Sabbath)

the Priests of Siva, who dedicate it to the sun god by marking a black round dot inside the symbol of the star.[2]

The Blazing Star

Freemasons, because they venerate the sun and its rays, know the star emblem as the "Blazing Star." Steve Worrall-Clare, a former Mason, in *Freemasonry — The Secret Language*, writes that in the Lodge:

> The blazing star points out the glory of the sun. It is central to all Masonic undertaking, for it enlightens the earth, and by its benign influence dispenses its blessings to mankind…It is found in the 28th degree and is the symbol of truth. It is found in the 4th degree as a symbol of light and in the 9th degree it is a symbol of divine providence. It is sometimes symbolically installed as the letter "G"…It is a door, an entrance to knowledge…[3]

Satan, The Goat of the Sabbath

High-sounding words, but deceptive. To gain a more direct perspective, we turn to Frenchman Eliphas Levi, a nineteenth-century satanist whose works inspired the writings of Albert Pike, the Sovereign Grand Commander of international Freemasonry. Levi enthusiastically reports:

> The pentagram with two horns in the ascendant represents Satan, or the goat of the Sabbath. (The horn) downward naturally represents the demon, that is, intellectual subversion, disorder and folly. [4]

In *Hidden Secrets of the Eastern Star*, one of the best guides ever published on the subject of the satanic star and other symbols of Masonry, Dr. Cathy Burns explains that the Blazing Star, or pentagram, has many meanings germane to the doctrines of Illuminism and the occult.[5]

Esoterically, the star symbolizes man as deity, as the universe embodied. It also stands for Sirius, the *"Dog Star"* or planet where Satan dwells. It stands for "Thor," the ancient Nordic god, and it stands for Baal, or Bel, the demonic god so often mentioned in derisive terms in the Old Testament.

This same star god was worshipped in Egypt, and the children of Israel, while wandering in the desert, fell under his hypnotic powers. They called him Moloch, Chiun, and Remphan. The prophet Amos castigated the Jewish idolaters for this unholy sacrilege:

But ye have borne the tabernacle of your Moloch and Chiun your images, the star of your god, which ye made to yourselves. (Amos 5:20)

A Magical Charm and Talisman

To Illuminists everywhere, the pantacle star, or pentagram, is considered a powerful charm, a talisman, and an emblem of favor with the Deity of the Underworld. Oh, how the Communists, founded by Karl Marx, a high priest of Satan, cherished their red stars!

In degree rituals of Freemasonry, an appropriate "Jewel" is awarded the rising initiate. It is believed that this Jewel holds magical powers. It can be used to invoke, or invite, spirits and to work spells. Albert Pike thus advised:

Another Jewel is necessary for you, and in certain undertakings cannot be dispensed with. It is what is termed the Kabalistic pantacle (pentagram)...This carries with it the power of commanding the spirits of the elements. It is necessary for you to know how to use it. [6]

In other words, Pike is recommending the star be the vehicle to invoke demon powers and cause them to do magical work.

Now, before you dismiss Pike's suggestion and imagine he was just some silly, insane occult nut, let me remind you that so respected is this man by the Illuminati of today, that a statue of Albert Pike stands in front of the Department of Justice building, the offices of the U.S. Attorney-General, in Washington, D.C. Displayed on public land, that statue is carefully tended to by the National Park Service. Moreover, the body of the much-revered former Sovereign Grand Commander Albert Pike, who died in 1891, is entombed in the Scottish Rite's House of the Temple, exactly 13 blocks from the White House.

Technically, there are several different types of occultic stars, each having its own set of doctrinal characteristics. The enneagram, for example, a nine-pointed star, is popular as a spiritual talisman in the Bahai faith and Theosophy and in other New Age occult sects.

The *pentagram*, from the Greek "*pente*," meaning five, and "*gramma*," a letter (thus the "letter five") is a five-pointed star. A *pentalpha* is more blatantly satanic. It is the form of a triple triangle. The pentagram star can also be called the pentacle, pentalpha, the Star of Isis, the Star of Venus and by other names. Its usage can be traced back to Babylon and it has often been employed in magical rites and activities.

It is sometimes said that the inverted pentagram, when it has two points ascendant, connotes evil and two points descendant, or down, indicates good, but this is not so. Either direction can be evil.

Israel's Six-Pointed Star

The six-pointed star, known as the Seal of Solomon, as the *Magen David* of the Jews, or as the hexagram, is considered by witches and occultists of all stripes as a powerful tool of witchcraft and magic. With this image, one can cast spells, curse victims, and otherwise wreak havoc. Or so it is said.

The six-pointed star was especially beloved by the cabalistic rabbis of the medieval era. The Rothschild Dynasty later adopted this star as a magical device and was instrumental in persuading (money talks!) the fledgling Zionist entity, Israel, to adopt the six-pointed star as the national emblem. It is the symbol of the Israel national flag, even though a more appropriate device undoubtedly would be the Torah, the Menorah, or some other historic or religious symbol.[7]

Geometrically and numerically (points, lines, triangles) the six-pointed star translates into the number 666. Thus, it is very possible that the six-pointed star could become the Mark of the Beast, the Antichrist, as prophesied in *Revelation 13*.

The Illuminists, cabalists, and Masons cunningly have also chosen the six-pointed star as symbol because of its hidden sexual meanings. It is made up of two triangles, integrated together, one superimposed on the other. The triangle pointing downward *(Delta)* represents the female vagina; the triangle pointed upward the male phallus. Joined, or yoked, the two triangles represent the generative sex act.[8]

Illuminati Stars Around the World

The Illuminati have cleverly designed architecture and art over the face of the whole earth to integrate their star talismans into global culture. For example, Texas is called the "Lone Star State," a choice of the Masons—Sam Houston, James Bowie, David Crockett, Stephen F. Austin, and others—who wrested political control of the state in an internecine struggle with Mexican Masonry (Mexican President, General Santa Anna, was also a Mason). Today, the five-pointed Texas star, actually an Illuminati icon, is displayed across the state.

The stars on the U.S. flag are of Masonic origination. The music later used for our national anthem, the Star-Spangled Banner, was composed by a Mason, John Stafford Smith, a member of Royal Somerset House and Inverness Lodge No. 4, London. Another Mason, Francis Scott Key, set the words to the music, and it became recognized as America's national anthem.[9]

Stars have, since World War II, been prominently painted on U.S.A. military equipment—on tanks, jeeps, aircraft—and as badges and emblems on the uniforms of American servicemen.

The Communists in Russia, China, and elsewhere—Illuminists all—adopted the Red Star as a dominant icon of totalitarian dictatorship and emblazoned it on everything, from their flags and monuments to works of art and items of clothing.

None of this is by accident. Always remember, the whole planet is a ritual stage for these mad-men. They have planted evil seeds everywhere one turns. In the scriptures, Paul and John warn that until Jesus our Lord finally puts a stop to this insanity, Satan is god of this world *(2 Corinthians 4:4)*. But Christians are not subject to the demonic powers of this world. Christians are unaffected by spells, rituals and magic cast by the servants of Satan. Only Christians—true, Bible-believing, blood-bought Christians—are immune from Satan's wiles and schemes. The star is one of those wiles. Its prevalence reminds us of how interlaced and permeated this world is with satanic artifices.

For whatsoever is born of God overcometh the world: and this is the victory that overcometh the world, even our faith. Who is he that overcometh the world, but he that believeth that Jesus is the Son of God?

I John 5:4, 5

The Egyptian supreme goddess wears on her head the diabolical, inverted pentagram star. Notice that rays of light emanate from the two "horn" points, creating a "V" effect. See Chapter 25 of *Codex Magica* for discussion of the satanic "V." (Illustration "Isis Recording Her Mysteries." From *Histoire de la Magie*, by Paul Christian, Paris, France.)

The *pentagram* is an ancient and modern magical, occult symbol of prime importance to Illuminists, satanists, and members of secret societies. In its upright form (left), the five-pointed star is said to be an indicator of *white magic*. In its inverted form (center) the same star becomes the sign of consummate evil and hellish intentions. In other words, *black magic*. Above, the pentagram at far right is simply the same as the star at center turned upside down. In each star, evil is found in the form of the goat-headed god of darkness, Baphomet. However, in the star in the center, the Baphomet goat has what appears to be his beard pointed downward, and in the star at right (reversed image), the supposed beard becomes the torch of fire emanating from the top of the beast's head.

Dr. (Colonel) Michael Aquino, Ipsissimus and founder of the Temple of Set, with his wife and High Priestess, Lilith Sinclair. The occultic star is dominant in this scene of Aquino with all his regalia.

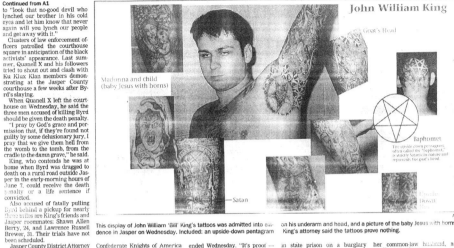

A12 Thursday, February 18, 1999   **FROM PAGE ONE**   Austin American-Statesman

Jasper proceedings focus on suspect's tattoos, activities

Continued from A1

to "look that no-good devil who lynched our brother in his cold eyes and let him know that never again will you lynch our people and get away with it."

Clusters of law enforcement officers patrolled the courthouse square in anticipation of the black activists' appearance. Last summer, Quanell X and his followers tried to shout out and clash with Ku Klux Klan members demonstrating at the Jasper County courthouse a few weeks after Byrd's slaying.

When Quanell X left the courthouse on Wednesday, he said the three men accused of killing Byrd should be given the death penalty.

"I pray by God's grace and permission that, if they're found not guilty by some delusionary jury, I pray that we give them hell from the womb to the tomb, from the cradle to the damn grave," he said.

King, who contends he was at home when Byrd was dragged to death on a rural road outside Jasper in the early-morning hours of June 7, could receive the death penalty or a life sentence if convicted.

Also accused of fatally pulling Byrd behind a pickup for nearly three miles are King's friends and Jasper roommates: Shawn Allen Berry, 24, and Lawrence Russell Brewer, 31. Their trials have not been scheduled.

Jasper County District Attorney Guy James Gray on Wednesday also showed the jury photos of the tattoos on Berry and Brewer.

Berry, who owned the pickup that allegedly dragged Byrd, has a tattoo of a skull with devil horns and the word "Brotherly" in ... d above it ...

Confederate Knights of America logo.

Gray argues that King was a racist who orchestrated Byrd's murder to gain recognition for a new hate group he was forming in Jasper. King's tattoos are proof of his hatred towar... cks, Gray

John William King

Madonna and child (baby Jesus with horns)

Goat's Head

Baphomet
The upside-down pentagram, often called the "Baphomet," is strictly Satanic in nature and represents the goat's head.

Satan

Upside Down

This display of John William 'Bill' King's tattoos was admitted into evidence in Jasper on Wednesday. Included: an upside-down pentagram on his underarm and head, and a picture of the baby Jesus with horns. King's attorney said the tattoos prove nothing.

ended Wednesday. "It's proof — state of mind, hate, anger — the kind of thing in somebody's mind it takes to commit this kind of act."

King's attorneys say the young man's tattoos prove nothing. "I don't think just the tattoos themselves make him ... ist," said court-appoi...

in state prison on a burglary charge.

Testimony early in the day linked all three men to the pickup on the night of Byrd's death and revealed that King may have occupied himself that evening with romance and betrayal. He twice ...ised his pregnant girlfriend to a ...

her common-law hu.band, according to testimony.

The former lover, Keisha Adkins, told a jury she spent about three hours with King in his apartment while Brewer turned away King's girlfriend, who had come to the apartment twice to look for hi...
Adki...

on June 7, she saw King, Brewe and Berry drive away in Berry' pickup.

Adkins, her voice often waver ing, also said she saw King's cig: rette lighter at his apartment th night of the dragging death. Th lighter is inscribed with his nick name, "Possum."

Law officers told the jury lighter with the word "Possum" o it was found at the remote locatio where Byrd was allegedly beate before being chained to a picku and dragged until he wa beheaded.

Offering a hint of their strategy King's defense lawyers challenge the manner in which detective gathered evidence from th dragging-death site and King apartment. Under questionin, detectives acknowledge they di not change gloves each time the collected a new piece of evidence

Prosecutors say they have co lected cigarette butts, beer bottle watches, the "Possum" lighte shoes and other items belonging t the three white men that link the to the bloody r ad where Byrd w: dragged.

Gray, the prosecutor, said t defense was tr ing to raise "an O theory" that evidence had be: contaminated, a reference to t defense strategy in O.J. Simpson murder trial.

"I'm satisfied there has not be any contamination," Gray said.

Missing from court on Wedn: day was King's father, who cou be heard moaning during some the testimony on Tuesday. B more than a dozen members Byrd's family again occu... front t...

The media gleefully devoted maximum attention to the killing of a black man in Jasper, Texas by three white men. The three chained the mutilated victim to the bumper of their pickup truck and drug him behind until he was dead. The media reported the grotesque murder as a racial crime, a horrible incident of racial prejudice and hate. In fact, the motive for the murder was satanic, not racial. John William King, one of the accused white men, had tattoos of a baby Jesus with horns, of the satanic pentagram, the goat's head, and more. Even King's hair was cut into symbols of evil. (*Austin American-Statesman*, February 18, 1999, p. A12)

This 5-pointed star is the seal, or logo of the Fraternal Order of The Police, an association much like a union of police and law enforcement personnel. The Masonic symbols gives convincing proof of the origins of this group. Many other police organizations have similar logos and, indeed, the "star" itself, in its numerous variations, is in widespread, almost universal use by law enforcement. Is this the elite's way of telling the whole world, *"We are the law!"*?

Parents in Pearland, Texas, objected after a police officer handed out calendars to students that featured this image of a Baphomet goat's head with a star. The calendar also had explicit details on satanic and sexual rituals for every day of the month. The police officer was presenting a talk about teen gang activity. (*Worldnetdaily.com*, December 13, 2004)

Charles Schrader, a practicing Wiccan, tears a Holy Bible in half during the Marion County Commission meeting Tuesday morning. Schrader asked for the removal of the Bible from the shelves of the Marion County Public Library because of its pornographic and crude verses.

DOUG ENGLE /STAR-BANNER

Making a point

Man protests Bible to discourage censorship by county

By CHRISTOPHER LLOYD
STAFF WRITER

OCALA – An outspoken Wiccan and community activist held up a Bible, called it pornographic and torn it in

Bible removed from the Marion County Public Library. His move came in response to a recent effort by commissioners to restrict access to "It's Perfectly Normal," a sex-education book by Robie ... e have dubbed obscene. ... about his

rape, and called it "a regimen of hate disguised as family values."

"If the home-schoolers really got into this book and started reading this and found what was between these holy pages, their m...mmas would do the

A practicing Wiccan (witchcraft advocate) tears a Holy Bible in half at a meeting of county commissioners in Florida. The man was demanding the Bible be removed from the public library. Notice above the star hanging from his neck, a symbol which he said represents sun worship. At left, the same man sits in the audience reportedly performing a pagan prayer while displaying a symbol with both hands. Still, the witch advocate protested he does not practice satanism or black magic.

Maggio undici MCMXCIIX

United Fascist Union

P.O.B. 26020
WILMINGTON, DE 19899-6020
(302) 764-5099

Ms. Wanda Marrs
c/o Living Truth Ministries
1708 Patterson Rd.
Austin, Texas. 78733-6507

Dear Ms. Marrs:

Thank you for your letter of Marzo venticinque MCMXCIIX, I'm sorry for the tardy reply but, I had to do two radio shows between then and now. I also had to get the United Fascist Union listed in two more directories of political associations & send out the usual batch of mailers to various radio & T.V. shows U.F.U. agents have been on in the past. We try as best we can to keep up with mail, it's not always easy but, being that we're trying to revive Pagan Rome we've become quite good at record keeping, so you will always get some sort of a reply even if it's only a standard form letter.

I have no desire to waste your time with idle chit-chat so I'll get straight to the point. We're asking the various talk shows, maga- zines & broadcast companies we sent courtesy copies of our propaganda short "THE DAWN OF THE NEW MILLENNIUM"to, to let us know what they think of the moving picture. Please, tell us what you like or didn't like about the film so we can improve it the next time we make a movie.

I am also enclosing an outline of the book "A New World Order for the New Millennium" that I co-authored with Sally Parker,because I read in one of your newsletters that you publish books for authors at times. I don't think you would agree with the fascist's about reviving Pagan Rome being that your Christians but, I do think you'd atleast agree with part of the United Fascist Union's doctrines concerning the present government. At what points Ms. Parker & I saw fit to quote Rev. Marrs in the text, we quoted him verbatim from the text of "Project L.U.C.I.D." without any embellishment of any sort.

Viva Nova Roma
HOLY IS BABYLON!!!

http://www.geocities.com/area51/chamber/7344
Mr. J. Grimes
Director & C.E.O.
of the UNITED FASCIST UNION

When the wife of the author of *Codex Magica* sent a letter to the United Fascist Union requesting information for our files about the group's purpose and activites, we received this letter in return. Notice that two pentagram symbols are prominently displayed as symbolic artwork on the letterhead of the United Fascist Union, a U.S.A.-based group headquartered in Wilmington, Delaware. Also observable is the fasces (ax and wheat bundled by X insignia). In the signature block of the letter, the "Director and CEO" of the United Fascist Union has typed the phrases *"Viva Nova Roma"* (Long live the New Rome) and *"Holy is Babylon!"*

De
LAPIDE PHILOSO-
PHICO
PERBREVE OPUS.
CULUM,
QUOD AB IGNOTO ALIQUO GER-
manico Philofopho, pene ante ducentos annos,
confcripum & LIBER ALZE nuncupatum fuit,
nunc vero in lucem editum.

FRANCOFVRTI
Apud HERMANNUM a SANDE.

Anno M DC LXXVII.

From *Muſæum Hermeticum Reformatum et Amplificatum.*

THE TITLE PAGE OF THE BOOK OF ALZE.
This title page is a further example of Hermetic and alchemical symbolism. The seven-pointed star of the sacred metals is so arranged that one black point is downward, thus symbolizing Saturn, the Destroyer. Beginning in the space immediately to the left of the black point, a reading clockwise discloses the cryptic word VITRIOL formed by the capital letters of the seven Latin words in the outer circle.

Left: A mysterious example of hermetic and alchemic teachings. This seven-point star is so arranged that one point of the star—painted black—is pointed downward, symbolizing adoration of he who rules Saturn, the sixth planet from the sun (i.e. Lucifer). (From Manly Hall's *Secret Teachings of All Ages*)

Baphomet Goat Head
Wall plaque made of ceramic, painted light steel gray with distressed finish, & attached wall hanger. Baphomet goat head, inverted pentacle & symbols are in 3-D relief. *Approx. 10" diam.*
⁴#SBGO **$34.95**

From a recent catalog offering a multitude of talismans and charms, were these two products offered for sale.

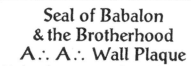

Seal of Babalon & the Brotherhood A∴A∴ Wall Plaque
Made of ceramic with attached wall hanger. Black painted background with characters in slight relief, painted red. *Approx. 10" - 11" diam.*
⁴#SBAB
$25.95

In this ad (left) in *Magical Blend*, a New Age magazine, we see many occultic and pagan symbols, including the 5-pointed star above the goddess' head. The shell represents the love goddess Aphrodite who, mythology says, rose out of the sea (see *Revelation 13:1* for a prophecy about the beast that rises up out of the sea). The goddess figure in this ad sits in the familiar lotus position with the flame in her genital area and her arms and hands arranged symbolically.

IMAGINE
THE BEAUTY.

FEEL
THE POWER.

PURE QUARTZ CRYSTAL BLADE,
NATURAL STAG ANTLER &
BLACK OAK HANDLE,
SOLID SILVER HILT
IN THE SHAPE OF A PENTACLE.
EXQUISITELY BALANCED.

*Individually handcrafted
with love in Vermont.*

$1,400.

Call ▓▓▓▓▓▓▓▓▓ *for credit card purchases
or send a check or money order to*

COMPASS GROVE

Write for a free catalog and discover our other fine offerings.

Size shown is 12"
and will vary due to
use of natural materials.
Please allow 4 to 6 weeks
for handcrafting
and delivery.

© copyright 1991

This ad in *Magical Blend* magazine touts that for just $1,400 you can order this pentacle star-shaped dagger, suitable for ceremonies and rituals. The ad also says that the product is "handcrafted with love in Vermont."

A wax talisman created by occultist Edward Kelley, using directions obtained in the angelic language he called "Enochian" (*Enigma* magazine, Issue 6).

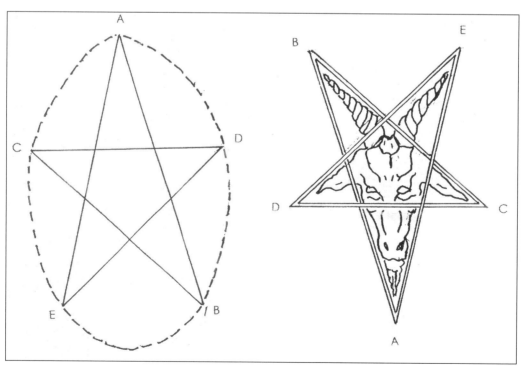

A friend of Texe Marrs' ministry sent this drawing of Baphomet incorporated in an oval shaped, irregular pentagram. He noted that such an arrangement indicates the revolving of Venus (the goddess, or feminine principle) around the sun in an elliptical orbit. The irregular pentagram is a sign of black magic when shown inverted and enclosing the horned head of the goat.

Elephant Feathers
by Ron Barrett III'

While attending the Set X Conclave in New Orleans last summer, an initiate posed a question to me which went something like this: "If we, as Black Magicians, are consciously existing outside of the natural order, and affect magical change soley by the Will within ourselves, why, then, do we go through all the trouble of employing all these rituals and symbols in our magical Work?"

Arrgh.

Just kidding. My answer at the time was that he was correct in theory, but that at the ... of most ... s.

provides a good azimuth into the issue of the role of symbol and ritual in initiation. I will therefore give the elephant a run for his money.

Picture, if you will, the Constellation of the Thigh scintillating brightly on a clear and windy summer night. Somewhere on the side of a mountain, underneath a pile of rocks, is a strange creature wearing a black camel-hair robe, fumbling with a pack of matches. That creature is an initiate who recently joined the Temple of Set and is now attempting to execute a Working with flaw ... His intenti ...

The masthead of the periodic *"Scroll of Set"* newsletter, published by Dr. (Colonel) Michael Aquino, High Priest of the Temple of Set. Aquino claims to be an initiate of the "Left-handed Path," which indicates Lucifer worship.

The empty sanctuary of the Order of the Solar Temple shows signs of satanic worship—candles on the floor arranged in a triangular pattern and a satanic hexagram drawn out on the floor. In October 1994, the 53 adults and children who participated in the unholy rituals of this cult—headquartered in Switzerland but operating in Canada as well—were found dead, victims of mass, joint suicide and murder. The official logo of the "Solar Temple" (not shown) is a triangle with 4-pointed Maltese cross.

AVON BOOKS • 0-380-01539-0 • (CANADA $5.95) • U.S. $4.95

The Satanic Bible
Anton Szandor LaVey

Above: Cover of the bestselling *The Satanic Bible*, by Anton LaVey, High Priest of the Church of Satan. Published by Avon Books, a major publisher, the title has long been a brisk seller in the large bookstore chains. On page 25 of the book, LaVey lists his suggested "Nine Statements," or principles of the Church of Satan (at right). *The Satanic Bible* is upfront with its hideous recommendations to worship Satan as "His infernal Majesty," and LaVey garnered many hundreds, if not thousands, of open followers, including politicians, Hollywood actors, actresses, and producers, singers and entertainers, etc. Among the devotees: black entertainer Sammy Davis, Jr. and blond bombshell actress Jayne Mansfield.

THE NINE SATANIC STATEMENTS

1   Satan represents indulgence, instead of abstinence!

2   Satan represents vital existence, instead of spiritual pipe dreams!

3   Satan represents undefiled wisdom, instead of hypocritical self-deceit!

4   Satan represents kindness to those who deserve it, instead of love wasted on ingrates!

5   Satan represents vengeance, instead of turning the other cheek!

6   Satan represents responsibility to the responsible, instead of concern for psychic vampires!

7   Satan represents man as just another animal, sometimes better, more often worse than those that walk on all-fours, who, because of his "divine spiritual and intellectual development," has become the most vicious animal of all!

8   Satan represents all of the so-called sins, as they all lead to physical, mental, or emotional gratification!

9   Satan has been the best friend the church has ever had, as he has kept it in business all these years!

25

High Priest LaVey and followers at a 1966 ritual. Observe the pentagram on the wall.

In the 1990s, President George Bush's National Endowment for the Arts (NEA) gave photographer Robert Mapplethorpe a $15,000 grant from the tax trough (that's my money and yours!) to produce photographs. Regrettably classified as "art," some of Mapplethorpe's photographs depicted homosexuals "enjoying" violent, degrading sex acts. Mapplethorpe also produced vulgar and unseemly pictures of little boys and girls displaying their sexual genitals.

Extremely satisfied with Robert Mapplethorpe's pornographic art, the NEA's artist community promptly arranged for his lewd photographs to be put on exhibit in some of America's finest art museums. All this, of course, was funded by the taxpayers through that gracious government cultural agency, the NEA.

Well, tragically, Robert Mapplethorpe is no longer with us. He has died of the AIDS virus, a result of his homosexual lifestyle. But he left behind a very revealing photograph that he had taken of himself. The photograph, entitled "Self-Portrait," shows Mapplethorpe in a terrorist/ gangster leather overcoat, machine gun in hands. On the wall behind the posed artist is a satanic pentagram, the five-pointed star so revered by occultists.

Frankly, my heart goes out to the late Robert Mapplethorpe. He was a deceived, sick man. But I have little sympathy for the politicians who year after year fund the wicked tastes of the NEA's art crowd. Neither do I have a soft spot in my heart for the liberal clergy who insanely support and applaud the homosexual lifestyle.

Yes, Robert Mapplethorpe was personally responsible for his actions. He must now answer to an almighty God. But he had many accomplices to his immoral crimes. And the blood of Robert Mapplethorpe and thousands of other desperate and confused young men is on their hands!

Jack Roper, a friend of Texe Marrs who is a law enforcement consultant and an expert on satanic rituals and crimes, sent Texe this photo of a satanic altar and worshipper.

The United Kingdom's Mick Hucknell, lead singer of the soul group *Simply Red.* Fans call him a "stage-strutting sex god" in his red vest wearing a six-pointed silver star as talisman around his neck. The band has sold over 20 million albums. (Photo: *The European Magazine*, December 6, 1995, p. 17)

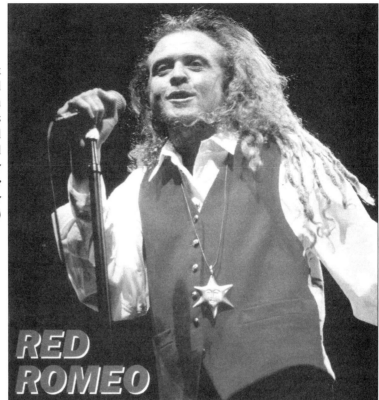

The teachers of "The Craft" claim that a skyclad (nude) witch draws "energy" from forces unleashed by the pentagram star as she lies inside of it while spells are performed (photo from book, *Heartbeat of the Dragon*).

Cover of music album by rock group *Rush* has a naked man compelled by the energy forces of a pentacle star.

Fortean Times (March 2000), a magazine specializing in the bizarre and strange that is real, devoted its cover and feature article to the documented story of Jack Parsons, the American rocket scientist and genius who made space travel possible with his scientific inventions and discoveries. Parsons was a Luciferian priest and an initiate of the Ordo Templi Orientis (O.T.O.), an occultic order made infamous by Englishman Aleister Crowley ("the beast, 666"). Parsons died in a mysterious explosion some 50 years ago, but his name and legend continue to be honored by Illuminists around the world. NASA, America's space agency, even named a crater on Mars after Parsons. Parsons conducted sex rituals designed to invoke the coming of the antichrist. Satanists call these perverted, dark rituals *"Babalon Working."*

BIRTH OF A NEW
CITY STAR

CREATORS: JULIAN LAVERDIERE AND
PAUL MYODA
COMMUNITY: CITIES AFFLICTED BY
LIGHT POLLUTION
PROJECT: SYNTHETIC STAR

The designers of the magnificent Tribute in Light memorial for the World Trade Center turned their attention to urban night blindness: the blankness of the city skies. Urban Lodestar is a light-emitting five-pointed star designed to float serenely above a city center and pulse gently at the same rate as a resting heart to calm the city folk below. Lodestar hovers with the aid of helium-filled polymer balloons; propellant tanks and directional boosters attached to a GPS-equipped positioning system keep it from going AWOL. During the day, photovoltaic film panels harness energy from the Sun and store it in batteries; at night, electroluminescent strips in the shape of a star glow with that stored energy. Graphite composite struts provide stability, and a battery-powered xenon strobe creates the pulsing effect. Intermittent green flashes differentiate the Urban Lodestar from natural celestial bodies.

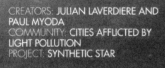

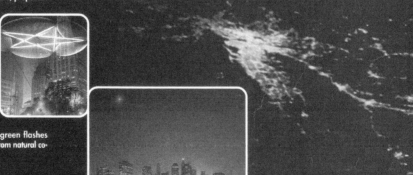

Popular Science magazine (July 2004) published this artist's conception of a proposed Synthetic Star, pentagram star of light to be beamed over the city of New York as a memorial to World Trade Center 9/11 victims. The designers believe the five-pointed star, designed to float serenely above a city center and pulse quietly at the same rate as a beating human heart—will calm the city folk below. Would you like to look up into the sky each evening and see a huge satanic pentagram like this hovering over *your* community?

This incredibly revealing official poster was unveiled and distributed by the Council of Europe, sub-organization of the European Community. It depicts the Tower of Babylon being rebuilt with the announcement, "Europe: Many Tongues, One Voice." Above the Tower is a circular constellation of satanic pentagram stars. The Masons have long given themselves the nickname, "The Builders." In the book of *Genesis* in the Bible, we are told that the original building of the Tower of Babylon came to naught after God confounded the wicked inhabitants by causing them to speak many different languages. As this poster demonstrates, however, it's *déjà vu* all over again.

Communist Chinese dictator Mao Tse Tung often wore a cap with a red star. Mao may have slaughtered as many as 100 million people during his long reign. His barbarism stemmed from his following the insane ideology of Illuminati puppet Karl Marx, a Jewish high priest of Satan worship.

"The Great Experiment" was the title of this mural painted by Russian artist Ilya Glazunov. The mural claims to picture the history of 20th century Russia. The Bolsheviks' satanic star is the overall container and inside it is found the satanic pentacle star along with pictures of Lenin, Trotsky, Gorbachev, and others.

TWENTY-SEVEN

Lightning Fall From Heaven

And he said unto them, I beheld Satan as lightning fall from heaven. Behold, I give unto you power to tread on serpents and scorpions, and over all the power of the enemy: and nothing shall by any means hurt you.

—Jesus *(Luke 10:18-19)*

Lightning has long been a supreme symbol of Lucifer, whom the Illuminati deem to be their "enlightener." In the Bible, Jesus states, "I beheld Satan as lightning fall from heaven" *(Luke 10:18)*. We also discover in the scriptures that Lucifer is called the "Prince of the Power of the Air" *(Ephesians 2:2)*.

The pagan Mystery Religions—from which the modern Illuminati have borrowed—pictured their supreme god as a fiery, flying serpent, bringing lightning and thunder in his wake. The Greeks and the Romans worshipped angry deities, Zeus and Jupiter, sitting on a throne at the hub of the heavens throwing lightning bolts and booming thunder at enemies. The modern revival of the use of the lightning symbol is seen by the Nazis, the symbols of rock music groups, and in the Harry Potter books and movies.

Once again we also see the *phallic symbol* recognized—this time as lightning—in the Illuminist religion. This originated from the tantric tradition, in which it is taught that lightning is a phallic scepter, jewel, lingam, or magical wand of the gods. Lightning especially symbolizes the Hindu fire god, Agni, whose mark is given by his High Priests and Priestess in the Third Eye region of the forehead between the eyes.

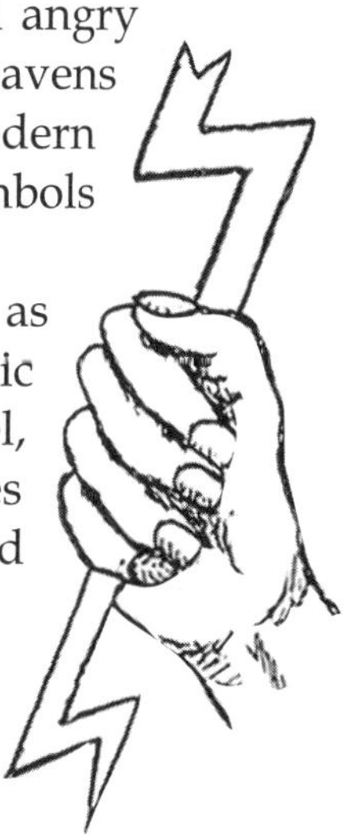

The lightning bolt is the Sign of Zeus, the Father of the mythological deities of Greece. The Nordic peoples worshipped him as Odin.

In this classic oil painting we see mighty Thor, the Nordic god, with his hammer and lightning strikes. At bottom, the black color of the horned goats and the hand's grasping on the rock ledge have much occult significance. In Masonry, the use of a gavel, or hammer, is said to be a sign of authority. The Communists in the U.S.S.R. adopted the hammer and sickle as official state logos.

The bugle corps of the Hitler Youth fly the banner of the lightning bolt, an occultic symbol of the ancient Mystery Religions. The lightning bolt is designed as a rigid "S", meaning the secret adoration of Satan.

A German Nazi concentration camp doctor helps in the processing of new arrivals. He's wearing a white doctor's smock with the runes symbol (two satanic "S" lightning bolts) inside a circle. (From the book, *Kinsey: Crimes & Consequences*, by Dr. Judith Reisman)

Sir Oswald Mosley, founder of Britain's splinter *New Party*, leading a march in London in 1939. The New Party said its lightning flash stood for Action and the circle (wreath) around it for Unity, or Union. Fascists rallied around this banner, and many of the goals of the Party were Socialist.

Over 30,000 people attended this rally in Britain under Mosley's New Party and its banner of the lightning bolt and circle. The British flag also is interesting in its Masonic design of the Osiris X intersecting a horizontally elongated cross.

SEPTEMBER 20, 1999 $3.50   www.time.com

TIME

The MAGIC of
HARRY
POTTER

Hero of three best sellers, he's not just for kids. Here's why the books have captured our imagination

```
#BXBDJLX**********CARR-RT-SORT**R073
#78733MRRPT708W91#3 T3 TX23D**0 FEB00
WANDA MARRS                      0003
                              #01472
1708 PATTERSON RD             P0014B
AUSTIN          ,TX 78733-6507
```

The lightning bolt has long been a satanic symbol. Its use stems from Jesus' statement in the Holy Scriptures: *"I beheld Satan as lightning fall from heaven" (Luke 10:18).* The Harry Potter books were cleverly packaged to introduce tens of millions of kids to satanic symbols, rituals, and concepts. Here we see Harry Potter, on the cover of *Time* (September 20, 1999) with the lightning bolt on his forehead. Inside, in the feature article, is a picture of two tattooed young fans also with thunderbolts on foreheads.

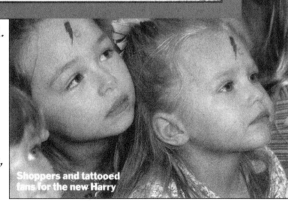

Shoppers and tattooed fans for the new Harry

A Harry Potter bookstore display. Again, note the satanic symbol, or mark, on Harry's forehead.

This full page color ad in *Time* magazine (October 23, 2000) by FTD Florist exemplifies how witchcraft has excited the public imagination. In the upper right corner it is indicated that this ad is based on Disney's Winnie the Pooh, a popular kids creation.

Charles Colson, of Prison Fellowship, received the million dollar, "Progress in Religion" prize at the Parliament of the World's Religions in Chicago. Now he's helping to promote the Harry Potter witchcraft books. Still, official Christendom holds Colson up as the very epitome of Christian example, and his books are sold in almost every Christian bookstore.

Most Christian parents are not hesitating to buy Harry Potter sorcery witchcraft books for their kids. Witchcraft has now virtually conquered the whole of the Christian establishment.

TWENTY-EIGHT

Blood Red—Red Stars, Clenched Fists, Hammers and Sickles, and Other Signs and Symbols of Communist Murderers and Thugs

How is the hammer of the whole earth cut asunder and broken! how is Babylon become a desolation among the nations!…This is the work of the Lord God of hosts…

— *Jeremiah 50:23, 25*

Communism was solely the invention of the Jews.

— Sir Winston Churchill
London Illustrated Herald
(February 8, 1920)

The most brutal, murderous, and monstrous gang of all time was the Communist regime in Soviet Russia, the U.S.S.R. According to noted historian Aleksandr Solzhenitsyn, sixty-six million people perished in the Soviet gulag concentration camps and in the liquidation of the farmers and small businessmen.[1] In contrast, the notorious Adolf Hitler and his Nazis were pikers. The real holocaust happened in the Soviet Union, and many of those deaths and torments occurred before the Nazis had built a single camp. Hitler and Himmler must have been green with envy.

What is most surprising—at least to the uninformed general public—is that few today are even aware of the Soviet Holocaust. Because of the Jewish ownership of the Western media, all the emphasis is put on the crimes of the Nazis. The horrors of the Red Terror are neglected. Maybe more remarkable, in many media and academic circles, the monsters who committed the atrocities in Soviet Russia—led by Lenin, Trotsky, Stalin, Kaganovich, Beria and others—are often adored, being cast in a favorable light. This is especially true of Lenin and, to a lesser extent, the theoretical, so-called "founder" of Communist ideology, the German Karl Marx.

Communist Leaders of Jewish Bloodline

The reason why the Western media, owned and run as it is by Jewish interests, fails to expose the Communist butchery is easy to discern. The instigators and leaders of Communism were virtually all of the Jewish race and bloodline! The Lenin Museum in Russia today admits that Vladimir Lenin was a crypto-Jew (a crypto Jew is a Jew who keeps his race hidden from public knowledge). Trotsky, his deputy in crime and mass murder, was a Jew who had lived in the Bronx, New York under his real name, Lev Bronstein. Stalin, the third leg of the Soviet troika, was half-Jew, and Yiddish was the only language spoken in his boyhood home in Georgia. Stalin's real surname was Dzhugashvilli—Jewish.[2]

Karl Marx was a German Jew whose grandfather was a rabbi, and the entire Communist Bolshevik revolution was financed by the Jewish Rothschilds and Jewish Warburgs in Germany, in partnership with the Jewish Warburgs and Jewish Schiffs in the United States.

Communism was Jewish from the ground up. Marx's view and his classic texts, *The Capitalists* and *The Communist Manifesto*, were ideological expressions of the Jewish Cabala, which is also the basis for Marx's theory of dialectical materialism and economic class evolution, specific throwbacks to Hegelian dialectics and Weishaupt's Illuminism. Albert Pike's writings in *Morals and Dogma* are also right out of the Jewish Cabala aquarium. It seems that the piranhas, the killer "fish" of humanity, all swam in the same polluted pond: Jewish Cabalism and rabbinical magic and despotism.

From Lenin to Putin, we have a straight-line succession of Jewish Cabalism under the guise of Communism and now, "Democratic Capitalism" under Gorbachev, Yeltsin and Putin.[3]

Writing in his provocative, fact-filled exposé, *Bloodlines of the Illuminati*, researcher Fritz Springmeier reveals how incestuously Jewish the rulers of Russia have been, including their spouses. First, he notes that Stalin married the daughter of his number 2 man, the Jew Kaganovich. Also:

> The wife of Boris Yeltsin is the daughter of Joseph Stalin from Stalin's marriage with Rosa Kaganovich. Rosa's father was Illuminati…Boris Yeltsin and Rosa are secretly Jewish.

> Lenin was married to a Jewish wife, Krupsakaya. Molotov married a Jewess, too. And Stalin was married to Jewess Kaganovich. Kaganovich's powerful brother

Lazar is in the Politburo, and Lazar's son, Mikhail Kaganovich, married Stalin's daughter, Svetlana. Boris Yeltsin's original (Jewish name) was Baruch Ellia. He in turn is a good friend of David Rockefeller.[4]

Communism the Invention of Jews

So dominant was the Jewish influence in the Communist regime and its bloody Red Terror that Sir Winston Churchill, in the *London Illustrated Herald* newspaper, stated that, "Communism was solely the invention of the Jews."[5] And, he added, it is not a new thing, for the Jews are historically the people who have fomented bloody revolutions and horrors. Churchill said the Jewish global revolutionary plot can be traced back to the days of Adam Weishaupt and his Bavarian Order of the Illuminati (1776).

Churchill went on to emphasize that this "worldwide conspiracy for the overthrow of civilization, and the reconstruction of society...has been steadily growing." Now, he warns, this band of thugs and murderers "have become the undisputed masters of the enormous Russian empire."[6]

Solzhenitsyn records that over 60 percent of the Commissars who headed Gulag camps in the U.S.S.R. were Jewish. Other historians estimate the number at 80 percent. Every leader of the dreaded Checka, KGB and secret police was Jewish, including the butcher Beria.

May Day—Illuminism and Communism

It is interesting to note that that Adam Weishaupt, infamous founder of the Illuminati, founded his group on May 1. It was exactly that day that the Communists under Lenin celebrated. Annually on May 1, the huge May Day parade is held in Moscow.

Is it a mere accident that the most holy day of paganism and witchcraft, Beltane, is also celebrated on May 1? On that day, in pagan Europe, children and adults celebrated around the phallus symbol known as the May Pole, even as witches howled at the moon.[7]

Of Wolves and Freemasons

In his exposé of Communism, *Under the Sign of the Scorpion*, Swedish writer and researcher Jüri Lina, writes how in his last months, a mad Vladimir Lenin, his body and brain racked with the sexually transmitted disease syphilis, demanded each night to be taken out on his balcony in his wheelchair. There, for hours, the angry Lenin would howl and bay at the moon like a wounded wolf.[8]

Lenin, Stalin, Marx and all the other top Communist leaders were all Freemasons. Gorbachev, too, and Yeltsin were Masons, members of the Grand Orient Lodge of France as well as the Soviet Consistory.

Albert Mackey, 33°, former Sovereign Grand Commander, in his authoritative *Encyclopedia of Freemasonry*, states that Alexander Kerensky (Lenin's immediate predecessor) and the other plotters of the 1917 revolution against the Czar were

Masons: "The first Revolution in March 1917 is said to have been operated from these (Masonic) Lodges and all the members of Kerensky's government belonged to them."[9]

All Masonic organizations throughout the world are secretly run by Jewish masters operating behind-the-scenes.[10]

I also have documentation to prove that Marx, Lenin, and most other Communist leaders were homosexual perverts. Most, like Beria, were pedophiles as well, and they all enjoyed brutalizing and degrading women. The wives of these homosexual deviants led miserable lives. One of Stalin's wives committed suicide.[11]

Signs and Symbols of Communism

Seeing as how the Communist founders and leaders have all been apostate Jews into Cabalism, Freemasonry, and blatant satanism (Marx was an official High Priest in a satanic church), we can be sure the signs and symbols of Communism are also of cabalistic/Masonic/satanic origins, as is the color red so fanatically adored by the Communist wackos. Let us now examine these signs and symbols of the Red Murderers, e.g. the Communists.

The Clenched Fist

In all nations where Communist politicians and insurgents operate, these evil men and women invariably identify themselves by making the sign of the clenched fist. Some biblical authorities say that, "The clenched fist represents the (rebellious) attitude of the people of Babylon toward God."[12]

The closed, or clenched fist is, in the Illuminist Philosophy, the symbol of secrecy, dissimulation, and hermeticism. It veils and conceals secrets from the "profane" and the "vulgar" (the non-Illuminists). Interestingly, the meaning is the same in the canons of Buddhism.[13]

Dr. Peter Ruckman, in his fascinating study of things occulticly black and evil, mockingly titled *Black is Beautiful*, comments about the raised, clenched fist:

> You will find this 'salute' being given by all members of the Communist Party in New York, in the 1920s and by the (Stalinist) Abraham Lincoln Brigade, during the civil war in Spain in the 1930s.
>
> By some quirk of 'fate,' this salute was adopted by the Black Panthers in America during the 1960s...the followers of Martin Luther King called it the 'BLACK POWER' salute.[14]

Liberal Afro-American leaders continue to employ this salute to this day. Jesse Jackson does it almost as an automatic response.

The clenched fist salute, or hand sign, is well-known in Freemasonry. The First Sign, or Due-guard, in the ritual of the Select Master Degree is the holding up, or raising, of both arms in an "L" (square) position with the fists of both hands clenched. The lecture for this degree in *Richardson's Monitor of Freemasonry* states:

The signs of a Select Master are then given as follows: The first is similar to the sign of a Master Mason. The fists are both clenched, in allusion to one of the penalties of the obligation, which is to have both hands chopped off to the stumps.[15]

How interesting. Ironically, according to the Masons, the symbol of the clenched fist relates to having the hand chopped off at the stump. Communists out there: Maybe you should listen to what your cronies in Freemasonry are teaching you.

In the initiation for the Secret Monitor Degree of the Lodge, the sign of the clenched fist is given in remarkably similar fashion to the Communist salute, with one hand and arm.

The First Sign in the Select Master's Degree. (From *Richardson's Monitor of Freemasonry*, p. 84)

This illustration comes from *Richardson's Monitor of Freemasonry* (p. 93) and demonstrates the clenched-fist sign which is learned by the initiate of the Secret Monitor Degree.

Hammer and Sickle

The sickle is a universal symbol of the Grim Reaper; that is, a symbol of death. However, the Communists would maintain that the hammer and sickle represent workers, or laborers, the proletariat, or common people whom the Communist leadership represents.

Perhaps the hammer has other relevant meanings, however, which are concealed by the satanic Illuminists who sponsored—and continue to sponsor Communism. *The Herder Dictionary of Symbols* says the hammer "symbolizes power and strength" and notes, "In some cultures magical protective powers against evil are ascribed to ritually forged hammers."

Every Masonic Lodge has a gavel, or hammer, wielded by the "Worshipful Master" or other potentate in charge. In her celebrated dark work, *The Secret Doctrine*, Theosophy founder Helena Blavatsky reveals that the god of forces (Lucifer) renders the "divine hammer" and it is the "mallet or gavel of the Grand Masters of Masonic Lodges."[16]

Sarah Terry, a member of the Masonic-aligned group, the Eastern Star, traces the gavel, or hammer, back to the hammer of the Nordic sun god, Thor, and says it is an emblem of power.[17]

If we realize that the Illuminati's chief goal is the rebuilding of Babylon in a desperate bid to undo what God did as recorded in the *Book of Genesis*, the significance of this Bible verse relating to the prophesied destruction of Babylon by God's might becomes clear:

A sound of battle is in the land, and of great destruction. How is the hammer of the whole earth cut asunder and broken. How is Babylon become a desolation among the nations…The Lord hath opened his armory, and hath brought forth the weapons of his indignation; for this is the work of the Lord God of Hosts. (Jeremiah 50:22-25)

Red Star

The Red Star is perhaps Communism's best-known symbol. I have examined the occultic meaning of the five-pointed star in previous chapters, so I simply reiterate here that the star is a sign of false gods and specifically of the god of Illuminism,

134   RICHARDSON'S MONITOR OF FREE-MASONRY.

PERFECT MASTER

The Lodge is hung with green tapestry, on eight columns, four on each side, placed at equal distances; illuminated with sixteen lights, placed at the four cardinal points. A table stands before the canopy covered with black. A pyra-

Grand Marshal informs the Tyler, and then reports that the Lodge is duly tyled.

Master raps three, and the Warden and Master of Ceremonies rise.

Master—Brother Stolkyn, are you a Perfect Master?

Warden—I have seen the tomb of our respectable Master, Hiram Abiff, and have in company with my brethren shed tears at the same.

Master—What is the hour?

Warden—It is four.

Master then knocks four, upon which all the brethren rise.

Master—If it is four, it is time to set the workmen to labor. Give notice that I am going to open a Lodge of Perfect Masters by fou...

In the Perfect Master Degree, the Masons assembled in the Lodge all simulate the drama of lamenting the mythical death of their "brother," the false Christ-figure, the Grand Master Hiram Abiff. Observe the red star on the coffin here. (From *Richardson's Monitor of Freemasonry*, p. 134)

Lucifer, the solar deity who comes disguised and is worshipped by the deceived Illuminati as "Angel of Light" and as the "Blazing Star."

Incidentally, so popular is the Red Star in Russia that in late 2000, under pressure from military brass and segments of public opinion, Vladimir Putin, Russia's President, brought back the Soviet red banner as the military's flag and agreed to reinstate the Soviet-era *red star* as the Russian military's official emblem.

"The star is sacred to all servicemen," said Defense Minister Sergei Ivanov, who spoke at a meeting of Putin's top generals attended by Putin.[18]

Oddly enough—or understandably enough for those in the know—the red star is often seen on U.S.A. military vehicles and uniforms. It became a staple during World War II, under the direction of the Pentagon's "red brass" leadership put in place by Zionist fanatic President Franklin D. Roosevelt and his ever watchful guardian, Jewish financier Bernard Baruch. (No wonder General Eisenhower's West Point yearbook called Ike the "Swedish Jew.")

The Color Red

But why the color red? Could it have a relationship with the Bible's identification of the whore of Babylon as the woman in scarlet?

Also in the Bible, we find that Esau was born red (Genesis 25:25), and God says, "I have hated Esau."

The color red has a long and non-illustrious history of whoredom and violence. In pre-Vedic India the people worshipped a primitive form of Shiva as the "red god" and as "the howler." The god and planet Mars was known by the ancients as the red god.

In Scandinavia, the major god, Odin, had clothing, shield symbols and runes of red color. A hero Viking's death became celebrated on the calendar as a "red-letter day," and thus we have this phrase in common use today.

Robin was the god of witches in the forest and when human sacrifices were made, they were dedicated to Robin redbreast, or the slain Cock Robin.

Updated to more recent times, we find that in her occult book, *A Treatise On The Seven Rays*, Lucis Trust director Alice Bailey taught the occult importance of colors. "The three major rays," she said, "are red, blue, and yellow." The color red, Bailey explained, has to do with "Will, or Power."[19]

In *The Symbolism of Color*, Faber Birren points out the primacy of the color red. He notes:[20]

- ❖ In ancient Egyptian religion, the god Shu was red, and red animals symbolized Seth.

- ❖ The red poppy was sacred to Ceres, the goddess of the harvest.

- ❖ The face of the wine-god Dionysus was sometimes painted red.

In my researches of occult traditions, the color red is always the color of fire and blood, of evil and destruction, and of immorality. Even the Devil is sometimes conceived of as a red beast.

And isn't that what Communism has proven to be — A *red beast*? Even a *Red Dragon?*

Earl Browder, head of the United States Communist Party for sixteen years (1931-1946), giving the Communist salute at the 1936 convention. Browder was a friend of Soviet dictator Joseph Stalin and worked behind the scenes to get President Franklin D. Roosevelt re-elected.

Standing before a U.S. flag displayed for propaganda effect, presidential candidate John Kerry gives the classic Communist, clenched fist salute.

Democratic presidential nominee John Kerry at annual meeting of NAACP.

U.S. Senator John Edwards, 2004 vice presidential running-mate to Senator John Kerry, gives Communist salute during political campaign speech.

General Wesley Clark giving the traditional clenched fist salute of Marxists at a political rally in Texas. (Photo: *Austin American-Statesman*, September 30, 2003)

President Bill Clinton giving the Communist fist in 1993.

From boyhood, the elite managed and groomed the young Bill Clinton for stardom. How many young men at age 16 got the opportunity to go to Washington, D.C. and have the photo opportunity of shaking hands with President John F. Kennedy? A few years later, college student Clinton marched in communist protest demonstrations.

Bill Clinton, an Illuminatus, was made the youngest governor in the history of Arkansas. Here he is in 1982 with Hillary after winning the governor's mansion.

The late New York Congresswoman Bella Abzug was a hardened lesbian, a feminist, and a dedicated Communist. Abzug and Hillary Clinton were dear friends.

Mandela was released after serving 27 years for sabotage and treason

South Africa

The incredible background to the betrayal of South Africa (from 1652 to the present) was concisely summarized by Warren L. McFerran in THE NEW AMERICAN for October 22, 1990. During this past year the key step in that ongoing betrayal was Nelson Mandela's release from prison and his subsequent glorification by the major media and political figures of a life sentence (he was convicted of sabotage and treason in 1964), Mandela was released on February 11th. On February 2nd, President F.W. De Klerk had lifted his government's 30-year ban on the communist-dominated African National Congress (ANC), of which Mandela is a top leader, and had also legalized the South African Communist Party (SACP) and Pan-Africanist Congress

the taping of an ABC News "town meeting," moderated by Ted Koppel and broadcast later that evening. At one point he refused to criticize Palestine Liberation Organization chairman Yasir Arafat, Cuban dictator Fidel Castro, or Libyan strongman Muammer Qaddafi, all of whom he said "support our struggle to the hilt." Later in the day, he attended a rally in Manhattan's Harlem section. Among those specially invited were three Puerto Rican nationalists who had shot and wounded five congressmen in 1954. Asked about their presence, Mandela defiantly asserted: "We support the cause of anyone who is fighting for self-determination, and our attitude is the same no matter who it is. I would be honored to sit on the platform with the ... comrades you refer to."

On June 22nd, he addressed the Special Committee Against Apartheid at UN headquarters. He received a number of standing ovations from Secretary General Javier Perez de Cuellar and the others in attendance.

In a speech to black journalists in Washington DC on June 24th, Mandela condemned United States m

South African leader Nelson Mandela, a devoted Communist, with Communist radical wife, Winnie and the head of the Communist Party.

Nelson Mandela and wife, Winnie, give the Marxist salute. Winnie Mandela was known to participate in torture sessions and directed a number of "necklace parties"— events at which a tied-up victim has a tire full of gasoline around his neck which is lit by fire. (Photo: from book, *In The Words of Nelson Mandela*, edited by Jennifer Williams, Carol Publishing Group, 1998, p. 43)

"Black Power" symbol.

POLITICS

ADIOS
Having fallen into disarray, the International Brigades were disbanded in 1938. Here, a farewell ceremony outside Barcelona.

fronted earlier he "might not have needed to demonstrate his worthiness." But now, remembering Dallet, Osheroff says flatly, "There were very few tears lost on him."

For a long time, Osheroff concedes, he avoided the dark side of Spain, the compromises, the deceptions. "If you're driven by the blinding force of passion, you're not going to criticize it," he explains. "It's a religion, a crusade." Shortly after the war, Osheroff read *Homage*

to have been a sham. The republic had shipped gold reserves to Moscow for safekeeping. Stalin simply impounded the treasure, deeming it payment for arms and supplies, for which he charged exorbitant prices. Meanwhile, even as Russian propaganda mills spun out the gossamer of "the Popular Front" and maintained that the first order of business was to defeat Franco, Moscow's people on the ground were burrowing deeper into the government, seizing hold of other power centers (the military,

In other words, had Stalin prevailed, Spain would have become a dictatorship depressingly similar to the one Franco ultimately installed. It is an appalling irony.

But it isn't news to Osheroff. Long years of hard thought have led him to the same conclusion. He recalls a seminar he taught some years back at the University of Washington. The students "asked me a tough question: 'Would it have been better if your side had won?' I had to go home and think about that one. Now I think it

The Communist Party's International Brigades fought a bloody civil war in Spain. Here are some of the merciless Red thugs at a rally in Barcelona in 1938 (Photo: *Vanity Fair*, September 2001, p. 302)

Islamic cleric Ayatollah Khomeni, his hand clenched in the Communist style in this poster, led the nation of Iran until his death.

Performers of the Cirque du Soleil give the clenched fist salute. Cirque du Soleil (Circus of the Sun) is a big hit with their dazzling theatre in shows in Las Vegas. The demonic influence in their performances is thick.

Communist hatred of Jesus and of Christianity is evidenced by this disgusting Soviet depiction of The Last Supper, with Jesus and His disciples having a drunken orgy. The Soviet leadership was made up of Revolutionary Jews.

The resemblance of the monstrous Communist butcher Leon Trotsky (right) to the shadow devil creature created by the hand of British satanic high priest Aleister Crowley (left) is remarkable. The drawing of Trotsky is from a Greek publication while the photo of Crowley is found in an unrelated British-published book. In fact, Trotsky, whose real name was Bronstein (Jewish) was a satanist, which is why he was so thrilled to see countless thousands of Russian and other Christians arrested, tortured, killed, or sent to gulag concentration camps. Trotsky was himself murdered in Mexico City by an assassin wielding an axe.

Star god of Communism? This 1920 propaganda poster by a Communist artist depicts Trotsky as Saint George slaying the dragon of capitalism. In reality, Jewish capitalists, the Warburgs and Rothschilds, were the ones who put Trotsky, Lenin, and Stalin and their Red Terror in power in Moscow in 1917. Trotsky and his cohorts *were* servants of the dragon!

Vanishing Comrades: The Illuminati throughout the centuries have falsified history. Want proof? Check out these two sets of Soviet-era photographs. Compare the first photo in each set with the corresponding second photo. Notice someone missing? The second photo is the touched-up, "remaking of history" photo. Having purged and killed off certain "comrades," the Illuminati-inspired Soviet leaders felt obligated to remove all traces of the disgraced comrades from history. Textbooks, library archives, press accounts all had to be changed, much like Orwell's *1984* black hole procedures. Today, in both the East and the West, the same historical falsification process continues, with the true accounts of cardinal events like Pearl Harbor attack, the JFK assassination and the 9/11 World Trade Center disaster being doctored and retouched by the elite's media puppets. (Note: For the eye-opening account of Soviet Communist falsification of history, see the book, *The Commissar Vanishes*, Metropolitan; Also see *Newsweek*, November 10, 1997, p. 80)

General Vo Nguyen Giap was North Vietnam's legendary guerilla leader whose rag-tag armies successively drove the Japanese, the French and the Americans out of Vietnam. Giap co-founded the Vietnamese Communist Party. (Note: The design of the Vietnam flag is a 5-pointed star against a red background.)

Russian President Boris Yeltsin displays the fist of Soviet Communism while speaking in 1992 to a joint session of the U.S. Congress. The Senators and Representatives responded with prolonged applause. (Photo and story: *The Washington Post*, June 18, 1992, p. 1)

The Communists adopted both the hammer and sickle and the red star for their official logos, or symbols. The ancient god Saturn, depicted here in a 15th century drawing, was said to carry the sickle as the symbol of death. Note also the radiant star in Saturn's genital area, the horns of the goat (Satan) and the water bearer (Satan's astrological Age of Aquarius). Occultists view the planet Saturn as representing Satan, because it is the *sixth* planet from the sun and because of Saturn's role as taught in the mythologies.

The similarity of the USSR emblem and the United Nations emblem is undeniable. A friend tells me a resemblance is also found on products and in commercials for *Cadillac* automobiles, *Lenox* china, *George Dickel* whiskey, *Winston* cigarettes, and on the design of "wheat" pennies.

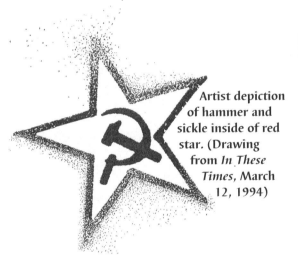

Artist depiction of hammer and sickle inside of red star. (Drawing from *In These Times*, March 12, 1994)

The Shriners, an Islamic-oriented Freemasonry organization whose members take an oath at the altar of Allah, erected and dedicated The Peace Monument in Toronto, Canada in 1930. Observe how the globe, the angel's arms position and the sheathes in the angel's hands are elements found in both the U.S.S.R. and the U.N. emblems. The statue is called "Lady of Peace," just as the U.S.S.R. called itself a peace-loving country and the U.N. proclaims itself to be devoted to world peace. (Photo: from book, *Parade to Glory—The Shriners and Their Caravan to Destiny*, by Fred van Deventor)

In his thoughtful, eye-opening book, *Scarlet and the Beast*, knowledgeable Christian author and conspiracy researcher John Daniel illustrates the communist connection with Freemasonry. The most prominent emblem of universal Freemasonry is the square and compass with the letter "G" inside the internal triangle. Daniel notes that this represents the tools used by the Lodge's Great Architect (false God) to create the heavens and the earth. In reality, the letter "G" represents Gnosticism, the core doctrine of Masonry, and the Generative process (sex act). Masonry is, as Daniel notes, a sex cult.

However, English Freemasonry (the United Lodge of Britain) substitutes a human arm wielding a hammer in place of the "G." This arm and hammer represents the Mason as the Builder, as "man at work" creating the heavens and the earth. Thus, man becomes God. The arm and hammer is of socialist/communist origins. The same symbol is found on a bestselling brand of baking soda. Noted communist financier and oil corporation CEO Armand Hammer was given his name in honor of the communist movement. Note, too, that the arm and hammer symbol inside the square and compass is configured as a "G."

Finally, we come to the modified square and compass of French Freemasonry and its Grand Orient Lodge. This Lodge and its membership are decidedly anti-Christian and are markedly pro-communist. In 1877, the Grand Orient Lodge declared, "There is no god but humanity." Embracing Reason as their God, they replaced the "G" with the now-familiar communist symbol of the hammer and sickle. This represents collective common man, the proletariat. John Daniel points out that the French Lodge's substituted symbol inside the typical square and compass forms the letter "G" backward, "which is symbolic of the negation of God." It was Albert Pike who wrote, in *Morals and Dogma*, that there is no real person or entity named "Satan." Pike claimed that Satan is simply a Force, the negation of God. (Illustrations: *Scarlet and the Beast*, by John Daniel, published 1994, JKI Publishing, P. O. Box 131480, Tyler, TX 75713)

In a vain and failing effort to lionize and deify their bloodthirsty founder, the communist Jew Vladimir Lenin, the U.S.S.R. planned to build this gigantic memorial to the dead Soviet dictator. Josef Stalin, Lenin's successor, in 1931, commissioned architect Boris Iofan to do the design work. It was to be the largest building in the world and was to be called the Palace of the Soviets. The design favors that of Mayan pyramids and the ziggurats of Babylon. The site chosen for the Lenin monument was a piece of land on which a closed-down Christian church building sat, the 19th century Cathedral of Christ the Savior. Stalin ordered the church blown-up and the debris removed, and it was. However, World War II intervened and the gargantuan, monstrous structure was never completed. At the top of the planned monument, a statue of Lenin was to tower above the people and landscape, his right hand and finger vertically pointed upward toward the heavens. Possibly this was a fulfillment of scripture. In Isaiah 14, Lucifer vainly boasts that his kingdom will ascend to the stars and that he will be like the Most High. But Lucifer's true destiny is the pit of hell!

Black magic holds sway over a paranoid Kremlin

A fanatic of the occult is now dictating Russian policy, writes **Miranda Anichkina**

WORLD leaders gathering in Moscow this month will be treated to gala concerts, receptions and dinners in the Kremlin Palace. They will be hosted by a beaming, if stressed, President Boris Yeltsin, eager to boost his electoral chances by putting some grand guests on display. But behind the carefully orchestrated parade of Russian pomp, an almost Stalinesque paranoia and hysteria is gripping the country's top officials.

The president's men are now reduced to communicating via slips of paper which they burn in ashtrays, while the entire staff lives in terror of the man known as the Black Magician – a KGB general who apparently studies the occult in order to determine national policy.

He is General Georgy Georgievich Rogozin, who is said to prepare daily horoscopes for top Kremlin officials, as well as scanning space to determine budget issues, using spinning saucers in his Kremlin office and punctuating his working day with repeated mantras. He also goes to great lengths to create favourable magnetic fields around the president, even to the extent of determining an exact north-south position for Yeltsin's bed. The general is reported to decide appointments to high office by consulting black magic tables.

He is loathed by Kremlin staff and is thoroughly feared. Ludmila Pikhoya, an experienced presidential aide and speech writer who is known for her iron strength of character and calm temperament, turned on Rogozin during a recent stormy Kremlin meeting, dragging him outside a conference room and screaming: "Don't you try to control my subconscious ever again".

The unreal atmosphere is compounded by the widespread belief among staff

AFP

Three wise men (from left, at front): Boris Yeltsin, Defence Minister Pavel Grachev and Alexander Korzhakov

that they are now subject to a level of surveillance undreamt of even during the worst days of the KGB. Well-connected Kremlin correspondents tell of sources pointing to air-conditioning systems and light bulbs, while conducting conversations about the weather.

Meanwhile, they are feverishly scribbling notes on scraps of paper. One top-ranking official stuffed pencils inside the keyholes of his safe while talking to *Sevodnya* newspaper correspondent Sergei Parkhomenko, suspecting video cameras to be installed inside. Others insist on meeting journalists in the same parks that were the scene of many a clandestine Cold War encounter.

Even Yeltsin's own chief of staff Sergei Filatov has publicly admitted that he and his colleagues are afraid to talk freely.

"You can't even breathe without being watched," confirms a member of the president's analytical centre. "The 'neighbours' are always with us," he adds darkly, employing a euphemism that once stood for the intelligence service. "But I'm not talking about the Lubyanka. I mean the Rogozin people."

The mysterious and alarming Rogozin officially heads an analytical team whose intelligence is so jealously guarded that it is delivered by a courier whose arrival is heralded by a coded telephone call. Rogozin reports to General Alexander Korz-

hakov, a shadowy figure in charge of the presidential bodyguard who is widely reported to control the president.

Rogozin is one of only three generals in the presidential team along with Korzhakov and Admiral Zakharov, the man who masterminded the 1993 storming of the White House. Born in 1942 in Vladivostok, the Black Magician joined the KGB at 21 and enjoyed a meteoric rise. From 1989 to 1991 he was the chief scientist in the first division of the institute dealing with security problems.

It was at this point that his obsession with the occult became more than just a hobby. He persuaded his colleagues that they should be looking for a scientific breakthrough in the field of the paranormal. Then the general pursued a programme which included mind-reading from a distance, control of the subconscious by telepathy and information-gathering from the deceased by scanning brain waves from the skull.

A colleague from this period is certain that Rogozin is continuing to

develop his bizarre techniques. "Georgy is a complete fanatic of the occult and I am sure that he has got the necessary equipment for his experiments.

"In any organisation you are bound to get a few people who get paranoid," said Sergei Parkhomenko, the Russian journalist who has put together a dossier of the strange goings-on, "but *everybody* I talk to at the Kremlin confirms the nightmare. Sane people are all drained by the atmosphere of petty and humiliating surveillance and people reporting on each other."

Both Rogozin and his boss Korzhakov are accountable to the secretive GUO, the security service for all state buildings. In one year the number of staff at the GUO has risen to 44,000. Now, some members of the Duma have begun to demand that the GUO should be subjected to the legal constraints of the constitution.

Members of the Russian Parliament question what kind of influence is being wielded by this former KGB officer with his projects and what proportion of state funds are being squandered on black magic.

The mere fact that these rumours are circulating so wildly reveals the paranoid state of mind into which Russia's democratic government has slipped; and it calls into question its ability to responsibly run a nuclear armed, former superpower.

A highly placed officer of the electronic surveillance service FAPSI warned: "It cannot be permitted that parquet [deskbound] generals from the Kremlin guard are allowed to usurp power in this country. If no one stops them, anything could happen."

The occult magic of the Czar is also back! Or did it ever leave? In *The European* (May 5-11, 1995, p. 4) was found this story reporting on "Black Magicians" among the highest ranks of Russian military and political circles. Among the magic techniques common in the Kremlin: Mantras, meditation, astrology and horoscopes, mind powers, telekinesis, spinning saucers, coded messages, remote viewing, tarot cards, and energy fields.

Actress holds up an icon of Vladimir Lenin during Russian occult stage production, *The Fourteen Red Huts.*

The Scarlet Island, another Russian production.

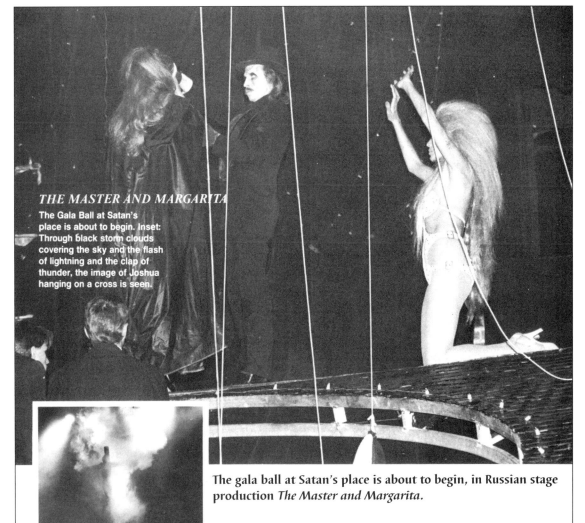

THE MASTER AND MARGARITA
The Gala Ball at Satan's place is about to begin. Inset: Through black storm clouds covering the sky and the flash of lightning and the clap of thunder, the image of Joshua hanging on a cross is seen.

The gala ball at Satan's place is about to begin, in Russian stage production *The Master and Margarita.*

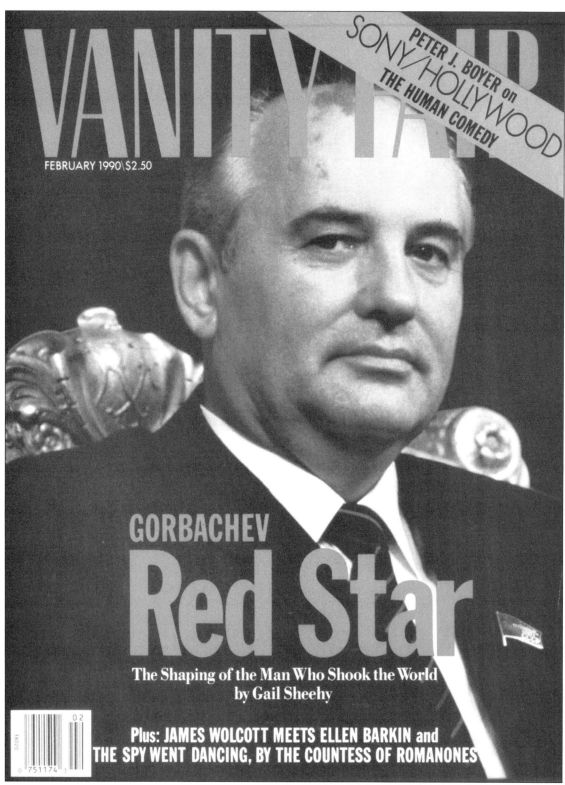

Gorbachev Red Star" trumpeted this cover of *Vanity Fair* magazine (February 1990). Ink type, appropriately, was colored red.

The red star is universally recognized as a sign of hard-core Communism. So, why has Macy's department stores adopted it also as its logo, as shown on these Macy's plastic shopping bags?

In what is clearly a staged photo in *Newsweek* magazine (January 4, 1999), then U.S. Senator and later Attorney-General, John Ashcroft is called "The True Believer." In the photograph, Ashcroft sits in a red chair with golden stars emblazed on the fabric. On the wall behind him are a series of framed United States flags. Each has the same gold star prominent inside the blue field of 50 white stars of the states. The star and the colors red and gold have special significance for Illuminists.

Was Lee Harvey Oswald playing the part of a Communist secret agent when he displayed the clenched fist shortly after his arrest for the alleged assassination of President Kennedy?

Senator John Kerry, failed presidential candidate, giving his favorite hand sign.

Back to Senate

Sen. John Kerry returns to Capitol Hill today, 'changed forever' by his White House run ■ 5A

By Amy Sancetta, AP

When Bush nominee John Ashcroft, a Freemason, was sworn in as Attorney-General of the United States, he did not swear on the Holy Bible. In this revealing photo published in *Criminal Politics* magazine, Lawrence Patterson, foremost authority on the global conspiracy and on secret societies, points out that Ashcroft—whom the White House and the press promoted as an "evangelical Christian"—placed his hands and swore on a mysterious stack of books. Were they law books or books of the Jewish Talmud or...?

FOOTNOTES AND REFERENCES

Introduction: The Occult Script—A Colossal and Monstrous Conspiracy

1. Henry Makow, "Lucifer is the Secret God of Secular Society—Occult Agents Control Humanity," internet, *savethemales.ca*, October 13, 2003.

2. Ibid

3. William L. Cummings, "Rites and Rituals," *Royal Arch Mason*, Winter 1994, p. 107.

4. Ray V. Denslow, quoted in *Ibid*.

Chapter 1:   Caution!—You Are Now Entering the Forbidden Zone

1. Christopher Mark, "Grand Deception: The Theft of America and the World," *South East Christian Witness*, Issue #4, PO Box 8129, South Australia 5291, 2003.

2. *Ibid.*

3. *Ibid.*

4. Thomas Mann, Famous Quotes.

5. Paul Huston, *Mastering Witchcraft* (New York: Wideview/Perigee Books/Putnam & Sons), p. 21.

6. *Ibid.*

7. Manly P. Hall, *Lectures on Ancient Philosophy* (Los Angeles, CA., The Philosophical Research Library, 1984), p. 433.

8. Robert Guffey, in *The Conspiracy Reader* (New York: Citadel Press/Carol Publishing, compiled by Al Hidell and Joan D. Arc, editors, *Paranoia* Magazine).

9. Emile Grillot: DeGivry, Picture Museum of *Sorcery, Magic, and Alchemy* (Hyde Park, NY: University Books, 1963).

10. Marie Roberts and Hugh Ormsby-Lennon, *Secret Texts: The Literature of Secret Societies* (New York: AMS Press, 1995).

11. Thomas Carlyle, *Sartor Resartus*, quoted by Piers Compton, *The Broken Cross: The Hidden Hand in the Vatican* (Australia: Veritas Publishing, 1984), p. 11.

12. Cathy Burns, *Hidden Secrets of the Eastern Star* (Mt. Carmel, PA: Sharing, 1994), p. 292.

13. *Ibid.*, p.291.

14. *Ibid.*

15. Alex Horne, *Sources of Masonic Symbolism* (Missouri Lodge of Research, 1981).

16. Foster Bailey, *The Spirit of Freemasonry* (New York: Lucis Press, 1957).

17. Henry C. Clausen, *Emergence of the Mystical* (Washington, D.C.: The Supreme Mother Council of the World, Ancient and Accepted Scottish Rite of Freemasonry, Southern Jurisdiction, U.S.A., 1981).

18. Albert Mackey, *Encyclopedia of Freemasonry and Kindred Sciences*, Volume Two (Chicago, IL: The Masonic History Company, 1929).

19. Helena Blavatsky, *The Secret Doctrine*, quoted in column of Edith Kermit Roosevelt, IKR Syndicate, Washington, D.C., 1962.

20. Albert Pike, *Morals and Dogma of the Ancient and Accepted Scottish Rite of Freemasonry* (Richmond, VA: L.H. Jenkins, Inc., 1871).

21. George Steinmetz, *Freemasonry: Its Hidden Meaning* (New York: Macoy Publishing and Masonic Supply Co., 1948), pp.43-44.

22. Albert Pike, quoted by J.D. Buck, *The Lost Word Found in the Great Work* (Chicago, IL: Indo-American Book Co., 3d ed., 1913), pp. 14-15; and see Cathy Burns, *Hidden Secrets of the Eastern Star* (Mt. Carmel, PA: Sharing, 1994) pp. 136-137.

23. Lynn F. Perkins, quoted by Cathy Burns, op.cit., p. 17.

24. Martin Short, *Inside the Brotherhood*, (London: Harper Collins Publishers, 1990), p. 22.

25. Jüri Lina, *Architects of Deception* (Stockholm: Referent Publishing, 2004), p. 11.

26. *Ibid.*

27. *Ibid.*

28. Peter Ruckman, Bible Believers Bulletin, Pensacola, Florida, 2005.

29. *Ibid.*

30. *Ibid.*

31. Bob Whitaker, "Situation Terminal…But Not Serious," *The Barnes Review*, September-October, 2002, p. 6.

Chapter 2: The Megalomania of the Psychopaths—Why the Illuminati Do What They Do

1. Essi Viding, quoted by Nic Fleming, "Psychopaths Inherit Anti-social Traits," *The Telegraph*, United Kingdom; May 25, 2005.

2. William Krasner, "Neurotica", quoted by Texe Marrs, *Big Sister is Watching You*, p. 48 (Austin, TX: Living Truth Publishers, 1993).

3. *The New Encyclopedia Brittanica, Volume 7, 15th ed.* (London: 1989), p. 671.

4. Michael A. Hoffman, II, *Secret Societies and Psychological Warfare* (Coeur d'Alene, ID: 2001).

5. George Bernard Shaw, quoted by Dave Hunt, *The Cult Explosion* (Eugene, OR: Harvest House, 1980).

6. F. Aster Barnwell, *The Meaning of Christ For Our Age* (Llewellyn Publications: St. Paul, MN, 1984).

7. Newt Gingrich, quoted in *The Washington Post*, January 3, 1985.

8. Jim Keith, *Mind Control and UFOs: A Casebook on Alternative 3* (Lilburn, GA: Illuminet Press).

9. *Ibid.*

10. Israel Shahak, quoted by Normany F. Dacey, *Democracy in Israel* (Torrance, CA: Institute for Historical Review).

11. Barry McWaters, *Conscious Evolution* (San Francisco: Evolutionary Press, 1983), p. 10.

12. *Ibid*, p. 111.

13. *Ibid.*, p. 57.

14. Albert Pike, quoted by Brian Garlin in *Global Checkmate* (New Zealand, 1983), and see Lady Queensborough, *Occult Theocracy, Volume 1*, 1933.

15. Eliphas Levi, quoted by David Carrico, *Lucifer – Eliphas Levi – Albert Pike and the Masonic Lodge* (Evansville, IN: Followers of Jesus Christ, 1991); and see A. Ralph Epperson, *Masonry: Conspiracy Against Christianity* (Tucson, AZ: Publius Press, 1997).

16. Vera Stanley Alder, *The Initiation of the World* (York Beach, ME: Samuel Weiser, Inc., 1972).

17. Paul Huston, *Mastering Witchcraft* (New York: Wideview/Perigee/Putnam & Sons, 1970), p. 32-33.

18. *Ibid.*

19. C.W. Leadbetter, quoted by Ted Flynn, *Hope of the Wicked: The Master Plan to Rule the World* (Herndon, VA: Maxkol Communications, 2000), p. 48-49.

20. Ibid.

21. Alice Bailey, *The Rays and the Initiations*, Volume V (New York: Lucis Publishing, 1960).

22. C. Fred Kleinknecht, "A Brave New World of Heroes," *The Scottish Rite Journal,* March 2002.

23. Vera Stanley Alder, op. cit., p. 164.

24. Jack Parsons, *The Collected Works of Jack Parsons* (Falcon Press, O.T.O, 1989).

Chapter 3: Concealed Messages—The Importance of Hand Signs to the Illuminati

1. *Coil's Masonic Encyclopedia*, edited by Henry Wilson Coil (Richmond, VA: Macoy Publishing and Masonic Supply House, 1961 & 1996).

2. J.C. Cooper, *An Illustrated Encyclopedia of Traditional Symbols* (London: Thames & Hudson, 1978), p. 78-79.

3. Manfred Adler, *The Freemasons and The Vatican* (Germany), p. 163.

4. *Ibid.*

5. Juan Maler, *The Victory of Reason: The World Model of Freemasonry* (Buenos Aires, Argentina, 1978), p. 77.

6. Johannes Rothkranz, *Did You Already Know?* (Germany), pp.11, 44.

7. *Ibid.*

8. *The Herder Dictionary of Symbols* (Wilmette, IL: Chiron Publications, 1986).

9. *Ibid.*

10. James Curl, *The Art and Architecture of Freemasonry* (Woodstock, NY: Overlook Press, 1993), p. 238.

11. *A Dictionary of Symbols*, edited by Jean Chevalier and Alain Gheerbant (New York: Penguin Books, 1996).

12. *Ibid.*

Chapter 4: Hidden Hand of the Men of Jahbuhlun

1. Malcolm A. Duncan, *Duncan's Masonic Ritual and Monitor, 3d. ed.* (New York: Crown Publishers), p. 226.

2. Ed Decker, *The Dark Side of Freemasonry* (Lafayette, LA: Huntington House Publishers, 1994), p. 18.

3. C.C. Zain, *Ancient Masonry: The Spiritual Significance of Masonic Rituals, Degrees, and Symbols* (Los Angeles: The Church of Light, 1994).

4. W.L. Wilmshurst, *The Meaning of Masonry* (New York: Gramercy Books & Crown Publishers, 1980), p. 143.

5. *Ibid.*

6. Malcolm C. Duncan, op. cit.; also see Decker, op. cit.

7. Christopher Knight and Robert Lomas, *The Hiram Key* (New York: Barnes and Noble, 1996).

8. Malcolm C. Duncan, op. cit. p. 254.

9. C.C. Zain, op. cit

Chapter 5: For He's A Jolly Good Fellow—Sign of the Devil's Claw By the Men of the Craft

1. Henry W. Coil, *Coil's Masonic Encyclopedia* (New York: Macoy Publishing & Masonic Supply Company, Inc., 1961)

2. *Witchcraft, Magic, and The Supernatural* (Hong Kong: Mandarin Publishers/Octopus Books, 1974).

3. Albert Mackey, *Encyclopedia of Freemasonry and Kindred Sciences* (Chicago: The Masonic History Company, 1929).

4. *Ibid.*, p. 352.

5. *Ibid.*

Chapter 6: Baphles Me!—Horned Beasts, Leaping Goats, Satanic Beards, and Other Messages of Evil

1. Israel Regardie, *The Eye in the Triangle: An Interpretation of Aleister Crowley* (Phoenix, AZ: Falcon Press, 1986); also see Aleister Crowley, *Confessions of a Heretic.*

2. Aleister Crowley, *Confessions of A Heretic*, p. 629.

3. Judith Reisman, *Kinsey: Crimes and Consequences* (U.S.A.: The Institute for Media Education, 1998).

4. Aleister Crowley, *Magic in Theory and Practice*, p. 559-561.

5. Anton LaVey, *Satan Speaks* (Los Angeles: Feral House, 1997).

6. *South East Christian Witness* newsletter, Australia, January 1992, p. 5; also see Peter Sawyer, *Inside News*, Australia, November, 1981.

Chapter 8: Secret Handshakes of the Illuminati

1. Cathy Burns, *Hidden Secrets of the Eastern Star* (Mt. Carmel, PA: Sharing, 1994); also see Albert Mackey, *A Manual of The Lodge* (New York: Charles E. Merrill Co., 1870), p. 40-41.

Chapter 9: A Show of Hands—Illuminists Employ The Grand Hailing Sign and the Sign of Admiration and Astonishment

1. Jabez Richardson, *Richardson's Monitor and Freemasonry* (1860).

2. Malcolm C. Duncan, *Duncan's Masonic Ritual and Monitor*, 3d. ed. (New York: Crown Publishers), p. 216.

3. *Time*, January 4, 1993.

4. John J. Robinson, *Born in Blood: The Last Secrets of Freesmasonry* (New York: M. Evans & Co., 1989).

5. *Ibid.*, p. 217.

6. Jack Harris, *Freemasonry* (New Kensington, PA: Whitaker House, 1983).

Chapter 11: "Cross My Heart and Hope to Die"—The Mysterious "X" Factor

1. C. J. Koster, *Come Out of Her My People* (South Africa: Institute for Scripture Research, 2004).

2. Jim Tresner, "Seventeenth Degree, Knight of the East and the West," *Scottish Rite Journal*, June 2000.

3. *Ibid.*

4. *Ibid.*

5. *Ibid.*

6. *Ibid.*

7. *Ibid.*

8. Jabez Richardson, *Richardson's Monitor of Freemasonry* (1860), p. 161.

9. *Ibid.*

10. *The Monitor of Work, Lectures and Ceremonies of Ancient Craft Masonry for the Grand Lodge of the State of New York* (New York: J.J. Little & Ives Co., 1910).

11. Texe Marrs, *Dark Majesty: The Secret Brotherhood and the Magic of a Thousand Points of Light* (Austin, TX: RiverCrest Publishing, 2004).

Chapter 12: That Ravenous Dark Bird—Sublime Mysteries of the Illuminati's Double-Headed Eagle

1. Albert Pike, *Morals and Dogma of the Ancient and Accepted Scottish Rite of Freemasonry* (Richmond, VA: L.H. Jenkins, Inc., 1871), p. 861.

2. Texe Marrs, *Circle of Intrigue: The Hidden Inner Circle of the Global Illuminati Conspiracy* (Austin, TX: RiverCrest Publishing, 2000).

3. Anton LaVey, *Satan Speaks* (Los Angeles: Feral House, 1997).

4. Gareth Knight, *The Rose and the Goddess* (New York: Destiny Books).

5. Albert Pike, *Morals and Dogma of the Ancient and Accepted Scottish Rite of Freemasonry* (Richmond, VA: L.H. Jenkins, Inc., 1871), p. 734.

6. Francis Adams, "The Invisible Sun," *The Beacon*, published by Lucis Trust, July/August 1986, No. 10, Volume LT, p. 312.

7. *Ibid.*

8. Paul Huston, *Mastering Witchcraft*.

9. Peggy Noonan, *The Wall Street Journal*, August 25, 2001.

10. *Ibid.*

Chapter 13: The Riddle of the Great Seal of the United States, and the All-Seeing Eye of the Serpent of Wisdom

1. *Strange Stories, Amazing Facts of America's Past*, Readers Digest Books, 1989, p.56-57.

2. Albert Pike, *Morals and Dogma of the Ancient and Accepted Scottish Rite of Freemasonry* (Richmond, VA: L. H. Jenkins, Inc., 1871), p. 477.

3. *Ibid.*, p. 506; also see A. Ralph Epperson, *Masonry: Conspiracy Against Christianity* (Phoenix, AZ: Publius Press, 1997).

4. Rex Hutchens, *A Bridge to Light* (Washington, D.C.: Supreme Mother Council, 33° of Scottish Rite Freemasonry, 1988).

5. G. H. Pember, *Earth's Earliest Ages* (Grand Rapids, MI: Kregel Publications, 1987).

6. Helena P. Blavatsky, *The Secret Doctrine* (Covina, CA: Theosophical University Press, 1947, 4th ed.).

7. *Ibid.*

8. Barbara G. Walker, *The Woman's Encyclopedia of Myths and Secrets* (San Francisco: Harper & Row Publishers, 1983), p. 753.

9. A.S. Raleigh, *Occult Geometry* (Marina del Rey, CA: DeVorss & Co., 1932 & 1981).

Chapter 14: *"Silence, Slaves, or We'll Cut Your Throat From Ear to Ear!"*

1. Malcolm C. Duncan, *Duncan's Masonic Ritual and Monitor* (New York: Crow Publishers); also see Jabez Richardson, *Richardson's Monitor of Freemasonry* (1860), especially p. 142-143.

2. Jabez Richardson, *Ibid.*, p. 81.

3. *Ibid.*

4. *Ibid.*, p. 133.

5. "Grand Commander Kleinknecht Presents Revised Standard Pike Ritual to the Northern and Southern Prince Hall Supreme Councils," *The Scottish Rite Journal*, June 2001, p. 34-35.

6. *Ibid.*

7. David Fideler, *Jesus Christ, Sun of God* (Wheaton, IL: Quest Books, 1993); also Manly P. Hall, *The Adepts in the Esoteric Classical Tradition* (Los Angeles: Philosophical Research Library, 1988).

8. Jim Keith, *Secret and Suppressed* (Feral House, 1993).

9. David Ovason, *The Secret Architecture of Our Nation's Capitol* (New York: Harper Collins Publishers, 1999), p. 372.

10. Lewis Spence, *The Encyclopedia of the Occult* (London: Bracken Books, 1988).

Chapter 15: *Up to Their Necks in Mischief*

1. Albert Mackey, *Encyclopedia of Freemasonry and Kindred Sciences* (Chicago: The Masonic History Company, 1929), p. 373.

2. *Ibid.*, p. 374.

3. Malcolm C. Duncan, *Duncan's Masonic Ritual and Monitor*, 3d ed. (New York: Crown Publishers), p. 269

4. *Ibid.*, p. 101

Chapter 16: *Hand on Heart—Sign of Devotion to Chiefs*

1. Rex Hutchens, *A Bridge to Light* (Washington, D.C.: Supreme Mother Council, 33° of the Scottish Rite of Freemasonry, 1988).

Chapter 17: *Triangles Up, Triangles Down, Triangles, Triangles All Around*

1. Barbara G. Walker, *The Woman's Encyclopedia of Myths and Secrets* (San Francisco: Harper & Row Publishers, 1983), p. 1016-1017.

2. *Ibid.*

3. Rex Hutchens, *A Bridge to Light* (Washington, D.C.: Supreme Mother Council, 33° of Scottish Rite Freemasonry, 1988).

4. Joan Quigley, *What Does Joan Say? – My Seven Years As White House Astrologer to Nancy and Ronald Reagan* (New York: Pinnacle Books, 1990), p. 91.

5. *Ibid.*, p. 79.

6. Telephone interview with historian of Alcoholics Anonymous, New York, 1989; also see Cathy Burns, *Alcoholics Anonymous Unmasked: Deception and Deliverance* (Mt. Carmel, PA: Sharing, 1991), pp.78-82.

7. S.L. McGregor Mathers, *The Kabbalah Unveiled*.

Chapter 18: *Black Magic, Masonic Witchcraft and Triangle Powers*

1. Dr. O.J. Graham, *The Six-Pointed Star* (Ontario, Canada: The Free Press 777, 1984).

2. Henry W. Coil, *Coil's Masonic Encyclopedia* (New York: Macoy Publishing and Masonic Supply House Company, 1961).

3. Albert G. Mackey, *Mackey's Masonic Ritualist* (New York: Clark and Magnard, 1873).

4. Jim Keith, *Secret and Suppressed* (Feral House, 1993), p.63.

5. Jim Tresner, *The Scottish Rite Journal*, (March, 2000, p. 63.

6. Arkon Daraul, *A History of Secret Societies* (Secaucus, NJ: Citadel Press, 1961), p. 193.

7. "Triangles," Lucis Trust, Geneva, September, 1994.

8. Alice Bailey, *Telepathy*, quoted in *Ibid*.

9. *Ibid*.

10. Aleister Crowley, *The Book of the Law* (1904)

11. John Yarker, translation of French manuscript, *Letters of a Chapter, Senate, and Council* (London: J. Hogg, 1882), p. 86.

Chapter 20: *The Merovingian Dynasty, The Priory of Sion, and The Spear of Longinus*

1. *Paranoia*, Fall 2001, Issue 27, p. 11.

2. Milton William Cooper, *Behold A Pale Horse* (Sedona, AZ: Light Technology Publishers, 1991).

3. *Ibid*.

4. Anton LaVey, *Satan Speaks* (Los Angeles: Feral House, 1998), p. 32

5. *Ibid*.

6. D.C. Yermak, *The Axis of Death: Vatican, Masonry, Zionism, Enemies of God* (Greece).

7. Dean Grace, letter to Texe Marrs, June 20, 2001.

8. *Ibid*.

Chapter 21: *Magical Signs of the Jewish Cabala—The Six-Pointed Star, Babylonian Witchcraft, and the Hollywood Perdition of Jerry Seinfield and Associates*

1. "Kabbalah The Cure-All," *New York Post, online edition,* 2005.

2. *Ibid*; also see "Roseanne Makes Nice in Reality TV," *The Jewish Journal of Greater Los Angeles*, July 25, 2003, p.1; "Personality Parade," *Parade*, February 8, 2004, p. 4; "Kabbalah goes Hollywood Like A Prayer," by Yossi Klein Halevi, *The New Republic*, May 10, 2004, p. 21; and "Once Secretive Jewish Mysticism Gains Popularity," by Rachel Graves, *Associated Press*, January 18, 1998.

3. *Scottish Rite Journal*, cover, September, 2000.

4. "Gestures and Handshakes: Mr. Spock's Vulcan Greeting," www.tvacres.com/greetings.

5. *Cauldron of Abaddon*, Video (VHS or DVD), RiverCrest Publishing, Austin, TX, 2004.

6. Albert Pike, quoted by Faber Birron, *The Symbolism of Color* (Seacaucus, NJ: 1988), p. 36.

7. Ed Decker, *Free the Masons Ministry*, newsletter, PO Box 1077, Issaquah, WA 98027, June, 1992.

8. James L. Holly, *The Southern Baptist Convention and Freemasonry* (Beaumont, TX: Mission and Ministry to Men, 1992)

9. Jabez Richardson, *Richardson's Monitor of Freemasonry* (1860), p. 143.

10. Isaac Wise, quoted in *Masonic Lodge Over Jerusalem* video (VHS or DVD), RiverCrest Publishing, Austin, TX, 2004.

11. "Freemasonry Is Based On Judaism," *The Jewish Tribune*, circa 1927.

12. Ray Novosel, "Freemasonry Historic Links to Zionism/Judaism," www.rense.com, March 8, 2004.

13. "Judaism and Freemasonry," www.harrystruman.org, April 21, 2003.

14. Albert Pike, *Morals and Dogma of the Ancient and Accepted Scottish Rite of Freemasonry* (Richmond, VA: L.H. Jenkins, 1871).

15. *Ibid.*

16. Lady Queensborough (Edith Starr Miller), *Occult Theocracy, Volume I* (1933), p. 184-187.

Chapter 22:   Scorched By The Sun—Solar Signs, Circles, and Serpents

1. John Yarker, *Notes on the Scientific and Religious Mysteries of Antiquity* (London, 1872), p.8.

2. G.H. Pember, *Earth's Earliest Ages* (London: Hodder & Stoughton, 1907).

3. Reginald Haupt, Jr., *Gods of the Lodge* (Savannah, GA: Victory Publishing Company, 1990).

4. Albert G. Mackey, *Encyclopedia of Freemasonry and Kindred Sciences* (Chicago: The Masonic History Company, 1873 and 1912), p. 572-573.

5. *Ibid.*

6. Cathy Burns, *Hidden Secrets of the Eastern Star* (Mt. Carmel, PA: Sharing, 1994).

7. *Ibid*; p. 192-193.

8. Bill Schnoebelen, in *The Dark Side of Freemasonry*, edited by J. Edward Decker (Lafayette, LA: Huntington House Publishers, 1994), p. 174.

Chapter 23:   "I Fell In To a Burning Ring of Fire"—Arnold Schwarzenegger's Masonic Ring, Newt Gingrich's T-Rex Dinosaur, and Other Mysterious Messages on Rings and Neckties of the Elite

1. David Roach, "If You Only Knew What This Ring Means to Me," *The Louisiana Freemason*, April 2001.

2. *Ibid.*

3. Bill Schnoebelen, in *The Dark Side of Freemasonry*, edited by J. Edward Decker (Lafayette, LA: Huntington House Publishers, 1994), p. 173.

4. Barbara G. Walker, *The Woman's Dictionary of Symbols and Sacred Objects* (San Francisco: Harper & Row Publishers), p. 12.

5. Albert P. Mackey, *Encyclopedia of Freemasonry and Kindred Sciences* (Chicago: The Masonic History Company, 1873 and 1912), p. 12.

Chapter 25: Victory For the Devil—Fabulous Exploits of Sir Winston Churchill and Other Druid Priests and Illuminati Servants

1. *Paranoia*, Winter 1995/1996, p. 23.
2. Cathy Burns, *Masonic and Occult Symbols Illustrated* (Mt. Carmel, PA: Sharing, 1998).
3. *Complete Book of Witchcraft*, quoted in *Ibid*, p. 233.
4. *Ibid*.
5. Stephen Knight, *The Brotherhood* (London: Granada/Grafton, 1984).
6. Stanley Monteith, *Radio Liberty* newsletter, October, 1999. Also Winston Churchill's Jewish bloodline was examined in Criminal Politics magazine, Lawrence Patterson, publisher, February, 1995, p. 22.
7. Miranda J. Green, *The World of the Druids* (London: Green, Thames and Hudson, 1997), p. 170; also see John Daniel, *Scarlet and the Beast* (Tyler, TX: JKI Publishing).
8. For comparison, see Lady Queensborough (Edith Starr Miller), *Occult Theocracy* (1933).

Chapter 26: "Every Man and Woman Is A Star"

1. Aleister Crowley, *The Book of The Law* (1904).
2. Helena P. Blavatsky, *The Voice of the Silence* (Pasadena, CA: Theosophical University Press, 1889).
3. Steve Worrall-Clare, *Freemasonry — The Secret Language* (Dorset, England: Freedom Ministries International).
4. Eliphas Levi, quoted in Cathy Burns, *Hidden Secrets of the Eastern Star* (Mt. Carmel, PA: Sharing, 1994), p. 316.
5. Cathy Burns, *Ibid*.
6. Albert Pike, quoted in *Ibid*, p. 314.
7. O.J. Graham, *The Six Pointed Star* (Ontario, Canada: The Free Press 777, 1984).
8. Albert P. Mackey, *Encyclopedia of Freemasonry and Kindred Sciences* (Chicago: Masonic History Company, 1896 and 1912).
9. *Royal Arch Mason*, Fall 1993.

Chapter 28: Blood Red—Red Stars, Clenched Fists, Hammers and Sickles, and Other Signs and Symbols of Communist Intrigue

1. Aleksandr Solzhenitsyn, *Two Hundred Years Together* (Russia); also see Solzhenitsyn, *The Gulag Archipelago*.
2. "Was Stalin A Rothschild?," by Clifford Shack, www.geocities.com/cliff-shack/stalinrothschild.html.
3. "Truth About The World's Bankers," Myron C. Fagan (cassette tape series).
4. Fritz Springmeier, *Bloodlines of the Illuminati* (Austin, TX: Ambassador House, 2002).
5. Winston Churchill, *London Illustrated Herald*, February 8, 1920.
6. *Ibid*.
7. John Sharkey, *Celtic Mysteries: The Ancient Religion* (London: Thames and Hudson, 1924), p. 18.
8. Jüri Lina, *Under The Sign of the Scorpion* (Stockholm: Referent Publishing, 2002).
9. Albert G. Mackey, *Encyclopedia of Freemasonry and Kindred Sciences* (Chicago: Masonic History Company, 1896 and 1912).

10. Don Bell, "And the Barbarians Captured the Beloved Country," *Don Bell Reports* #55, November 12, 1955; also see *The Axis of Death*, by D. C. Yermak (Greece).

11. Richard Wurmbrand, *Marx and Satan* (Bartlesville, OK: Living Sacrifice Book Company, 1986), also see Robert Payne, *Marx: A Biography*; and Jüri Lina, op.cit.

12. Allen Bonck, *America: The Daughter of Babylon* (Chichester, England: New Wine Press, 1989).

13. *A Dictionary of Symbols*, edited by Jean Chevalier and Alain Gheerbandt (New York: Penguin Books, 1996).

14. Peter Ruckman, *Black is Beautiful* (Pensacola, FL: Bible Believers Press, 1995).

15. Jabez Richardson, *Richardson's Monitor of Freemasonry* (1860), p. 84

16. Helena P. Blavatsky, *The Secret Doctrine* (Covina, CA: Theosophical University Press, 1947).

17. Cathy Burns, *Hidden Secrets of the Eastern Star* (Mt. Carmel, PA: Sharing, 1994).

18. Sergei Ivanov, quoted by Vladimir Isachenkov, "Putin Brings Back Soviet Red Star," *Associated Press*, November 26, 2000.

19. Alice Bailey, *A Treatise On the Seven Rays* (New York: Lucis Publishing), p. 127.

20. Faber Birren, *The Symbolism of Color* (Seacaucus, NJ: Citadel Press, 1988).

INDEX

10,000 Famous Freemasons (book), 67
120 degrees, 328
1984 (book), 578
555 (symbolism), 376
6 (symbolism), 475, 497
666 (symbolism), 181, 206, 362, 363, 433, 466, 501, 502, 522, 540
700 Club, The, 88, 152, 462

A

A Pilgrim's Path (book), 39
AARP magazine, 415
Abaddon, 18, 207, 268
Abbas, Mahmoud, 152, 509
ABC News, 416
ABC-TV, 536
abdomen, 396
Abdullah, King, 163
Abel, 18
Abiff, Hiram, 268, 568
abortion, 243
Abraham Lincoln Brigade, 566
Abraxas, 257
Abzug, Bella, 573
Academy of Sublime Masters of the Luminous Ring, 484
Acheson, Dean, 488
Achtenberg, Roberta, 126
Ackerman, Duane, 380
Active Meditation, 271
Acton, Lord, 33
Adams Moore, Francis, 246
Adams, Gerry, 148
Adams, John, 266
Adams, John Quincy, 190, 192, 478
Adepts In the Esoteric Classical Tradition, The, 290
Adler, Manfred, 47
Age of Aquarius, 17, 373, 529, 580
Ageless Wisdom, The, 246
Aghora, 130
Agni, 557

Ahepa, Order of, 12
Ahern, Bertie, 170
AIDS, 551
Ain Soph, 515
Aiwass, 107
ajna center, 272
Al-Aqsa Martyr's Brigade, 391
Albright, Madeleine, 212
Alchemy, 20, 242, 264, 426
Alcoholics Anonymous, 329, 385, 388
Alder, Vera Stanley, 40, 43
Aldrich, Winthrop, 398
Aldrin, Buzz, 383, 393, 402
Aldworth, Elizabeth, 309
Alexander of Yugoslavia, Crown Prince, 75
Alexander the Great, 111, 477
Alexander, Jason, 421, 452, 453
Allah, 581
All-Mother Demeter, 327
all-seeing eye, 268, 270, 271, 273, 274, 282, 373, 378, 399, 406, 472, 485
Alta Vendita, 12
altars, 461
Altman, Robert, 360
Alumbrados, 291, 318
Amaterasu, 535
Ambassador to France, 401
America First Party, 476
American Bar Association, 284
American Civil Liberties Union (ACLU), 174
American Federation of Astrologers, 387
American Revolution, 267
Americans United, 174
AMORC, 372
amulet, 101, 501
ananta, 462
Ancient Cymric Medicine (book), 462
Ancient Masonry, 53, 58
Ancient Mystery Religions, 459
Anderson, Major Robert, 65
Anderson, Philip, 284
Andreessen, Marc, 340
androgyne, 264, 445

androgynous figure, 273
angel of light, 465, 568
angel pin, 510
angel wings, 270
angels, 426
Angerona, 289
Angleton, James Jesus, 233, 302
ankh, 78, 238
Annan, Kofi, 166
Anno Lucis, 428
Annuit Coeptus, 282, 501, 502
antichrist, 282, 386, 540
Antidefamation League (ADL), 174, 278, 424, 439
Antonelli, Cardinal Giacomo, 76
A-OK, 501
Aphrodite, 546
Apollo, 459
Apollo 11, 383
apron, 363
Aqua Toffeta, 16
Aquarian energies, 364
Aquino, Dr. Michael A., 97, 100, 281, 321, 492, 542, 549
Arab, 430
Arafat, Yasser, 67, 148, 391, 438, 441, 450, 455, 509, 529
arch, 399
Archangels, 426
Archbishop of Canterbury, 522
Arch-Druid, 462
Architects of Deception (book), 23
Areopagite degree, 73
Ark of the Covenant, 440
Armstrong, Lance, 144
Armstrong, Neal, 383
Army of the Confederacy, 403
Army of the Potomac, 65
Arrow of Re, or Ra, 406
Art and Architecture of Freemasonry, The (book), 49
As Above, So Below, 243, 246, 249, 254, 255, 257, 258, 274, 421, 426, 452, 492, 523
Asclepius, 250
Ashcroft, John, 413, 587
ashlar altar, 377
Ashmole, Elias, 404
Asmodeus, 484
Assad, Hafez, 378
astrology, 426, 584
Astrum Argentinium, Order of, 13
Atlantean Brotherhood, 107
Atlantis, 74
Atlas, Rabbi Seymour, 424
Austin, Stephen F., 540

Avedon, Richard, 220
Axis of Death, The, 383, 406
Ayin, 98

B

B'nai B'rith, 424
Baal, 54, 55, 56, 99, 110, 376, 460, 484, 538
Babalon Working, 98, 554
Babylon, 20, 21, 55, 57, 230, 241, 249, 362, 421, 425, 539, 563, 566, 567, 568
Bacchus, 363
Bahai, 539
Bailey, Alice, 364, 373, 432, 569
Bailey, Foster, 19
Bakula, Scott, 411
Bank of America, 217
Baphomet, 39, 50, 55, 98, 99, 100, 101, 102, 131, 246, 335, 406, 408, 409, 410, 417, 418, 422, 452, 542, 543, 548
Barak, Ehud, 163, 211, 438, 445
Barnum, P.T., 22
Barnwell, F. Aster, 31
Barr, Roseanne, 420
Bartholdi, Frédéric-Auguste, 72
Barton, William, 266
Baruch, Bernard, 497, 568
Bassiouny, Mohammed, 171
Bay, David, 13
BBC News, 468
Beacon, The (publication), 246
Beatles, The, 142, 466, 467
BeeGees, The, 142
Beethoven, Ludwig van, 337
Begin, Menachem, 168
Behold a Pale Horse (book), 405
Bel, 538
Belgium, 163
Bell, Charlie, 127
BellSouth Corporation, 380
Beltane, 565
Benediction, 527
Berg, David
Beria, 564, 565, 566
Berle, Milton, 457
Berlusconi, Silvio, 120, 126
Bernhard, Sandra, 420
Berry, Marion, 126
Besant, Annie, 41, 82, 83, 89, 194
Bhagavad Gita, 30
Bilderberger, 313, 530
Birren, Faber, 569
bisexual, 382
black and red, 495

black and white, 399
Black Book of Honorius, 368
Black Crowes, 276
black hand, 462
Black is Beautiful (book), 566
black is white, 242
black lodge, 406
black magic, 29, 48, 361, 537, 542, 544, 548
Black Muslims, 443
Black Panthers, 566
Black Pope, 76
Black Power, 566
black sabbat ritual, 110
Black's Law Dictionary (book), 206
Blair, Tony, 147
Blake, William, 103
Blavatsky, Helena, 20, 65, 89, 134, 265, 269, 300, 363, 493, 567
Blazing Star, 268, 538, 568
Blevins, Gary, 9, 14
blood, 569
blood ritual, 431
bloodline of Jesus, 405
Bloodlines of the Illuminati (book), 13, 119
Blue Lodge of Freemasonry, 18, 22, 54, 82, 227, 399
blue-stone, 499
Blumenthal, Sidney, 532
Boaz, 212
Bodh Gaya, 513
body posture, 116
body quartered, 297
body severed in two, 286
body signs, 41
Bohemia, 282
Bohemian Club, 13, 189
Bohemian Grove, 494
Bolger, Jack, 414
Bolshevik, 71, 332, 357, 556, 564
Bolshevism, 427
Bonaparte, Josephine, 49
Bonaparte, Napoleon, 30, 44, 56, 73, 74, 98, 179, 185
Book of The Law, The (book), 107, 335, 537
Book People, 474
Booth, Edwin, 90
Booth, John Wilkes, 66, 83, 90
Borman, Frank, 169
Born in Blood (book), 39, 180
Boteach, Rabbi Shmuley, 447
Bowie, James, 540
Bradley, Bill, 251, 372
Brady, Nicholas, 317
Brahma, 328
Brave New World of Heroes, A (article), 42

Brazil, 502
breast torn open, 286
Breyer, Stephen, 169
Bridge to Light, A (book), 258, 328
Brill's Content, 500
British Military Intelligence, 337
British National Party, 167
Bronfman, Edgar, 37, 278, 432
Bronfman, Jr., Edgar, 446
Bronstein, Lev (Leon Trotsky), 564, 577
Brookings Institute, 359
Broomstick, 471
Brosnan, Pierce, 137
Brotherhood of Darkness (book), 22
Brotherhood of Light, The (book), 54, 58
Browder, Earl, 570
Brown, Jerry, 535
Brown, Rodney Howard, 132
Bruno, Joseph, 164
Bua, Swami, 226
Bucharest, Hungary, 98
Buddha, 122, 506, 513, 515, 516
Buddhism, 535, 566
Buddhist, 469
Buffett, Warren, 494
burned to ashes, 286
Burns, Dr. Cathy, 13, 199, 462, 484, 492, 538
Bush, George Herbert Walker, 100, 108, 168, 261, 450, 487, 507, 530, 551
Bush, George W., 120, 121, 122, 162, 170, 184, 247, 248, 332, 341, 380, 507, 509
Bush, Jenna, 120, 122
Bush, Laura, 122, 184
Bush, Mrs. Barbara, 124, 184
Butcher of Lebanon, 433
Buy, Richard, 343
By Deception We Conduct War, 434

C

Cabala, 50, 113, 207, 264, 269, 270, 273, 329, 419, 420, 421, 422, 423, 424, 425, 426, 434, 436, 445, 447, 452, 487, 515, 564
cabalism, 420, 426, 427, 566
cabalist, 530
cabalistic, 421
Cabalistic Judaism, 329
cabalistic magic, 430, 458
Cabrinovic, 43
Cadillac, 581
caduceus, 250
Caesar, 95, 177
Cagliostro, Count, 255
Cain, 18

Calvary, 351
Calvinist, 320
Campbell, Joseph, 356
Canaanite, 56
Canada, 278, 549
Cantalupo, Jim, 127
Capitol building, 361
capstone, 362
Captain of the Guard, 59
Carlos, King Juan, 255
Carlyle, Thomas, 18
Carnegie Institute, 359
Carter, Jimmy, 190, 191
Carville, James, 445
Casolaro, Danny, 15
cast spells, 540
Castro, Fidel, 38, 44, 165, 190, 191, 378, 528
Catholic World Report, The, 330
Cauldron of Abaddon (video), 421
Caushun, 343
CBS, 341
CBS News, 410
Ceausescu, 147
Ceerfbeer, 427
Celtic, 282
Celts, 484
Ceres, 569
Cernunnos, 105, 232
Chagall, Marc, 116
Chaldean Magic, 434
Chaplin, Charlie, 220
Charlemagne, 30
charm, 41, 501, 546
Chase-Manhattan Bank, 398, 449
Checka, 565
Cheney, Dick, 407, 412
Cheney, Lynn, 412
Cheops, 85
Chernobyl, 420
Chernomyrdin, Viktor, 508
Chi, 206
Chick, Jack, 14
China, 21, 166, 468, 540
Chinmoy, Sri, 377
Chirac, Jacques, 170, 509
Chiun, 537, 539
Choctaw, 317
Christ, Cosmic, New Age, 373, 376
Christian Coalition, 462, 530
Christian Intelligence Resource Network, 205
Church of England, 522
Church of Satan, 83, 94, 98, 100, 101, 119, 131, 252, 321, 492, 550

Church of Scientology, 208
Churchill, Sir Winston, 401, 521, 565
CIA, 302, 466, 498, 509
circle, 427, 459, 472, 501
circle inside a triangle, 332
circle of the earth, 459
circle with a point inside, 535
circles, 476
circular, 400
circumambulation, 460
Cirque du Soleil, 576
Civil War, 526
Clarinex, 206
Clark, Wesley, 571
Clausen, Henry C., 19, 20, 115
Clenched fist, 47, 201, 397
Cleo, Miss, 355
Clinton, Bill, 37, 44, 114, 120, 125, 147, 148, 166, 169, 172, 177, 179, 183, 212, 236, 247, 284, 292, 394, 401, 409, 410, 420, 432, 438, 441, 486, 487, 504, 510, 535, 572, 573
Clinton, Hillary Rodham, 356, 408, 510, 573
Clooney, George, 324
cloven hooves, 369
cobra, 280, 515
Coca-Cola Company, 469
cocaine, 466
Cochrane, Thomas, 74
Cock Robin, 569
coffin, 59, 366, 376
Coil's Masonic Encyclopedia, 247, 369
color magic, 426
Colson, Charles, 561
Columbus, Christopher, 309, 311
Co-Mason, 300
Communist Manifesto, The (book), 564
Communist Party, 182, 312, 332, 570, 574, 575
Communist salute, 570, 571, 572, 573, 574, 575, 576
Communists, 99, 540, 563, 566, 567
Companion Select, 308
CompUSA, 217
concentric circles, 479
Confederate Army, 65
confederate flag, 234, 235
Confessions of a Heretic (book), 97
Congress Hall, 525
Conscious Evolution, 36
Conspiracy Reader, The, 18
Constitution, 62
Continental Congress, 266, 267
Cooper, J.C., 47
Cooper, William, 405

Copeland, Kenneth, 132
Cosa Nostra, 462
Cosmic Man, 451
cosmic reorganization, 374
Council of Princes of Jerusalem, 287
Council on Foreign Relations (CFR), 26, 67, 170, 182, 182, 359
counterclockwise, 49
crescent moon, 377, 535
Criminal Politics (magazine), 497
Crockett, David, 540
cross, Celtic, 476
Cross my heart and hope to die, 206
cross of Baphomet, 488
Cross of Burgundy, 234
Cross Saltire, 208
cross, occult, 472
Crowley, Aleister, 13, 31, 97, 98, 99, 321, 335, 347, 373, 466, 488, 537, 577
Crown of Purity, 484
Crown Royal (bourbon), 278
cryptocrats, 18
Crystal Cathedral, 203
Crystals, 333
Cuba, 191, 378, 528
Cuddy, Dr. Dennis, 14, 172
Cummings, Dr. William L., 12
Cuomo, Mario, 126, 382
Curl, James, 49
curse victims, 540
Czar Nicholas, 583
Czechoslovakia, 360

D

Dae-Jung, Kim, 148
Dagon, 229
Dagon Fish God hat, 328
Daily Mail (newspaper), 513
daisy flower, 463, 490
Dalai Lama, 360
Daniel, book of, 515
Daraul, Arkon, 247, 363
Darboy, Georges, 231
Darcis, 271
Dark Majesty, 205, 209
Dark Side of Freemasonry, The (book), 54
darkness and light, 470
Dashwood, Sir Francis, 81, 82, 289
David, Larry, 420
Davis, Jr., Sammy, 50, 100, 252, 550
Dawn Horse, The (book), 476
Day, Doris, 346
de Grande Pré, Donn, 14

de Lafayette, Marquis, 61
de Lancre, Pierre, 110
de Molay, Jacques, 50
de Valera, Eamon, 149
De Villepin, French Foreign Minister, 506
Dean, Howard, 203
Dean, James, 78
death's head, 376
Debs, Eugene V., 83, 95
December 25, 491
Decker, Ed, 14, 54, 422
Declaration of Independence, 62, 266, 379
Defense Department, 418
DeGivry, Emile Grillot, 18
Degrelle, Leon, 234
DeLay, Tom, 461
Delors, Jacques, 293
delta, 362
Democrat Party, 198, 203, 245
Democratic Capitalism, 564
demon possessed, 55
Denslow, Ray V., 12
Der Golem (movie), 436
Der Spiegel (magazine), 583
Dern, Laura, 420
dervish, 321
devas, 426
devil's horns, 505
Deyo, Jeff, 438
Diabolicus, 119
diamond, 262, 278, 427, 449, 479, 500, 582
diamond in the lotus, 417
Diana, Princess, 210
Diana (goddess), 247, 535
Dictionary of Symbols, A (book), 50
Dietrich, Marlene, 220
Diffie, Whitfield, 418
dinosaur, 490, 491
Dionysius the Ariopagite, 523
Dionysus, 569
disk, 459
Disney Corporation, 215, 341, 385, 561
Disney Studios, 74
Divine King, 502, 512
Divine Man, 521
Diwali ritual, 261
Do As Thou Wilt Shall Be the Whole of the Law, 99
Dog Star, 538
Doggett, Lloyd, 485
Dole, Bob, 236
dollar bill, 485
Donaldson, Sam, 407, 416
Donnelly, Ignatius, 74
Doors, The, 489

Dostum, Rashid, 339
double circle sign, 510
double-headed eagle, 56, 179, 183, 243, 245,
    248, 249, 250, 253, 256, 259, 262, 263, 264,
    355, 375, 393, 402, 526, 582, 583
Double-Headed Eagle, The Supreme
    Symbol, The (painting), 244
Doyle, Roddy, 505
dragon, 279, 282, 492
Dragon's Eye, 328, 407
Dreamworks, 382
drinks wine from a human skull, 56
Drucker, Peter, 301
druid, 247, 487, 521, 522, 523
Du Simitiére, Pierre Eugene, 266
dual polarity, 245
dualism, 243, 328
Duke of Kent, 167
Duncan's Masonic Ritual and Monitor
    (book), 54
Duodecim Claves, 284
Duplantis, Jesse, 132
Dzhugashvilli, 564

E

eagle, 266, 363
Eagle Sovereign Prince Rose Croix of
    Heredom, 308
ear smitten off, 286
Earth Day, 529
earth energy powers, 328
Earth First, 118
Earth's Earliest Ages (book), 460
Eastern Europe, 502
Eastern Star, 19, 567
Eating Raoul (movie), 326
Edinburgh University, 233
Edwards, Edwin, 342
Edwards, John, 570
egg, 274, 505
egg-shaped, 524
Egypt, 171, 185, 249, 363, 425, 539
Egyptian Book of the Dead, The (book), 307
Egyptian Royal Cubit, 460
Ein Soph, 268
Einhorn, Ira, 529
Eisenhower, General Dwight, 506, 568
Eisner, Michael, 215
El Diablo, 105, 119, 120, 421, 452, 505
elementals, 426
Elijah, 56
Ellia, Baruch, 565
emblems, 423, 540

Encyclopedia of Freemasonry (book), 20
Endara, Guillermo, 316
Energy System Parameters, 374
enneagram, 539
Enochian, 548
Enron Corporation, 343
Ensler, Eve, 531
Entered Apprentice, 22, 82, 145, 199, 285
Ephram, Veitesl Heine, 427
Epidaurus, 481
Epperson, Ralph, 13, 97
Epstein, Jacob, 105
equilibrium, 207, 245, 246, 328, 399
Erlichman, John, 189
Erwin, James, 217
Esau, 569
Eternal Madonna, The, 389
eternity sign, 270
Europe, 431
European Community, 293, 313, 556
European, The (newspaper), 584
Euston, Mark, 205
evil eye, 48, 502
Excalibur, 378
Exodus, 58
Eye of Horus, 335
Eye of the Dragon, 328

F

faces toward the east, 460
Fahd, King, 168
Falun Gong, 468
Falwell, Jerry, 168
Family of Man, 105
Farrahkan, Louis, 206, 264, 443
Fascists, 559
Father of Unitarianism, The, 320
Fatima, 50
Fatone, Joey, 534
FBI, 277
Federal Reserve, 478, 497
Fellow Craft Mason, 81, 82, 83, 191, 286
female trinity, 327
feminist, 573
Ferdinand, Archduke, 43
fertility, 501
Fideler, David, 460
Fides, 146
finger to the head, 442
finger touching head, 50
finger touching the lip, 50
finger, index, 50
fingernail of left pinkie, 50

fingers, 50
Finkelstein, Arthur, 445
Fiorina, Carly, 352
fire, 328, 521, 569
First Sign of a Select Master, 427
Fischler, Franz, 163
fist, 83
five-pointed, 551
five-pointed star, 368, 406, 436, 535, 537, 539, 542, 543, 546, 555, 568
flame, 476, 546
fleur de lis, 407
Florentine Man, 103
flower, 491
Flower Power, 463
Fludd, Robert, 319
Following The Sun Association, 467
Fonda, Jane, 531
Ford, Gerald, 488
Fordham University, 492
forefinger of the right hand upon the lips, 286
Foreign Affairs, 182
Forrest, Nathan B., 235
Fortean Times (magazine), 554
Four Horsemen of the Apocalypse, 182
Fox, Vicente, 528
Fox-TV, 275, 433
France, 167, 176, 271, 293, 509
Frankist, 266
Franklin, Benjamin, 62, 81, 255, 266, 268, 289, 295, 298, 362, 372
Fraternal Order of The Police, 543
Free the Masons Ministries, 422
Freemason Street Baptist Church, 88
Freemasonry Exposed (book), 192
Freemasonry-The Secret Language (book), 538
Freemasons and The Vatican, The (book), 47
freepressinternational.com, 465
French Revolution, 255, 271, 310
Frew, Donald, 342
Friedlander, 427
Frontiers (magazine), 331
Funke, Karl-Heinz, 163

G

G (letter or symbol), 523
Gacy, John Wayne, 27
Gaelic Wars, 178
Ganesha, Lord, 261
Garden of Eden, 269
gargoyle, 76

Garret-Evangelical Theological Seminary, 233
gave their hearts, 307
gavel, 567
gay, 382, 448
gay liberation, 328
gay marriages, 448
Gay Pride Parade, 382
Geffen, David, 382
Geller, Uri, 299, 420
General Grand Council of Cryptic Masons International, 390
generative sex act, 540
Genesis, 556
genital, 418
Geometry, 366, 484
Georgetown University, 394, 401
Gephardt, Richard, 357, 399
German, 558
Germany, 33, 313, 502, 532
Gest, David, 414
Getz, Rabbi Yehuda, 440
Giap, Vo Nguyen, 579
Gingrich, Newt, 32, 180, 236, 420, 489, 491
Ginott, Alice Cohn, 358
Ginsberg, Allen, 218
Ginsberg, Ruth Bader, 169
GIs and Vets For Peace, 532
Giuliani, Rudy, 382, 531
Giza, Egypt, 86
Glazunov, Ilya, 556
Glendon, Mary Ann, 345
Glover, Danny, 415
gnostic duality, 247
goat, 369, 548, 558, 580
Goat of Mendes, 108, 246
Goat of Sabbath, 538
goat's head, 108, 543
goatee, 91, 99
goatheads, 524
God of Forces, 41
God of Prosperity and Riches, 249
God of the Arch, 249
God of the Mysteries, 249
God's Eye Pendant, 388
Goddess, 117, 118, 180, 307, 329, 362, 407, 471, 501, 546, 548
Goddess of Oaths and Honesty, 146
goddess of the harvest, 569
goddess worship, 470
Gods of the Lodge (book), 460
Golden Dawn, 335
Goldsmid, Benjamin and Abraham, 427
Golem, 264, 436, 445
Golgotha, 351

good and evil, 399
good is evil, 242
Goodman, Jr., Lt. Robert O., 378
Gorbachev, Mikhail, 148, 173, 176, 182, 261, 263, 302, 556, 564, 565, 583, 586
Gore, Al, 190, 198, 236, 251, 487, 508
Grace, Dean, 13, 406
Grace, J. Peter, 126, 382
Graham, Billy, 82, 87, 174, 175, 504
Graham, David, 507
Graham, Donald E., 213
Graham, Dr. O.J., 14
gramma, 539
Grand Deception: The Theft of America and the World, 16
Grand Hailing Sign of Distress, 179, 180, 186
Grand Lodge of Jerusalem, 45, 171, 173
Grand Lodge of Pennsylvania, 61
Grand Lodge of Rhode Island, 66
Grand Lodge of the Orient, 12
Grand Lodge of the State of Montana, 59
Grand Masonic Lodge of Israel, 12
Grand Master Elect, 62, 296, 297, 396, 567
Grand Orient Lodge of Paris, 45, 72, 98, 167, 170, 176, 256, 261, 295, 565
Grand Plan, 19
Grand Scottish Knight of St. Andrew, 239
grand trine, 328, 329
graphology, 426
Great Architect, 209
Great Architect of the Universe, 268, 389
Great Britain, 153, 167, 338, 521
Great Experiment, The, 556
Great Goddess, 329
Great Pyramid of Giza, 85
Great Pyramid of the Americas, 454
Great Seal, 183, 243, 265, 266, 267, 268, 270, 282, 362, 498
Great Serpent, 265, 269
Great White Brotherhood, 29, 41, 335
Great Work, 19, 81, 242, 297, 308
Great Work of the Initiation of the World, 249
Greece, 21, 281, 355, 368, 557
Greek, 155, 156
Greek Orthodox, 193
Greeks, 491
Green Man, the, 99, 104, 523
Green Room, 295, 298
Greenpeace, 188, 201
Griffin, Des, 14, 147
Griffin, Nick, 167
Grim Reaper, 567
grimoires, 426

grip, 50, 145
group energies, 374
Group of Eight, 533
Grove, Andy, 346
Guardian Angels, 270
Gueverra, Ché, 99, 106
Guffey, Robert, 18
Guggenheim Museum, 116
guillotine, 295, 310
Gurion, David Ben, 427

H

Hades, 337
Haldemann, Robert, 189
Hall, Manly P., 18, 20, 22, 39, 118, 244, 268, 290, 322, 478, 500, 523, 546
Halos, 400, 461, 465
Hamas, 316
hammer, 558, 567
hammer and sickle, 558, 580, 581
hand of blessing, 50
hand of punishment, 50
Hand on Breast, 47, 50
Hand on Heart, 307, 308
Hand on neck, 47, 50
hand raised with palm outward, 178
hand signs, 41, 47, 51
hand with all five fingers showing, palm outward, 178
hand, closed , 48
hand, hidden, 57, 67
hands together, 50
hands, three people linking, 50
handshake, 45, 47, 50, 51, 145
Hard Rock Café, 480
Harmony Lodge #9, 66
Harpocrates, 288, 290, 294
Harriman, Averell, 393, 400, 401
Harriman, E.H., 400
Harriman, Pamela, 393, 401
Harriman, Roland, 400
Harris, Jack, 180
Harris, Katherine, 420
Harrison, George, 466
Harry Potter and the Order of the Phoenix (book), 334
Harvard Law School, 345
Harvard University, 104, 212, 292
hashish, 466
Hastert, Dennis, 357
Hathor, 307
Haupt, Jr., Reginald, 14, 460
Havel, Václav, 360

Hawaii, 515
Hawn, Goldie, 420
Hayek, Salma, 136
Hayes, Charles, 498
Hayes, Rutherford B., 56, 67, 248
Hays, Moses M., 424
Hazelden, 388
HBO-TV, 531
Hearst, Patty, 277
heart plucked out, 286
hearts were eaten, 307
Hebrew, 444
Hegelian dialectic, 212, 259, 263, 385, 527,
    583
Hegelian, 37, 167
Hegelian Dialectical, 30
Heimbichner, Craig, 425
Heinz, John, 359, 372
Heinz-Kerry, Teresa, 359
Hell Fire Club, 81, 82, 289
Herder Dictionary of Symbols, The (book),
    48, 247
hermaphrodite, 264, 335, 445
Hermes, 104, 478
hermetic monk, 271
Hermeticism, 20, 264, 445
Herod, 433
heroin, 466
Hersheim, Moses, 427
Hewlett-Packard, 352
hexagram, 361, 362, 432, 435, 472, 484, 538,
    540, 549
hidden codes, 426
Hidden Secrets of the Eastern Star (book),
    13, 462, 538
Hidell, Al, 77
Higashi, Tetsuro, 164
Higher Power, 329
Hillman, James, 356
Hilton, Paris, 420
Himmler, Heinrich, 525
Hindu, 65, 226, 272, 300, 307, 327, 328, 377,
    451, 466, 467, 476, 501, 514, 515, 535, 537,
    557
Hinduism, 130
Hindus, 461, 463, 468
Hinn, Benny, 132
Hippacratic Oath, 250
Hislop, Alexander, 459
History of Secret Societies, A (book), 247
History of the Garter (book), 404
History of The World, The (book), 273
Hitler, Adolf, 30, 38, 147, 197, 220, 300, 405,
    461, 468, 495, 525, 563
Hobson's choice, 245

Hoffman, II, Michael, 13, 200, 326
Holly, James L., 422
Hollywood, 499, 550
holocaust, 563
Holy Blood, Holy Grail (book), 405, 407
Holy Door, 327
Holy Empire of true Masonic Brotherhood,
    241
Holy Grail, 405
Holy Serpent, 426
homosexuals, 330, 551, 566
Hong Kong, 469
hoodwink, 20, 22
Hoover, J. Edgar, 189
Hope For Healing, 333
Hope, Bob, 381
Hormiga, 35
horn, 541
Horne, Alex, 19
horned symbol, 544
horns, 501, 513, 535, 543
horoscopes, 478, 584
Horus, 107, 258, 268, 276, 289, 290, 406
House of the Temple, The, 174, 235, 246,
    250, 307, 397, 539
Houston, Jean, 356
Houston, Sam, 540
Howard, Charles, 334
Hubbard, L. Ron, 98, 99, 107, 321
Hubble space telescope, 274
Hucknell, Mick, 553
Hugo, Victor, 72
human sacrifice, 368
human skull, 56, 393
Hunt brothers, 384
Hussein, King, 455
Hussein, Saddam, 147
Huston, Paul, 17, 40, 41, 247
Hutchens, Rex, 258, 268, 328
Hutchinson, Kay Bailey, 304
Hynkel, Adenoid, 220

I

I Am That I Am, 56
Il Cornuto, 105, 119, 202, 255
Il Vecchio, 103
Illie, 147
Order of the Illuminati, 60, 62, 64, 81, 97,
    163, 255, 318, 427, 462, 463, 565
Illustrated Encyclopedia of Traditional
    Symbols, An (book), 335
In The Words of Nelson Mandela (book),
    574

incantations, 426
India, 440, 468, 513
Indiana University, 358
infant as sacrifice, 110
infinity, 501
Initiation of The World, The (book), 43
Inside the Brotherhood (book), 22
Institute For Planetary Synthesis, 379
Institute for Scripture Research, 206
Intel, 346
International Brigades, 575
International Forum for a Non-nuclear
    World and the Survival of Humanity, 174
Intifada, 528
Intimate Secretary Degree, 208, 362
Inverness Lodge No. 4, 540
inverted pentagram, 537, 538, 541
involution, 270
Ipsissimus, 542
Iran, 314
Ireland, 473, 511
Iron Curtain, 92
Isis, 238, 276, 307, 361, 541
Islam, 201, 210, 430, 575, 581
Israel, 150, 152, 163, 166, 168, 170, 171, 173,
    362, 421, 427, 433, 435, 438, 440, 441, 445,
    454, 504, 512, 540
Italy, 533
Itzig, Daniel, 427
Ivanov, Sergei, 568
Iverson, Allen, 221

J

Jabotinsky Award, 168
Jackson, Andrew, 150
Jackson, Jesse, 264, 378, 566
Jackson, Michael, 140, 299, 420, 447, 527
Jacob, 421
Jacobins, 310
Jagger, Mick, 420
Jahbuhlun, 18, 45, 46, 54, 57, 58, 59, 64, 68,
    70, 209, 267, 268, 329, 460
James, Frank, 83, 90
James, Jesse, 83, 90
Janklow, Morton L., 170
Janus, 264
Japan, 467, 468, 502, 506
Jaquin, 212
Jay, John, 67
Jefferson, Thomas, 62, 266, 267
Jerry Seinfeld Show, The, 420
Jerusalem, 181, 362, 421, 440, 460
Jerusalem Post, The, 152

Jesuit, 62, 64, 76, 318, 492, 535
Jesus, 62
Jesus Christ, Sun of God (book), 460
jewel, 362, 483, 557
jewelry, 483
Jewish American Grand Masters, 424
Jewish cabalists, 249
Jewish Kingdom, 427
Jewish mysticism, 425
Jewish supremacism, 419
Jewish Utopia, 427
John, DaFree, 476
Johnson, Ladybird, 395
Johnson, Lyndon B., 150, 189, 393-397
joint suicide, 549
Jones, Alex, 13
Jones, John Paul, 322
Jong-Il, Kim, 148
Jordan, 163, 316
Jordan, Vernon, 442
Jung, Carl, 472
Jupiter, 557

K

Kabbalistic, 422, 539
Kabbalah, 419, 421, 425
Kabbalism, 419
Kabbalists, 419
Kadmon, Adam, 264, 445
Kaganovich, Mikhail, 564
Kaganovich, Rosa, 564
Kahn, A. Q., 201
Kai, 86
Kali, 227, 337
Kali Yantra, 327
Kallidai, Ramesh, 468
Kaplan, Philip, 291
Karloff, Boris, 221
Karmazin, Mel, 341
Katkov, Mikhail, 65
Katzenberg, Jeffrey, 382
Keaton, Dianne, 420
Keith, Jim, 13, 32, 35, 363
Keller, Helen, 120, 134
Kelley, Edward, 548
Kennedy, Claudia, 345
Kennedy, Jackie, 395
Kennedy, John F., 189, 247, 394, 488, 572
Kepler, Johannes, 91
Kerensky, Alexander, 256, 565
Kerry, John, 147, 179, 184, 359, 570
Key, Francis Scott, 540
KGB, 565

Kharchev, Konstantin, 174
Kharrazi, Kamel, 314
Khomeni, Ayatollah, 575
Khufu, 85, 87
King David, 362
King of Jerusalem, 255
King Peter, 75
King, John William, 543
King, Martin Luther, 566
King, Stephen, 209, 221, 438
Kinsey Institute, 98
Kinsey, Alfred, 98, 99, 358
Kinsey: Crimes & Consequences (book), 558
Kirov, Sergei, 71
Kissinger, Henry, 32
KKK, 235
Kleinknecht, C. Fred, 42, 115, 287
Knesset, 512
knife under the chin, 297
Knight of the East, 363
Knight of the East and West, 206, 207
Knight of the Pelican, 308
Knight of the Sword, 363
Knight, Gareth, 245
Knight, Stephen, 153
Knights of Columbus, 12
Knights of Kadosh, 422
Knights of Malta, 12, 126, 406, 505, 530
Knights of the Christian Mark, 58
Knights of the Golden Circle, 90
Knights Templar, 12, 39, 50, 59, 90, 99, 102, 224, 251, 303, 311, 376, 406, 422
Kohl, Helmut, 47, 313
Koolhaas, Rem, 116
Kosher Sex, 447
Koster, Dr. C.J., 206
Krasner, William, 26
Kremlin, 584
Krishna, 30
Krishnamurti, 194
Ku Klux Klan, 90
Kundalini, 31
Kutcher, Ashton, 420
Kwakiutl, 290

L

La Raison, 271
Ladd, Diane, 420
Lady Freemason, 309
Lagash, 19
Laksmi, 261
lapel pins, 388
Laskoff, Michael, 217

Last Supper, 405
Last Trumpet (newsletter), 13
Latter-Day Saints (LDS), 180
Lau, Chief Rabbi Yisrael, 173, 455
LaVey, Anton, 83, 94, 98, 99, 100, 101, 109, 120, 131, 245, 246, 252, 321, 406, 550, 551
LaVey, Zeena, 101
Law, Cardinal Bernard, 154
Lazare, Bernard, 427
le Pen, Jean-Marie, 167
Leadbeater, C.W., 41, 493
Learning Channel, The, 272
Lebed, Alexander, 380
Lectures on Ancient Philosophy, 18
Lee, Robert E., 403
Lee, Tommy, 221
left eye, 48
left hand, 48, 49, 50, 308, 396
left triangle, 74
left-handed (dark) path, 48, 73, 196, 311, 448, 549
Lenin Museum, 564
Lenin, Krupsakaya, 564
Lenin, Vladimir, 44, 56, 69, 182, 253, 256, 263, 332, 357, 556, 564, 565, 566, 577, 583
Lennon, John, 142, 466, 512
Lenox, 581
lesbian, 573
lesbian sex novels, 412
Letters on Freemasonry (book), 190, 192
Levandovsky, Mikhail, 71
Levi, Eliphas, 39, 106, 107, 274, 538
Leviathan, 283
Levy, David, 166
Lewinsky, Monica, 409, 487
Lewis and Clark, 64
Liberty, Equality, Fraternity, 43
Lieberman, Joseph, 454
light and darkness, 399
lightning, 557, 558, 559, 560, 561
lightning and thunder, 557
lightning bolt, 336, 370, 406
Limbaugh, Rush, 420
Lincoln, Abraham, 64, 83, 90, 341
Lina, Jüri, 14, 23, 565
lingam, 557
Lion King, The (movie), 385
Lion's grip, 238
Lion's Paw, 147, 148, 197
Lir, 19
Lodge of the Doubleheaded Eagle, 402
Lodge of the Nine Sisters, 62, 295
lodge sanctuary, 366
Longinus, 405
Lord of Death, 269

Lord of Light, 502
Lord of the Rings (book), 483
Lost Continent of Atlantis, 74
Lost Messiah, The (book), 321
lotus, 288, 290, 375, 514, 546
Lotz, Anne Graham, 504
Louis X, 206
Louis-Dreyfuss, Julia, 453
Louvre, 257
Lovett, Lyle, 202
Loyola, Ignatius, 309, 318
Lucent Technologies, 400
Luciano, Lucky, 497
Lucifer, 18, 40, 49, 55, 56, 117, 120, 179, 206,
    209, 242, 289, 329, 426, 460, 485, 501, 557,
    568
Luciferian doctrine, 39
Luciferianism, 426
Lucis Trust, 246, 337, 363, 373, 432
Lukoil, 582
Luna, 226
Luna, Diego, 418
Luther, Martin, 322, 372

M

Mackey, Dr. Albert G., 20, 82, 146, 268, 309,
    363, 367, 565
MacLaine, Shirley, 420
Macoy Masonic Publishing, 496
macrocosm, 426
Madonna, 420
Mafia, 462
Magen David, 361, 362, 427, 540
magic, 242
Magic Circle, 463
magic cords, 426
Magic Flute, The, 336
Magic in Theory and Practice (book), 98
Magic Mirror, 429
magic symbols, 426
magic water, 426
magic word, 436
Magical Blend, 546, 547
Magical Charm, 539
Magical Mystery Tour (album), 466
magical wand, 557
Magus, 258
Ma-Ha-Bone, 18, 57, 147, 148, 268
Maharishi Mahesh Yogi, 466, 467
Makow, Henry, 9
Malavalli, Kumar, 440
Malcolm X, 206, 443
male and female, 470

Malediction, 527
Malcr, Juan, 47
Maltese, 73
Maltese Cross, 406
Malthus Principle, 36
Mammon-Ra, 249, 259
Man of the Year, 491
Manchurian Candidate, 10, 466
Mandela, Nelson, 164, 215, 456, 574
Mandela, Winnie, 574
man-gods, 465
Mann, Thomas , 17
mano figo, 204
Mansfield, Jayne, 100, 109, 550
Manson, Charles, 44, 179
Manson, Marilyn, 94
Mansueto, Joe, 339
mantra-like chants, 426
Mao, 38
Mapplethorpe, Robert, 551
Mari, 535
marigold (flower), 463
Mark Master, 286, 308, 443, 444
Mark of the Beast, 540
Mark, Christopher, 16
marriage, 243
marriage of opposites, 452
Mars, 210, 554, 569
Marshal, E. G., 194
Martin, Margie, 426
Martin, Phillip, 317
Marvel Comics, 210
Marx and Satan (book), 69
Marx, Groucho, 10, 289
Marx, Harpo, 289, 294
Marx, Karl, 56, 69, 99, 539, 556, 565, 566
Marxist, 415
Mary Magdalene, 405
Mashaal, Khaled, 316
Masloff, Sophie, 372
Masonic and Occult Symbols Illustrated
    (book), 13
Masonic apron, 367
Masonic emblems, 428
Masonic grip/handshake, 156, 168, 169, 170,
    172, 174, 176, 273, 366
Masonic handsigns, 158
Masonic Temple, 368
masonic tracing board, 376
Masonry: Conspiracy Against Christianity
    (book), 13
Master and Margarita, The, 585
Master degree, 238
Master Mason, 82, 150, 180, 196, 286, 390,
    394, 397, 423, 484, 491, 567

Master of the Second Veil, 57, 58
Master's Grip, 197, 198
Mastering Witchcraft (book), 17, 247
Masters Carpet, 375
Matthews, Dave, 347
May Day, 565
McCartney, Paul, 142, 512
McCarty, Burke, 76
McClellan, Barr, 394
McClellan, General George, 65
McClenachan, Charles T., 367
McDonald's, 127
McGinly, Reverend, 492
McKenney, Tom, 13
McKinnell, Hank, 444
McQuaig, C. F., 83
McVeigh, Timothy, 190, 204
McWaters, Dr. Barry, 36
Meacham, Stewart, 529
Meaning of Masonry, The (book), 55
Media Bypass (magazine), 498
meditation, 426
Medusa, 280
Meet the Press, 489
Mega, 341
Megalomania, 25, 26
Mekhonoshin, Konstantin, 71
Memphis, Tennessee, 454
Mendelsohn, Moses, 427
Mephistopheles, 118
Mercury, 250, 276
Meriwether, John, 202
Merovingian Dynasty, 405, 407
Mesopotamian, 479
Metallica, 139
Mexican Scottish Rite, 98
Mexico, 528
Meyer, David, 13, 418
MI5, 337
Michaelangelo, 99, 103
Middle Eastern Lodges, 454
Midsummer Nights Dream, 116
Mighty Ones, 41
Milosevic, Slobodan, 179, 183
Minelli, Liza, 414
mirror, 417
Miss America, 132
Mithra, 459
Mithraism, 146
Mitterrand, Francois, 257
Mocatta, Moses, 427
Modrow, Hans, 48
Mohammed, 50
Mohammed VI, King, 151
Moloch, 537, 539

Molotov, 564
Molten Image, The (book), 426
Monitor of the Work, Lectures, and Ceremonies of Ancient Craft Masonry for the Grand Lodge of the State of New York, The (book), 208
Monroe, Marilyn, 100
Monteith, Dr. Stanley, 14, 22
Montessori, Maria, 187
moon, 281, 368, 383, 402, 445, 471
moon goddess, 60
Moore, Demi, 420
Moore, Michael, 341
Moors, 318
Moose, Charles, 254
Morals and Dogma (book), 39, 235, 237, 238, 239, 242, 246, 258, 259, 268, 500, 564
Morgan, Captain William, 15, 189, 192
Mormon, 161, 179, 180, 199
Mormon Church, 146, 288
Mormonism, Masonry and Godhood (book), 199
Mormonism's Temple of Doom (book), 161
Morningstar, 339
Morocco, 151
Morrison, Jim, 489
Mosaic, 340
Moscow Gazette, 65
Moses, 58, 99, 112, 421, 422
Moslem coat-of-arms, 247
Moslems, 318
Mosley, Sir Oswald, 559
Mossad, 341, 434, 509
Most Excellent Master, 181, 198, 286
Most Worshipful Grand Master, 167
Mother Delta, 327
Mother Mary, 329
Mother Supreme Council, 206
Mozart and Freemasonry, 336
Mozart, Wolfgang Amadeus, 16, 336, 337, 526
MTV, 341
Mubarek, Hosni, 252, 446, 455
mudra, 501, 513, 514, 515
Mueller, Robert, 162
Muhammed, Elijah, 206
Mummy, The, 221
Munn, Sheldon A., 66
Murdock, Rupert, 433
Murphy, Brittany, 503
Murrah Federal Building, 33
Murray, Arthur, 457
Murry, Chad Michael, 137
Musharraf, General Pervez, 148, 210
Mussolini, 38, 44

My Religion (book), 134
Myers, John, 206
Mysteries, 460
Mystery of the Balance, The, 242
Mystery Religions, 267, 282, 289, 327, 406,
    460, 463, 557
Mystery, Babylon the Great, Mother of
    Harlots, 502
mystic tie, 145
Mystical Divinity, The (book), 523
Mystics and Mysteries of Alexandria
    (book), 523

N

NAACP, 570
Nahum Goldman Medal, 432
Nakamaru, Kaoru, 467
naked man, 553
NAMBLA, 154, 218
Naphtali, 180
Napoleon, 405
NASA, 274, 393, 554
Nastase, Adrian, 147
National Center for Supercomputing
    Applications, 340
National Endowment for the Arts, 551
National Geographic (magazine), 274
National Museum, Paris, 271
National Park Service, 539
Native American Indian, 461, 468, 479
Nature Conservancy, The, 487
nature worship, 491
Nawaz, Mian Mohammed, 315
Nazi, 461, 469, 558
Nazis, 557, 563
NBC, 489
Nebo, 157
Nebuchadnezzar, 157
necklace parties, 574
necktie, 417, 483, 484, 485, 486, 487, 488, 491,
    492, 500
Nehushstoan, 385
Neo-Nazi, 532
Neptune, 337
Nero's Cross, 480
Netanyahu, Benjamin, 504
New Aeon, 117
New Age, 364, 419
New Age Bible Interpretation, 389
New Age Bible Versions (book), 13
New Encyclopedia of Freemasonry, A
    (book), 206

New Man of Reason, 99
New Millennium, The (book), 462
New Mobilization Committee, 529
New Moon Rising, 280
New Party, 559
New Rome, 545
New World Order, 364
New World Order, The (book), 462
New York, 408
New York Times, 34
Newsom, Gavin, 448
Newsweek (magazine), 202, 345
Nicaragua, 166
Nicholas II, Czar, 256, 263, 357
Nicholas, Albert, 440
Nicholson, Dr. Nancy L., 497
Nickelback, 140
Nicoll, Maurice, 472
Night Ranger, 139
Nimbus, 400, 461
Nimoy, Leonard, 421, 444, 458
nine-pointed star, 539
Ninus, 273
Nixon, Richard, 189, 195, 502, 533
Noonan, Peggy, 247, 249
Noriega, Manuel, 316
North American Man-Boy Love
    Association, 218
North Vietnam, 579
Notes on the Scientific and Religious
    Mysteries of Antiquity (book), 460
Novosel, Ray, 423
Novus Ordo Seclorum, 209, 267, 282
NSYNC, 534
Nubian temple, 78
Numa, 146
Numerical hand signs, 47
numerology, 47, 426
Nuremberg, 525

O

oath, 285, 286
Oath of Freemasonry, 285
obelisk, 376, 427
obverse, 362
Occult Geometry (book), 270
Occult Theocracy (book), 427
Odd Fellows, 12, 165, 191
Odin, 557, 569
OK sign, 501, 502, 505, 514, 515
Olcott, Colonel, 89
Oman, 168

Omega Energy Work, 378
On, 460
on the square, 190, 194, 308
one dollar bill, 265
One World Church, 423
One World Government, 423
Oppenheimer, J. Robert, 30, 150, 164
Orbis Miraculum, 429
Order of Cincinnati, 61
Society of the Cincinnati, 61
Order of Knights Templar, 366
Order of Saturn, 385
Order of the Garter, 404
Order of the Solar Temple, 549
Ordo ab Chao, 33, 207, 226, 242, 268, 308
Ordo Saturnus, 385
Ordo Templi Orientis (OTO), 13, 31, 42, 44,
    45, 53, 98, 99, 107, 147, 335, 425, 488, 554
Ormsby-Lennon, Hugh, 18
Oroboros, 89, 258, 268, 269, 270, 274, 275,
    281, 282, 283, 367, 385, 400, 472, 475, 500
Orwell, George, 24, 578
Osbourne, Ozzy, 184, 194
Osiris, 54, 55, 60, 209, 222, 225, 236, 238, 240,
    258, 268, 269, 276, 282, 290, 376, 406, 485,
    500, 502, 559
Oswald, Lee Harvey, 394, 487, 488
Our Lady of Grace Chapel, 228

P

P2 Lodge, 12
Padre Pio, 228
pagan goddess, 458
pagan religion, 426
paganism, 565
Pain in the Neck, 297
Pakistan, 201, 315
Palestine, 316, 391, 528
Palestinian, 152, 168, 341
Palestinian Liberation Organization, 529
palms down, 180
palms forward, 180
Paltrow, Gwyneth, 420
Pan, 99, 104, 487
Panama, 316
pantacle, 539
Parade (magazine), 345, 360
Parade to Glory-The Shriners and Their
    Caravan to Destiny (book), 581
Paranoia magazine, 77
paranoid, 19
Parliament of the World's Religions, 342,
    479, 561

Parsons, Jack, 44, 107, 554
Past Master, 286, 287, 297, 303
Pataki, George, 164
Patterson, Lawrence, 13, 497
Pazuzu, 225
Peace Monument, The, 581
peace sign, 480
peace symbol, 201
Peale, Norman Vincent, 174
Pearl Harbor, 19, 33
Pearland, Texas, 543
pedophiles, 243, 330, 566
Pei, I.M., 257
Pell, Claiborne, 299
Pember, G.H., 269, 460
Penn & Teller, 137
pentacle, 427
Pentagon, 33
pentagram, 245, 387, 427, 436, 437, 471, 492,
    500, 537, 538, 539, 542, 543, 544, 545, 547,
    548, 551, 553, 555, 556
pentagram, inverted, 406
pentalpha, 539
pente, 539
People For the American Way, 174
Peres, Shimon, 170, 171
Perestroika, 267
perfect ashlar stone, 267
Perfect Master, 181, 568
Perkins, Lynn F., 21, 22
Persia, 501
Peru, 460
Perusha, 451
Pfizer, 444
phallic symbol, 99, 407, 557
phallus, 248, 461, 462, 484, 540, 565
Pharaoh Amenhotep IV, 84
Pharaoh Netjerykhet Djoser, 85
Philosophia Reformata, 226
Phoenix, 268
Phoenix Wealth Management, 354
Phoenix, River, 77
Pickle, Jake, 485
Pierce, Franklin, 56, 67
Pike, Albert, 20, 21, 22, 39, 115, 235, 237,
    239, 242, 245, 258, 259, 264, 268, 288, 422,
    424, 425, 500, 526, 538, 539, 564
Pike, Ted, 14
Pilgrims Path, A (book), 39
Pilgrims Society, 13
pin (jewelry), 484
Pink, 140
Planet X, 206
Plato, 91
Playboy (magazine), 521

Playboy Club, 219
Pledge of Allegiance, 309
Plimpton 322, 327
Pluto, 337
Poe, Edgar Allen, 27
point within the circle, 387, 461, 462, 470, 472, 481
Polk, James K., 414
Pollard, Red, 334
Polly, Stephen, 217
Polo, 325
Pope John Paul II, 154, 166, 172, 173, 228, 229, 230, 350, 424
Pope John XXIII, 154, 372
Pope Paul VI, 155
Pope Pius IX, 76
Pope Pius XII, 154
Popular Science (magazine), 555
pornographic art, 551
Portland, Oregon, 283
Poseidon, 337
Potok, Chaim, 458
Potter, Harry, 101, 557, 560, 561
Powell, Colin, 67, 151, 291
Pravda, 196
presidential seal, 179, 247
Presley, Lisa Marie, 240
Prieure de Sion, 405
Prince (singer), 142
Prince Hall Freemasonry, 443
Prince Hall Mason, 206
Prince of the Power of the Air, 49, 182, 557
Prince William, 126
Princess Diana, 210
Priory of Sion, 72, 405, 406, 407, 408, 409, 410, 417, 418
Prison Fellowship, 561
Pritzker, Tom, 414
profane, 20
Progress in Religion, 561
Proletarian Revolution, 332
prostrate, 476
Protestant Reformation, 318, 322
Protocols of the Learned Elders of Zion (book), 283
Prozac, 475
Prussian Guard, 189
psychological trauma, 466
psychopath, 17, 25, 26
Public Broadcasting System (PBS), 356
Putin, Vladimir, 262, 263, 500, 564, 568, 582, 583
Pyramid, 85, 265, 266, 267, 268, 282, 284, 307, 377, 472, 485
pyramid of fire, 335

Pyramids of Giza, 185
Pythagoras, 91, 451
Pythagorean, 484
Pythagorean Signet Ring, 500
Pythagorean triplets, 327

Q

Qadhaffi, Muammar, 147
Quaballah, 421
Qaboos, Sultan, 168
Quayle, Dan, 125
Queen Elizabeth, 210
Queensborough, Lady, 427
Quigley, Joan, 328

R

R.E.M., 347
Ra, 460
Rabbi Löw, 436
Rabin, Yitzhak, 148, 441, 455
radiant star, 580
raised hand, 47
Raleigh, A.S., 270
Raleigh, Sir Walter, 273
Rameses I, 224
Rameses the Great, 223
Harry Ransom Center, 103
Rasputin, Grigori, 190, 193, 511
Rather, Dan, 410
Reagan, Nancy, 125, 328, 329, 350, 351
Reagan, Ronald, 79, 125, 148, 247, 261, 328, 329, 351
Real Grip of a Master Mason, 362, 423
Rebagliati, Ross, 143
Rectified Rite, 12
red, 400
Red (the color), 569
Red Dragon, 569
red poppy, 569
red roses, 248
red star, 540, 556, 568, 587
red string wristband, 420
Red Terror, 564, 577
red velvet, 363
red-letter day, 569
Redon, Odilon, 294
Redstone, Sumner, 341
Reed, Ralph, 530
Reign of the Wise, The, 274
reincarnation, 78, 406
remote viewing, 584

Remphan, 539
Renaissance, 274
Reno, Janet, 16, 284
Rense, Jeff, 14, 394
Rense.com, 465
Republican Party, 79, 88, 245
Revere, Paul, 299
Revolutionary War, 61
Rex, 491
Rhea, 307
Rhodes, Cecil, 32
Rhodes, Elisha Hunt, 66
Rice, Anne, 458
Richards, Michael A., 303, 421, 453
Richardson's Monitor of Freemasonry
    (book), 207
right hand, 45, 48, 49, 50, 73, 146
right hand on the heart, 308, 396
right-hand (light or good) path, 48, 448
ring, 484, 485, 492, 493, 494, 495, 497, 498,
    499
Ring of Fire (song), 483
rings, 483, 496
RIP (magazine), 338
Riplinger, Dr. Gail, 13
Ritchie, Guy, 420
Rite of Memphis, 12, 98
Rite of Misraim, 98
rituals, 424, 560
Roach, David, 484
Roberts, Julia, 499
Roberts, Marie, 18
Robertson, Pat, 82, 88, 152, 462, 505
Robespierre, 44, 310
Robin redbreast, 569
Robin, god of witches, 569
Robinson, John J., 39, 180
Rock of Sion, 407
Rockefeller, 164, 342
Rockefeller foundation, 479
Rockefeller, David, 189, 398, 448, 449
Rockefeller, Nelson, 506
Roerich Museum, Nicholas, 472
Rogers, Will, 393, 403
Rolling Stone (magazine), 138
Roman Catholicism, 329
Romanov Dynasty, 259, 357
Romans, ancient, 491
Rome, 21
Rongji, Zhu, 152
Roosevelt Arch, 59
Roosevelt, Franklin D., 19, 33, 37, 44, 248,
    282, 472, 497, 530, 568, 570
Roosevelt, Theodore, 56, 68
rooster god, 257

Roper, Jack, 552
Rose Cross and the Goddess, The (book),
    245
Rosicrucian, 11, 12, 42, 53, 62, 72, 81, 84, 145,
    147, 165, 183, 197, 220, 226, 243, 276, 284,
    295, 298, 305, 319, 322, 361, 363, 372, 383,
    385, 389, 406, 470
Rosicrucian Orders, 245
Roth, Alain, 270, 283
Rothkranz, Johannes, 47
Rothschild Dynasty, 247, 540
Rothschild, Edmund de, 100, 131
Rothschild, Jacob, 494
Rothschild, Salomon, 56, 75
Rothschild, Sir James, 82, 93
Rothschilds, 37, 73, 164, 266, 362, 401, 497,
    529, 577
rough ashlar stone, 267
Round Towers of Atlantis, The (book), 78
Rove, Karl, 170
Royal Arch, 46, 208, 368, 423
Royal Arch Mason, 12, 54, 55, 56, 57, 73, 74,
    267, 291, 312, 399
Royal Arch Mason, The (magazine), 390
Royal Arch Masonry, 181, 189, 195
Royal Arch Banner, 369
Royal Master, 286
Royal Order of the Freemasons, 428
Royal Secret, 241, 242
Royal Somerset House, 540
Rubin, Robert, 504
Ruby, Jack, 487
Ruckman, Dr. Peter, 23, 24, 566
Ruda, Manuela, 129
Rumsfeld, Donald, 168, 344, 503
runes, 558, 569
Rush, 553
Russia, 33, 92, 332, 344, 357, 380, 400, 431,
    502, 540, 583, 585
Russian mystic, 472
Russo, Patricia, 400
Rwanda, Africa, 194

S

S (letter or symbol), 474
Sabazios, 49
Sabbatai Sevi, 321
Sabbatian, 266
Sabbatic Goat, 107
sacred geometry, 451
Sacred Geometry (book), 375
sacred sex rituals, 445
sacred word, 207

sacrifice, 431
Saint Andrews, 234, 239
Saint George, 577
Salomon, Haym, 266, 267, 268
Salt Lake City, 333
San Marga Sanctuary, 515
Sanat, 364
Sanders, Alex, 186, 338
Sanhedrin, 309
Santa Anna, 540
sapphire, 493
Sartor Resartus, 18
Satan, 18, 39, 55, 265, 328, 426, 460, 539, 550, 560
Satan Speaks (book), 94, 99, 406
Satan Wants You (book), 386
Satanic Bible, The (book), 98, 550
Satanic Witch, The (book), 101
Satanicide, 139
Satanism, 21, 501, 566
satanists, 361
Saturn, 580
Saudi Arabia, 168
Sayegh, Selim, 302
Scandinavia, 569
scarab beetle, 367
Schiffs, 564
schizophrenic, 19
Schnoebelen, William J., 13, 419, 425, 463, 484
Schuller, Robert, 174, 176, 203
Schumer, Charles, 439, 440
Schwarzenegger, Arnold, 493, 494, 495
science, 484
Scientology, 98, 107, 321
scorpions, 557
Scottish Rite, 19, 42, 55, 56, 66, 67, 76, 79, 81, 82, 115, 146, 148, 197, 245, 258, 264, 268, 299, 303, 328, 363, 397, 402, 422, 539
Scottish Rite flag, 393, 402
Scottish Rite Freemasonry, 45, 174, 234, 235, 237, 238, 245, 488, 500
Scottish Rite Journal, The (magazine), 42, 59, 63, 205, 206, 287, 366, 372, 374, 421, 424, 497, 526
Scroll of Set, 549
Seabiscuit, 334
Seagram, 278, 446
Seal of Babalon, 107
seal of Black Magic, 368
seal of Great Work, 368
Seal of Solomon, 246, 361, 362, 427, 540
Seal of the Grand Master of the O.T.O., 107
Secret Doctrine, The (book), 21, 89, 134, 265, 269

Secret Master degree, 286
Secret Monitor degree, 567
Secret of the Universal Equilibrium, 241, 242
Secret Societies and Psychological Warfare (book), 13, 200, 326
Secret Teachings of All Ages, The (book), 118, 244, 500
Secret Texts: The Literature of Secret Societies (book), 18
Seinfeld, Jerry, 447, 452
Select Master, 208, 297, 308, 566, 567
Semiramis, 273
Sephira, 329
Sephiroth, 207, 329
Serbia, 183, 410
serpent, 276, 278, 279, 281, 282, 283, 377, 459
Serpent devouring his own tail, 246
Serpent of Wisdom, 270
serpents, 492, 557
Servetus, Michael, 320
Set, 258, 363
seven-point star, 546
Seventh-day Adventists, 174
sex, 361
sex (perverted), 243, 523
sex cult, 361
sexual intercourse, 484
sexual rituals, 543
Shahak, Dr. Israel, 35
Shakespeare, William, 32, 42
Shamballa, 29
Shanley, Priest Paul, 154
Sharon, Ariel, 44, 152, 341, 433, 442
Shas political party, 512
Shaw, George Bernard, 31
Shaw, Jim, 13
Shearer, Lloyd, 78
Shekina, 444
Shepherd, The (poem), 103
Sherman, Roger, 379
Sherman, William Tecumseh, 78
Shevardnadze, Eduard, 302
Shibboleth Grip, 148
Shield of David, 362
Shield of the Trinity, 407
Shimon Peres Peace Center, 441
shin, 421, 423, 458
Shin sign, 444
Shintoists, 461
Shiva, 105, 307, 328, 337, 515, 569
Shlenker, Sidney, 454
Short, Martin (actor), 358
Short, Martin (author), 22
Shriners, The, 581

Shriver, Maria, 493
Shu, 569
sickle, 567
Sign of Admiration, 181, 181
Sign of an Arrow, 406
Sign of Astonishment, 181-183, 185
Sign of the Ram, 454, 455
Sign of the Spear Point, 406, 407
Silence, 294
silver sword, 522
Simply Red, 553
Sinclair, Lilith, 542
Sirius, 538
six-pointed star, 246, 274, 328, 362, 427, 435, 436, 472, 540, 553
Skull and Bones, Order of, 13, 45, 59, 99, 168, 189, 233, 359, 372, 394, 400, 401
skull cap, 420, 433
Smith, Joseph, 44, 161, 179, 199
Smith, Luther A., 402
Smithsonian, 491
snake, 278, 280
Socialist, 559
Socialist Party, 95
socialist power, 397
Sodano, Cardinal Angelo, 165
Sodom and Egypt, 421
sodomy, 422
Sohar, 242
Sol, 226
solar, 274
solar blaze, 335
Solar Deity, 389, 460, 476
solar disk, 271
Solar Logos, 373
Solar Order of the Temple, 12
Solomon, 177, 181, 362, 484
Solomon's Temple, 177, 363, 376
Solzhenitsyn, Aleksandr, 563, 565
sorcerers, 419
Sorcery, 426
Souder, Judge, 168
Sources of Masonic Symbolism, 19
South Africa, 164, 167
Southern Baptist Convention and Freemasonry, The (book), 422
Sovereign Grand Commander, 115, 264, 488, 500, 526
Sovereign Military Order of the Knights of Malta, 88, 381
Soviet Holocaust, 564
Soviet Union, 150, 563
Spacey, Kevin, 135
Spain, 502, 575
Spear of Destiny, 405, 406

Spear of Longinus, 405, 418
Spears, Britney, 281, 420
Spellman, Cardinal, 154, 492
spells, 426, 540
Spencer, James, 13, 161
Sphinx, 307
Spielberg, Steven, 382
Spirit of Freemasonry, The, 19
spiritual magic, 328
Springmeier, Fritz, 13, 119, 283, 385, 564
square, 370, 376, 377, 399, 459, 524, 526
square and compass, 366, 432, 523
Sri Yantra, 375, 376
SS, 525, 558
St. Patrick's Day, 473
Stafford, John, 540
Stage of manhood, 82
Stalin, Joseph, 30, 38, 44, 56, 71, 180, 190, 196, 312, 400, 564, 565, 570, 577
Stalin's Shadow (book), 312
star, 100, 476, 500, 537, 543
Star of Baphomet, 538
Star of David, 89, 186, 246, 328, 341, 423, 432, 434, 435, 437, 538
Star of Initiation, 537
Star of Isis, 539
Star of Venus, 539
Star Wars, 101, 118, 353
Starr, Kenneth, 510
Star-Spangled Banner, 540
Statue of Liberty, 72, 513
Steinem, Gloria, 219
Steiner, Rudolf, 197
Steinmetz, George, 21, 22
Stelle Group, The, 356
Stiles, Ezra, 318
Stiller, Ben, 448
stone temples, 463
Story, Christopher, 147
Streep, Meryl, 202
Streisand, Barbra, 420
Strong Delusion, 39
Sublime Knights Elected, 308, 396, 403
Sufi Moslem, 146, 247, 321
Sumeria, 21, 501
Sumerian, 19
Summers, Lawrence, 212, 292
sun, 184, 187, 279, 281, 282, 318, 373, 386, 427, 445, 459, 460, 466, 467, 468, 470, 471, 473, 475, 476, 477, 478, 479, 480, 488, 491, 501, 535, 544, 548
Sun God, 257, 406, 460, 466
Sun Goddess, 535
Sun Microsystems, 418
sun rays, 248

sun signs, 304
sunflower, 463, 466
sunwheel, 476
Super-Excellent Master Mason, 45, 46, 48, 208
Super-Excellent Master's Degree, 59
supernatural, 19
superstition, 363
Suppressed Truth About the Assassination of Abraham Lincoln, The (book), 76
Supreme Architect of the Universe, 180
Supreme Court, 67
Supreme Grand Master, 180
Supreme Mother Council, 67
Supreme Mother Lodge of Freemasonry, 402
swastika, 89, 256, 461, 468, 469
Swedenborg, Emmanuel, 134
Swedenborgian Rite, 12, 134
Swinton, John, 34
Switzerland, 549
Sword and The Grail, The (book), 376
swords, 304
Symbionese Liberation Army, 277
Symbolism of Color, The, 569
symbols, 424, 426, 560
synthesis of opposites, 446, 527
Syria, 378

T

Taiyo no Kai, 467
talisman, 41, 121, 405, 539, 540, 546, 548
Talisman of the United States, The, 407
talismanic jewelry and clothing, 426
Talmud, 35, 421, 422, 430, 439
Talmudic, 421
Tambo, Oliver, 164
Tammuz, 491
Taniguchi, Yoshio, 216
tantric, 327, 418
tantric tradition, 557
Tantric Way, The (book), 375
tantric yoga, 501
Tara, Shrine of Mother Earth, 49
Target department store, 462
Tarot Card, 355, 584
tau, 107, 276, 368, 372, 374, 375, 491
tau, triple, 56, 390
Taylor, Elizabeth, 420
Teichman, Arthur (Arthur Murray), 457
telekinesis, 584
Temple Mount, 440

Temple of Reason, 83
Temple of Set, The, 97, 100, 281, 321, 542, 549
Temple of Solomon, 57, 180, 429, 460
Temple Room of the Scottish Rite, 250
Terry, Sarah, 567
The Great American Pyramid, 480
The Royal Arch Banner, 369
Theosophical Society, 41
Theosophy, 20, 65, 83, 89, 134, 194, 337, 363, 539, 567
They Live (movie), 16
Third Eye, 557
Thirty-Nine Steps, The (movie), 378
Thomas, Albert, 395
Thomas, Clarence, 191
Thompson, Charles, 266
Thor, 538, 558
Three candelabra, 363
three Centres, 364
three points, 270
Three Snakes, 276
Three Times Three, 46
three triangles, 417
three-headed serpent, 336
throat cut, 285
tie tacks, 483
Tigrett, Isaac, 480
Tikkun Olam, 42, 267
Time (magazine), 179, 184, 491, 492, 560
Times Square New Years Eve, 333
tokens, 145, 423
Tolkien, J.R.R., 483
tongue split from tip to root, 286, 297
tongue torn out, 285
torch and hand, 387
torch of fire, 542
Torch of Liberty, 99
Torrell, John, 425
totem poles, 461
Tower of Babel, 282
Tower of Babylon, 556
Transcendental Magic, 274
transvestite, 382
Treatise On The Seven Rays, A (book), 569
Tree of Life, 207, 432
Tresner, Jim, 205, 206, 209, 363
Triad, 329, 363
triangle, 262, 270, 327, 361, 377, 397, 427, 433, 582
triangle, double, 332, 361, 362
triangle, down, 330, 334, 341, 357, 358, 368, 372, 375, 381, 453
triangle, pink, 327, 330, 331

triangle, radiant, 367
triangle, up, 330, 335, 336, 338, 339, 342, 343, 344, 348, 366, 369, 370, 373, 375, 378, 379, 380, 385
triangle inside the circle, 329, 387, 389
Triangle of Life, 327
triangle within a circle, 364, 385, 386, 390
triangle within a circle, with a single dot, 364
triangle, rainbow-colored, 331
triangle, triple, 362, 363, 407, 452, 539
Triangles, 364, 373, 486, 500
triangles, six, 362
triangular chain, 362
triangular pose, 396, 397, 398, 399, 400, 402
triceps, 328
triceratops, 490
Trident, 337
Trilateral Commission, 398, 449
trinity as unity, 284
Trinity Gate of the Kremlin, 234
triple phallus, 337
triple power, 390
Triple Tau, 56, 390
Trotsky, Leon, 69, 256, 332, 357, 556, 564, 577
True Ivorites, Order of the, 51
Truman, Harry S., 30, 37, 175, 188, 247, 249, 390, 488
Trump, Donald, 417
Tubal Cain, 484
Tung, Mao Tse, 556
Turkey, 321
Turner, Ted, 487
Tutsi, 194
twenty-seven days, 55
Two Babylons, The (book), 264, 279, 459
two feet, 476
two fingers, 45, 48
two heads, 241
two-headed eagle, 445
Tyrannosaurus Rex, 491

U

U.S. flag, 493
U.S.S.R., 558
ubique, 182
UN Meditation Room, 377
Uncle Sam, 91
Under the Sign of the Scorpion (book), 565
unholy trinity, 271, 501
union of opposites, 207
United Fascist Union, 545

United Lodge, 12
United Mine Workers Union, 273
United Nations, 345, 377, 506, 581
Universal Agent, 246
Universal Mind, 37
universal motion, 242
University of Texas, 120
Unseen Hand, The (book), 13
up to their necks in mischief, 295, 296
USSR, 581

V

V (letter or symbol), 201, 206, 376, 453, 520, 521, 522, 523, 524, 525, 526, 527, 528, 529, 530, 531, 532, 534, 535, 536, 541
V, double, 456, 533
vagina, 248, 461, 462, 540
Vagina Monologues, The, 531
Vajpayee, Atal, 148
vajra, 208
Vatican, 76, 88, 328, 424
V-design, 295
veil of secrecy, 17
Venus, 548
Viacom, 341
Victoria, Queen, 248
Viding, Dr. Essi, 26
Vietnam War, 480
Vintras, Eugene, 320
Virginia Slims, 370
Vishnu, 328
Voice of America (radio show), 24
Voltaire, 296
Von Hindenburg, Paul, 70
Von Knigge, Baron, 81
Vulcan, 520
vulva, 329, 407

W

Waddesdon Manor, 93
Wagner, Mayor, 149, 492
Waite, Arthur Edward, 206
Waldorf schools, 197
Wales, 522
Walken, Christopher, 323
Walker, Barbara, 484
Walker, Reverend Canon John T., 76
Wall Street, 440
Wallace, Henry, 472
Wallonien Waffen SS Division, 234
Warburgs, 564, 577

Wardens, 460
Warren Commission, 488
Warren, Earl, 488
Washington Monument, 376
Washington Post, The, 213
Washington, D.C., 126, 361
Washington, George, 55, 60, 267, 332, 524
Watchers, 41
Waterford, 333
Way of Initiation, The (book), 197
Way of the Sacred, The (book), 290
Weishaupt, Adam, 35, 44, 62, 81, 82, 99, 427, 462, 463, 491, 564, 565
Welles, Orson, 37
Wep-em-nefret, 86
Wescott, Kay, 514
Wessely, Naphtali, 427
Westbook, Ph.D., Charles, 407
wheat bundle, 545
wheat pennies, 581
Wheel of Fortune-tarot card, 472
Whitaker, Bob, 24
white horse, 446, 476
White House, 295, 298
white magic, 29, 48, 537, 542
Whitestone, Heather, 132
Whitney Museum, 116
whore of Babylon, 569
wicca, 232, 463
Wiccan, 544
Wilcher, Paul, 15
Williams, Dr. Rowan, 522
Wilmington, Delaware, 545
Wilmshurst, W.L., 55
Wilson, Bill, 329
Wilson, Neal, 174
Wilson, Woodrow, 189
Winnie the Pooh, 561
Winter Olympics, 333
Wise, Rabbi Isaac, 423
witch, 540
witch, male, 463
witchcraft, 21, 361, 419, 445, 463, 540, 565
Witchcraft, Magic and the Supernatural (book), 186
witches, 104, 361, 419, 565
Wizard of Oz, The (movie), 414
Wolcott, Louis Eugene, 206
Woman's Dictionary of Symbols and Sacred Objects, The (book), 208, 484
World Goodwill, 373
World Jewish Congress, 278, 432
World Trade Center, 33, 555
World War I, 70
World's Fair, New York, 378

Worrall-Clare, Steve, 538
Worshipful Master, 66, 295, 567
Wotan's spear point, 406
wreath, 559
Wurmbrand, Richard, 69

X

X (letter or symbol), 156, 205, 206, 208, 209, 305, 337, 343, 372, 385, 449, 453, 485, 500, 510, 545, 559
Xmas, 206
XXX, 205

Y

Y (letter or symbol), 328
Yah, 54
Yahweh, 54, 55
Yale University, 99, 104, 124, 233, 318
Yarker, John, 460
Ye shall be as gods, 82
Yellow Springs Institute for Contemporary Studies and Arts, 369
Yellowstone National Park, 59
Yeltsin, Boris, 82, 83, 92, 263, 564, 565, 579, 583
Yermak, D.C., 53, 406
yin/yang, 243, 247, 361, 375, 468, 470, 481, 535
YMCA, 504
Yoda, 118
Yoga, 451
Yoga Institute and Bookshop, 514
Yogi, 307
Yom Kippur, 426
yoni, 427, 461
York Rite, 45, 54, 55, 56, 57, 81, 286, 297
Yosefa, 358
Yugoslavia, 410

Z

Z (letter or symbol), 206
Zain, C.C., 53, 54, 58
Zeus, 557
Zhirinovsky, Vladimir, 263, 583
Zionism, 430
Zionist interests, 397
zodiac, 478
Zohar, 257
Zoroastrians, 463

More Resources For You

Books:

Circle of Intrigue — The Hidden Inner Circle of the Global Illuminati Conspiracy, by Texe Marrs (304 pages) $20.00

Dark Majesty — The Secret Brotherhood and the Magic of a Thousand Points of Light, by Texe Marrs (304 pages) $20.00

Mystery Mark of the New Age — Satan's Design for World Domination, by Texe Marrs (288 pages) $17.00

Project L.U.C.I.D. — The Beast 666 Universal Human Control System, by Texe Marrs (224 pages) $17.00

Letters on Freemasonry, by John Quincy Adams (334 pages) $22.00

Masonic and Occult Symbols Illustrated and Exposed, by Dr. Cathy Burns (553 pages) $22.00

Hidden Secrets of the Eastern Star — The Masonic Connection, by Dr. Cathy Burns (491 pages) $20.00

Bloodlines of the Illuminati, by Fritz Springmeier (623 pages) $40.00

The Six-Pointed Star, by Dr. O.J. Graham (122 pages) $10.00

Secret Societies and Psychological Warfare, by Michael Hoffman (215 pages) $20.00

Brotherhood of Darkness, by Dr. Stanley Monteith (144 pages) $14.00

The Elite Don't Dare Let Us Tell the People, by Robert Gaylon Ross (382 pages) $36.00

Gods of the Lodge, by Reginald Haupt Jr. (195 pages) $14.00

The Globalists, by Dr. Dennis Cuddy (318 pages) $18.00

Videos:

Masonic Lodge Over Jerusalem — The Hidden Rulers of Israel, the Coming World War in the Middle East, and the Rebuilding of the Temple (VHS or DVD) $27.00

Cauldron of Abaddon—"From Jerusalem and Israel Flow a Torrent of Satanic Evil and Mischief Endangering the Whole World" (VHS or DVD) $27.00

Thunder Over Zion—Illuminati Bloodlines and the Secret Plan for A Jewish Utopia and a New World Messiah (VHS or DVD) $27.00

Freemasonry—From Darkness to Light? (VHS) $22.00

Secrets of the Kabbalah-4 Video Set (VHS) $75.00

The Secret Brotherhood (VHS) $27.00

"The Eagle Has Landed!"—Magic, Alchemy and the Illuminati Conquest of Outer Space (VHS or DVD) $27.00

Dark Secrets Inside the Bohemian Grove (VHS) $27.00

Illuminati Mystery Babylon—The Hidden Elite of Israel, America, and Russia, and Their Quest for Global Dominion (VHS or DVD) $27.00

The Other Israel (VHS or DVD) $25.00

Leviathan In Space—Strange Mysteries, Oddities, and Monstrosities of the U.S. Space Program (VHS or DVD) $27.00

ALL PRICES INCLUDE SHIPPING AND HANDLING

To order, phone 1-800-234-9673, or send check or money order to:

Power of Prophecy
1708 Patterson Road, Austin, TX 78733

Visa/Mastercard/Discover Accepted

Check Out These Web Sites for more invaluable books, videos, audiotapes, and for breaking news and informative articles:

www.conspiracyworld.com
www.powerofprophecy.com

About the Author

Well-known author of the #1 national bestseller, *Dark Secrets of The New Age*, Texe Marrs has also written 37 other books for such major publishers as Simon & Schuster, John Wiley, Prentice Hall/Arco, Stein & Day, and Dow Jones-Irwin. His books have sold over two million copies.

Texe Marrs was assistant professor of aerospace studies, teaching American defense policy, strategic weapons systems, and related subjects at the University of Texas at Austin for five years. He has also taught international affairs, political science, and psychology for two other universities. A graduate *summa cum laude* from Park College, Kansas City, Missouri, he earned his Master's degree at North Carolina State University.

As a career USAF officer (now retired), he commanded communications-electronics and engineering units. He holds a number of military decorations including the Vietnam Service Medal, and has served in Germany, Italy, and throughout Asia.

President of RiverCrest Publishing in Austin, Texas, Texe Marrs is a frequent guest on radio and TV talk shows throughout the U.S.A. and Canada. His monthly newsletter, *Power of Prophecy*, is distributed around the world, and he is also heard globally on his popular, international shortwave radio program, *Power of Prophecy*.

For Our Newsletter

Texe Marrs offers a *free* sample copy of his newsletter about Bible prophecy, conspiracies, the Illuminati, world events, secret societies, mysteries, scandals, political intrigue, the New Age Movement, cults, and the occult challenge to Christianity. If you would like to receive this newsletter, please write to:

Power of Prophecy
1708 Patterson Road
Austin, Texas 78733

You may also e-mail your request to:
customerservice@powerofprophecy.com

For Our Website

Texe Marrs' newsletter is published monthly on our websites. These websites have descriptions of all Texe Marrs' books, and are packed with interesting, insight-filled articles and information about prophecy and world events. You also have the opportunity to order an exciting array of books, tapes, and videos through our online *Catalog and Sales Stores*. Visit our websites at:

www.powerofprophecy.com
www.conspiracyworld.com

Our Shortwave Radio Program

Texe Marrs' international radio program, *Power of Prophecy*, is broadcast weekly on shortwave radio throughout the United States and the world. *Power of Prophecy* can be heard on WWCR at 5.070 Saturdays at 7:00 p.m. Central Time. A repeat of the program is aired on Sunday nights at 9:00 p.m. Central Time.